ENGLISH LINGUISTICS
1500—1800

(A Collection of Facsimile Reprints)

Selected and Edited by

R. C. ALSTON

No. 318

THE SCOLAR PRESS LIMITED
MENSTON, ENGLAND
1972

JOHN COWELL

THE INTERPRETER

1607

A Scolar Press Facsimile

THE SCOLAR PRESS LIMITED
MENSTON, ENGLAND
1972

THE SCOLAR PRESS LIMITED
20 Main Street, Menston, Yorkshire, England

SBN 85417 647 0

Printed in Great Britain by
The Scolar Press Limited
Menston, Yorkshire, England

NOTE

Reproduced (original size) by permission of the Curators of the Bodleian Library. Shelf-mark: Douce C 276.

John Cowell (1559-1611) was one of the most distinguished professors of law in the Elizabethan period and amongst other positions held the Regius Professorship at Cambridge from 1594 until the year before his death. His two great works are undoubtedly his *Institutione Iuris Anglicani* (1605) – translated into English in 1651 – and the work here reproduced. Legal lexicography begins in England with John Rastell's vocabulary of *ca.* 1525 (*Expositiones terminorum legum Anglorum,* frequently reprinted throughout the sixteenth century) and Sir John Skene's glossary of Scottish law (*De verborum significatione,* 1597). Cowell's work was, however, a much larger and more comprehensive endeavour than either of these, and was not superseded until Giles Jacob's *New Law Dictionary* of 1729.

Cowell's absolutist opinions were censured in a Royal Proclamation issued on March 25, 1610 (STC 8446) and the work was temporarily suppressed. Two editions appeared, however, in 1637 and the work was subsequently revised in 1658, 1684 (by Thomas Manley), and 1701 (White Kennet). An eighth edition was published in 1727, two years before Jacob's great work.

Reference: STC 5900.

THE INTERPRETER:

OR

BOOKE CONTAINING the Signification of Words:

Wherein is set foorth the true meaning of all, or the most part of such Words and Termes, as are mentioned in the *Lawe VVriters, or Statutes of this victorious and renowned Kingdome, requiring any Exposition or Interpretation.*

A Worke not onely profitable, but necessary for such as desire throughly to be instructed in the knowledge of our Lawes, Statutes, or other Antiquities.

Collected by IOHN COWELL Doctor, and the Kings Maiesties Professour of the Ciuill Law in the Vniuersitie of *Cambridge*.

In Legum obscuritate captio.

AT CAMBRIDGE
Printed by IOHN LEGATE. *Anno:* 1607.

To the most reuerend Father in God, *his especiall good Lord, the Lord Archbishop* of Canterburie, Primate and Metropolitan of all En- *gland, and one of his Maiesties most Ho- nourable Priuy Councell.*

AFTER long deliberation, I hardly induced my selfe to craue your gracious protection toward this simple worke: valewing it at so lowe a price, as I thinke it hardly woorth the respect of any graue man, much lesse the fauourable aspect of so honorable a personage. Yet the remembrance of those your fatherly prouocations, whereby, at my comming to your Grace from the Vniuersitie, you first put me vpon these studies, at the last by a kind of necessitie inforced me to this attempt: because I could not see how well to auoide it, but by adventuring the hatefull note of vnthankfulnesse. For I cannot without dissimulation, but confesse my selfe perswaded, that this poore Pamphlet may proue profitable to the young Students of both Lawes, to whose aduancement that way, I haue of late addicted mine indeuours: else were I more then madde to offer it to the world: and to offer it without mention of him, that by occasioning of this good, more or lesse, deserueth the prime thankes, were to proue my selfe vnworthie of so graue advice.

And therefore howsoeuer I accompt this too much boldnesse in respect of the subiect: yet could I be exceedingly glad, it might please your Grace to ascribe mine intention to the integrity of my duty. For he that meaneth truly wel, & cannot perform much: must needes reioyce at the good acceptance of that litle which he performeth.

All I craue for this at your Graces hands, is patience and pardon for this enterprise, with the continuance of those your many fauours, that hitherto to my great comfort I haue enioyed. And so my long obseruation of your iudicious disposition, hauing taught me, what small delight you take in affected complements and verball commendation, without more words, in all true humblenes, I beseech the Almighty long to continue your Grace in health and prosperitie, to his glorie, and the good of his Church.

Your Graces at all Commaundment,

Io. Cowell.

To the Readers.

GENTLE Readers, I heere offer my selfe to your censures, with no other desire, then by you to be admonished of my faults. For though I doe professe the amplifying of their workes, that haue gone before me in this kinde, and haue both gathered at home, and brought from abroade some ornaments for the better embellishing of our English lawes: yet am I *neither so vaine, as to denie mine imperfections, nor so passionate, as to be offended at your charitable reformation. Nay, my true ende is the aduauncement of knowledge; and therefore haue* I *published this poore worke, not onely to impart the good thereof to those young ones that want it: but also to drawe from the learned the supply of my defects: and so by degrees, if not my selfe to finish this modell, yet at the least, by the heate of emulation to incense some skilfuller architect thereunto. Yea,* I *shall thinke my paines sufficiently recompensed, if they may be found but worthy to stirre vp one learned man to amend mine errours.*

The Ciuilians of other nations, haue by their mutuall industries raised this kinde of worke in their profession, to an inexpected excellencie. I haue seene many of them that haue bestowed very profitable and commendable paines therin: and lastly one Caluinus *a Doctor of* Heidelberge, *like a laborious Bee, hath gathered from all the former, the best iuyce of their flowers, and made vp a hiue full of delectable honie. And by this example would I gladly incite the learned in our common lawes and antiquities of England, yet to lend their aduice, to the gayning of some comfortable lights & prospects toward the beautifying of this auncient palace, that hitherto hath bene accoumpted (howsoeuer substantiall) yet but darke and melancholy.*

Whosoeuer will charge these my traueiles with many ouer-

sights, he shall neede no solemne paines to prooue them. For I will easily confesse them. And, vpon my view taken of this booke sithence the impression, I dare assure them that shall obserue most faults therein, that I by gleaning after him, will gather as many omitted by him, as he shall shew committed by me. But I learned long sithence out of famous Tullie; *that as no mans errours ought to be folowed, because he sayeth some things well: so that which a man saith well, is not to be reiected, because he hath some errours. No man, no booke is voide of imperfections. And therefore reprehend who will, in Gods name: that is, with swveetnes, and vvithout reproche. So shall he reape hartie thankes at my hands: and by true imitation of the most iudicious that euer vvrote, more soundly helpe on this pointe of learning to perfection in a fevve moneths, then I by tossing and tumbling my bookes at home, could possibly haue done in many yeares. Experience hath taught me this in mine Institutes lately set forth: by publishing vvhereof I haue gained the iudicious obseruations of diuers learned gentlemen vpon them, vvhich by keeping them priuate I could neuer haue procured. By vvhich meanes* I *hope one day to commend them to you againe in a more exact puritie, and so leaue them to future times for such acceptance, as it shall please God to giue them.*

I *haue in some tovvardnes a tract* (de regulis iuris) *vvherein my intent is, by collating the cases of both lavves, to shevve, that they both be raised of one foundation, and differ more in language and termes then in substance, and therefore vvere they reduced to one methode (as they easily might) to be attained (in a maner) vvith all one paines. But my time imparted to these studies, being but stolne from mine emploiments of greater necessitie,* I *cannot make the hast* I *desire, or perhaps that the discourse may deserue. VVherefore vntill my leisure may serue to performe that,* I *intreate you louingly to accept this.*

One thing I *haue done in this booke, vvhereof, because it may seeme straunge to some,* I *thinke to yeld my reason: and that is the inserting not onely of vvords belonging to the art of the lavve, but*

of

of any other also, that I *thought obscure, of what sort soeuer; as Fish, Cloth, Spices, Drugs, Furres, and such like. For in this* I *follow the example of our Ciuilians, that haue thought it their part to expound any thing they could meete with in their walke. And in deede a Lawyer professeth true Philosophy, and therefore should not be ignorant (if it were possible) of either beastes, foules, or creeping things, nor of the trees from the Cedar in* Lebanon, *to the Hyssop that springeth out of the wall. And therefore, if* I *haue either omitted any hard word within my circuit, or set it downe not expounded;* I *giue you good leaue to impute the one to my negligence, the other to mine ignorance: and so cōmend these my paines to your best profit, and you vnto God.* Nouember. 3. 1607.

IO. COVVELL.

These faults I haue noted (according to the words alphabetically) which of necessitie require emendation.

IN the word Rawnge, for Pouralleeses, read Pourallees. In the word Reasonable ayde, reade Claimeth of his tenents, houlding &c. For the word Remittere, read Remitter. In the word Returno habendo, for Expleuied, reade Repleuied. In the word Scot and Lot, for Aulote & Auscote, reade Anlote & Anscote. For the word Statutum de laboriis, reade Laborariis. In the word Terme, for Certifie, reade Rectifie. For the word Thrid with hawan man, reade Thrid nith. For the word Tost, read Toft In the word Tolle, for ζελόνια, or ζέλονια, read τελωνια, or τελωνεια. For ζελος, read τέλος. In the word Verdour, for Verdioir, read Verdeur. For the word Vicountie, reade Vicountiel. In the word Watlingstreat, for Tosse, read Fosse: in the word Widow, for Vide, read Vuide. For the word Woolferthfod, read Wolferhefod.

The ſignification of Words.

ABATE (*Intrudere*) ſeemeth to be taken from the French *Abatre*, i. *decutere, deſtruere, proſternere*. It is in the Writers of the Common law vſed both actiuely and paſſiuely, or rather neuterly: as to abate a caſtell or a fortlet, *Old.Nat.br.fo* 45. which in *Weſtm*.1.*cap*.17. is plainely interpreted to be as much, as to beate downe. And to abate a Writ, is by ſome exception to defeate or ouerthrow it, *Britton*. *cap*.48. And in this Actiue voice it hath two ſignifications: one generall, another ſpeciall: generall, as in the former examples: and againe in *Kitchin fol*.173. *Abater meaſon*, is to ruine or caſt downe a houſe: eſpeciall, as in the Old.*Nat br.fol* 115. A ſtranger abateth, that is, entreth vpon a houſe or lãd void by the death of him that laſt poſſeſſed it, before the heire take his poſſeſſion, and ſo keepeth him out. Whereſore as he that putteth out him in poſſeſſion, is ſaid to diſſeiſe: ſo he that ſteppeth in betweene the former poſſeſſor and his heire, is ſaid to abate. In the neuter ſignification it is vſed, *ann*.34.*Edw*.1.*ſtat*.2. of ioynt tenants, *viz*. the Writ of the demandant ſhall abate, that is, ſhall be diſabled, fruſtrated or ouerthrowne. So in *Stawnfords* plees of the crowne, *fol*. 148. In this caſe a man may ſay, that the appeale abateth by covin, that is, that the accuſation is defeated by deceit. See *Intruſion*.

Abatement (*Intruſio*) cõmeth alſo of the French (*abatement*) i. *deiectio, decuſſio, proſtratio*, and is likewiſe vſed as the verbe (*abate*) both actiuely and paſſiuely: ſomtime ſignifying the act of the abator; as the abatement of the heire into the land before he hath agreed with the Lord. *Old nat. br. fol*. 91. Sometime the affection or paſſion of the thing abated, as abatement of the writ. *Kitchin. fol*. 214. And in this ſignification it is as much as *exceptio dilatoria* with the Civilians, *Brit.cap*. 51. or rather an effect of it. For the exception alledged, and made good, worketh the abatement. And this exception may be taken either to the insufficiencie of the matter, or to the incertaintie of the allegation by the misnaming of the plaintiffe, defendant, or place, to the variance betweene the Writ and the specialtie, or record, to the incertaintie of the VVrit, count, or declaration, or to the death of the plaintiffe or defendant: new tearmes of the law, *verbo*, Abatement of Writ. And he that will reade more of this, may looke vpon the new booke of Entries, *verbo*, *Briefe*.

Abatour (*Intrusor*) is he that abateth, that is, thrusteth into a house or land, void by the death of the former possessor, and not yet entred or taken vp by his heire. *Old. nat. br. fol.* 115. *Perkins fol.* 76. If there be a disseissor, abator, or intrudor vpon any land by the deceipt of the woman, &c.

Abbot (*Abbas*) in French *Abbè*, is by skilfull Linguists said to come from the Syriacke word (*Abba*) i. *pater*, and in our common law is vsed for him that in the covent or fellowship of Canons hath the rule and preheminence. He is by *Iustinian. novel. constitut.* 115. §. ὑπολοιπον. tearmed *Archimandrita*, of others *Cœnobiarcha*, *vel Archimonachus*, *Hoto. in verbis feuda*. Of these some here in England were mitred, some not: *Stowes annals*, *pa.* 442. And those that were mitred, were exempted from the iurisdiction of the diocesan, hauing in themselues episcopal authoritie within their precincts, and being also Lords of the Parlament. Of this kind thus saith *Corasius*; *Aliqui Abbates habent iurisdictionem episcopalem, ad quos cum Ecclesia pleno iure pertineat, in eorum Monasteriis Episcopus nihil exercet, cap. Ea quæ. Vbi Panor. extra de statu Monacho. Hæc dictus author in Paraphrasi de sacerdotio. materia, parte pri. cap.* 9. And these were called Abbots soueraigne, *anno* 9. *R.* 2. *cap* 4. and Abbots generals, as *M. Fearne* noteth in his glory of generositie. *pag.* 126. The other sort were subiect to the diocesan in all spirituall gouernement, *cap. Monasteria*, 18. *quæst.* 2. *cap. Abbas. & cap. visitandi, cum quatuor sequentibus ibidem. ca. Omnes.* 16. *quæst.* 7. & *cap. Cùm venerabilis. extra. de religiosis domibus*. And as Abbots, so were there Lord Priors also, who both had exempt iurisdiction, & were Lords of the Parlament, as appeareth by *S. Edward Cooke de iure Ecclesiastico, fol.* 28. *a.*

Abeyance, seemeth to be derived from the French (*Abayer.* i. *allatrare*,) to barke at, as dogs do against a stranger, or spaniels at a Fesant put to the pearke. So children are said (*bayer à la mamme*) when seing the dug, they struggle and make meanes towards it. And they likewise (*bayer a l'argent*) *qui spe atque animo incumbunt pecuniæ*. This word in *Litleton, cap. Discontinuance*, is thus vsed. The right of Fee-simple lyeth in abeyance: that is, (as himselfe interpreteth) all onely in the remembrance, intendmẽt, and consideration of the law. Also in the same place: the Francke tenement of the glebe of the parsonage, is in no man during the time that the parsonage is void, but is in abeyance. And againe: It is a principle in lawe, that of euery land there is Fee-simple in some man, or the Fee-simple is in abeyance. Considering these places, and comparing them with the signification of the French word, I am driuen to thinke, that our auncient Lawyers would signifie hereby a kind of hope, or longing expectance: because that those things that be in abeyance, though for the present they be in no man, yet they are in hope and expectation belonging to him that is next to enioy them. For I find also in the French, that *vn bayard*, is *avidus spectator*, a greedy beholder. I cannot in mine owne opinion better compare this, then to that which the Civilians call *hæreditatem iacentem*. For as *Bracton* saith (*lib.* 1. *cap.* 12. *nu.* 10.) *Hæreditas iacens nullius est in bonis ante aditionem. Sed fallit in hoc quia sustinet vicem personæ defuncti, vel quia speratur futura hæreditas eius qui adibit*. So that (as the Civilians say) goods and lands do *iacere*, whilest they want a possessor, and yet not simply, because they had lately one, and may shortly haue another: so the common Lawyers do say, that things in like estate are in abeyance. Reade farther of this in the new tearmes of lawe, and in *Plowdens* reports, *casu VValsingham, fol.* 554. *a*.

Abet (*Abettare*) may without absurditie be said to proceed frõ the French (*bouter*) i. *ponere, apponere, impellere, propellere*. It signifieth in our common law as much as to encourage or set on. The substantiue (*abetment, abettum*) is vsed for an encouraging or setting on, *Stawnf. pl. cor. fol.* 105. And also (*abettour*) for him that encourageth or setteth on, *Old nat. br. fol.* 21. But both verbe and noune is alway vsed in the euill part.

Abishersing (according to *Rastall* in his Abridgement, *titulo* Exposition of law words) is to be quit of amerciaments before whom soeuer of transgression. The author of the new tearmes calleth it otherwise (*Mishersing*)

 and

and saith it is to be quit of amerciaments before whom soeuer of transgression proued. I am of opinion that the word originally signifieth a forfeiture, or an amerciament, and that it is much transformed in the writing by misprision and ignorance of Clerkes: thinking it very probable, that it proceedeth from the Germane verbe (*Beschetzen*) which is as much as *fisco addicere vel confiscare*. It seemeth by the former authors to be tearmed a freedome or libertie, because he that hath this word in any charter or grant, hath not onely the forfeitures and amerciaments of all others within his fee for transgressions, but also is himselfe free from all such controule of any within that compasse.

Abiuration (*Abiuratio*) signifieth in our common law a sworne banishment, or an oath taken to forsake the realme for euer. For as *Stawnford pl. coro. li. 2. cap.* 40. saith out of *Polydore Virgils* eleuenth booke of Chronicles, the deuotion toward the Church first in *S. Edward* a Saxon king, and so consequently in al the rest vntil *anno* 22. *H.* 8. was so earnest that if a man hauing committed felonie, could recouer a church or church yard before he were apprehended, he might not be thence drawne to the vsuall trial of lawe, but confessing his fault to the Iustices at their comming, or to the Coroner, before them, or him giue his oath finally to forsake the realme. Of this you may reade a touch, *anno* 7. *Hen.* 7. *cap.* 7. But the forme and effect of this you may haue in the old abridgement of *Statutes*, *titulo. Abiuration. nu.* 3. taken out of the auncient Tractate intituled, *De officiis coronatorum*: as also in *Cromptons* Tractate of the office of the Coroner, *fol.* 206. *b.* and in the new booke of entries, *verbo, Abiuration*: and in *Andrew Horns* myrror of Iustices, *lib. 1. cap. del office del coroner*. This part of our lawe was in some sort practised by the Saxons, as appeareth by the lawes of king *Edward* set out by *M. Lamberd, nu.* 10. but more directly by the Normans, as is euident by the grand customarie, *cap.* 24. where you haue these words in effect: He that flyeth to a Church, or holy place, may stay there for eight dayes. And at the ninth day he must be demaunded, whether he will yeeld himselfe to secular iustice, or hold him to the Church. For if he will, he may yeeld himselfe to the lay Court: if he will cleaue to the Church, he shall forsweare the countrie before the Knights and other people of credit, which may witnesse the act, if need require. The forme of the oath is likewise there set downe with the

the rest of the proceeding in this matter very agreable with ours. This mercie as well of the Saxōs as Normans deriued vnto vs, something resembleth that of the Romaine Emperors toward such as fled to the Church, *lib. 1. Co. titulo* 12. or to the images of themselues, *eodem titulo* 25. And also that of *Moses* tou hing the cities of refuge, *Exod. cap.* 21 *vers.* 13. *Numb. cap.* 35. *vers.* 6. 11 12. *Deut.* 19. *vers.* 2. *Ios.* 20. *vers.* 2. But as it was in our auncestors dayes larger by great oddes in this realme, so had it lesse reason, as it may appeare to all that will compare them. Of all circumstances belonging to this abiuration, you may farther reade the new tearmes of lawe: *Stawnford vbi supra*, and such others. But this grew at the last vpon good reason to be but a perpetual confining of the offender to some Sanctuarie, wherein, vpon abiuration of his liberty and free habitations, he would chuse to spend his life, as appeareth, *anno* 22. *Hen.* 8. *cap.* 14. And this benefite also by other statutes is at the last wholly taken away. So that abiuration at this day hath place but in few cases: and if it be inflicted vpon any, it is not a confining to a Sanctuarie (for there be no Sanctuaries remaining amongst vs) but a sworne banishment out of the Kings dominions. This the Civilians call *exilium*, or *deportationem*, *lib.* 28. *Digest. titulo* 22. *de interdictis, relegatis & deportatis.*

Abridge (*Abbreuiare*) cōmeth of the French (*abreger*) and in one generall language signifieth as much as to make shorter in words, holding still the whole substance. But in the common lawe it seemeth (at the least for the most part) to be more particularly vsed for making a declaration or count shorter by subtracting or seuering some of the substance therein comprised. As for example: a man is said to abridge his plaint in an Assise, or a woman her demaund in an action of dower, that hath put into the plee or demand any land not in the tenure of the tenant or defendant: and finding that by his answer, razeth those parcels out of the plee, praying answer to the rest. So that here (*abridger*) is not (*contrahere*) but rather *subtrahere*. Termes of the lawe. *Broke. titulo, Abridgement.* and *anno* 21. *Hen.* 8. *cap.* 3. Of this the Civilians haue no vse, by reason of certaine cautelous clauses, they ordinarily haue at the end of euery position or artic'e of their libell or declaration to this effect: *Et ponit coniunctim, divisim, & de quolibet, & de tali & tanta quantitate vel summa qualis & quanta per confessionem partis ad-*

versa, vel per probationes legitimas in fine litis apparebit. And againe, in the conclusion of all: *Non astringens se ad singula probanda, sed petens, vt quatenus probauerit in præmissis, aut eorum aliquo, eatenus obtineat.* By vertue of which clauses the plaintiffe faileth not in the end by any ouer or vnder demand, neither is driuen to begin his action againe, but obtaineth for so much as he proueth to be due, though not to the heithe of his demaund.

Abridgement (abbreuiamentum) see *Abridge.*

A C

Acceedas ad Curiam, is a Writ that lieth for him, who hath receyued false iudgement in a court Baron, being directed to the Sheriffe, as appeareth by *Dyer, fol.* 169. *nu.* 20. Like as the writ *De falso iudicio* lyeth for him that hath receiued false iudgement in the county Court: the forme whereof you may see in *Fitzh. nat. br. fol.* 18. *d.* and in the Register *fol.* 9. *b.* where it is said, that this writ lyeth for iustice delayed, as well as falsly giuen. It is a *species* of the writ called (*Recordare*) Register originall, *fol.* 5. *b.* and *Fitzh. vbi supra.*

Accedas ad Vicecomitem is a writ directed to the Coroner cōmanding him to deliuer a writ to the Sheriffe, that hauing a (*pone*) deliuered vnto him, doth suppresse it, *Regist. origin. fol.* 83.

Accessory (*Accessorius vel Accessorium*) is vsed in our common lawe, otherwise then among the Ciuilians. For whereas with them it is generally takē for any thing depending vpon another: here though it be so likewise, yet most commonly and notoriously it signifieth a man that is guiltie of a fellonious offence, not principally, but by participation: as by commandement, aduice, or concealement. And a man may be accessorie to the offence of another after two sorts: by the common lawe, or by statute: and by the common lawe two waies also: that is, before or after the fact. Before the fact, as when one commaundeth or aduiseth another to commit a felony, and is not present at the execution thereof. For his presence maketh him also a principall: wherfore there cannot be an accessorie before the fact in manslaughter, because man-slaughter is sodaine and not prepensed, *Cooke lib.* 4. *fol.* 44. *a.* Accessorie after the fact, is when one receiueth him, whom he knoweth to haue committed felonie. Accessorie by statute is he that abetteth, councelleth, or hideth any man committing or hauing committed an offence made felony by statute. For though the statute make no mention of abet-tours,&c. yet they are by interpretation included. Of all these consult with *Stawnf pl.cor. lib. 1. cap.* 45.46.47. 48. There is also an accessorie of an accessorie, as he that wittingly receiueth an accessorie to felonie. *lib. Assis.* 26. *pl.* 51. *Coron. Fitzh.* 196. *Stawnf. pl. cor. li. 1. cap.* 48. And the lawe of England is, that so long as the principall is not attainted, the accessorie may not be dealt with, *Stawnf. vbi supra.* The reason whereofyou may see, *Cooke lib.* 4. *fol.* 43. *b.* And this is also true by the ciuill lawe. *Claudius de Battandier. in pract. crim. regula* 101. at the least vntill the principall be certainely knowne. Of this subiect reade *M. Cromptons* Iustice, *fol.* 37. *b.* 38.39.

Acceptance, is a receiuing of a rent, whereby the receiuer bindeth himselfe for euer to allow a former fact done by another, whether it be in it selfe good or not. new tearmes of law.

Accompte (computus) is in the cōmon lawe taken for a writte or action brought against a man, that by meanes of office or businesse vndertaken, is to render an account vnto another: as a bailife toward his Master, a guardian in socage toward his ward, & such others, as you shall find particularly named by *Fitzh.* in his *nat. br. fo.* 116. where you may also haue the forme and further vse of this writte. See *ex parte talis.*

Accroche. See enchrochement. This word accroche is vsed. *ann.* 25. *Ed.* 3. *Stat.* 3. *ca.* 8.

Achat. commeth of the french (*achet.* 1. *emptio, nundinatio*) and is vsed for a contract or bargain. *Broke. tit. contract.*

Acquitall, signifieth in our cōmon law most ordinarily a deliuerance & setting free from the suspicion or guiltines of an offence: and is twofold: acquitall in law, or acquital in fact. Acquitall in law is , when two be appealed or endicted of felony, one as principall, the other as accessorie , the principall being discharged, the accessorie by consequent is also freed. And in this case as the accessorie is acquitted by law, so is the principall in fact. *Stawnf. pl. cor. fo.* 168.

Acquittance (Acquietantia) cōmeth from the french (*quicter* or *quitter.* i. *accepto ferre,* or *quictance.* i. *acceptitatio, apocha.*) and signifieth a release or discharge from a dept formerly due. But the verbe (acquite), the participle (acquited) & the nowne (acquital) signifie also a discharge or cleering from an offence obiected, as: acquited by proclamation. *Smith de rep. Anglo. pa.* 76. *Stawnf. pl. cor. fo.* 168. *Broke. tit. Acquitall.* See the new tearmes of lawe. *verbo,* acquitall & acquittance.

Acquietandis plegiis, is a Writ lying for a suretie against the creditour that refuseth to acquite him, after the debt is paid by the debtour, *Register ori. fol.* 158. where it appeareth that this is a Iusticies.

Acre (*acre*) is a certaine quãtitie of land containing in length 40. perches, and foure in breadth, or to that quantitie, be the length more or lesse. And if a man erect any new cotage, he must lay 4. acres of land to it after this measure, *anno* 31. *Eliza. cap.* 7. and with this measure agreeth *M. Crompton* in his iurisdiction of Courts, *fol.* 222. though he say also, that according to the diuers customes of diuers countries the perche differeth, being in some places, and most ordinarily, but 16. foot *dimid.* But in the Counties of *Stafford* 24. foote, as was adiudged in the case betweene *Sir Ed. Aston*, and *S. Iohn B.* in the Exchequer. In the Statute made of sowing of Flaxe, *ann.* 24 *H.8. cap.*4. eight score perches make an acre, which is 40. multiplied by 4. See also the ordinance of measuring land, made *anno* 34. *Ed.1. Stat.* 1. which agreeth with this accompt. The word (*acre*) seemeth to come from the Germane word (*acker*) which is all one with the Latine (*ager.*)

Action (*actio*) is defined by *Bracton lib.* 3. *cap.* 1. as it is by *Iustinian. li.* 4. *Instit. titulo. de actionibus, viz. Actio nihil aliud est quàm ius persequẽdi in iudicio quod alicui debetur.* Action is principally diuided by *Iustinian, in personalem & realem*: by *Bracton*, into personall, reall, and mixt: action personall is that, which belongeth to a man against another by reason of any contract, offence, or cause of like force to a contract or offence made or done by him or some other, for whose fact he is by law to answer, *Bract. lib.* 3. *cap.* 3. *nu.* 2. Action reall is defined to be that which is giuen to any man against another, that vpon any cause possesseth or occupieth the thing required or sewed for in his owne name, and none other mans: and in this onely respect, that he possesseth or occupieth the thing, and none other. *Bract. ibid. nu.* 3. and his reason is this: *quia habet rem vel possidet, quam restituere potest vel dominum nominare.* This definition & reason he farther exẽplifieth in the words there following, which he that wil may reade at large. Action mixt is that, which lyeth aswell against or for the thing which we seeke, as against the person that hath it: and is called mixt, because it hath a mixt respect both to the thing & the person, *Bract. lib.* 3. *cap.* 3. *nu.* 5. For exam-

example, the diuision of an inheritance betweene coheyres or copartners, called in the ciuill lawe (*actio familiæ exciscundæ:*) secondly, the diuision of any particular thing being common to more, called likewise (*actio de communi dividundo:*) this kind of action (saith *Bracton*) doth seeme to be mixt, because it lyeth as well against the thing, as the person: and indeed so do other excellent Civilians, as *Cuiacius* and *Wesenbecius* in their Paratitles. ꝟ. *finium regund.* And though *Iustinian* in his first diuision omitteth the third member: yet afterward in the same title, §. 20. he saith as these men do, *viz.* that there be certaine actions (naming these and other of like nature) that seeme to haue a mixture, &c. Of this you may also reade *Britton* at large in his chapter 71. And this diuision of action springeth frō the obiect or matter, wherabout it consisteth, *Wesenb. parat.* ꝟ. *de actio. & obliga.* The author of the new tearmes of law defineth a mixt action to be a suite giuen by the lawe to recouer the thing demaunded, and also the dammages for wrong done: as in Assise of nouel disseysin: the which writ, if the disseisour make a feoffment to another, the disseiseur shall haue remedie against the disseisour and the feoffer, or other land tenant, to recouer not onely the land, but the dammages also. See the rest. These words occasion me to shew, that *actio* is by the ciuill lawe called *mixta* in two respects: *Nam quædam mistæ sunt quòd in se, & actionis in rem, & actionis personalis naturam habeant, & in iis, & actor & reus vterque sit, l. actionis verbo. §. fina.* ꝟ. *de obliga. & actio. Tales sunt actio familiæ ercisc. communi diuidun. & finium regun. quædam verò mistæ sunt, quòd rem simul & pœnam persequantur, vt in actione vi bonorum rapt. legis Aquiliæ, & ea quæ datur contra eos qui legata vel fidei commissa sacrosanctis Ecclesiis relicta soluere distulerunt.* And of this later sort is the example that the said author bringeth of a mixt action.

Action, is also by the Civilians divided, of the efficient cause, *in civilem & prætoriam.* Whereof the one riseth out of the common civil lawe, the other from some edict of the Pretour. Who being cheife Iusticer, had authoritie for his yeare, to supply the defects of the generall law by his especial edicts. And a division not vnlike this may be made in the common law of England, one growing from the auncient customary law, the other from some statute. *Broke. tit. Action sur le statut.*

Action of the finall cause, is divided into *civil, pœnal, & mixt.*

Cooke vol.6.fo.61.a. Action civile is that, which tendeth onely to the recouerie of that which by reason of any contract or other like cause, is due vnto vs: as if a man by action seeke to recouer a summe of money formerly lent, &c. Action penall is, that aimeth at some penaltie or punishment in the partie sued, be it corporall or pecuniarie. As in the action *legis Aquiliæ* in the civile lawe: whereby in our common lawe the next frends of a man feloniously slaine or wounded, shall persue the law against the murderer, or him that wounded him, to condigne punishment. *Bract. li.* 3. *ca.* 4. Action mixt is that, which seeketh both the thing whereof we are depriued, and a penaltie also for the vniust deteyning of the same: as in an action of tithe vpon the statute. *anno.*2.& 3.*Ed.6.ca.*13.

Action is also, according to the forme of petion divided into such as are conceiued to recouer either the simple value of the thing chalenged, or the double, the triple, or quadruple. *Bract. li.* 3.*ca.*3.*nu.*6. So doeth *Decies tantum* lie against embracers. *Fitzh. nat.br.* fo.171. and against iurours that take mony for their verdict of one part, or the other, or both. And to be short, any other action vpon a statute that punisheth any offence by restitution, or fine proportionable to the transgression.

Action is preiudiciall (otherwise called preparatorie) or els principall: preiudiciall is that which groweth from some question or doubt in the principall: as if a man sue his younger brother for land descended from his father, and it be obiected vnto him that he is a bastard. *Bract. li.* 3.*ca.*4. *nu.* 9. For this pointe of bastardie must be tried before the cause can farder proceede, & therefore is termed *preiudicialis, quia prius iudicanda.*

Action is either awncestrell, or personall. *Stawnf. pl.cor.*59. Auncestrel seemeth to be that, which we haue by some right descending from our auncester vpon vs: and that personall, which hath the beginning in and from our selues.

Action vpon the case (*actio super casu*) is a generall action giuen for redresse of wrongs done without force against any man, and by lawe not especially prouided for. For where you haue any occasiõ of suite, that neither hath a fitte name, nor certaine forme alreadie prescribed: there the clerkes of the chauncerie in auncient time conceiued a fitte forme of action for the fact in questiõ: which the Civilians call *actionem in factum*, & our common lawyers action vpon the case.

cafe. *In factum actiones dicuntur ideo, quia quod nomine non possunt exprimere negotium, id rei gesta enarratione declarant citra formulā ac solennitatem ullā: Cuiacius & Gothofredus ad Rubricam de praescriptis verbis*. And whereas in the civile lawe there are two sorts (*actionis in factum*) one tearmed *actio in factum ex praescriptis verbis*, the other *actio in factum pratoria. Wesemb. parat. de praescrip. verb.* the former growing vpon words passed in contract, the other more genarally vpon any fact touching either contract or offence formerly not provided against, this action vpon the case seemeth in vse to bemore like to the pretours action *in factum*, then to the other: because in the perusall of the new booke of entries, and *Brookes* his abridgement heerevpon, I perceiue that an action vpon the case lieth as well against offenses, as breach of contract. Of this see more in the word *Trespas*.

Action vpon the statute (*actio super statuto*) is an action brought against a man vpon breach of a statute: to be resembled in mine opinion to any action giuen in the lawe imperiall, either vpon *edictum pratoris, plebiscitum*, or *senatusconsultum*. For as the Pretour, so the common people *in comitijs tributis*, & the Senatours or nobility *in curia vel senatu*, had power to make lawes, wherevpon the Pretour or other Iudges permitted action. And euen so our high court of Parlament maketh Statutes against such offẽces, as are either newly grown, or more and more increased: and our Iudges intertaine their plees, that commence actions against the breakers of them.

Action is perpetuall or temporall (*perpetua vel temporalis*) and that is called perpetuall, the force whereof is by no time determined. Of which sort were all ciuill actions among the auncient Romaines, *viz*. such as grew from lawes, decrees of the Senate, or constitutions of the Emperors: whereas actions granted by the Pretor, died within the yeare, *de perpet. & tempor. actio. in Institut.* So we haue in *England* perpetuall and temporarie actions: and I thinke all may be called perpetuall, that are not expresly limited. As diuers *Statutes* giue actions, so they be pursued within the time by them prescribed, namely, the Statute *anno 1. Ed. 6. cap.* 1. giueth action for 3. yeares after the offences therein shall be committed, and no longer: and the Statute *anno* 7. *H*. 8. *cap*. 3. doth the like for foure yeares, and that *anno* 31. *Eliz. cap*. 5. for one yeare & no more. But as by the ciuill lawe no actions were at the last so perpetual, but that by time they might be prescribed against: as *actiones in rem, decem aut viginti terminantur annis, personales vero triginta.* §. *1. de perpet. & temp. actio. in Institutio. & l. 3. Co. de praescript.* 30. *annorum*: so in our common law, though actions may be called perpetual in comparison of those that be expressely limited by statute: yet is there a means to prescribe against reall actions within fiue yeares, by a fine leuied, or a recouerie acknowledged, as you may see farther in the word, Fine, and Recouerie. And for this also looke Limitation of assise.

Action is farther diuided, *in actionem bona fidei & stricti iuris.* Which diuision hath good vse in our common lawe likewise, though the tearmes I find not in any of their writers. But of this, and such like diuisions, because they haue as yet no apparent acceptance amongst our Lawyers, but onely a hidden vse, I referre the reader to the Ciuilians, and namely to *Wesenb.* in his Paratitles. *ff. De obligatio. & actio.*

Addition (*additio*) is both the English and French word made of the Latine, and signifieth in our common law a title giuen to a man ouer and aboue his Christian and surname, shewing his estate, degree, occupation, trade, age, place of dwelling, &c. For the vse wherof in originall writs of actions personale, appeales, and indictments, it is prouided by Statute *anno 1. H. 5. cap. 5.* vpō the penaltie therein expressed. Tearmes of the lawe. *Broke* farder addeth, that it is likewise requisite in townes, and gates of townes; parishes in great townes and cities, where there may be any doubt, by reason of more townes, gates, or parishes of the same name, *titulo Addition*. See also *M. Cromptons* Iustice of peace, *fol.* 95. 96.

Adeling was a word of honor among the *Angles*, properly apertaining to the Kings children, whereupon king *Edward* being himselfe without issue, and intending to make *Eadgare* (to whome he was great Vnkle by the mothers side) his heire to this kingdome, called him *Adeling*. *Roger Houedine, parte poster. suorum Annal. fol.* 347. *a.*

Adiournment (*adiurnamentum*) is almost all one with the French (*adiournement. i. denunciatio vel diei dictio*) and signifieth in our cōmō law an assignement of a day, or a putting off vntill another day, *Adiournment in eyre*, (*anno* 25. *Ed.* 3. Statute of pourveyers, *cap.* 18.) is an appointment of a day, when the Iustices in *eyre* meane to sit againe. *Adiourn. anno 2. Edw. 3. cap.* 11. hath the like signification. And this whole title in *Broke* his abridgement

ment proueth the same. The bastard Latine word (*adiurnamentum*) is vsed also among the Burgundians, as *M. Skene* noteth in his booke *De verbo signi. verbo, Adiurnatus*, out of *Chassaneus de consuet. Burg.*

Ad inquirendum, is a writ iudiciall, commanding inquirie to be made of any thing touching a cause depending in the Kings court, for the better execution of iustice, as of bastardie, of bondmen, and such like: whereof see great diuersitie in the Table of the Register iudiciall, *verbo, Ad inquirendum.*

Admeasurement (*admensuratio*) is a writ, which lyeth for the bringing of those to a mediocritie, that vsurpe more then their part. And it lyeth in two cases: one is tearmed admeasurement of dower (*admensuratio dotis*) where the widow of the deceased, holdeth from the heire or his guardian more in the name of her dower, then of right belongeth vnto her. *Register orig. fol.* 171. *a. Fitzh. nat. br. fol.* 148. The other is admeasurement of pasture (*admensuratio pasturæ*) which lieth betweene those, that haue common of pasture appendant to their free-hold, or common by vicenage, in case any one of them, or more, doe surcharge the common with more cattell then they ought, *Register. orig. fol.* 156. *b. Fitzh. nat. br. fol.* 125.

Administer (*administrator*) in our common law is properly taken for him, that hath the goods of a man dying intestate, committed to his charge by the ordinary, & is accountable for the same, whensoeuer it shall please the ordinarie to call him thereunto. I finde not this word soe vsed in all the ciuile or canon lawe, but more generally for those, that haue the gouernment of any thing, as the Decrees. *can.* 23. *quæst.* 5. *c.* 26. *Administratores plane secularium dignitatum. &c.* and *extrava.com.ca.* 11. *Grangias autem, & alia loca Cistercien sium ordinis, & aliorum Regalium, in quibus Gubernatores, seu custodes vel administratores ponuntur, &c.* Howsoeuer the signification of this word grew to be restrained amongst vs, it greatly booteth not. But there was a statute made *anno.* 31. *Ed.* 3. *ca.* 11. whereby power was giuen to the ordinarie to appointe these administratours, and to authorize them as fully as executors, to gather vp, and to dispose the goods of the deceased: alway prouided, that they should be accountable for the same, as executors. And before that, *viz. Westm.* 2. *anno* 13. *Ed.* 1 *ca.* 19. it was ordeined, that the goods of those that died intestate, should be committed to the

the ordinarie his diſpoſition, and that the ordinarie ſhould be bound to anſwer his debts,ſo far forth as the goods would extẽd, as executors.And I perſwade my ſelfe that the committing of this burden vnto Biſhops,& to thoſe that deriue eccleſiaſticall authoritie from them, grew firſt from the cōnſtitution of *Leo* the Emperour. *Co.de Epiſco.& cleri. l.nulli licere.*28.Where it is ſaide,that if a man dying bequeath any thing to the redeeming of captiues,&c.and appoint one to execute his will in that point,the partie ſoe appointed ſhall ſee it performed: and if he appointe none to doe it, then the Biſhop of the citie ſhall haue power to demaund the legacie, and without all delay performe the will of the deceaſed.

Admirall (*Admiralius*) cometh of the frenche (*amerall*)and ſignifieth,both in France and with vs,an high officer or magiſtrate that hath the gouernement of the Kings navie,and the hearing and determining of all cauſes, as well ciuile as criminall belōging to the ſea. *Cromptons* diuers *iuriſd. fo.*88.and the ſtatutes *anno* 13.*R.* 2.*ca.*5.*& anno.*15. *eiuſdem.ca.*3. *& an.*2.*H.*4.*ca.*11.*& anno.* 2.*H.*5.*ca.*6.*& an.*28.*H.*8.*ca.*15. with ſuch like. This officer is in all kingdomes of Europe that border vpon the ſea:and his authoritie in the kingdome of Naples is called, *magna Curia Admirariæ quæ habet iuriſdictionem in eos qui viuunt ex arte maris. Vincent de Franch.deſci:ſ.*142 *nu.* 1.This Magiſtrate among the Romanes was called *præfectus claſſis*, as appeareth by *Tully in Verrem.*7.but his authoritie was not continuall, as the Admirals is in theſe daies, but onely in time of warre. Neither doe I finde any ſuch officer belonging to the Emperours in our Code.And *M. Guyn* in the preface to his reading,is of opinion that this office in England was not created vntill the daies of *Edward* the third:His reaſon is probable. *Britton* that wrote in *Edw.* the firſts time, and in the beginning of his booke taking vpon him to name all the courts of Iuſtice,maketh no mention of this courte or magiſtrate. And againe *Richard* the ſecond finding the Admirall to extend his iuriſdiction over farre, ordeined by ſtatute made the 10. yeare of his reigne, that the limits of the admirals iuriſdiction ſhould be reſtrained to the power he had in his grandfather *Edward* the thirds daies, whereby the ſaide *Maſter Gwin* coniectureth that he did nought els but reduce him to his originall.But contrarily to this it appeareth by auncient records, the copies whereof I have ſeene, that not onely in the daies of

Ed.

Ed.the first,but also of King *Iohn*, all causes of Merchants and mariners, and things happening within the fludde marke, were ever tried before the *Lord* admirall.

Ad iura Regis,is a writ for the Kings Clerke against him that seeketh to eiect him to the preiudice of the Kings title in the right of his crowne. Of this you may see diuers formes vpon divers cases.*Register.orig.fo.61.a.*

Admittendo clerico, is a writte graunted to him that hath recouered his right of presentation against the Bishop in the common bank: the forme whereof read in *Fitzh.nat.br.fo.* 38.& the *Register.orig.fo.33.a.*

Admittendo in socium, is a writ for the association of certaine persons to Iustices of assises formerly appointed, *Register. orig. fol.* 206. *a.*

Ad quod damnum,is a writ that lyeth to the eschcater to inquire what hurt it will be to the King, or other person,to graunt a Faire or market, or a mortmaine for any lands intended to be giuen in fee simple to any house of religion, or other body politicke. For in that case,the land so giuē is said to fal into a dead hād,that is, such an estate and condition, that the chiefe Lords do leese all hope of heriots,seruice of court, and escheates vpon any trayterous or felonious offence committed by the tenant. For a bodie politicke dieth not, neither can performe personall seruice, or commit treason or felonie, as a singular person may. And therefore it is reasonable, that before any such grant be made, it should be knowne, what preiudice it is like to worke to the graunter. Of this reade more in *Fitzh.nat.breu.fol.*221.and look *Mortmaine*.

Ad terminum qui praeteriit, is a writ of entrie, that lyeth in case where a man hauing leased lands or tenements for terme of life or yeers, and after the terme expired,is held from them by the tenant,or other stranger that occupieth the same, and deforceth the leassour. Which writ belongeth to the leassour and his heire also, *Fitzh.nat.br.fol.* 201.

*Aduent (aduentus)*is a certaine space of time comprising a moneth or thereabout, next before the feast of Christs natiuitie. Wherein it seemeth that our ancestors reposed a kind of reuerence for the neerenesse of that solemne feast: so that all contentions in lawe were then remitted for a season. Whereupon there was a statute ordained *Westm.* 1. *cap.* 48. *anno* 3. *Ed* 1. that notwithstanding the said vsuall solemnitie and time of rest, it might be lawfull in respect of iustice and charitie, which ought at all times to be regarded) to take assises of *nouell disseisin*, *mort d'auncester*, and *darrein presentment*, in the time of Aduent, Septuagesima, and Lent. This is also one of the times, from the beginning whereof vnto the end of the Octaues of the Epiphany, the solemnizing of mariage is forbidden, by reason of a certain spiritual ioy that the church, & so consequently euery member thereof, for that time, doth or ought to conceiue in the remembrance of her spouse Christ Iesus, and so abandon all affections of the flesh. See Rogation weeke, and Septuagesima.

Advocatione decimarum, is a writ that lyeth for the claime of the fourth part or vpward, of the tythes that belong to any Church, *Register orig. fol.* 29. *b.*

Advow, aliâs avowe (advocare) commeth of the French (*advoüer, aliâs avoüer*, and signifieth as much as to iustifie or maintaine an act formerly done. For example, one taketh a distresse for rent or other thing, and he that is destreyned, sueth a Replevin. Now he that tooke the distresse, or to whose vse the distresse was taken by another, iustifying or maintaining the act, is said to avowe. Teames of the lawe. Hereof commeth *advowant, Old.nat. br. fol.* 43. and *advowrie, eodem folio.* *Bracton* vseth the Latine word in the same signification, as (*advocatio disseisinæ*) *li* 4. *cap.* 26. And I find in *Cassanæus de consuet. Burg. pa.* 1210. (*advohare*) in the same signification, and pag. 1213. the Substantiue (*desavohamentum*) for a disavowing or refusall to avowe.

Advowzen (advocatio) signifieth in our common law a right to present to a benefice, as much as (*ius patronatus*) in the canon lawe. The reason why it is so tearmed, proceedeth from this, because they that originally obtained the right of presenting to any Church, were maintainers and vpholders, or great benefactors to that Church, either by building or increasing it: and are thereupon tearmed sometime *patroni*, sometime *Advocati, cap.* 4. *& cap.* 23. *de iure patronatus in Decretal.* And *advowzen* being a bastardly French word is vsed for the right of presenting, as appeareth by the Statute of *Westm.* the second *anno* 13. *Ed.* 1. *ca.* 5.

Advowsen is of two sorts: *advowsen in grosse*, that is, sole or principall, not adhering or belonging to any maner as parcell of the right thereof: *advowzen dependant*, which dependeth vpon a maner as appertinent vnto it, tearmed of *Kitchin* an incident, that may be separated from the subiect. Of this *M. Iohn Skeene de verbo .sig.* hath these wordes: *dicitur advocatio Ecclesiæ, vel quia patronus alicuius Ecclesiæ ratione sui iuris advocat se ad eandem Ecclesiam, & asserit se in eadem habere ius patronatus, eamque esse sui quasi clientis loco, vel potiùs cùm aliquis (nempe patronus) advocat alium iure suo ad Ecclesiam vacantē, eumque loco alterius (veluti defuncti) præsentat & quasi exhibet.* See *Advowè* next following:

Advowè, alias avowè (advocatus) is vsed for him that hath right to present to a benefice, *an. 25 Ed. 3. stat. 5. ca. vnico.* There haue you also (*Advowe paramount*) which is as much as the highest patron, and is spoken of the King. *Advocatus est ad quem pertinet ius advocationis alicuius ecclesiæ, vt ad ecclesiam, nomine proprio non alieno, possit præsentare. Fleta li. 5. ca. 14. §. i. Fitzh.* in his *nat. br. fo. 39.* vseth it in the same signification. *See Advowsen.* and *Avowè.*

Ætate probanda, is a writ that the Kings tenent holding in chiefe by chivalrie, and being warde by reason of his nonage, obteineth to the eschetour of the countie where he was borne, or some time, where the land lyeth, to enquire, whether he be of full age to haue deliverie of his lands into his owe hand. *Register orig. fo. 294. & 295. Fitzh. nat. br. fo. 253.* Who also *fo. 257.* saith that this writ is some time directed to the *Shireife* to empanell a iurie for this enquirie against a day certaine, before commissioners authorized vnder the broad seale to deale in such a cause.

Aërie of Goshawkes (*aëria accipitrum*) commeth from the french (*aiëre*) signifiing so much as (*par*) in latine or (*a paire*) in English. For the french man saying that one is (*vn houme de boun aiere*) signifieth that he commeth of a good paire, that is, a good father and a good mother. It is in our language the proper word in hawkes, for that which we generally call a nest in other birds. So is it vsed *anno 9. H. 3. ca. 13.* in the charter of the forest, and in divers other places.

Affeerours (afferatores, aliàs affidati) may probably be thought to proceede from the french (*affier. i. confirmare, affirmare*) It signifieth in our common lawe, those that be appointed in court leetes, &c. vpon oath to mulct such as haue committed faults arbitrablely punishable, & haue no expresse penaltie set downe by statute. The forme of their oathe you may see in *Kitchin. fo. 46.* The reason of this appellation may seeme to be, because they that be appointed to this office, do affirme vpon there oathes, what penaltie they think in conscience the offendour hath deserued. It may likewise probably be thought, that this commeth from (*feere*) an olde englifh word fignifying a companion, as (*gefera*) doeth among the Saxons by *M. Lamberds* teftimonie, *verbo* (*contubernalis*) in his explication of Saxon words. And fo it may be gathered that *M. Kitchin* taketh it. *ca. Amercements. fo.* 78. in thefe words. (*Mas fi le amercement foit affire per pares*) where (*pares*) be put for affeerors. And there may be good reafon of this, becaufe they are in this bufines made companions and equals. You fhall finde this word vfed. *an.* 25. *Ed.* 3. *fta.* 7. *viz.* And the fame Iuftices before their rifing in every feffions, fhall caufe to be affeered the amercements, as pertaineth, & alfo to the fame effect. *an.* 26. *H.* 8. *ca.* 6. *Kitchin. fo.* 78. ioyneth thefe. 3. wordes togither as *fynonyma.* (*Affidati, amerciatores, affirours. Affidare* in the canon lawe is vfed for *fidem dare. ca. fin. i. de cognatio. fpiritua. in Decretal. & ca. fuper eo. de teftibus. Bracton* hath *affidare mulierem*, for to be betrothed to a woman. *li.* 2. *ca.* 12. But I finde in the cuftomarie of Normandie. *ca.* 20. this word (*affeurer*) which the latine interpretour expreffeth by (*taxare*) that is, to fet the price of a thing, as (*aeftimare, indicare*, *&c.*) which etymologie of all the other pleafeth me beft, leauing euery man to his own iudgemēt.

Affirme (*affirmare*) commeth either of the latine, or frenche (*affirmer*) It fignifieth in our common law, as much as to ratifie or approue a former law or iudgement. So is the fubftantiue (*affirmāce*) vfed *anno.* 8. *H.* 6. *ca.* 12. And fo is the verb it felfe by *M. Weft. parte.* 2. *fymbolai. titulo, Fines. fect.* 152. And if the iudgement be affirmed, &c. as alfo by *M. Crompton* in his diuers *Iurifd. fo.* 166.

Afforeft (*afforeftare*) is to turne ground into foreft. *charta de forefta. ca.* 1. *&* 30. *an.* 9. *H.* 3. What that is, look more at larg in *Foreft.*

Affraye (*affreia*) commeth of the french (*effraier.* i. *horrificare, terrere*) It fignifieth in our common lawe a skirmifh or fighting betweene two or more. *M. Lamberd* in his *eirenarcha. lib.* 2. *cap.* 3. faith, that it is often times confounded with an affault, but yet he is of opinion that they differ in this, that where an affault is but a wrong to the partie, an affray is a common wrong: and therefore both enquirable and punifhable in a leete. It might be faid likewife, that an affault is but of one fide, and an affray of two or more. I thinke this word (affray) to be two wayes vfed, one, as I haue alreadie defcribed it, another, for a terror wrought in the fubiects by any vnlawfull fight of violence, or armor, &c. tending toward violence. For fo is it vsed, *anno* 2. *Ed.* 3. *cap.* 3.

Age (ætas) commeth from the French *(aage)* and signifieth in our language that part of a mans life, which is from his birth vnto his last day. But it is in the common lawe particularly vsed for those especiall times, which enable men or women to do that, which before for want of age, and so consequently of iudgement, they might not do. And these times in a man be two, in a woman sixe. The age of 21. yeres is termed the full age in a man, the age of fourteene yeares, the age of discretion, *Litleton li.* 2. *ca.* 4. In a woman there are sixe seuerall ages obserued, that seuerally enable her to do sixe seuerall things. *Broke. Gard.* 7. First, at 7. yeares of age the Lord her father may distraine his tenents for ayde to marry her: for at those yeares she may consent to matrimonie, *Bract. lib.* 2. *cap.* 36. *nu.* 3. Secondly, at the age of nine yeares she is dowable: for then, or within halfe a yeare after, is she able *promereri dotem, & virum sustinere. Fleta li.* 5. *cap.* 22. *Litleton lib. prim. cap.* 5. which *Bracton loco citato* doth notwithstanding limit at 12. yeares. Thirdly, at twelue yeares she is able finally to ratifie and confirme her former consent giuen to matrimonie. Fourthly, at 14. yeares she is enabled to receiue her land into her owne hands, and shall be out of ward, if she be of this age at the death of her ancestor. Fiftly, at sixteene yeares she shal be out of ward, though at the death of her auncestor she was within the age of fourteen yeres. The reason is, because then she may take a husband able to performe Knights seruice. Sixtly, at 21. yeares she is able to alienate her lands and tenements, *Instit. iure com. cap.* 24. Touching this mater, take further these notes perspicuously gathered. At the age of 14. yeares a striplin is enabled to chuse his owne guardian, and to claime his land holden in socage, *Dyer fol.* 162. which *Bracton* limiteth at fifteene yeares, *li.* 2. *cap.* 37. *num.* 2. with whom *Glanvile* also agreeth, *lib.* 7. *cap.* 9. And at the age of fourteene yeares, a man may consent to mariage, as a woman at 12. *Bracton. vbi supra.* At the age of fifteene yeres a man ought to be sworne to keepe the kings peace, *anno* 34. *Edw.* 1. *Stat.* 3. The age of 21. yeares compelleth a man to be knight, that hath twentie pounds land *per annum* in fee, or for tearme of life, *anno* 1. *Edw.* 2. *stat.* 1. and also enableth him to contract and to deale by himself, in all lawfull causes appertaining vnto his estate. Which vntill that time, he cannot with the security of those that deale with him.

This the *Lombards* settle at 18. yeares, as appeareth by *Hotomans* disputations *in libros feudorum, l.2. c. 53. ver. decimo. octauo anno.* which power the Romans permitted not *vsque ad plenam maturitatem,* and that they limited at 25. yeares. *lib. 1. in fine π. de maior. 25. an. l. fin. Co. de Legit. tut. in principio, titulo de curat. in Institut.* The age of twelue yeares bindeth to appearance before the Sheriffe and Coroner for enquirie after roberies, *an. 52. H. 3. cap.* 24. The age of 14. yeares, enableth to enter an order of religion without consent of parents, &c. *anno* 4. *H.* 4. *cap.* 17.

Age prier (*ætatem precari*) or (*ætatis precatio*) is a petition made in court by one in his minoritie, hauing an actiō brought against him, for lands coming to him by discent, that the action may rest vntill he come to his full age: which the Court in most cases ought to yeeld vnto. This is otherwise in the ciuill lawe, which inforceth children in their minoritie to answer by their tutors or curatours, *π. de minor.* 25. *an.*

Agenhine. See *Haghenhine.*

Agist (*agistare*) seemeth to come of the French (*gist.* i. *iacet*) hauing (*gisir*) in the Infinitiue moode, whence commeth the nowne (*gisme*) a lying in childbed: or rather of (*gister.* i. *stabulari*) a word proper to a Deare, cùm sub mensem Maium è locis abditis in quibus delituit emigrans, in loco delecto stabulari incipit, vnde commoda & propinqua sit pabulatio. *Budæus in posteriori libro philologiæ.* Where also he saith, that (*giste*) *est idem quod lustrum vel cubile.* Or it may be probably deduced from the Saxon word (*Gast.* i. *hospes.*) It signifieth in our common lawe, to take in and feede the catell of straungers in the kings forest, and to gather the money due for the same to the kings vse, *Charta de Foresta, an.* 9. *H.* 3. *cap.* 9. The Officers that do this, are called (*agistors*) in English, Guest-takers, *eodem. cap.* 8. *Cromptons iurisdic. fol.* 146. These are made by the kings leters patents vnder the great seale of *England*: of whom the King hath foure in number within euery forest, where he hath any pawnage, called *agistors*, or Gist-takers. And their office consisteth in these foure points: (*in agistando, recipiendo, imbreviando, certificando*) *Manwood parte prima.* Of Forest lawes, *p.* 336. & 337. whome you may reade more at large. Their function is tearmed *Agistment*, as agistment vpon the sea banks, *anno* 6. *H.* 6. *cap.* 5.

Agreement (*agreamentum.* i. *aggregatio mentium*) is the assent or cōcord of more to one thing: & this by the author of the newe tearmes of lawe, is either executed

ted or executory: which you may read more at large in him exemplified by cases.

Ayde (*auxilium*) is all one in signification with the French (*aide*) and differeth in nothing, but the onely pronunacitiõ, if we take it as it is vsed in our vulgar language. But in the common lawe, it is applied to divers particular significations, as sometime to a subsidie. *anno.* 14. *Ed.* 3. *stat.* 2. *ca.* 1. sometime to a prestation due from tenents to their Lords, as toward the releife due to the Lord Paramount, *Glanvile li.* 9. *cap.* 8. or for the making of his sonne knight, or the marying of his daughter, *idem, eodem*. This the King, or other Lord by the auncient lawe of *England*, might lay vpon their tenents, for the knighting of his eldest sonne at the age of 15. yeares, or the mariage of his daughter at the age of seuen yeares, *Regist. orig. fol.* 87. *a.* and that at what rate them selues listed. But the Statute, *Westmin.* 1. *anno* 3. *Edw.* 1. ordained a restraint for to large a demand, made by common persons being Lords, in this case, and tyed them to a certaine rate. And the Statute made *anno* 25. *Ed.* 3. *stat.* 5. *cap.* 11. prouideth, that the rate set downe by the former Statute, should hold in the King, as well as in other Lords. Of this I find mention in the Statute, *an.* 27. *H.* 8. *ca.* 10. This imposition seemeth to haue descended to vs from *Normandie*: for in the grand custumarie, *cap.* 35. you haue a Tractate intituled (*des aides chevelz.* i. *de auxilys capitalibus*) whereof the first is (*a faire l'aynè filz de son seigneur chevalier.* i. *ad filium primogenitum militem faciendum*) the second, (*son amee fille marier.* i. *ad filiam primogenitam maritandam.*) And the third, (*a rechapter le corps de son seigneur de prison quand il est prins per la guerre au Duc.* i. *ad corpus domini sui de prisona redimendum cùm captus fuerit pro bello Ducis Normandiæ.* Also I find in *Cassaneus de cõsuet. Burg.* *Quòd dominus accipit à subditis pro dotanda filia, pa.* 122. which seemeth to be all one with this our imposition: and also in *Vincentius de Franchis des. cis.* 131. where he calleth it *adiutorium pro maritanda filia*. Whence it appeareth, that this custome is within the kingdome of *Naples* also. Touching this likewise, you may reade these words in *Manochius, lib.* 2. *de arbitrat. Iud. quæst. centuria.* 2. *cap.* 181. *Habent sæpissimè feudorum possessores & Domini multa in eorum ditionibus privilegia, multasq; cum locorum incolis conuentiones: inter quas, illa vna solet nominari, vt possit Dominus collectam illis indicere, pro solutione dotium suarum filiarum, cum matrimonio collocantur.*

Hoc aliquando Romæ obſervatum à Caligula fuiſſe, in illius vita ſcribit Suetonius, cap. 42. Hodiè hic vſus in ſubalpina regione eſt frequens, vt ſcribit Iacobinus de Sancto Georgio, in tractu de homagiis. col. 8. Etiam pro filia quæ religionem ingreditur: & non modò pro vna filia, ſed pluribus filiabus, non tamen pro ſecundis nuptijs exigitur. In which place, the ſaid author maketh mention of diuers other Civilians and feudiſts, that record this cuſtome to be in other places. Of this aide, our *Fleta* writeth thus: *ſicut etiam quædam conſuetudines quæ ſervitia non dicuntur, nec concomitantia ſeruitiorũ, ſicut rationabilia auxilia ad filium primogenitum militem faciendum, vel ad filiam primogenitã maritandam: quæ quidem auxilia ſunt de gratia & non de iure, pro neceſſitate & indigentia domini capitalis. Et non ſunt prædialia ſed perſonalia, ſecundùm quod perpendi poterit in breui ad hoc prouiſo, &c.*

This word (*ayde*) is alſo particularly vſed in matter of pleading, for a petition made in court for the calling in of helpe from another, that hath an intereſt in the cauſe in queſtion, and is likely both to giue ſtrength to the party that prayeth in aide of him, and alſo to auoide a preiudice growing toward his owne right, except it be preuented. For example: when a tenent for terme of life, by courteſie, tenent in taile after poſſibility of iſſue extinct, for tearme of yeares, at will, by elegit, or tenent by ſtatute merchant being impleaded touching his eſtate, may *petere auxilium*, that is, pray in ayde of him in the reuerſion (that is) deſire or intreate the court, that he may be called in by writ, to alledge what he thinketh good for the maintenance both of his right, and his owne. Termes of the lawe. *Fitzh.* mentioneth both (*prier en ayde*) and (*prier ayde de patron, &c.*) *auxilium petere à patrono, nat. br. fol. 50. d.* and the new booke of entries, *verbo, Ayde de parcener, auxilium de parcionario, fol. 411. columna 4.* This the later practitioners in the ciuill lawe, call *authoris laudationem vel nominationem. Emericus in pract. titulo. 48.* This *ayde prier*, is alſo vſed ſometime in the kings behoofe, that there be no proceeding againſt him, vntill the kings Councell be called, and heard to ſay what they thinke good, for the auoyding of the kings preiudice or loſſe, touching the cauſe in hand. For example: if the kings tenent holding in chiefe, be demaunded a rent of a common perſon, he may pray in ayde of the king. Alſo a citie or borough that hath a fee ferme of the king, any thing being demaunded againſt them which belongeth thereunto, may pray in ayde of

the

the King,&c. Tearms of the law. of this thing you may read the statute (*de bigamis.a.4.Ed.1.ca.1.2.& 3.& anno.14.Ed.3.stat.1.ca.14.* The civile law in suites begunne betweene two, alloweth a third to come in (*pro interesse*) and he that commeth in for his interrest, commeth either *assistendo* or *opponendo, &c.* The former is like to this (*ayde prier*) the other to that which our common lawyers call *Receyte.* Looke *Receyte.*

Aile (*avo*) commeth of the French (*aieul.i. avus*) & signifieth a writ that lieth, where the grãdfather or great grandfather called of our common lawyers (*besayle*) but in true French (*bisaieul*) was seised in his demaines as of fee, of any land or tenement in fee simple, the day that he died, and a stranger abateth or entreth the same day, and dispossesseth the heire. *Fitzh.nat.br.fo.221.*

Alderman (*aldermannus*) is borrowed from the saxon (*Ealderman*) signifying as much as Senator in latine. *Lamb.* in his explica of Saxon words. *verbo senator.* See *Roger Hoveden parte poster. suorum.annal.fo 346.b.*

Aler sans iour, is *verbatim,* to goe without day: the meaning wherof is, to be finally dismissed the courte: because there is no day of farder appearãce assigned, *Kitchin.fo.140.*

Ale-taster, is an officer appointed in every court leete, and sworne to looke to the assise, and the goodnes of bread and ale or beere, within the precincts of that Lordship. *Kitchin. fo. 46.* where you may see the forme of his oath.

Alias v.Capias alias.

Alien (*alienare*) commeth of the French (*aliener*) and signifieth as much as to transferre the propertie of any thing vnto another man. To *alien* in *mortmaine,* is to make over lands or tenements to a religious companie, or other body politike. *Stawnf.præro.fo.48.* looke *Mortmayn.* To alien in fee, is to sel the fee simple of any land or tenement, or of any incorporeall right, *West.2.ca.25. anno.13. Ed. 1.*

Alien alias alion (*alienigena*) commeth of the latine (*alienus*) and signifieth one borne in a straunge country. It is ordinarily taken for the contrarie to (*Denizen*) or a naturall subiect, that is, one borne in a straunge country, and never heere infranchised. *Broke. Denizen.4.&c.* And in this case, a man born out of the land, so it be within the limits of the Kings obedience, beyond the sease, or of English parents, out of the Kings obedience (so the parents at the time of the birth, be of the Kings allegiance) is no alien in account, but a subiect to the King. *Statute.2.a.25.Ed.3.ca. unico.*

vnico. commonly called the Statute, *De natis vltra mare*. Also if one borne out of the kings allegiance, come and dwell in *England*, his children (if he beget any heere) be not aliens, but denizens. Termes of the lawe. See *Denizen*.

Allaye (*Allaia*) is vsed for the temper and mixture of siluer and gold, *anno* 9.*H*.5.*Stat*.2.*cap*.4.& *Stat*. 1.*eiusdem anni*, *cap*.11. The reason of which allay is, with a baser mettall to augment the waight of the siluer or gold so much, as may counteruaile the Princes charge in the coining. *Antonius Faber*.*de nummariorum debitorum solutionibus*, *cap*.1.

Allocatione facienda, is a writ directed to the *Lord* Treasurer, and Barons of the Exchequer, vpõ complaint of some accountant, commaunding them to allow the accountant such sums, as he hath by vertue of his office lawfully and reasonably expended, *Regißter*. *orig*. *fol*. 206.*b*.

Alluminor, seemeth to be made of the French (*allumer*, i. *accendere*, *incendere*, *inflammare*) it is vsed for one that by his trade coloureth or painteth vpon paper or parchment. And the reason is, because he giueth grace, light, and ornament by his colours, to the leters or other figures coloured. You shall find the word, *an*. 1. *R*.3.*ca*.9.

Almaine riuets, be a certaine light kind of armor for the body of a man, with sleeues of maile, or plates of iron, for the defence of his armes. The former of which words, seemeth to shewe the countrie where it was first invented: the other, whether it may come from the French verb (*reveßtir*, i. *superinduere*) to put on vpon another garment, I leaue to farther consideration.

Almner (*eleemosinarius*) is an officer of the kings house, whose function is, *fragmenta diligenter colligere*, *& ea distribuere singulis diebus egenis*: *ægrotos & leprosos*, *incarceratos*, *pauperesq́*, *viduas*, *& alios egenos vagosq́*, *in patria commorantes*, *charitative visitare*: *item equos relictos*, *robas*, *pecuniam*, *& alia ad eleemosynam largita*, *recipere & fideliter distribuere*. *Debet etiam regem super eleemosynæ largitione crebris summonitionibus stimulare*, *& præcipuè diebus Sanctorum*, *& rogare ne robas suas quæ magni sunt pretii*, *histrionibus*, *blanditoribus*, *adulatoribus*, *accusatoribus vel meneßtrallis*, *sed ad eleemosinæ suæ incrementum iubeat largiri*, *Fleta*. *lib*. 2.*cap*.22.

Almoine (*eleemosina*.) See *Frank almoyne*.

Almond (*amygdalum*) is well knowne to euery mans sight: it is the kirnell of a nut or stone, which the tree in Latine called (*amygdalus*) doth beare

with-

within a huske in maner of a walnut, of whose nature, and diuersities, you may reade *Gerards Herball, lib.* 3. *cap.* 87. This is noted among merchandize that are to be garbled, *anno* 1. *Iaco. ca.* 19.

Alnegeor, aliàs, aulnegeor (vlniger vel vlnator) cometh from the French *(aulne)* an elle, or elwand, and signifieth an officer of the Kings, who by himselfe or his deputie, in places conuenient, looketh to the assise of wollen cloth made through the land, and to seals for that purpose ordained vnto them, *an.* 25. *Ed.* 3. *Stat.* 4. *cap.* 1. *anno* 1. *R.* 2. *cap.* 2. who is accomptable to the king for euery cloth so sealed in a fee or custome therunto belonging, *anno* 17. *R.* 2. *cap.* 2. Reade of this more, *anno* 27. *Ed.* 3 *cap.* 4. *anno* 17. *R.* 2. *cap.* 2. & 5. *anno* 1. *H.* 4. *cap.* 13. *anno* 7. *eiusdem. cap.* 10. *anno* 11 *eiusd. cap.* 6. *anno* 13 *eiusd. cap.* 4. *anno* 11. *H.* 6. *cap.* 9. *anno* 31. *eiusdem. cap.* 5. *anno* 4. *Ed.* 4. *ca.* 1. *anno* 8. *eiusdem, cap.* 1. & *an.* 1. *R.* 3. *cap.* 8.

Ambidexter is that iurour or embraceour, that taketh of both parties for the giuing of his verdict. He forfeiteth ten times so much as he taketh, *anno* 38. *Ed.* 3. *cap.* 12. *Cromptons* iustice of peace, *fol.* 156. *b.*

Amendment (emendatio) commeth of the French *(amendement)* and signifieth in our common lawe, a correction of an error committed in a processe, and espyed before iudgment. Termes of the lawe. *Broke, titulo Amendement per totum.* But if the fault be found after iudgment giuen: then is the party that wil redresse it, driuen to his writ of errour. Tearmes of the lawe, *Broke titulo Error.*

Amerciament (amerciamentum) signifieth the pecuniarie punishment of an offendor against the King or other Lord in his court, that is found to be *(in misericordia)* i. to haue offended, and to stand at the mercie of the King or Lord. There seemeth to be a difference betweene amerciaments and fines, *Kitchin fol.* 214. And I haue heard cōmon Lawyers say, that fines, as they are taken for punishments, be punishments certaine, which grow expresly from some statute, and that amerciaments be such, as be arbitrably imposed by affeerors. This is in some sort confirmed by *Kitchin fol.* 78. in these words: *(l'amerciamēt est affire per pares.) M. Manwood* in his first part of Forest lawes, *pag.* 166. seemeth to make another difference, as if he would inferre an amerciamēt to be a more easie, or more mercifull penaltie, and a fine more sharpe and grieuous. Take his wordes: If the pledges for such a trespasse (saith he) do appeare by common summons, but not the defendant himselfe: then the pledges shall be imprisoned, for that default of the defendant: but otherwise it is, if the defendant himselfe do appeare, and be ready in Court before the Lord Iustice in *eyre*, to receiue his iudgment, and to pay his fine. But if such pledges do make default, in that case the pledges shall be amerced, but not fined, &c. The author of the new tearmes of lawe, saith, that amerciament is most properly a penalty assessed, by the peeres or equals of the partie amercied for an offence done, for the which he putteth himselfe vpon the mercie of the Lord. Who also maketh mentiō of an amerciament royal, and defineth it to be a pecuniarie punishment laid vpon a Sheriffe, Coroner, or such like Officer of the kings, amercied by Iustices for his offence. See *Misericordia*.

Amoveas manum. Looke *ouster le maine.*

An, iour, & waste (annus, dies, & vastum.) Looke yeare, day, and waste.

Ancaling of tile, anno. 17. *Ed.* 4. *ca* 4.

Annats, (Annates) seemeth to be all one with first fruites. *anno.* 25. *H.* 8. *ca.* 20. looke, First fruites. The reason is, because the rate of first fruites payed of spirituall liuings, is after one yeares profite. Of which *Polydore Virgil, de inuētione rerum, lib.* 8. *cap.* 2. saith thus: *Nullum inuentum maiores Romano Pontifici cumulavit opes, quàm annatum (quas vocant) vsus, qui omnino multò antiquior est, quàm recētiores quidam scriptores suspicantur. Et annates more suo appellant primos fructus vnius anni sacerdotii vacantis, aut dimidiam eorum partem. Sanè hoc vectigal iampridem, cùm Romanus Pontifex non habuerit tot possessiones quot nunc habet, & eum oportuerit pro dignitate, pro officio, multos magnosque facere sumptus, paulatim impositum fuit sacerdotiis vacantibus quæ ille conferret: de qua quidem re vt gravi, sæpe reclamatum fuisse testatur Henricus Hostiensis, qui cum Alexandro* 4. *Pontifice vixit, sic vt Franciscus Zabarellus tradat post hac in concilio Viennensi, quod Clemens quintus indixit (qui factus est Pontifex anno salutis humanæ,* 135.*) agitatum fuisse, vt, eo deposito, annatum onere vigesima pars vectigalium sacerdotalium penderetur quotannis Romano Pontifici, & id quidem frustrà. Quare Pontifex annatas in sua nassa retinuit, vt ne indidem exire possent: lege cætera.*

Annienied, commeth of the French *(aneantir.* i. *se abiicere, atque prosternere)* It signifieth with our lawyers, as much as frustrated or brought to nothing, *Litleton. lib.* 3. *cap. warrantie.*

Annua pensione, is a writte, whereby

wherby the king hauing due vnto him an annuall pension from any Abbot or Prior for any of his Chaplaines, whom he shal think good to name vnto him, being as yet vnprouided of sufficient liuing, doth demaund the same of the said Abbot or Prior for one, whose name is comprised in the same writ, vntill, &c. and also willeth him, for his Chaplaines better assurance, to giue him his leters patents for the same. *Register orig. fol.* 265. & 307. & *Fitzh. nat. br. fol.* 231. where you may see the names of al the Abbeyes and Priories bound vnto this, in respect of their foundatiõ or creation: as also the forme of the leters patents vsually graunted vpon this writ.

Annuitie (annuus reditus) signifieth a yearely rent to be paide for tearme of life or yeres, or in fee, and is also vsed, for the writ that lyeth against a man for the recouerie of such a rent, either out of his land, or out of his cofers, or to be receiued of his person, at a day certaine euery yere, not satisfying it according to the graunt. *Register. orig. fol.* 158. *Fitz. nat. br. fol.* 152. The author of the new tearmes of law defineth *(annuitie)* to be a certaine summe of money graunted to another in fee simple, fee taile, for tearme of life, or of yeares, to receiue of the graunter, or his heires, so that no Free-hold be charged therewith, whereof a man shall neuer haue assise or other action, but a writ of annuitie. *Saintgerman* in his booke intituled *(The Doctor and Student) dialogo primo, cap.* 3. sheweth diuers differences betweene a rent and an annuitie, whereof the first is, that euery rent, be it rent seruice, rent charge, or rent seck, is going out of land: but an annuity goeth not out of any land, but chargeth onely the person: that is to say, the graunter, or his heires that haue assets by descent, or the house, if it be granted by a house of religion, to perceiue of their coffers. The second difference is, that for the recouerie of an annuity, no action lyeth, but onely the writ of annuitie against the graunter, his heires, or successors: but of a rent, the same actions lye as do of land, as the case requireth. The third difference is, that an annuitie is neuer taken for assets, because it is no Free-hold in lawe, neither shall be put in execution vpon a statute Merchant, statute Staple, or elegit, as a rent may. *Dyer fol.* 345. *num.* 2. speaketh also to this effect:

Annise seede (semen Anisi) is a medicinall seed not vnknowne, so called of the hearbe *anisum*, whereof it is the fruite. Of this he that listeth may reade *Gerards tads herball.li.2.ca.* 397. It is noted among the garbleable drugs and spices. *anno.1.Iaco.ca.*19.

Anoisance, alias Noisance, alias Nusance (nocumentum) commeth of the French (*nuisance.* i *incommodum, noxa*) and hath a double signification, being vsed as well for any hurt done either to a publike place, as (high way, bridge, or common river) or to a private, by laying any thing, that may breede infection, by incroaching, or such like means: as also, for the writ that is brought vpon this transgression: whereof see more in *Nusance.* The word (*anoysance*) I finde, *anno* 22. *H.* 8. *ca.*5.

Apostata capiendo, is a writ that lyeth against one, that hauing entred and professed some order of religon, breaketh out againe, and wandereth the country, contrarily to the rules of his order. For the Abbot or Prior of the house, certifying this into the chawncerie, vnder their common seale, and praying this writ directed to the Shyreeue for the apprehensiõ of such offendour, and for the delivery of him again to his Abbot or Prior, or their lawful atturney, were wont to obtaine the same. The forme whereof, with other circumstances, you shall finde in the *Register. orig.fo.*71. & 267. and *Fitzh. nat. br. fo.* 233. C.

Apparelment, commeth of the French (*pareilement.* i. *similiter, perinde, itidem*) and signifieth a resemblance: as apparelment of warre. *anno* 2.*R.*2.*stat.*1.*ca.*6.

Appeale (*appellum*) commeth of the French (*appeller.*i.*accire, accersere, nominare, evocare, clamore aliquem flagitare*) It signifieth in our common lawe, as much as (*accusatio*) with the civilians. For as in the civile lawe, cognisance of criminal causes, is taken either vpon inquisition, denunciation, or accusation: so in ours, vpon indictment or appeale, indictment comprehending both inquisition, and denunciation. And accusation or apeale, is a lawfull declaration of another mans crime (which by *Bracton* must be felonie at the least in the common lawe) before a competent Iudge, by one that setteth his name to the declaration, and vndertaketh to prooue it, vpon the penaltie that may ensue of the contrary. To declare the whole course of an appeale, we are to much for this treatise. Wherefore for that, I must referre you to *Bractlon.li.*3. *tract.*2.*ca.*18.*cum sequent. Britton, ca.*22.23.24.25. and to *S. Thomas Smith.li.*3.*de repub. Anglo.ca.* 3. and lastly to *Stawnf.pl.cor.li.*2. *ca.*6.7.& *c.usq;* 17. An appeale is commenced two waies: either by writte, or by bill. *Stawnf. vbi supra.fo.*46. And it may be gathe-

red

red by him. *fo.* 148. that an appeale by writ is, when a writ is purchased out of the chauncerie by one to another to this ende, that he appeale a third of some felonie committed by him, finding pledges that he shall doe it, and deliuer this writ to the *Shyreeue* to be recorded. Appeale by bill is, when a man of himselfe giueth vp his accusation in writing to the Vicount or Coroner, offering to vndergoe the burden of appealing another therein named. This pointe of our lawe, among others, is drawne from the *Normans*, as appeareth plainly by the grand custumarie. *ca.* 68. where there is set downe a solemne discourse of both the effects of this appeale. *viz.* the order of the cōbate, & of the tryall by enquest: of which by the common lawe of England, it is in the ioyce of the defendant, whether to take. See the newe booke of entrise. *verbo Appel.* & the booke of Assises. *fo.* 78. *Appel.*

Appeale of *mahem* (*appellum mahemy*) is an accusing of one that hath maymed another. But that being no felony, the appeale thereof is but in a sort, an action of trespas: because there is noe thing recouered but dammages. *Bracton* calleth this (*appellum de plagis & mahemio*) and writeth of it a whole chapter. *li.* 3. *tract.* 2. *ca.* 24. See *S. Ed. Cook.* 4. *vol. fo.* 43. *a*

Appeale of wrong imprisonment (*appellum de pace & imprisonamento*) is vsed by *Bracton*, for an action of wrong imprisonment, whereof he writeth a whole *tractat. li.* 3. *tractat.* 2. *ca.* 25.

Appeale (*appellatio*) is vsed in our common law diuers times, as it is taken in the ciuile lawe: which is a remouing of a cause from an inferiour iudge to a superiour. as appeale to Rome. *an.* 24. *H.* 8. *ca.* 12. & *an.* 1. *Eliz. ca.* 1. But it is more cōmonly vsed, for the priuate accusation, of a murderer by a party, who had interest in the partie murdered or of any felon by one of his complices in the fact. See *Approver.*

Appendant (*appendens*) is any thing belonging to another, as *accessorium principali*, with the Ciuilians, or *adiunctum subiecto*, with the logicians. An hospitall may be appendant to a Maner. *Fitzh. nat. br. fo.* 142. Common of fishing appendant to a free hold. *Westm.* 2. *ca.* 25. *anno.* 13. *Ed.* 1.

Appertinances (*pertinentia*) commeth of the French (*appartenir*. i. *pertinere*) It signifieth in our common lawe, things both corporal, belonging to another thing, as to the more principal: as hamlets to a chiefe Maner, common of pasture, turbarie, piscarie, and such like; and incorporeal, as liberties and seruices of tenents. *Brit. ca.* 39. where I note by the way, that he accounteth common of pasture, turbarie, and piscary, to be things corporal. looke *Common*.

Apporcionment (*Apportionamentū*) is a dividing of a rent into parts, according as the land, whence the whole rent issueth, is divided among two or more. See the new termes of lawe.

Apprentice (*Apprenticius*) commeth of the French (*aprenti*. i. *tyro & rudis discipulus*) or of the verb (*apprendre*. i. *addiscere, discere*) and signifieth with vs, one that is bound by couenant in word or writing, to serue another man of trade for certaine yeares, vpon condition, that the artificer or man of trade, shall in the meane time endeavour to instruct him in his art or misterie. *S. Thomas Smith*, in his booke *de rep. Ang. li.* 3. *ca.* 8. saith, that they are a kinde of bond men, differing onely, in that they be seruants by couenant and for a time. Of these you may reade divers statutes made by the wisedome of our realme, which I thinke superfluous heere to mention.

Appropriation (*appropriatio*) proceedeth from the French (*approprier*. i. *aptare, accommodare*) and properly signifieth, in the lawe of England, a severing of a benefice ecclesiasticall (which originally and in nature is, *iuris diuini & in patrimonio nullius*) to the proper and perpetuall vse of some Religious house or Deane, &c. and Chapter, Bishoprick or Colledge. And the reason of the name I take to be this: because that whereas persons ordinarily be not accounted (*domini*) but (*vsufructuary*) hauing no right of fee simple. *Littleton. titulo Discontinuance*: these, by reason of their perpetuitie, are accounted owners of the fee simple, and therefore are called *proprietary*. And before the time of *Richard* the second, it was lawfull (as it seemeeth) simply, at the least by mans lawe, to appropriate the whole fruites of a benefice to an abbey or priory, they finding one to serue the cure. But that King made so euill a thing more tolerable by a lawe, whereby he ordeined, that in euery licence of appropriation made in chauncerie, it should expresly be contained, that the diocesan of the place should prouide a conuenient summe of money yearely to be paide out of the fruites, toward the sustenance of the poore in that parish, and that the Vicar should be well and sufficiently endowed. *anno.* 15. *Rich.* 2. *ca.* 6. Touching the first institution, & other things worth the learning about appropriations, reade *Plowden in Grendons case. fo.* 496. *b. & seqq.* as also the new termes of lawe, *verbo Appropriation*. To an appropriation, after the licence obteined of the King in chauncerie, the consent of the Diocesan, Patron, and incumbent are necessarie, if the Church be full: but if the Church be voide, the Diocesan and the Patron vpon the Kings licence may conclude it. *Plowden vbi supra.* To dissolue an appropriation, it is enough to present a Clerke to the Bishop. For, that once done, the benefice returneth to the former nature. *Fitzh. nat. br. fo.* 35. *F.*

Approvour (*approbator*) commeth of the French (*approuver*. i. *approbare, comprobare, calculum albo adijcere*) It signifieth in our common law, one that cõfessing felony of him self, appealeth or accuseth another, one or more, to be guilty of the same; & he is called so, because he must prooue that which he hath alleadged in his appeale. *Stawnf. pl. cor. fo.* 142. And that proofe, is by battell or by the countrey, at his election that appealed. The forme of this accusation, you may in part gather by *M. Cromptons* Iustice of peace. *fo.* 250. & 251. that it is done before the coroner, either assigned vnto the felon by the court, to take and record what he saith, or els called by the felon himselfe, and required for the good of the Prince & common wealth, to record that which he saith, &c. The oath of the approuer, when he beginneth the combate, see also in *Crompton* in the very last page of his booke, as also the proclamation by the Herald. Of the antiquity of this law, you may reade something in *Horns myrror of Iustices, l.* 1. *in fine cap. del office del coroner.* Of this also see *Bracton* more at large, *lib.* 3. *tract.* 2. *cap.* 21. & 34. and *Stawnf. pl. cor. lib.* 2. *cap.* 52. *cum seq.*

Approuers of the king (*Appruatores regis*) be such as haue the letting of the kings demeasnes in smal Manors to the kings best aduantage, *anno* 51. *H.* 3. *stat.* 5. See *Approue.*

Approue (*appruare*) commeth of the French (*approuer*, i. *approbare, comprobare, calculum albo adiicere*) it signifieth in the common lawe to augment, or (as it were) to examine to the vttermost. For example: to approue land, is to make the best benefite thereof by increasing the rent, &c. So is the Substantiue (*approuement*) vsed in *Cromptons iurisd. fol.* 153. for the profits them selues. So is it likewise in the statute of *Merton cap.* 4. *anno* 2. *H.* 3 land newly approued, *Old. nat. br. fol.* 79. So the Sheriffes called themselues the kings approuers, *anno* 1. *Ed.* 3. *cap.* 8. which is as much in mine opinion as the gatherers or exactors of the kings profits. And *anno* 9. *H.* 6. *cap.* 10.

Bailiffes

Bailiffes of Lords in their franchises be called their approuers. But *anno* 2. *Ed.* 3. *cap.* 12. Approuers be certaine men especially sent into seuerall counties of the Realme, to increase the Fermes of hundreds and wapentakes, which formerly were set at a certaine rate to the Sheriffes, who likewise dimised them to others, the countie Court excepted.

Approuement (*appruamentum*) see Approue. See the Register iudiciall. *fol.* 8. *br.* & 9. *a.* See the new tearmes of lawe, *verbo* (*Approuement.*)

Arbitratour (*arbiter*) may be taken to proceede from either the Latine (*arbitrator*,) or the French (*arbitre*) it signifieth an extraordinarie iudge in one or moe causes, betweene party and partie, chosen by their mutuall consents, *West. parte* 2. *Symb. titulo Compromisse. Sect.* 21. who likewise diuideth arbitrement, into generall, that is, including all actions, quarels, executions, and demands, and special, which is of one or moe matters, facts, or things specified, *eodem sect.* 2. 3. 4. The Civilians make a difference betweene (*arbitrum & arbitratorem*) *l.* 76. *ff. pro socio.* For though they both ground their power vpon the compromise of the parties: yet their libertie is diuers. For *arbiter* is tyed to proceede and iudge according to lawe with equitie mingled: *arbitrator* is permitted wholy to his owne discretion, without solemnitie of processe, or course of iudgement, to heare or determine the controuersie committed vnto him, so it be *iuxta arbitrium boni viri*.

Arches court (*Curia de arcubus*) is the chiefe and auncientest Cõsistorie, that belongeth to the Archbishop of *Canterburie*, for the debating of spiritual causes: and is so called of the Church in *London* dedicated to the blessed Virgin, commonly called *Bow* church, where it is kept. And the Church is called *Bow* church of the fashion of the Steeple or clocher thereof, whose toppe is raised of stone pillars builded arch-wise, like so many bent bowes.

The Iudge of this Court, is termed the Deane of the Arches, or the officiall of the Arches court. Deane of the *Arches*, because with this officialtie, is commonly ioyned a peculiar iurisdiction of thirteene parishes in *London* tearmed a Deanrie, being exempted from the authoritie of the Bishop of *London*, and belonging to the Archbishop of *Canterburie*: of which the parish of *Bow* is one & the chiefe, because the Court is there kept. Some others say, that he was first called *Deane of the arches*, because

cause the officiall to the Archbishop, being many times employed abroad, in ambassages for the king and realme, the Deane of the Arches was his substitute in his court, and by that meanes the names became confounded. The iurisdiction of this Iudge is ordinarie, and extendeth it selfe through the whole Prouince of *Canterburie*. So that vpon any appeale made, he foorthwith, and without any farder examinatiō of the cause, sendeth out his citation to the party appealed, and his inhibition to the Iudge, from whome the appeale is made. Of this he that will, may reade more in the booke intituled. *De antiquitate Eccelesiæ Britānicæ historia.*

Arma moluta, seeme to be sharpe weapons that doe cut, & not blunt that doe onely breake or bruise. *Bracton. li. 3. tract. 2. ca. 23. & Stawnf. pl. cor. fo. 78. & 79.* whereof *Bracton* hath these words: *arma moluta plagam faciunt, sicut gladius, bisacuta, & huiusmodi: ligna verò & lapides brusuras, orbes, & ictus, qui iudicari non possunt ad plagam ad hoc, vt inde veniri possit ad duellum.*

Armour (*arma*) in the vnderstanding of our common lawe, is extended to any thing, that a man in his anger or furie taketh into his hand, to cast at or strike another. *Cromptons* Iustice of peace. *fo. 65. a.* So, *armorum appellatio, non vtiq; scuta & gladios & galeas significat, sed & fustes & lapides. l. 42. ff. de verbo. significatione.*

Array (*arraia, aliàs arraiamentum*) commeth of the French (*array. i. ordo.*) which is an old word out of vse: or it may be well deduced from (*raye. i. linea*) It signifieth in our commō lawe, the ranking or setting forth of a iurie or enquest of men impaneled vpō a cause. *a. 18. H. 6 c. 14.* Thence is the verb to array a panel. *owld. nat. br. fo. 157.* that is, to set forth one by another, the men empaneled. The array shalbe quashed. *owld. nat. br. fo. 157.* By statute, every array in assise, ought to be made foure daies before. *Broke. titulo Panel. nu. 10.* to chalenge the array. *Kitchin. fo. 92.*

Arreyers, seemeth to be vsed in the *statut. anno. 12. Rich. 2. ca. 6.* for such officers, as had care of the souldiers armour, to see them duly appointed in ther kindes.

Arraine (*arraniare*) commeth of the French (*arranger. i. astituere, ordinare*,) that is, to set a thing in order, or in his place, and the same signification it hath in our common law. For example, he is saide to arraine a writ of *novel disseisin* in a countie, that fitteth it for triall, before the Iustices of that circuit. *owld nat. br. fo. 109. Litleton. fo. 78.* vseth the same word in the same sence. *viz.* the lease arraineth an assise of nouel disseisin. Also a prisoner is said to be arrained, where he is indighted and brought forth to his triall. Arrained within the verge vpon murder. *Stawnf. pl. cor. fo.* 150. The course of this arrainment, you may read in *S. Thomas Smith. de repub. Anglo. li.* 2. *ca.* 23.

Arrearages (arreragia) commeth of the French *(arrierages.* i. *reliqua)* It signifieth the remaine of an account, or a summe of mony remaining in the hands of an accoũtant. It is vsed sometime more generally, for any mony vnpaide at the due time: as arrearages of rent. That this word is borowed from France, it appeareth by *Tiraquel de vtroq; retractu. tomo.* 3. *pa.* 32. *nu.* 10.

Arrest (arestum) commeth of the French *(arrester.* i. *retinere, restare, subsistere)* or rather, it is a French word in it selfe, signifying a setling, stop, or stay, and is metaphorically vsed for a decree or determinatiõ of a cause debated or disputed to and fro, as *(arrest du Senat.* i. *placitum curiæ)* In our comon law, it is taken most of all for a stay or stoppe: as a man apprehended for debt, &c. is said to be arrested. To pleade in arrest of iudgment, is to shew cause why iudgment should be stayed, though the verdict of the 12. be passed. To plead in arrest of taking the enquest vpon the former issue, is to shew cause why an enquest should not be taken, &c. *Broke. tit. Repleder.* Take this of learned *M. Lambard* in his *eirenarch. li.* 1. *ca.* 2. *pa.* 94. *Buda.* (saith he) in his greeke commentaries is of opinion, that the French word *(arrest)* (which with them signifieth a decree or iudgment of court, tooke beginning of the Greeke (ἀρεστόν. i. *placitum)* and as we might say, the pleasure and will of a court. And albeit it were not out of the way to think that it is called an arrest, because it stayeth or arresteth the partie: yet I beleeue rather, that we receiued the same from the Normane lawes, because we vse it in the same sence with thẽ. For commonly with vs, an arrest is taken for the execution of the commaundement of some court, or of some officer in iustice. But howsoeuer the name began: an arrest is a certaine restraint of a mans person, depriuing him of his owne will and libertie, and binding it to become obedient to the will of the lawe. And it may be called the beginning of imprisonment. Precepts & writs of the higher courts of lawe, do vse to expresse it by two sundry words: as *(capias)* and *(attachies)* which signifie to take or catch hold of a man. But this our precept noteth it by the words *(duci facias)* that is, cause him to be conueyed, *&c.* For that the officer hath (after a sort) taken him before, in that he commeth vnto him, and requireth him to go to some Iustice of the peace. Thus farre *M. Lamberd*. And by like this word is spred farder then *France*. For *Gaile* a Germaine writer sheweth by his Tractate (*de arrestis imperii*) that it is vsed also in the imperiall territories, & in the same significatiō, *c.1.n.1.*

Arrestandis bonis ne dissipentur, is a writ which lyeth for him, whose catell or goods are taken by another, that, during the controuersie, doth, or is like to make them away, and will be hardly able to make satisfaction for thē afterward, *Reg. orig. fol.* 126.*b.*

Arrestando ipsum qui pecuniam recepit ad proficiscendum in obsequium Regis, &c. is a writ that lieth for the apprehension of him, that hath taken prest money towards the kings warres, and lieth hidden when he should goe. *Register. orig.* 24. *b.*

Arresto facto super bonis mercatorum alienigenorum, &c. is a writ that lyeth for a denizen against the goods of strangers of any other countrie, found within the kingdome, in recompence of goods taken frō him in the said countrie, after he hath bene denied restitution there. *Register. orig. fo.* 129.*a.* This among the aūciēt Civilians was called (*clarigatio*) now barbarously (*represalia*.

Arretted (*arrectatus*) is he that is conuented before a Iudge, and charged with a crime. *Stawnf. pl. cor. lib.* 2. 45. *quasi ad rectum vocatus*. It is vsed somtime, for (imputed or laid vnto) as, no folly may be arretted to him being vnder age. *Litleton cap. Remitter.* The Latine substantiue (*Rettum*) is vsed in the *Register orig.* *Chawcer* vseth the verb (arretteth) *id est*, layeth blame, as *M. Speight* interpreteth it. I may probably coniecture, that this word is the Latine (*rectum*.) For *Bracton* hath this phrase (*ad rectum habere malefactorem*) i. to haue the malefactor foorth cōming: so as he may be charged, and put to his triall. *lib.* 3. *tract.* 2. *cap.* 10. and in another place (*rectatus de morte hominis*) i. charged with the death of a man, *eod. cap.* 1. *num.* 3.

Articles of the Cleargie (*articuli Cleri*) be certaine statutes made touching persons and causes ecclesiasticall, *anno* 9. *Ed.* 2. Like vnto which there were other made, *anno* 14. *Ed.* 3. *stat.* 3.

Assay of measures and waights (*assaia mensurarum & ponderum*) *Register. orig. fol.* 279. is the examination vsed by the Clerke of the market.

Assayer of the king, is an officer of the mint, for the due triall of siluer, indifferently appointed betwixt the maister of the Mint, and the merchants that bring siluer thither for exchange. *anno* 2. *H.6. cap.* 12.

Assault, insultus, commeth of the French verb (*assailir.* i. *adoriri, appetere*, *invadere*) which French also proceedeth from the Latine (*assilire.* i. *vim afferre, oppugnare.*) It signifieth in our common lawe, a violent kind of iniurie, offered to a mans person, of a higher nature then batterie. For it may be committed by offering of a blowe, or by fearefull speech. *M. Lamberd* in his *eirenar. lib.* 2. *cap.* 3. whome reade. The feudists call this (*assultum*) and define it thus: *Assultus, est impetus in personam aut locum, siue hoc pedibus fiat vel equo, aut machinis, aut quacunque alia re assiliatur. Zasius de feud. parte* 10. *nu.* 38. And (*assilire*) *est, vim adferre, adoriri, oppugnare, li. feud.* 1. *tit.* 5. §. 1.

Assach, seemeth to be a Welch word, and to signifie so much, as a kind of excuse, or strange kind of purgation by the oathes of three hundred men. *anno* 1. *H.* 5. *cap.* 6.

Assart (*assartum*) in *M. Manwoods* iudgement, *parte.* 2. *ca.* 9. *nu.* 5. of his forest lawes, commeth of the French (*assortir*) signifying (as he saith) to make plaine, or to furnish; but rather indeede, to set in order and handsomly to dispose. *Assartum est, quod redactum est ad culturam. Fleta. li.* 4. *ca.* 21. §. *Item respondere.* It signifieth, as the said *M. Manwood* saith. *nu.* 1. *vbi supra*, an offence committed in the forest, by plucking vp those woods by the rootes, that are thickets or coverts of the forest, and by making them plaine, as earable land, where he also saith, that an *assart* of the Forest, is the greatest offence or trespasse of all other, that can be done in the forest, to vert or venison, containing in it as much as waste or more. For whereas the waste of the Forest, is but the felling and cutting downe of the couerts, which may grow againe in time: an *assart*, is a plucking them vp, &c. which he confirmeth out of the redde booke in the Exchequer, in these words: *Assarta verò, occasiones nominantur, quando sc: forestæ nemora vel dumeta, pascuis & latibulis ferarum oportuna, succiduntur: quibus succisis & radicitus avulsis, terra subvertitur & excolitur.* And again out of the Register *originall. fo.* 257. *a. b.* in the writ (*ad quod damnum*) sent out in case, where a man sueth for a licence, to assart his grounds in the Forest, and to make it severall for tillage. Soe that it is no offence, if it be done with licence. To this, may Bracton also be added. *li.* 4. *ca.* 38 *nu.* 11. where he saith, that these words (*boscus efficitur assartum*) signifie as much, as (*redactus in culturam*) of this you may read more in *Cromptons Iurisdictions.fo.* 203.and in *chart 2 de foresta,anno.* 9.*H.*3. *ca*.4. where the english word is not (*assart*) but assert, & in *Manwood,parte*.1. of his Forest lawes.*pa*.171. The word is vsed. *anno*.4.*Ed*.1. *stat*.1. in the same signification. That which we call (*assartum*) is els where tearmed *Disboscatio.Decis.Genu*.74.

Assembly vnlawfull, (*illicita assemblata*) cometh of the French (*assembler*.i. *aggregare*) whence also is the substantiue (*assemblee*.i. *coitio, congregatio*) It is in our common lawe (as *M. Lamberd* defineth it,*eiren. li*.1.*ca*.19.) the companie of 3.persons (or more) gathered together to doe an vnlawfull act, although they doe it not. See vnlawfull assemblie.

Assets (*quod tantundem valet*) *Bract.li*.5.*tract*.3.*ca*.8.*nu*.2.is nothing but the French (*assez*. i.*satis*) For though this word masque vnder the vizard of a substantiue, it is in truth but an adverb. It signifieth in our common lawe, goods enough to discharge that bruden, which is cast vpon the executour or heire, in the satisfying of the testators or aunceestors debts or legacies. See *Brooke,titulo Assets per discent*: by whome you shall learne, that whosoeuer pleadeth assets, sayeth nothing, but that he against whome he pleadeth, hath enough descended or come to his hands, to discharge that which is in demaūd. The author of the newe tearmes of lawe, maketh.2. sorts of assets, *viz.assets par discent*, & *assets enter mains*. the former, being to be alleaged against an heire, the other, against an executor or administrator.

Assigne(*assignare*) both it selfe, and the French (*assigner*) come of the latine. It hath two significations: one generall: as to appoint a *depute*, or to set ouer a right vnto another. In which signification, *Britton*. *fo*.122. saith this word was first brought into vse, for the fauour of Bastards; because they cannot runne vnder the name of heires to their fathers, and therefore were, & are comprised vnder the name of (*assignees*) The other signification of this word is especial, as to appointe at, or set forth. *viz*.to assigne errour.*old.br.nat.fo*.19.is to shew in what part of the proces errour is committed. To assigne false iudgement.*eodem.fo* 17.that is, to declare how and where the iudgement is vniust. To assigne a false verdict. *eodem.fo*.112.and to assigne an oath to be false. *anno*. 9.*R*.2.*ca*.3. To assigne the cessor, *old.nat.br.fo*.134.1. to shew how the plaintife had cessed, or giuen ouer. To assigne wast, is to shewe, wherein especially the wast is cōmitted.*Reg. orig f*.72.

Assigne, in the generall signification is vsed. *anno* 20. *Ed* 1. *&* *anno* 11. *H. 6. cap.* 2. in these words: Iustices assigned to take assises. And the Substantiue (*assignement*) hath the same signification. *Wests symb. parte* 1. *lib.* 2. *sect.* 496. *& seq.* In which maner is also vsed the adiectiue (*assignee, assignatus*) *viz.* for him that is appointed or deputed by another to do any act, or performe any businesse, or enioy any commoditie. And an *assignee* may be either in deed, or in law. *Assignee* in deed, is he that is appointed by a person, an *assignee* in lawe is he, whom the lawe so maketh without any appointment of the person. *v. Dyer fol.* 6. *num.* 5. *Perkins* in *Grauntes* saith, that an *assignee* is he, that occupieth a thing in his owne right, and *depute*, he that doth it in the right of another.

Assise (*assisa*) commeth of the French (*assise*) which in the grand custumarie of *Normandy*, *cap.* 24. is defined to this effect. *Assise* is an assembly of Knights and other substantiall men, with the Bailiffe or Iustice in a certain place, and at a certaine time appointed. And againe, *cap.* 55. *Assise* is a court, in the which whatsoeuer is done, ought to haue perpetuall strength. This Normane word (*assise*) commeth of the French (*asseoir*. i. *collocare*) to settle or bestow in some place certaine: as (*s'asseoir*) is to sit downe by another. And metaphorically it is vsed of things incorporeall: as (*asseoir son iugement sur quelque lieu*) is, *interponere iudicium suum*. Of this verbe commeth the participle (*assis*) as (*estre assis*) i. *sedere*. And this Participle in the grand custumarie of *Normandie*, *cap.* 68. is vsed, as we would say: appointed, limited, or determined, *viz.* (*au iour qui est assis à faire la battaille, se doibuent les champions offrir á la iustice*) that is: at the day which is appointed for the combat, the champions ought to offer themselues to the Iustice. So that by all these places compared together, it is euident whence the original of this word (*assise*) floweth. How diuersly it is vsed in our common lawe, it followeth that we declare. First *Litleton* in the chapter, *Rents.* saith, that it is *aequivocum*: where he setteth downe three seuerall significations of it: one, as it is taken for a writ: another, as it is vsed for a Iurie: the third, as for an ordinance. And him, he that listeth, may reade more at large. My collections haue serued me thus: first (*assise*) is taken for a writ directed to the Shyreeue, for the recouerie of possession of things immoueable, whereof your selfe, or your auncestor haue bene

disseised.

disseised. And this is as well of things corporall as incorporeall rights, being of foure sorts: as here they follow in their order.

Assise of novel disseisin (*assisa novæ disseisina*) lyeth where a tenent in Fee-simple, Fee-taile, or for tearme of life, is lately disseised of his lands or tenements, or else of a rent seruice, rent seck, or rent charge, of common of pasture, of an office, of tolle, tronage, passage, pownage, or for a nusance leuied, and diuers other such like. For confirmation whereof, you may reade *Glanvile lib.* 10. *cap.* 2. *Bracton lib.* 4. *tract.* 1. *per totum. Britton cap.* 70. *& seqq. Register orig. fol.* 197. *Fitz. nat. br. fol.* 177. 178. 179. new booke of entries. *fol.* 74. *col.* 3. *West.* 2. *cap.* 25. *anno* 13. *Ed.* 1. And to this may aptly be added the Bill of fresh force (*friscæ fortiæ*) which is directed to the officers or magistrates of Cities or Townes corporate, being a kinde of assise for recovery of possession in such places within 40. daies after the force, as the ordinarie assise is in the countie. *Fitzh. nat. br. fo.* 7. c. This the Civilians call, *iudicium possessorium recuperandi*.

Assise of mort d' auncester (*assisa mortis antecessoris*) lyeth, where my father, mother, brother, sister, vncle, aunte, &c. died seised of lands, tenements, rents, &c. that he had in fee simple, and after his death a straunger abateth: an it is good, as well against the abatour, as any other in possession: How likewise this is extended, see *Bracton. li.* 4. *tract.* 3. *per totum. Britton. ca.* 70. *cum multis sequent. Fitzh. nat. br. fo.* 114. *Register. orig. fo.* 223. This the Civilians call, *Iudicium possessorium adipiscendi*.

Assise of darrein presentment (*assisa vltima præsentationis*) lieth, where I, or mine auncestor haue presented a Clerke to a Church, and after (the Church being voide by the death of the said Clerke or otherwise) a straunger presenteth his Clerke to the same Church, in disturbance of me. And how otherwise this writ is vsed, See *Bracton. li.* 4. *tract.* 2. *Register. orig. fo.* 30. *Fitzh. nat. br. fo.* 195.

Assise de vtrum (*assisa vtrum*) lieth either for a parson against a lay man, or a lay man against a parson, for land or tenement doubtfull, whether it be lay fee, or free almes. And of this, see *Bracton. li.* 4 *tract.* 5. *cap.* 1. *& seqq. Brit. ca.* 95. The reason why these writs be called assises, may be diuers. First, because they settle the possession, and so an outward right in him that obteineth by them. Secondly, they were originally spedde and executed at a certaine time and place formerly appointed. For by the Norman law, the time and place must

must be knowne 40.daies before the Iustices sate of them: and by our lawe, there must be likewise 15.daies of preparation, except they be tried in those standing courts of the king in *Westminster*: as appeareth by *Fitzh. nat.br.fo.* 177.*D. E.* Lastly, they may be called assises, because they are tried most commonly by especial courts, set & appointed for the purpose: as may be well proved not onely out of the custumarie of Normandie, but our bookes also: which shew, that in auncient times, Iustices were apointed by especiall commission, to dispatch controversies of possession, one or more, in this or that onely countie, as accasion fell out, or disseisins were offered, & that as well in terme time, as out of terme: whereas of later daies, wee see that all these commissions of assises, of *eyre*, of *oyer* & *terminer*, of *gaol deliuerie*, and of *nisi prius*, are dispatched all at one time, by two severall circuits in the yeare, out of terme, and by such as haue the greatest sway of Iustice, being al of them, either the Kings ordinarie Iustices of his benches, Sergeants at the lawe, or such like.

Assise, in the second signification (according to *Litleton*) is vsed for a Iurie. For (to vse his owne example) it is set downe in the beginning of the record of an assise, of *novel disseisin*. *Assisa venit recognitura*; which is as much to say, as *Iuratores veniunt recognituri*. The reason why the Iurie is called an assise, he giueth to be this: because by the writte of assise, the Shyreeue is commaunded, *quòd faciat duodecim liberos & legales homines de viceneto &c. videre tenementum illud, & nomina eorum imbreviari, & quod summoneat eos per bonas summonitiones, quòd sint coram Iustitiarijs, &c. parati inde facere recognitionem, &c.* This is (as if he should haue spoken shorter) *metonymia effecti*. For they are called the *assises*, because they are summoned by vertue of the writ so termed. And yet the Iurie summoned vpon a writ of right, is likewise called the assise, as himself there confesseth: which writ of right is not an assise. But this may be said to be καταχρηστικῶς, or abusiuely so tearmed. *Assise*, in this signification, is diuided *in magnam & parnam. Glanvile lib.* 2.*ca.* 6.7.*&c.* and *Britton.c.* 12.where it appeareth, wherein the great assise differeth from the petit assise: whome I wish to be read, by those that would be furder instructed in this point. For this place, thus much in short. The former 4.kindes of assises vsed in actions only possessory, be called petit assises, in respect of the graund assise. For the law of feese is groũded vpon two rights: one of possession, the other of propertie: and as the grand assise serueth for the right of property, so the petit assise serueth for the right of possession. *Horns* myrror of Iustices, *lib.* 2. *cap. de novel. disseisin.*

Assise in the third signification according to *Litleton*, is an ordinance or statute: as the statute of bread and ale made, *anno* 51. *H.* 3 is termed the assise of bread and ale (*assisa panis & ceruiciæ*, *Regist. orig. fol.* 279.*b.* The assise of *Clarendon*, (*assisa de Clarendon*) wherby those that be accused of any hainous crime, and not able to purge themselues by fire and water, but must abiure the realme, had libertie of 40. daies to stay, and trie what succour they could get of their friends, toward their sustenance in exile. *Stawnf. pl. cor. fol.* 118. out of *Bracton li.* 3. *tract.* 2. *cap.* 16. *num.* 2. Of this also *Roger Hoveden* maketh mention, and more particularly then any that I haue read, *parte poster. suorum annalium, fol.* 313.*b. in Henrico secundo.* Assise of the Forest, (*assisa de Foresta*) which is a statute or constitution touching orders to be obserued in the kings forest. *Manwood parte.* 1. of his Forest lawes, *pag.* 35. *Crompton* in the Court of the Iustices of the Forest *per totum, fol.* 146. *& seq.* And the assise of the king, *anno.* 18. *Ed.* 3. *stat.* 1. called the statute for view of Francke pledge. And these be called assises, because they set downe and appoint a certaine measure, rate, or order in the things which they concerne. Of assise in this signification doth *Glanvil* also speake, *lib.* 9. *cap.* 10. *in fine. Generaliter verum est quod de quolibet placito quod in comitatu deducitur & terminatur, misericordia quæ inde prouenit, vicecomiti debetur: quæ quanta sit, per nullam assisam generalem determinatum est.* And thus much touching *Litletons* diuisiõ. But if we marke well the writers of the lawe, we shall find this word (*assise*) more diuersly vsed, then this author hath noted. For it is vsed sometime for the measure or quantity it selfe, (and that *per Metonymiam effecti*) because it is the very scantline described or commaunded by the ordinance: as for example we say, when wheate, &c. is of this price, then the bread, &c. shall be of this assise. This word is furder taken, for the whole processe in court vpon the writ of assise, or for some part therof, as the issue or verdict of the Iury. For example, assises of new disseisin, &c. shall not be taken, but in their shires, and after this maner, &c. *mag. char. cap.* 12. And so it seemeth to signifie, *Westm.* 2. *cap.* 25. *anno* 13. *Ed.* 1. in these words:

let the disseissours alledge no false exceptions, whereby the taking of the assises may be deferred,&c. And *anno* 34. *Ed.* 1. *stat.* 2. if it be found by assise: the assise is arrained: to averre by the assise: the assise by their default shal passe against them: and also *an.* 1. *H.* 6. *cap.* 2. assises awarded by default of the tenents,&c. Lastly, by *Merton, cap.* 4. *anno* 20. *H.* 3. certified by the assise, quite by the assise,&c. And in this signification, *Glanvile* calleth it, *magnam assisam domini regis: quæ ex duodecim ad minus legalium hominum sacramentis consistit .lib.* 2. *cap.* 7. *Bracton* vseth it in like sort: as *assisa cadit in transgressionem. lib.* 4. *cap.* 30. *& assisa cadit in perambulationem. eodem. cap.* 31. *num.* 2. *Fleta* defineth an assise in this signification, thus: *Assisa in iure possessorio, est quædam recognitio duodecim hominum iuratorum, per quam Iusticiarij certiorantur de articulis in breui contentis.* An assise also thus signifying, is said sometime to passe, (*per modum assisæ*) and sometime *in modum iuratæ.* in maner of an assise, when onely the disseisin in question, is put to the trial of the twelue: in maner of a iurie, when as any exception is obiected to disable the interest of the disseisee, and is put to be tryed by the twelue, before the assise can passe. As for example: *Quæstio status, causa successionis, causa donationis, pactum siue conditio vel cōuentio, voluntas & dissimulatio, transactio, vel quietaclamatio vel remissio, confirmatio siue consensus, propria vsurpatio rei propriæ, difficultas iudicij, iustum iudicium, finis, chirographum, intrusio in rem alienam, vel disseisina, si incontinenti reijciatur, negligentia quæ per transitum temporis excludit actionem. Fleta. lib.* 4. *cap.* 10. §. 1. whome reade also to this point, *cap.* 11. §. *Si autem à Domino:* and at large, *cap.* 16. *eiusdem libri. & lib.* 5. *cap.* 6. §. *Item vertitur assisa & seq.* And note that assise in this signification, is taken foure waies, *Old nat. br. fol.* 105. The first, is assise at large, which is taken aswell vpon other points, as vpon the disseisin. For example, where an infant bringeth an assise, and the deed of his auncestor is pleaded, whereby he claimeth his right or foundeth his title: then the assise shall be taken at large: that is, the Iurie shall enquire, not onely whether the plaintiffe were disseised or not by the tenent, but also of these other points: *viz.* whether his auncestor were of full age, of good memorie, and out of prison, when he made the deed pleaded. Another example out of *Kitchin, fol.* 66. The tenent pleadeth a forraine release, in barre to an assise, whereupon the cause was adiourned. At the

day

day the tenent maketh default. Therefore the asise was taken at large: that is, not onely whether the plaintiffe were disseised, but also whether there be any such forraine release. A third example you may reade in *Litleton. cap.* Estates vpon condition. The second maner of asise in point of asise (*assisa in modum assisæ*) which is, when the tenent, as it were, setting foote to foot with the demandant, without furder circumstance, pleadeth directly contrarie to the writ, no wrong, no disseisin. The third manner is, asise out of the point of asise (*assisa extra assisam, vel in modum iuratæ.*) *viz.* when the tenent alledgeth some by exception, that must be tried by a Iurie, before the principall cause can proceed: as if he pleade a foreine release, or foreine mater tryable in another countie. For in this case, the Iustices referre the record to the Court of common plees, for the triall of the foreine plee, before the disseisin can come to be discussed. Of this sort reade diuers other examples in *Bracton, lib.* 4. *part.* 1. *cap.* 34. For there be of them (as he saith) and *Britton* also, *cap.* 52. both dilatorie and peremptorie. The fourth and last manner is: asise of right of dammages, and that is, when the tenent confessing a putting out, and referring it to a demurrer in lawe, whether it were rightly done or not, is adiudged to haue done wrong. For then shall the demandant haue a writ to recouer dammages, which is called asise to recouer dammages, as also the whole processe.

Assise, is further taken for the court, place, or time, where and when the writs and processes of asise be handled or taken. And in this signification asise is generall: as when the Iustices passe their seuerall circuits, euery couple with their commission, to take all asises twice in the yeare. For he that speaketh of any thing done, at that time, and in that place, will commonly say, that it was done at the generall asise. It may likewise be speciall, in this signification: as if an especiall commission should be granted to certaine (as in ancient times they often were, *Bracton. lib.* 3. *cap.* 11. *in fine*) for the taking of an asise vpon one disseisin or two: any thing done in the court before them, a man would say, it was done at such an especiall asise. And in this very signification doth *Glanvil* vse it, *lib.* 9. *cap.* 12. in these words: *Si contra dominum suum & non infra assisam, tunc distringitur ipse occupator, &c.* and *lib.* 13. *cap.* 32. in these words: *cùm quis itaque infra assisam domini regis.i. infra tempus à domino rege de consilio procerum ad hos constitutum, quod quandoq; maius, quandoq; minus censetur, alium iniustè & sine iudicio disseisiverit, &c.* Of this word asſiſe, you may reade in *M. Skene, de verbo. signif. verbo. Asſiſe*, and by him vnderſtand, that in *Scotland* alſo it is diuerſely vſed, *viz.* in 5. ſeuerall ſignifications. And touching the fifth ſignification, he hath theſe words: An aſſiſe is called a certaine number of men lawfully ſummoned, receiued, ſworne and admitted to iudge and diſcerne in ſundrie civil cauſes, ſyke as perambulations, cognitions, moleſtations, *pourpreſture*, diviſion of lands, ſeruing of brieues, and in all and ſundrie criminall cauſes decided and tried by an aſſiſe: whereof there are two kinds: one ordinarily in vſe, which may be called a litle aſſiſe of the number of 13. or 15 perſons: the other, called a great aſſiſe, which conſiſteth of 25. perſons, &c. The reſt is very worthe the reading.

Aſſiſa continuanda, is a writte directed to the Iuſtices aſſigned to take an aſſiſe, for the continuance of the cauſe, in caſe where certaine records alleaged, cannot in time be procured by the party that would vſe it. *Reg orig. f.* 217.

Aſſiſa proroganda, is a writ directed to the Iuſtices of aſſiſe, for the ſtay of proceeding, by reaſon of the Kings buiſnes, wherein the partie is imploied. *Regiſter. orig. fo.* 208. and *fo.* 221.

Aſſociation (*aſſociatio*) is a patent ſent by the King, either of his owne motion, or at the ſuite of the plaintife, to Iuſtices appointed to take aſſiſes of *novel diſſeiſin*, or of *oyer* and *terminer*, &c. to take others vnto them as felowes and collegues in that buſines. The dirivation is plaine: the examples, and ſundrie vſes hereof you may finde, in *Fitzh. nat. br. fo.* 185. *E.* & *fo* 111. *B.* but more particularly in the *Reg. orig. f.* 201. 202. 205. 206. 207. 223. 224.

Aſſoile (*abſolvere*) commeth of the French (*abſouldre*) and ſignifieth to deliuer or ſet free from an excommunication. *Stawnf. pl. cor. fo.* 72. in words to this effect: Otherwiſe the defendãt ſhould remaine in priſon, vntill the plaintiffe were aſſoyled, that is, deliuered from his excommunication.

Aſſumpſit, is a voluntarie promiſe made by word, whereby a man aſſumeth or taketh vpon him to performe or pay any thing vnto another. This word containeth any verball promiſe made vpon conſideration, which the Civilians expreſſe by divers words, according to the nature of the promiſe, calling it ſometime *pactum*, ſometime *ſponſionẽ*, ſometime *promiſſionem, pollicitationem* or *conſtitutum*, the word ſeemeth to be drawne from the latine

tine (*assumptio*) *quæ significat professionem. l. π. ad municipalem.*

Attache (*attachiare*) cõmeth of the French (*attacher.* i. *figere, nectere, illigare, defigere, alligare*) In our common lawe it signifieth, to take or apprehend by commaundement or writte. And *M. Lamberd* in his *eirenarch. li.* 1. *cap.* 16. maketh this difference betweene an arrest and an attachement, that an arrest proceedeth out of lower courts by precept, and an attachment out of higher courts by precept or writ: and that a precept to arrest hath these formall words (*duci facias &c*) and a writ of attachment these words: (*præcipimus tibi quòd attachies talem, & habeas eum coram nobis &c.* whereby it appeareth, that he which arresteth, carrieth the party arrested to another higher person to be dispozed of forthwith, he that attacheth, keepeth the party attached, and presenteth him in court at the day assigned in attachement. yet I obserue out of *Master Kitchin*, that an attachement issueth out of a court baron, which is a lowe court. *cap*: *Attachment in court baron, fo.* 79. Another difference there is, that an arrest lieth onely vpon the body of a man, and an attachement sometime vpon his good, as shalbe shewed in the sequele. It may be likewise asked how an attachement and a (*capias*) doe differ: & how an attachement and a (*cape*) and an attachement and a distresse. First that an attachement differeth from a (*capias*) it appeareth by *Kitchin* in these words: *fo.* 79. Note that in a court Baron a man shalbe attached by his goods; and a (*capias*) shall not goe out thence. wherby I gather, that an attachement is more generall, taking hold of a mans goods, and a (*capias*) of his body onely. Then an attachement differeth from a (*cape*) in this, because a (*cape*) be it (*cape magnum*) or (*cape parvum*) taketh hold of immoveables, as lands or tenements, and are properly belonging to action reall: as you may gather out of their formes, in *Fitzh. nat. br.* whereas attachemẽt hath rather place in actions personall, as *Bracton* plainly setteth downe. *li.* 4. *tracta.* 4. *ca.* 5. *nu.* 3. Where neuerthelesse it appeareth, that a (*cape*) may be likewise vsed in an action personall. An attachement (as it is formerly said) taketh hold of moueable goods or the bodie. For it appeareth, by *Kitchin. fo.* 263. that a man may be attached by a hundred sheepe. Reade *Skene, de verbo. signific. verbo attachiamentum.*

Now it followeth to shew how attachement differeth from a distresse. For so it doth, as may be shewed out of *Kitchin, fo.* 78.

where he saith, that processe in co[u]rt baron, is summons, attachment, and distresse, out of the *owld.nat.br.fo.*27. where it is said, that a processe in a (*quare impedit*) is summons, attachement, and one distresse, and, againe *fo.* 28. wheare (speaking of the writ) *ne admittas*) he saieth thus: and the processe is one prohibition, and vpon the prohibition an attachment and distresse, and *fo.* 32. in a writ of (*Indicauit*) you haue these words: and after the attachment returned, the distresse shall goe out of the rols of the Iustices. *Bracton* on the other side, *li.* 5. *tract.* 3. *ca.* 4. *nu.* 2. sheweth, that both (*attachiamentum, & magnum cape, districtiones sunt*). of which opinion *Fleta* also is, *li.* 5. *ca.* 24. §. *si autem ad.* But there also he saith, that (*attachiamentum est districtio personalis, & cape magnum districtio realis.* So that by his opinion, *districtio is* (*genus*) to attachement. *Britton* in his 26. chapter, hath words to this effect: but in attachement of felony, there commeth no distresse, otherwise then by the body. And if the Shyreeue return in the cases aforesaid, that the trespassours haue nothing in his baylywick, by the which they may be distreined, it must be awarded that he take their bodies, &c. In which place, an attachement is plainly vsed, for an apprehension of an offender by his goods. So that to conclude, I finde no difference between an attachment, and a distresse, but these two; that an attachement reacheth not to lands, as a distresse doth, and that a distresse toucheth not the bodie (if it be properly taken) as an attachement doth. yet are they diuers times confounded, as may appeare by the places formerly alleadged, and by *Glanvile.li.* 10. *ca.* 3. and *Fleta. li.* 2. *ca.* 66. *& seqq.* How be it, in the most common vse, an attachment is an apprehẽsion of a man by his body, to bring him to answer the action of the plaintiffe: a distresse is the taking of another mans goods, for some reall cause, as rent, seruice, or such like, whereby to driue him to replevie, and so to be plaintiffe in an action of trespas, against him that distreined him. And so much for the difference, and coherẽcie of these words. See also Distres.

I finde in *West. parte.* 2. *symbolaio. titulo* proceedings in chauncerie. *sect.* 22. 23. that attachemẽt out of the chaũcery is two-fold, one simple, and originally decreed for the apprehension of of the partie: the other, after return made by the Shyreeue *quod defendens non est inventus in baliva sua*, with proclamations made through the whole countie, in such places, as he shall thinke

meete,

meete, that the partie appeare by a day assigned, and that he attached never the lesse, if he may be found. This second kinde hath an affinitie with the canonists (*vijs & modis*) at the which if the partie apppeare not, he is excommunicate: or with the Civilians (*vijs & modis vnâ cum intimatione*) For in the chāucerie, if he com not vpō this, he is forthwith pressed with a writ of rebellion.

There is an attachment of priviledge, which is a power to apprehend a man in a priviledged place, or els, by vertue of a mans priuiledge, to call another to this or that courte, whereunto he himselfe belongeth, and in respect whereof, he is priviledged. Newe booke of entrise. *verbo priviledge. fo 431. col. 2.* There is also a foreine attachement, which is an attachement of a foriners goods found within a libertie or citie, to satisfie some creditour of his within the citie. There is also an attachement of the forest, which is a court there held. For (as *M. Manwood* saith) in his first parte of forest lawes, *p. 90. 92. 99.* there be three courts of the forest, wherof the lowest is called the (*Attachement*) the meane, the (*swaynemote*) the highest, the (*Iustice seate in eyre.*) This court of attachement seemeth so to be called, because the verderours of the forest haue therein no other authoritie, but to receiue the attachements of offenders against vert and venison, taken by the rest of the officers, and to enrol them, that they may be presented and punished at the next Iustice seate. *Manwood. parte. 1. pa. 93.* And this attaching is by three meanes, by goods and cate's, by body, pledges, and mainprise, or by the body onely. The courte is kept euery. 40. daies throughout the yere. And he that hath occasion to learne more of this, I refer, him to *M. Manwood, loco quo supra,* & to *M. Crompton* in his courte of the forest. Attachement is commaunded in writs, the diversitie whereof you may see, in the *Register originall* vnder the word *Attachiamentum in indice.*

At large, see assise at large in the word assise, and *owld nat. br. fo. 105.* Verdict at large. *Lutleton. fo. 98.* To vouch at large. *owld. nat. br. fo. 108.* To make title at large. *Kitchin. fo. 68.* See *Barre.*

Attaint (*attincta*) commeth of the French, as you shall see in the word (*attainted*) But as it is a substantiue, it is vsed for a writ that lyeth after iudgement, against a Iurie that hath giuen a false verdict in any court of record (be the action reall or personall) if the debt or dammages surmount the summe of 40. shillings: what the forme of the writ is, and how in in vse it is extended, see *Fitz. na. br. fol.* 105. and the new booke of entries, *fol.* 84. *colum.* 1. The reason why it is so called, seemeth to be, because the partie that obtaineth it, endeuoureth thereby to touch, deprehend, or staine the Iurie with periurie, by whose verdict he is grieued. What the punishment of this periurie is, or of him that bringeth the writ against the Iurie, if he faile in his proofe, see *Glanvile lib.* 2. *cap.* 19. *Fitz. nat. br. fol.* 109. *K. L.* & 110. *A. B. C. D.* &c. the termes of the lawe, *verb. Attaint. Fortescue cap.* 26. *Smith de rep. Anglo. lib.* 3. *cap.* 2. and *anno* 11. *H.* 7. *cap.* 21. & *an.* 23. *H.* 8. *cap.* 3. and others. In what diuersitie of cases this writ is brought, see the *Register orig. in Indice.*

Attainted (*attinctus*) commeth of the French (*teindre.* i. *tingere:* the participle whereof is (*teinct.* i. *tinctus,*) or else of (*attaindre.* i. *assequi, attingere.*) It is vsed in our common lawe, particularly for such as are found guiltie of some crime or offence, and especially of felonie or treason. How be it a man is said to be attainted of of disseisin. *Westm.* 1. *cap.* 24. & 36 *anno* 3. *Ed.* 1. And so it is taken in French likewise (as *estre attaint & vayncu en aucun cas*) is to be cast in any case. Which maketh me to thinke that it rather cometh from (*attaindre*) as we would say in english catched, ouertaken, or playnly deprehended. And *Britton ca.* 75. vseth the participle (*attaint*) in the sence that we say (attained vnto) A man is attainted by two meanes: by appearance or by proces. *Stawnf. pl. cor. fo.* 44. Attaynder by by apparence, is by confession, by battelll, or by verdict. *idem. fo.* 122. Confession whereof attaynt groweth, is double: one at the barre before the iudges, when the prisoner vpon his endictment read, being asked guilty or not guilty, answeareth guilty, neuer putting himselfe vpon the verdict of the Iurie: the other is before the coroner in sanctuarie, where he vpon his confession was in former times constreyned to abiure the Realme. which kinde also of the effect, is called attaynder by abiuration. *Idem. fo.* 182. Attaynder by battel is, when the party appealed by another, and chusing to trie the the truth by combat rather then by Iurie, is vanquished. *Idem. fo.* 44. Attaynder by verdict is, when the prisoner at the barre answering to the endictment, not guilty: hath an enquest of life and death passing vpon him, and is by their verdict or doome pronounced guiltie. *Idem fo.* 108. & 192. Attainder by processe (otherwise called attainder by de-

default, or attainder by outlagarie) is where a partie flieth, and is not found vntill he haue bene fiue times called publikely in the countie, and at the last out-lawed vpon his default. *Idem fol.* 44. I find by the same author. *fol.* 108. that he maketh a difference betweene attainder and conuiction, in these words: And note the diuersitie betweene attainder and conuiction, &c. And with this agreeth the Statute, *anno* 34. & 35. *H.* 8. *cap.* 14. *in ipso principio*, and *anno* 1. *Ed.* 6. *cap.* 12. in these words: that then euery such offender being duly thereof conuicted or attainted, by the lawes of this realme, &c. And againe, in these words: Euery woman that is, or shall fortune to be wife of the person so attainted, conuicted, or outlawed, &c. To this you may likewise adde the stat. *anno* 2. & 3. *Edw.* 6. *cap.* 33. And I find by *Stawnf. pl. cor. fol.* 66. that a man by our ancient lawes, was said to be conuicted presently vpon the verdict (guiltie) but not to be attainted, vntill it appeared that he was no clerke: or being a clerke, and demanded of his ordinarie, could not purge himselfe. So that a man was not attainted vpon conuiction, except he were no Clerke: and, in one word, it appeareth, that attainder is larger then conuiction; conuiction being onely by the Iurie.

And *attainder* is not before iudgement, *Perkins Graunts num.* 27. 29. Yet it appeareth by *Stawnf. fol.* 9. that conuiction is called *attainder* sometime. For there he saith, that the verdict of the Iurie doth either acquit or attaint a man: and so it is, *Westm. pr. cap.* 14. *anno* 3. *Ed.* 1. This auncient lawe touching the conuiction and purgation of Clerkes, is altered, by *anno* 23. *Eliz. cap.* 2. as you may farder reade in *Clergie*.

Attainder (*Attinctus*) though it be most vsed in matters of felonie and treason: yet is it likewise applied to inferior transgressions, as to disseisin, *Westm.* 1. *cap.* 36. *anno* 3. *Ed.* 1. and *Britton cap.* 26. See *Attaint*, and *Attainted*.

Attendant (*attendens*) commeth of the French (*attendre.* i. *demorari, opperiri, expectare, praestolari,*) it signifieth in our common law, one that oweth a dutie or seruice to another, or after a sort dependeth of another. For example, there is Lord, mesn, and tenent: the tenent holdeth of the mesn by a peny; the mesn holdeth ouer by two pence. The meane releaseth to the tenent all the right he hath in the land, and the tenent dyeth. His wife shall be endowed of the land, and she shall be attendent to the heire of the third part of the peny, and not of the third part of the two pence. For she shall be endowed of the best possession of her husband. Another hath, *Kitchin, fol.* 209. in these words: where the wife is endowed by the gardian, she shal be attendant to the gardian, and to the heire at his full age: with whome agreeth *Perkins* also, in *Dower.* 424.

Atturney (atturnatus) cometh of the French *(tourner.* i. *vertere)* as, *tourner son esprit à faire quelque chose,* i. *animum ad rem aliquam inclinare.)* Thence commeth the participle *(tournè.* i. *versus, conversus,)* and the Substantiue *(tour.* i. *vices, vicissitudo)* as, *chacun à son tour,* i. *quilibet sua vice.)* It signifieth in our common lawe, one appointed by another man to do any thing in his steade, as much as *(procurator)* or *(syndicus)* in the ciuill lawe, *West. parte* 1. *Symbolaeogr. lib.* 2. *sect.* 559. defineth it thus: Atturneys be such persons, as by the consent, commandement, or request, do take heed, see to, and take vpon them the charge of other mens busines in their absence, by whome they are commaunded or requested. And where it seemeth that in auncient time, those of authoritie in Courts, had it in their arbitriment, whether they would suffer men to appeare, or sue by any other then themselues, as is euident, by *Fitz. nat. br. fol.* 25. in the writ. *Dedimus potestatem de atturnato faciendo,* where it is shewed, that men were driuen to procure the kings writs or letters patents to appoint Atturneys for them: it is sithence prouided by Statutes, that it should be lawfull so to do without any such circuit, as by the Statute. *anno* 20. *H.* 3. *cap.* 10. *anno* 6. *Ed.* 1. *cap.* 8. *anno* 27. *eiusdem. stat.* 2. *an.* 12. *Ed.* 2. 1. *anno* 15. *eiusdem cap. vnico. anno* 7. *Ric.* 2. *cap.* 14. *anno* 7. *H.* 4. *cap.* 13. *anno* 3. *H.* 5. *cap.* 2. *anno* 15. *H.* 6. *cap.* 7. & *anno* 17. *H.* 7. *cap.* 2. is to be proued. And you may see great diuersitie of writs, in the table of the *Regi. origin.* wherein the king by his writ commaundeth the Iudges to admit of Atturneys. Wherby there grew at the last so many vnskilfull Atturneys, and so many mischiefes by them, that prouision for restraining them was requisite. Wherefore *anno* 4. *H.* 4. *cap.* 18. it was ordained, that the Iustices should examine them, and displace the vnskilfull. And againe, *anno* 33. *H.* 6. *cap.* 7. that there should be but a certaine number of them in *Northfolke* and *Southfolke.* In what cases a man at this day may haue an Atturney, and in what not, see *Fitz. vbi supra.* Atturney is either generall or speciall: Atturney generall is he, that by generall authoritie is appointed to all our affaires

faires

faires or suites : as the Atturney generall of the king. *pl. cor. fol.* 152. which is as much as (*Procurator Cæsaris*) was in the Romane Empire. Atturney general of the Duke, *Cromptons Iurisd. fol.* 105. Atturney speciall or particular is he, that is employed in one or more causes particularly specified. Atturneys generall be made after two sorts: either by the kings leters patents before him or the Lord Chancelour, or by our appointment before Iustices in *eyre* in open court, *Glanvile li.* 11. *cap. pri. Britton. cap.* 126. whome of this thing you may reade more at large. There be also in respect of the diuers courts, Atturneys at large, and Atturneys special, belonging to this or that court onely. The name is borrowed of the Normanes, as appeareth by the custumarie, *cap.* 65. And I find the word (*attornati*) or as some reade (*tornati*) in the same signification in the title (*de statu regularium*) *ca. vnico.* §. *Porrò i. n sexto.*) where the glosse saith, that *Atturnati dicuntur Procuratores apud acta constituti.* Our old Latine word for this seemeth to be (*responsalis*) *Bract. lib.* 4. *cap.* 31. *& lib.* 5. *parte* 2. *cap.* 8. and so it is in *Scotland* at this day, but especially for the Atturney of the defendant, as (*prolocutor*) is for the persewer. *M. Skene de verb. significatione.* *Responsalis*, as *Sigonius* witnesseth, in his first booke *de regno Italiæ*, was in auncient time, the title of the Popes ambassadour, *pag.* 11.

Atturney of the court of wards and Liueries (*Atturnatus regis in curia Wardorum & Liberaturarũ*) is the third officer in that Court, who must be a person learned in the lawes of the land, being named and assigned by the king. At his admission into the office, he taketh an oath before the Master of the said court, well and truly to serue the king, as his Atturney in all courts, for and concerning any mater or cause, that toucheth the possessions and hereditaments limited to the suruey and gouernement of this court, and to procure the kings profite thereof: truly to councell the king, and the Master of the Court, in all things concerning the same, to the best of his cunning, witte, and power: and with all speed and diligence from time to time at the calling of the Master, to endeuour himselfe for the hearing and determination indifferently of such matters & causes, as depend before the Master: not to take any gift or reward in any mater or cause depending in the court, or else where, wherein the king shall be partie, whereby the king shall be hurt, hindred, or disinherited: to do to his power, wit, and cunning, all and euery thing that appertaineth to his office.

Atturney of the Court of the Duchie of Lancaster, (*Atturnatus curiæ Ducatus Lancastriæ*) is the second officer in that Court, and seemeth, for his skill in law, to be there placed as (*assessor*) to the Chanceler of that court, being for the most part, some honorable man, and chosen rather for some especiall trust reposed in him to deale betweene the king and his tenents, then for any great learning, as was vsuall with the Emperors of *Rome*, in the choice of their Magistrates.

Attournment (*attornamentum*) commeth of the French (*tourner. i. vertere*) and in our common lawe, is an yeelding of the tenent to a new Lord, or acknowledgement of him to be his Lord. For otherwise he that buyeth or obtaineth any lands or tenements of another, which are in the occupation of a third, cannot get possession: yet see the statute, *an.* 27. *H.* 8. *cap.* 16. The words vsed in atturnment are set downe in *Litleton*. I agree me to the graunt made to you, &c. But the more common atturnment is to say: Sir, I attourn to you by force of the same graunt: or, I become your tenent, &c. or else deliuer vnto the grauntee a peny, halfepeny, or farding, by way of attournment, *Litleton lib.* 3. *cap. Attournment*. 10. whome you may reade more at large, and find that his definition proceedeth from more lawe then Logicke: because he setteth downe diuers other cases in the same chapter, whereto attournment appertaineth as properly as vnto this. But you may perceiue there, that attournment is the transposing of those duties that the tenent ought to his former Lord, vnto another, as to his Lord: and also, that attournment is either by word or by act, &c. Also attournment is voluntarie, or else compulsorie, by the writ tearmed *Per quæ seruitia*, *Owld. nat. br. fol.* 155 or sometime by distresse. *Fitzh. nat. br. fol.* 147. Lastly, attournment may be made to the Lord himselfe or to his Steward in Court, *Kitchin. fol.* 70. And there is attournment in deede, and attournment in lawe. *Coke vol.* 6. *fo.* 113. *a.* Attournment in lawe, is an act, which though it be no expresse attournment, yet in intendment of law is all one.

(*Atturnato faciendo vel recipiendo*) is a writ which a man oweing suite to a countie, hundred, weapon take, or other court, and desiring to make an attourney, to appeare for him at the same court, whome he doubteth whether the Shyreeue or bailiffe will admit or not for his Attourney there,

there, purchaseth, to commaund him to receiue such a man for his attourney, and admit his appearance by him. The forme and other circumstances whereof, see in *Fitzh.nat.br.fo* 156.

Audiendo & terminando, is a writ, but more properly tearmed a commission, directed to certaine persons, when as any great assembly, insurrectiō, or heinous demeanure or trespasse is committed in any place, for the appeasing, and punishment thereof. which you may read at large, in *Fitzh.nat.br.fo.*110. See also *oyer & terminer.*

Audience courte (*Curia audientia Cantuariensis*) is a court belonging to the Archbishop of *Canterburie*, of equall authoritie with the Arches court, though inferior both in dignity and antiquitie. The originall of this court was, because the Archeb. *of Canterbury* heard many causes extra iudicially at home in his owne palace, in which, before he would finally determine any thing, he did vsually commit them to be discussed by certaine learned men in the ciuile & canon lawes, whome thereupon be termed his auditors. And so in time it grew to one especiall man, who at this day is called (*Causarum negotiorumq́, audientia Cantuariensis auditor seu officialis.* And with this office hath heretofore commonly bene ioyned the Chancelership of the Archbishop, who medleth not in any point of cōtentious iurisdiction, that is, deciding of causes betweene party and party (except such as are ventilated *pro forma* onely, as the confirmation of bishops elections, or such like) but onely of office, and especially such as are *voluntaria iurisdictionis*, as the granting of the custody of the spiritualties, during the vacation of Bishoprickes, Institutions to benefices, dispensing with banes of matrimonie, and such like. But this is now distinguished in person from the Audience. Of this Audience court, you may reade more in the booke, intituled *De antiquitate ecclesiæ Brittannicæ historia.*

Audita querela, is a writ, that lieth against him, who hauing taken the bond called (statute Merchant) of another, and crauing or hauing obteined execution of the same at the Maior & Bayliffes hands, before whome it was entred, at the complaint of the partie who entred the same, vpon suggestion of some iust cause why execution should not be graunted; as a release, or other exception. This writ is graunted by the Chaunceler of England, vpon veiwe of the exception suggested, to the Iustices of the common banke, or of the

the Kings benche, willing them to graunt summons to the Shyreeue of the countie, where the creditour is, for his appearance at a certain day before them. See more in *owld.nat.br.fo. 66.* and *Fitzh.nat.br.fo.102.*

Auditour (*auditor*) commeth of the French (*auditeur*) and in our lawe, signifieth an officer of the king, or some other great personage, which yearely by examining the accounts of all vnder officers accountable, maketh vp a generall booke, that sheweth the difference betweene their receipts or burden, and their allowances, commonly called (*allocations*): as namely, the auditours of the exchequer, take the accounts of those receiuers, which receiue the revenewes of the augmentation: as also of the Shyreeues, eschcatours, collectours, and customers, and set them downe and perfect them. Him that will read more of this, I referre to the *Statut. anno.* 33. *H.* 8. *c.* 33.

Auditours of the Prests, are also officers in the exchequer, that doe take and make vp the great accounts of Ireland, Berwick, the mint, & of any mony imprested to any man.

Auditour of the receipts, is an officer of the exchequer, that fileth the Tellers bils, and maketh an entrie of them, and giueth to the Lord Treasurer a certificate of the mony receiued the weeke before. He maketh also (*Debenturs*) to euery Teller, before they pay any mony, & taketh their accounts. He keepeth the blacke booke of the receipts, and the Treasurers key of the treasurie: and seeth euery Tellers monies locked vp in the new treasury.

Auenture. is a mischance, causing the death of a man without felony: as when he is sodenly drowned, or burnt, by any soden disease falling into the water or fire. *Britton. ca.* 7. where you may see, what it differeth from Misadventure. See *Misadventure*.

Average (*averagium*) by *M. Skenes opinion* (*verbo arage*) *de verborum significatione*, commeth of the word (*averia.*) i. a beast, and so consequently signifieth seruice which the tenent oweth to to the Lord, by horse or cariage of horse. I haue heard others probably deriue it from the French (*euvrage*) or (*euvre.* i. *opus.*) It seemeth with vs to haue two diuers significations; for the first, *Rastall. titulo Exposition of words.* maketh mention of the Kings averages, which I take to be the kings cariages by horse or cart. Then *anno.* 32. *H.* 8. *ca.* 14. and *anno.* 1. *Iacobi, ca.* 32. it is vsed for a certaine contribution that merchants and others doe every man pro-

proportionably make toward their losses , who haue their goods cast into the sea for the safegard of the shippe, or of the goods and liues of them in the shippe in time of a tempest. And this contribution seemeth to be so called, because it is proportioned, after the rate of euery mans average or goods caried.

Averijs captis in withernam, is a writ for the taking of catell to his vse, that hath his catell taken vnlawfully by another, and driuen out of the countie where they were taken, that they cannot be repleuied. *Register. originall. fo.* 82.*a b.* See *Withernam.*

Averment (*verificatio*) cōmeth from the French (*averer.i. testari*) as *averer quelque meschācete.*i *extrahere scelus aliquod in lucem ex occultis tenebris.* It signifieth (according to the author of the termes of lawe) an offer of the defendant to make good, or to iustifie and exception pleaded in abatement or barre of the plaintifs actiō. But me thinketh it should rather signifie the act, thē the offer of iustifying the exception, by diuers places where I finde it vsed. For example. *an.* 34.*Ed.*1 *stat.*2. And the demaundant will offer to averre by the assise or Iurie. where to offer to averre and to averre must needes differ: and againe in the same *statut.* and the demaundaunt will offer to averre by the countrie, &c. thirdly in the english *nat. br. fo.*57. These errours shallbe tried by averment, &c.

Averpennie (*quasi Average pennie,*) is mony contributed toward the Kings averages. *Rastall* exposition of words. *See Average.*

Augmentation (*augmentatio*) was the name of a court, erected the 27 yeare of *H.*8. as appeareth by the 27. chapter of that yeares parlament. And the end thereof was, that the king might be iustly delt with touching the profits of such religious howses and their lands, as weare giuen vnto him by an act of parlament the same yeare not printed. For the dissolving of which courte, there was authoritie giuen to Queene *Mary*, by the parlament held the first yeare of her raigne. *ses.*2. *ca.* 10. which shee afterward put in execution by her leters patents. The name of the courte grewe from this, that the revenewes of the crowne were augmented so much by the suppression of the said houses, as the king reserved vnto the crowne, and neither gaue nor sold away to others.

Aulne of *Renish wine. a.* 1.*Ed.* 6.*ca.* 13. *alias, Awme of Renish wine.* 1.*Iaco.ca.*33. is a vessell that conteineth 40. gallons.

Aulnegeowr. See *Alneger.*

Avo; is the name of a writ for the

the which see (*Ayle*).

Awncell weight, as I haue beene informed, is a kinde of weight with scoles hanging, or hookes fastened at each end of a staffe, which a man lifteth vp vpon his forefinger, or hand and so discerneth the equalitie or difference betweene the weight and the thing weied. In which, because there may, and was wont to be great deceipt, it was forbidden. *anno.* 25. *Ed.* 3. *stat.* 5. *ca.* 9. & *anno.* 34. *eiusdem. ca.* 5. and the euen ballance onely commanded. yet a man of good credit, once certified me, that it is still vsed in leaden hall at London among butchers &c. In the deriuation of this word, I dare not be ouer confident. But it may probably be thought to be called (*awnsell weight, quasi hand sale weight*) because it was and is performed by the hand, as the other is by the beame. And if I should draw it from the greeke, ἀγκών. i. *cubitus.* the parte of the arme from the elbowe to the fingers ends, I might chalenge a good warrand of this from the Romaines; whoe thence derived their (*ancile*). i. the luckie shield, that was saide to be sent from heauen in a tempest to *Numa Pompilius*, together with a voice, that the citie of *Rome* should be the mightiest of all others, soe long as that shield remained in it.

Auncient demeasne, (*antiquum dominicum*) is called (more at large auncient demeasn of the king or of the crowne. *Fitzh. nat. br. fo.* 14. *d.* It cometh of .2. *French* words (*auncien*. i. *veter, vetus, veteranus, antiquus*) and of (*demaine, alias domaine*. i. *publicum vectigal*) It signifieth in our common lawe, a certaine tenure, whereby all the maners belonging to the crowne, in the daies of *Saint Edward* the Saxon king, or of *William* the conquerour, did hold. The number & names of which maners, as all other, belonging to common persons, he caused to be written into a booke, after a survey made of them, now remaining in the exchequer, and called Domes day booke. And those, which by that booke doe appeare, to haue belonged to the crowne at that time, and are conteined vnder the title (*Terra regis*) be called auncient demeasn. *Kitchin. fo.* 98. and *M. Gwin.* in the preface to his readings. Of these tenents there were two sorts, one that held their land frankely, by charter, and another that held by copy of court rolle, or by verge, at the will of the Lord, according to the custome of the maner. *Fitzh. nat. br. fo.* 14. *d.* of which opinion also *Britton* is, *ca.* 66. *nu.* 8. The benefite of this tenure, consisteth in these points: first, the tenents of a manner holding freely by charter in this sort, cannot be impleaded, out of the same maner: and if they be, they may abate the writ, by pleading their tenure before or after answer made. *Secondly*, they be free of tolle for al things concerning their sustenãce & husbãdry. Thirdly, they may not be ẽpaneled vpõ any ẽquest. Terms of the law. but more at large by *Fitzh. nat. br. fo.* 14. *d.* whome reade, as also *fo.* 128.*a. &c.* And as it appeareth by him. *eodem. fo.* 4 *B. C.* these tenents held by the service of plowing the kings land, by plashing his hedges, or by suche like, toward the maintenance of the kings houshold; in which regard they had such liberties giuen them, wherin, to avoide disturbance, they may haue writs to such as take the duties of tolle in any market or feire; as likewise for immunitye of portage, passage, & such like. *Fitzh. nat. br. f.* 228. *A. B. C. D.* by which author it also appeareth, that no lands be to be accompted auncient demeasn, but such as are holden in socage. *fo.* 13. *D. et.* 14. *B. C.* See *Monstraverunt, and Fitzh. fo.* 14. and *Dessendo quietum de telonio. fo.* 226. *Fleta* maketh three tenures holding of the crowne: auncient demeasn, by escheate, & by purchase. *li.* 1 *ca.* 20. See *Demaine.*

Auncient Demesn arere (antiquum dominicum à retro) is that aũcient demesn, which the king graunteth ouer to hold of a maner. *Kitchin. fo.* 67.*b.*

Avowè (advocatus) see *Advowe*; *Britton* saith that *Avowè* is he, to whome the right of advowzen of any Church appertaineth; so that he may present thereunto in his owne name, and is called *avowè* for a difference from those, that sometime present in another mans name: as a gardiã that presenteth in the name of his warde, and for a difference also from them, which haue the lands whereunto an advowzen appertaineth, but onely for tearme of their liues, or of yeares, or by intrusion or desseisin. *ca.* 92.

Avowrie. See *Advowrie.*

Avoir de pois, is in true French *(avoir du poix. i. habere pondus, aut iusti esse ponderis)* It signifieth in our common lawe, two things: first, a kinde of weight divers from that, which is called Troy weight conteining but 12. ounces to the pound, where as this conteineth sixteene. And in this respect it may be probably coniectured, that it is so called, because it is of more weight then the other. Then also it signifieth such merchandize, as are waied by this weight, and not by Troy weight. as in the statute of *York. anno* 9. *Ed.* 3. *in procem. anno.* 27. *Ed.* 3. *Statuto* 2 *ca.* 10. *at anno.* 2

Rich. 2. *cap.* 1. See *Weights.*

Auxilium ad filium militem faciendum, & filiam maritandam, is a writ directed to the Shyreeve of euery countie, where the king or other lord hath any tenents, to leuye of them reasonable ayde toward the knighting of his son, and the mariage of his daughter. See *Ayde*, and *Fitz. nat. br. fol.* 82.

B

BAcheler (*Bachalaureus*) cometh of the French (*Bachalier.* i. *tyro*) and thereupon I thinke, those that be called Bachelers of the Companies in *London*, be such of each company, as be springing toward the estate of those that be imployed in Coũcel, but as yet are inferiors. For euery cõpany of the twelue, consisteth of a Master, two Wardens, the Liuerie, which are assistants in matter of Councell, or at the least, such as the Assistants be chosen out of, and the Bachelers, which are yet but in expectance of dignitie among them, and haue their function onely in attendance vpon the Master and Wardens. I haue read in an old monument, this word *Bacheler*, attributed to the Lord Admirall of *England*, if he be vnder a Baron, in French words to this effect: and it is to weet, that when the Admirall rideth to assemble a shippe of warre, or other, for the businesse and affaires of the Realme, if he be a Bacheler, he shall take for his day wages, 4.s. sterling: if he be an Earle or Baron, he shall take wages after the rate of his estate and degree. This word is vsed, *anno* 13. *R.* 2. *stat.* 2. *cap.* 1. & signifieth as much as Bacheler Knight doth, *anno* 3. *Ed.* 4. *cap.* 5. that is, a simple Knight, not a Knight baneret. See *Banaret.* Touching the farder etymologie of this word, *Bachalarii, teste Renano, à bacillo nominati sunt, quia primi studii authoritatem, quæ per exhibitionem baculi concedebatur, iam consecuti fuissent. Vt fuerit velut quoddam mancipationis signum in huiusmodi aliquod studium baculi traditio. Alciat* writeth the word (*baccalaurei, eosque dicit visos à bacca laurea nomen sumpsisse in l. cui præcipua* 57. *ꝛ. de verbo. significa.*

Backberond. is a Saxon word. and almost English at this day, signifying as much as bearing vpon the backe, or about a ma . *Bracton* vseth it for a signe or circumstance of manifest theft, which the Civilians call, *furtum manifestum.* For dividing (*furtum, in manifestum, & non manifestum*) he defineth (*furtum manifestum*) in this sort: *Furtum verò manifestũ est, vbi latro deprehensus est seisitus de aliquo latrocinio: sc. hand habend & backberend, & insecutus fuerit per aliquem cuius res illa fuerit. li.* 3

tract.

tract. 2. cap.32. Master Manwood in the second part of his forest lawes, noteth it for one of the 4. circumstances or cases, wherein a Forester may arrest the bodie of an offender against vert or venison in the Forest. For by the assise of the Forest of *Lancaster* (saith he) taken with the maner is, when one is found in the kings Forest in any of these foure degrees: *sc.* stable stand, dogge drawe, backe beare, and bloudie hand. In which place you may find all these interpreted.

Badger, cometh of the French (*bagage*, i. *sarcina*, *impedimentū*,) It signifieth with vs, one that buyeth corne or victuals in one place, and carieth it into another. See *Cromptons* Iustice of peace, *fol. 69. & 70.*

Baye or *penne* is a pond head made vp of a great heith, to keep in a great quantitie or store of water, so that the wheeles of the fornace or hammer belonging to an Iron mill, may stand vnder them, and be driuen by the water comming out of them by a passage or flud-gate (called the penstocke) and falling vpon the said wheeles. This word is mentioned in the statute, *anno 27. El. cap. 19.*

Bayle (*Ballium*, *plevina*, *manucaptio*) commeth of the French (*bailler*, i. *attribuere*, *tradere*, *tribuere*.) It is vsed in our common lawe, properly for the freeing or setting at liberty of one arrested or imprisoned vpon action either civill or criminall, vnder suretie taken for his apparence at a day and place certainely assigned. *Bracton lib. 3. tract. 2. cap. 8. num. 8. & 9.* The reason why it is called *Bayle*, is, because by this meanes the party restrained, is deliuered into the hands of those that bind themselues for his forth-comming. There is both common and speciall baile. Cōmon baile, is in actions of small preiudice, or slight proofe: being called common, because any sureties in that case are taken: whereas vpon causes of greater weight or apparent specialtie, speciall baile or suretie must bee taken: as subsidie men at the least, and they according to the value. *Master Manwood* in his first part of Forest lawes, *pag.* 167 maketh a great difference betweene bayle and mainprise, in these words: and note that there is a great diuersitie betweene bayle and maniprise. For he that is mainprised, is alwaies said to be at large, and to go at his own libertie out of ward, after that he is let to mainprise, vntill the day of his appearance, by reason of the said common summons or otherwise. But otherwise it is, where a man is let to bayle, by foure or two men, by the Lord chiefe Iustice in *eyre* of the Forest, vntill a certaine day. For there he is alwaies accompted by the lawe, to be in their ward and custodie for the time. And they may, if they wil, keepe him in ward or in prison at that time, or otherwise at their will. So that he which is so bailed, shall not be said, by the lawe, to be at large, or at his owne libertie. See *Lamberds eirenarcha. lib. 3. cap. 2. pag.* 330. *Bayle*, is also a certaine limit within the forest, accordingly as the Forest is diuided into the charges of seuerall Foresters. *Crompton* in the oath of the bow-bearer, *fol.* 201. See *Maynprise*.

Baylife (*ballivus*) commeth of the French (*bailif*. i. *diacetes, nomarcha, præfectus Prouinciæ*) and as the name, so the office it selfe, in auncient time, was very aunswerable to that of *Fraunce* and *Normandie*: for as in *France* there be sixteene Parlaments, (*Lupanus de Magistratibus Francorum, lib.* 2. *cap. Parlamentum*) which be high courts, whence lyeth no appeale: & within the precincts of those seuerall parts of that kingdome, that belong to each Parlament, there be seueral prouinces, vnto which, within themselues, iustice is ministred by certaine officers called bayliffes: so in *England* we see many seuerall counties or shires, within the which iustice hath bene ministred to the inhabitants of each countie, by the officer whome we now call Shyreeue or Vicount (one name descending frõ the Saxons, the other from the Normans.) And though I cannot expressely proue, that this Shyreeue was euer called a bailiffe: yet is it probable, that that was one of his names likewise, because the countie is called many times (*balliva*) that is a Baylywicke: as namely, in the returne of a writ with (*non est inuentus*,) he writeth thus: (*A. S. infra scriptus, non est inventus in balliva mea, post receptionem huius brevis*) Kitchin *returna brevium. fol.* 258. and againe in *Bracton, lib.* 3. *tract.* 2. *cap.* 33. *num.* 3. and *anno* 5. *Eliz. cap.* 23. and *anno* 14. *Ed.* 3. *stat.* 1. *cap.* 6. And I thinke the word (*bailife*) vsed *cap.* 28. of *Magna charta*, compriseth as well Shyreeues, as bailiffes of hundreds: as also *anno* 14. *Ed.* 3. *stat.* 1. *cap.* 9. But as the realme is diuided into Counties: so euery Countie is againe diuided into hundreds, within the which it is manifest, that in auncient times, the kings subiects had iustice ministred vnto them, by the seuerall officers of euery hundred, which were called bailiffes, as those officers were and are in *Fraunce* and *Normandie*, being chiefe officers of iustice within euery Prouince. *Lupanus de Magistratibus Francorum, lib. 2. cap. Balivi.* and the grand custumary of *Normandie, cap. 1.* And that this is true among many others, I bring *Bracton* for my witnes, *li. 3. tract. 2. cap. 34. n. 5.* where it appeareth that bailiffes of hundreds might hold plee of appeale and approuers. But sithence that time, these hundred courts (certain franchises excepted) are by the statute *anno 14. Ed. 3. stat. 1. cap. 9.* swalowed into the Countie courts, as you may reade in countie and hundred. And the Bailiffes name & office is growne into such contempt, at the least, these bailiffes of hundreds, that they are now but bare messengers and mandataries within their liberties to serue writs, and such like base offices: their office consisting in 3. points onely: which see in *Cromptons* Iustice of peace, *fol. 49. a.* Yet is the name still in good esteeme some other way. For the chiefe Magistrates in diuers townes corporate be called Bailiffes, as in *Ipswitch*, *Yarmouth*, *Colchester*, and such like. And againe, there be certaine, to whom the kings castels be committed, which are called Bailifs, as the Bailiffe of *Dover* castell.

These ordinary bayliffes are of two sorts: baylifs errant, and baylifs of franchises. Baylifes errant *(ballivi itinerantes)* be those which the *Shyreeue* maketh, and appointeth to goe hither & thither in the countie to serue writs, to summon the countie, sessions, assises, and such like. Baylifs of franchises (*ballivi franchesiarum aut libertatum*) be those, that are appointed by euerie lord within his libertie, to doe such offices within his precincts, as the baylife errant doth at large in the countie. Of these read *S. Thomas Smith. de repub. Anglo. li. 2. ca. 16.* There be also baylifes of the forest. *Manwood parte 1. pa. 113.* There be likewise baylifes of husbandrie, belonging to priuate men of great substance, who seeme to be so called, bycause they dispose of the vnder seruants euery man to his labour and taske, check them for misdoing their buisenes, gather the profits of their lord and master, and deliuer an accompt for the same at the yeares end, or otherwise as it shallbe called for. The word baylife or *balivus*, is by *Rebuffus* deriued from (*Baal*, *dominus, quia ballivi dominantur suis subditis, quasi eorum magistri & domini. Rebuf. in constitut. regias. de senten. executionis. art. 7. glos. 1.* The office or dutie of a bayliffe of a manor or houshold (which in aunciet time seemeth to haue beene all one) *Fleta* well describeth, *li. 2. ca. 72. & 73.* This word is allso vsed in the canon lawe. *ca. dilecto. de sentent. excom. in sexto. & ca. pri. de pœnis in clement.* wher the glossographer saith, it is a French word, signifiing as much as (*prapositus*) & (*balia*) or (*balivatus*) is vsed among our later interpreters of the civile & canon law, for *provincia*, as *balliua* heere in England, is vsed for a countie or shire.

Baleors See *Conders*.

Ballivo amovēdo, is a writ to remooue a baylife out of his office, for want of sufficient liuing with in his bayliwick. *Reg orig. f.* 178.

Bane, seemeth to signifie the destruction or ouerthrow of any thing. *Bracton. li.* 2. *tracta.* 2. *ca.* 1. *nu.* 1. as he which is the cause of of another mans drowning, is said there to be *la bane*. i. *malefactor*. In that *Bracton*, in the place aforesaid, prefixeth a French article to this word, it should seeme by his opinion, that the word is French, but I finde it not in any French writer that euer I read.

Baneret (*banerettus*) in *M. Skenes* opinion, seemeth to be compounded of (*baner*) and (*rent*) whome reade more at large of this, *verbo. Baneret. de verbo. signi.* but our *M. Camden*, rather draweth the word from the *German* (*bannerheires. Brittan. pa.* 109. *in meo libro. S. Thomas Smith de repub. Anglo. li.* 1. *ca.* 18. saith, that baneret is a Knight made in the field, with the ceremonie of cutting of the point of his standard, and making it, as it were, a baner. And they being before bachelers, are now of greater degree, allowed to display their armes in a baner in the Kings armie, as barons doe. *M. Camden vbi supra*, hath these words of this matter, *Baneretti, cùm vasallorum nomen iam desierat, a baronibus secundi erant: quibus inditum nomen a vexillo. Concessum illis erat militaris virtutis ergo, quadrato vexillo (perinde ac barones) uti. vnde & equites vexillarii a nonnullis vocantur, &c.* Of creating a knight baneret, you may read farder, in *M. Segar. Norrey* his booke. *li.* 2. *ca.* 10. That they be next to barons in dignitie, it appeareth by the statut. *an.* 14. *R.* 2. *c.* 11. & by *anno.* 5. *R.* 2. *stat.* 2. *ca.* 4. it may be probably coniectured, that they were auncien tly called by summons to the court of parlament. and *anno.* 13. R. 2. *stat.* 2. *ca.* 1. we finde, that a baneret for praying a pardon for a murderer, contrarie to that statut, is subiect to all one punishment with a baron. *Iohan: Gregorius Tholosanus. li.* 6. *ca.* 10. *sui syntagmatis. nu.* 9. hath these words: *In Gallia sunt duæ species affines nobilium & feudorum, quas dicunt de benneretz & barons. Benneretus iure suæ dignitatis, antequam talis dici mereatur, nobilis esse debet genere, in quarto gradu, possidens*

dens in ditione decem scutarios bachalarios armorũ: id est, decem vasallos, habens sufficiens patrimonium, quo possit secum ducere quatuor aut quinque nobiles comites continuos, cum equitibus duodecim aut sexdecim. Fit autem Benneretus, cum princeps huiusmodi persona concedit vexilli ius, & ex vexillo peditum in acie, vel extra, de solenni, sacris peractis, adimit acumina. Vocant la queve de pennon, fitq́; labarum, id est, equitum vexillum, vocant cornette eumq́; equitem facit, si iam non est. Quòd si ditior his fiat benneretus, & habet vnam benneretam, aut sex equites bachalarios, qui possideant singuli in censum sexcentas libras ex eius ditione seu feudo, tunc possunt ex licentia principis, baronis nomen sibi adsciscere.

Bans (*bannus vel bannum*) signifieth a publike notice giuen of any thing. The word is ordinarie among the feudists, and growne from them to other vses: as to that which we heere in England call a proclamation, whereby any thing is publikely commaunded or forbidden. *Vincentius de Franchis. descis.* 521. & 360. *Hotoman verbo bannus, in verbis feudalibus* saith that there is both (*bãnus*) and (*bannum*) and that they signifie two divers things. His words are these: *Bannus siue bannum duo significat: Edictũ, qua die vasalli equis armisq; instructi, ad comitatum adesse debent: & sanctionẽ, hoc est, mulctam edicto non parentis.* which he confirmeth by divers authorities. This word (*bans*) we vse heere in England, especially in the publishing of matrimoniall contracts in the church, before mariage, to the end that if any man can say against the intẽtion of the parties, either in respect of kindred or otherwise, they may take their exception in time. And in the canon lawe, *Banna, sunt proclamationes sponsi & sponsæ in ecclesijs fieri solita ca.* 27. *extra de sponsal. & ca. vlt qui matrimonium. accus. pos. & ca. vlt de clan. despons.* Yet our word (*banning*) seemeth to come thence, being nothing but an exclamation of another. Onely *Bracton*, once maketh mention of *bannus regis*, for a proclamation, or silence made by the crier, before the congresse of the champions in a combate. *li.* 3 *tracta.* 2. *ca.* 21.

Bank (*bancus*) commeth of the French (*banque. i. mensa*) In our common lawe, it is most vsually taken for a seate or bench of iudgement, as *bank le roy* the kings bench. *bank de commũ plees:* the bench of comon plees, or the common bench. *Kitchin. fo.* 102. called also in latine *bancus regius, & bancus communium placitorum. Crompt. iuris. fo.* 67. & 91. *Camden* in his *Britannia. pag.* 112. & 113. *in meo.* calleth them also *bancum regium & bancum communem.*

See.

See *frank bank.*

Bankrupt,(alias bankrowte.) cometh of the french *(banque route)* and *(faire banqueroute)* with the French, is as much as *(foro cedere, solum vetere)* with the Romanes. The composition of the French word I take to be this *(banque.* i. *mensa)* & *(route.*i.*vestigium)* metaphorically taken from the signe left in the earth, of a table once fastened vnto it, & now taken away. So that the original seemeh to haue sprung frō those Romain *(mensary)* which (as appeareth by many wrighters) had their *(tabernas & mensas)* in certaine publique places, whereof, when they were disposed to flie, & deceiue men that had put them in trust with their monies, they left but the signes or carcases behinde them. I know that others of good learning (and *M.Skene* for one) bring this *(a bancorupto)* but the French word worketh in me this other opinion, for after their sence, the French should rather be *banque rompu*. Bankrupt with vs signifieth him or his act, that hauing gotton other mens goods into his hands, hideth him selfe in places vnknowne, or in his owne priuate house, not minding to pay or restore to his creditours their duties. *anno.* 34.*H.* 8.*ca.*4. where the french phrase *(faire banque route)* is translated to the word, to make bankrupt. A bankrupt, *anno.* 1.*Iacobi.ca.*15, is thus described: All and euery such person and persons, vsing, or that shall vse the trade of merchandise, by way of bargaining, exchange, bartrey, cheuisance, or otherwise in grosse, or by seeking his, her, or their trade of liuing by buying and selling, and being a subiect borne of this Realme, or any the kings dominions, or denizen, who at any time sithence the first day of this present parlament, or at any time hereafter, shall depart the Realme, or begin to keepe his or her house or houses, or otherwise to absent him or her selfe, or take sanctuarie, or suffer him or her selfe willingly to be arrested for any debt or other thing, not growne or due for mony deliuered, wares sould, or any other iust or lawful cause, or good consideration or purposes, or hath or will suffer him or her selfe to be outlawed, or yeld him or her selfe to prison, or willingly or fraudulently hath or shall procure him or her selfe to be arrested, or his or her goods, money, or chatels to be attached or sequestred, or depart from his or her dwelling house, or make, or cause to be made any fraudulent graūt or conueyance of his, her, or their lands, tenements, goods or chatels, to the intent or whereby his, her, or their creditours being subiects borne, as aforeforcsaide, shall or may be defeated or delayed for the recouery of their iust and true dept: or being arrrested for debt, shall after his or her arrest, lye in prison sixe monethes or more, vpon that arrest, or any other arrest or detention in prison for debt, and lye in prison sixe monethes vpon such arrest or detention, shall be accompted and adiudged a bankrupt to all intents and purposes.

Banishment (exilium, abiuratio) commeth of the French *(bannissement)* and hath a signification knowne to euery man. But there be two kinds of banishments in *England*: one voluntarie and vpō oath, whereof you may reade *(Abiuration:)* the other vpon cōpulsion for some offence or crime: as if a lay-man succor him that, hauing taken sanctuarie for an offence, obstinately refuseth to abiure the realme, he shall loose his life aud member: if a Clerke do so, he shall be banished, *Stawnf. pl. cor. fol.* 117. This punishment is also of our moderne Civilians called *(bannimētum)* which was auinciently tearmed *(deportatio)* if it were perpetuall, or *(relegatio in insulam,)* if for a time. *Vincentius de Franchis. Petrus de Belluga in suo speculo. fol.* 125. *num.* 4.

Barbaries (Oxycantha) is a thornie shrub knowne to most men to beare a bery or fruite of a sharpe taste. These beries (as also the leaues of the said tree) be medicinable, as *Gerard* in his herball sheweth, *lib.* 3. *cap.* 21. You find them mentioned among drugs to be garbled, *anno* 1. *Iacob. cap.* 19.

Bard, aliâs, Beard. See *Clack.*

Bargaine and sale, as it seemeth by *West. part.* 1. *symb. lib.* 2. *sect.* 436. is properly a contract made of maners, lands, tenements, hereditaments, and other things, transferring the propertie thereof from the bargainer to the barganee. But the author of the new termes of lawe addeth, that it ought to be for money: saying farder, that this is a good contract for land, &c. and that fee-simple passeth thereby, though it be not said in the deed (To haue and to hold the land to him and to his heyres,) and though there be no liuerie and seisin made by the seller, so it be by deed indented, sealed, and enrolled, either in the Countie where the land lyeth, or within one of the kings courts of Records at Westminster, within sixe moneths after the date of the deed indented, *anno* 27. *H.* 8. *cap.* 16.

Barkarie (Barkaria) is a heath house. New booke of Entries, *titulo. Assise corp. polit.* 2. Some call it a Tanne house.

Baron (*Baro*) is a French word, and hath diuers significations here in *England*. First, it is taken for a degree of Nobilitie next vnto a Vicount. *Bracton. lib.* 1. *cap.* 8. *num.* 4. where he saith, they be called *Barones, quasi robur belli*. And in this signification it is borowed from other nations, with whom *Baronia* be as much as *Prouinciæ*. *Petrus Belluga in speculo princip. fol.* 119. So *Barones* be such, as haue the gouernment of Prouinces, as their fee holden of the king: some hauing greater, some lesser authoritie within their territories, as appeareth by *Vincentius de Franchis* in diuers of his desceisions, and others. Yet it may probably be thought, that of old times here in England all they were called Barons that had such Seigniories, as we now call court-barons, as they be at this day called Seigneurs in *France*, that haue any such manor or lordship. Yea, I haue heard by men very learned in our Antiquities, that neere after the conquest, all such came to the Parlament, and sate as Nobles in the vpper house. But when by experience it appeared, that the Parlament was too much pestered with such multitudes: it grew to a custome, that none shold come but such, as the king, for their extraordinarie wisedome or qualitie, thought good to call by writ; which writ ranne (*hac vice tantum*) After that againe men seeing this estate of Nobilitie to be but casuall, and to depend meerly vpon the Princes pleasure, they sought a more certain hold, and obtained of the King, leters patents of this dignitie to them and their heyres male. And these were called Barons by leters patents or by creation: whose posterity, be now by inheritance and true descent of Nobilitie, those Barons that be called Lords of the Parlament: of which kind the king may create more at his pleasure. It is thought neuerthelesse, that there are yet Barons by writ, as wel as Barons by leters patents, and that they may be discerned by their titles: because the Barons by writ are those, that to the title of *Lord* haue their owne surnames annexed, as *Compton*, *North*, *Norice*, &c. whereas the Barons by leters patents, are named by their Baronies. These Barons which were first by writ, may now iustly also be called Barons by prescription, for that they haue continued Barons in themselues and their auncestors time, beyond the memorie of man. The originall of Barons by writ *Master Camden* in his *Britannia pag.* 109. *in meo*. referreth to *Henry* the third: Barons by leters patents or creation, (as I haue heard among our Antiquaries) were first created about the dayes of *Henry* the sixth: the maner of whose creation reade in *Master Stowes* Annales, *pag.* 1121. Of all these you may also reade *Master Ferns* glorie of Generositie, *pa.* 125 & 126. And see *M. Skene de ver. signif. verb. Baro.* with *Sir Thomas Smith, lib. 1. de rep. Anglor. cap. 17.* who saith, that none in England is created Baron, except he can dispend a thousand pound by yeare, or a thousand markes at the least. To these former, *Master Seager* (by office) *Norrey, lib. 4. cap. 13.* of *Honour ciuill and militarie*, addeth a third kind of Baron, calling them barons by tenure, and those be the Bishops of the land: all which by vertue of baronries annexed to their bishoprickes, haue alwaies had place in the vpper house of Parlament, and are tearmed by the name of Lords spirituall.

Baron in the next significatiō is an Officer: as barons of the Exchequer be to the king: of which the principall is called Lord chiefe Baron *(capitalis Baro)* and the three other (for so many there be) are his assistants in causes of iustice, betweene the king and his subiects, touching causes appertaining to the *Exchequer*.

The Lord chiefe Baron at this day, is the chiefe Iudge of the court, and in matter of lawe, information, and plea, answereth the barre, and giueth order for iudgment thereuppon. He alone in the terme time doth sit vpon *Nisi prius*, that come out of the Kings Remembrancers office, or out of the office of the clerke of of the please, which cannot be dispatched in the mornings for want of time. He taketh recognisances for the Kings debts, for appearances, and obseruing of orders. He taketh the presentation of all the officers in court vnder himselfe, and of the Mayor of London, and seeth the Kings Remembrancer to giue them their oathes. He taketh the declaration of certaine receiuers accompts of the lands of the late augmentation, made before him by the Auditors of the shires. He giueth the two parcel makers places by vertue of his office.

The second Baron in the absence of the Lord chiefe baron, answereth the barre in matters aforesaid: he also taketh recognisances for the kings debts, apparences, and obseruing of orders. He giueth yearely the oath to the late Maior and escheatour of *London* for the true accompt of the profits of his office. He taketh a declaration of certaine receyuers accompts. He also examineth the letters and summes of such Shyreeues foraine accompts, as also the accompts of Eicheatours and Collectours of Subsidies and Fifteens, as are brought vnto him by the auditors of the Court.

The third Baron, in the absēce of the other two, answereth the barre in matters aforesaide, he also taketh recognisances, as aforesaide. He giueth yerely the oath of the late Mayor and gawger of *London* for his true accōpting. He also taketh a declaration of certaine receiuers accompts: and examineth the leters and sūmes of such of the former accountants, as are brought vnto him.

The fourth barons is alwaies a coursetour of the court, and hath bene chosen of some one of the clerks in the remembrancers offices, or of the clerke of the pipes office. He at the daies of prefixion, taketh oth of al high shyreeus and their vndershyreeues, and of all escheatours, baylifs, and other accountāts, for their true accounting. He taketh the oath of al collectours, controlers, surueyours and serchers of the custome houses, that they haue made true entrances in their bookes. He apposeth all shyreeues vpon their sūmons of the pipe in open court. He informeth the rest of the Barons, of the course of the court in any mater that concerneth the kings prerogatiue. He likewise, as the other Barons, taketh the declaration of certaine receiuers accompts: and examineth the leters and summes of such of the former accountants, as are brought vnto him.

These barons of the exchequer, are auncient officers: for I finde them named, *westm.* 2.*ca.* 11.*anno.* 13. *Ed.* 1. and they be called barons, because barons of the realme were wont to be employed in that office. *Fleta.li.* 2.*ca.* 24. S. *Thomas Smith* saith of them, that their office is to looke to the accompts of the Prince: and to that end they haue auditors vnder them: as also to descide all causes, appertaining to the Kings profits, comming into the exchequer by any meanes. This is in part also proued, by the statut *anno.* 20.*Ed.* 3.*ca.* 2.*&. anno.* 27.*eiusdem.stat.* 2.*ca.* 18.*& anno.* 5.*R.* 2. *stat.* 1.*ca.* 9. *&* 12.*& anno.* 14. *eiusd ca.* 11. And hereupon they be of late, men learned in the common lawe of the realme: wheras in auncient times, they were others: *viz. maiores & discretiores in regno, siue de clero essent, siue de curia. Ockam* in his lucubrations *de fisci regij ratione. Horn* in his *mirrour* of Iustices saieth, that barons were wont to be two, and they Knights. *ca. De la place del Eschequer.*

Then be there in this signification, Barons of the Cinque portes. *anno.* 31. *Ed.* 3. *stat.* 2.*ca.* 2.

*et anno.*33.*H* 8.*ca.* 10. which are twoof euery of the seuen towns, *Hastings,Winchelsey, Ry, Rumney, Hthe, Douer,& Sandwiche,* that haue places in the lower house of Parlament. *Cromptons iurisd. fo.* 28.Baron in the the third signification,is vsed for the husband in relation to his wife: which is so ordinary in all our lawe writers, that wright in french, as it were superfluous to confirme it by any one.

Baronet. I reade this word,*anno.*13.*R.*2.*stat.*2.*ca.*1.but I hould it falsely printed for *Baneret*, or els to signifie all one with it.

Baronye (baronia, baronagium) is the fee of a baron. In which accompt are not only the fees of temporall Barons, but of Bishops also: who haue two respects: one, as they are spirituall men, without possessions, as was the tribe of Levy among the Israelites,being susteined by the only first frutes and tenthes of the other tribes. *Iosue.ca.* 13. *versue.*14.The other respect they haue, groweth from the bountie of our english Kings, whereby they haue baronies at the least, & are thereby Barons or Lords of the Parlament. This baronie (as *Bracton* saith, *li.*2. *ca.*34.is a right indiuisible:and therefore if an inheritance be to be divided among coparceners: though some capitall messuages may be divided: yet, *si capitale messuagium sit caput Comitatus, vel caput Baronia*,he saith they may not be parcelled, The reason is,*ne sic caput per plures particulas dividatur, & plura iura comitatuum & baroniarum deveniant ad nihilum: per quod deficiat Regnum, quod ex Comitatibus & Baronys dicitur esse constitutum.*

Barre (barra) commeth of the French*(barre)* or *barriere*(.i.*repagalum, obex, vectis)* It is vsed in our common law, for a peremptory exception against a demaund or plaint:and is by the author of the Termes of law,defined to be a plee brought by the defendant in an action, that destroieth the action of the plaintiffe for euer. It is divided into a barre to common intent,and a barre speciall. Abarre to a common intendment,is an ordinarie or generall barre, that ordinarily disableth the declaration or plee of the plaintiffe: a barre speciall is, that, which is more then ordinarie,& falleth out in the case in hand or question,vpon some speciall circumstance of the fact. *Plowden. casu Colthirst. fo.* 26.*a.b.*For exāple,an executor being sued for his testators debt, pleadeth that he had no goods left in his hands,at the day when the writ was purchased or taken out against him. This is a good barre to common intendment,or *(pri-*

mi facio)But yet the case may so fall out, that more goods might come to his hands sithence that time: which if the plaintiffe can shew by way of replication, then excep the haue a more especiall plee or barre to alleadge, he is to be condemned in the action. See also *Plowden* in the case afore named. *fo.* 28.*a.b.* and *Brooke. titulo. Barre. nu.* 101. & *Kitchin. fo.* 215. Barre also in the same signification, is devided into barre materiall, and barre at large. *Kitchin. fo.* 68. A barre materiall (as it seemeth) may otherwise be called a barre speciall: as when one in the stoppe of the plaintiffes action, pleadeth some particular mater, as a descent from him that was the vndoubted owner, a feofment made by the auncester of the plaintiffe, or such like. A barre at large is, when the tenent or defendant by way of exception, doth not traverse the plaintifes title by pleading *not guiltie*, ncr confesse and avoid it, but onely maketh to himselfe a title in his barre. As if in an Assise of *novel disseisin*, the tenent pleade a feofment of a straunger vnto him, and giues but a colour onely to the plaintiffe. Of this there is an apt example to be found. 5. *H.* 7. *fo.* 29.

Barre, is also in regarde of the effect, diuided into *barre perpetuall* & *barre pro tempore*. *Perpetuall* is that, which overthroweth the actiõ for euer. *Barre pro tempore* is that, which is good for the present, and may faile heereafter: looke an example or two in *Broke titulo. Barre. nu.* 23. where he saith, that to plead (*plene administrauit*) is good, vntill it may appeare, that more goods come to the executors hands afterward, which also holdeth for an heire, that in an action of his auncesters debt pleadeth (*rien per discēt.*) This word is also vsed for a materiall *bar*: as the place where Sergeants or Cōucelers stand to pleade causes in courte, or prisoners to aunswere to their endictments. Of which our cōmon lawyers, that be lycēced to plead, in other contries called *licentiati*) are termed *barristers. anno.* 24. *H.* 8. *ca.* 24.

Barrator (*barectator*) commeth from the French (*barat.* i. *astutia*) and is neere the French it selfe in significatiõ. For (*barateur*) in that tong betokneth a deceiver: and a barator in our common law, is a common wrangler, that setteth men at ods, and is himselfe never quiet, but at brawle with one or other. To this effect you may read *M. Lamberds eirenarcha. pa.* 342. who saith likewise, that *barettor* (for so he writeth is) may seeme to come from the latine (*baratro*) or (*balatro*) that is, a vile knaue or vnthrift, and (by a metataphor) a spot in a cōmon wealth See. the statute of *champerty. an.* 33. *Ed.* 1. *stat.* 2. *ca. vnico.* and *West.* 1. *ca.* 32. *anno.* 3. *Ed.* 1. *M. Skene de verb. signif. verbo barratrie*, saith that barratours be Symonists called of the Italian word (*barrataria*) signifying corruption or briberie in a Iudge giuing a false sentence for mony: whome you may read more at large: as also *Hortensius Cavalcanus*, in his tractat *de brachio regio. parte.* 5. *nu.* 66. whose words are: *Barataria verò dicitur, quando Iudex aliquid petit indebitum, vt iustitiam faciat.* Who also. *nu.* 195. *partis* 5. saith thus: *barraterii appellātur, qui pratorium nimis frequentāt.* And in another place of the same worke. *Baratria dicitur, quia fit quoddam barratrum .i. commutatio pecunia cum iustitia, &c.* See also *Ægidius Bossius in practica criminali. titulo de officialibus corrupt. &c. nu.* 2. *&* 6. *Baratariam committunt, Iudices, qui iusticiā auro vendunt. Paris Puteola. de syndicatu. verbo Barataria. pa.* 217.

Barre fee, is a fee of 20. ꝺ. that euery prisoner acquited of felonie payeth to the gaoler. *Crompt. Iustice of peace. fo.* 158. *b.*

Barrell, is a measure of wine, oyle, &c. conteining the 8. parte of a tonne, the 4. of a pipe, and the second of a hogshead, that is, 31. gallons and a halfe. *anno.* 1. *R.* 3. *ca.* 13. But this vessel seemeth not to conteine any certaine quantitie, but differeth according to the liquor: for a barrell of beere conteineth 36. gallons, the Kilderkin, 18. and the firkin, 9. a barrell of ale 32. gallons. the kilderkin 16. and the firkin. 8. gallons. *anno.* 23. *H.* 8. *ca.* 4.

Barriers, commeth of the French (*barres*) and signifieth with vs that which the French men call (*ieu de barres .i. palastrā.*) a martial sport or exercise of mē, armed and fighting together with short swords, within certain limits or lists, whereby they are severed from the beholders.

Barter, may seeme to come of the French (*barater .i. circumvenire.*) It signifieth in our statutes, exchange of wares with wares. *an.* 1. *R.* 3. *ca.* 9. & so battry the substantiue. *anno.* 13. *Eliza. ca.* 7. The reason may be, because they that choppe and change in this maner, doe what they can for the most part, one to ouer-reach the other. See *barratour.*

Base estate, is in true French (*bas estat*) It signifieth in our cōmon law, that estate which base tenents haue in their lands. Base tenents be they (as *M. Lamberd* saith in his explica. of Saxō words. *verbo Paganus*) which do to their lords villeinous service. The author of the termes of law in his Tractat of old termes, saith that to hold in fee base, is to hold at the

the will of the lord. *Kitchin.fo.* 41.seemeth to make base tenure and franck to be contraries: where it appeareth, that he putteth copy holders in the number of base tenents. And out of these, I thinke, that it may be probably coniectured, that everie base tenent holdeth at the will of the lord, but yet, that there is a difference betweene a base estate, and and villenage, which *Fitzh.* in his *nat.br.fo.*12.*B.C.* seemeth to cōfound. For the aboue named author of the termes of law saith in the place before cited, that to hold in pure villenage, is to doe all that the lord will commaund him. So that if a copie holder haue but base estate, he not holding by the performance of everie commandement of his lord, cannot be saide to hold in villenage. Whether it may be said, that copy holders, be by custome and continuāce of time, growne out of that extreame servitude, wherein they were first created, I leaue to others of better iudgement: but *Fitzh. loco citato* saith, tenure by copie is a terme but lately invented.

Base courte, is any court that is not of record, as the court baron. Of this read *Kitchin.f.*95.96.&c.

Base fee, See *base estate.*

Baselard (*baslerdus*) in the *statut.anno.*12.*R.*2.*ca.*6. signifieth a weapon, which *M. Speight* in his exposition vpon *Chaucer*, calleth *pugionem vel sicam.*

Bastard (*bastardus*) See *Bastardy*. and See *Skeene de verbo.signif. verbo Bastardus.*

Bastardy (*bastardia*) commeth of the French (*bastard.i. nothus*) *Cassanaus de consuetu.Burg.pa.*1116. saith (*bastard*) and (*filius naturalis*) be all one. *Bastardy* in our common law, signifieth a defect of birth, obiected to one begotten out of wedlock. *Bract.li.*5.*ca.*19.*per totum.* How bastardie is to be prooued, or to be inquired into, if it be pleaded, see *Rastalls* booke of Entrise.*tit. Bastardie fo.*104. *Kitchin.fo.*64. maketh mention of bastardie speciall, and bastardie generall. The difference of which is, that bastardie generall is a certificate from the Bishop of the dioces to the Kings Iustices, after iust enquiry made, that the party inquired of, is a bastard or not a bastard vpon some question of inheritance. Bastardy speciall, is a suite commenced in the Kings court, against him that calleth another bastard: so termed (as it seemeth) because bastardy is the principall and especiall case in triall, and no inheritance contended for. And by this it appeareth, that in both these significations, bastardy is rather taken for an examination or triall, whether a mans birth be defectiue or illegitimat,

then

it selfe. See *Broke.titulo.* Bastardy. *n.29.* and *Doctor Ridlies* booke. *pa.*203.204.

Baston , is in french a staffe, club, or coulestaffe. It signifieth in the statuts of our realme, one of the warden of the fleets his seruants or officers, that attendeth the Kings court with a red staffe, for the taking of such to warde, as be committed by the court. So it is vsed. *anno* 1.*R.*2. *ca.* 12. *anno* 5.*Eliz.ca.*23.

Batable ground, seemeth to be the ground in question heeretofore, whether it belōged to *England* or *Scotland*, lying betweene both the kingdomes. *anno.*23.*H.*8.*ca.*16. as if we should say debatable ground . For by that name. *M.Skene.de verbo.sign.verbo Plegius.* calleth ground, that is in controuersie betweene two.

Battell(*duellum*) commeth of the French (*bataille*.i. *bellum, prælium*) and signifieth in our cōmon lawe, a triall by combate. The maner whereof because it is long, and full of ceremonies, I doe for the better and more full vnderstanding of it, referre you to *Glanvile, lib.* 2. *cap.*3.4.5. to *Bracton, lib.*3.*tract* 2 *cap.*21.*fol.*140 to *Britton, cap.*22. and to *S. Thomas Smith de repub. Anglorum, li.* 2. *cap.* 7. & *lib.* 3. *cap.* 3. See *Bombat.*

Battery cōmeth of the French (*batre.* i. *verberare, cudere, percutere*) and signifieth in our common lawe, a violent striking of any man, which the Civilians call *iniuriam personalem, quia persona infertur per verbera, cruciatū, &c. Wesemb. parat.* π. *de Iniur.& fam. libel.*

Baubels (*baubella*) is an old word, signifying Iewels. *Ro. Hoveden parte poster. suorum annal.fo.* 449. *b.*

Bearding, aliàs, Barding of wooll. See *Clack.*

Bearers, signifie all one with Maintainers, *anno* 20. *Edvar.* 3. *cap.* 5.

Beconage (*Beconagium*) signifieth money paid for the maintenance of Becons.

Bewpleder(*pulchrè placitando*) is made of. 2. french words (*beau.* i. *decorus, formosus, pulcher*) and (*pleder.* i. *disputare, & causam agere*) It signifieth in our common law, a writ vpon the statute of *Marlbridge* or *Marlborow*, made the 52. yeare of *H.*3.*ca.* 11. whereby it is provided, that neither in the circuit of Iustices, nor in Counties, Hundreds, or Courts-baron, any fines shall be taken of any man for faire pleading, that is, for not pleading fairely or aptly to the purpose. Vpon which Statute, this writ was ordained against those, that violate the lawe herein. See *Fitz. nat. br. fol.* 270. *A.B.C.* whose definition is to this effect: The writ vpon the Staute of *Marlebridge* for not faire pleading, lyeth where the Shyreeue or other Bailiffe in his court, will take fine of the party plaintiffe or defendant, for that he pleadeth not fairely, &c.

Bedell (*Bedellus*) commeth of the French (*bedeau*.i. *apparitor*) & it signifieth with vs, nothing else but a messenger or seruitour belonging to a Court, as a Courtbaron or Leet, *Kitchin fol.* 46. where you may see his oath: or to the Court of the Forest, *Manwood parte pri.* of his Forest lawes. *pag.* 221. in these words: A Bedell is an officer or seruant of the Forest, that doth make all maner of garnishments of the Courtes of the Forest, and also all maner of Proclamations, as well within the Courts of the Forest as without: and also doth execute all the processes of the Forest. He is like to a Bailiffe errant of a Shyreeue in a countie, &c.

Benefice (*Beneficium*) is generally taken for all ecclesiasticall liuings, be they dignities or other, as *anno* 13. R. 2. *stat.* 2. *ca.* 2 where benefices are diuided into electiue, and benefices of gift. So is it vsed in the Canon lawe also. *Duarenus de beneficiis. lib.* 2. *cap.* 3.

Beneficio primo ecclesiastico habendo, is a writ directed from the King to the Chanceler, to bestow the benefice that first shall fall in the kings gift, aboue or vnder such a valew, vpon this or that man, *Regist. orig. fol.* 307. *b.*

Beneuolence (*Beneuolentia*) is vsed both in the Chronicles and Statutes of this realme, for a voluntarie gratuitie giuen by the subiects to the King. Looke *Stowes annals pag.* 701. That it hath bene some thing auinciently accustomed, it appeareth by him and by the Statute *anno* 1. *Ric.* 3. *cap.* 2. where it is called a newe imposition: and in that respect reprehended by that tyrant in his predecessors: whether iustly or not I cannot say, nor mind to dispute. But *Stowe*, *pag.* 791. saith, that the inuention grewe from *Edward* the fourths dayes. You may find it also, *anno* 11. *H.* 7. *ca.* 10. to haue bene yeelded to that worthy Prince, in regard of his great expences in wars and otherwise. This is also mentioned and excepted out of the pardon, *anno* 1. *Ed.* 6. *cap.* 15. It is in other nations called (*subsidium charitativum*) giuen somtime to Lords of the fee, by their tenents, somtime to bishops by their Clergy. *Matthaeus de Afflictis, decis.* 136. *Cassan. de consuet. Burg. pag.* 134. 136. *Baldus consitio.* 120. *vol.* 6. *pag.* 230. Of this *Manochius* maketh mention, *lib.* 2. *centur.* 2. *ca.* 178. & 179. shewing, when it is lawful for a Prelate *charitatiuum subsidium à sibi subditis exigere, &*

quanta

quanta debeat esse eius summa, setting downe eight iust causes of this exaction.

Besaile (proavus) is borowed of the French (*bisayeul*. i. *le pere de mon pere grand*) the father of my grandfather. In the common law it signifieth a writ, that lieth, where the great grandfather was seised in his demesne as of fee, of any lands or tenements in fee-simple, the day that he dyed, and after his death a strãger abateth, or entreth the same day vpon him, and keepeth out his heyre, &c. The forme and farder vse of this writ, reade in *Fitz. nat. br. fol.* 221. *D. E. F. &c.*

Beastes of chace (Feræ campestres) be fiue of the Forest, chace, or parke: that is, the Bucke, the Doe, the Foxe, the Martron, and the Roe, *Manwood parte prim.* of his Forest lawes, *pag.* 342. *& parte 2. cap.* 4. *num.* 2.

Beasts of the forest (feræ sylvestres) are the Hart, the Hind, the Hare, the Boare, and the Wolfe, *Manwood parte* 2. of his Forest lawes, *cap.* 4. *num.* 1.

Beasts and Fowles of Waren, are the Hare, Conie, Fesant, and the Pertridge, *Manwood parte* 2. *cap.* 4. *num.* 3.

Bestaile, commeth of the French (*bestial*. i. *pecus*) it seemeth with vs to signifie all kind of catell taken for the kings provision, *anno* 4. *Ed.* 3. *cap.* 3. And bestiall is generally vsed for all kind of catell, *anno* 1. *Iacobi cap.* 33.

Bidding of the bedes, was a charge or warning, that the parish Priest gaue to his parishioners, at certaine especiall times, to say so many *Pater nosters, &c.* vpon their beades, *anno* 27. *H.* 8. *cap.* 26.

Bigamie (bigamia) signifieth a double mariage. It is vsed in the common lawe, for an impediment that hindreth a man to be a Clerke, by reason that he hath bene twice maried. For vpon those words of *S. Paule* to *Timothie* the first. *cap.* 3. *vers.* 2. (*Oportet ergo Episcopum irreprehensibilem esse, & unius uxoris virum:*) the Canonists haue founded their doctrine, that he that hath bene twice maried, may not be a Clerke. And also him that hath maried a widow, they by interpretation, take to haue bene twice maried. And both these they do not onely exclude from holy orders, but also deny them all priuiledges that belong vnto Clerkes. But the author of the new termes of lawe well saith, that this lawe is abolished by *anno* 1. *Ed.* 6. *cap.* 12. And to that may be added the statute, *anno* 18. *Elizab. cap.* 7. which alloweth to all men that can read as Clerkes, though not within orders, the benefite of Clergie in case of felonie not especially excepted by some other statute.

Bilanciis deferendis, is a writ directed to a corporation, for the carying of weights, to such or such a hauen, there to weigh the wools that such a man is licenced to trãsport, *Reg. orig f.* 270. *a.*

Bilawes, are orders made in court leets or court Barons by common assent, for the good of those that make them, farder then the publique lawe doth binde. *Coke vol.6.fo.63.a.Kitchin fo.*45.& 79. These in *Scotland* are called (*burlawe*) or (*birlawe*) *Skene de verbo: sign. verbo Burlawe*: where he saith thus: Lawes of *burlawe*, are made and determined, by consent of neighbours elected and chosen by common consent, in the courts called *birlawe* courts. In the which cognition is taken of compleints betwixt neighbour and neighbour: which men so chosen, are iudges and arbitratours to the effect aforesaide, and are called *birlawe men*, For (*bawr*) or (*bawrsman*) in Dutch is (*rusticus*) and so (*birlaw*) or (*burlaw*) *leges rusticorum*. Hetherto *M. Skene*.

Bilinguis, though it signifie in generality a double tounged man; yet in our common lawe, it is vsed for that Iury, that passeth betweene an english man and an alien. Wherof part must bee Englishmen, and part straungers. *anno.*28.*Ed.*3.*ca.*13.

Bille (*billa*) is diuersly vsed among our cõmon lawyers. First (as *West.* saith *pa.* 1. *symb.li.* 2.*sect.* 146. it is al one with an obligation, sauing that whẽ it is in ẽglish, it is commonly called a bill, and when it is in latine, an obligation. But I heare other good lawyers say, that a bill, though it be obligatorie, yet is without condition or forfeiture for *non payment*: and that the obligation hath both. Bille secondly, is a declaration in writing, that expresseth either the griefe and the wrong that the complaynant hath suffered, by the party complained of, or els some fault, that the party complayned of, hath committed against some lawe or statute of the common wealth. This bille is sometime offered vp to Iustices errants in the generall assises: sometime, and most of all, to the Lord Chanceler of England, especially for vnconscionable wrongs done, sometime to others hauing iurisdiction, accordingly as the law, wherupon they are grounded, doeth direct. It containeth the fact complained of, the dammages thereby suffered, and petition of processe against the defendant for redresse. *West. parte.* 2.*Simbol. titulo supplications.sect.*52. whom you may reade at large touching

this

this mater.

Billa vera, is (as it were) a word of arte in our common lawe. For the grand enquest empaneled and sworne before the Iustices in *eare* &c. indorsing a bill, whereby any crime punishable in that court, is presented vnto them, with these two words; do signifie thereby, that the presentor hath furnished his presentment or denunciation with probable euidence, and worthy of farder consideration. And thereuppon, the party presented by the same bill, is said to stand indicted of the crime, and so tyed to make answer vnto it, either by confessing, or trauersing the indictment. And if the crime touch the life of the party indicted, it is yet referred to another enquest, called the enquest of life and death: who if they finde him guilty, then he standeth conuicted of the crime, and is by the Iudge to be cōdemned to death. See *Ignoramus*, see *Indictment*.

Billets of gold, commeth of the french (*billot*. I. *massa auri*. *anno*. 27. *Ed* 3. *stat*. 2. *ca*. 14.

Bynny peper. *anno*. 1. *Iaco*. *ca*. 19.

Blacke maile, is halfe english, halfe french. For in french (*maille*) signifieth a smal peece of mony, which we cal a halfepeny. It signifieth, in the counties of *Cumberlād*, *Northumberland*, *Westmerland*, and the bishopricke of *Durisme*, a certaine rate of mony, corne, catell, or other consideration, paide vnto some inhabiting vpon or neere the borders, being men of name and power, allied with certaine, knowne to be great robbers and spoile-takers within the saide counties, to the end thereby to be by them freed, protected, and kept in safty, from the daunger of such as doe vsually robbe and steale in those partes. *an*. 43. *Eliza*. *ca*. 13.

Blacke rodde, is the huissier belonging to the order of the Garter, so called of his blacke rodde that he carrieth in his hand. He is of the kings chamber, and also huissier of the parlament.

Blanks, cōmeth of the french (*blanc*. I. *candidus*, *albus*) It signifieth a kind of coine that was coined in the parts of Frāce 5. by *K*. *H*. that were subiect to England: the valew whereof was eight pence. *Stowes annals*. *pa*. 586. These were forbidden to be current within this realme. *a*. 2. *H*. 6. *ca*. 9. The reason why they were called blankes may be, because at the time these were coyned in France, there was also a peece of gold coyned, which was called a (*Salus*) of the value of 22. shillings from which this siluer was in name distinguished by the colour.

Bloody hand. See *Backberend*.

Blomary, is one of the forges

belonging to an iron mill (which also seemeth otherwise to be tearmed a *Finary.*) The vse wherof if you will vnderstand, you must knowe, that first there is a fornace, wherin the mine-stones are melted and cast into a raw iron, fashioned into long wedges three square. that be called sows. Then be there two forges like vnto smithes forges, but much bigger, the one whereof is called the blomary or (as it seemeth) the finary, into the which being maintained with a charcole fire blowne with bellowes, made to goe by water, are cast the saide sowes of raw iron, and melted againe, and by a workman called the finary man, are wounde and wrought rounde, and afterwarde beaten by a hammer into little wedges about a yarde long, which are called bloomes. Then is there another forge called the Hammer, into which these bloomes are cast, and by a workman (called the hammer man) againe chafed and made soft in a charcole fire, blowne likewise with bellowes caused to goe by the water: and after caried by the saide hammer man, and put vnder the great hammer driuen also by the water. And so the saide bloomes are drawen, fashiõed, and made into such barres of iron of diuers sortes and formes, as we see commonly sould. Of these you may reade in the statut. *anno.* 27. *Elizab. ca.* 19. *See Baye.*

Bloodwit (*blodwita*) is compoũded of 2. Saxon words (*blout.* i. *sanguis*) and (*wit*) for the which we haue the word (*wite*) still in the West parts of *England* signifying a charging of one with a fault, or an vpbraiding. And *Speight* in his expositions vpon *Chawser* saith that (to wit) is as much as to blame. (To twit) in some other places of this land signifieth as much as (to hitte in the teeth) or to vpbraide. This bloodwit is a word vsed in charters of liberties auncietly grãted, and signifieth an amercement for shedding of blood. So that whosoeuer had it giuen him in his charter, had the penaltie due for shedding of blood graunted vnto him. *Rastall* in his exposition of words. *Skene de verbo. signif.* writeth it (*bludveit*) and saith that (*veit*) in englishis *iniuria vel misericordia:* and that (*bludveit*) is an amercement or (vnlawe) as the *Scottish men* call it, for wrong or iniurie, as bloodshed is. For he that is *infest* with (*bludveit*) hath free libertie to take all amercements of courts for effusion of blood. *Fleta* saith, *quod significat quietantiam misericordiæ pro effusione sanguinis. li.* 1. *ca.* 47.

Bockland, See *Charterland.* See

Copie hould and *Free hould*.

Bonis arrestandis, is a writ, for the which See *Arrestandis bonis*.

Bonis non amovendis, is a writ to the *Shyreeues* of *London*, &c. to charge them, that one condemned by judgement in an action, and prosecuting a writ of errour, be not suffered to remooue his goods, vntill the errour be tried. *Register. orig. fo.* 131. *b*.

Borow (*burgus vel burgum*) may either come from the French (*burg*. i. *pagus*) or from the Saxon (*borhoe*. i. *vadium, pignus*.) It signifieth here in England a corporate towne that is not a Citie. *anno*. 2. *Ed*. 3. *ca*. 3, namely all such as send *Burgesses* to the Parlament: the number whereof you may see in *M. Cromptons Iurisd. fo.* 24. It may probably be thought, that it was auncientlyly taken for those companies consisting of ten families, which were combyned to be one anothers pledge or borhoe: See *Bracton. li*. 3. *tractat*. 2. *ca*. 20. See Headborowe, and Borowhead, and *M. Lambard* in the duties of constables. *pa*. 8. *Lynwood* vpon the prouinciall (*vt singula de censibus*), speake to this effect: *Aliqui interpretantur burgum esse castrum, vel locum vbi sunt crebra castra. vel dicitur burgus, vbi sunt per limites habitacula plura constituta*.) But then setting downe his owne opinion, he defineth it thus: *Burgus dici potest villa quaecunque alia a ciuitate, in qua est vniuersitas approbata*. And that he proueth oute of the 11. booke of *Instinians Codex. titulo de fund. rei priuatae*. 65. *et. l*. 6. *eius tituli*. where *burgus* is termed *corpus*. some deriue it from the *greeke* (πυργος. i. *turris*) see *M. Skene de verbo signif. verbo. Borghe*. The late author *M. Verstegan*. in his restitution of decaied intelligences, saith, that (*burg*) or (*burgh*) whereof we say yet (*Borough*) or (*Bourrow*) metaphorically signifieth a towne, hauing a wall, or some kinde of closure about it: also a Castell. All places that in old time had among our auncesters the name of borrough, were places one way or other fensed or fortified.

Bordlands, signifie the demeasns, that lords keepe in their hands, to the maintenance of their bord or table. *Bract. li*. 4. *tractat*. 3. *ca*. 9. *nu*. 5.

Borowhead alias Headborowe, (*capitalis plegius*) by *M. Lamberds* opinion in his treatise of *Constables*, is made vp of these two words. (*borhoe*. i. *pledge* and (*head*) and signifieth a head or chiefe pledge. And in explication of this, and other Saxon words of this nature, he maketh an excellent rehearsall of some auncient customes of England, during the reigne of the *Saxons*, which you may reade. This borowhead (*in short*) was

was the head or cheife man of the Decurie or *Borhoe*, that there he speaketh of, chosen by the rest to speake, & to doe in the name of the rest, those things that concerned them. See *Borowholders*.

Borowhowlders, alias Bursholders, be *quasi borhoe ealders*, signifing the same officers that be called borowheads. (*Lamb.* in the duties of *Constables.*) *Bracton* calleth them (*Borghie Aldere*) *li.* 3. *tractat.* 2. *ca.* 10.

Borow english, is a custumarie descent of lands or tenements, whereby in all places where this custome holdeth, lands and tenemenrs descend to the yongest sonne: or, if the owner haue no issue, to his yongest brother: as in *Edmunton. Kitchin. fo.* 102. And the reason of this custome, as (*Litleton* saith) is, for that the yongest is presumed in lawe, to be least able to shift for himselfe.

Borow goods divisable, I finde these words in the statute of *Acton. Burnel. anno* 11. *Ed.* 1. *statuto vnico.* and dare not confidently set downe the true meaning of them. But as before the statute of 32. & 34. *H.* 8. no lands weare diuisable at the common law, but in auncient baronies: so perhaps, at the making of the foresaide statute of *Acton burnel*, it was doubtfull, whether goods were deuisable but in auncient borowes For it seemeth by the writ. *de rationabili parte bonorum.* that auncieutly the goods of a man were partible betwene his wife and children.

Bote, signifieth compensation. *Lamb. explication of Saxon words.* Thence cometh (*manbote, aliâs monbote*) that is compensation or amends for a man slaine, which is bound to another. For farder vnderstanding whereof, it is to be seene in *K. Inas* lawes, set out by *M. Lamberd. ca.* 96. what rate was ordeined for the expiation of this offence: See *Hedgebote, Plowbote, Housebote.* & reade *M. Skene de verbo. signif. verbo. Bote.*

Botiler of the king (*pincerna regis*) *anno* 43. *Ed.* 3. *ca.* 3. is an officer that prouideth the Kings wines: who (as *Fleta li.* 2. *ca.* 21. saith) may by vertue of his office out of euery shippe loaden with sale wines, *vnum doleum eligere in prora navis ad opus regis, & aliud in puppi, & pro qualibet pecia reddere tantùm* 20. *solid. mercatori. Si autem plura inde habere voluerit, bene licebit: dum tamen precium fide dignorum iudicio pro rege apponatur.*

Bowbearer, is an vnder officer of the forest (as *M. Crompton* in his *iurisdict fo.* 201. setteth downe, sworne to the true performance of his office in these words: I will true man be to the master forister

ſter of this foreſt,& to his lieutenent: and in the abſence of them,I ſhall truly overſee, and true inquiſition make,as well of ſwornemen as vnſworne in euerie bayliwick,both in the north bayle. and ſouth bayle. of this foreſt,and of all maner of treſpaſſes done, either to vert or veniſon, I ſhall truly endeavour my ſelfe to attach, or cauſe them to be attached,in the next court Attachement, there to be preſented,without any concealment had to my knowledge: ſo helpe me God,&c.

Bracton (otherwiſe called *Henry* of *Bracton*) was a famous lawyer of this land, renowmed for his knowledge both in the common and civill lawes, as appeareth by his booke every where extant. He liued in the daies of *Henry* the third. *Stawn.praro.fo.* 5.*b*. and as ſome ſay, Lord cheife Iuſtice of *England*.

Bread of treate, and bread of coket. *anno*.51.*H*.3.*ſtatuto*. 1. of bread and ale.

Bred, ſignifieth broade. This word *Bracton* vſeth, *li*..3.*tracta*.2. *ca*.15.*nu*.7. proverbially thus: to lange and to bred: the meaning whereof you may there finde, word for word it is, as we now ſpeake, two long and two broad: or two in length, and two in breadth.

Breuibus, & rotulis liberandis, is a writ or mandat to a Shyreeue to deliuer vnto the newe Shyreeue choſen in his roome, the county with the appertenances, together with the rols, briefes, remembrances, and all other things belonging to that office. *Regiſter.original.fo.* 295.*a*.

Bribours, commeth of the french (*bribeur*.i.*mendicus*) It ſeemeth to ſignifie with vs, one that pilfreth other mens goods. *anno* 28.*Ed*.2.*ſtat*.1.*ca*.*vnico*.

Brief (*breve*) commeth from the French (*bref ou breif*. i. *brevis*) and in our common lawe, ſignifieth a writ, whereby a man is ſummoned to anſwer to any action: or (more largely) any precept of the king in writing, iſſuing out of any court, whereby he commaundeth any thing to be done, for the furtherance of iuſtice or good order. The word is vſed in the ciuile lawe, ſome time in the ſingular number and maſculine gender. as *l.vlt.Cod. de conueniendis fiſci debitoribus.li.* 10. *tit*.2. you haue theſe words: *Inter chartulas confiſcati brevis, quidam adſeueratur inventus, qui nomina cōtinebat debitorũ*. Where it is vſed for a ſhort note. Again, I finde a title reſtored by *Gothofred*, in the firſt booke of the *Code. de quadrimenſtruis brevibus. Quadrumenſtrui autem breves erant, qui de ſingulis indictionum penſionibus, quarto quoq; menſe ſolutis, conficiebantur.*

Alſo *Lampridius* in *Alexandro* hath it ſingularly thus: *notarium, qui falſum cauſæ brevem in conſilio imperatori oretuliſſet, &c.* And in the *Authētiques Novel.* 105.*ca.* 2. you haue this word (*breviatores.* i. *brevium proſcriptores*). *Breves autem, brevia, brevicula, ſunt chartæ ſive libelli breves*, as *Gothofred.* there noteth. Where he noteth likewiſe out of *Zonaras in Carthagin: Cōcilio*, that this is a greeke word, thus: βρέβιον ἡ ἐπίτομη λέγεται καὶ σύντομος γραφή. See *Skeno de verbo. ſignif. verbo Breue*. Of theſe breifes ſee alſo *Bracton. li.* 5. *tract.* 5. *ca.* 17. *nu.* 2. *Breve quidem cùm ſit formatum ad ſimilitudinem regulæ iuris, quia breviter & paucis verbis intentionem proferentis exponit & explanat, ſicut regula iuris rem quæ eſt breviter enarrat. Non tamen ita breve eſſe debet, quin rationem & vim intentionis contineat. &c.*

Brigandine (*lorica*) is the french (*brigandine*) that is a coate of maile. This is vſed. *anno* 4. & 5. *Ph. & Mar. ca.* 2.

Brig*bote*, *ſignificat quietantiam reparationis pontium. Fleta. li.* 1. *ca.* 47. It is compounded of (*brig*) a bridge and (*bote*) which is a yeelding of amends or ſupplying a defect. See (*Bote*) and *Bruckbote*.

Britton, was a famous Lawyer, that liued in the daies of *K. Edward* the firſt, at whoſe commandemēt, & by whoſe authority he writ a learned booke of the lawe of this realme. The tenure wherof runneth in the Kings name, as if it had beene penned by himſelfe, anſwerably to the Inſtitutions, which Iuſtinian aſſumeth to himſelfe, though compoſed by others. *Stawnf. prær. fo.* 6. & 21. *S. Edward Cooke* ſaith, that this *Britton* writ his booke in the fifte yeare of the ſaid Kings reigne. *li.* 4. *fo.* 126. *a.* & *lib.* 6. *fo.* 67. *a. M. Guin.* in the preface to his reading, mencioneth, that this *Iohn Britton* was biſhop of *Hereford*.

Broke, commonly called *S. Robert Broke*, was a greate lawyer and lord chiefe Iuſtice of the cōmon plees in *Queene Maries* time. *Cromptons* Iuſtices of peace. *fo.* 22. *b.* he made an abbridgement of the whole lawe, a booke of highe accoumpt.

Broker (*brocarius.*) ſeemeth to come from the French (*broieur.* i. *tritor*) that is a gryneder or breaker into ſmall peeces. Becauſe he that is of that trade, to deall in maters of mony and marchandiſe betwene Engliſhe men and Strangers, doth draw the bargaine to particulars, and the parties to concluſion, not forgetting to grinde out ſomthing to his owne profit. Theſe men be called broggers. *anno.* 10. *R.* 2. *ca.* i. It may not improbably be ſaid, that this word commeth from

(*bra-*

carder. i. *cavillari.)* because these kinde of men, by their deceitfull speeches and abusing their true trade, many times inuegle others. In *Scotland* they be called *(broccary)* and in their owne idiome, blockers or brockers, that is, mediators or intercessors in any trãsaction, paction, or contract: as in buying or selling, or in contracting mariage. *Skene de verbo. signi. verbo. broccary*.

He that will know what these brokers were wont & ought to be, let him read the *statut. anno*. 1. *Iacobi. ca*. 21. These in the civile lawe are called *(proxenetæ)* as also of some *(licitatores & mediatores. titulo. de proxeneticis. in Digestis*. This kind of dealer is also of the Romanes called *(pararius)* *Seneca. li. 2. de benef. ca*. 22. *Cælius Rhodoginus, libro. 6. ca*. 32. *& li* 3. *cap*. 15.

Broderers (commeth of the French *(brodeur)* and that commeth of *(bordure. i. fimbria, limbus)* the edge or hemme of a garmẽt. And that because it is distinguished frõ the rest, most cõmõly, by some conceipted or costly worke; he that worketh it, is called *(brodeur)* in French, and broderer or embroderer with vs.

Brodehalpeny, commeth of the three Saxon words *(bret*, or *bred,)* i. *a boord*: and *(halve)* that is, for this or that cause *(cuius rei gratia)* as the Latinists speake; and *(penning)* it signifieth a tolle or custome for setting vp of tables or boords in a Faire or Market. From the which they that are freed by the Kings Charter, had this word mentioned in there leters patents. In so much, as at this day the freedome it selfe (for shortnesse of speech) is called by the name of *brodehalpenie*.

Broggers. See *Brokers*.

Bruckbote (Pontagium) is compounded of two German words *(bruck*. i. *pons,)* and *(bote*. i. *compensatio.)* It signifieth with vs, a tribute, contribution, or ayde toward the mending or reedifiing of bridges; whereof many are freed by the kings charter. And thereupon the word is vsed for the very libertie or exemptiõ from this tribute. See *Pontage & Brigbote*.

Bull (bulla) seemeth to come from the Greeke, (βουλη) .i. *consilium*) as *Polidorus Virgilius* saith, *de inventio. rerum. lib*. 8. *cap*. 2. It signifieth the leters, by the Canonists called Apostolique, strengthened with a leaden seale, and containing in them the decrees or commandements of the Pope or bishop of Rome. The word is vsed many times in our *Statutes*: as *anno* 28. *H*. 8. *cap*. 16. *& anno* 1. *&* 2. *Ph. & Ma. ca*. 8.

Bullion, cometh of the French *(billon)* that is, the place where gold is tried. It signifieth with vs, gold or siluer in the masse or billet, *anno 9. Ed. 3. stat. 2. cap. 2.* and sometime the Kings exchange or place, whether such gold in the lumpe is brought to be tryed or exchanged, *anno 27. Ed. 3. stat. 2. cap. 14. & anno 4. H. 4. cap. 10.* See *Skene de verbo. signif. verbo Bullion.*

Burgbote, commeth of (*burg.* i. *castellum*) and (*bote.* i. *compensatio*) and signifieth a tribute or contribution toward the building or repairing of castels, or walles of defence, or toward the building of a borow or city. Frō this diuers had exemption by the auncient charters of the Saxon kings. Whereupon it is taken ordinarily for the exemption or libertie it selfe. *Rastals expos. of words. Fleta* hath these words of it: *Significat quietantiam reparationis murorum ciuitatis vel burgi li. 1. cap. 47.*

Burgh English. See *Borow English.*

Burgage (*burgagium*) is a tenure proper to cities & townes, whereby men of cities or borowes, hold their lands or tenements of the King, or other Lord for a certaine yearely rent. *Old Tenures* It is a kind of socage. *Swinborn. parte 2. §. 3. nu. 6.*

Burglarie (*burglaria*) is compounded of two French words, (*bourg.* i. *pagus, villa*) and (*larecin,* i. *furtum,*) or of (*bourg & laron*) *Coke lib. 4. fol. 39. b.* It is, according to the acceptance of our common lawe, thus defined: Burglarie is a felonious entring into another mans dwelling house, wherein some person is, or into a Church in the night time, to the end to commit some felonie therein: as to kill some man, or to steale somewhat thence, or to do some other felonious act there, albeit he execute not the same. If the intent, or fact of this offender, be to steale, this is like robberie, if to murder, it differeth not much from murder, and so of other felonies. *West. parte 2. symbol. titulo. Indictments. Sect. 56.* Burglarie, in the naturall signification of the word, is nothing, but the robbing of a house: but as it is (*vox artis*) our common Lawyers restraine it to robbing a house by night, or breaking in with an intent to robbe, or to do some other felonie. The like offence committed by day, they call house-robbing, by a peculiar name. How many wayes burglarie may be committed, see *Cromptons Iustice of peace, fol. 28. b. & fol. 29. 30.*

Butlerage of wines, signifieth that imposition of sale wine brought into the land, which the Kings butler, by vertue of his office, may take of euery shippe, *anno 1. H. 8. cap. 5.* For the which see more in *Boyler*.

C

CAblish (*cabiscia*) among the writers of the Forest lawes, signifieth brush wood, *Manwood parte pag.* 84. *Cromptons Iurisd. fol.* 165.

Calamus, is a cane, reed, or quill, the diuers kinds wherof, you haue set downe in *Gerards Herball. lib.* 1. *cap.* 24. This is comprized among merchandize and drugs to be garbled, in the statute *anno* 1. *Iacobi, cap.* 19.

Calendrin of Worsseds. anno 5. *H.* 8. *cap.* 4. *& anno* 25. *eiusdem. cap.* 5.

Cantred, is as much in *Wales*, as an hundred in *England*. For *Cantre* in the Brittish tongue signifieth *centum*. This word is vsed *anno* 28. *H.* 8. *cap.* 3.

Cape, is a writ iudiciall touching plee of land or tenements, so tearmed (as most writs be) of that word in it selfe, which carieth the especiallest intention or end thereof. And this writ is diuided in (*Cape magnum, & Cape parvum*:) both which (as is before said in Attachment) take hold of things immoueable, and seeme to differ betweene themselues in these points. First, because (*cape magnum*) or the (*grand Cape*) lyeth before appearance, and (*Cape parvum*) afterward. Secondly, the (*Cape magnum*) summoneth the tenent to aunswer to the default, and ouer to the demaundant: (*Cape parvum*) summoneth the tenent to aunswer to the default onely: and therefore is called (*Cape parvum*) or in French English (*petit Cape*.) *Old. nat. br. fol.* 161. 162. Yet *Ingham* saith, that it is called (*petit Cape*) not because it is of small force, but that it consisteth of few words. (*Cape magnum*) in the *old nat. br.* is thus defined. This writ is a iudiciall, and lyeth where a man hath brought a (*Pracipe quod reddat*) of a thing that toucheth plee of land, and the tenent make default at the day to him giuen in the writ originall: then this writ, shall goe for the king to take the land into the kings hands: and if he come not at the day giuen him by the (*grand Cape*) he hath lost his land, &c. A president and forme of this writ you may see in the *Register iudiciall, fol.* 1. *b.* It seemeth after a sort to containe in it the effect (*missionis in possessionem ex primo & secundo decreto*) among the Civilians. For as the first decree seiseth the thing, and the second giueth it from him, that the second time defaulteth in his appearance: so this (*Cape*) both seiseth the land, and also assigneth to the partie a farder day of appearance, at which if he come not in, the land is forfeited. Yet is there difference betweene these two courses of the ciuill and cōmon lawe: first, for that (*missio in possessionem*) toucheth both moueable and immoueable goods, whereas the (*cape*) is extended only to immoueable: secondly, that the partie being satisfied of his demaund, the *remanet* is restored to him that defaulted: but by the (*cape*) all is seised without restitution: thirdly, (*missio in possess:*) is to the vse of the partie agent, the (*cape*) is to the vse of the king. Of this writ, and the explication of the true force and effect thereof, reade *Bracton lib.* 5. *tract.* 3. *cap.* 1. *num.* 4. 5. & 6. See Cape *ad valentiam.*

Cape parvum, in the *Old. na. br. fol.* 162. is thus defined: This writ lyeth, in case where the tenent is summoned in plee of land, and commeth at the summons, and his appearance is of record, and after he maketh default at the day that is giuen to him: then shall goe this writ for the king, &c. Of this likewise you haue the form in the Register iudiciall, *fol.* 2. *a.* Why it is called *cape parvum*, see in *cape magnum.* Of both these writs, reade *Fleta lib.* 6. *cap.* 44. §. *Magnum* & *seqq.*

Cape ad Valentiam, is a species of *cape magnum*, so called of the end whereunto it tendeth. In the *Old nat. br. fol.* 161. 162. it is thus defined or described: This writ lyeth, where any impleaded of certaine lands, and I vouch to warrant another, against whom the summons *ad warrantizandum*, hath bene awarded, and the Shyreeue commeth not at the day giuen: then if the demandant recouer against me, I shall haue this writ against the vouchee, and shall recouer so much in value of the land of the vowchee, if he haue so much: and if he haue not so much, then I shall haue execution of such lands and tenements, as descend vnto him in fee-simple: or if he purchase afterward, I shall haue against him a resummons: and if he can nothing say, I shall recouer the value. And note ye, that this writ lyeth before apparence. Thus farre goeth the booke. Of these, and the diuers vses of them, see the Table of the Register iudiciall, *verbo. Cape.*

Capias, is a writ of two sortes, one before iudgement called (*Capias ad respondendum*) in an action personall, if the Shyreeue vpon the first writ of distresse returne (*nihil habet in balliva nostra:*) and the other is a writ of execution after iudgement, being also of of diuers kindes (*viz. Capias ad satisfaciendum, Capias pro fine, Capias vtlagatum, Capias vtlagatũ & inquiras de bonis & catallis*).

Capias ad satisfaciendum, is a writ of execution after iudgement, lying where a man recouereth in an action personall, as debt, or dammages, or detinew in the kings court: and he against whome the debt is recouered, and hath no lands nor tenemẽts, nor sufficient goods, wherof the debt may be leuied. For in this case, he that recouereth, shal haue this writ to the shreue, commanding him that he take the body of him, against whome the debt is recouered: and he shalbe put in prison, vntill satisfaction be made vnto him that recouered.

Capias pro fine, is where one being by iudgement fined vnto the king, vpon some offence committed against a statut, doth not discharge it according to the iudgement. For by this is his body taken, and committed to prison, vntill he content the king for his fine. *Coke. li. 3 fo.* 12 *a.*

Capias vtlagatum, is a word of execution, or after iudgement, which lyeth against him that is outlawed vpon any suite: by the which the shyreue vpon the receite thereof, apprehendeth the party outlawed, for not appearing vpon the (*exegend*) and keepeth him in safe custodie vntill the day of returne assigned in the writ: and then presenteth him vnto the court, there farder to be ordered for his contempt.

Capias vtlagatum, & inquiras de bonis & catallis, is a writ al one with the former, but that it giueth a farder power to the shyreue, ouer and beside the apprehension of the body, to inquire of his goods and cattels. The forme of all these writs see in the *ould nat. br. fo.* 154. and see the Termes of law, *verbo Proces.* Lastly you may finde great variety of this kinde, in the table of the Register iudiciall *verbo Capias.*

Capias in Withernamium de averys, is a writ lying for catell in *Withernam. Register orig. fo.* 82. & 83. see *Withernam.*

Capias in Withernamium de homine, is a writ that lyeth for a seruant in *Withernam. Regist. or. fo.* 79. & 80. see *Withernam:*

Capias conductos ad proficiscendum, is a writ that lieth for the taking vp of such, as hauing receiued prest mony to serue the king, slink away, and come not in at their time assigned. *Register. orig. fo.* 191.

Captaine, alias capitayne (*capitaneus*) commeth of the French (*capitaine*) and signifieth with vs, him that leadeth, or hath charge of of a companie of souldiers: and is either generall, as he that hath the gouernance of the whole host: or speciall, as he that leadeth one only band. The word (*capitanei*) in others nations signifieth more generally those, that are in latine called (*principes*) or (*proceres*) because, as *Hottoman* saith *in verbis feudalibus: tanquã caput reliquo corpori, sic hij reliquis civibus præsunt*. He divideth them into two sorts: and to vse his words. *aliĩ sunt capitanei regni: quo verbo Duces, Comites, Marchiones intelligũtur. li.1. feudo. tit.1. §.1. & ti.7. Alii improprie, qui vrbiũ præfecti sunt, quibus plebs ab aliquo superiorum gubernanda committitur: qui & vallasores regii, & maiores appellantur. l.1. feud. tit.1. §.1. & tit.7. & tit.17.* So we haue captaines of castels heere in *England*, and other places, as of the Isles of *Gearsey* and *Gearnsey*, of the Isle of *Weight, &c.*

Capite, is a tenure, which holdeth immediately of the king, as of his crown, be it by knights seruice or socage: *Broke. tit. Tenures. 46. 94. Dyer. fo.123. nu. 38 & fo. 363. nu.18.* & not as of any Honour, castell, or maner: and therefore it is otherwise called a tenure, that holdeth meerely of the king, because as the crowne is a corporation, and seigneury in grosse (as the common lawyers terme it) so the King that possesseth the crowne, is in accõpt of lawe, perpetually King, and neuer in his minoritie, nor neuer dieth: no more then (*populus*) doth, whose authoritie he beareth. See *Fitzh. nat. br. fo.5. F.* Note by the way, that a man may hold of the king, and not (*in Capite*) that is, not immediately of the crowne in grosse, but by meanes of some Honour, castel, or maner belonging to the Crowne, wherof I hold my land. Whereof *Kitchin* saith well, that a man may hold of the King by Knight seruice, and yet not in *capite*, because he holdeth happily of some honour by Knights seruice, which is in the kings hands (as by descent from his auncesters) and not immediately of the king, as of his crowne. *fo.129.* with whome agreeth *Fitzh. nat. br. f.5. K.* whose words are to this effect: So that it plainely appeareth, that lands which be held of the king, as of an honour, castell, or maner, are not held in *capite* of the King: because that a writ of right, in that case, shallbe directed to the bayliffe of the honour, castell, or maner, &c. but when the lands be held of the King, as of his crowne, then they be not held of honour, castell, or maner, but meerely of the King, as King, and of the Kings crowne, as of a seigneury of it selfe in grosse, and the cheife aboue all other seigneuries,

ries,&c. And this tenure in *capite* is otherwise called tenure holding of the person of the King. *Dyer.fo.44.n.37.* Author of the new termes.*verb.Tenure in capite. Broke.titulo.Tenures.nu. 65. 99.* And yet *M.Kitchin.fo.208.* saith, that a man may hould of the person of the King, and not in *capite.* His example is this: if the King purchas a maner that *I. S.* houldeth, the tenent shall hould as he held before, and shall not render liuery or *primier seisin*, nor hould in *capite*: And if the king graunt that maner to *W.N.* in fee, excepting the seruices of *I. S.* then *I.S.* holdeth of the king, as of the person of the king, and yet houldeth not in *capite*, but as he held before. So that by this booke, tenuere houlding of the person of the king, and tenure in *capite*, are two diuers tenures. To take away this difficulty, I thinke *M. Kitchin* is in that place to be taken, as if he saide, not in *capite* by Knights seruice, but by socage, folowing the vsuall speech: because most commonly where we talke of tenure in *capite*, we meane tenure by Knights seruice.

Carno, Cromptons iurisd. fol. 191. is an imunity

Carke, seemeth to be a quantitie of wolle, whereof thirtie make a Sarpler.*anno.27.H.6.ca. 2.*See *Sarpler.*

Carrack, alias Carrick, seemeth to be a shippe of burden, so called of this Italian (*carrico*) or (*carco*) a burden or charge, or of the spanish (*cargo*) you haue this word. *anno 2.R.2.ca.4.& anno 1.Iaco.ca.33.*

Carroway seedes, alias Carruway seedes (*semen cari vel carei*) is a seed springing of the herbe so called, of whose operation you may read in *Gerards herball.li. 2.ca.396.* It is reckoned among the merchandize, that ought to be garbled.*anno.i. Iaco.ca. 19.*

Carue of land (*carucata terræ*) commeth of the French(*charue. i.aratrum*) and with vs is a certaine quantitie of land, by the which the subiects haue some time bene taxed: wherevpon the tribute soe leuied, is called(*Carvage Caruagium.*)*Bracton.li. 2. ca. 16.nu.8.* It is all one with that, which the same author. *lib. 2. ca. 17.* calleth(*carucatam terra*) For *Litleton ca Tenure in socage.* saith, that(*hæc soca soca, idem est quod carruca*) *sc*, one sok or one plow land. Yet one place I finde in *Stowes annals*, that maketh me doubt. *pag. 271.* where he hath these words: The same time king *Henry* tooke carvage, that is to say, two merks of siluer of euery knights fee, toward the mariage of his sister *Izabell* to the Emperor: where carvage cannot be taken for a plow land, except there were some other farder division, whereby to raise of euery plowe land so much: and so consequently of euery *Knights* fee: that is, of euery 680. acres, two merkes of siluer. *Rastall* in his *Exposition of words* saith, that caruage is to be quite, if the lord the King shall taxe all the land by carues: that is, a priuiledge, whereby a man is exempted frõ caruage. *Skene de verb. signif. ver. Carucata terra*, deriueth it from the French (*charon*. i. a plough, and saith, that it containes as great a portion of land, as may be tilled and laboured in a yere and day with one plough: which also is called (*hilda*) or (*hida terræ*) a word vsed in the old Britaine lawes. *M. Lamberd* among his precedents, in the end of his *Eirenarcha*, translateth (*carucatũ terræ*) a plough land.

Caruage (*caruagium*,) see *Carue*.

Cassia Fistula, is a tree that beareth certaine blacke, round, and long cods, wherein is contained a pulpe, soft & pleasantly sweet, seruing for many vses in Phisick. This tree with her vertues you may find described in *Gerards* Herball, *lib.* 3. *cap.* 77. The fruite is mentioned in the statute, *anno* 1. *Iacob. cap.* 19. among drugges and spices, that be to be garbled.

Cassia lignea, is a sweet wood not vnlike to Cynamom, and sometime vsed in steede of Cynamom. Whereof you may read in *Gerards* Herball, *lib* 1. *ca.* 141. This is called *Cassia lignum*, in the Statute *anno* 1. *Iacob. cap.* 19 and is comprised among merchandize that are to be garbled.

Castellain (*castellanus*) is a keeper or a Captaine, sometime called a Constable of a castell, *Bracton lib.* 5. *tractat.* 2. *cap.* 16. & *lib.* 2. *cap.* 32. *num.* 2. In like maner is it vsed, *anno* 3. *Ed.* 1. *cap.* 7. In the bookes (*de feudis*) you shall find (*guastaldus*) to be almost of the same signification, but something more large: because it is also extended to those that haue the custodie of the Kings mansion houses, called of the *Lumbards* (*curtes*) in *England* (Courts,) though they be not places of defence or strength. *M. Manwood, part.* 1. of his Forest lawes, *pag.* 113. saith, that there is an officer of the Forest called *Castellanus*.

Castelward (*castelgardum, vel wardum castri*) is an imposition laide vpon such of the kings subiects, as dwell within a certaine compasse of any castell, toward the maintenance of such, as doe watch and ward the castell. *Magna charta, cap.* 20. & *anno* 32. *H.* 8. *cap.* 48. It is vsed sometime, for the very circuit it selfe, which is inhabited by such as are subiect

iect to this seruice, as in *Stowes annals, pag.* 632.

Casu consimili, is a writ of entrie, graunted where the tenent by courtesie, or tenent for terme of life, or for the life of another, doth alien in fee, or in tayle, or for tearme of anothers life. And it hath the name of this, for that the Clerkes of the Chauncerie did, by their common consent, frame it to the likenesse of the writ, called (*In casu proviso*) according to their authoritie giuen them by the Statute, *Westm.* 2. *cap.* 24. which, as often as there chanceth any new case in Chancerie, something like to a former case, and yet not especially fitted by any writ, licenceth them to lay their heads together, and to frame a new forme aunswerable to the new case, and as like some former case as they may. And this writ is graunted to him in the reuersion, against the party to whom the said tenent so alienateth to his preiudice, and in the life time of the said tenent. The forme and effect whereof reade more at large in *Fitz. nat. br. fol.* 206.

Casu proviso, is a writ of entry, giuen by the Statute of *Glocester, cap.* 7. in case where a tenent in dower alieneth in fee or for tearme of life, or in taile, and lyeth for him in reuersion against the alienee. Whereof reade *Fitz. nat. br.* more at large, *fol.* 205.

Catals (*catalla*) *alias chatels*, cōmeth of the *Normans.* For in the 87. chapter of the grand Custumarie you shal find, that al moueable goods with them, are called chatels: the contrary whereof is (*fief*) *ibid.* which we do call fee. But as it is vsed in our common law, it comprehendeth all goods moueable and immoueable, but such as are in the nature of free hould, or parcell thereof, as may be gathered out of *Sawns. prar.* *ca.* 16. and *anno. Eliza.* 1. *ca.* 2. How be it *Kitchin* in the chapter *catalla. fo.* 32. saith, that ready mony is not accompted any goods or catels, nor haukes, nor houndes. The reason why hawks and hounds be not, he giueth, because they be (*fera natura*) why money is not, though he set not downe the cause: yet it may be gathered to be, for that money of it selfe, is not of worth, but as by cōsent of men, for their easier traficke, or permutation of things necessary for common life, it is reckoned a thing rather consisting in imagination, then in deede. *Catals* be either personall or reall. Personall may be so called in two respects: one, because they belong immediatly to the person of a man, as a bowe, horse, &c. the other, for that being any way withheld iniuriously from vs, we haue no meanes to recouer them, but by personall action. *Chatels* reall be such, as either appertain not immediatly to the person, but to some other thing, by way of dependencie: as a boxe with charters of land, the body of a ward, apples vpon a tree, or a tree it selfe growing on the ground. *Cromptons Iustice of peace, fo.* 33. *B*, or els such as are necessary issuing out of some immoveable thing to a person: as a lease or rent for tearme of yeares. Also to hould at will, is a chatell reall. *New tearmes. verbo Chatell.* The ciuilians comprehend these things, as also lands of what kin de or hould so euer, vnder *bona*; *bona autē diuiduntur in mobilia & immobilia: mobilia verò in ea quæ se movent vel ab aliis moventur. v. legem.* 49. *& l.* 208 *ff. de. verb. significa. & interpretes ibidem. Bract.* also *ca.* 3. *li.* 3. *nu.* 3. *&* 4. seemeth to be of the same iudgement.

Catallis captis nomine districtionis, is a writ which lyeth within a borowe, or within a house, for rent going out of the same, and warranteth a man to take the doores, windowes, or gates, by way of distresse, for the rent. *Old nat. br. fo.* 66.

Catallis reddendis, is a writ, which lyeth where goods being deliuered to any man to keepe vntill a certaine day, and be not vpon demande deliuered at the day. And it may be otherwise called a writ of detinew. See more of it in the *Register orig. fo.* 139. and in the *ould nat. br fo.* 63. This is answerable to *actio depositi*, in the ciuile lawe.

Catchepolle, though it now be vsed as a word of contempt, yet in auncient times, it seemeth to haue bene vsed without reproch, for such as we now call sergeants of the mace, or any other that vse to arrest men vpon any cause. *anno.* 25. *Ed.* 3. *stat.* 4. *ca.* 2.

Cathedrall. See church.

Casu matrimonii prælocuti, is a writ which lyeth in case where a woman giueth lands to a man in fee simple, to the intent he shall mary her, and refuseth so to doe in reasonable time, being required thereunto by the woman. The forme, and farder vse hereof, learne in the *Register orig. fol.* 233. and in *Fitzh. nat. br. fo.* 205.

Causam nobis significes, is a writ which lyeth to a *Mayor* of a towne or city, &c. that formerly by the kings writ being commaunded to giue seisin vnto the kings grantee of any land or tenements, doth delay so to do do, willing him to shew cause, why he so delayeth the performance of his charge. *Coke. li. 4. casu communalty des Sadlers. fo. 55 b.*

Cautione admittenda, is a writ that lyeth against the Bishop, houlding an excommunicate person in prison for his contempt, notwithstanding that he offereth sufficient caution or assurance to obey the commandments and orders of holy church from thence forth: The forme and farder effect whereof, take out of the *Regist. orig. pa. 66.* and *Fitzh. nat. br. fol. 63.*

Century (centuria) See *Hundred.*

Cepi corpus, is a returne made by the Shyreue, that vpō an (exigēd) he hath taken the bodie of the partie. *Fitzh nat. br. fo. 26.*

Certiorari, is a writ issuing out the chauncerie, to an inferiour courte, to call vp the records of a cause therein depending, that conscionable iustice therein may be ministred, vpon complaint made by bill, that the partie which seeketh the said writ, hath receiued hard dealing in the said court. *Termes of the lawe.* See the diuers formes and vses of this, in *Fitzh. nat. br. fo. 242.* as also the Register, both originall and iudiciall in the tables. *verbo. Certiorari. Cromptō* in his *Iustice of peace fo 117.* saith, that this writ is either returnable in the Kings bench, and then hath these wordes (*nobis mittatis*): or in the chauncerie, and then hath (*in cancellaria nostra*) or in the common bench, and then hath (*Iusticiariis nostris de banco.*) The word (*certiorare*) is vsed diuers times in the *digest* of the ciuile lawe: but our later *Kritiques* think it soe barbarouse, that they suspect it rather to be foisted in by *Tribonian*, thē to be originally vsed by those men, of whose workes the saide *digest* is compiled. *Prataus in suo lexico.*

Certificat (certificatoriū) is vsed for a wirting made in any courte, to giue notice to another courte of any thing done therein. *As* for example, a certificate of the cause of attainte, is a transcript made briefely and in few words, by the clerke of the Crowne, clerke of the peace, or clerke of assise, to the courte of the Kings benche, conteyning the tenure and effect of everie endictment, outlawrie, or conviction, and clerke attained, made or pronounced in any other court. *an. 34. H. 8. c. 14.* Of this see more in *Certificat d'evesque.* Broke. f. 119.

Certification of assise of novel disseisin, &c (Certificatio assisæ novæ disseisinæ. &c.) is a writ graunted for the re examining or reuew of a mater passed by assise before any Iustices, and is called (*certificatione novæ disseisinæ*) *Old. nat. br. fo. 181.* Of this see also the Regi-

*ster.original.fo.*200.and the newe booke of entrise,*verbo. Certificat of assise* . This word hath vse, where a man appearing by his bayliffe to an assise brought by another, hath lost the day : and hauing something more to pleade for himselfe, as a deede of release,&c.which the bayliffe did not,or might not pleade for him, desireth a farder examination of the cause either before the same Iustices, or others : and obteineth leters patents vnto them to that effect.(The forme of these leters patents, you may see in *Fitzh.nat. br. fo.* 181.) and that done, bringeth a writ to the Shyreeue, to call both the party for whome the assise passed, and the Iurie that was empaneled vpon the same, before the said Iustices at a certaine day and place. And it is called a certificate, because in it there is mention made to the Shyreeue, that vpon the parties complainte of the defectiue examination, or doubts yet remaining vpon the assise passed, the King hath directed his leters patẽts to the Iustices,for the beter certifiing of themselues,whether all points of the said assise were duly examined,yea or not. See farder *old. nat.br.*and *Fitzh. vbi supra.* Of this also you may reade *Bracton.li.*4.*ca.*19.*nu.*4. *in fine.* & 5. 6.where he discusseth the reason of this pointe very learnedly.and lastly *Horn* in his *Myrrour* of Iustices.*li.*3 *ca.finali.* §.*en eyde des memoyres, &c.*

Certificando de recognitione Stapulæ , is a writte directed to the *Mayor* of the *staple,&c.* cõmaunding him to certifie the chaunceler of a statute of the *staple,* taken before him betweene such and such,in case where the partie himselfe deteineth it,and refuseth to bring it in. *Regist. orig. fo.* 152. *b.* In like maner may be said of (*certificando de statuto mercatorio*)*eodem.fo.*148. and (*de certificando in cancellarium de inquisitione, de idemptitate nominis*) *fo.* 195. and (*certificando quando recognitio,*)*&c.*and (*certificando quid actum est de breui super statutum mercatorium.*)*fo.*151 & *certificando si loquela Warantiæ.fo.*13.

Cessor, is he that ceseth or neglecteth so long to performe a dutie belonging vnto him , as that by his cesse or cessing he incurreth the daunger of lawe, and hath, or may haue the writ (*cessavit*) brought against him. *Old.nat.br.fo.*136.And note, that where it is saide in diuers places(the tenent cesseth) without any more words, such phrase is so to be vnderstood, as if it were said : the tenent ceseth to doe that which he ought , or is bound to doe by his land or tenement.

Ces-

Cessavit, is a writ that, lyeth in diuers cases, as appeareth by *Fitzh.nat.br. fo.* 208. vpon this generall grounde, that he against whome it is brought, hath for 2. yeares foreslowne to performe such seruice, or to pay such rent, as he is tied vnto by his tenure, and hath not vpon his land or his tenement, sufficient goods or catells to be distreined. Consult more at large with *Fitz.* vpon this *vbi supra.* with *Fleta. li.5.ca.34.§. visa sunt.* and with the *Termes of lawe.* See *Cessauit de cantaria. Register orig. fo.* 238. *Cessavit de feodi firma. eodem fo.* 237. *Cessavit per biennium. eodem. folio etiam eodem.* See the newe booke of entrise. *verbo Cessavit.*

Cestui qui vie, is in true French (*cestui a vie de qui*). i. he for whose life any land or tenement is graunted. *Perkins graunts.97.*

Cestui qui vse (*ille cuius vsui vel ad cuius vsum*) is broken french, and thus may be bettered: (*Cestui al vse de qui*) It is an ordinarie speech among our common lawyers, signifying him, to whose vse any other man is infeoffed in any lands or tenements. See the newe booke of entrise. *verbo. vses.* and in Replevin. *fo.508. colum.3. & verbo Trespas fo.606. & fo.123.a b. colum.3.nu.7.*

Chafe waxe, is an officer in chauncery, that fitteth the waxe for the sealing of the writs, and such other instruments as are there made to be sent out. This officer is borowed from the French. For there (*calefactores ceræ sunt, qui regiis literis in Cancellaria ceram imprimunt. Corasius.*

Chase (*chacea*) commeth of the French (*chasser. i. sectari belluas, apros, cervos*) It signifieth two things in the commõ lawe. *First*, as much as (*actus*) in the civil lawe, that is a dryving of catell to or from any place: as to chase a distresse to a fortlet, *Old nat.br. fo.45.* Secondly, it is vsed for a receite for deere and wilde beasts, of a middle nature betweene a forest, and a parke: being commonly lesse then a forest, and not endued with so many liberties, as the courtes of *attachment*, *Swaine mote*, and *Iustice seate*: and yet of a larger compas, and stored with greater diuersity both of keepers and wilde beasts or game, then a park. And *Crompton* in his booke of *Iurisdictions.fo.148.* saith, that a forest cannot be in the hands of a subiect, but it forthwith looseth the name, and becommeth a chase. and yet *fo.197.* he saith, that a subiect may be lord and owner of a forest. which though it seeme a contrariety, yet be both his sayings, in some sort, true. For the king may giue or alienate a forest to a subiect: yet so, as when it is once in the subiect, it leeseth the true propcity of a Forest: because that the courts, called the Iustice seate, the Swain mote, and Attachment, foorthwith doe vanish: none being able to make a Lord chiefe Iustice in *Eyre* of the Forest, but the king: as *M. Manwood* well sheweth *parte* 2. of his Forest lawes, *cap.* 3. & 4. And yet it may be granted in so large a maner, that there may be Attachement and Swainemote, and a court equiualent to a Iustice seat, as appeareth by him in the same chapter, *num.* 3. So that a chase differeth from a Forest in this, because it may be in the hands of a subiect, which a Forest in his proper & true nature cannot: and from a Parke, in that that it is not inclosed, and hath not onely a larger compasse, and more store of game, but of Keepers also and ouerseers. See *Forest*.

Chalenge (calumnia) commeth of the French (*chalanger*, i. *sibi asserere*) and is vsed in the commõ lawe for an exception taken either against persons or things: persons, as in assise to the Iurors, or any one or more of them: or in a case of felonie by the prisoner at the barre. *Smith de rep. Anglor. lib.* 2. *cap.* 12. *Britton. ca.* 52. *Bracton lib.* 2. *tract.* 2. *cap.* 22. Against things, as a declaration, *old nat. br. fol.* 76. Chalenge made to the Iurours, is either made to the array, or to the polles. Chalenge to the array is, when the whole number is excepted against, as partially empaneled: chalenge to or by the polle, when some one, or more are excepted against, as not indifferent. *Termes of the law*. Chalenge to the Iurours, is also diuided into Chalenge principall, and Chalenge *per* cause. i. vpon cause or reason. Chalenge principall (otherwise by *Stawnf. pl. cor. fol.* 157. & 158. called (peremptorie) is that, which the lawe alloweth without cause alledged or farder examination. *Lamberd. Eirenar. lib.* 4. *cap.* 14. as a prisoner at the barre, arraigned vpon felonie, may peremptorily chalenge to the number of 20. one after another, of the Iurie empaneled vpon him, alledging no cause, but his owne dislike: and they shall be still put off, and new taken in their places. But in case of high treason no Chalenge peremptorie is allowed, *an.* 33. *H.* 8. *cap.* 23. *Fortescue* saith, that a prisoner in this case may chalenge, 35. men *c.* 27. but that law was abridged by *anno* 25. *H.* 8. *cap.* 3. I cannot here omit to note some difference, that (in mine opinion) I obserue betweene Chalenge principall, and Chalenge peremptorie, finding peremptorie to be vsed onely in maters criminall, and barely without cause alledged more then the prisoners owne phantasie, *Stawnf. pl. cor. fol.* 124. but principall in ciuill actions for the most part, and with naming of some such cause of exception, as being found true, the lawe alloweth without farder scanning. For example: if either partie say, that one of the Iurors is the sonne, brother, cousin, or tenent to the other, or espoused his daughter, this is exception good and strong enough (if it be true) without farder examination of the parties credit. And how farre this chalenge vpon kinred reacheth, you haue a notable example, in *Plowden, casu Vernon.* against *Maners. fol.* 425. Also in the plee of the death of a man, and in euery action reall, as also euery action personall, where the debt or dammages amount to 40. merks, it is a good chalenge to any man, that he cannot dispend 40. shillings by the yeare of Freehold, *anno* 11. *H.* 7. *cap.* 21. and Termes of the lawe, *verbo Chalenge.* The ground of this chalenge you may see farder in *Fleta lib.* 4. *cap.* 8. Chalenge vpon reason or cause is, when the partie doth alledge some such exception against one or more of the Iurors, as is not forthwith sufficient vpon acknowledgement of the truth thereof, but rather arbitrable and considerable by the rest of the Iurors: as, for example: if the sonne of the Iuror haue maried or espoused the daughter of the aduerse partie. Termes of lawe, *vbi supra.* This chalenge *per cause*, seemeth to be tearmed by *Kitchin, chalenge for fauour, fol.* 92. or rather Chalenge for fauour is said there to be one *species* of chalenge *per cause*: where you may read what chalenges be commonly accounted principall, and what not. See the new booke of Entries, *verbo, Chalenge.* and the *old nat. br. fol.* 158. & 159. That this word (*chalenge*) is long sithence latined by the word (*calumnia*) appeareth by *Bracton. lib.* 3 *tract.* 2. *cap.* 18. & *li.* 4. *tract.* 3. *cap.* 6. & *lib.* 5. *cap.* 6. But I doubt, *Priscian* will neuer forgiue him that first strooke this blowe at him. Of *chalenge* you may farder read *Fleta. lib.* 1. *cap.* 32. §. *Ad quem diem, & seqq.*

Chamberdekins, are Irish beggers, *anno* 1. *H.* 5. *cap.* 8.

Chamberer, is vsed for a chamber maide, *anno* 33. *H.* 8. *cap.* 21.

Chamberlaine (*camerarius vel camberlingus*) commeth of the French (*chambellan.* i. *cubicularius, vel praefectus cubiculi.*) It is diuersly vsed in our Chronicles, Lawes, and Statutes: as Lord great Chamberlaine of *England*, Lord Chamberlain of the kings house, the kings Chamberlaine, *anno* 13. *Ed.* 1. *cap.* 41. *anno* 17. *R.* 2. *cap.* 6. to whose office it especially appertaineth to looke to the kings chambers and wardrobe, and to gouerne the vnder ministers belonging vnto the same. *Fleta lib.* 2. *cap.* 6. & 7. Chamberlaine of any of the kings courts, *anno* 7. *Ed.* 6. *cap.* 1. Chamberlaine of the Exchequer, *anno* 51. *H.* 3. *stat.* 5. & *anno.* 10. *Ed.* 3. *cap.* 11. & *anno* 14. *eiusdem. cap.* 14. & *anno* 26. *H.* 8. *cap.* 2. Chamberlaine of north *Wales*, *Stow. pag.* 641. Chamberlaine of *Chester*. *Cromptons iurisd. fol.* 7. This Officer is commonly the receiuer of all rents and reuenues belonging to that person or citie, whereunto he is chamberlaine. *v. Fletam li.* 2. *cap.* 70. §. *Si autem.* The Latine word seemeth to expresse the function of this officer. For (*camerarius dicitur à camera.* i. *testudine sive fornice:*) *quia custodit pecunias quæ in cameris præcipuè reservantur. Onyphrius de interpret. vocum ecclesiasticarum.* It seemeth to be borowed from the *Feudists*, who define the word (*camera*) thus: *Camera est locus in quem thesaurus recolligitur, vel conclave in quo pecunia reservatur. Zasius de feudis. part.* 4. *num.* 7. and *Peregrinus, de iure fisci. lib.* 6. *tit.* 3. saith, that *camerarius vel camberlingus* (*quē quæstorem antiqui appellarunt,*) *in rebus fisci primum locum tenet, quia thesaurarius & custos est publicæ pecuniæ. Sane officium hoc primipilatus fuisse nonnulli senserunt.* There be two officers of this name in the kings Exchequer, who were wont to keepe a controlment of the pels of *receipt* and *exitus*, & kept certaine keyes of the treasurie cofers, which is not now in vse. They keepe the keyes of the Treasurie, where the leagues of the Kings predecessors, and diuers auncient bookes doe remaine. There is mention of this officer, in the Statute *anno* 34. & 35. *H.* 8. *cap.* 16. There be also vnder-chamberlaines of the Exchequer, which see in *Vnder-chamberlaine*.

Champártie, (*cambipartita*) *aliàs champertie*, seemeth to come from the french (*champart.* i. *vectigal*) and signifieth, in our common lawe, a maintenance of any man in his suit depending, vpon condition to haue part of the thing (be it lands or goods) when it is recouered. *Fitzh. nat. br. fo.* 171. and *champertours* be they, that moue plees or suites, or cause to be moued, either by their owne procurement, or by other; and persyew at their proper costs, for to haue part of the land in variance, or part of the gaines. *anno.* 33. *Ed.* 1. *stat.* 2. in *fine*.

fine. Whereunto adde the third statut made the same yeare. This seemeth to haue bene an auncient fault in our realme. For notwithstanding these former statutes, and a forme of writ framed vnto them, yet *anno*.4. *Ed*. 3. *ca*.11. it was againe inacted, that whereas the former statute prouided redresse for this in the kings bench onely (which in those dayes folowed the court) from thence forth it should be lawfull for Iustices of the common plees likewise, and Iustices of assises in their circuits, to inquire, heare, and determine this and such like cases, as well at the suite of the king, as of the party. How farre this writ extendeth, and the diuers formes therof, applied to seuerall cases, see *Fitzh.nat.br.fo*. 171. and the *Register orig.fo*. 183. and the new booke of entrise.*verbo. Champertie*. Euery *champertie* employeth maintenance. *Cromptons iurisd fo*. 39. See also his Iustice of peace. *fo*.155.*b &c*. These with the Romans were called *redemptores litium, qui sc. quotidianas lites mercantur, aut quipartem litis paciscuntur l. si remunerandi*. §. *Maurus.π. Mandati.l.si contra. &.l. per diuersas.Co.eodem*. 13.

Champion, (*campio*) is thus defined by *Hotoman, in verbis feudalibus*. *Campio est certator pro alio datus in duello: a campo dictus, qui circus erat decertantibus definitus*. In our common lawe, it is taken no lesse for him that trieth the combat in his owne case, then for him that fighteth in the place or quarell of another. *Bracton li*.3.*tracta*.2.*ca*.21.*nu*.4. who also seemeth to vse this word for such, as hould by sergeanty, or some seruice, of another, as: *campiones faciunt homagium domino suo. li*. 2.*ca*.35. Of this reade more in *Battell* and *Combat*. 30.

Chanceler, (*cancellarius*) commeth of the french (*chancelier*) *Vincentius Lupanus de magistratibus Francorum* saith, that (*cancellarius*) is no latine word: howbe it he citeth diuers latine writers that doe vse it. With him agreeth that excellent man *Petrus Pithaeus, libro*. 2. *aduersariorum.ca*. 12. and whereas *Lupanus* would deriue it from the verb (*cancello*) *Pithaeus* confesseth, he hath good colour for his opinion, though he thinke it not sound; and therefore rather deduceth it (*a cancellis*). (*Cancellare*) is (*literas vel scriptum linea per medium ducta damnare*) and seemeth of it selfe likewise to be deriued (*a cancellis*) which signifie all one with (*κιγκλιδες*) in greeke, which we in our tong call a letis: that is, a thing made of woode or iron barrs laide crosse waies one ouer another, so that a man may see through them in and out. And it is to be thought, that iudgement seates in ould time, were compassed in with those barres, being founde most necessary to defend the iudges and other officers from the presse of the multitude, and and yet neuer the more to hinder any mans view, that had a desire or cause to obserue what was done. *Cancellarius* at the first by the opinion of *Lupanus*, signified the regisiters or actuaries in court, (*grapharios sc: qui conscribendis & excipiendis iudicum actis dant operam*) *Pithœus* saith, they were such as we now call (*Secretarios*) But this name in our daies is greatly advanced, and not onely in other kingdomes, but in ours also, is giuen to him, that is the cheife man for mater of iustice (in priuate causes especially) next vnto the prince. For whereas all other Iustices in our common wealth, are tied to the lawe, and may not swerue from it in iudgement: the Chanceler hath in this the kings absolute power, to moderate and temper the written lawe, and subiecteth himselfe onely to the lawe of nature and conscience, ordering all things *iuxta æquum & bonum*. And therefore *Stawnford* in his *Prerogatiue.ca.* 20.*fo.* 65. saith, that the Chanceler hath two powers: one absolute, the other ordinary: meaning that though by his ordinary power in some cases, he must obserue the forme of proceeding, as other ordinarie Iudges: yet that in his absolute power he is not limited by the written law, but by conscience and equitie, according to the circumstances of the mater in question. But how long he hath had this power, some would doubt. For *Polidorus Virgilius*, *lib.* 9. *historiæ Anglicæ.* hath these words of *William* the Conqueror: *Instituit item Scribarum Collegium, qui diplomata scriberent, & eius Collegii magistrum vocabat Cancellarium, qui paulatim supremus factus est Magistratus, qualis hodie habetur.* And see *Fleta*, *lib.* 2. *cap.* 13. This high Officer, seemeth to be derived from *Fraunce* vnto vs, as many other Officers and vsages be. For of this thus writeth *Boërius* in his Tractate *De authoritat. Magni Concilii.num.* 8. *Consistorio Franciæ post Principem Dominus Franciæ Cancellarius, cui velut excelsum iudicii tribunal hoc in regno (sub Principe tamen nostro) moderanti, sigillumq; authenticum, quo sine publicis & patētibus regiis literis nulla fides adhibetur, liberam administrationem habenti, omnes & singuli regii Iusticiarii, quocunque nomine nuncupentur, ac quavis authoritate fungantur, eo inferiores sunt. Et meritò: Succedit enim in quæstoris locum, &c.*

He

He that ... beareth this magistracie, is called the Chanceler of *England. anno 7. R. 2. cap. 14.* and by the Statute *anno 5. Eliz. cap.* 18. the Lord Chanceler and Keeper haue all one power. Note farder that diuers inferior Officers, are called Chancelers, as Chanceler of the Exchequer. *an. 25. H. 8. cap. 16.* whose office hath bene thought by many, to haue bene created for the qualifying of extremities in the Exchequer. He sitteth in the court, and in the Exchequer chamber, and with the rest of the court ordereth things to the kings best benefit: he is alwaies in cōmission with the Lord Treasurer for the letting of the lands that came to the crowne by the dissolution of Abbeyes: and hath by priuie seale from the king, power with others to compound for forfeitures of bonds, and forfeitures vpon penall statutes. He hath also much to doe in the reuenue come by the dissolution and first fruites, as appeareth by the acts of vniting them to the Crowne. Chanceler of the Duchie of *Lācaster, anno 3. Ed 6. cap. 1. & an. 5. eiusdem. cap. 26.* whose office is principall in that court to iudge and determine all controuersies betweene the king and his tenents of the Duchie land, and otherwise to direct all the kings affaires belonging to that court. Chanceler of the Order. i. of the Garter, *Stowes annals pag.* 706. Chanceler of the Vniversity, *anno 9. H. 5. cap. 8. & anno 2. H. 6. cap.* 8. Chaunceler of the court of Augmentations, *anno 27. H. 8. cap. 27. & anno 32. eiusdem. cap. 20. & anno 33. eiusd. cap.* 39. Chaunceler of the first fruites, *anno 32. H. 8. cap.* 45. Chaunceler of courts, *anno 32. H. 8. cap.* 28. Chaunceler of the Diocesse, *anno 32. H. 8. cap.* 15.

Chancerie (*cancellaria*) is the court of equitie and conscience, moderating the rigour of other courtes, that are more streightly tyed to the leter of the lawe, whereof the Lord *Chancelor* of *England* is the chiefe Iudge. *Cromptons iurisd. fol.* 41. or else the Lord Keeper of the great Seale, sithence the statute 5. *Eliz. cap.* 18. It taketh the name from the Chaunceler, as *M. Camden* noteth in his *Britannia, pag.* 114. *in meo.* The Officers belonging to this court, are (as is abouesaid) the Lord *Chaunceler* or Keeper of the broade Seale, twelue Masters of the Chancerie, whereof the Master of the rolles is one and the chiefe, the sixe Clerkes, the Examiners, a Sergeant at armes, the Marshall, and cryer of the court, the clerks of the courts, otherwise called *Coursiters*, the clerkes of the petie bagge, the clerke of the crowne, the clerk of the hanaper, the protonotary or regiſter, the controller of the hanaper, the clerk of appeales, the ſealer, the chafe waxe, the clerke of the faculties, the clerk of the patents, clerk of the ſtarre chamber, clerk of preſentations, clerk of diſmiſſions, clerk of licenſes to alienate, clerkes of the enrolments, clerk of the protections, clerk of the court of wards, clerk of the ſub penaes, which ſee deſcribed in their places.

Chapell,(*capella*) commeth of the French (*chapelle.*i.*ædicula*) and is of 2. ſorts, either adioining to a Church, as a parcel of the ſame, which men of worth doe build, *vt ibidem familiaria ſepulchra ſibi conſtituant*, to the vſe of the Romans. *l.*5.*π. de religio.* or els ſeparate from the mother church, where the pariſh is wide, and is commonly called a chappell of eaſe: becauſe it is builded for the eaſe of one or more pariſhioners that dwell ouer farre from the Church, and is ſerued by ſome inferiour curate prouided at the charge of the rector, or of them that haue benifite by it, as the compoſition or cuſtome is. Whence the word is deriued the *Canoniſts* differ in opinion. *Rebuffus de pacif poſſeſ. nu.*104. ſaying, that ſome take it (*à capiendo laicos*) others (*à capra*) becauſe it repreſenteth thoſe cotages, which men were wont to couer ouer with goates skins. *Petrus Gregorius in ſuo ſyntagmate.li.*15.*ca.* 29. hath theſe words of this thing: *Capellanus à capellania & capella, cui præficitur, nominatur: item ab officio ſeu beneficio & capellania. Capella aliquibus dicta, quaſi capiens* λαυς *ſeu populos, vel capiens laudem: vel ſecundùm præpoſitum, a cappa Diui Martini, aut à caprinis pellibus, quibus olim altaria tegebantur ſecundùm Archidiaconum. Arbitrarer & a ſimplici tecto, quo oratorium campeſtre operitur, lateribus vndiquaque patentibus & patulis. Tectum enim Gallis ſimpliciter dicitur (chapelle,) a capite. Vnde & formata aliqua nomina (chapean, cape, &c) Aut capella locus qui minoris ſpatii ſit quam eccleſia, quòd tot homines non capiat, vt eccleſia. Ita altare capella eſt. ca. quæſitum, & ca. penult. i. quæſt.* 3. *Ioan. Andreas. in ca.* i. *de ſucceſ. ab inteſta. & præbenda cum onere quotidie celebrandi ſacram liturgiam. ca. ſignificatum.* 11. *de præbend & oratorium. ca. authoritate: de priuilegiis. in* 6. *quòd in eo loco orationes non alia res profanæ peragi debeant. ca. pen. & fina.* 42. *diſtinct.* The ſame author in his booke *de beneficiis. ca.* 11. *nu.* 10. hath theſe words: *Dicti porro primitùs capellani, a cappa Sancti Martini, quam Reges Francorum ob adiutorium in prælus ſolebant ſecum habere: quam ferentes*

tes & custodientes cum cæteris sanctorum reliquiis clerici, capellani cæperunt vocari. vt omnia refert Valafridus Strabo. Abbas Augensis. ca. fina. de incrementis rerum ecclesiastica.

There is of these chapels one kinde called a free chapell, which seemeth to be such as hath maintenance perpetuall toward the vphoulding thereof, and wages of the curate, by some land charitablely bestowed on it, without the charge of the rector or parishe. *anno.* 37. *H.* 8. *cap.*4.*anno.* 1. *Ed.* 6. *ca.* 14.

Chapellaine, (*capellanus*) is he that performeth diuine seruice in a chappell. and therefore in our common law, it is vsed most ordinarily for him, that is depending vpon the king, or other man of worth, for the instruction of him and his family, the executing of praiers and preaching in his priuate house, where commonly they haue a chappell for that purpose. as *anno.* 21.*H.*8.*ca.* 13. where it is set downe what persons may priuiledge one or moe chaplaines, to discontinew from their benefices, for their particular seruice.

Chapiters, (*capitula*) commeth of the French (*chapitre.* i. *caput libri*) It signifieth in our common lawe, a summary or content of such matters, as are to be inquired of or presented before Iustices in *Eyre*, Iustices of assise, or of peace in their sessions. Soe is it vsed., *anno.* 3. *Ed.* 1. *ca.* 27. in these words: and that no clerke of any Iustice, Escheatour, or Commissioner in *Eyre*, shall take any thing for deliuering chapiters, but onely clerkes of Iustices in their circuits: and againe *anno.* 13.*eiusdem.ca.*10. in these words: and when the time commeth, the shyreeue shall certifie the chapiters before the Iustices in *Eire,* how many writs he hath and what &c. *Britton* likewise vseth the same worde in this signification. *ca.* 3. *Chapiters* or (*capitula*) be now called articles most ordinarily, and are deliuered as well by the mouth of the Iustice in his charge, as by the clerks in wrighting to the enquest; whereas in auncient times (as appeareth by *Bracton* and *Britton*) they were after an exhortation giuen by the Iustices for the good obseruation of the lawes and kings peace, first red distinctly and opely in the whole court, and then deliuered in writing to the grand enquest. And the same order doth *M. Lamberd* wish to be kept in these daies also. *Eirenar. li.* 4. *ca.*4. *pa.* 393. *Horn* in his mirrour of Iustices calleth them articles, and expresseth what they were wont to containe. *li.* 3. *ca. des articles* in *Eire.* An exãple of these chapichapters or articles, you haue in the booke of assises, *fo* 138. *nu.* 44. as also in *Roger Hoveden, parte poster. suorum annal. in* Richar*do primo. fo.* 423.

Chapter. (*capitulum*) signifieth in our common lawe (as in the canon lawe, whence it is borowed) *congregationem clericorum in ecclesia cathedrali, conuentuali, regulari, vel collegiata*: and in another signification, *locum in quo fiunt communes tractatus collegiatorum.* It hath other significations, though not greatly worth the repeating in this place, which you may read in *Linwods prouincials. glos. in ca. quia in continētia. de constitutionibus. verb.* Capi*tulis.* Why this collegiat companie should be called (*capitulum*) of the canonists, a man may make a question: and for answer, it may be said, that it is metaphorically so termed the word originally signifiing a litle head. For this companie or corporation is a kinde of head, not onely to rule and gouerne the dioces in the vacatiō of the Bishoprick, but also in many things to aduise the Bishop, when the See is full. See *Panormitan. in ca. capitulum. extra de rescriptis.*

Charta perdonationis se defendendo, is the forme of a pardon for slaying another in a mans owne defence. R*egister. original. fo.* 287.

Charta perdonationis vtlagariæ, is the forme of a pardon for a man that is outlawed. *Reg. orig. fo.* 288. 388.

Charter (*charta*) commeth of the French (*chartres*. i. *instrumenta*) It is taken in our lawe, for written evidence of things done betweene man and man, whereof *Bracton lib.* 2. *ca.* 16. *num.* 1. saith thus: *Fiunt aliquando donationes in scriptis, sicut in chartis, ad perpetuam rei memoriam, propter brevem hominum vitam, &c.* & a litle after: *nu.* 12. *Et sciendum, quòd chartarū alia regia, alia privatorum; & regiarum alia privata, alia communis, & alia vniuersalis. Item priuatorum, alia de puro feoffamento & simplici, alia de feoffamento conditionali siue conventionali: & secundùm omnia genera feoffamentorum fieri potest. Item privatorum alia de recognitione pura vel conditionali. Item alia de quiete-clamantia: Item alia de confirmatione, &c.* and so thorough the chapter. *Britton* likewise in his 39. chapter, diuideth charters into the charters of the King, and charters of priuate persons. Charters of the King are those, whereby the King passeth any graunt to any person or more, or to any bodie politique: as a charter of exemption that a man shall not be empaneled vpon any Iurie. *Kitchin. fo.* 114. & *fo.* 177. charter of of pardon, whereby a man is forgiuen a felonie, or other offence committed against the Kings crowne and dignitie. *Broke. tit. charter* of *pardon.* Charter of the forest, wherein the lawes of the forest are comprised. *anno.9. H.3. Cromptons Iurisd. fo.147. Pupilla oculi. parte. 5.ca. 22. Manwood. parte.1.* of his forest lawes. *fo.* i. where he setteth downe the charters of of *Canutus.* and *fo.* 17. where he hath set downe that which was made. *anno 9.H.3.* with the charter of the forest which we vse, *M. Skene* saith, that the lawes of the forest in Scotland doe agree. *de verbo. signif. verbo. Venison.* Charter of land. *Broke. eodem titulo.* That which we call a charter, the *Lombards in libris feudalibus*, call *præceptũ(præceptionem) Hotoma. verbo præceptũ. in verbis feudalibus.* Of these charters you haue also a long discourse in *Fleta.li.3.ca.* 14. who expoundeth euery substantiall part of a deede of gift particularly in order.

Charter land, (terra per chartam) is such as a man holdeth by charter, that is, by euidence in writing; otherwise called freehold. *anno* 19.*H.7.ca.* 13. and *Kitchin.fo.*86.& these in the *Saxons* time, were wont to be called *(bockland) Idem.fo.* 89. and *Lamberd* in his explication of Saxon words. *verbo Terra ex scripto* which was held, as he there saith, with more commodious & easier conditions, then *(folkland)* was: that is land held without writing. And the reason he giueth, because that was *hæreditaria, libera, atq; immunis:* whereas *fundus sine scripto censum pensitabat annuum, atq; officiorum quadam seruitute est obligatus. Priorē viri plerunq; nobiles atque ingenui, posteriorem rustici ferè & pagani possidebant. Illam nos vulgò* freehold *& per chartam, hanc ad voluntatem domini appellamus.* Thus farre *M. Lamberd.*

Charter partie (charta partita) is nothing but that which we call a paire of indentures, conteining the couenants and agreements made betweene merchants, or sea faring men touching their marine affaires. *anno* 32. *H.*8. *cap.*14.

Chartis reddendis, is a writ, which lyeth against him that hath charters of feofment deliuered him to be kept, and refuseth to deliuer them. *old.nat.br. fo.66.Register orig.fo.*159.

Chase: See *Chace.*

Chatell. See *Catell.*

Chaunce medley (Infortunium) commeth of 2. french words *(chance.i. lapsus)* and *(mesler.i. miscere)* It signifieth in our common lawe, the casuall slaughter of a man, not altogether without the fault of the slayer. *Stawnf. pl.cor.li.*1.*ca.*8. calleth it *homicide* by misaduenture, *West.* calleth it *homicide mixt.parte.*2.*symbol. titulo Indictments.sect.*50.and there defineth it thus: *Homicide mixt* is, when the killers ignorance or negligence is ioyned with the chaunce: as if a man loppe trees by an high way side, by which many vsually trauell, and cast doune a bowe, not giuing warning to take heede thereof, by which bowe one passing by is slaine: In which case he offendeth, because he gaue noe warning, that the party might haue taken heede to himselfe. See *Skene de verbo:signifi. verbo Melletum.*

Chaungeour, is an officer belonging to the Kings mint, whose function seemeth especially to consist, in exchanging coine for gold or siluer in the masse, brought in by merchants or others. *anno 2. H.6.ca.*12.

Chawntery, (*cantaria*) is a Church or chapell endewed with lands or other yearely revenewe, for the mantenance of one or moe priests, daily to sing masse for the soules of the donours, and such others, as they doe appointe. *anno* 37. *H.* 8. *ca.*4.*anno* 1. *Ed.*6. *ca.* 14.

Check rolle, seemeth to be a rolle or booke, that conteineth the names of such, as are attendants and in pay to great personages, as their houshold seruants. It is otherwise called the chequer rolle. *anno* 24. *H.* 8.*ca.* 13.*anno* 3. *H.*7.*ca.* 13. & seemeeth to haue one etymologie with eschequer. Which see.

Chevage, (*cheuagium*) commeth of the French (*chef.*i. *caput*) It signifieth with vs, a summe of money paid by villeins to their Lords, in acknowledgment of their slauerie. Whereof Bracton *li.*1.*ca.*10. saith thus: *chevagium dicitur recognitio in signum subiectionis & dominij de capite suo.* It seemeth also to be vsed, for a summe of a mony, yearely giuen by a man to another of might & power, for his avowement, maintenance, and protection, as to their head or leader. *M.Lamberds li.* 2. *ca.* 5. *eirenarch.* writeth it (*chivage*) or rather (*chiefage*)

Chevisance, commeth of the French (*chevir.* i. *venir a chef de de quelque chose*) to come to the head or end of a busines, to perfect a mater. This word is vsed for bargayning. *anno* 37.*H.* 8.*ca.* 9.& *anno.*13.*Eliza.ca.*5.& 8.*an.* 10.R.2.*cap.* 1.& *anno* 3. *H.* 7. *cap.*5.

Chief. See *Capite.*

Chiefe pledge (*plegius, vel vas capitalis*)*an.*20.*H.*6.*ca.*8. For the vnderstanding of this word, See Borowhead.

Childwit, commeth of the Saxon word (*child*), and (*wit*) which some say, in that tongue, is a terminatiō of certain words without signification, as (*dom*) in (*christendom*) or (*hood*) in (*childehood*) with vs. But for the signification of (*wit*) see *Bloodwit*) *Childwit* signifieth a power to to take a fine of your bondwoman begotten with child without your consent. *Rastall. exposit.* of *words*.

Chimin, (*chiminus*) commeth from the French (*chemin*.i.*aditus*, *via*) and signifieth in our common lawe, a way. It is diuided into two sorts: the Kings high way, and a priuate way. *Kitchin. fo.* 35. The Kings highe way (*chiminus regius*) is that, by which the Kings subiects, and all others vnder his protection, haue free libertie to passe, though the propertie of the soyle of each side, where the way lieth, may perhaps belong to some priuate man. A way priuate is that, by which one man or more haue libertie to passe, either by prescription or by charter, through another mans ground. And this is diuided into *chymin* in *grosse*, and *chymin appendant. Kitchin. fo.* 177. *Chymin* in grosse is that way, which a man holdeth principally and solely in it selfe: *chimin* apendant is that, which a man hath adioyned to some other thing as appertinent thereūto. For example, if a man hire a close or pasture, and couenāt for ingresse and egresse to and from the said close, through some other ground, by the which otherwise he cannot passe. Or *chimin* in grosse may be that, which the Civilians call personall: as when one covenanteth for a way through another mans ground, for himselfe and his heires: *chimin* appendant, on the otherside, may be that which they call reall: as when a man purchaseth a way through another mans ground, for such as doe or shall dwell in this or that house for euer, or be owners of such a maner.

Chiminage, (*chimmagium*) signifieth a tolle for wayfarage thorough the forest. *Cromptons. Iurisd. fo.* 189. and *Manwood. parte.* 1. of his forest lawes. *pa.* 86. See *Chimin*. The *Feudists* call it, *pedagium*. See *Chimin*.

Chirographer of fynes (*chirographus finium & concordiarum*) commeth of the greeke (χειρόγραφον) which signifieth a wrighting of a mans owne hand, whereby he acknowledgeth a dept to another. It signifieth in our common lawe, him in the common bench office, that ingrosseth fines in that court acknowledged, into a perpetuall record, after they be acknow-

 ledged,

ledged, and fully passed by those officers, by whome they are formerly examined; and that writeth and deliuereth the indentures of them vnto the party. *anno.* 2. *H.* 3. *ca.* 8. and *West Symbol: parte.* 2. *titulo. fines. sect.* 114. & 129. *Fitzh. nat. br. fo.* 147. *A.* This officer also maketh two indentures, one for the buier, another for the seller; and maketh one other indented peece, containing also the effect of the fine, which he deliuereth ouer to the *custos breuium*, that is called the foote of the fine. The *Chirographer* also, or his debuty, doth proclaime all the fines in the court euery tearme, according to the Statute; and then repayring to the office of the *custos breuium*, there indorseth the proclamations vpō the backside of the foot thereof: and alwaie keepeth the writ of couenant, as also the note of the fine.

Chivage. See *Chevage.*

Chivalrie, (seruitium militare) commeth of the French (*chevalier.* i. *eques*) and signifieth in our common lawe, a tenure of land by knights seruice. For the better vnderstanding whereof, it is to be knowne, that there is noe land, but is holden mediatly or immediatly of the Crowne, by some seruice or other: and therfore are all our free-houlds that are to vs and our heires, called (*feuda*) feese, as proceeding frō the benefit of the King, for some small yearely rent and the performance of such seruices, as originally were laid vpon the land at the donation thereof. For as the king gaue to the great Nobles his immediat tenents, large possessions for euer, to hold of him for this or that rent and seruice: so they againe in time parcelled out to such as they liked, their lands so receiued of the kings bountie, for rents and seruices, as they thought good. And these seruices are all by *Litleton* diuided into two sorts: chivalry, and socage. The one is martiall and military, the other clownish and rusticall. Chivalrie therefore is a tenure or seruice, whereby the tenent is bound to performe some noble or military office vnto his Lord, and is of two sorts: either regall, that is, such as may hold onely of the king: or such as may also hold of a common person, as well as of the king. That which may hold onely of the *King*, is properly called *seruitium*, or *sergeantia*: and is againe diuided into *grand* or *petit*, i. great or small. Great, commonly called *grand sergeantie*, is that where one holdeth lands of the King by seruice, which hee ought to doe in his own person vnto him: as to beare the kings baner,

baner or his speare, or to leade his hoast, or to be his Marshall, or to blow a horne, when he seeth his enemies inuade the land, or to find a man at armes to fight within the foure Sease, or else to do it himselfe, or to beare the kings sword before him at his coronation, or at that day to be his sewer, caruer, butler, or chamberlaine. *Litleton tit. Sergeantie*. *Petit Sergeantie*, is where a man holdeth land of the king, to yeeld him yearely some small thing toward his warres, as a sword, dagger, bowe, knife, speare, paire of gloues of maile, a paire of spurs, or such like. *Litleton. titulo petit Sergeanty. Chivalry*, that may hould of a common person as well as of the king, is called (*scutagium*) *escuage*, that is seruice of the shield. And this is either vncertaine or certaine. *Escuage* vncertaine is likewise twofold: first, where the tenent by his tenure, is bounde to follow his lord going in person to the kings wars against his enemies, either him selfe, or to send a sufficient man in his place, there to be maintained at his cost so many daies, as were agreed vpon betweene the lord and his first tenent at the graunting of the fee. And the daies of such seruice seeme to haue bene rated by the quantity of the land so houlden: as if it extend to a whole knights fee, then the tenent was bounde thus to follow his lord fourty dayes. And a knights fee, was so much land, as in those dayes was accoumpted a sufficient liuing for a knight: and that was 680 acres, as some opinion is, or 800 as others thinke: or 15 pounds *per annum*. *Camdens Brittan. pa.* 110. *in meo.* S. *Thomas Smyth* sayeth, that *census equestris* is 40. poundes reuenew in free lands. If the law extend but to halfe a knights fee, then the tenent is bounde to follow his lord, as aboue is said, but twenty dayes. If to a fourth part, then ten daies. *Fitzh. nat. br. fo.* 83. *C. &* 84. *C. E.* The other kinde of this escuage vncertaine is called castelward: where the tenent by his land is bound, either by him selfe, or by some other, to defend a castell, as often as it shall come to his course. Escuage certaine, is where the tenent is set at a certaine summe of money, to be paide in lieu of such vncertaine seruice, as that a man shall yerely pay for a Knights Fee, 20. shillings, *Stow annal. pag.* 238. for halfe a Knights Fee, tenne shillings, or some like rate. And this seruice, because it is drawne to a certaine rent, groweth to be of a mixt nature: not meerely socage, for that it smelleth not of the plough, and yet socage in effect: being now neither personall seruice, nor vncertaine, *Litleton, titulo Socage*. This tenure called chiualry, hath other conditions annexed vnto it; as homage, fealty, wardship, reliefe, and mariage. *Bracton. li. 2. ca. 35.* which what they signifie, looke in their places. *Chilualry* is either generall or especiall. *Dier. fo. 161. nu. 47.* Generall seemeth to be, where only it is said in the feofment, that the tenent houldeth *per seruitium militare*, without any specification of sergeanty, escuage, &c. Speciall, that which is declared particularly what kinde of knights seruice he houldeth by.

Chorall, (choralis) seemeth to be any that by vertue of any of the orders of Clergie, was in auncient time admitted, to sit and serue God in the Quier, which in Latine is tearmed *Chorus*.

Chose, (res) is the French word as generall as *(thing)* is with vs. It is in the common lawe, vsed with diuers epithites worthie the interpretation: as, *chose* locall, is such a thing as is annexed to a place. For example: a mill is *chose* locall, *Kitchin fol. 18.* *Chose* transitorie, in the same place seemeth to bee that thing which is moueable, and may be taken away, or caried from place to place. *Chose* in action, is a thing incorporeall, and onely a right: as an annuitie, an obligation of debt, a couenant, or vowcher by warrantie. *Broke titulo. Chose in action.* And it seemeth, that *chose in action*, may be also called *chose in suspence*, because it hath no reall existence or being, neither can be properly sayde to bee in our possession. *Broke ibid.*

Churchwardens (Ecclesiarum gardiani) be Officers yearely chosen, by the consent of the Minister and parishioners, according to the custome of euery seuerall place, to looke to the church, church-yard, and such things, as belong to both, and to obserue the behauiours of their parishioners for such faults as appertaine to the iurisdiction or censure of the court ecclesiasticall. These be a kind of corporation, inabled by lawe, to sue for any thing belonging to their church, or poore of their parish. See *Lamberd* in his pamphlet of the duty of *Churchwardens*.

Churchesset, is a word that I find in *Fleta. lib. 1. cap. 47 in fine.* whereof he thus writeth: *Certam mensuram bladi tritici significat, quam quilibet olim sanctæ Ecclesiæ die Sancti Martini tẽpore tam Britonum quàm Anglorum contribuerunt. Plures tamen magnates, post*

Roma-

Romanorum adventum, illam contributionem secundum veterem legem Moysi nomine primitiarum dabant: prout in brevi regis Knuti, ad summum Pontificem transmisso, continetur, in quo illam contributionem, (chirchsed) appellant, quasi semen Ecclesiæ.

Cinamom (cinamomum) is a tree, whereof the barke is knowne to be a pleasant, comfortable, and medicinall spice, which you haue described in *Gerards Herball. lib. 3 cap. 142.* This is reckoned among garbleable spices, *an. 1. Iac. cap. 19.*

Cinque portes (quinque portus) be those speciall hauens, that lye toward *Fraunce*, and therfore haue bene thought by our kings, from time to time, to be such, as ought most vigilantly to be obserued against invasion. In which respect, the places where they be, haue an especiall gouernor or keeper, called by his office Lord Warden of the Cinque ports: and diuers priuiledges graunted vnto them, as a particular iurisdiction, their Warden hauing the authoritie of an Admirall among them, and sending out writs in his owne name. *Crompton* in his Iurisdictions, *fol.* 28. nameth the Cinque ports, *Douer*, *Sandwich*, *Rye*, *Hastings*, *Winchelsea*, *Rumney*, *Hithe*: whereof some, because the number exceedeth fiue, must either be added to the first institution, by some later graunt, or be accompted as appendents to some of the rest. See *Gardein of the Cinque ports*: and the Statute *anno 32. H. 8. cap.* 48.

Circuit of action, (circuitus actionis) is a longer course of proceeding, to recouer the thing sued for, then is needfull. See the new Tearmes of lawe.

Circumstantibus, is a word of art, signifying the supply or making vp of the number of Iurors, (if any empaneled appeare not, or appearing, be chalenged by either partie) by adding vnto them so many other of those that are present or standing by, as will serue the turne, *v. ann.* 35. *H.* 8. *cap.* 6. and *anno* 5. *Elizab. cap.* 25.

Citie (civitas) commeth of the French *(citè)* and signifieth with vs, as it doth in other regions, such a towne corporate, as hath a Bishop and a cathedrall church. For *Lucas de Penna lege vnica, tituli, De Metropol. Beryto. ti. 21. lib. 10. Cod.* hath these words: *Idem locus, vrbs, civitas, & oppidum appellatur. (Pro quo est etiam infra. De spectaculis. l. Nemo.) Civitas enim dicitur, quatenus cum institia & magistratuum ordine gubernatur, oppidum, quatenus est ibi copia incolarum: & vrbs, quatenus muris debito more cingitur. Propriè autem*

dici-

dicitur civitas, quæ habet Episcopũ. Supra de Episcop. & Cleri. l. Nulli. Aliàs dicitur generaliter omnis habitatio plurimorum, quæ muro cingitur. ff. de verb. signif. lib. 2. & de penu lega. l. Nam quod. §. Si ita. Sed stricte loquendo, si Episcopo caret, dicitur vrbs. ff. de verb. signif. l. Pupillus. §. Oppidum, &c. Yet *M. Crompton* in his Iurisdictions, where he reckoneth vp the cities, leaueth out *Elye*, though it haue a bishop and a cathedrall Church, and putteth in *Westminster*, though now it haue no bishop. And *anno 35. Eliza. ca. 6. Westminster* is called a citie, *anno 27. eiusd. cap.* 5. Of the Statutes not printed, it is alternatiuely tearmed a citie or borow. It appeareth by the Statute, 35. *H.* 8 *cap.* 10. that then there was a bishop of *Westminster. Ciuitas*, according to *Aristotle, lib.* 3. *politicorum. ca. pri.* is defined to be a certaine or vniforme gouernment of the inhabitants. *& Cæsar ciuitatem vocat populum eodem iure vtentem. Camd. Brittan. pa.* 310. But this is the generall definition of a common wealth, and not of a city, at the least, as we now a daies particularly take it. For ouer and beside that which is aboue saide, *Cassaneus in consuetudi. Burg. pa.* 15. saith, that France hath within the teritories of it, 104. cities, and giueth reason of this his saying, because there be there so many seates of Archbishops and bishops.

Clack, as to clack, force, and bard, *alias*, beard good wools, *anno. 8. H. 6. ca.* 22. whereof the first, *viz.* to clack wooll, is to cut of the sheepes marke, which maketh it to waigh lesse, and so yeld the lesse custome to the king, to force wooll, is to clip of the vpper and more heary part of it, to bard or beard it, is to cut the head and necke from the rest of the fleece.

Clamea admittenda in itinere per Atturnatum, is a writ whereby the king commandeth the Iustices in *eyre* to admitte of ones claime by Atturney, that is employed in the kings seruice, and cannot come in his owne person. *Regist. orig. fol.* 19. *b.*

Clayme (*clameum*) is a chalenge of interest in any thing that is in the possession of another, or at the least out of his owne: as, claime by charter, clayme by descent, *old nat. br. fol.* 11. *Si dominus infra annum clameum qualitercunque apposuerit: Bracton. lib.* 1. *cap.* 10. See the definition & diuers sorts of claime in *Plowden. Casu Stowel. fol.* 359. *a.*

Clarentius. See *Herald.*

Clergie (*clerus, clericatus*) is diuersly taken: sometime for the whole number of those, that are

(de

de Clero domini) of the Lords lot or ſhare, as the tribe of *Leuy*. was in *Iudæa*: ſome time for a plee to an indictment, or an appeale, and is by *Stawnf.pl.cor.li.*2. *ca.*41. thus defined. Clergie is an auncient liberty of the church, which hath bene confirmed by diuers parlaments, and is, when a prieſt, or one within orders, is arraigned of felony, before a seculer iudge, he may pray his clergie. which is as much, as if he prayed to be deliuered to his ordinarie, to purge him ſelfe of the offence obiected. And this might be done in caſe of murder. *Coke. li.* 4. *fo.* 46. *a.* This liberty is mentioned in *articulis cleri. anno.* 9. *Ed.* 2. *ca.* 16. and what perſons might haue their clergy, and what not, ſee *Stawnf. pl. cor. li.* 2. *ca.* 42. & 43. Howbeit there be many ſtatuts made ſithence he writ that booke, wherby the benefite of clergy is abridged. as *anno.* 8. *El. ca.* 4. *anno.* 14. *eiuſdem. ca.* 5. *anno.* 18. *eiuſd. cap.* 4.6.7. & *anno* 23. *eiuſd. cap.* 2. *a.* 29. *eiuſd. c.* 2. *anno* 31. *eiuſd. ca.* 12. *a.* 39. *eiuſd. ca.* 9. & *ca.* 15. Of this ſee *Cromptons* Iuſtice of peace, *fo.* 102. 103. 104. 105. and *Lamberds Eirenarcha. li.* 4. *ca.* 14. *pa.* 543. And note by the way, that the auncient courſe of the law in this point of clergy, is much altered. For by the ſtatute *anno.* 18. *Eliza. ca.* 7. clerks be no more deliuered to their ordinaries to be purged, but now euery man, though not within orders, is put to reade at the barre, being founde guilty, and conuicted of ſuch felonie as this benefit is ſtill granted for: and ſo burnt in the hand and ſet free for the firſt time, if the ordinaries commiſſioner or *deputè* ſtanding by do ſay: (*legit vt clericus*) or otherwiſe ſuffereth death for his tranſgreſſion.

Clerico addmittendo, is a writ directed to the biſhop, for the admitting of a clerk to a benefice vpon a (*Ne admittas*) tryed & founde for the party that procureth the writ. *Regiſt. orig. fo.* 31. 6.

Clerico capto per ſtatutū mercatorum, &c. is a writ for the deliuery of a clerk out of priſon, that is impriſoned vpon the breach of a ſtatut merchant. *Regiſter orig. fo.* 147.

Clerico conuicto commiſſo gaolæ in defectu ordinarii deliberando, &c is a writ for the deliuery of a clerk to his ordinary, that formerly was conuicted of felony, by reaſon his ordinary did not chalenge him according to the priuiledge of clerks. *Regiſter. orig. fo.* 69. *a.*

Clerico infra ſacros ordines conſtituto non elegendo in officium, is a writ directed to the baylifs, &c. that haue thruſt a bayliwick or bedelſhip vpō one in holy orders, charging them to releaſe him againe.

gaine. *Register orig. fo.* 187. *b.*

Clerk, (*clericus*) hath two significations: one, as it is the title of him, that belongeth to the holy ministery of the church, that is (in these daies) either minister, or deacon, of what other degree or dignity soeuer: though according to former times, not only *sacerdotes & diaconi*, but also, *subdiaconi*, *cantores*, *acolyti*, *exorcistæ*, *& ostiarii* were within this accoumpt, as they be at this daye, where the canon law hath full power. And in this signification, a clerk is either relegious (otherwise called *regular*) or *secular*. *anno.* 4. *H.* 4. *ca.* 12. The other signification of this word, noteth those, that by their function or course of life, practise their penne in any court or otherwise; as namely, the clerk of the rolles of parliament, clerks of the Chancery, and such like, whose peculiar offices I purpose to set downe in order, according to that knowledge that I could procure of them.

Clerke of the parlament rolles, (*clericus rotulorum Parlamenti*) is he that recordeth all things done in the high court of Parlament, and engrosseth them fairely into parchement rolles, for their better keeping to all postetitie. Of these there be two, one of the higher, another of the lower or common house, *Cromptons Iurisd. fol.* 4. *&* 8. *Smith de rep. Anglor. pag.* 38. See also *Vowels* booke touching the order of the Parlament.

Clerke of the crowne in the chācerie (*clericus Coronæ in Cancellaria*) is an officer there, that by himselfe or his deputie, is continually to attend the Lord Chanceler, or Lord Keeper, for speciall matters of estate by commission, or the like, either immediatly from his maiestie, or by order of his priuy councell, as well ordinary as extraordinary. *viz.* commissions of lieutenancies, of Iustices errant, and of assises, of *oyer* and *terminer*, of gaol deliuery, of the peace, and such like, with their writs of association, and *dedimus potestatem*, for taking of oathes. Also all generall pardons vpon graunts of them at the kings coronation, or at a parlament, where he sitteth in the higher house at the Parlament time; the writs of parlament, with the names of knights and burgesses, which be to be returned into his office. He hath also the making of all speciall pardons, and writs of execution, vpon bonds of statute of the *Staple* forfeited: which was annexed to his office in the raigne of Queene *Mary*, in consideration of his continuall and chargeable attendance: both these before being common for euery coursitour, and clerk of court to make.

Clerk of the Crowne (*clericus Coronæ*) is a clerk or officer in the Kings bench, whose function is to frame, reade, and record all indictments against traitours, felons, and other offenders there arraigned vpon any publique crime. He is otherwise termed Clerke of the Crowne office. And *anno.2.H.4.ca.*10. he is called clerk of the crowne of the kings bench.

Clerk of the extreates (*clericus extractorum*) is a clerk belonging to the exchequer, who termely receiueth the extreats out of the Lord treasurers remembrancer his office, and writeth them out to be levied for the king. He also maketh ceduls of such summes extreated, as are to be discharged.

Clerk of assise (*clericus assisæ*) is he, that writeth all things iudicially done by the Iustices of assise in their circuits. *Cromptons Iurisd. fo.*227.

Clerke of the pele (*clericus pellis*) is a clerk belonging to the exchequer, whose office is, to enter euery tellers bille into a parchement rolle called (*pellis receptorum*) and also to make another rolle of paiments, which is called (*pellis exituum*) where in he setteth downe, by what warrent the monie was paid.

Clerk of the warrants (*clericus warrantorum*) is an officer belonging to the court of common plees, which entreth all warrants of atturney for plantiffe and defendant, and enrolleth all deedes of indentures of bargaine and sale, which are acknowledged in the court, or before any iudges out of the court. And he doth extreate into the exchequer, all issues, fines, and amercements, which growe due to the king any way in that court, and hath a standing fee of ten pound of the king, for making the same extreats. See *Fitzh.nat.br.fo.*76. *in prin.*

Clerk of the petit bagge (*clericus parvæ bagæ*) is an officer of the chawncerie, of which sort there be three, and the master of the Roles their cheife. Their office is to record the returne of all inquisitions out of euerie shire, all liveries granted in the courte of wardes, *all ouster les mains*, to make all patents of customers, gawgers, controllers, and aulnegers, *all conge d' eslires* for Bishops, *all liberateis* vpon extents of statute staples, the recouerie of Recognisances forfeited, and all Elegits vpon them, the summons of the nobilitie, clergie, and burgeses to the Parlament; commissions directed to knights and other of euery shire for seassing of the subsidies. Writs for the nominations of collectours for the fiftenthes, and all traverses vpon any office, bille or otherwise, and to recieue the money due to the king for the same. This officer is mentioned. *anno* 33. *H.* 8. *ca.* 22.

Clerk of the Kings great wardrobe (clericus magnæ garderobæ regis) is an officer of the Kings house, that keepeth an account or Inventarie in writing, of all things belonging to the kings wardrobe. This officer is mentioned. *anno* 1. *Ed.* 4. *ca.* 1.

Clerk of the market (clericus merketi) is an officer of the kings house. *anno* 1. *Ed.* 4. *cap.* 1. & *anno* 13. *R.* 2. *ca.* 4. whose dutie is to take charge of the kings measures, and to keepe the standards of them, (that is) the examples of all the measures that ought to be through the land: as of elns, yards, lagens, as quarts, pottels, gallons, &c. of weights, bushels, and such like, and to see, that all measures in euerie place, be answerable vnto the said standard, *Fleta. li.* 2. *ca.* 8. 9. 10. 11. 12. of which office, as also of our diuersitie of weights and measures, you may there finde a treatise worth the reading. *Britton* also in his 30. chapter saith in the Kings person, to this effect: we will that none haue measures in the realme but we our selues: but that every man take his measures and weights from our standards: and so goeth on with a tractat of this mater, that well sheweth the auncient law and practise in this poynt. Touching this officers dutie, you haue also a good statut. *anno* 13. R. 2 *cap.* 4.

Clerk of the Kings siluer (clericus argenti Regis) is an officer belonging to the court of common plees, vnto whome euerie fine is brought, after it hath beene with the *custos brevium*, and by whome the effect of the writ of couenant is entred into a paper booke; and according to that note, all the fines of that terme are also recorded in the rolles of the court. And his entrie is in this forme: He putteth the Shire ouer the margen, and then saith. *A. B. dat domino regi dimidiam merkam* (or more, according to the value) *pro licentia concordandi. C. cum C. D. pro talibus terris, in tali villa, & habet chirographum per pacem admissum &c.*

Clerk of the peace (clericus pacis,) is an officer belonging to the sessions of the peace. His dutie is, in the sessions to reade the endictments, to enrolle the acts, and drawe the proces: to record the proclamations of rates for servants wages, to enrolle the discharge of apprentices, to keepe the counterpaine of the indenture of armour, to keepe the

the regiſter booke of licences, giuen to badgers and laders of corne,& of thoſe that are licenſed to ſhoote in guns,& to certify into the kings bench tranſcripts of indictments, outlawries, attainders, and conuictions had before the Iuſtices of the peace, within the time limited by ſtatute. *Lamberds eirenarcha. li.4. ca. 3. fo. 379.*

Clerk of the ſignet (*clericus ſignetti*) is an officer attendant continually on his maieſties principall ſecretary, who alwaies hath the cuſtodie of the priuie ſignet, as well for ſealing his maieſties priuate leters, as alſo ſuch graunts as paſſe his maieſties hands by bill aſſigned. Of theſe there be fower that attend in their courſe, and haue their diet at the Secretaries table. More largely you may reade of their office, in the ſtatute made *anno* 27. *H.* 8. *ca.* 11.

Clerk of the priuie ſeale (*clericus priuati ſigilli*) is an officer (whereof there be foure in number) that attendeth the *Lord* keeper of the priuie ſeale, or if there be none ſuch, vpon the principal *S*ecretarie, writing and making out all things that be ſent by warrant from the ſignet to the priuie ſeale, and are to be paſſed to the great ſeale: as alſo to make out (as they are tearmed) privie ſeales, vpon any eſpeciall occaſion of his maieſties affaires; as for loane of mony, or ſuch like. Of this officer, and his function, you may read the ſtatute *anno.* 27. *H.* 8. *ca.* 11. He that is in theſe daies called the Lord keeper of the privie ſeale, ſeemeth in auncient time to haue beene called clerke of the priuie ſeale, and to haue beene reckoned in the number of the great officers of the realme. Read the ſtatute. *anno.* 12. R. 2. *ca.* 11.

Clerk of the Iuries or *iurata writs* (*clericus iuratorum*) is an officer belonging to the court of the common plees, which maketh out the writs called (*habeas corpora*) and (*diſtringas*) for appearance of the Iurie, either in court or at the aſſiſes, after that the Iurie or panell is returned vpō the (*venire facias*). He entreth alſo into the rols the awarding of theſe writs, and maketh all the continuance from the going out of the (*habeas corpora*) vntill the verdict be giuen.

Clerk of the pipe (*clericus pipæ*) is an officer in the kings exchequer, who hauing all accounts and debts due to the king delivered and drawne downe out of the Remembrancers offices, chargeth them downe into the great rolle: who alſo writeth ſūmons to the Shyreeue, to levie the ſaid debts vpon the goods and catels of the deptors: and if they

they haue no goods, then doth he drawe them downe to the *L.* treasurers remembrancer, to write extreats against their lands. The awncient revenew of the Crowne, remaineth in charge afore him, & he seeth the same answered by the fermers & shyreeues to the King. He maketh a charge to al Shyreeues of their summons of the pipe and greenwax, and seeth it answered vpon their accompts. He hath the drawing and ingrossing of all leases of the Kings land.

Clerk of the hamper or hanaper (clericus hanapery) is an officer in chawncerie, *anno* 2. *Ed.* 4. *ca.* 1. otherwise called warden of the hamper, in the same statute, whose functiō is, to receiue al the mony due to the kings maiestie, for the seales of charters, patēts, commissions, and writs, as also feese due to the officers for enrolling & examining the same, with such like. He is tied to attendance on the lord Chanceler, or lord keeper, daily in the terme time, and at all times of sealing: hauing with him leather bags, wherein are put all charters, &c. after they be sealed by the Lord Chanceler, and those bags being sealed vp with the lord Chancelers priuate seale, are to be deliuered to the controller of the hanaper, who vpon receipt of them, doth as you shall reade in his office. This hanaper representeth a shadowe of that which the Romanes termed (*fiscum*) that conteined the Emperours treasure.

Clerk of the plees (clericus placitorum) is an officer in the exchequer, in whose office all the officers of the court (vpon especiall priuiledge belonging vnto them) ought to siew or be siewed vpon any action.

Clerk of the treasurie (clericus thesauraria) is an officer belonging to the common plees, who hath the charge of keeping the records of the courte, and maketh out all the records of *Nisi prius*, hath the fees due for all searches, and hath the certifiing of all records into the the kings bench, when a writ of errour is brought; and maketh out all writs of (*Supersideas de non molestando*) which are graunted for the defendants, while the writ of errour hangeth. Also he maketh all exemplications of records being in the treasurie. He is taken to be the seruant of the chiefe Iustice, and remoueable at his pleasure: whereas al other officers are for terme of life. There is also a Secondarie, or vnder clerk of the treasurie for assistance, which hath some allowances. There is likewise an vnder keeper, who alway keepeth one key of the treasury doore, & the chiefe

chiefe clerke of the Secundarie another:so the one cannot come in without the other.

Clerk of essoines, (*clericus essoniorum*) is an officer belonging to the courte of common plees, who onely keepeth the essoines rolle, and hath for entring everie essoine, sixe pence, and for every exception to barre the essoine, in case where the partie hath omitted his time, sixe pence. *He* hath also the providing of parchment, and cutting it out into rols, and marking the numbers vpon them, and the deliuerie out of all the rols to euerie officer, and the receiuing of them againe, when they be written, and the binding and making vp of the whole bundels of euerie terme: and this he doth as seruant to the cheife Iustice. For the cheife Iustice is at charge for all the parchemét of all the rols.

Clerk of the outlawries, (*clericus vtlagariarum*) is an officer belonging to the court of common plees, being onely the seruant or deputie to the kings atturney generall, for making out the writs of (*capias vtlagatum*) after outlawrie. And the kings atturneis name is to euerie one of those writs. And whereas seuen pence is paide for the seale of everie other writ betwixt partie & party, there is but a peny paid for the seale of this writ, because it goeth out at the Kings suite.

Clerk of the sewers, (*clericus suerarum*) is an officer appertei-ning to the commissioners of sewers, writing all things that they doe by vertue of their cõmission, for the which See *Sewers*: and see the statute *anno* 13. *Elizabe.ca.9.*

Clerk controller of the kings house, (whereof there be two) is an officer in court, that hath place and seate in the compting house and authoritie to allow or disallow the charges and demands of pursuivants or messengers of the greene cloth, purveiours, or other like. He hath also the ouersight and controlling of all defaults, defects and miscariages of any the inferiour officers, and to sit in the counting house with the superiour officers, *viz.* the *L.* Steward, treasurer, controller and coferer. either for correcting or bettering things out of order; and also for bringing in country provision requisite for the Kings houshold: and the censure for faylling of cariages and carts warned & charged for that purpose. This officer you haue mentioned. *anno.* 33. *H.*8. *ca.*12.

Clerk of the Nihils (*clericus nihilorum*) is an officer in the Exchequer, that maketh a rolle of all such summes, as are nihiled by the shyreeues vpon their estreats of greene waxe, and deliuereth vereth the same into the *Lord* treasurers remembrancer his office, to haue execution done vpon it for the king.

Clerk of the check, is an officer in court, so called, because he hath the check and controlment of the yeomen of the gard, and all other ordinary yeomen and huissiers belonging either to his maiesty, the *Queene*, or Prince, either giuing leaue, or allowing their absences or defects in attendance, or deminishing their wages for the same. He also nightly by himselfe or depute, taketh the view of those that are to watch in the court, and hath the setting of the watch. This officer is mentioned. *anno.* 33. *H.* 8.*ca.*12.

Clerk marshiall of the kings house, seemeth to be an officer that attendeth the marshiall in his court, and recordeth all his proceedings, *anno* 33. *H.* 8.*cap.* 12.

Clothe of raye. anno 27.*Ed.* 3.*sta.* 1.*cap.* 4.

Closhe, is an vnlawfull game forbidden by the statute, *anno* 17. *Ed.* 4. *cap.* 3. which is casting of a bowle at nine pinnes of wood, or nine shanke bones of an oxe or horse.

Clove is the 32. part of a weigh of cheese i. 8. pound, *anno* 9. *H.* 6. *cap.* 8.

Cloues (*caryophylli*) are a spice knowne by sight to euery man. They be flowers of a tree called (*caryophyllus*) gathered and hardened by the Sunne. Of their nature you may reade in *Gerards Herball. lib.* 3. *cap.* 144. This is cōprised among such spices, as be to be garbled, *anno* 1. *Iacob. cap.* 19.

Cocket (*cokettum*) is a seale appertaining to the kings custome house, *Regist. orig. fol.* 192. *a.* & also a scrow of parchement sealed and deliuered by the officers of the custome house to merchants, as a warrant that their merchandize be customed, *anno* 11. *H.* 6. *cap.* 16. which parchment is otherwise called *litera de coketto*, or *litera testimoniales de coketto. Regist. vbi supra. fol.* 179. *a.* So is the word vsed. *anno* 5. & 6. *Ed.* 6. *cap.* 14. and *anno* 14. *Ed.* 3. *stat.* 1. *cap.* 21. This word is also vsed for a distinction of bread in the statutes of bread & ale, made *anno* 51. *H.* 3. where you haue mention of bread coket, wastell bread, bread of trete, and bread of commen wheate.

Coferer of the Kings houshold, is a principal officer of his Maiesties court, next vnder the Controller, that in the counting house and else where at other times, hath a speciall charge and ouersight of other officers of the houshold, for their good demeanure and cariage in their offices, to all

which,

which one and other, being either Sergeants, Yeomẽ, groomes, pages, or children of the kitchin, or any other in any roome of his Maiesties seruants of houshold, and payeth their wages. This officer is mentioned. *anno* 39. *Elizab. cap.* 7.

Cogs anno 23. *H.* 8. *cap.* 18.

Conisour of a fine, is he, that passeth or acknowledgeth a fine in lands or tenemẽts to another: *Cognisee* is he to whom the fine is acknowledged, *West. parte* 2. *symbol. titulo Fines. sect.* 2.

Cognizance, commeth from the French (*cognisance.* i. *intelligentia, intellectus, notio, cognitio,*) with vs it is vsed diuersly: somtime signifying a badge of a seruingmans sleeue, whereby he is discerned to belong to this or that Noble or Gentleman: somtime an acknowledgement of a fine, or confession of a thing done: as *cognoscens latro, Bracton. lib.* 3. *tract.* 2. *cap.* 3. 20. 32. *cognoscere se ad villanum. Idem lib.* 4. *tractat.* 3. *cap.* 16. As also to make cognisance of taking a distresse: somtime as an audience or hearing of a mater iudicially, as to take cognisance: sometime a power or iurisdiction, as cognisance of plee, is an habilitie to call a cause or plee out of another court: which no man can doe but the king, except he can shew charter for it. *Manwood parte* 1. Of his Forest lawes, *pag.* 68. See the new tearmes of the lawe, and the new booke of Entries, *verbo, Conusance.*

Cognatione. See *Cosenage.*

Cognisour, see *Conisour.*

Cognitionibus mittendis, is a writ to a Iustice, or other, that hath power to take a fine, who hauing taken knowledgement of a fine, deferreth to certifie it into the court of common plees, commanding him to certifie it. *Regist. orig.* 68. *b.*

Coin (*cuneus, vel cuna*) seemeth to come from the French (*coin.* i. *angulus*) which probably verifieth the opinion of such, as doe hould the auncientest sort of coyne to be cornered and not round. Of this Lawyers substantiue (*cuna*) commeth the Lawyers verbe (*cunare*) i. to coyne. *Cromptons* iustice of peace *fol.* 220.

Coliander seede, or rather *Coriander seede* (*Semen coriandri*) is the seede of an herbe so called, medicinable and wholesome for diuers good purposes, which see in *Gerards Herball. lib.* 2. *cap.* 379. It is numbred among the drugges that be to be garbled, *anno* 1. *Iacob. cap.* 19.

Collaterall (*collateralis*) commeth of the Latine (*laterale*) i. that which hangeth by the side. *Lateralia viatoria.* ꝟ. *de lega. & fideium, tertio l.* 102. seeme to sig-

signifie a budget or capcase to hang by a saddle pomel. *Collaterall*, is vsed in the common law, for that which commeth in, or is adhering of the side: as, collaterall assurance, is that which is made ouer and beside the deede it selfe. For example, if a man couenant with another, and enter bond for the performance of his couenant, the bond is termed collaterall assurance: because it is externall, and without the nature and essence of the couenant. And *Crompton* in his Iurisd. *fol.* 185. saith, that to be subiect to the feeding of the kings Deere, is collateral to the soyle within the Forest. In like maner may we say, that the libertie to pitche boothes or standings for a Faire in another mans ground, is collaterall to the ground. The priuate woods of a common person within a Forest, may not be cut without the kings licence. For it is a prerogatiue collaterall to the soyle. *Manwood parte 1.* of his Forest lawes, *pag.* 66. *Collaterall warrantie.* See *Warrantie.*

Collation of a benefice (collatio beneficii) signifieth properly the bestowing of a benefice by the Bishop, that hath it in his owne gift or patronage: and differeth from Institution in this, for that Institution into a benefice, is performed by the Bishop at the motion or presentation of another, who is patron of the same, or hath the patrons right for the time. *Extra de Institutionibus. & De concessione prebendarum. &c.* And yet is collation vsed for presentation. *anno.* 25. *Ed.* 3. *stat.* 6.

Collatione facta vni post mortem alterius, &c. is a writ directed to the Iustices of the cōmon plees, commanding them to direct their writ to a *Bishop*, for the admitting of a clerk in the place of another presented by the king, that during the suit betweene the king and the Bishops clerk, is departed. For iudgment once passed for the kings clerk, and he dying before he be admitted, the king may bestow his presentation vpon another, *Register orig. fo.* 31. *b.*

Collatione heremitagii, is a writ whereby the king conferreth the keeping of an ermitage vpon a clerk. *Register orig. fo.* 303 308.

Colour, (color) signifieth in the common law, a probable plee, but in truth false, and hath this end, to draw the triall of the cause from the Iury to the Iudges. Of this see two apt examples in the author of the new tearms. *Verbo Colour.* who also referreth you to the Doctor and student. *fo.* 158. *&c.* See *Broke tit. Colour in assise, trespas &c. fol.*

fo. 140.

Collusion, (*collusio*) is in our common law, a deceitfull agreemēt or compact between two or more, for the one party to bring an action against the other to some euill purpose; as to defraude a third of his right, &c. See the new tearms. and *Broke titulo. Collusion.* See also one case of collusion in the *Register orig. fo.* 179. *a.*

Combat, (*duellum*) is a french word signifiing as much as (*certamen, decertatio, dimicatio, discrimen, prælium, pugna*) but in our common law, it is taken for a formall triall of a doubtfull cause or quarrell, by the sword or bastons of two champions. Of this you may reade at large both in diuers ciuilians, as *Paris de Puteo, de re militari & duello. Alciat de duello, Hotomam disputatio. feudalium. ca.* 42. and others: as also in our common lawyers of England, namely *Glanuile. li.* 14. *ca.* 1. *Bracton. li.* 3. *tracta.* 2. *ca.* 3. *Britton ca.* 22. *Horns mirrour of Iustices li.* 3. *ca. des exceptions in fine proxime ante c. Iuramentū duelli. Dier. fo.* 301. *nu.* 41. & 42. That this also was aunciently the law of the *Lombards*, before they inuaded Italy (which was about the yeare of our Lord 571. appeareth by *Sigonius*, in his historie *De regno Italiæ. lib.* 2. *de Arioaldo rege.* who there reporteth, that the said king, hauing put away his wife *Gundeberga*, vpon a surmise of adulterie with *Tato* Duke of *Etruria*, at the priuate suggestion of *Adalulphus*, a great man among the *Lombards*, and being charged by *Clotharius* the king of *France* his Ambassadors, of whose bloud she was, that he had done her wrong: he answered, that he had done her no wrong. Whereupon *Ansoaldus* one of the ambassadors replyed, that they would easily beleeue him, if he would suffer the truth to be tried by combat, betweene some one of the Queens friends, and her accuser, according to the custome of the *Lombards*. And the king yeelding vnto this, *Adalulphus* was vanquished by one *Pitto*, otherwise called *Charles*, set foorth for the Queenes chāpion, and she restored to her former place and honour.

Cominseede, aliâs, Cuminseed, (*Semen cumini*) is a seede brought foorth by an hearbe so called, which you may see described in *Gerards Herball, lib.* 2. *cap.* 416. This is placed among the garbleable drugges, *anno* 1. *Iacob. cap.* 19.

Comitatu commisso, is a writ or a commission, whereby the Shyreeue is autherized to take vpon him the swaye of the countie. *Regist. orig. fol.* 295. *a.* & *b.* and *Cokes Reports. li.* 3. *fol.* 72. *a.*

Comitatu & castro commisso, is a writ whereby the charge of a countie, together with the keeping of a castell, is committed to the Shyreeue, *Reg orig. fol. 295.a.*

Commaundrie (præceptoria) was by some mens opinion, a maner or chiefe mesuage, with which lands or tenements were occupied, belonging to the Priorie of *S. Iohns* in *Hierusalem* in *England*: and he which had the gouernement of any such maner or house, was called the commaunder, who had nothing to dispose of it, but to the vse of the Priorie, taking onely his sustenance thence, according to his degree, and was vsually a brother of the same Priorie. Author of the new tearmes of lawe. *verbo, Commaundrie*. By some other bookes it appeareth, that the chiefe Prior of *S. Iohns*, was a cōmaunder of a Nunnerie, and cōstituted the Priores of the said Nunnerie, who was vnder his obedience, and remoueable at his will, notwithstanding that shee had covent, and common seale, and had her possessions seuerall, and was wont to lease the land for terme of yeares. *Fulbecks Paralels, fol. 2. a.* Of these commādries also *Petrus Gregorius lib. de beneficiis cap. 11. num. 11.* hath these words: *Præceptoriæ dictæ commendæ sacrorum militum, veluti ordinis hospitalis Sancti Ioannis Hierosolymitani, beneficia quidem secundùm quid Ecclesiastica dicuntur à Barbatia ad Clement. causam col. 51. de Electione. Tamen non propriè dicuntur ex genere communium beneficiorum, eo quòd personæ conferentes, & quibus conferuntur, non sunt laicæ vel ecclesiasticæ, sed tertii ordinis. De hiis beneficiis fit mentio. cap. exhibita de priuilegiis. in extravag. com. in cap. Dudum. de decimis.* These in many places of our realme are termed by the name of temples, because they sometime belonged to the Templers. Of these you reade *ann. 26 H. 8. cap. 2. & anno 32. eiusd. ca 24.* And of these the said *Gregorius Tolosanus. li. 15. sui syntagmatis. cap. 34.* hath these words: *Monuimus superiori capite, crescente numero peregrinorum, iuxta Tēplum Hierosolymitanum Xenodochium ædificatum, tit. Diui Iohannis, quo exciperentur peregrini, quos cœnobia capere non possent. Huius ergo ministerio quoque viri pij nobiles se devoverunt, qui & peregrinos tutarentur, & à latronum seu Agarenorum incursu defenderent. Horum professio est votum solenne paupertatis, & abdicationis propriorum, castitatis, & obedientiæ. Proinde propter primum votum nihil proprii habent, vel habere debent, sed accipiunt annonam, quàm diu viuunt, vel præceptorias (quas vocant Commanderies) administrant, quàm diu eas possident, & optione mutant,* vel

vel ex magistri licentia permutant reddituri morientes quæ apud eos reperientur, societati Of these *Corasius* in his paraphrase *Ad sacerd. mat. parte prim. cap.* 3. saith thus: *Præceptoriæ Rhodienses, cùm non nisi fratribus Hierosolymitanis, atque ita personis ecclesiasticis conferantur, beneficiis ecclesiasticis annumerari meritò debent.*

Commaundement (*præceptum*) is vsed diuersely in the common lawe: some time for the commaundement of the king, when vpon his meere motion, and from his owne mouth, he casteth any man into prison. *Stawnf. pl. cor. fo.* 72. or of the Iustices. And this commãdement of the Iustices, is either absolute or ordinary: absolute, as when vpon their owne authority in their wisedome and discretion, they commit a man to prison, for a punishment: Ordinary is, when they commit one rather for safe custody then punishment. And a man committed vpon an ordinary commandemẽt, is repleuisable. *pl. cor. fo.* 73. Cõmandement is againe vsed for the offence of him, that willeth another man to transgresse the lawe, or to doe any such thing, as is contrary to the lawe, as murder, theft, or such like. *Bract. li.* 3. *tra.* 2 *ca.* 19 And this the ciuilians call (*mandatum*) *Angelus de maleficiis.*

Commen (*communia*) commeth from the french (*commun.* i. *quod ad omnes pertinet*) and signifieth in our common lawe, that soile or water, whereof the vse is common to this or that towne, or lordship; as common of pasture (*communia pasturæ.*) *Bract. li.* 4. *ca.* 19. & 40. commen of fishing. *communia piscariæ. Idem. li.* 2. *ca.* 34. commen of *turbary.* i. of digging turues (*communia turbariæ*) *Idem. li.* 4. *ca.* 41. cõmen of *estouers* (*communia estouerio rum.*) *Kitchin. fo.* 94. *Comen*, is deuided into *commen* in grosse, *commen appendant, commen appertinent*, and *commen per cause de vicinage.* i. by reason of neighbourhood. *Cõmen* in grosse, is a liberty to haue *cõmen* alone (that is) without any land or tenement, in another mans land, to him selfe for life, or to him and his heires. And this is commonly passed by deede of graunt or specialty. *Old nat. br. fo.* 31. & 37. *Commen appendant* and common appertinent, be in a maner confounded: as appeareth by *Fitzh. nat. br. fo.* 180. and be defined to be a liberty of common, appertaining to, or depending of such or such a freehould. Onely *Kitchin. fo.* 94. seemeth to make this difference, that he which hath *commen* appertinẽt, hath it without limitation of this or that kinde of beastes: but that is controlled by *Dyer. fo.* 70. *b.*

nu. 19. He that hath *commen* appendant, hath it but for beastes commenable, as horses, oxen, kine, and sheepe, being acompted fittest for the plowman: and not of goates, geese and hogs. whereunto the author of the new teaams of law addeth another difference: which is, that common appertinent may be seuered from the land, wherunto it is appertinent, but not common appendant. The originall of common appendant *S. Ed. Coke li.* 4. *fo.* 37. thus expresseth: Common appendant, by the auncient lawe, had beginning in this maner, when a lord infeoffed another in erable lands, to hould of him in socage (*id est, per seruicium socæ*) as all tenure in the beginning (according to *Litleton*) was: the feoffee, to maintaine the seruice of his plough, had cōmō in the wasts of his lord, for his necessary beasts to gaine and compas his land: & that for two causes: one for that, as then it was taken, it was (*tacitè*) implyed in the feofment, by reason the feoffee could not gaine or compas his land without catell, and catell could not be sustained without pasture. anb so by consequent the feoffee had (as a thing necessary and incident) common in the wastes and land of the lord. And this appeareth by aunciēt books *tempore. Ed.* 1. *tit.* common 24. & 17. *E.* 2. *tit.* common. 23. & 20. *Ed.* 3. *tit.* Admesurement. 8, & 18. *Ed.* 3. and by the rehersall of the statute of *Merton. ca.* 4. The second reason was for maintenance, and aduancement of tillage, which is much regarded and fauoured in the lawe, Thus farre S. *Edward.*

Commen per cause de vicinage, is a libertie, that the tenents of one lord in one towne, haue to common with the tenents of another lord in another towne. which kinde of common they that chalenge, may not put their catell into the common of the other towne. For then they be distreinable. But turning them into their owne fields, if they strey into the neighbours commen, they must be suffered. See the *termes of lawe*. Common of pasture the Civilians call *ius compascendi, cum sc: plures ex municipibus qui diversa prædia possidebant, saltum communem, vt ius compascendi haberent, mercarentur. l. penul. π. si servit, vendicetur.* It is also called *ius compascuum. ibidem.*

Commendam (*commenda*) is a benefice, that being voide, is cōmended to the charge & care of some sufficient clerk, to be supplied, vntill it may be conveniently provided of a pastor. And that this was the true originall of this practise, you may read at large in *Duarenus de sacris ecclesiæ ministeriis & beneficiis li.5.ca.7.* And whereas the glosse, *in verbo commendare.in ca. Nemo deinceps:de electione. in sexto.* defineth *commendam esse ecclesiæ custodiam alicui commissam: Iohannes Andreas* therevpon saith thus: *huic definitioni necessariò hæc adijcienda putem: in tempus gratiâ evidentis necessitatis & vtilitatis. Idq; docuit textus in dicto capite. Nemo. Corrasius in his paraphrase de sacerdotiorum materia. parte prima. ca.6.nu.3.& seqq.* thus describeth the mater: *In commendam conceditur beneficium, cùm Romanus Pontifex, Legatus, aut Episcopus (Neque enim inferioribus, qui ex privelegio aut alio iure spirituali conferunt, concessum est, ca. cum omnes basilicæ. 16.quæst.7.) ecclesiæ vacantis custodiam alicui committit, administratorem generalem eius tempori eum constituens, ca. nemo.de electio.in sexto. Commendare enim aliud est nihil, quàm deponere.l. publius.π. depositi.l. cōmēdare.π. de verb: signif.) Hoc autē, ad tempus sex mensium, & pro evidenti necessitate aut vtilitate ecclesiæ lex permittit, (d ca. Nemo.) Quare commendatarius qui ecclesiæ vacantis & fructuum, ad tempus duntaxat custodiā habet, nec tenere beneficiū, iusve habere in beneficio, aut canonicum titulum censebitur: vti nec depositarius in re deposita.* wherof also *Petrus Gregorius de beneficiis, ca.10.nu.13.* thus writeth. *In hac quarta divisione, potest addi tertium genus beneficii, quod citra præscriptionem qualitatis a persona alterius qualitatis quàm beneficium exigat naturâ, possidetur, sed sine præiudicio naturæ beneficii, & per dispensationem, eo commendato olim ad tempus certum certæ personæ, hodie, vt plerunq;, quàm diu commendatarius vixerit. Vocant hoc beneficium commendatum commendam: vt si regulare beneficium à Summo Pontifice conferatur, nomine commēdæ, sæculari. Nam ideo non mutatur beneficii natura, nec fit ideo sæculare, &c.* And a little after, *Interim annotabimus duplici de causa fieri commendam ecclesiæ, nempe vel in vtilitatem ecclesiæ, vel commendatarii. In primo commenda titulum non dat beneficii commendatario, & dicitur potius custodia quæ revocari potest: quod repugnat naturæ beneficii, quod est perpetuum. In secundo autem casu beneficium censetur in vtilitatem commendatarii commēda facta, quam possidere potest quàm diu vixerit, &c.* whome you may also read. *ca.2.li.13.*

Commissarie (*cōmissarius*) is a title of ecclesiasticall iurisdiction, appertaining to such a one as exerciseth spirituall iurisdiction (at the least, so farre as his commission permitteth him) in places of the dioces so farre distant from the cheife citie, as the chanceler cannot call the subiects

iects to the *Bishops* principall consistorie, without their to great molestation. This commissarie is of the canonists termed *commissarius* or *officialis foraneus. Lyndwoods provin.ca.1.de accusatio.verbo. Mandatum archiepiscopi.in glos.* and is ordeined to this especiall end, that he supply the bishops iurisdiction and office in the out places of the dioces, or els in such parishes as be peculiars to the bishop, and exempted from the iurisdiction of the Archdeacon. For where either by prescription or composition, there be archedeacons that haue iurisdiction within their archdeaconries, as in most places they haue, there this commissarie is but superfluous, and most commonly, doth rather vexe and disturb the country for his lucre, then of conscience seeke to redresse the liues of offenders. And therefore the Bishop taking prestation mony of his archdeacons yearely *pro exteriori iurisdictione*, as it is ordinarily called, doeth by superonerating their circuit with a commissarie, not onely wrong archdeacons, but the poorer sort of subiects much more, as common practise daily teacheth to their great woe.

Cōmission, (commissio) is for the most part, in the vnderstanding of the common lawe, as much as (*delegatio*) with the Civilians. (*See Broke. titulo commission.*) and is taken for the warrant or letters patents, that all men exercising iurisdiction either ordinarie or extraordinarie, haue for their power to heare or determine any cause or action. Of these see diuers in the table of the *Register originall. verbo. Commissio.* yet this word sometime is is extended farder, then to maters of iudgement: as the commission of purveiours or takers. *anno.*11. *H.* 4. *ca.*28. But with this epitheton (*high*) it is most notoriously vsed for the honourable commission court, instituted and founded vpon the statute 1.*Eliza.ca.*1. for the ordering and reformation of all offences, in any thing appertaining to the iurisdiction ecclesiasticall: but especially such as are of higher nature, or, at the least, require greater punishment, then ordinarie iurisdiction can afford. For the world being growne to that loosenes, as not to esteeme the censure of excommunicatiō, necessitie calleth for those censures of fynes to the prince and imprisonment, which doe affect men more neerely.

Commission of rebellion (Commissio rebellionis) is otherwise called a writte of rebellion, (*breue rebellionis*) and it hath vse, when a man after proclamation made by the *Shyreeue* vpon an order of of the chauncerie, or court of Starre chamber, vnder penaltie of his allegance, to present himselfe to the court by a certaine day, appeareth not. And this commission is directed by way of commaund to certaine persons, to this end, that they, or three, two, or one of them, doe apprehend, or cause to be apprehend, the party as a rebell and contemner of the kings lawes, wheresoeuer they find him within the kingdome, and bring him, or cause him to be brought to the courte, vpon a day therein assigned. The true copie of this commission or writ, you haue in *Cromptons* diuers Iurisdictions. *Court de Starre chamber:* as also in *West. tractat.* touching proceedings in Chancerie, *Sectio* 24.

Commissioner (commissionarius) is he that hath commission, as leters patents, or other lawfull warrant, to execute any publike office: as commissioners of the office of fines and licenses. *West. parte. 2. symbol: titulo Fines. sect.* 106. commissioners in eyre. *an.* 3. *Ed.* 1. *ca.* 26. with infinite such like.

Committee, is he to whome the consideration or ordering of any mater is referred, either by some court, or consent of parties, to whome it belongeth. As in Parlament, a bille being read, is either consented vnto and passed, or denied, or nether of both, but referred to the consideration of some certaine men, appointed by the house farder to examine it: who thereupon are called *committees*. Committee of the King. *West. par. 2. symbo. titulo Chancerie. sect.* 144. This word seemeth to be something strangely vsed in *Kitchin. fo.* 160. where the widow of the kings tenent being dead, is called the cōmittee of the king, that is, one committed by the auncient law of the land, to the kings care and protection.

Common bench (bancus communis) is vsed some time for the court of common plees. *anno.* 2. *Ed.* 3. *ca.* 11. So called, as *M. Camden* saith in his *Britannia. pa.* 113. *quia communia placita inter subditos ex iure nostro, quod communia vocant, in hoc disceptantur,* that is, the plees or controuersies tryed betweene common persons.

Common fine (finis communis) of this *Fleta* hath these words: *Quibus expeditis* (speaking of the businesse finished by Iustices in eyre) *consueverunt Iusticiarii imponere villatis, iuratoribus, hundredis, & toti comitatui concelamētum, & omnes separatim amerciare: quod videtur voluntarium, cùm de periurio & concelamento non fuerint convicti, sed potius dispensandum esset cum eis quod animus in statera posuerint pro pacis conservatione. li.* 1. *cap.*48. §. *Quibus.* And a litle following. §. *Et provisum,* he hath these words: *Et provisum est, quòd communes misericordiæ vel fines comitatuum amerciatorum in finibus itinerum Iusticiariorum ante recessum ipsorum Iustitiariorum per sacramenta militum, & aliorum proborum hominum de commitatu eodem, affidantur super eos qui contribuere debent: vnde particulæ Iusticiariis liberentur, vt cum aliis extractis suis ad Scaccarium liberare valeant.* These last words of his haue relation to the statute, *Westminst. pr.cap.* 18. which reade. See *Fine.*

Common plees (*communia placita*) is the kings Court now held in *Westminster* hall, but in auncient time moueable, as appeareth by the statute called *Magna charta. cap.* 11. as also *anno* 2. *Ed.* 3. *cap.* 11. and *Pupilla oculi, parte* 5. *cap.* 22. But *M. Gwin* in the Preface to his readings saith, that vntill the time that *Henry* the third granted the great charter, there were but two courts in all, called the Kings courts: whereof one was the Exchequer, and the other, the kings bench, which was then called (*curia Domini regis*) and (*aula regia*) because it followed the court or king: and that vpon the grant of that charter, the court of common plees was erected and setled in one place certaine: viz. at *Westminster.* And because this court was setled at *Westminster*, wheresoeuer the king lay: thereupon *M. Gwin, vbi supra,* saith, that after that, all the writs ranne, *Quòd sit coram Iusticiariis meis apud Westmonasterium:* whereas before the partie was cōmanded by thē, to appeare *coram me vel Iusticiariis meis,* simply without addition of place, as he well obserueth out of *Glanvile* and *Bracton,* the one writing in *Henry* the seconds time, before this court was erected, the other in the later end of *Henry* the thirds time, who erected this court. All ciuill causes both reall and personall are, or were in former times, tryed in this court, according to the strict lawe of the realme: and by *Fortescue, cap.* 50. it seemeth to haue bene the onely court for reall causes. The chiefe Iudge thereof is called the Lord chiefe Iustice of the common plees, accompanied with 3. or 4. assistants or associates, which are created by leters patents from the king, and (as it were) enstalled or placed vpon the bench, by the Lord Chaunceler and lord chiefe Iustice of the court, as appeareth by *Fortescue, cap.* 51. who expresseth all the circumstances of this admission. The rest of the officers belonging to this court, are these: the *custos breuium*, three Protonotaries, otherwise called Prenotaries, Chirographer, Filazers 14. Exigenters, 4. Clerke, of the warrants, Clerke of the Iuries or iurata writs, Clerke of the Treasurie, Clerke of the kings siluer, Clerke of the essoins, Clerke of the outlawries. Whose distinct functions looke in their places. See *Common bench*.

Common day in plee of land, an. 13. *R.* 2. *stat.* 1. *cap.* 17. signifieth an ordinarie day in the court as *Octauis Michaelis*, *quindena pasca.&c.* as you may see in the statute made *anno* 51. *H.* 3. concerning generall dayes in the bench.

Common house of parlament, is vsed for the nether house: because the commōs of the realme, that is, the knights of the shires and burgeses, possesse that house. *Crompton iurisd.* 9.

Commotes, seemeth to be compounded of the prepositiō (*con*) and (*mot.* i. *dictio, verbum*) and signifieth in Wales a part of a shire, as a hundred. *anno.* 28. *H.* 8. *ca.* 3. It is written *commoithes. anno.* 4. *H.* 4. *ca.* 17. and is vsed for a gathering made vpon the people (as it seemeth) of this or that hundred, by welsh minstrels.

Common law (comunis lex) hath three diuers significatiōs. which see in the author of new termes of law. *verbo. Common law.*

Communi custodia, is a writ that lyeth for that lord, whose tenent houlding by knights seruice, dyeth, and leaueth his eldest sonne vnder age, against a straunger that entreth the land, and obtaineth the ward of the body. It may seeme to take the name from the common custom or right in this case: which is, that the lord haue the wardship of his tenent, vntill his full age, or because it is common for the recouery both of land and tenent, as appeareth by the forme thereof. *Old nat. br. fo.* 89. See also the *Register orig. fo.* 161. *a.*

Communi placito non tenendo in scaccario, is a writ directed to the treasurer and barons of the exchequer, forbidding them to hould plee betweene two common persons in that court, neither of them belonging toward the said court. *Register orig. fo.* 187. *b.*

Companion of the garter, is one of the knights of that most noble and honourable order. *anno.* 24. *H.* 8. *ca.* 13. See *Garter.*

Compromis, (compromissum) is a mutuall promise of two or more parties at difference, to referre the ending of their controuersies, to the arbitriment and equitie of one or more arbitratours. *West* defineth is thus, *parte.* 2. *Symbol. titulo Compromise. sect.*

pri. A compromiſe or ſubmiſſion (*arbitrium, compromiſſum, ſubmiſſio*) is the faculty or power of pronouncing ſentence betweene perſons at controuerſie, giuen to arbitratours by the parties mutuall priuate conſent, without publique authority.

Computo, is a writ ſo called of the effect: becauſe it compelleth a baylife, chamberlaine, or receiuer to yeld his accoumpt, *Old nat. br. fo.* 58. It is founded vpon the ſtatut of *Weſtm.* 2. *ca.* 2. *anno.* 13. *Ed.* 1. which for your beter vnderſtanding you may read. And it lyeth alſo for executours of executours. *anno.* 15. *Ed.* 3. *ſtatut. de prouiſ. victuall. ca.* 5. Thirdly, againſt the garden in ſocage for waſte made in the minority of the heire. *Marlb. ca.* 17. And ſee farder in what other caſes it lyeth. *Regiſter orig. fo.* 135. *old nat. br. vbi ſupra.* & *Fitzh. nat. br. fo.* 116.

Concealers, be ſuch as finde out concealed lands, that is, ſuch lands as priuily are kept from the king by common perſons, hauing nothing to ſhew for them. *anno.* 39. *Eliza. ca.* 22. They be ſo called a *concelando, as mons a mouendo. per antiphraſin.*

Concord, (*concordia*) is in the common law, by a peculiar ſignification, defined to be the very agreement betweene parties, that intend the leuying of a fine of lands one to the other, how and in what maner the land ſhall paſſe. For in the forme thereof many things are to be conſidered. *Weſt. parte.* 2. *Symbol. titulo. Fines and concords*, *ſect.* 30. whome read at large. Concord is alſo an agreement made vpon any treſpas cōmitted betweene two or more: and is diuided into a concord executory, and a concord executed. See *Plowden. caſu* Reniger, & *Fogaſſa fo.* 5. & 6. where it appeareth by ſome opinion, that the one bindeth not as being imperfect: the other abſolute and tyeth the parties: and yet by ſome other opinion in the ſame caſe, it is affirmed that agreements executory be perfect, and doe noe leſſe binde, then agreements executed. *fo.* 8. *b.*

Concubinage, (*concubinatus*) is an exception againſt her, that ſheweth for her dower, whereby it is alleadged, that ſhee was not a wife lawefully maried to the party, in whoſe lands ſhee ſeeketh to be endowed, but his concubine. *Britton. ca.* 107. *Bract. li.* 4. *tract* 6. *ca.* 8.

Condition, (*conditio*) is a rate, maner, or lawe, annexed to mens acts, ſtaying or ſuſpending the ſame, and making them vncertaine, whether they ſhall take effect or no, *Weſt. parte* 1. *ſymb. li.* 2. *Sect.* 156. In a leaſe there may be two sorts of conditions: condition collaterall, or condition annexed to the rent. *Sir Edward Coke. lib. 3. Pennants case. fol. 64.* Collaterall condition is that, which is annexed to any collaterall act: as that the leassee shall not go to *Rome, ibi fol. 65.* Condition is also diuided, into condition in deed or fact, and condition in lawe: which otherwise may be tearmed, condition expressed, and condition implyed. *Perkins. Conditions. 722.* These and other like diuisions of conditions you may reade in the author of the new Tearmes of law. *verbo. Condition.* and in *Litleton. li. 3. cap. 5.*

Conders, may seeme to proceed from the French, (*conduire.* i. *deducere, gubernare*) they be such as stand vpon high places neere the sea coast, at the time of herring fishing, to make signes with bowghes, &c. in their hand vnto the fishers, which way the shole of herrings passeth. For that may beter appeare to such as stand vpon some high cliffe on the shore, by a kind of blew colour, that the said fish causeth in the water, then to those that be in the shippes. These be otherwise called huers, by likelihood of the French (*huyer.* i. *exclamare*) and balkers: as appeareth by the statute, *anno 1. Iacob. cap. 23.*

Cone & key. Bracton. lib. 2. ca. 37. num. 3. looke *Cover* and *Key.*

Confirmation (*confirmatio*) is a strengthening of an estate formerly had, and yet voydable, though not presently voide. For example, a Bishop graunteth his Chancelershippe by patent for the terme of the patentee his life: this is no voide graunt, but voydable by the bishops death, except it be strengthened by the confirmation of the *Deane* and chapter. See more of this, in *West. parte prim. symb. lib. 2. sect.* 500. and *Fitz. nat. br. fol. 169.* B. 226. *H.* 271. *D.* 163. *G.* and *Litleton lib. 3. cap. 9.*

Confiscate (*confiscatus*) may be said to come either from the Latine (*confiscare*) or the French (*confisquer.* i. *in publicum addicere.*) All these words are drawne from (*fiscus*) which originally signifieth a hamper, pannyer, basket, or freyle: but metonymically the Emperours treasure: because it was anciently kept in such hampers, &c. And though our king keepe not his treasure in such things: yet as the *Romanes* said, that such goods as were forfeited to the Emperors treasurie for any offence, were *bona confiscata*: so do we those that are forfeited to our kings Exchequer. See more of these goods confiscate. *in Stawnf. pl. cor. lib. 3. cap. 24.*

Congè d'eslire (*venia eligendi*) is very French, and signifieth in our common lawe, the kings permission royall, to a Deane and chapter in time of vacation, to chuse a bishop: or to an Abbey or Priorie of his owne foundation, to chuse their Abbot or Prior. *Fitz. nat. br. fol.* 169. *B.* 170. B. C. *&c.* Touching this mater, *M. Gwin* in the preface to his readings saith, that the king of *England*, as soueraigne patron of all Archbishoprickes, Bishoprickes, and other Ecclesiasticall benefices, had of auncient time, free appointment of all ecclesiasticall dignities, when soeuer they chaunced to be voide: inuesting them first (*per baculum & annulum*) and afterward by his leters patents: and that in proces of time he made the election ouer to others, vnder certaine formes and conditions: as namely, that they should at euery vacation before they chuse, demaund of the king (*congè d'eslire*) that is, licence to proceede to election, and then after the election, to craue his royall assent &c. And furder he affirmeth by good proofe out of common lawe bookes, that King Iohn was the first that graunted this, and that it was afterward confirmed by *Westm. pri. ca.* i. which statute was made *anno.* 3. *Ed. pri.* and againe by the statut (*Articuli cleri*) *ca.* 2. which was ordained. *anno.* 25. *Ed.* 3. *statuto tertio.*

Congeable, commeth the of french (*conge* i. *venia*) It signifieth in our common law, as much as lawfull or lawfully done; as the entry of the disseisee is congeable. *Litleton. fo.* 91. *in meo.*

Conisance, See *Cognisance.*

Conizour, *aliàs cognizour* (*recognitor*) commeth of the French (*cognoistre*. i. *cognoscere, cernere*) and is vsed in the passing of fynes' for him, that doth acknowledge the fyne; and the conizee is hee, to whome it is acknowledged. *West. parte.* 1. *symbol. li.* 2. *sect.* 49. *& parte* 2. *titulo. Fines sectio.* 114. See *Recognizour.*

Coniuration (*coniuratio*) is the very French word drawne from the latine, which as it is compounded of (*con & iuro*) so it signifieth a compact or plot, made by men combining themselues together by oath or promise, to doe some publique harme. But in our common lawe, it is especially vsed for such as haue personall conference with the deuill or evill spirit, to know any secret, or to effect any purpose. *anno* 5. *Eliza. ca.* 16. And the difference that I haue obserued (how truly let those iudge that be beter skilled in these maters) betweene coniuration and witchcraft, is because

the

the one seemeth, by prayers and invocation of Gods powerfull names, to compell the devill, to to say or doe what he commandeth him: the other dealeth rather by a friendly and voluntarie conference or agreement betweene him or her and the deuill or familiar, to haue her or his desires and turnes serued in lieu of blood, or other gift offered vnto him, especially of his or her soule. And both these differ from inchawntments or sorceries, because they are personall conferences with the deuill, as is said: but these are but medicines and cerimoniall formes of words (called commonly charmes) without apparition.

Consanguineo, is a writ, for the which *See Avo*: and See the *Register orig. De auo, proavo, & consanguineo. fo. 226. a.*

Conseruatour of the truce and safe conduicts (*conservator induciarum & saluorum regis conductuum*) was an officer appointed in euery port of the Sea, vnder the Kings leters patents, and had 40. pound for his yearely stipend, at the least. His charge was to enquire of all offences done against the Kings truce & safe conduicts, vpon the maine sea out of the countries, and out of the franchises of the Cinque ports of the king, as the admirals of custome were wont and such other things as are declared. *anno 2. H. 5. ca. 6.* Touching this mater you may read another statut. *anno 4. H. 5 cap. 7.*

Conseruatour of the peace (*conseruator vel custos pacis*) is he that hath an especiall charge by vertue of his office, to see the kings peace kept. which peace learned *M. Lamberd* defineth, in effect, to be a withholding or abstinence from that iniurious force and violence, which boysterous and vnruly persons are in their natures prone to vse toward others, were they not restrained by lawes and feare of punishment. Of these conservators he farder saith thus: that before the time of K. Edward the third, who first erected Iustices of peace, there were sundrie persons, that by the common lawe had interest in keeping of the peace. Of those some had that charge as incident to their offices, which they did beare, and so included within the same, that they were neuer the lesse called by the name of their office only: some others had it simply as of it selfe, and were thereof named *custodes pacis*, wardens or conservators of the peace. The former and later sort he againe subdivideth. Which read in his *eirenarcha. li. 1. ca. 3.*

Consideration, (*consideratio*) is that with vs, which the *Grecians* called συναλλαγμα: that is, the materiall cause of a contract, without the which no contract bindeth. This consideration is either expressed, as if a man bargain to giue 20. shillings for a horse: or els implyed, as when the law it selfe inforceth a consideration; as if a man come into a common Inne, and there staying sometime, taketh both meat and lodging, or either for himselfe and his horse: the lawe presumeth, that he intendeth to pay for both, though nothing be farder couenanted betweene him and his host: and therefore if he discharge not the house, the host may stay his horse. *Fulb: parel: tracta. Contracts fo. 6. a. b.*

Consistory (*consistorium*) is a word borowed of the *Italians*, or rather *Lombards*, signifiing as much as (*pratorium*) or *tribunal. vocab. vtriusq; iur.* It is vsed for the place of iustice in the courte christian.

Convocation house (*domus convocationis*) is the house, wherein the whole clergie is assembled, for consultation vpon maters ecclesiasticall in time of parlament. And as the house of Parlament, so this consisteth of two distinct houses, one called the higher conuocation house, where the Archebishops and Bishops sitte seuerally by themselues: the other the lower conuocation house, where all the rest of the clergy are bestowed. See *Prolocutor*.

Conusance. See *Cognisance*.

Conuzour, See *Cognizour*.

Consolidation (*consolidatio*) is vsed for the combining, and vniting of two benefices in one. *Brooke titulo. Vnion.* This word is taken from the civile lawe, where it signifieth properly an vniting of the possession, occupation, or profit with the propertie. For example, if a man haue by legacie *vsumfructum fundi*, and after ward buy the propertie or fee simple (as we call it) of the heire, *hoc casu consolidatio fieri dicitur* §. 3. *De vsufructu in Institut.* See *Vnion*, and *Vnitie of possession*.

Conspiracie (*conspiratio*) though both in Latine and French, it be vsed for an agreement of men, to doe any thing either good or bad: yet in our lawyers bookes, it is alway taken in the evill part. It is defined. *anno. 34. Ed. pri. statut.* 2. to be an agreement of such, as doe confedre or binde themselues by oath, covenant, or other allyance, that everie of them shall beare and ayde the other falsly and malitiously to indight, or falsly to moeue or maintaine plees, and also such as cause childrẽ within age, to appeale mẽ of of felonie, whereby they are imprisoned, and sore grieued: and such as reteine men in the contries with liueries or feese, to maintaine their malitious enterprises. And this extendeth as well to the takers, as to the giuers. And Stewards and baylifes of great lords, which by their seignorie, office, or power, vndertake to beare or maintaine quarels, plees, or debates that concerne other parties, then such as touch the estate of their lords, or themselues. *anno* 4. *Ed.* 3 *cap.* 11. *anno.* 3. *H.* 7. *ca.* 13. & of this see more. *an.* 1. *H.* 5. *c.* 3. & & *an.* 18. *H.* 6. *c.* 12. as also in the new book of ẽtries. *ver. Cõspiracy.*

Conspiracie, in the places before mentioned, is taken more generally, and is confounded with maintenance and champertie. But in a more speciall signification, it is taken for a confederacie of two at the least, falsly to endict one, or to procure one to be indicted of felonie. And the punishment of conspiracie, vpon an endictment of felonie, at the kings suyte, is that the partie attainted, leese his franke lawe, to the intent that he be not empaneled vpon iuries or assises, or such like employments, for the testifiing of truth. And if he haue to doe in the kings court, that he make his atturney: and that his lands, goods and chatels be seysed into the kings hands, his lands estreaped (if he finde no better fauour) his trees raced, and his body committed to prison. 27. *lib. assis.* 59. *Cromptons Iustice of peace. fo.* 156. *b.* This is called vilanous iudgement or punishment. See *Vilanous iudgement*. But if the partie greiued siew vpon the writ of conspiracie, then see. *Fitzh. nat. br. f.* 114. *D.* 115. I. Conspiracie may be also in cases of lesse weight. *Idem. fo.* 116. *A.* &c. See *Franke law.*

Conspiratione, is a writ that lieth against conspiratours. *Fitz. nat. br. fo.* 114. *d. Cromptons iurisd. fo.* 209. See also the *Regist. fo.* 134.

Constable (*constabularius vel conestabulis*) is a Saxon word, compounded of (*cuning or cyng*) and (*staple*) which doe signifie the stay and hold of the king. *Lamb. duties of constables. nu.* 4 But I haue heard it made heretofore of these two words, (*comes stabuli*) which seemeth to me the more probable, because we haue this officer from France, as most others, and not from the Saxons. And *Tilius* in his commentaries (*de rebus gallicis*) *li.* 2. *ca. de conistabili*, hath the same etymologie, giuing the reason thereof, (*quia praeest stabulo.* i. *equili regis*) which office is auncient heere in England, and mentioned by *Bracton*, seeming to answere him,that was called (*tribunus celerum*) vnder the first kings of Rome, and (*Magister equitum*) afterward. The *Germans* that inhabite the side of the riuer *Rhene*,note him by this title (*die constofler*) and in counterfeit latine (*constofelerus*) and in owlder time (*constafolarius*) that the Romanes were wont to tearme (*assessorem iudicij*) And (as *Spiegelius* in his lexicon noteth, deriue the word (*a stafolo comitis*. i.*gradu Iudicis fiscalis*. For *staffel* in their language (as he saith) signifieth a grees or steppe of a paire of staires. And therevpon (*staffelstein*) being a word vsed in their very awncient writings, signifieth as much as *prætorium*. But a man many times may shew in this kinde more curiositie then discretion: as perhaps some will iudge me heere to haue done. And therefore enough of this. This word is diuersly vsed in our common law:first for the cunstable of England, who is also called marshiall.*Stawn.pl.cor.fo.65*.of whose great dignitie and authoritie a man may find many arguments and signes both in the statutes and chronicles of this realme. His sway consisteth in the care of the common peace of the land, in deedes of armes, and maters of warres.*Lamb. vbi supra* with whome agreeth the *statut. anno.13.R. 2.ca. 2.statu.1. Smith de Repub. Anglo.li.2.c.25*. Of this officer or magistrate *M.Gwyn* in the preface to his readings saith to this effect: The court of the constable and marshiall determineth cōtracts touching deeds of armes out of the realme, and handleth things cōcerning wars within the realme, as combats, blasōs of armorie,&c.But it may not deale with battel in appeales, nor generally with any other thing that may be tried by the lawe of the land. And reade *Fortescue ca.32*.This office was belonging heeretofore to the lords of certaine maners,*iure feudi*:and why it is discontinued, see *Dyer.fo.258.nu. 39*. Out of this high magistracie (saith *M. Lamberd*) were drawen these lower constables, which we call constables of hundreds & franchises, and first ordeined by the statute of *Winchester, anno. 13. Ed. 1*. which appointeth for the conseruation of the peace, and view of armour, two constables in euerie hundred and franchise, which in latine are called *constabularii capitales*. And these be nowe a daies called high constables: because continuance of time,and increase both of people and offenses, hath againe vnder these made others in euery towne called petit constables, in latine (*subconstabularios*) which are of like nature but of inferiour authoritie to the other, as you may read at large in that learned mans treatise before named. Of these also read S. *Thomas Smith li. 2. ca. 22.* Beside these there be officers of particular places, called by this name; as constable of the tower. *Staunf. pl. cor. fol. 152. & anno. 1. H. 4. ca. 13. Stowes annals pa. 812. iurisdict. fo. 132.* constable of the exchequer. *anno. 51. H. 3. statute. 5.* Constable of *Douer castel. Camdeni Britan. pa. 239. Fitzh. nat. br. fo. 240.* otherwise called *castellane. Westm. 1. ca. 7. anno. 3. Ed. 1.* But these be *castellani* properly. as *M. Lamberd.* noteth, though conioined in name with the others. See the *statute. anno. 32. H. 8. ca. 38. M. Manwood parte. prima. ca. 13.* of his forest lawes, maketh mention of a constable of the forest.

Consuetudinibus & seruitiis, is a writ of right close, which lyeth against the tenent, that deforceth his lord of the rent or seruice dew vnto him. Of this see more at large the *Old nat. br. fo. 77. Fitzh. eodem. fo. 151.* and the *Register orig: fo. 159.*

Consultation, (consultatio) is a writ whereby a cause, being formerly remoued by prohibition from the ecclesiasticall court, or court christian, to the kings court, is returned thither againe. For the Iudges of the kings court, if vpon comparing the libell with the suggestion of the party, they do find the suggestion false, or not proued, and therefore the cause to be wrongfully called from the court christian; then vpon this consultation or deliberation, they decree it to be returned againe, wherevpon the writ in this case obtained, is called a consultation. Of this you may reade the *Register orig. fo. 44. 45. &c. vsq. fol. 58. Old nat. br. fo. 32. & Fitzh. eodem. fo. 50.*

Contenement, (contenementum) seemeth to be the free hould land, which lyeth to a mans tenement or dwelling house, that is in his owne occupation. For in *magna charta. ca. 14.* you haue these words: A free man shall not be amerced for a small fault, but after the quantity of the fault: and for a great fault, after the maner thereof, sauing to him his contenement or free hould. And a merchant likewise shalbe amerced sauing to him his merchandies: and any other villaine then owers, shalbe amerced sauing his wainage, if he take him to our mercy. And *Bracton. li. 3. tracta. 2. ca. 1 nu. 3.* hath these words: *& sciendum, quod miles & liber homo non amerciabitur, nisi secundum modum delicti. secundum quod delictum* *fuit magnum vel parvum, & saluo contenemento suo: mercator vero non nisi salua merchandiza sua, & villanus nisi saluo Waniagio suo.* which mercy seemeth to haue bene learned from the ciuile lawe: whereby (*executio non potest fieri in boues, aratra, aliaue instrumenta rusticorum.l. executores & Authen. Agricultores. Co: quæ res pign. obliga.nec in stipendia, arma, & equos militum. l. stipendia. Co. de executio. rei iudica. & ibi doctores. nec in libros scholarium. glos. in. l. Nepos Proculo. verbo. dignitate. ff. de verbo: significa. Quæ tamen rusticorum, militum, & scholarium priuilegia circa executionem vera esse, & eatenus obtinere intelligenda sunt, quatenus alia bona habent. Iohan. Eimericus in processu iudiciario: cap. de Executione senten. 79. num.* 11.

Continuance, seemeth to bee vsed in the common law, as *prorogatio* is in the ciuile lawe. For example: Continuance vntil the next assise. *Fitz. nat. br. fol.* 154. *F.* and 244. *D.* in both which places it is sayde, that if a record in the treasurie be alledged by the one partie, and denyed by the other: a (*certiorari*) shall be sewed to the Treasurer, and the chamberlaine of the Exchequer: who, if they certifie not in the Chauncerie, that such a record is there, or that it is likely to be in the Tower: the king shall send to the Iustices repeating the (*certificate*) and will them to continue the assise. In this signification it is likewise vsed by *Kitchin. fol.* 202. & 199. and also *anno* 11. *H.* 6. *cap.* 4.

Continuall claime (*continuum clameum*) is a claime made from time to time. Within euery yere and day, to land or other thing, which in some respect we cannot attaine without daunger. For example, if I be disseised of land, into which, though I haue right vnto it, I dare not enter for feare of beating: it behooueth me to hold on my right of entry to the best oportunitie of me & mine heyre, by approching as neare it as I can, once euery yere, as long as I liue: and so I saue the right of entry to mine heire. *Termes of law*. Againe, if I haue a slave or villein broken from me, and remaining any where within the auncient demesn of the king, being in the handes of the king, I cannot maintaine the writ *de natiuo habendo*, as long as he continueth there: but if I claime him within the yeare and the day, and so continue my claime, vntill I can find him within that compasse: I may lawfully lay hold of him as mine owne. *Fitz. nat. br. fol.* 79. See more in *Litleton, verbo Continuall claime.* And the new booke of Entries. *Ibid.* and *Fleta. lib.* 6. *cap.* 53.

Con-

Contract (*contractus*) is a couenant or agreement with a lawfull consideration or cause. *West. parte prim. symbol. lib.* 1. *Sect.* 10. and *lib.* 19. *x. de verbo: Significa.* with other places, it is thus defined: *Contractus est negotium inter duos pluresve data opera gestum, vt vel vterque inuicem, vel alteruter obligetur.* Who so will throughly examine the difference betweene this and (*pactū*) and such other words something like in signification: let him search the civilians, and he shall find worke both pleasant and profitable, and well fitting the common lawe also.

Contra formam collationis, is a writ that lyeth against an abbot or his successor, for him (or his heire) that hath giuen land to an Abbey, to certaine good vses, and findeth that the Abbot or his successour hath made a feofment thereof, with the assent of the tenents, to the disherison of the house or church. This is founded vpon the statute of *Westm.* 2. *cap.* 41. And of this see the *Regist. orig. fol.* 238. and *Fitzh. nat. br. fol.* 210. And note that the author of the Termes of law saith, that this is not brought against the tenent or alienee.

Contra formam feoffamenti, is a writ, that lyeth for the heire of a tenent infeoffed of certain lands or tenements, by charter of feofment by a Lord, to make certain seruices and suites to his court, and is afterward distreined for more, then is contained in the said charter. *Regist. orig. fol.* 176. *old nat. br. fol.* 162. and the Tearmes of the lawe.

Contributione facienda, is a writ that lieth in case where more are bound to one thing, & one is put to the whole burden. *Fitz. nat. br. fo.* 162. bringeth these examples. If tenēts in cōmon or ioynt, hold a mill (*pro indiuiso*) & equally take the profits therof, the mill falling to decay, & one or more of thē, refusing to contribute toward the reparation therof, the rest shall haue this writ to cōpell thē. And if there be 3. coparceners of land, that owe suite to the lords court, & the eldest perform the whole: then may she haue this writ to compell the other two to a cōtributiō of the charge or to one of them, if one only refuse. The *old nat br.* frameth this writ to a case, where one onely suite is required for land, & that land being sold to diuers, suite is required of them all, or some of them by distresse, as intirely, as if all were still in one. *fol.* 103. See the *Regist. orig. fol* 176.

Controller (*contrarotulator*) cōmeth of the French (*contrerouleur.* i. *antigraphus, graecè* ἀντιγραφεύς.) which in *Rome* was vsed for him, *cui id muneris iniunctum erat,* vt *vt observaret pecuniam, quam in vsum Principis vel civitatis collegerunt exactores. Budæus in annota. prio. in pand. titulo* De officio *quæstoris.* In *England* we haue diuers officers of this name: as controller of the kings house, *pl. cor. fol.* 52. *& anno* 6. *H.* 4. *cap.* 3. controller of the nauie. *anno* 35. *Elizabeth. cap.* 4. controller of the custome. *Cromptons Iurisd. fol.* 105. controller of *Calis. anno* 21 *Rich.* 2. *cap.* 18. controller of the Mint. *anno* 2. *H.* 6. *cap.* 12. controller of the hamper, (*Contrarotulator Hamperii*) which is an officer in the Chauncerie attending on the Lord Chauncelor or Keeper daily in the terme time, and dayes appointed for sealing. His office is to take all things sealed from the clerke of the hanaper, inclosed in bags of lether, as is mentioned in the said clerkes office, and opening the bags to note the iust number, & especiall effects of all thinges so receiued, and to enter the same into a speciall booke, with all the duties appertaining to his Maiestie, and other officers for the same, and so chargeth the clerke of the hanaper with the same. Controller of the Pipe, (*contrarotulator Pipæ*) who is an officer of the Exchequer that writeth out summons twice euery yeare to the Shyreeues, to levie the Fermes and debts of the Pipe, and also keepeth a contrarolment of the Pipe. *Controller of the pell*, is also an officer of the Exchequer, of which sort there be two, *viz.* the two chamberlaines clerkes, that do or should keepe a contro'ment of the pell of receipts and goings out. And in one word, this officer was originally one, that tooke notes of any other officers accompts or receipts, to the intent to discouer him, if he dealt amisse, and was ordained for the Princes beter securitie, howsoeuer the name sithence may be in some things otherwise applyed. To the proofe whereof you may take these few words out of *Fleta. lib.* 1. *cap.* 18. *in prin. Qui cùm fuerint ad hoc vocati & electi,* (speaking of the coroners) *attachiari præcipiant appella: qui & capitula coronæ in comitatu præsentēt contra quos vicecomes loci habeat contrarotulum, tam de appellis & inquisitionibus, quàm aliis officium illud tangentibus, &c.* Which (*contrarollum*) is nothing else, but a paralel of the same quality and contents with the πρωτότυπον, or originall. This also appeareth by *anno* 12. *Ed.* 3. *ca.* 3. And this signification it seemeth to haue also in *Fraunce*. For there the king hath his receyuers of taylles in euery prouince, and controllers, *qui ad maiorem fidem susceptoribus accedunt, describuntq́;*

in tabulis quæ colliguntur. Gregorii syntagn. lib. 3. cap. 6. num. 6.

Conuentione, is a writ, that lyeth for the breach of any couenant in writing. *Register orig. fo.* 185. *Old nat. br. fo.* 101. *Fitzh.* calleth a writ of couenant. *nat. br. fo.* 145. who deuideth couenants into personall and reall, making a sufficient discourse of them both: as also how this writ lyeth for both.

Conuict, (conuictus) is he that is founde guilty of an offence by the verdict of the iurie. *Stawnf. pl. cor. fo.* 186. yet *Master Crompton* out of Iudge *Dyers* commentaries 275. saith, that conuiction is, either when a man is outlawed, or appeareth and confesseth, or els is founde guilty by the inquest. *Crompt. Iust.* of peace. *fo.* 9. *a.* Conuiction and attainder are often confounded. *li.* 4. *fo.* 46. *a. b.* See *Attaint.*

Coparceners, (participes) be otherwise called parceners: and in common law, are such as haue equall portion in the inheritance of their auncestour. and, as *Litleton* in the beginning of his third booke saith, parceners be either by law or by custome. Parceners by law, are the issue femall, which (noe heyre male being) come in equality to the lands of their auncestours. *Bract. li.* 2. *ca.* 30. Parceners by custome, are those that by custome of the country, chalenge equall part in such lands: as in *Kent* by the custome called *(Gauel Kinde)* This is called *adæquatio* among the *Feudists. Hot. in verbis feuda. verbo. Adæquatio.* And among the ciuilians it is tearmed *familiæ erciscundæ iudicium. quod inter cohæredes ideo redditur, vt & hæreditas diuidatur, & quod alterum alteri dare facere oportebit, præstetur. Hotoman.* Of these two you may see *Litleton* at large in the first and second chapters of his third booke, and *Britton cap.* 27. *intituled De heritage diuisable.* The crowne of England is not subiect to coparcinory. *anno.* 25. *H.* 8. *ca.* 22.

Copie, (copia) commeth from the french *copia.* i. *le double de quelque escripture, latinè descriptio, græcè* ἀπογραφον, and signifieth in our common language, the example of an originall writing: as the copie of a charter, the copie of a court rolle.

Copia libelli deliberanda, is a writ that lyeth in case where a man cannot get the copie of a libell at the hands of the Iudge ecclesiasticall. *Register orig. f.* 51.

Copiehould, (tenura per copiam rotuli curiæ) is a tenure, for the which the tenent hath nothing to shew, but the copie of the rols made by the steward of his lords court. For the steward, as he inrolleth, and maketh remembrances

membrances of all other things done in the lords court: so he doth also of such tenents, as be admitted in the court, to any parcell of land or tenement belonging to the maner: and the transcript of this, is called the court rowle: the copie whereof the tenent taketh from him, and keepeth as his onely euidence. *Coke. li. 4. fo. 25. b.* This tenure is called a base tenure, because it houldeth at the wil of the lord. *Kitchin. fo.* 80. *chap:* copihoulds. *Fitzh. nat. br. fo.* 12. *B. C.* who there saieth, that it was wont to be called tenure in villenage, and that this copihould is but a new name. Yet is it not simply at the will of the lord, but according to the custome of the maner. So that if a copie houlder breake not the custome of the maner, and thereby forfeit his tenure, he seemeth not so much to stand at the lords courtesie for his right, that he may be displaced hand ouer head at his pleasure. These customes of maner be infinit, varying in one point or other, almost in euery seuerall maner. First, some copiehould is fineable, and some certaine: that which is fineable, the lord rateth at what fine or incom he pleaseth, when the tenent is admmitted vnto it: that which is certaine, is a kinde of inheritance, and called in many places custumary: because the tenent dying, and the hould being void the next of the blood paying the custumarie fine, as two shillngs for an acre or such like, may not be denied his admission. Secondly, some copihoulders haue by custome, the wood growing vpon their owne land, which by law they could not haue. *Kitchin vbi supra.* Thirdly, copiholders, some be such as hold by the verge in ancient demesn: & although they hold by copy, yet are they in accompt a kind of Free-holders. For if such a one commit felonie, the king hath (*annum, diem, & vastum*) as in case of Freehold. Some other hold by common tenure, called meere copy hold: and they committing felonie, their land escheateth to the *Lord* of the maner foorthwith. *Kitchin fol.* 81. *chap. Tenents per verge in auncient demesn.* What auncient demesn is, see in the right place. See *Tenent by copie of court rolle.*. This is the land that in the *Saxons* time, was called Folk land. *Lamberd, explicat.* of Saxon words. *verbo, Terra ex scripto. West. parte prim. symbol. lib.* 2. *Sect.* 646. defineth a copiholder thus: Tenent by copie of court rolle, is he which is admitted tenent of any lands or tenements within a maner, that time out of the memory of man, by vse and custome of the said maner, haue bene dimisable, and dimised to such, as will take the same in fee, in fee-taile, for life, yeares, or at will, according to the custome of the said maner, by copie of courtrolle of the same maner. where you may read more of these things.

Coraage (coraagium) is a kinde of imposition extraordinarie, & growing vpon some vnusuall occasion, and it seemeth to be of certaine measures of corne. For *corus tritici*, is a certaine measure of corne. *Bracton libro 2. ca. 16. nu. 6.* who in the same chapter. *nu. 8.* hath of this mater these words: *Sunt etiam quædam communes præstationes, quæ seruitia non dicuntur, nec de consuetudine veniunt, nisi cùm necessitas interuenerit, vel cùm rex venerit: sicut sunt hidagia, coraagia, & caruagia, & alia plura de necessitate & ex consensu communi totius regni introducta, & quæ ad dominum feudi non pertinent, & de quibus nullus tenetur tenentē suū acquietare, nisi se ad hoc specialiter obligauerit in charta sua. &c.*

Cordiner, commeth of the French (*cordoüannier. i. sutor calcearius*) a shoomaker, and is so vsed in diuers statutes. as *anno. 3. H. 8. ca. 10, & anno. 5. eiusdem. ca 7.* and others.

Cornage (cornagium) commeth of the French (*cor .i. cornu*) and in our common law, signifieth a kinde of grand sergeantie, the seruice of which tenure, is to blow a horne, when any inuasion of the northern enemie is perceiued. And by this many men hold their land northward, about the wall, commonly called the Picts walle. *Camd. Britan. p. 609.* hence commeth the word (*cornuare*) to blow a horn. *pupil. oculi, parte. 5. ca. 22. in charta de Foresta.* This seruice seemeth to haue proceeded from the Romanes. For I finde (*cornicularios*) mentioned in the ciuile lawe. *viz. li. 1. Cod. de officio diuerso. Iud. 48. lege. 3. & lib. 12. titulo de apparitoribus præfectorum pretorio. 53. lege. 1. & 3.* where *Lucas de Penna* defineth them (*eos qui cornu faciunt excubias militares.* And *Brissonius. libro. 3. de verbo significat.* saith thus of them: (*hi militum quoddam genus fuere, qui corniculo merebant, vnde nomen habent.* Where it appeareth by him out of *Suetonius, Plinie*, and *Liuie*, that the horne was an honour & reward giuen for seruice in war.

Corner tile. See *Gutter tile.*

Corodye (corodium) commeth of the Latine verb (*corrodo*) and signifieth in our common lawe, a summe of mony or allowance of meate and drinke due to the king from an abbey, or other house of religion, whereof he is the founder, toward the reasonable sustenãce of such a one of his seruants, being put to his pension, as he thinketh good to bestowe it on. And the difference betweene a corodie and a pension seemeth to be, that a corodie is allowed toward the maintenance of any the kings seruants, that liueth in the abbey: a pension is giuen to one of the kings chaplaines, for his better maintenance in the kings seruice, vntill he may be prouided of a benefice. Of both these read *Fitzh. nat. br. fo.* 230. 231. 233. who there setteth downe all the corodies and pensions certaine, that any abbey, when they stoode, was bound to performe vnto the king. There is mention also of a corodie in *Stawnf. prarogatiue. fo.* 44. And this seemeth to be awncient lawe. For in *Westm.* 2. *ca.* 25. it is ordeined, that an assise shall lie for a corodie. It is also apparent by the statute. *anno.* 34. & 35. *H.* 8. *ca.* 16. that corodies belonged some time to Bishops from monasteries: & by the new termes of lawe, that a corodie may be due to a common person by graunt from one to another, or of common right, to him that is founder of a religious house, not holden in frank almoyn. For that tenure was a discharge of all corodies in it selfe. By which booke it appeareth also, that a corodie is either certaine or vncertaine, and that it may be for life, yeares, in taile, or in fee.

Corodio habendo, is a writ whereby to exact a corodie of any abbey or religious house. See *Corodie*. See the *Register originall. fo.* 264.

Coronatore eligendo, is a writte which after the death or discharge of any coroner, is directed to the shyreeue out of the Chãcery, to call togither the free holders of the countie, for the choice of a new coroner, to certifie into the chanceries both the election, and the name of the partie elected, and to giue him his oath. See *Westm.* 1. *ca.* 10. and *Fitzh. nat. br. fo.* 163. and the *Register orig. fo.* 177.

Coroner (coronator) is an auncient officer of this land, so called, because he dealeth wholly for the king and crowne. There be fower of them commonly in euery countie, and they are chosen by the freeholders of the same vpon writ, and not made by leters patents. *Crompt. Iurisd. fo.* 126. This officer, though now he be some inferiour gentleman, that hath some smattering in the lawe: yet if we looke to the statute of *Westm.* 1. *ca.* 10. we shall finde, that he was wont, and ought to be, a sufficient man: that is, the most wise and discreete knight, that best will and may

may attend vpon such an office. Yea there is a writ in the *Register, Nisi sit miles.fo.177.b.* whereby it appeareth, that it was sufficient cause to remooue a coroner chosen, if he were not a knight, and had not a hundred shillings rent of freehold. And the Lord cheife Iustice of the kings bench, is the soueraigne coroner of the whole realme in person. i. wheresoeuer he remaineth *Libro assisarum fo.49.5.coron. Coke.li.4.casu.de Wardens,&c.* of the Sadlers.*fo.57.b.* His office especially concerneth the plees of the crowne: but if you will reade at large, what auncientlly belonged vnto him: reade *Bracton.li.3.tra.2.c.5.de officio coronatorum circa homicidium.* and *ca. 6. de officio coronatoris in thesauris inventis.*& *ca.6.de officio coronatorum in raptu virginium.* and *ca. 8. de officio coronatorum de pace & plagis.* and *Britton* in his first chapter, where he handleth it at large. *Fleta* also in his first booke *cap.* 18. and *Andrew Horns mirrour of Iustices. li. 1.ca. del office del coroners.* but more aptly for the present times, *Stawnf.pl.cor li. 1. ca.* 51. Note there be certaine coroners speciall within diuers liberties, as well as these ordinarie officers in euerie countie: as the coroner of the verge, which is a certaine compas about the kings court. whome *Crompt.* in his *iurisd.fo.* 102. calleth the coroner of the kings house: of whose authoritie see *S. Ed. Cokes reportes. lib. 4.fo.46. a.b.* And I know certen charters belonging to colledges and other corporations, whereby they are licēsed to appoint their coroner within their owne precincts. Farder of this office see also *Fitzh. nat.br.fo.76. A. B. S. Thomas Smith.li.2.ca.ca.21.de repub. Anglo.* and *Lamb. eirenarcha. li.4.ca.* 3.*pa.*380. And the office of the coroner in *Scotland.* what it is, read *M.Iohn. Skene de verbo. signifi.verbo.Iter.*

Corporation (*corporatio*) is that which the civile law calleth *universitatem, or collegium*. a bodie politique authorised by the kings charter, to haue a common seale, a head officer, one or more, and members able by their common consent, to graunt or to receiue in law any thing within the compas of their charter: euen as one man may doe by law all things, that by lawe he is not forbidden: and bindeth the successours, as a single man bindeth his executour or heyre. See *Brokes* his abridgment. *titulo Corporation*, and the newe Tearmes of lawe. *eodem.*

Corpus cum causa, is a writ issuying out of the Chauncerie, to remoue both the bodie and the record touching the cause of any man lying in execution, vpō a iudgement for debt into the Kings bench, &c. there to lye vntill he haue satisfied the iudgement. *Fitzh. nat. br. fol.* 251. *E.*

Corrector of the staple, is an officer or clerke belonging to the staple, that writeth and recordeth the bergains of Merchants there made, *anno* 27. *Ed.* 3. *stat.* 2. *cap.* 22. & 23. The Romanes called them *Mensarios*.

Corruption of blood, is an infection growing to the estate of a man attainted of felonie or treason, and to his issue. For as he leeseth all to the Prince, or other lord of the fee, accordingly as his case is, so his issue cannot be heires to him, or to any other auncester, of whom they might haue claimed by him. And farder if he were noble, or a gentleman before, he and his children are made vnnoble and vngentle in respect of the father. Newe Tearmes of the lawe.

Corse present, are words borrowed from the French, signifying a mortuarie. *anno* 21. *H.* 8. *ca.* 6. The true French is (*corps præsentè*) i. the bodie presented or tendered. The reason why the mortuarie is thus also tearmed, seemeth to be, for that where a mortuarie was wont to be due, the bodie of the best beast was according to the law or custome offered or presented to the priest.

Corselet, is a French word signifying a litle bodie, in Latine (*corpusculum.*) It is vsed with vs, for an armor to couer the whole bodie, or trunke of a man. *anno* 4. & 5. *Ph.* & *Mar. cap.* 2. wherewith the pikemen, commonly set in the front and flanks of the battaile, are armed, for the beter resistance of the enemies assaults, and the surer guard of the gunners placed behind or within them, being more sleightly armed, for their speedier issuing in and out to discharge their peeces. See *Barrets* discourse of Warre. *lib.* 3. *dialog.* 2.

Cosenage, (*cognatione*) is a writ, that lyeth where the tresaile (that is, tritavus, the father of the besaile, or of the great grandfather) is seysed in his demesn as of fee, at the day of his death, of certaine lands or tenements, and dyeth: and then a straunger entreth and abateth. For then shall his heyre haue this writ of *cosenage*: the forme whereof see in *Fitz. nat. br. fol.* 221. Of this also reade *Britton* at large. *cap.* 89.

Cosening, is an offence vnnamed, whereby any thing is done guilefully in or out of contracts, which cannot be fitly termed by any speciall name. *West. parte.* 2. *simbolæogr. titulo. Indictments. sect.* 68. It is called *stellionatus* in the ciuile lawe of (*stellio*) the beast

beast, which is *lacertæ genus versutissimum*, as *Cuiacius* in his *paratitles* calleth it, and, *quo nullum animal homini invidet fraudulentius. Plinie li.3.ca.10.*

Cotage (*cotagium*) is a house without land belonging vnto it. *anno.4.Ed.pri.statut.primo.* And the inhabitant of such a house is called a cotager. But by a later statute, no man may builde a cotage, but he must lay 4. acres of ground vnto it. 31.*Eli ca.7.*

Cote, is a kind of refuse wolle clung or clotted together, that it cannot be pulled asunder. *anno.* 13.R.2.*stat.1. ca. 9.* It signifieth also as much as cotage in many places, as also it did among the Saxons. *Verstegan* in his *Restitut. of decayed intelligẽce in antiquities.*

Covenable (*rationabilis*) is a French word, signifying fitte or convenient, or suteable. covenably endowed *an.o.4.H.8.ca.* 12. It is auncienctly written (convenable) as in the *stat.an. 27.Ed. 3. stat.2. ca.17.*

Couenãt. conuẽtio, is the consẽt of two or more in one self thing, to doe or giue somwhat. *West.part. 2. symbol. li.1.sect.4.* It seemeth to be as much as (*pactum. conventum*) with the ciuilians. which you read often times in *Tullie. Pactum conuentum, quod & vulgo vestitum vocant, opponitur nudo pacto, velut ab omni iuris solennitate destituto. Huius exempla ponere difficile esse Iason existimavit. Conventum aiunt, quod vestitur, aut re, aut verbis, aut literis, aut contractus cohærentiâ, aut rei interuentu. Oldendorpius.* And couenant in this signification, is either a covenant in lawe, or a couenant in fact. *Coke.lib.4.Nokes case. fo.* 80. or couenant expresse & couenant in lawe. *idem. li. 6.fo. 17.a.* Couenant in law is that, which the law intendeth to be made, though in words it be not expressed: as if the lessour doe dimise and graunt. &c. to the lessee for a certaine tearme, the lawe intendeth a couenant of the lessours part, that the lessee shall, during his whole terme, quietly inioy his lease against all lawfull encumbrance. Covenant in fact is that, which is expressely agreed betweene the parties. There is also a couenant meerely personall, and a couenant reall. *Fitzh.nat.br.fo.* 145. And he seemeth to say, that a couenant reall is, whereby a man tieth himselfe to passe a thing reall, as land or tenements, as a couenant to levie a fyne of land, &c. a couenant meerely personall of the other side, is where a man couenanteth with another by deede, to build him a house, or any other thing, or to serue him, or to infeoffe him &c. Couenant is also the name of a writ, for the which see *Conuentione*. Instruments

ments of couenants you may see good store in *West parte*.i. *Symbolaog.li. 2.sectio.* 100. See also the new booke of entries. *verbo. Couenant.*

Couent, (conuentus) signifieth the society or fraternity of an abbie or priorie, as *(societas)* signifieth the number of fellowes in a colledge. *Bracton. li. 2.ca.* 35. It commeth of the french *(conuent.* i. *cœnobium).*

Couerture, is a french word signifying any thing that couereth, as apparell, a couerlet, &c. and deduced from the verb *(couvrir.*i. *tegere)* It is particularly applied in our common lawe, to the estate and condition of a maried woman, who by the lawes of our realme, is in *(potestate viri)* and therefore disabled to contract with any, to the preiudice of her selfe or her husband, without his consent and priuity; or at the least, without his allowance and confirmation. *Broke. hoc tit. per totum.* And *Bracton* saith, that *omnia quæ sunt vxoris, sunt ipsius viri, nec habet vxor potestatem sui, sed vir. li.* 2. *ca.* 15. and that *(vir est caput mulieris) li.* 4. *ca.* 24. and againe, that in any law mater, *sine viro respondere non potest. li.* 5. *tract.* 2. *ca.* 3. and *tract.* 5. *ca.* 25. *eiusdem libri.* he hath words to this effect: *vir & vxor sunt quasi vnica persona: quia caro vna & sanguis vnus. Res licet sit propria vxoris, vir tamen eius custos, cùm sit caput mulieris.* and *li.* 1. *ca.* 10. *nu.* 2. *Vxores sunt sub virga viri.* And if the husband alienate the wifes land, during the mariage, shee cannot gainesay it during his life. See *Cui ante diuortium.* and *Cui in vita.*

Covine, (covina) is a deceitfull assent or agreement betweene two or more, to the preiudice or hurt of another. New tearms of lawe. It commeth of the french verb *(conuenancer.*i. *depacisci.)* or rather *(conuenir.*i. *conuenire.)*

Corcher, signifieth a factour that continueth in some place or country for trafique. *anno.* 37. *Ed.* 3. *ca.* 16. It is vsed also for the generall booke, into which any corporation entreth their particular acts for a perpetuall remembrance of them.

Counte, cōmeth of the french *(coumpte.*i. *subductus, cōputatio, ratio)* or of *(cōte.*i. *narratio.)* It signifieth as much as the originall declaratiō in a proces, though more vsed in reall actions then personall, as declaration is rather applied to personall then reall. *Fitzh. nat. br. fo.* 16. *A.* 60. *D.* 71. *A.* 191. *E.* 217. *A. (Libellus)* with the ciuilians comprehendeth both. And yet count and declaration be confounded sometimes; as count in debt. *Kitchin: fo.* 281. count or declaration in appeale. *pl. cor. fo.* 78.

Count

Count in trespasse. *Britton. cap.* 26 count in an action of trespasse vpon the case for a slaunder. *Kit. fol.* 252. This word seemeth to come from *France* & *Normandy*. For in the grand Custumarie, *c.* 64. I find (*conteurs*) to be those, which a man setteth to speake for him in court, as aduocates: & *cap.* 63. (*pledeurs*) to be another sort of spokes men, in the nature of Atturneys, for one, that is him selfe present, but suffereth another to tell his tale. Where also in the 65. chapter, Atturney is said to be he, that dealeth for him that is absent. See this text and Glosse vpō those 3. chapters. *Countours* (by *Horn* in his Myrror of Iustices. *li.* 2. *ca.* *Des loyers*) are Sergeants skilfull in the lawe of the Realme, which serue the cōmon people, to pronounce and defend their actions in iudgement for their fee, when occasiō requireth: whose duty, if it be as it is there described, and were obserued, men might haue much more comfort of the lawe then they haue.

Countenance, seemeth to be vsed for credit or estimation, *old na. br. fol.* 111. in these words: Also the attaint shall be graunted to poore men that will sweare, that they haue nothing whereof they may make fine, sauing their countenance, or to other by a reasonable fine. So is it vsed, *anno* 1. *Ed.* 3. *stat.* 2. *cap.* 4. in these words: Shyreeues shall charge the kings depters with as much as they may leuie with their oathes, without abating the depters countenance.

Counter (*computatorium*) seemeth to come of the *Latin* (*computare*) or the French (*counter.*) For we vse it for the name of a prisō, wherinto he that once slippeth, is like to accompt ere he get out.

Counter plee, is compounded of two French words (*contre*. i. *contra, adversus*) and (*pleder*. i. *causam agere.*) It signifieth properly in our common lawe, a replication to (*ayde prier.*) For when the tenent by courtesie, or in dower, prayeth in ayde of the king, or him in the reuersion, for his beter defence: or else if a stranger to the action begun, desire to be receiued to say what he can for the safegard of his estate: that which the demandant alledgeth against this request, why it shuold not be admitted, is called a counter plee. See *Broke* h t. And in this signification it is vsed. *anno*. 25. *Ed* 3. *stat.* 3. *cap.* 7. See also the new termes of the law, and the statute *anno* 3. *Ed.* 1. *cap.* 39.

County, (*comitatus*) signifieth as much as (*shire*,) the one descending from the French, the other from the Saxons, both conteining a circuit or portion of the realme, into the which the whole land

land is diuided,for the beter gouernment thereof, and the more easie administration of iustice. So that there is no part of the kingdome,that lieth not within some countie,and euery county is gouerned by a yerely officer,whom we cal a Shyreeue,which among other duties belonging to his office,putteth in execution all the commandements & iudgments of the kings courts,that are to be executed within that compasse. *Fortescue cap.24.* Of these counties there be foure of especiall marke,which therefore are tearmed countie Palatines, as the county Palatine of *Lancaster, of Chester,of Durham,*& of *Ely,ann.* 5.*Eliz.* 1.*c.2*3.I read also of the county Palatine of *Hexam.an.*33 H.8.*ca.*10.*Vnde quare.* And this county Palatine is a Iurisdiction of so high a nature, that whereas all plees touching the life or mayhem of man, called plees of the crowne, be ordinarily held & sped in the kings name, & cannot passe in the name of any other;the chiefe gouerners of these, by especiall charter from the king,did heretofore send out all writs in their owne name,and did all things touching iustice, as absolutely as the Prince himself in other counties, only acknowledging him their superiour and Soueraigne. But by the statute. *anno* 27. *H.* 8.*c.*25. this power is much a bridged, vnto the which I refer the reader,as also to *Crom. Iuris.fo.*137.for the whole course of this court. Besides these counties of both sorts,there be likewise counties corporate, as appeareth by the statute.*anno* 3. *Ed.*4.5.and these be certaine cities,or auncient boroughs of the land, vpon which the *Princes* of our nation haue thought good to bestow such extraordinary liberties. Of these the famous city of *London* is one, and the principall, *Yorke* another, *an.* *32.H.*8.*cap.*13.the city of *Chester* a third,*an.42.Eliz.cap.* 15. *Canterburie* a fourth.*Lamb.Eiren. l.1. cap.* 9. And to these may be added many moe:but I haue onely obserued out of the statutes & other writers, the county of the towne of *Kingston vpon Hull,anno* 32. H. 8.*cap.* 13. the county of the towne of *Hauerford.West.anno* 35. H. 8. *cap.* 26. and the county of *Litchfield. Cromptons Iustice of peace.fo.*59.*a.* County is in another significatiō vsed for the County court, which the Shyreeue keepeth euery moneth within his charge either by himselfe or his deputie,*anno* 2.*Ed.6 ca.* 25. *Cromptons Iuris.fo.*221.*Bract.li.*3.*c.*7.& *li.* 3. *tract.*2.*cap.* 12. Of these counties or shires one with another, there are reckoned in *England* 37. beside twelue in *Wales.*

county court. The word (*comitatus*) is also vsed for a iurisdiction or territorie among the Feudists.

Countie court (*curia comitatus*) by *M. Lamberd* is otherwise called (*conuentus*) in his explication of Saxon words, and diuided into two sorts: one retaining the generall name, as the county court held euery moneth by the Shyreeue, or his deputie the vnder-shyreeue, whereof you may reade in *Cromptons iurisd. fol.* 231. the other called the Turne, held twice euery yeare, which see more at large in his place: and *Cromptons Iurisd. fol.* 231. This countie court had in auncient times the cognition of these and other great maters, as may appeare by *Glanvile. lib.* 1. *cap.* 2 3. 4. by *Bracton* and *Britton* in diuers places, and by *Fleta. li.* 2. *cap.* 62. But that was abridged by the statute of *Magna charta. cap.* 17. and much more by 1. *Ed.* 4. *cap. vnico.* It had also, and hath the determination of certaine trespasses, and debts vnder forty shillings. *Britton. cap* 27. & 28. what maner of proceeding was of old vsed in this court, see *Fleta vbi supra.*

Coursitour. See *Cursetour*.

Court (*curia*) commeth of the French (*court*) which signifieth the kings palace or mansion, as (*curtis*) doth among the *Lombards*. All these spring of the Latine (*curia*) which signifieth one of thirty parts, into which *Romulus* diuided the whole number of the Romaines: sometime also the Senate house, as appeareth by *Tully* in his Offices (*nihil est quod dignum nobis, aut in foro aut in curia agere possumus*: which in his oration (*pro Milone*) he calleth, *Templum sanctitatis, amplitudinis, mentis, consilii publici, caput vrbis, &c.* Court, with vs, signifieth diuersly: as the house where presently the king remaineth with his ordinarie retinue, and also the place where iustice is iudicially ministred: of which you finde 32. seueral sorts in *M. Cromptons* booke of *Iurisdictions* well described. And of them most be courts of record: some be not, and therefore are accompted base courts in comparison of the rest. Beside these also there are courts Christian. *Smith de repub. Anglor. lib.* 3. *cap.* 9. which are so called, because they handle maters especially appertaining to Christianitie, and such as without good knowledge in diuinity cannot be well iudged of, being held heretofore by Archb. and *Bishops*, as from the Pope of Rome: because he chalenged the superioritie in all causes spirituall: but sithence his eiection, they hold them by the kings authoritie (*virtute magistratus sui*) as the Admirall of *England* doth his court. Whereupon

upon it proceedeth, that they send out their precepts in their owne names, and not in the kings, as the Iustices of the kings courts doe. And therefore as the appeale from these courts did lie to *Rome:* now by the statute *an.* 25. *H.* 8. *cap.* 19. it lyeth to the king in his Chauncerie.

Court baron (*curia baronis*) is a court that euery lord of a maner (which in auncient times were called barons) hath within his owne precincts. Barons in other nations haue great territories and iurisdiction from their Soueraignes: as may be proued out of *Cassanæus de gloria mundi. parte* 5. *consideratio.* 56. by *Vincentius de Franchis decisi.* 211. and many others. But here in *England* what they be, and haue bene heretofore, see in *Baron.* Of this court Baron you may reade your fill in *Kitchin*, that writeth a large booke of it, and of a court leete. *S. Edward Coke* in his fourth booke of Reports, amongst his copyhold cases. *fol.* 26. *b.* saith, that this court is two after a sort: and therefore if a man hauing a maner in a towne, and do graunt the inheritance of the copyholders thereunto belonging, vnto another: this grantee may keep a court for the custumarie tenents, and accept surrenders to the vse of others, and make both admittances and graunts: the other court is of Freeholders, which is properly called the court baron, wherein the suyters, that is, the Freeholders be Iudges: whereas of the other the Lord or his steward is Iudge.

Court christian (*curia christiana*) See *Court.*

Court of Pypowders. See *Pypowders.*

Court of Requests (*curia requestarum*) is a court of equitie, of the same nature with the Chancerie, principally instituted for the helpe of such petitioners, as in conscionable cases deale by supplication with his Maiestie. This court, as *M. Gwin* saith, in the preface to his readings, had beginning from commission first graunted by *Henry* the 8. to the masters of Requests: whereas before that time (by his opinion) they had no warrant of ordinary iurisdiction, but trauelled betweene the king and the petitioner by direction from the kings mouth. But *Sir Iulius Cæsar* in a Tractate of his, painefully and very iudiciously gathered from the records of the same court, plainely sheweth that this court was 9. *Henrici septimi*, though then following the king, and not setled in any certaine place, neither swayed particularly by the Masters of requests, (as now it is) but more at large by others of of the kings most Honourable Councell, whom he pleased to employ in this seruice: For *pag*. 148. of the said Tractate, you haue the forme of the oath then ministred to those that were Iudges in this court: and *à pag. prim. vsque ad pag*. 46. causes of diuers natures, which in the said kings dayes were there handled and adiudged. This court, as that right Honorable and learned Knight, in a briefe of his vpon the same court plainely proueth, was and is parcell of the kings most Honorable Councell, and so alwaies called and esteemed. The Iudges thereof were alwaies of the kings most Honourable Councell, appointed by the king to keepe his Councell board. The keeping of this court was neuer tyed to any place certaine, but onely where the Councell sate, the suyters were to attend. But now of late for the ease of suiters, it hath bene kept in the White hall at *Westminster*, and onely in the Tearme time. It is a court of Record, wherein recognizances are also taken by the kings Councell. The forme of proceeding in this court, was altogether according to the processe of summarie causes in the ciuile lawe. The persons plaintiffes and defendants, were alwaies either priviledged, as officers of the court, or their seruants, or as the kings seruants, or as necessarie attendants of them: or else where the plaintiffes pouertie, or meane estate was not matchable with the wealth or greatnesse of the defendant: or where the cause meerely contained mater of equitie, and had no proper remedie at the common law: or where it was specially recommended from the king to the examination of his Councell: or concerned Vniuersities, Colledges, Hospitals, and the like. The causes wherwith they deale, and wherof they iudge, are of all sortes: as maritime, vltra marine, ecclesiasticall, temporall; but properly temporall causes, and onely of the other sort, as they are mixt with temporal. The maner of proceeding in the said court, is first, by priuie seale, leters missiue, or Iniunction, or messenger, or bond. Secondly, by attachement. Thirdly, by proclamation of rebellion. Fourthly, by commission of rebellion: fiftly, by Sergeant at armes. The effect of the defendants apparence is, that he attend *de die in diem* on the councell, till he haue made his answer to the plaintiffes bill, and be licenced to depart vpon caution *de iudicio sisti & iudicato solvendo*, and constitution of his Atturney and councell by name. The authoritie of this court is such, as vppon cause to graunt iniunctions for barring the defendant from syewing the plaintiffe at the common lawe: and to stay the suyte at the common lawe before commencement, and not to arrest the bodie of the plaintiffe, till furder order be taken by the Kings councell: and the execution of a decree in this court may be done, either by imprisonment of the person disobeying, being partie, or claiming vnder the partie: or by levie of the summe adiudged vppon his lands.

Courtesie of England (lex Angliæ) commeth of the french (*Courtesie*. i. *benignitas, humanitas*) but with vs hath a proper signification, being vsed for a tenure. For if a man marie an inheretrice, that is, a woman seised of land in fee simple, or fee taile generall, or seised as heire of the taile speciall, and getteth a childe of her that commeth aliue into the world, though both it and his wife die forthwith, yet, if she were in possession, shall he keepe the land during his life, and is called tenent *per legem Angliæ*, or by the courtesie of England. *Glanvil.li.* 7. *ca.* 18. *Bracton. li.* 5. *tracta.* 5. *ca.* 30. *nu.* 7. 8. 9. *Britton. ca.* 51. *fo.* 132. *Fleta. li.* 6. *ca.* 56. §. *lex quædam. Fitzh. nat. br. fo.* 149. *D. Littleton. li.* 1. *ca.* 4. It is called the law of England. *Westm.* 2. *ca.* 3. This is in Scotland called (*curialitas Scotiæ. Skene de verbo. sign. verbo Curialitas:* who there saith that this is vsed in these two realmes onely, and maketh a large discourse of the custome.

Couthcutlaughe, is he that wittingly receiueth a man outlawed, and cherisseth or hideth him. In which case he was in auncient times subiect to the same punishment, that the outlawe himselfe was. *Bracton. li.* 3. *tracta.* 2. *ca.* 13. *nu.* 2. It is compounded of (*couthe*. i. knowne, acquainted, familiar, and (*vtlaughe*) an outlaw, as we now call him.

Courtilage, aliàs curtilage (*curtilagium, aliàs curtilegium*) signifieth a garden, a yard, or a feeld, or peece of voide ground lying neere and belonging to a mesuage, *West. parte.* 2. *Symbolæo. titulo fines. sect.* 26. And so is it vsed *anno.* 4. *Ed.* i. *ca. vnico. anno.* 35. *H.* 8. *ca.* 4. & *anno.* 39. *Eliza. ca.* 2. and *Coke vol.* 6. *fo.* 64. *a.* Of this also *Lindwood* thus writeth. *Curtilegium vulgare nomen est, non omnium patriarum, sed certarum. Est enim curtis mansio vel manerium ad habitandum cum terris, possessionibus, & aliis emolumentis ad tale manerium pertinentibus,*

tibus, prout satis colligitur in libro feudorum, titulo. de controuersia investiturae. § *si quis de manso. Coll.* 10. *Vnde curtilegium dicitur locus adiunctus tali curti, vbi leguntur herbae vel olera: sic dictus a (curtis) & (lego legis) pro colligere.* Thus farre *Linwood. titulo de decimis. ca. Sancta.* §. *omnibus, verbo Curtelegiorum.* So that in effect, it is a yard or a garden adioyning to a house.

Creansour, (creditor) commeth of the french *(croyance.* i. *persuasio)* and signifieth him, that trusteth another with any debt, be it in mony or wares. *Old nat. br. fo.* 67.

Cranage, (cranagium) is a liberty to vse a crane for the drawing vp of wares from the vessels, at any creek of the sea or wharfe, vnto the land, and to make profit of it. It signifieth also the mony paide and taken for the same. New booke of Entries. *fo.* 3. *col.* 3.

Creeke, (creca, crecca, vel crecum) seemeth to be a part of a hauen, where any thing is landed or disburdened out of the sea. So that when you are out of the mayne sea within the hauen, looke how many landing places you haue, so many creeks may be said to belong to that hauen. See *Cromptons iurisdictions. fo.* 110. *a.* This word is mencioned in the statute, as *anno* 5. *El. ca.* 5. and diuers others.

Creast Tile. See Roofe tile.

Croft, (croftum) is a litle close or pitle ioyning to a house, that sometimes is vsed for a hemp ground, sometime for corne, and sometime for pasture, as the owner listeth. It seemeth to come of the ould english word *(Creaft)* signifiing handy craft: because such groundes are for the most part extraordinarily dressed and trimmed by the both labour and skill of the owner.

Croises, (cruce signati) be vsed by *Britton. ca.* 122. for such as are pilgrimes: the reason may be, for that they weare the signe of the crosse vpon their garments. Of these and their priuileges reade *Bracton. li.* 5. *parte* 2. *ca.* 2. & *parte* 5. *ca.* 29. and the grand custumary of *Normandy ca.* 45. Vnder this word are also signified the knights of the order of *Saint Iohn* of *Ierusalem,* created for the defence of pilgrims. *Grego. Syntag. li.* 15. *ca.* 13. & 14.

Cucking stoole, (tumbrella) is an engine inuented for the punishment of scolds and vnquiet women, called in auncient time a tumbrell. *Lamb. eirenarcha. li.* 1. *ca.* 12. *po.* 62. *in meo. Bracton* writeth this word *(tymborella.) Kitchin,* where he saith, that euery one hauing view of Frank-pledge, ought to haue a pillorie and a tumbrell, seemeth by a tumbrell to meane the same thing. *cap. Charge in court leete. fol.* 13.*a.*

Cuth, other, vncuth (*privatus vel extraneus.*) These be old English words, not yet worne out of knowledge, for the which see *Roger Hoveden. parte poster. suorum annalium. fol.* 345.*a.*

Cudutlaghe. See *Conthutlaughe.*

Cui ante divortium, is a writ, that a woman diuorced from her husband, hath to recouer lands or tenements from him, to whome her husband did alienate them during the mariage: because during the mariage, she could not gainesay it. *Regist. ori. fol.* 233. *Fitzh. nat. br. fol.* 204.

Cuinage, is a word vsed for the making vp of tinne, into such fashion, as it is commonly framed into for the cariage thereof into other places, *anno* 11. *H.* 7. *cap.* 4.

Cui in vita, is a writ of entrie, that a widow hath against him, to whome her husband aliened her lands or tenements in his life time: which must containe in it, that during his life time, she could not withstand it. *Regist. orig. fol.* 232. *Fitz. nat. br. fol.* 193. See the newe booke of Entries. *verbo. Cui in vita.*

Cuntey cuntey is a kind of triall, as appeareth by *Bracton* in these words: *Negotium in hoc casu terminabitur per cuntye cuntey, sicut inter cohæredes. Bracton. lib.* 4. *tra.* 3. *cap.* 18. And againe, in the same place: *In brevi de recto negotium terminabitur per cuntey cuntey.* And thirdly, *lib.* 4. *tract.* 4. *cap.* 2. *Terminabitur negotium per breve de recto: vbi nec duellum, nec magna assisa, sed per cuntey cuntey omnino*: which in mine opinion is as much, as the ordinarie Iurie.

Curfew, commeth of two French words, (*couvrir.* i. *tegere,*) and (*feu.* i. *ignis.*) We vse it for an euening peale, by the which the Conquerour willed euery man to take warning for the raking vp of his fire, and the putting out of his light. So that in many places at this day, where a bell customably is rung toward bed time, it is said to ring curfew. *Stowes annals.*

Curia avisare vult, is a deliberation, that the court purposeth to take, vpon any point or points of a cause, before iudgement be resolued on. For this, see the new booke of Entries. *verbo. Curia avisare vult.*

Curia claudenda, is a writ, that lyeth against him, who should fence and close vp his ground, if he refuse or deferre to doe it. *Regist.*

*Register.orig.fo.*155.*Fitzh.nat. br. fo.*127.See also the newe booke of Entrise. *verbo. Curia clauden-da.*

Cursiter (*clericus de cursu, vel cursista curiæ cancellariæ*) is an officer or clerke belonging to the chancerie, that maketh out originall writs. *anno.*14 & 15. *H.*8. *ca.* 8. They be called clerks of course in the oathe of the clerks of the chancerie appointed *anno* 18. *Ed.*3. *stat.*5. *ca.vnico.* There be of these 24. in number, which haue allotted vnto every of them certaine shires, into the which they make out such originall writs, as are by the subiect required, and are a corporation among themselues.

Curteyn (*curtana*) was the name of King *Edward the sainct* his sword, which is the first sword, that is caried before the kings of this land at their coronation. *Mathæus Parisiens. in Henrico tertio.* And I haue heard say, that the point thereof is broken: which may argue an embleme of mercie.

Curtilage. See *Courtelage.*

Custode admittendo, & *Custode amouendo*, are writs for the admitting or remouing of gardians. *Register.original.in indice.*

Custom (*consuetudo*) is all one in signification with our common lawyers and Civilians, being by them both accounted a part of the lawe. *Consuetudo quandoq; pro lege seruatur* (saith *Bracton*) *in partibus vbi fuerit more vtentium approbata. Longævi enim temporis vsus & consuetudinis non est vilis authoritas. li.* 1. *ca.* 3. It may be thus not vnaptly defined: Custom is a lawe or right not written, which being established by long vse and the consent of our awncesters, hath beene and is daily practised: our awncesters, that is (*maiores,*) and those of our kindred that are *vltra tritavum. li.*4. §.*parentem.ff.de in ius vocando.l.vlt.* §.*parentes.ff. de gradibus & affini. & nominibus eorum.* So that allowing the father to be so much owlder then his sonne, as (*pubertas*) or the yeares of generation doe require, the grandfather so much elder then him, and soe forth *vsque ad tritavum*: we cannot say that this or that is a custom, except we can iustifie, that it hath continued so one hundred yeares. For *tritavus* must be so much elder then the party that pleadeth it: yet because that is hard to prooue: it is enough for the profe of a custom by witnesses in the common lawe (as I haue credibly heard) if two or more can depose, that they heard their fathers say, that it was a custome all their time, and that their fathers heard their fathers also say, that it was likewise a custome in their time. If it be be to be prooved by record, the continuance of a hundred yeares will serue. Custom is either generall or particular: generall I call that, which is current thorough England: whereof you shall read diuers in the *Doctor* and *Student. li. pri. ca. 7.* very worthy to be knowne. Particular is that, which belongeth to this or that countie, as *Gavelkind* to *Kent*, or to this or that *Lord*-ship, citie, or towne. Custom differeth from prescription, for that custom is common to more, and prescription (in some mens opnion) is particular to this or that man. Againe, prescription may be for a farre shorter time then a custom, *viz.* for fiue yeare, or for one yeare, or lesse. Example of fiue yeares prescription you haue in the levying of a fine. For if a fine duly levied of lands &tenements be not impugned within fiue yeres, it excludeth all claime for euer. And if a man omit his continuall claime for a yeere and a day: then the tenent in possession prescribeth an immunity against the entrie of the demandant and his heyre. *Fitzh. nat. br. fo.79. Terms of the law. verbo. Continuall clayme.* Out of our statutes you may haue greater diuersitie, which see collected in mine Institutes. *titulo de Vsucapio: & longi tempo. præscript*. So that *Brissonius* in his 14. *de verbo signif.* seemeth to say truly, that prescription is an exception founded vpon so long time runne and past, as the lawe limiteth for the pursuite of any action. An example may be taken from those statutes. *anno.* 1.*H.* 8.*ca.*4. which inacteth, that in all actions populer, informati-on shall be made within three yeares after the offence committed, or els be of no force. Of like nature is the *statute. anno* 7.*H.* 8.*ca.*3. which in some cases maketh one yeeres prescription sufficient against informations. Custome is also vsed for the tribute or tolle, that merchans pay to the king for carying in and out merchandise. *anno* 14.*Ed.*3.*stat.* 1.*ca.* 21. in which signification it is latined (*custuma*) *Regster. orig. fo.* 138.*a.* 129.*a.* and lastly for such seruices, as tenents of a maner owe vnto their lord. New booke of entries, *verbo Custome.*

Customary tenents, (tenentes per consuetudinem) are such tenents, as hould by the custome of the maner, as their especiall euidence. See *Copihoulds.*

Custos breuium, is the principall clerk belonging to the court of common plees: whose office is to receiue and keepe all the writs, and put them vpon files, euery returne by it selfe, and at the end of euery terme to receiue of of the protonotaries all the records of (*Nisi prius*) called the (*postea*) For they are first brought in by the clerk of assise of euery circuit to the protonotarie that entred the issue in that mater, for the entring of the iudgement. And then doe the protonotaries get of the court peremptory day, for euery party to speake what he hath to alleage in arrest of iudgement: which day being past, he entreth the verdict and iudgement thereupon into the rols of the court: and that done, he doth in the end of the tearme deliuer ouer to the *custos breuium*, all the records of (*Nisi prius*) which came to his hand that terme: which receiued he bindeth into a bundle and bestoweth them. The *custos breuium* also maketh entry of the writs of couenant, and the concord vpon euery fine: and maketh forth exemplifications and copies of all writs and records in his office, and of all fines leuied. The fines after they be ingrossed, the parts therof are diuided betwen the *custos breuium* and the *chirographer*: whereof the *chirographer* keepeth alwaies with him the writ of couenant and the note, the *custos breuium* keepeth the concord and the foote of the fine, vpon the which foote the chirographer doth cause the proclamations to be indorsed, when they be all proclaymed. This office is in the princes gift.

Custos placitorum coronæ. Bracton.li.2.ca.5. This seemeth to be all one with him, whome we nowe call (*custos rotulorum*) of this officer I finde mention in the writ (*odio & atia*) *Register. originał.fo.133.b.*

Custos rotulorum, is he, that hath the custodie of the rols or records of the sessions of peace: and (as some thinke) of the commission of the peace it selfe. *Lamb.Eirenarch.li.4.ca.pa.3.373.* He is alway a Iustice of Peace and *Quorum*, in the countie where he hath his office. *Idem. eodem.* and by his office he is rather termed an officer or minister then a iudge: because the commission of the peace layethe, by expresse words this especiall charge vpon him: *quòd ad dies & loca prædicta, breuia, præcepta, processus, & indictamenta prædicta coram te & dictis sociis tuis venire facias. Idem. eodem.* where read a competent tract of other things belonging to this office.

Custos of the spiritualties (*custos spiritualitatis vel spiritualium*) is he that exerciseth the spirituall or ecclesiasticall iurisdiction of any dioces, during the vacancie of the See: the appointment of whome by the canon lawe apperteineth to the deane and chapter. *ca ad abolendam, Extra. Ne sede vacante aliquid innovetur.* but with vs in England to the Archbishop of the province by prescription. How be it diuers deanes and chapters (if *M. Gwin* say truly in the preface to his readings) doe chalenge this by awncient charters from the kings of this land.

Cutter of the talyes, is an officer in the exchequer, that prouideth wood for the talyes, and cutteth the summe paid vpon them, and then casteth the same into the Court to be written vpon.

D A

D*Ammage*, commeth of the french (*dam*) or (*domage*) signifiing generally any hurt or hinderance, that a man taketh in his estate: But in the common lawe, it particularly signifieth a part of that the Iurours be to inquire of, passing for the plaintiffe or demandant in a ciuile action, be it personall or reall. For after verdict giuen of the principall cause, they are likewise asked their consciences touching costs (which be the charges of suite, called of the Civilians (*expensa litis*) and dammages, which conteine the hindrance that the plaintiffe or demandant hath suffered by meanes of the wrong done to him by the defendant or tenent.

Dane guilt, Danegold, or Danegelt (*Danegeldum*) is compounded of (*Dane* and *gelt.* i. *pecunia*) and was a tribute laide vpon our ancesters of 12. pence for euerie hide of land through the realme by the Danes, that once got the masterie of vs, in regard (as they pretended) of clearing the sease of pyrates, which greatly annoyed our land in those daies. *Cambd. Brittan.* 83. with whome agree the lawes of *Edward* set out by *M. Lamberd. ca.* 11. *Stowe in his annals, pa.* 118. saith, that this tribute came to 40000. pownds by the yeare, and that it was released by *Edw.* the confessour. *The author of the newe Terms of law* saith, that this tribute began in the time of king *Etheldred*, who being sore distressed by the continuall inuasion of the *Dane*, to procure his peace, was compelled to charge his people with importable payments. For first he gaue them at fiue severall paiments 113000. poundes, and afterward graunted them 48000. poundes yeerely. See *Roger Houeden parte poster. suorum annalium in Henrico secundo fo.* 344. *a.*

Dareyn continuance, See *Continuance. Darein* is a corrupt word of of the French (*dernier.* i. *vltimus.)*

Darrein presentment (*vltima præsentatio.)* See *Assise or darreyn presentment.*

Dates(dactyli) is the plumme or fruite of the tree in latine called *palma* , in english the Date tree well knowne to most men by sight. And he that will farder vnderstand the nature or diuersities of this fruite, may repaire to *Gerards* herball. *li.* 3.*ca.* 131. They be numbred among spices and drugs to be garbleled. 1. *Iaco.*19.

*Day(dies)*is sometime vsed in the lawe, for the day of appearance in court, either originally, or vpon assignation; and sometime for the returnes of writs. For example, daies in bank, be daies set downe by statute or order of the court, when writs shall be returned, or when the partie shall appeare vpon the writ serued . And of this you may read the statutes,*anno* 51.*H.* 3. *ca.*1.& 2. *Marlb.ca.* 12.*anno.* 52.*H.*3. and the statute *de anno bissextili.anno* 21.*H.* 3. and lastly *anno* 32. *H.*8.*ca.* 21.To be dismissed with out day,is to be finally discharged the court. *Kitchin.fo.*193.He had a day by the rolle.*Kitchin.* *fo.*197.that is, he had a day of appearance assigned him.*Day*, yeere, and waste.Sea *Dies, and yeare.*

Deadly feude (feuda) is a profession of an vnquencheable hatred,vntill we be reuenged,euen by the death of our enemie. It is deduced from the German word (*Feed*)which, as *Hotoman* saith, *in verbis feudalibus, modo bellum, modo capitales inimicitias significat.* This word is vsed.*anno.*43. *Eliz. cap.*13.

Dead pledge(mortuum vadium) See *Mort gage.*

Deane, (decanus) is an ecclesiasticall magistrate, so called of the greeke (δέκα) because he hath power ouer ten *Canons* at the least. How be it in England we vse to call him a deane, that is next vnder the bishop, and cheife of the chapter ordinarily in a cathedrall church: and the rest of the societie or corporation we call *Capitulum*, the chapter. But this word how diuersly it is vsed,read *Lindwood. titulo de iudiciis ca.pri. verbo Decani rurales.*where deane rurals are saide to be certaine persons that haue certaine iurisdiction ecclesiasticall ouer other ministers and parishes neere adioyning, assigned vnto them by the Bishop and archdeacon,being placed & displaced by them. As there be two foundations of cathedrall churches in England, the old,& the new(the new be those which *Henry* the 8. vpon suppression of abbeyes transformed from abbot or prior & couēt to deane and chapter) so be there two meanes of creating these deanes. For these of the old foundation, are brought to their dignitie much like Bishops: the king first sēding out his *congè d' eslire* to the chapter, the chapter then chusing, the king yeelding his royal assēt, and the Bishop confirming him, and giuing his mandate to installe him. Those of the newe foundation are by a shorter course installed by vertue of the kings leters patents, without either election or confirmation. This word is also applyed to diuers, that are the chiefe of certaine peculiar Churches, or chapels, as the deane of the kings chapell, the deane of the Arches, the deane of Saint George his chapell in *Windsour*, the deane of *Bockin in Essex*.

Debet & solet: These words are diuers times vsed in the writers of the common lawe, and may trouble the minde of a young student, except he haue some aduertisement of them. For example, it is saide in the *old.nat. br.fo.*98. This writ *(de secta molendini)* being in the *(debet)* and *(solet)* is a writ of right, &c. and againe. *fo.*69. A writ of *(Quod permittat)* may be pleaded in the countie before the shyreeue, and it may be in the *(debet)* and in the *(solet)* or the *(debet)* with out the *(solet)* according as the Demandāt claymeth. wherfore note, that those writs that be in this sort brought, haue these words in them, as formall words not to be omitted. And according to the diuersity of the case, both *(debet)* and *(solet)* are vsed, or *(debet)* alone: that is, if a man siew to recouer any right by a writ, whereof his awncester was disseised by the tenent or his awncester, then he vseth onely the word *(debet)* in his writ: because *(solet)* is not fit by reason his awncester was disseised, and the custome discontinued: but if he siew for any thing, that is now first of all denied him, then he vseth both these words *(debet & solet)* because his awncesters before him, and he him selfe vsually inioyed the thing siewed for: as suite to a mille, or common of pasture vntill this present refusall of the tenent. The like may be saide of *(debet)* and *(detinet)* as appeareth by the *Register.orig.* in the writ *de debito.fo.* 140. *a.*

Debito, is a writ which lieth, where a man oweth to another a certaine summe of mony vpō an obligation or other bargain, for any thing sold vnto him. *Fitz.nat br.fo.* 119. This writ is made somtime in the *Detinet*, & not in the *Debet*. which properly falleth out, where a man oweth an annuitie: or a certaine quantity of wheat,

wheat, barley, or such like, which he refuseth to pay. *old.nat. br.fo.* 75. See *Debet & Solet.*

Denelage (*denelagia*) is the law that the Danes made heere in England, out of which and *Merchenlage*, and *West Sexonlage, the Conquerour* compounded certaine ordinances for his subiects. *Camdeni Britan.pa.* 94. *& pa.* 183.

Decem *tales.* See *Tales.*

Decies *tantum*, is a writ that lieth against a Iurour, which hath taken mony for the giuing of his verdict, called so of the effect, because it is to recouer ten times so much as he tooke. It lieth also against embracers that procure such an enquest. *anno* 38. *Ed.* 3. *ca.* 13. *Reg. orig.fo.* 188. *Fitzh.nat.br.fo.* 171. *New booke of Entrise. verbo* Decies tantum.

Deceyte (*deceptio fraus, dolus*) is a subtile wilie shift or deuise, hauing noe other name. Hereunto may be drawen all maner of craft, subtiltie, guile, fraude, wilynes, slightnes, cunning, couin, collusion, practise, and offence, vsed to deceiue another man by any meanes, which hath none other proper or particular name, but offence. *West. parte. 2. symbol. titulo. Indictments. sect.* 68. See *Cosening.*

Decenniers. See *Deciners.*

Deceptione, is a writ that lieth properly against him, that deceitfully doth any thing in the name of another, for one that receiueth harme or dãmage therby. *Fitzh.nat. br. fo.* 95. This writ is either originall or iudiciall, as appeareth by the *old.nat.br.fo.* 50. where you may reade the vse of both. For some satisfaction, take these words of that booke: This writ of deceit, when it is original, then it lieth in case, where deceit is made to a man by another, by which deceit he may be disherited, or otherwise euill intreated: as it appeareth by the *Register*, &c. And when it is iudiciall, then it lieth out of the rols of record: as in case where (*scire facias*) is sent to the Shyreeue, that he warne a man to be before the Iustices at a certaine day, and the Shyreeue returne the writ serued; whereas the said man was not warned, by which the partie that sueth the (*scire facias*) recouereth, then the party which ought to haue beene warned, shall haue the saide writ against the Shyreeue. *The author of the termes of lawe. verbo* Deceite, saith that the originall writ of deceite lieth, where any deceit is done to a man by another, so that he hath not sufficiently performed his bargaine or promise, In the writ iudicial he concurreth with the former booke. See the *Reg.orig.fo.* 112. and the *Reg.iudiciall in the table. verbo* Deceptione.

Decimis solvendis pro possessionibus alienigenarum, is a writ or leters patents, yet extant in the Register, which laye against those, that had fermed the Priors aliens lands of the king, for the Rector of the Parish, to recouer his tythe of them. *Regi. orig. fol.* 179.

Deciners, aliàs, desiners, aliàs, doziners, (decennarii) commeth of the French, *(dizeine.* i. *decas)* tenne in number, or else of *(disenier.* i. *decearchus.)* It signifieth, in the auncient monuments of our lawe, such as were wont to haue the ouersight and checke of ten friburgs, for the maintenance of the kings peace. And the limits or compasse of their iurisdiction was called *(decenna) Bracton lib.* 3. *tract.* 2. *cap.* 15. of whom you may also reade, *Fleta lib.* 1. *cap.* 27 and a touch in the *Regist. orig. fol.* 68. *b.* These seemed to haue large authoritie in the Saxons time, taking knowledg of causes within their circuite, and redressing wrongs by way of iudgement, as you may reade in the lawes of king *Edward*, set out by *M. Lambard. num.* 32. In later times I find mention of these, as in *Britton cap.* 12. who saith in the kings person (as he writeth his whole booke) in this maner: We will, that all those which be 14. yeares old, shall make oath, that they shall be sufficient and loyall vnto vs, and that they will be neither felons, nor assenting to felons: and we will, that all be *(en dozeine & plevis per doseniers)* that is, professe themselues to be of this or that dozein, and make or offer suretie of their behauiour by these or those doziniers: except religious persons, clerks, knights, and their eldest sonnes, and women. Yet the same author in his 29. chapter, some thing toward the end, doth say, that all of 12. yeares old and vpward, are punishable for not comming to the Turne of the Shyreeue, except Earles, Prelats, Barons, religious persons, and women. *Stawnf. pl. cor. fol.* 37. out of *Fitzh.* hath these wordes: The like lawe is, where the dozeniers make presentment, that a felon is taken for felonie, and deliuered to the Shyreeue, &c. And *Kitchin*, out of the Register, and *Britton*, saith thus. Religious persons, clerkes, knights, or women shall not be deceniers. *fol.* 33. So that hereby I gather, that of later times, this word signifieth nothing but such an one, as by his oath of loyaltie to his Prince, (for suretie none ordinarily findeth at these dayes) is setled in the combination or societie of a dozein. And a dozein seemeth now to extend so farre, as euery leete extendeth: because in leetes onely this oathe is

ministred

ministred by the steward, and taken by such as are twelue yeares old and vpwards, dwelling within the compasse of the leete where they are sworne. *Fitz. nat. br. fol.* 161. *A.* The particulars of this oath you may reade in *Bracton. lib.* 3. *tract.* 2. *cap.* 1. *num.* 1. in these words: *Quibus propositis* (that is, the commission of the Iustices being read, and the cause of their comming being shewed) *debent Iusticiarii se transferre in aliquem locum secretum, & vocatis ad se quatuor vel sex, vel pluribus de maioribus de comitatu, qui dicuntur Busones Comitatus, & ad quorum nutum dependent vota aliorum, et sic inter se tractatum habeant Iusticiarii ad inuicem, & ostendant qualiter a Domino Rege & eius concilio prouisum sit, quod omnes tam milites, quam alii qui sunt quindecim annorum & amplius, iurare debent, quod vtlagatos, murditores, robbatores, & burglatores non receptabunt, nec eis consentient, nec eorum receptatoribus, & si quos tales nouerint, illos attachiari facient, & hoc Vicecomiti & baliuis suis monstrabunt: & si hutesium vel clameum de talibus audiverint, statim audito clamore, sequantur cum familia & hominibus de terra sua.* Here *Bracton* setteth downe 15. yeares, for the age of those that are sworne to the kings peace, but *lib.* 3. *tract.* 2. *cap.* 11. *num.* 5. he nameth 12. yeares. *See Inlaughe.* A man may note out of the premisses, diuersities betweene the auncient and these our times, in this point of law and gouernement, as well for the age of those that are to be sworne, as also that *Decenner* is not now vsed for the chief man of a *Dozen*, but for him him that is sworne to the kings peace: and lastly, that now there are no other Dozens but leetes, and that no man ordinarily giueth other security for the keeping of the kings peace, but his owne oathe: and that therefore none aunswereth for anothers transgression, but euery man for himselfe. And for the general ground this may suffice. *See Frankepledge.*

Declaration (*declaratio*) is properly the shewing foorth, or laying out of an action personall in any suite, howbeit it is vsed sometime and indifferently for both personall and reall actions. For example, *anno* 36. *Ed.* 3. *c.* 15. in these words: By the auncient termes and formes of declarations, no man shall be preiudiced: so that the mater of the action be fully shewed in the demonstration & in the writ: *See* the new Termes of lawe. See *Cownte.*

Dedimus potestatem, is a writ, whereby commission is giuen to a priuate man for the speeding of some act appertaining to a Iudge. The Ciuilians call it (*Delegationem.*) And it is graunted most commonly vpon suggestiō, that the partie, which is to doe something before a Iudge, or in court, is so feeble, that he cannot trauell. It is vsed in diuers cases: as to make a personall aunswer to a bill of complaint in the Chauncerie, to make an Atturney for the following of a suite in the Countie, *Hundred*, Wapentake, &c. *Old nat. br. fol.* 20. To levie a fine. *West. part.* 2. *symbol. titulo. Fines. sect.* 112. and diuers other effects, as you may see by *Fitzh. nat. br.* in diuers places noted in the *Index* of the booke: In what diuersitie of cases this writ or commission is vsed, see the table of the *Regist. orig. verbo Dedimus potestatem.*

Deedes, (*Facta*) signifie in our commō law wrightings, that containe the effect of a contract made betweene man and man, which the ciuilians call (*literarum obligationem*) And of deeds there be two sorts, deeds indented and deeds poll. Which diuision, as *M. West.* saith *parte.*1. *Simbol: lib.* 1. *sect.* 46. groweth from the forme or fashion of them; the one being cut to the fashion of teeth in the toppe or side, the other being plaine. And the definition of a deede indented he expresseth thus *Sect.* 47. A deed indented, is a deede consisting of two partes or more, in which it is expressed, that the parties to the same deede, haue to euery parte thereof interchangeabely, or seuerally set there seuerall seales. See the rest, where at the last he sheweth the cause of the name: *viz*: for that consisting of more partes, eche parte is indented or cut one of them into the other, that by the cut it may appeare, they belonge to one busines or contract. A deede poil or polled he describeth thus: *Sect.* 46. Q. A polled deede, is a deede testifying, that onely the one of the parties to the bargaine, hath put his seale, thereunto, after the maner there by him described: which reade for your beter vnderstanding. See the newe Tearmes of lawe, *verbo Fait*, where he sheweth, that each deed consisteth of 3. points: writing, sealing, and deliuerie.

Deere Hayse. anno 19. *H.* 7. *cap.* 11. seemeth to be an Engine of cords, to catch Deere.

De essendo quietum de telonio, is a writ that lyeth for them which are by priuiledge freed from the payment of tolle, which reade at large in *Fitzh. nat. br. fol.* 226.

Defalt (*defalta*) commeth from the French (*Defaut*) and is an offence in omitting that, which

which we ought to doe. *West. part. 2. symbol. titulo. Indictment. sect. 2.* Of this hath *Bracton* a whole tractats, *lib. 5. tractat. 3.* By whome it appeareth that a default is most notoriously taken for *non* appearance in court, at a day assigned. Of this you may reade also in *Fleta. lib. 6. cap. 14.*

Defeisance (defeisantia) commeth of the French *(Deffaire)* or *Deffaire)* i. *infectum reddere quod factum est*, and signifieth in our common lawe, nothing but a condition annexed to an act, as to an obligation, a recognizance or statute, which performed by the obligee or recognizee, the act is disabled and made voide, as if it neuer had bene done, whereof you may see *West* at large. *part. 1. symb. li. 2. sect. 156.*

Defendant (defendens) is he that is siewed in an action personall: as tenent, is he which is siewed in an action reall. Tearmes of the lawe.

Defendemus, is an ordinarie word in a feofment or donation, and hath this force, that it bindeth the donour and his heyres, to defend the Donee, if any man goe about to laye anie seruitude vpon the thing giuen, other then is contained in the donation. *Bract. lib. 2. cap. 16. num. 10.* See also *Warrantizabimus & Acquietabimus.*

Defender of the faith (defensor fidei) is a peculiar title giuen to the King of *England* by the Pope, as *(Catholicus)* to the king of *Spaine*, and *Christianissimus* to the French king. It was first giuen by *Leo decimus* to king *Henry* the 8. for writing against *Martin Luther*, in the behalfe of the Church of *Rome*, then accounted *Domicilium fidei Catholicæ. Stowes annals. pag. 863.*

Deforsour, (Deforciator) commeth of the french *(For ceur. i. expugnator)*. It is vsed, in our common law, for one that ouercommeth and casteth out by force, and differeth from disseisour first in this, because a man may disseise another without force, which act is called simple disseisin. *Britton. ca. 53.* next, because a man may deforce another, that neuer was in possession: as for example: if more haue right to lands, as cōmō heires and one entring keepeth out the rest, the law saith, that he deforceth them, though he doe not disseise them. *Old nat: br: fol: 118.* and *Litleton* in his chapter *(Discontinuance) fol. 117.* saith, that he which is infeoffed by the tenent in taile, and put in possession, by keeping out the heire of him in reuersion being dead, doth deforce him, though he did not disseise him; because he entred, when the tenent in taile was liuing, and the heire had noe present right. And a deforsour differreth from an Intrudour, because a man is made an Intrudour by a wrongfull entry only into land or tenement voide of a possessour. *Bracton li*: 4: *ca*: *pri*. and a deforsour is also by houlding out the right heire, as is abouesaide.

Deliuerance, See *Repligiare*.

Demaund, (*Demanda vel Demandum*) commeth of the french (*Demande*. i. *postulatio*, *postulatus*) and signifieth a calling vpon a man for any thing due. It hath likewise a proper signification with the common lawyers opposite to plaint. For the pursiute of all ciuill actions are either demaunds or plaints: and the persyewer is called demaundant or plaintife: *Viz*: Demandaundant in actions reall, and plaintife in personall. And where the party persiewing is called demaundãt, there the party persiewed is called tenent: where plaintife, there defendant. See terms of law, *verbo Demaundant*.

Demy haque, See *Haque*, and *Haquebut*.

Demaine, (*Dominicum*) is a french word, otherwise written (*Domaine*) and signifieth (*Patrimonium domini*) as *Hotoman* saith *in verbis feudalibus*. *verbo Dominicum*. where by diuers authorities he proueth those lands to be *dominicum*, which a man holdeth originally of himselfe, and those to be *feodum*, which he holdeth by the benefite of a superiour Lord. And I find in the ciuill law (*Rem dominicam*) for that which is proper to the Emperour. *Cod. Ne rei dominicæ vel templorum vindicatio temporis præscriptione submoueatur*, being the 38. title of the 7. booke. And (*res dominici iuris*. i. *reipub*. in the same place. And by the word (*Domanium*) or (*Demanium*) are properly signified the kings lands in *Fraunce*, appertaining to him in propertie, *Quia Domanium definitur illud, quod nominatim consecratum est, vnitum, & incorporatum Regiæ coronæ, vt scripsit Chopinus de domanio Franciæ tit. 2. per legem. Si quando 3. Cod. de bon. vacan. lib. 10. & Mathæus de Afflictis in constit. Siciliæ li. 1. tit. De locatione Demanii*. 82. which may be called *Bona incorporata & in corpus fisci redacta*. *Skene de verborum signif. verb. Terræ Dominicales*. In like maner doe we vse it in *England*: howbeit, we here haue no land (the Crowne land onely excepted) which holdeth not of a superior. For all dependeth either mediatly or immediately of the Crowne, that is, of some honour or other belonging to the Crowne, and not graunted in fee to any inferior person. Wherefore no common person hath

hath any demaynes, simply vnderstood. For when a man in pleading would signifie his land to be his owne, he saith, that he is or was seised thereof in his demaine as of fee. *Litleton li.* 1. *cap.* 1. Whereby he signifieth, that though his land be to him and his heyres for euer, yet it is not true demaine, but depending vpon a superior Lord, and holding by seruice, or rent in liewe of seruice, or by both seruice and rent: Yet I find these words vsed in the kings right, *anno* 37. *H.*8. *cap.* 16. and 39. *Eliz. cap.* 22. But the application of this speech to the king and crowne land, is crept in by errour and ignorance of the word *(Fee,)* or at least by vnderstanding it otherwise then of the Feudists it is taken. But *Britton. cap.* 78. sheweth, that this word *(Demeyne)* is diuersly taken: sometime more largely, as of lands or tenements held for life, &c. and sometime more strictly as for such onely as are generally held in fee. This word somtime is vsed for a distinction between those lands, that the Lord of a maner hath in his owne hands, or in the hands of his leasee, dimised vpon a rent for tearme of yeares or life, and such other lād appertaining to the said maner, which belongeth to free or copy-houlders. Howbeit, the copyhold belonging to any maner, is also in the opiniō of many good lawyers accounted Demeines. *Bracton* in his fourth booke *tract.* 3. *ca.* 9. *nu.* 5. hath these words: *Item dominicum accipitur multipliciter. Est autē dominicum quod quis habet ad mensam suam & propriè, sicut sunt Bordlands anglie. Item dicitur dominicum villenagium, quod traditur villanis, quod quis tempestiuè & intempestiue resumere possit pro voluntate sua, & reuocare.* Of this *Fleta* likewise thus writeth: *Dominicum est multiplex. Est autem Dominicum propriè terra ad mensam assignata, & villenagium quod traditur villanis ad excolendum, & terra precariò dimissa, quæ tempestiuè & pro voluntate domini poterit reuocari: & sicut est de terra commissa, tenenda quam diu commissori placuerit. poterit & dici Dominicum, de quo quis habet liberum tenementum, & alius vsumfructum: & etiam vbi quis habet liberum tenementum, & alius curam, sicut de custode dici poterit & curatore; & vnde vnus dicitur a iure, alius quoque ab homine. Dominicum etiam dicitur ad differentiam eius quod tenetur in seruitio. Dominicum est omne illud tenementum, de quo antecessor obiit seisitus vt de feudo, nec refert cum vsufructu vel sine, & de quo si eiectus esset, si viueret, recuperare posset per assisam nomine disseisinæ, licet alius haberet vsum* *fructum: sicut dici poterit de illis qui tenent in villenagio, qui vtuntur, fruuntur non nomine proprio sed nomine Domini sui. Fleta: l.5. c: 5.§. Dominicũ autē.* And the reasō why copyhold is accoūted Demeanes, is because they that be tenents vnto it, are iudged, in law, to haue nor other right, but at the will of the lord. Soe that it is reputed still after a sort to be in the Lords hands. And yet in common speach, that is called ordinarily Demeanes, which is neither free nor copy. It is farder to be noted, that Demaine is sometime vsed in a more speciall signification, and is opposite to Franck fee. For example, those lands, which were in the possession of King *Edward* the confessor, are called auncient Demaine, & all others be called Franck fee. *Kitchin. fol*: 98. and the tenents which hould any of those lands, be called tenents in auncient demaine, the others tenents in franck fee. *Kitchin vbi supra*. And also tenents at the common lawe. *West. parte 2. Simbol: titulo Fines. Sect* 25. The reason is, because tenents in auncient Demaine, cannot be syewed out of the Lords court: Tearmes of the Lawe. *verbo Auncient Demaine*. And the tenents in aunciēt demaine, though they hould all by the verge, and haue none other euidēce but copy of court rolle, yet they are saide to haue free hould. *Kitchin. fol.* 81. See *Auncient demame*.

Demayne cart of an Abbot, seemeth to bee that cart, which the Abbot vseth vpon his owe *Demaine: Anno.6.H.3.cap.21.*

Demurrer (*Demorare*) commeth of the French (*Demeurer. i.manere in aliquo loco vel morari*) It signifieth in our common lawe, a kinde of pawse vpon a pointe of difficultie in any action, and is vsed substantiuely. For in euery action, the controversie consisteth either in the fact, or in the lawe, if in the fact, that is tried by the Iurie, if in lawe, then is the case plaine to the Iudge, or so hard and rare, as it breedeth iust doubt. I call that plaine to the Iudge, wherein hee is assured of the lawe, though perhaps the partie and his councell yeeld not vnto it. And in such, the Iudge with his Assessors proceedeth to Iudgement without farder worke: but when it is doubtfull to him and his Associates, then is there stay made, and a time taken, either for the court to thinke farder vpon it, and to agree if they can: or els for all the Iustices to meete together in the Chequer chamber, and vpon hearing of that which the sergeants shall say of both partes, to advise and set downe what is lawe. And whatsoeuer they conclude,

clude, standeth firme without farder remedie. *Smith. de Repub. Anglo.lib.2.cap.13.West.* calleth it a *Demurrer* in chauncery likewise, when there is question made whether a parties answer to a bille of complaint, &c. be defectiue or not: and thereof reference made to any of the bench for the examination therof, & report to bee made to the court.*parte. 2.symb.tit.Chauncery. sect.29.*

Denariata terræ. See *Farding deale of land.*

Denizen, commeth of the French (*Donaison.* i.*Donatio*) and signifieth in our common lawe, an Alein that is infrāchised here in England by the Princes charter, and inabled, almost in all respects, to doe as the kings natiue subiects doe: namely to purchas, and to possesse lands, to be capable of any office or dignitie. Yet it is saide to be short of naturalisation, because a straunger naturalised, may inherit lands by descent, which a man made onely a denizen cannot. And againe, in the charter whereby a man is made denizen, there is commonly conteined some one clause or other, that abridgeth him of that full benefite, which naturall subiects doe inioy. And when a man is thus infranchised, he is saide to bee vnder the kings protection, or, *esse ad fidem Regis Angliæ*, before which time he can inioy nothing in England. *Bracton.lib.5. tractat.5.cap.25.nu. 3.* Nay, hee and his goods might bee seised to the kings vse. *Horn in his mirrour of Iustices. li.1.ca. de la Venue de franc plege.*

Deodand (*Deodandum*) is a thing giuen or forfeited (as it were) to God for the pacification of his wrath in a case of misaduenture, whereby any Christian soule commeth to a violent ende, without the fault of any reasonable creature. For example, if a horse should strike his keeper and so kille him; if a man in dryuing a cart, and seeking to redresse any thing about it, should so fall, as the cart wheele running ouer him, should presse him to death: if one should be felling of a tree, and giuing warning to one cōming by, whē the tree were neere falling, to looke to themselues, and any of them should bee slaine neuerthelesse by the fall of the tree. In the first of these cases the horse, in the second the cart wheele, carte and horses, and in the third the tree is to be giuen to God; that is, to be sold and distributed to the poore, for an expiation of this dreadfull euent, though effected by vnreasonable, yea sensles & dead creatures. *Stawnf.pl.cor.lib.1.ca. 2.* whereof alſo read *Bracton. lib.* 3. *tractat.* 2. *cap.* 5. and *Britton. cap.* 7. and *West. parte.* 2. *ſymbolaog. titulo Indictments. ſect.* 49. And though this be giuen to God: yet is it forfeited to the king by lawe, as ſuſteining Gods perſon, and an executioner in this caſe, to ſee the price of theſe diſtributed to the poore, for the appeaſing of God ſtirred vp euen againſt the earth and place, by the ſhedding of innocent blood thereupon. *Fleta*, ſaith that this is ſould, and the price diſtributed to the poore for the ſoule of the king, his auncеſters, and of all faithfull people departed this life. *lib.* 1. *cap.* 25. *verbo. De ſubmerſis.* And it ſeemeth that this law hath an imitation of that in *Exodus. cap.* 21. *Si cornu petierit bos virum vel mulierem, ita vt moriatur, lapidabitur bos, neq; comedetur caro eius, at Dominus eius erit innocens.*

De Deonerando pro rata portionis, is a writ that lieth where one is diſtrained for a rent, that ought to be paid by others proportionally with him. For exāple, a man holdeth ten Oxegangs of land by fealty, and ten ſhillings rent of the king, and alienateth one Oxegang thereof to one, another to another in fee. Afterward the Shyreeue or other Officer commeth and diſtraineth onely one of them for the Rent: he that is diſtrained may haue this writ for his helpe. *Fitzh. nat. br. fo.* 234.

Departer, is a word properly vſed of him, that firſt pleading one thing in barre of an action, and being replied thereunto, doth in his reioynder ſhew another mater contrary to his firſt plea. *Plowden in Reniger* and *Fogaſſa, fo.* 7. & 8. And of this ſee diuers examples in *Brooke. titulo Departer de ſon plee &c.*

Departers of gold and ſiluer. See *Finours.*

De quibus ſur diſſeiſin, is a writ of entry. See *Fitzh. nat. br. fol.* 191. C.

Dereyne (*Diſrationare, vel Dirationare*) may ſeeme to come of the French (*Diſarroyer.* i. *confundere, turbare*) to confound or turne out of order, or (*deſranger.* i. to ſet out of order, or laſtly of the *Norman* word (*deſrene*) for with the *Normans* (*deſrene*) is nothing elſe but a proofe of the deniall of a mans owne fact. For *Rubigineus in his grand cuſtumarie cap.* 122. & 123. maketh mention of (*lex probabilis*) and (*lex deraiſnia*) *legem probabilem* or (*probationem*) he defineth to bee a proofe of a mans owne fact, which he ſaith he hath done, & his aduerſarie denieth. His example is this: *A.* ſueweth *R.* for a hogge: ſaying, thou ſhouldeſt deliuer mee a hogge for 2. ſhillings ſixe pence: which mony *F.* paid thee: wherefore I demande my hogge. *R.* anſwereth. It is true that thou ſaieſt, and I deliuered thee thy hog, which I am ready to prooue. *Deraiſniã* he defineth, to be a proofe of a thing that one denieth to be done by himſelfe, which his aduerſarie ſaith was done, defeating or confounding his aduerſaries aſſertion (as you would ſay) and ſhewing it to be without and againſt reaſõ or likelyhood, which is auouched. In our commõ lawe it is vſed diuerſly, firſt generally, for to prooue: as *Dirationabit ius ſuum hæres propinquior. Glanuile li.* 2. *cap.*6. and *Habeo probos homines, qui hoc viderunt & audierunt, & parati ſunt hoc dirationare. Idem lib.*4.*cap.* 6. and (*Dirationauit terram illam in curia mea*) *Idem lib.* 2. *cap.* 20. i. hee prooued that land to bee his owne, &c. and (*pertinentiam eam dirationauit in vita ſua, vel alio modo iuſte perquiſivit*) *Idem, lib.* 6. *cap.* 12. and *Bracton* vſeth it after the ſame ſort, in theſe words: *Habeo ſufficientem diſrationationem & probationem. lib.* 4. *tracta:* 6 *cap.* 16. and ſo he vſeth (*diſrationare*) *lib.* 4. *cap.* 22. and ſo in *Weſtm.* 2. *anno.* 13. *Ed. pri: ca.* 32. an to dereine the warrantie *old. nat. br. f.*146. & to dereine the warrãty paramoũt. *an.*31. *H.*8.*c. primo*. And *dereigner le Warranty in Plowd. caſu Baſſet in fine.* 2.*partis fo.* 6. 7. & 8.*a.* hath the ſame ſignification. So it is vſed, *Weſtm.* 2. *cap.* 5. *anno.* 13. *Ed.* 1. in theſe words: And when the perſon of any Church is diſturbed to demaund tithes in the next pariſh, by a writ of (*Indicauit*) the patron of the Parſon ſo diſturbed to demaund tithes, ſhall haue a writ, to demaund the Advowſen of the tithes being in Demaund: and when it is deraigned, then ſhall the plee paſſe in the court chriſtian, as farre forth as it is deraigned in the kings court. *Bracton* alſo, *li.*3.*tracta.*2.*cap.* 3. *nu.* 1. ſpeaking of him that appealeth another for any treaſon or felonie, hath theſe words. *Proponat accuſans appellum ſuum in hunc modum, ſc: debet dicere ſe interfuiſſe, & vidiſſe certo loco, certo die, certa hora, & ſciviſſe ipſum accuſatum prælocutum fuiſſe mortem regis, vel ſeditionem ſuam, vel exercitus ſui, vel conſenſiſſe, vel auxilium & conſilium impendiſſe, vel ad hoc authoritatem præſtitiſſe: & hoc ego iuxta conſiderationem curiæ diſrationare paratus ſum.* He vſeth it likewiſe as the *Normans* vſe (*Deraiſniam*) for him, that offereth to iuſtifie his deniall: as *lib.* 3. *tracta.* 2.*cap.* 28. *nu.* 1. in theſe words. *Rex conſilio epiſcorum & bonorum miſit propter comitem, vt ſtatuto die veniret ad curiam, ad diſrationandum vel defendendum* *se, si posset.* Lastly, in some places I find the substantiue (*deremement*) vsed in the very literall signification of the french (*Disrayer*) or (*desranger*) that is, as a man wold say, turning out of course, displacing or setting out of order: as *dereinement* or departure out of religion. *anno* 31. *H.* 8. *cap.*6. and dereinment or discharge of their profession. *anno* 33. *H.*8. *cap.* 29. which is spoken of those religious men, that forsooke their orders and professions: as also *anno* 5. & 6. *Ed.* 6. *cap.* 13. Soe doth *Kitchin* vse the verb *fo.*152. in these words: the leassee entreth into religion, and afterward is deraigned. And *Britton* vseth these words (*Semounse desrenable*) for a summons that may be chalenged as defectiue or not lawfully made, *cap.* 21. Of this you may reade something more in *Skene de verb. signif. verbo Disrationare*, where in one signification he confoundeth it with our waging and making of lawe.

De son tort demesne, seeme to be certaine words of forme in an action of trespasse, vsed by way of reply to the plee of the *Defendant*. For example: *A.* sieweth *B.* in action of trespasse, *B.* answereth for himselfe, that he did that which *A* calleth a trespasse, by the commaundement of *C.* his maister. *A* saith againe, that B. did it *de son tort demesne, sans ceo que. C. luy commaunda modo & forma*, that is: *B.* did it of his owne wrong, without that that *C.* commaunded him in such forme, &c.

Detinet. See *Debito* and *Debet.*

Detynew (*detinendo*) is a writ that lyeth against him, who hauing goods or chatels deliuered him to keepe, refuseth to deliuer them againe. See of this *Fitzh. nat. br. fol.* 138. To this is answerable in some sort (*actio depositi*) in the ciuile lawe. And hee taketh his action of ditinew, that intendeth to recouer the thing deliuered, and not the dammages sustained by the detinew. *Kitchin fol.* 176. See the new booke of Entries. *verbo, Detinew.*

Devastaverunt bona testatoris, is a writ lying against executors, for paying Legacies and debts without specialties, to the preiudice of the creditours that haue specialties, before the debt vpon the said specialties be due. For in this case, the executers are as lyable to action, as if they had wasted the goods of the testatour riotously or without cause. New termes of lawe.

Devest (*devestire*) is contrarie to Invest. For as *Investire* significth *possessionem tradere.* So (*devestire*) is (*possessionem auferre*) *feud. lib.*

libro primo cap. 7.

Deviſe, aliàs, diviſe commeth of the French (*deviſer*, i. *diſpertiri, diſcernere, ſeparare, diſtinguere*) as (*deviſer par ci & par la, diſtribuere.*) This word is properly attributed in our common lawe to him, that bequeathes his goods by his laſt will or teſtament in writing: and the reaſon is, becauſe thoſe that now appertain onely to the *Deviſour*, by this act are diſtributed into many parts. Wherefore I thinke it better written *diviſe* thē *deviſe*, howbeit, it were not abſurd, to deriue this word from the French (*deuiſer*) i. *ſermocinari, fabulari, conſilium conferre*. For in this ſence it agreeth in ſome ſort with the nature of the act of the teſtator, and with the Etymologie of a teſtament ſet downe by *Iuſtinian*, who ſaith, that *teſtamentum* is (*quaſi mentis teſtatio. titulo. de Teſta. ordinan. in Inſtitut.* and *teſtatio mentis* cannot be ſo well, as by talke and conference with our wiſe and skilfull friends.

Devoires of Cales, anno 2. *R.* 2. *Stat.* 1. *cap.* 3. *& anno* 5. *eiuſdem, ſtat.* 2. *cap.* 2. were the cuſtomes due to the king for merchandize brought to or caried out from *Caleis*, when our Staple was there. The word is French, ſignifying as much as (*officium*) dutie.

Devorce, aliàs, divorce (*divortium*) is with our common Lawyers, accompted that ſeparation betweene two *de facto* maried together, which is *à vinculo matrimonii, non ſolùm à menſa & thoro.* And therefore the woman ſo divorced, receiueth al againe that ſhee brought with her. This is not, but onely vpon a nullitie of the mariage through ſome eſſentiall impediment, as conſanguinitie or affinity within the degrees forbidden, precontract, impotencie, or ſuch like. See the new Tearmes of lawe.

Diem clauſit extremum, is a writ that lyeth for the heyre of him that holdeth land of the Crowne, either by Knights ſeruice or in ſoccage, and dyeth, be he vnder or at full age, directed to the eſcheatour of the county for inquirie to bee made by him, of what eſtate the partie deceaſed was ſeiſed, and who is next heyre vnto him, and of what valew the land is. The forme thereof and other circumſtances, you may learne in *Fitzh. nat. br. fol.* 251.

Dyer, was a learned Lawyer, and Lord chiefe Iuſtice of the Common plees, in the dayes of Queene *Elizabeth*: who writ a booke of great accompt, called his Commentaries or Reports.

Dies datus, is a reſpight giuen to the tenent [illegible]fendant before the court. *Brooke titulo. Continuance.*

Dicker of lether, is a quantitie consisting of tenne hides. The name may seeme to come from the Greeke (*decas*) which is also a Latine word signifying tenne in number.

Dignitie ecclesiasticall (dignitas ecclesiastica) is mentioned in the statute *anno* 26. *H*. 8. *cap*. 3. and is by the Canonists defined to be (*administratio cum iurisdictione & potestate aliqua coniuncta. Glos. in cap*. 1. *de consuet. in sexto.*) whereof you may reade diuers examples in *Duarenus de sacris eccles. minist. & benefic. lib*. 2. *cap*. 6.

Doces (*diœcesis*) is a Greeke word compounded of (*διὰ*) and (*οἴκησις,*) and signifieth with vs, the circuit of euery Bishops iurisdiction. For this realme hath two sorts of diuisions, one into Shyres or Counties, in respect of temporall policie, another into Diocesses in respect of iurisdictiō ecclesiasticall.

Dieta rationabilis, is in *Bracton* vsed for a reasonable daies iourney. *lib*. 3. *parte*. 2. *chap*. 16. It hath in the ciuile law diuers other significations, not needfull heere to be set downe. *v. vocab: vtriusque iuris.*

Dimy haque. See *Haque*.

Disalt, signifieth as much as to disable. *Litleton* in his chapter of *Discontinuance*.

Disceite, See *deceite* and *deceptione*. See the new booke of Entry, *verbo Disceit.*

Discent, (*Discensus*) in the french (*Descente*) signifieth in the common law, an order or means whereby lands or tenements are deriued vnto any man from his auncestours: as to make his discent from his Auncestours. *Old nat. br. fol.* 101. is to shew how, and by what degrees, the land in question cam to him from his auncestours: as first from his great grandfather to his grandfather, from his grandfather to his father, and so to him. Or in such other like sort: This discent is either lineall or collaterall. *Lineall* discent is conueied downeward in a right line from the Grandfather, to the father, and from the father to the sonne, and from the sonne to the Nephew, &c. Collaterall discent is springing out of the side of the whole blood: as Grandfathers brother, fathers brother, &c. See the new Tearmes of law.

Disclamer, (*Disclamium*) is a plee containing an expresse deniall or refusall: as if the tenent sew a replevin vpon a distresse taken by the lord, and the lord avow the taking of the distresse, saying that he houldeth of him as of his Lord, and that he distreined for rent not paid, or seruice not perfourmed: then the

tenent

tenent denying himselfe to hould of such *Lord*, is said to disclaime: and the Lord prouing the tenent to hould of him, the tenant leeseth his land. Tearmes of law. Of this see *Skene de verb: signif: verbo Disclamation.* Also if a man deny himselfe to be of the blood or kindred of another in his plee, he is said to disclaime his blood: *Fitzh: nat: br: fol,* 197. *G.* See *Brooke, titulo Disclai mer* If a man arraigned of felonie do disclaime goods, being cleared he leeseth them. *Stamnf. pl. cor. fol.* 186. See the new booke of *Entries. verbo, Disclamer.*

Discontinuance, (*Discontinuatio*) commeth of the french (*Discontinuer*).i. *cessare, intermittere*) and signifieth in the common law, nothing els but an interruption or breaking of: as discontinuance of possession, or discontinuance of proces. And the large discourse that *Litleton* hath about this (*Discontinuance*) is rather to shew cases wherein it is, or wherein it is not, then to define the thing. The effect of discontinuance of possession is this, that a man may not enter vpon his owne land or tenement alienated, whatsoeuer his right be vnto it, of his owne selfe, or by his owne authority, but must bring his writ, and seeke to recouer possession by law. Examples you may haue store in his Terms of law, *verbo Discontinuance.* And in *Litleton eodem capite,* with whom agreeth another in these words: But discontinuance of possession is indeed an impediment to a man for entring into his owne land or tenements, caused by the fact of one, that alienated them contrary to right, and gaue Liuery and seisin of them, whereby the true owner is left only to his action. See the new tearmes of law, and the Institutes of the Common Law. *ca:* 43. & see *S. Ed. Cokes* reportes. *l.* 3. the case of *Fines. fo.* 85. *b.* The effect of discontinuance of plee is, that the instance is fallen, and may not be taken vp again, but a by new writ to begin the suite a fresh. For to be discontinued, and to be put without day, is all one; and nothing els, but finally to be dismissed the court of that instance. *West. parte* 2. *Simbol: titulo. Fines. sect:* 115. So *Crompton* in his diuers Jurisdictions, *fol:* 131. vseth it in these words: If a Iustice seate be discontinued by the not comming of the Iustices, the king may renew the same by his writ, &c. In this signification *Fitzh:* in his *nat. br.* vseth the word diuers times: as discontinuance of a corody, *f.*193.*A.* To discontinew the right of his wife. *fol.* 191. *L.* &. 193. *L.* *Discontinuance* of an assise, *fol.* 182. D. 187. *B.*

Disgrading, (*Degradatio*) is the punishment of a Clerk, that being deliuered to his Ordinary, cannot purge himselfe of the offience, whereof he was conuicted by the Iury: and is nothing but the depriuation of him from those orders of Clerkship that he had, as Preisthood, Deaconship. &c. *Stawnf. pl: cor: fol.* 130. & 138. There is likewise disgrading of a knight. *Stowes Annals. pag.* 865. And it is not to be omitted, that by the Canon law, there be two sorts of disgrading: one summary by word onely, and another solemne by deuesting the party degraded of those ornaments and rites, which be the ensignes of his order or degree.

Dismes (*Decimæ*) is made of the french (*Decimes*) and signifieth tithe or the tenth part of all the fruites, either of the earth, or beastes, or our labour, dew vnto God, and so consequently to him that is of the Lords lot, and hath his share: *viz.* our pastour. It signifieth allso the tenthes of all spirituall liuings, yearly giuen to the Prince (called a perpetuall *Disme. anno.* 2. & 3. *Ed.* 6. *ca.* 35) which in auncient times, were paid to the Pope, vntill Pope *Vrbane* gaue them *to Richard* the second, to aide him against *Charls* the french king, and those other that vpheld *Clement* the seuenth against him. *Polidor Virgil. Angl. hist: lib.* 20. Lastly it signifieth a tribute leuied of the Temporalty. *Holinshed. in Henry.* 2. *fol.* 111.

Disparidgment, *Disparagatio*, is by our common lawyers, vsed especially for matching an heire in mariage vnder his or her degree. or against decencie. See my *Institutes. titulo de nuptiis*. §. 6.

Disseisin (*Disseisina*) commeth of the french (*Desseisir*) and signifieth in the common lawe, an vnlawfull dispossessing of a man of his land, tenemēt or other immoueable or incorporeall right, *Institut. of the the com. lawe ca.* 15. And how farre this extendeth, See *Bracton, libro quarto, cap. tertio*. And therefore the Assises bee called writs of disseisin, that lie against disseisours in any case. whereof some bee termed little writs of disseisin. being *vicontiel*, that is, sewable before the Shyreeue in the countie court, *old. nat. br. fol.* 109. because they are determined by the Shyreeue without assise. *Register Orginal. fo.* 198. *b.* as for Nuissances of no great preiudice. *Disseisin* is of two sorts; either simple disseisin, committed by day without force and armes. *Bracton. li.* 4. *ca.* 4. *Britton. ca.* 42. & 43. & 44. where you shall finde in what especially it is lawfull, in what not *Britton. ca.* 53. And *Disseisin* by force

force, for the which see *Deforsour*. See *fresh Disseisin*. See *Redisseisin*, and *Postdisseisin*. See *Skene de verbo. significat. verbo Dissaisina. Disseisin* how many waies it is committed. *See Fleta.li. 4. ca.* 1. §. *Fit autem,&c.* & when it is lawfull. *ca.* 2.

Distresse (*Districtio, Districtus*) cometh of the French (*Distresse, angustiæ*) It signifieth most commonly in the common law, a compulsion in certaine reall actions, whereby to bring a man to appearance in courte, or to pay debt or dutie denied. The effect whereof most commonly is, to driue the party distreined to replevie the distresse, and so to take his action of trespasse against the distreiner, or els to compound neighbourly with him for the debt or dutie, for the which he distreineth. In what cases a distresse is lawfull, see *the newe termes of lawe*. The Civilians call it (*pignorum captionem*) *Brissonius de verbo. significa. lib.* 14. This compulsion is by *Britton. ca.* 71. diuided into a distresse personall and distresse reall: distresse personall, is made by surprising a mans moueable goods, and deteining them for the securitie of his appearance to the suite, and to make him plantiffe. A distresse reall, is made vpon immoveable goods, as the *Grand Cape & Petit Cape*. And thus it is interpreted by *Hotoman de verb. feudal: verbo Districtus.* This differeth from an attachement in this point (among others) that a distresse cannot bee taken by any common person, without the compasse of his owne fee. *Fitzh. nat. br. fol.* 904. except it bee presently after the catell or other thing is driuen or borne out of the ground by him that perceiueth it to bee in danger to be distreined. *New termes of the lawe. verbo distresse.*

Districtus, is sometime vsed for the circuit or territorie within the which a man may be thus compelled to apperance. *Cane Romani. de electione in Clem:* and *Cassan. de consuetud: Burgund. pa.* 90. *Britton. ca.* 120. and so likewise is *Districtio* in the Register originall. *fol.* 6. *b.* And so it seemeth to bee vsed in *pupilla oculi: parte.* 5. *c.* 22. *Charta de foresta.* See also *Mynsing.* in the chapter. *licet causam.* 9. *extra de probationibus. nu.* 5. & *Zasius* in his 16. *councell. nu.* 47. Distresse, in the former signification, is diuided first into finite and infinite. Finite is that which is limited by lawe, how often it shall be made to bring the partie to triall of the action, as once, twice. *Old. nat. br. fo.* 43. Distresse infinite is without limitation vntill the partie come: as against a Iurie that refuseth to appeare *super certificatione Assisæ*, the

the processe is a (*venire facias*) (*habeas corpora*) and distresse infinite. *Old.nat.br.fol.* 113. Then it is diuided into a graund distresse. *anno.* 52. *H.* 3. *ca.* 7. which *Fitzherbert* calleth in latine *magnam districtionem, nat. br. fol.* 126. *A.* and an ordinarie distresse. A graund distresse is that, which is made of all the goods and catels, that the partie hath within the Countie. *Britton. ca.* 26. *fol.* 52. but see whether it be sometime not all one with a distresse infinite. *Idem. fol.* 80. with whom also the Statute of *Marlbridge* seemeth to agree. *anno* 52. *H.* 3. *ca.* 7. & *ca.* 9. & *ca.* 12. See *old.nat. breu. fol.* 71. *b.* See grand distresse, what things bee distreinable, and for what causes. See the newe *Termes of lawe. verbo* *Distresse*. Of this also see more in *Attachment*.

Distringas, is a writ directed to the Shyreeue, or any other of-officer, commanding him to distreine one for a debt o the king, &c. or for his appearance at a day. See great diuersitie of this writ in the table of the Register iudicial, *verbo Distringas*.

Deuise. See *Deuise*.

Diuidends in the Exchequer, seemeth to be one part of an Indenture. *anno* 10. *Ed.* 1. *ca.* 11. & *anno* 28. *eiusdem. Stat.* 3. *ca.* 2.

Dyuorce. See. *euorce*.

Docket, is a brife in writing. *anno.* 2. & 3. *Ph.* & *Mar. ca.* 6. *West* writeth it (*Dogget*) by whome it seemeth to be some small peece of paper or parchement, conteining the effect of a larger writing. *Symbol. parte.* 2. *titulo Fines. sect.* 106.

Doctor and Student, is a booke conteining certaine dialogues, betweene a *D.* of *Diuinitie*, and a Student at the common Law, wherein are conteined questions and cases, as well of the equitie and conscience vsed in the common *Lawe*, as also a comparison of the Civile, Canon, and common lawe together, very worthy the reading. The author is said by *D. Cosin* in his Apologie, to bee a gentleman, called *Saint German*, The booke was writen in the daies of *H.* 8.

To do lawe (*facere legem*) is as much as to make lawe. 23. *H.* 6. *ca.* 14. See. *Make*.

Dogge drawe, is a manifest deprehension of an offender against venison in the forest. There bee foure of these noted by *M. Manhood. parte.* 2. of his forest lawes. *ca.* 18. *nu.* 9. *viz. Stablestand Dogge drawe*, *Back beare*, and *Bloodie hand*. Dogge drawe, is when one is found drawing after a deere, by the sent of a hound, that he leadeth in his hand.

Dogger, a kinde of shippe. *an.* 31. *Ed.* 3. *Stat.* 3. *ca. pri.*

Doggerfish, *ibid. c.* 2. seemeth to

bee

bee fish brought in those ships to *Blackeney hauen, &c.* Dogger men. *anno 2.H.8.ca.4.*

Dogget, See Docket.

Domo reparanda, is a writ that lyeth for one against his neighbour, by the fall of whose house he feareth hurt toward his owne house. *Register originall. fol.* 153. for this point. The ciuilians haue the action *de damno infecto.*

Dole fishe, seemeth to be that fish, which the fisher men, yerely imployed in the north sease, doe of custome receiue for their allowance, See the statute. *a.* 35. *H.* 8. *ca.* 7.

Donatyue, is a benefice meerely giuen and collated by the Patron to a man, without either presentation to the Ordinary, or Institution by the ordinarie or Induction by his commandement. *Fitzh.nat.br.fol.*35.*E.* See the statute, *anno* 8.*R.*2.*cap.* 4. Of this *Petr.Gregor. de beneficiis cap.* 11.*nu.*10. hath these words: *Si tamen Capellaniæ fundatæ per Laicos non fuerint à Diœcesano approbatæ, & vt (loquuntur) spiritualizatæ, non censentur beneficia, nec ab Episcopo conferri possunt, sed sunt sub pia dispositione fundatoris. Ioh. Faber ad* §. *Nullius. De rerum diuis: Ideo fundatores & heredes eorum, possunt tales Capellanias donare sine Episcopo, cui voluerint, tanquam profana beneficia. Guido Papæus decis.* 187. See also *Gregorius. lib.*15.*ca.* 29. *sui syntagmatis. nu.* 11. I finde in the preface of *M. Gwins* readings, that as the king might of auncient times found a free Chapell, and exempt it from the iurisdiction of the Diocesan: so hee might also by his leters patents licence a common person, to found such a chapell, and to ordeine, that it shalbe donatiue & not presentable, and that the Chaplaine shall be depriueable by the founder and his heires, and not by the Bishop. And this is likest to bee the originall of these *Donatiues in England. Fitzh.* saith, that there be certaine Chauntries, which a man may giue by his leters patents. *nat. br. fol.* 33.*C.* See him also, *fol.* 42. B. All *Bishopricks* were donatiue by the king, *Coke. li.* 3 *fo.* 75.*b.*

Doomes day, (Rotulus Wintoniæ) (domus Dei. Coke in Præfatione ad librum suum) is a booke that was made in king *Ed.* the Confessors dayes, as the author of the *old. nat. br.* saith, *f.* 15. containing in it not onely all the lands through *England,* but also all the names of those, in whose hands they were at that time when the book was made. *M. Lamberd* in his explication of Saxon wordes *(verbo, Ius Dacorũ, &c.)* proueth out of *Geruasius Tilburiensis,* that this booke was made in *William* the Conquerors time: with whome agreeth *M. Camden* in his

his *Britan. pag.* 94. prouing it out of *Ingulphus*, that flourished the same time. And for the beter commendation of the booke, it is not amisse to set downe the words of *Ingulphus*, touching the contents thereof. *Totam terram descripsit. Nec erat hyda in tota Anglia, quin valorem eius & possessorem scivit, nec lacus nec locus aliquis, quin in Regis rotulo extitit descriptus, ac eius reditus & proventus, ipsa possessio, & eius possessor regiæ notitiæ manifestatus, iuxta taxatorum fidem qui electi de qualibet patria territorium proprium describebant. Iste rotulus vocatus est Rotulus Wintoniæ, & ab Anglis pro sua generalitate, quòd omnia tenementa totius terræ continuit (Domesday) cognominatur.* So it is called in the Statute *anno pri. Ric.* 2.*cap.*6. And in *Ockhams lucubrations de fisci Regii ratione*, which seemeth to be taken out of the Booke called (*Liber rubeus*) in the Exchequer. It is termed (*liber Iudicatorius*) and the reason why, *quia in eo totius Regni descriptio diligens continetur: & tam de tempore Regis Edwardi, quàm de tempore Regis Willhelmi, sub quo factus est, singulorum fundorum valentia exprimitur.*

Dorture (*Dormitorium*) *anno.* 25. *H.*8.*ca.*11. is the common roome, place or chamber, where all the friers of one couent slept, and lay all night.

Dote assignanda, is a writ that lieth for a widowe, where it is found by office, that the kings tenent was seised of tenements in fee, or fee taile, at the day of his death, &c. and that hee holdeth of the king in cheife, &c. For in this case the widowe commeth into the Chauncerie, and there maketh oath, that shee will not mary without the kings leaue. *Anno* 15.*Ed.*3. *ca.*4. and herevpon shee shall haue this writte to the Escheatour, for which see the Register originall *fol.*297. and *Fitzh. nat. br. f.*263. And this sort of widowes is called the kings widowe. See *Widowe*.

Dote vnde nihil habet, is a writ of dower, that lyeth for the widow against the tenent, which hath bought land of her husband in his life time, whereof he was seised solely in fee simple, or fee taile, in such sort as the issue of them both might haue inhereted it. *Fitzh. nat. br. fol.* 147. *Register fol.* 170.

Dotis *admensuratione*, See *Admesurement*. See the *Register. fol.* 171.

Dotkins, a kinde of coine. *pl: cor: fol:* 37. It seemeth to come of the *Dutch* word *Duytken*, that is, the eight part of a *Stufer*, or French *Shilling*, which in latine is called *Solidus Gallicus*.

Doubles. anno 14. *H. 6. cap.* 6. signifie as much as leters patents, being as it seemeth a French word made of the Latine (*diploma.*)

Double plee, (duplex placitum) is that, wherein the defendant alledgeth for himselfe two seuerall maters, in barre of the action, whereof either is sufficient to effect his desire in debarring the plaintiffe. And this is not to be admitted in the common lawe: wherefore it is well to be obserued, when a plee is double, and when it is not. For if a man alledge seuerall maters, the one nothing depending of the other, the plee is accounted double. If they be mutually depending one of the other, then is it accompted but single. *Kitchin fo.* 223. See *Broke hoc titulo.* But why this doublenes (for so *Kitchin* calleth it, *fol.* 234.) should bee debarred, I see no reason (vnder correction all things being spoken.) For a man may haue two good defences: and happily in the issue he shall contrarily to his hope faile in prouing the one, and yet be able to carie the cause by the other. And therefore not onely the Civilians, but *Bracton* also saith: *Pluribus exceptionibus uti nemo prohibetur. lib.* 5. *tract.* 5. *cap.* 5. *num.* 4. whom also reade, *libro*, 4. *cap.* 17. And Sir *Thomas Smiths* reason of this scantly satisfieth me, alledging this to be the course of our proceeding, because the triall is by twelue rude men, whose heades are not to be troubled with ouer many things at once. *lib. 2. de Repub. Anglor. cap.* 13.

Double quarell (duplex querela) is a complaint made by any Clerke or other vnto the Archbishop of the Prouince, against an inferiour ordinarie for delaying of iustice in some cause ecclesiasticall: as to giue sentence or to institute a clerke presented, or such like. The effect whereof, is that the said Archbishop taking knowledge of such delay, directeth his leters vnder his authenticall seale, to all and singular clerkes of his Prouince, therby commaunding and authorizing them and euery of them, to admonish the said Ordinarie, within a certaine number of dayes, namely, 9. dayes, to doe the iustice required, or otherwise to cite him to appeare before him or his officiall, at a day in the said leters prefixed, and there to alledge the cause of his delay. And lastly, to intimate to the said Ordinarie, that if he neither performe the thing enioyned, nor appeare at the day assigned, he himselfe will, without farder delay, proceed to perform the iustice required. And this seemeth to be tearmed a double because it is most commonly made against both the Iudge, and him at whose petition iustice is delayed.

Dower *(dos)* commeth of the French *(douaire)* and signifieth in our common lawe, two things: first, that which the wife bringeth to her husband in mariage, otherwise called *maritagiũ*, mariage good: next, and more commonly, that which she hath of her husband, after the mariage determined, if she out-liue him. *Glanvile. lib.* 7. *cap.* 1. *Bracton. lib.* 2. *cap.* 38. *Britton. cap.* 101. *in princ.* And in *Scotland, (dos)* signifieth iust as much. *Skene de verb. signif. verbo. Dos.* The former is in French called *(dot)* the other *douayre*, and by them latined *doarium.* I likewise once thought it not vnreasonable, to call the former a *Dowrie*, & the other a *Dower*: but I find them confounded. For exãple: *Smith de rep. Anglo. p.* 105. calleth the later a *dowrie*, and *dower* is sometime vsed for the former: as in *Britton vbi supra.* yet were it not inconuenient to distinguish them being so diuers. The Ciuilians call the former *(dotem)* and the later *(donationem propter nuptias.)* Of the former the common law bookes speake very litle. This onely is to be noted, that whereas by the ciuile lawe, instruments are made before mariage, which containe the quantitie of the wiues dowrie, or substance brought to her husband, that he hauing the vse of it, during mariage, may, after certaine deductions, restore it againe to his wiues heires or friends, after the mariage dissolued: the common lawe of *England*, whatsoeuer chatels moueable or immoueable, or readie money she bringeth, doth make them foorthwith her husbands owne, to be disposed of, as he will, leauing her at his courtesie, to bestow any thing or nothing of her at his death. The reason whereof is said to be, the holding of the wife in obedience to her husband. Onely if she be an inheretrice, her husband holdeth the land but during her life, except he haue issue by her: but then he holdeth it by the courtesie of *England* during his owne life. *See Courtesie.* And againe, if he haue any land in fee, wherof he was possessed during the mariage, she is to haue a third therof during her life, though she bring nothing to him, except she doe by fine release her right, during the mariage. So that here is no great mater to bee spoken of, but touching *dower* in the later signification. You must know therfore, that vpon speech of mariage betweene two, the parents of both sides are commonly more carefull in prouiding each for his childe, then the parties themselues: and that by their meanes there bee diuers bargaines made, sometime for the conueiance of lands, &c. to them and their issue: and this is said to be giuen in franke mariage: sometime to her during her life, and that before, or at the mariage: if before mariage, then it is called a Ioynture. For a Ioynture is a couenant, whereby the husband, or some for him is tyed (*ratione iunctura*) in consideration of the mariage, that the wife suruiuing him, shall haue during her life, this or that tenement or lands, or thus much rent yearely payable out of such land, &c. with clause of distresse: and this may be more or lesse, as they doe accord. *Britton, cap.* 101. whome read also *ca.* 102. 103. 104. for *conventio vincit legem. Bracton. lib.* 5. *tract.* 4. *cap.* 9. The diuersitie of these Ioyntures, you may see in *West. parte prima symbol. lib.* 2. *sect.* 128. 129. 130. 131. 132. 133. But if none of these former bargaines passe before mariage, then must the wife stick to her Dower: and that is sometime giuen at the Church doore or the Chappell doore, if the mariage bee by licence, but not the chamber doore; and may bee what the husband will: so it exceede not a third part of his lands. *Glanvile libro.* 6. *cap. pri.* Or the halfe, as some say. *Fitzh. nat. br. fol.* 150. *N. P.* And this Dower is either certainly set downe and named, or not named but onely in generalitie, as the law requireth: if it be not named, then is it by lawe, the third part, and called (*dos ligitima*) *Bracton. lib.* 4. *tracta.* 6. *cap.* 6. *nu.* 6. & 10. *Magna. Charta. c.* 7. or the halfe by the custome of some countries, as in *Gavelkinde. Fitzh. nat. br. fol.* 150. O. And though it bee named, it seemeth that it cannot bee aboue halfe the lands of the husband. *Fitzh. nat. br. fol.* 150. *P.* And the woman that will chalenge this dower, must make 3. things good, *viz.* that shee was maried to her husband, that he was in his life time seised of the land, whereof shee demaundeth dower, and that he is dead. *Cokes reportes li.* 2. *Binghams case. fo.* 93. *a.* Of these things see *Glanvile. li.* 6. *cap.* 1. 2. & 3. *Bracton lib.* 2. *ca.* 38. 39. & *lib.* 4. *tracta.* 6. *cap.* 1. & 6. and *Britton cap.* 101. 102. 103. 104. and *Fitzherb. natur. brev. fol.* 147. 148. 149. & 150. And this custumary dower, seemeth to be obserued in other nations, as well as in ours. *Hotoman verbo* Dotalitium *in verbis feudal: Cassan. de consuetud. Burg. pag.* 580. 676. 677. & *de conventionali. p.* 720. And to these ioyne the graund Custumarie of *Normandie*, *cap*. 102. where you shall perceiue, that in a maner all our lawe in this point is taken from the *Normans:* See *Endowment*. Of dower reade *Fleta* likewise, who writeth largely thereof, and hath many things worth the learning. *li*. 5. *ca*. 22 *& seqq*.

Dozenne. See *Decennier*.

Drags. *ano*. 6. *H*. 6. *ca*. 5. seeme to be wood or timber so ioyned together, as swimming or floting vpon the water, they may beare a burden or load of other wares downe the river.

Drawe latches. *anno*. 5. *Ed*. 3. *ca*. 14. *& anno*. 7. *Rich*. 2. *ca*. 5. *Master Lamberd*, in his *Eirenarch lib:* 2. *ca*. 6. calleth them miching theeues, as Wasters and *Roberdsemen* mighty theeues, saying that the words be growne out of vse.

Dreit Dreit, signifieth a double right, that is *ius possessionis*, *& ius Domini*. *Bracton*. *lib:* 4. *cap*. 27. *& lib*. 4. *tracta*. 4. *cap:* 4. *& lib*. 5. *tracta*. 3. *cap*. 5.

Drye exchaunge. *an*. 3. *H*. 7. *ca*. 5. (*Cambium siccum*) seemeth to be a clenly terme inuented for the disguising of foule vsury, in the which some thing is pretended to passe of both sides, wheras in truth, nothing passeth but on the one side: in which respect it may well be called drie. Of this *Ludouicus Lopes tractat: de contract: & negotiatio*. *lib:* 2. *ca*. *pri*. §. *Deinde postquam*. writeth thus: *Cambium est reale vel siccum*. *Cambium reale dicitur, quod consistentiam veri Cambii realem habet, & Cambium per trans, & Cambium minutum*. *Cambium autē siccum est Cambium non habens existentiam Cambii, sed apparentiam ad instar arboris exsiccatæ, quæ humore vitali iam carens apparentiam arboris habet, non existentiam*. *Summa Sylv: Verbo Vsura*. *quæst:* 6. *Est ergo Cambium siccum iuxta hanc acceptionem (in qua etiam accipitur in Extrau*. *Pii quinti) idem quod Cambium fictū*. *Non autē habet propriam naturam Cambii, sed mutui & vsuræ*. *At verò secundum Laurentium de Nauarra in Cōmento de vsuris & Cambiis citatam, Cambium siccum in alia acceptione minùs communi sumptum est Cambium, in quo Campsor prius dat quam accipiat*. *Dicitur autem isto modo siccum, quia sine præuia acceptione dat Campsor*. *Quod tamen, vt sic acceptum (autore Siluestro) licitè celebratur aliquando*. *Quia tunc verum & reale Cambium est differens genere ab eo Cambio, in quo Campsor prius recipit*. *Quia in isto Campsor semper primò dat & deinde accipit*.

Drift of the Forest, seemeth to be nothing but an exact view or examination, what catell are in the forest: that it may be known. whether it be ouercharged or not, and whose the beastes be. This drift, when, how often in the yeare, by whome, and in what maner it is to be made, see *Manwood parte. 2.* of his forest lawes. *cap: 15.*

Droit d' Advowzen. See *Recto de aduocatione Ecclesiæ.*

Droit close. See. *Recto clausum.*

Droit de dower. See *Recto dotis.*

Droit sur Disclaimer. See *Recto sur disclaimer.*

Droit patent. See *Recto patens.*

Duces *tecum,* is a writ commaunding one to appeare at a day in the chauncery, and to bring with him some peece of euidence, or other thing, that the court would view. See the new booke of Entries, *verb.* Duces *tecum.*

Duke (Dux) commeth of the french *(Duc)* It signifieth in auncient times among the Romaines *Ductorem exercitus)* such as led their armies, who if by their prowes they obteined any famous victory, they were by their souldiers saluted *(Imperatores) as Hotoman verbo Dux, de verbis feudal:* proueth out of *Lyvy, Tully*, and others. Sithence that they were called *(Duces)* to whome the king or people committed the custodie or regiment of any prouince. *Idem. eod.* And this seemeth to proceede from the *Lombards or Germans*, *Sigon de regno Ital. l. 4.* In some natiōs at this day, the Soveraignes of the country, are called by this name, as *Duke of Russia, Duke of Swethen.* Heere in England, *Duke* is the next in seculer dignitie to the Prince of Wales. And as *(M. Camden* saith) heretofore in the *Saxons* times, they were called *Dukes*, without any addition, being but meere officers, and leaders of armies. After the Conquerour came in, there were none of this title vntil *Edward* the thirds daies, who, made *Edward* his son *Duke of Cornwayle.* After that there were more made, and in such sort, that their titles descended by inheritance to their posteritie. They were created with solemnitie *(per cincturam gladii, cappæq; & circuli aurei in capite impositionem, vide Camd. Britan. pa. 166 Zasium de feudis parte. 4. nu. 7. & Cassan. de consuetud. Burg pag. 6. & 10. and Ferns glory of generosity. pag. 139.*

Dutchy court, is a court, wherein all maters appertaining to the *Dutchy* of *Lancaster*, are descided the decree of the Chauncelour of that Court. And the originall of it was in *Henry* the fourthes daies, who obtaining the crown, by deposing *Richard* the second, and hauing the *Dutchy* of *Lancaster* by discent in the right of his mother, he was seised thereof as king, and not as *Duke.* So that all the liberties, fraunchises, and

Iurisdictions of the said *Dutchy* passed from the king by his graund seale, and not by liverie, or attournment: as the possessions of *Everwicke*, and of the *Earldome* of *March*, and such others did, which had descended to the king, by other Auncesters then kings. But at the last, *Henry* the 4. by authoritie of *Parlament* passed a charter, whereby the possessions, liberties, &c. of the said *Dutchy* were seuered from the Crowne: Yet *Henry* the 7. reduced it to his former nature, as it was in *Henry* the fifts daies. *Crompton Iurisdict. fol.* 136. The officers belonging to this Court are the Chauncellour, the Atturney, Receiuer generall, Clerke of the court, the Messenger. Beside these, there be certain Assistantes of this Court: as one Atturney in the Exchequer: one Atturney of the Dutchy in the Chauncery, foure learned men in the lawe, reteined of councell with the King in the said court. Of this Court *M. Gwin.* in the prefase to his readings thus speaketh: The court of the Duchy (or Countie Palatine of Lancaster) grew out of the graunt of king *Edward* the third, who first gaue the Dutchy to his sonne *Iohn of Gawnte*, and endowed it with such royall right, as the Countie Palatine of Chester had: and for as much, as it was afterward extinct in the person of king *Henry* the fourth, by reason of the vnion of it with the Crowne: the same king suspecting himselfe to bee more rightfully *Duke of Lancaster*, then king of England, determined to saue his right in the *Dutchy*, whatsoeuer should befal of the Kingdome: and therefore hee separated the *Dutchy* from the Crowne, and setled it so in the naturall persons of himselfe and his heires, as if he had bin no king or Politique bodie at all: In which plight it continued, during the reigne of *K. Henry* the 5. and *Henry* the 6. that were descended of him. But when *King Edw.* the 4. had (by recouery of the Crowne) recontinued the right of the house of *Yorke*, hee feared not to appropriate that *Dutchy* to the Crowne againe: and yet so, that hee suffered the Court and Officers to remaine as he founde them. And in this maner, it came together with the Crowne, to *King Henry* the 7. who liking well of that policy of *King* H. the 4. (by whose right also hee obteined the *Kingdome*) made like separation of the *Dutchy*, as hee had done, and so left it to his posterity which doe yet inioy it.

Dum fuit infra aetatem, is a writ which lyeth for him, that before hee came to his full age, made a fea feofment of his land in fee, or for terme of life, or in taile, to recover them againe from him, to whome he conveied them. *Fitzh. nat.br.fol.* 192.

Dum non fuit compos mentis, is a writ that lieth for him, that being not of sound memory, did alien any lands or tenements in fee simple, fee tayle, for terme of life, or of yeeres, against the alienee. *Fitzh.nat.br.fol.* 202.

Duplicat, is vsed by *Crompton*, for a second leters patent grãted by the Lord Chauncelour, in a case, wherein he had formerly done the same: and was therefore thought void. *Cromptons Iurisd.fol.* 215.

Dures (*Duritia*) commeth of the French (*dur*.i.*durus*, *vel durete*. i.*duritus*) and is in our common lawe, a plee vsed in way of exception, by him that being cast in prison at a mans suite, or otherwise by beating or threats hardly vsed, sealeth any bond vnto him during his restraint. For the lawe holdeth this not good, but rather supposeth it to be constrained. *Brooke* in his *Abridgement* ioyneth *Dures* and *Manasse* together. i. *duritiam & minas*, hardnes and threatning. See the newe booke of Entries, *verbo Dures*: and the *new Termes of law*.

E A

E*Alderman* (*Aldermannus*) among the *Saxons*, was as much as Earle among the *Danes*. *Camden*. *Britan.pag*. 107. If yee goe to the true etimologie of the word, mee thinketh, it shoud sound more generally, so much as πρεσβυς with the *Græcians*, or *Senator* with the Romanes: who were rather Councellers at large, then bestowed vpon any particular office, as *Comites* were. See *Countie*. And that signification we retaine at this day almost in all our Cities, and Borowes, calling those Aldermen, that are Associates to the Chiefe Officer in the common councell of the Towne. *anno* 24. *H*. 8. *ca*. 13. or sometime the cheife officer himselfe, as in *Stawnford*.

Earle (*Comes*) *in M. Camdens* opinion. *pag*. 107. is a word made by the *Danes* of (*Ealderman*) a word of the *Saxons*. *M. Lamberd* seemeth notwithstanding to acknowledge, that *Earle* is originally a Saxon word. *Explica. of Sax. words. verbo Paganus*: and interpreteth it (*Satrapam*) which word the Romaines borowing of the Persians, applied to those that were *præfecti provinciarum*. *M. Verstegan in his restitution of decaied intelligence*, deriueth it from two *Netherland words* (*ear*. i.*honor*) and (*ethel* i.*nobilis*) where-in I leaue the reader to his owne iudgement. This title in auncient time, was giuen to those, that were associates to the king in his coun-

councels and Marshall actions (as *Comes* was to those that folowed the Magistrates in *Roome*, and executed their offices for them as their deputies, and died alwaies with the man. *Zasius* hath of this word thus much. *Comitũ originem in Doctoribus non inveniminus: sed noveris eam dignitatem vetustissimam esse. Nam Cor. Tacitus in libello de Germania scribit apud priscos vsu fuisse receptum, vt cuilibet principi seu Duci exercitus duodecim comites assignarentur: ideo dictos, quia comitarentur eos, & à Ducum latere non decederent. Comitũ itaq; originẽ Germanis moribus ortum esse, dictus receptissimus autor testis est. Quapropter quod in duodecimo libro Codicis aliqui tituli de Comitibus largitionum &c. inscribuntur, usurpationem Imperatoris ex Germanorum ritibus sumptam credo.* But the Conquerour (as *M. Camd.* saith) gaue this dignitie in fee to his nobles, annexing it to this or that countie or province, and allotted them, for their maintenance, a certaine proportion of monie rising from the Princes profits, for the pleadings and forfeitures of the province. For example, he bringeth an auncent Record in these words. *Henricus 2. Rex Angliæ his verbis Comitem creauit: Sciatis nos fecisse Hugonet Bigot Comitẽ de Nortfolk. sc: de tertio denario de Norwic. & Northfolke, sicut aliquis comes Angliæ liberius comitatum suum tenet.* Which words (saith the same author) an ould booke of *Battell Abbie* thus expoundeth: *Consuetudinaliter per totam Angliam mos antiquitùs inoleverat, Comites provinciarum tertium denarium sibi obtinere, inde Comites dicti.* And another booke without name more fully. *Comitatus a Comite dicitur, aut vice versa. Comes autem est, quia tertiam portionem eorum, quæ de placitis proveniunt, in quolibet Comitatu percipit. Sed non omnes Comites ista percipiunt: sed hii quibus Rex hæreditariò aut personaliter concessit.* You may reade *M. Fern in Lacyse* nobility, something to this effect. *pa.* 12. But he saith, that one *Duke* or *Earle* had diuers Shires vnder his gouernment, as a viceroy, and had lieuetenants vnder him in euery particular Shire, called a Shyreeue. That one *Earle* was dignified by the appellation of more then one Shyreeue, it appeareth by diuers of our auncient *Statutes*, as namely by the sentẽce of excommunication pronounced by the Bishops against the infringers of the great Charter, & charter of the forest. *anno.* 38. H.3. *Roger Bigot* is named Earle both of *Northfolke* and *Southfolke*, and *anno* 1. *Ed.* 3. *Thomas* Earle of *Lancaster* and *Leycester*. *Humfrey Bohum*. *Earle of* Hereford

*ford and Essex.Dyer.fo.*285.*nu.*39. At these daies, as long since, the kings of England make Earles by their charters, of this or that Countie, giuing them no authoritie ouer the Countie, nor any part of the profit rising of it, but onely some annuall stipend out of the Exchequer, rather for honours sake, then any great commoditie. And these bee in other nations accompted *Earles* improperly. *Quia illi dicuntur verè Comites, quibus datur Comitatus in feudum: illi Comites abusivè, qui non habent administrationem. Vincentius de Franchis. descis.* 115.*nu.*7. The maner of creating Earles is by girding them with a sword. *Camden.pag.* 107. but see the solemnitie thereof described more at large in *Stowes annals.pa.*1121 The occasion why these Earles in later time haue had no swaye ouer the Countie, whereof they beare their name, is not obscurely signified in *Sir Thomas Smith. lib.* 2. *cap.*14. where he saith, that the Shyreeue is called *Vicecomes*, as (*Vicarius Comitis*) following all maters of iustice, as the Earle should do: and that because the Earle is most commonly attendant vpon the king, in his warres or otherwise. So that it seemeth that Earles by reason of their high employments, being not able to follow also the businesse of the countie, were deliuered of all that burthen, and onely enioyed the honour, as now they doe. And the Shyreeue, though he be still called *Vice-comes*, yet all he doth, is immediatly vnder the king, and not vnder the *Earle*. See *Countie*, & see *Hotoman.de verb.feudal.verbo Comes*: and *Cassan.de consuetud.Burg.p*12.

Easement, (*esamentum*) is a seruice that one neighbour hath of another by charter or prescription, without profite, as a way through his ground, a sinke, or such like. *Kitchin. fol.* 105. which in the ciuill lawe is called *Seruitus prædii.*

Eele fares, aliàs, Eele Vare. an. 25. *H.* 8. *cap.*7. be the frie or brood of Eeles.

Egyptians (*Egyptiani*) are in our statutes and lawes of *England*, a counterfeit kinde of roagues, that being English or Welch people, accompany thẽselues together, disguising themselues in straunge roabes, blacking their faces and bodies, and framing to themselues an vnknowne language, wander vp and downe, and vnder pretence of telling of Fortunes, curing diseases, and such like, abuse the ignorant common people, by stealing all that is not too hote or too heauie for their cariage. *anno* 1. *&* 2. *Phi. & M. cap.* 4. *anno* 5. *Eliz. cap.* 20. These are very like to those, whom the Italians call *Cingari*: of whom *Franciscus Leo in suo thesauro fori ecclesiastici parte prim. cap.* 13. thus writeth: *Cingari, qui corrupto vocabulo, quandoque etiam* Saraceni *nominantur, & permissione principũ ac aliorum dominorum, per Italiam vagantur, nec vnquam viderunt partes infidelium, minusq́, legem Mahometi noverunt: sed sunt ferè omnes Itali, & malè habituati, ex rebus furtivis vivunt, ac fraudulentis earum permutationibus & ludis, in quibus vt plurimum fraudes committunt, & sunt baptizati.*

Eiectione custodiæ, Eiectment de gard, is a writ which lyeth properly against him, that casteth out the Gardian from any land, during the minority of the heire. *Register origin. fol.* 162. *Fitz. nat. br. fol.* 139. Tearmes of the law. *verbo. Gard.* There be two other writs not vnlike this: the one is tearmed *Droit de gard*, or right of guard, the other *Rauishment de Gard.* Which see in their places.

Eiectione firmæ, is a writ, which lyeth for the Leassee for terme of yeares, that is cast out before the expiration of his tearme, either by the leassour, or a straunger. *Register fol.* 227. *Fitz. nat. br. fo.* 220. See *Quare eiecit infra terminum.* See the new booke of Entries. *verbo Eiectione firme.*

Einecia, is borowed of the French (*Aisne.* i. *primogenitus*) and signifieth in our common lawe, Eldership. *Statute of Ireland. anno* 14. *Hen.* 3. Of this see *M. Skene de verb. signif. verbo. Eneya.*

Eyre, aliàs, Eyer, (*Iter. Bracton lib.* 3. *cap.* 11. *in Rubrica*) commeth of the old French word (*Erre.* i. *iter*) as (*à grand erre.* i. *magnis itineribus.*) It signifieth in *Britton cap.* 2. the court of *Iustices itinerants*: and *Iustices in Eyre*, are those onely, which *Bracton* in many places calleth (*Iusticiarios itinerantes*) of the *Eyre*, reade *Britton vbi supra*, who expresseth the whole course of it. And *Bracton. lib.* 3. *tractat.* 2. *cap.* 1. & 2. The *Eyre* also of the Forest is nothing, but the Iustice seate otherwise called: which is or should by auncient custome, be held euery three yeare by the Iustices of the forest, iourneying vp and downe to that purpose. *Cromptons Iurisd. fol.* 156. *Mannwood parte prima* of his Forest lawes. *pag.* 121. See *Iustice in Eyre.* Reade *Skene de verborum significa. verbo. Iter*: whereby, as by many other places you may see great affinitie betweene these 2. *Kingdomes* in the administration of Iustice and gouernment.

Election de Clerke (*Electione clerici*) is a writ, that lyeth for the choyce of a clerke, assigned to take and make bonds called *statute Merchant*: and is graunted out of the Chauncerie vpon suggestion

gestion made, that the Clerke formerly assigned, is gone to dwell in another place, or hath hinderance to let him from following that businesse, or hath not land sufficient to answer his transgression, if he should deale amisse, &c. *Fitzh. nat. br. fol.* 164.

Elegit, is a writ Iudiciall, and lyeth for him, that hath recouered debt or dammages in the kings court, against one not able in his goods to satisfie: and directed to the *Shyreeue*, commaunding him that he make deliuery of halfe the parties lands or tenements, and all his goods, oxen and beasts for the plough excepted. *Old nat. br. fol.* 152. *Register originall fol.* 299. *&* 301. and the Table of the Register Iudiciall, which expresseth diuers vses of this writ. The author of the new terms of law saith, that this writ should be siewed within the yeare, whom read at large for the vse of the same.

Elk, a kinde of ewe to make bowes of. *anno* 33. *H* 8. *cap.* 9.

Empanel (*Impanellare, Ponere in assisis & Iuratis*) commeth of the french (*Panne.* 1. *pellis*) or of (*Panneau*) which signifieth some time as much as a pane with vs, as a pane of glasse, or of a windowe. It signifieth the wrighting or entring the names of a Iury into a parchment schedule or Rolle or paper, by the *Shyreeue*, which he hath sommoned to appeare for the perfourmance of such publique seruice, as Iuries are imployed in. See *Panell.*

Emparlance, commeth of the french (*Parler*) and signifieth in our common lawe, a desire or petition in court of a day to pause, what is best to doe. The ciuilians call it (*petitionem induciarũ*) *Kitchin fol.* 200. interpreteth it in these words: If he imparle or pray continuance. For praying continuance is spoken *interpretatiuè* in that place, as I take it. The same author maketh mention of *Emparlance* generall. *fol.* 201. and *Emparlance* speciall *fol.* 200. *Emparlance* generall seemeth to be that which is made onely in one word, and in generall terms. *Emparlance* speciall, where the party requireth a day to deliberate, adding also these words: *saluis omnibus aduantagiis tam ad iurisdictionem Curiæ quàm ad breue & narrationem*, or such like: *Britton* vseth it for the conference of a Iury vpon the cause committed vnto them. *ca.* 53. See *Imparlance*.

Emprouement, See *Improuement*.

Encheson. *A.* 50. *Ed.* 3. *ca.* 3. is a french word, signifiing as much as occasion, cause, or reason wherefore any thing is done, See *Skene de verbo. significa: verbo Encheson.*

Encrochement or *Accrochemēt*, commeth of the french (*Accrocher. i. apprehendere, inuncare, harpagare*) and that commeth of (*Crochure. i. aduncitas*) or (*crochu. i. aduncus*) *Encrochement*, in our common law, signifieth an vnlawfull gathering in vpon another man. For Example, if two mens grounds lying togither, the one presseth too farre vpon the other: or if a tenent owe two shillings rent seruice to the Lord, & the *Lord* taketh three: So *Hugh* and *Hugh Spencer* encroched vnto them royall power and authoritie, *anno prim. Ed.* 3. *in procem.*

Enditement (*Indictamentum*) commeth of the French (*Enditer. i. deferre nomen alicuius, indicare*) or from the Greeke ἐνδείκνυμι, because *M. Lamberd* will haue it so. *Eirenar. lib.* 4. *cap.* 5. *pag.* 468. It signifieth in our common lawe, as much as (*Accusatio*) in the ciuile lawe, though it haue not in all points the like effect. *West parte* 2. *symb. titulo*, *Inditements*) defineth it thus: An Inditement is a Bill or declaration made in forme of lawe, (for the benefite of the common wealth) of an accusation for some offence, either criminall or penall, exhibited vnto Iurours, and by their verdict found and presented to be true, before an Officer hauing power to punish the same offence. It is an accusation, because the Iury that inquireth of the offence, doth not receiue it vntill the party that offereth the Bill, appeare so farre in it, as to subscribe his name, and offer his oth for the truth thereof. It differeth from an Accusation in this, that the preferrer of the Bill is no way tyed to the proofe thereof vpon any penalty, if it be not proued, except there appeare conspiracy. Wherefore, though moued by *M. Wests* authority, I call it an Accusation: yet I take it to be rather (*Denuntiatio*) because it is of office done by the great enquest, rather then of a free intent to accuse. Of this you may reade. *S. Tho. Smith de Repub. Anglor. lib.* 2. *cap.* 19. and *Stawnf. pl. cor. lib.* 2. *cap.* 23. 24. 25. 26. *&c. Vsq;* 34. and *M. Lamberds Eirenarcha. li.* 4. *ca.* 5. whence you may receiue good satisfaction in this mater.

Endowment (*Dotatio*) commeth of the french (*Doüare*) and signifieth the bestowing or assuring of a *Dower. See Dower.* But it is sometime vsed metaphorically, for the setting forth or seuering of a sufficient portion, for a vickar toward his perpetuall maintenance, when the benefice is appropriated. *See* Appropriation. And the statute *A.* 15. *R.* 2. *cap.* 6.

Endowment de la plus Belle part. is where a man dying seised of some lands, houlding in knights seruice, and other some in socage, the widow is sped of her dower, rather in the lands houlding in socage, then knights seruice. Of this reade *Litleton* more at large. *li.* 1. *ca.* 5.

Enfranchisement, cōmeth of the french (*Franchise.* 1. *libertas*) and is in a maner a french word of it selfe: It signifieth in our common law, the incorporating of a man into any societie, or body politicke. For example, he that by charter is made Denizen of *England*, is said to be enfranchised; and so is he that is made a citizen of London, or other city, or Burges of any towne corporate, because he is made partaker of those liberties that appertaine to the corporation, whereinto he is enfranchised. So a villaine is enfranchised, when he is made free by his Lord, and made capable of the benefites belonging to freemen.

Englecerie (*engleceria*) is an old abstract word, signifying nothing else but to be an English man. For example, if a man bee priuily slaine or murthered, he was in old time accompted (*Francigena*) which word comprehendeth euery alien, vntil *Englecerie* was proued: that is, vntill it were made manifest, that he was an English man. A man may maruell, what meaning there might be in this: but *Bracton* cleareth the doubt, who in his third booke *tract.* 2. *cap.* 15. *num.* 3. telleth vs, that when *Canutus* the Danish king, hauing setled his estate here in peace, did at the request of our Barons, disburden the land of his armie, wherein he accompted his greatest safetie: and conditioned with them, that his countrimen which remained here, should continue in peace: and the more to secure that, that for euery *Francigena* (vnder which word (as is aboue said) he comprehended all outlandish men and women, and especially *Danes*) that was secretly murthered, there should be leauied to his Treasurie 66. merkes out of the village, where the murder was cōmitted, or out of the hundred, if the village were not able to pay it: and further, that euery man murdered should be accompted *Francigena*, except *Englecery* were proued: which how it was to be proued, looke the 7. number in the same chapter. And see also *Horns* myrror of Iustices. *lib.* 1. *cap. del office del coroner*, and *Fleta lib.* 1. *cap.* 30. This *Englecerie* for the abuses and troubles that afterwarde were perceiued to grow by it, was cleane taken away, by a statute made *anno*

14. *Ed.* 3. *capite quarto.*

Enheritance. See *Inheritance.*

Enquest (*Inquisitio*) is all one in writing with the french word, and all one in signification both with the *French* and *Latine*. Howbeit, it is especially taken for that Inquisition, that neither the *Romanes*, nor *French* men euer had vse of, that I can learne. And that is the *Enquest* of Iurors, or by Iurie, which is the most vsuall triall of all causes both ciuile and criminall in our realme. For in causes ciuill after proofe is made of either side, so much as each partie thinketh good for himselfe, if the doubt be in the fact, it is referred to the discretion of twelue indifferent men, empaneled by the Shyreeue for the purpose: and as they bring in their verdict, so iudgement passeth. For the Iudge saith, the Iurie findeth the fact thus: then is the law thus: and so we iudge. For the enquest in causes criminall, see *Iurie.* and see Sir *Thomas Smith de Repub. Anglor. lib.* 2. *cap.* 19. An enquest is either of office, or at the mise of the partie. *Stawnf. pl. cor. lib.* 3. *cap.* 12.

Entendment, commeth of the French (*entendement.* i. *intellectus, ingenium.*) It signifieth in our common lawe so much, as the true meaning or signification of a word or sentence. See of this *Kitchin, fol.* 224.

Entayle (*feudum talliatum*) commeth of the French (*entaillé.* i. *inscisus*) and in our cōmon lawe, is a substantiue abstract, signifying *Fee*-tayle, or *Fee*-intayled. *Litleton* in the second chapter of his book, draweth *Fee*-tayle from the verbe *Talliare*, (which whence it commeth, or whether it will I know not) whereas in truth it must come from the *French* (*taille.* i. *sectura*,) or (*tailler.* i. *scindere, secare*) And the reason is manifest, because fee-tayle in the law, is nothing but fee abridged, scanted or curtelled, (as you would say,) or limited and tyed to certaine conditions. *Taille* in *Fraunce* is metaphorically taken for a tribute or subsidie. *v. Lupanum de Magistratibus Francorū. lib.* 3. *cap. Talea.* See *Fee.* See *Tayle.*

Enterpleder (*Interplacitare*) is compounded of two french words: (*entre.* i. *inter*) and (*pleder.* i. *disputare*) and it signifieth in our common law, as much as *cognitio praeiudicialis* in the ciuile law: that is, the discussing of a point incidently falling out, before the principall cause can take end. For example, two seuerall persons being found heires to land by two seuerall offices in one countie, the king is brought in doubt to whether liuery ought to be made: and therefore be-

fore

fore liuery be made to either, they must enterpleade, that is, formerly try betweene them selues, who is the right heire. *Stawnf. prærога. chap.* 19. See more examples in *Brooke. titulo Enterpleder.*

Entiere tenancie, is contrary to seuerall Tenency, signifiing a sole possession in one man: wheras the other signifieth ioynt or common in more. See *Brooke* seuerall tenancy. See the new booke of *Entries, verbo Entier tenancy.*

Entry (Ingressus) commeth of the french (*Entree.i. introitus ingressus, aditus*) and properly signifieth in our common lawe, the taking possession of lands or tenements. See *Plowden.* Assise of fresh force in *London. fo.* 93. *b.* It is also vsed for a writ of possession, for the which See *Ingressu.* And read *West* also, *parte.* 2. *Symbol. titulo Recoueries. sect:* 2. & 3. Who there sheweth for what things it lyeth, and for what it lyeth not. Of this *Britton* in his 114. chapter writeth to this effect. The writs of entrie fauour much of the right of propertie. As for example: some be to recouer customes and seruices: in the which are contained these twoe words (*solet & debet*) as the writs *Quo iure, Rationabilibus diuisis, rationabili estouerio*, with such like. And in this plee of entrie there be three degrees: The first is, where a man demandeth landes or tenements of his owne seisin, after the terme is expired. The second is, where one demaundeth lands or tenements let by another after the terme expired. The third, where one demaundeth lands or tenements of that tenent, that had entry by one, to whom some auncestor of the plaintife did let it for a term now expired. According to which degrees the writs for more fit remedie are varied. And there is yet a fourth forme, which is without the degrees, and in case of a more remote seisin, whereunto the other three degrees do not extend. The writ in the second degree is called a writ of entrie *in le per*: and a writ in the third degree is called a writ of entrie *in le per & cui*: and the fourth forme without these degrees, is called a writ of *entry in le post*, that is to say, after the disseisin which such a one made to such a one. And if any writ of entry be conceiued out of the right case, so that one forme be brought for another, it is abatable. The form of the first degree is such. *Precipe Willielmo quod reddat Petro manerium de B. cum pertinentiis quod ille dimisit pro termino, qui est elapsus.* The second is such: *Pracipe Petro quod reddat Willielmo manerium,*

rium &c. in quod ille non habuit ingressum nisi per patrem aut matrem, avunculum, vel amitam, vel cognatum, avum vel proavum dicti Petri, qui dictum manerium dimisit pro termino qui est elapsus. The third forme is such: *Præcipe Iohanni quod reddat Petro manerium de S. in quod ille non habuit ingressum nisi per T. cui talis pater vel mater, vel alius antecessor aut cognatus idem dimisit, cuius hæres est ipse Petrus, pro termino, qui est elapsus.* And the forme without the degrees is such: *In quod non habuit ingressum, nisi post lessam, quam talis pater aut mater (sic vt supra) cuius hæres ille est, inde fecit pro termino, qui est elapsus.* And in those foure degrees be comprehended all maner writs of entry, which be without certaintie and number. Thus farre *Britton*: by whome you may perceiue, that those words (*solet & debet*) and also those other words (*in le per*) (*in le per & cui*) and (*in le post*) which we meete with many times in bookes shortly and obscurely mentioned, do signifie nothing else, but diuers formes of this writ, applyed to the case, whereupon it is brought, and each forme taking his name from the said words contained in the writ. And of this reade *Fitz.* in his *nat. br. fol.* 193. & 194. This writ of entry differeth from an assise, because it lyeth for the most part, against him, who entred lawfully, but houldeth against lawe: whereas an assise lyeth against him that vnlawfully disseised: yet sometime a writ of entrie lyeth vpon an intrusion. *Regist. orig. fol.* 233. *b.* See the new booke of Entries, *verbo Entre Brevis. fol.* 254. *colum.* 3. I reade of a writ of entry in the nature of an assise. Of this writ in all his degrees, reade *Fleta lib.* 5. *cap.* 34. & *seqq.* 5.

Entrusion (*Intrusio*) in our cōmon lawe, signifieth a violent or vnlawfull entrance into lands or tenements, being vtterly voide of a possessour, by him that hath no right nor sparke of right vnto them. *Bracton lib.* 4. *cap.* 2. For example, if a man steppe in vpon any lands, the owner whereof lately died, and the right heire, neither by himselfe nor others, as yet hath taken possession of them. What the difference is betweene *Abator* and *Intrudor*, I do not well perceiue, except an Abatour be he that steppeth into land voide by the death of a tenent in fee, and an Entrudour that doth the like into lands, &c. voide by the death of the tenent for termes of life or yeares. See *Fitz. nat. br. fol.* 203. *F.* The authour of the new Termes of law would haue abatement latined, (*Interpositionem, aut Intrusionem per interpositionem*) and to be restrained

ſtrained to him that entreth before the heyre after the deceaſe of a tenent for life, though the new booke of Entries *fol.* 63.C. & 205. *D.* & 519. *C.* by his confeſſion doth Latine (*Abatement*) by this word (*Intruſionem.*) See *Abatement.* See *Diſſeiſin.* See *Britton,cap.* 65. *Entruſion* is alſo taken for the writ brought againſt an Intrudour, which ſee in *Fitzh. nat. br. fol.* 203.

Entruſion de gard, is a writ, that lyeth where the Infant within age entred into his lands, and houldeth his Lord out: for in this caſe, the Lord ſhall not haue the writ (*De communi cuſtodia*) But this. *Old nat. br. fol.* 90.

Envre, ſignifieth to take place or effect, to be avaylable, Example: A Releaſe ſhall *envure* by way of extinguiſhment. *Litleton. cap: Releaſe:* And a releaſe made to a tenent for terme of life, ſhall inure to him in the Reuerſion.

Erius, alius Iris, is the flower *de-luce.* whoſe diuers kindes you haue expreſſed in *Gerards herball. lib.* 1. *ca.* 34. The roote of this is mentioned among merchandize or drugs to be garbled. *anno.* 1. *Iaco. ca.* 19.

Ermins, ſeemeth to come of the french (*Ermine.* i. *mus araneus*) it ſignifieth a furre of great price.

Erminſtreate. See *Watlingſtreate.*

Errant (*Itinerans*) commeth of the french (*Errer*) .i. *errare*) or the ould word (*Erre* .i. *iter*) It is attributed to Iuſtices of circuit. *pl.cor: f:* 15. and *Baylifes* at large. See Iuſtices in *Eyre.* and *Baylife.* See alſo *Eyre.*

Errour (*Error*) commeth of the french (*Erreur*) and ſignifieth more ſpecially in our common law, an errour in pleading or in the proces. *Brooke, titulo Errour.* And thereuppon the writ, which is brought for remedy of this ouerſight, is called a writ of error, in Latine, *De errore corrigendo*: thus defined by *Fitz.* in his *nat. br. fol.* 20. A writ of errour is that properly, which lyeth to redreſſe falſe iudgement giuen in any court of record, as in the common bench, *London,* or other citie, hauing power (by the kings charter or preſcription) to hold plee of debt. See the new booke of Entries. *verbo. Error.* or treſpaſſe aboue the ſumme of twenty ſhillings. This is borowed from the French practiſe, which they call (*propoſition d'erreur.*) Wherof you may reade in *Gregorius De appellation. pag.* 36. In what diuerſitie of caſes this writ lyeth, ſee the *Regiſter originall* in the Table, *verb. Errore corrigendo,* and *Regiſter iudiciall. fol.* 34. There is likewiſe a writ of errour to reuerſe a fine. *Weſt parte* 2. *ſect. ſymbol. titulo. Fines* 151.

Errore corrigendo. See *Errour.*

Escambio, is a licence graunted to one, for the making over of a Bill of Exchange to a man ouer Sea. *Register. original. fol.* 194.*a.*

Escape (*Escapium*) commeth of the French (*Eschapper.*i. *aufugere effugere*): and signifieth in the lawe, a violent or priuie euasion out of some lawfull restraint. For example, if the Shyreeue vpon a *Capias* directed vnto him, take one, and indeavour to carie him to the Gaol, and he in the way, either by violence or by flight, breake from him: this is called an *Escape.pl.cor.fol.* 70 Many examples might bee brought out of him and others, but the thing is plaine: *Stawnford lib.* 1.*c.a.* 26. *pl. cor* nameth two kindes of *Escapes, voluntarie & negligent*: *Voluntarie* is, when one arresteth another for felonie or some other crime, and afterwards letteth him goe whither he listeth. In which escape the partie that permitteth it, is by lawe guiltie of the fault committed by him that escapeth, be it felonie, treason, or trespas: *Negligent* escape is, when one is arrested, and afterward escapeth against his wil that arrested him, and is not pursued by fresh suite, and taken againe, before the partie pursuing hath lost the sight of him: *Idem, cap.* 27. but there read more of this mater. for there be doubts worth the consideration. And of the course of punishment by the ciuill lawe in this point, reade in *practica criminali Claudii de Battandier. reg.* 143. reade also *Cromptons Iustice. fol.* 35.*b. & fol.* 36. *&* 37. and read the *newe Termes of lawe.* There is an escape of beasts likewise: and therefore he that by charter, is *quietus de escapio* in the forest, is deliuered of that punishment, which by order of the forest, lieth vpon those whose beasts be found within the land forbidden: *Cromptons Iurisdict.fo.* 196.

Eschequer (*Scaccarium*) commeth of the French (*Eschequier.* i.*abacus, tabula lusoria*) and signifieth the place or court of all receipts belonging to the crowne, and is so termed, as I take it, by reason that in auncient times, the accomptants in that office vsed such tables as *Arithmeticians* vse for their calculations, for that is one signification of (*Abacus*) amonst others. *Polidor.Virgil. lib.* 9. *histo. Anglo.* saith that the true word in latine is *Statarium*, and by abuse called *Scaccarium.* In mine opinion, it may well seeme to be taken from the German word (*schatz*) signifiing as much as (*thesaurus*) or (*fiscus*) And from this fountaine (no doubt) sprin-

springeth the Italian word (*Zeccha*) signifiing a mynt: and *Zeccherii aliàs Zecchieri*) the officers thereunto belonging, *Descis. Gemuen* 134. *M.Cam.* in his *Britan.p.* 113. saith that this court or office tooke the name *à tabula ad quam assidebant*, proouing it out of *Geruasius Tilburiensis*, whose words you may read in him. This court is taken from the *Normans*, as appeareth by the *grand Custumarie. cap.* 56. where you may finde the *Eschequier* thus described. The *Eschiquier* is called an assemblie of high *Iusticiers*, to whome it appertaineth to amend that which the Baliffes and other meaner Iusticiers haue euill done, and vnaduisedly iudged: and to doe right to all men without delaie, as from the princes mouth: *Skene de verbo. significatione: verbo* (*Scaccarium*) hath, out of *Paulus Æmilius* these words: *Scaccarium dicitur quasi Statarium, quòd homines ibi in iure sistantur, vel quòd sit stataria & perennis Curia, cum cetera curiæ essent indictivæ, nec loco nec tempore statæ*: where he saith also of himselfe, that in *Scotland* the *Eschequer* was stable, but the other session was deambulatorie, before *Iames* the 5. *qui instituit Statariam curiam, cum antea esset indictiva*: he addeth farder: Others thinke that *Scaccarium* is so called *a similitudine ludi Scaccorum*, that is the play of the chests: because many persons meete in the Chequer, pleading their causes one against the other, as if they were fighting in an arraied battaile. Others think that it commeth from an old Saxon word (*Scata*) as writeth *S. Thomas Smith*, which signifieth treasure, taxation, or imposts, whereof accompt is made in the Chequer: This court consisteth, as it were, of 2. parts: whereof one is conuersant especially in the iudiciall hearing and deciding of all causes appertaining to the princes cofers, auncientl y called *Scaccarium computorum*, as *Ockam* testifieth in his *lucubrations*: the other is called the receipt of the *Eschequer*, which is properly imploied in the receiuing and paiment of money. *Crompton in his Iurisdictions, fo.* 105. defineth it to be a court of record, wherein al causes touching the reuenewes of the crown are handled. The officers belonging to both these, you may find named in *M. Camdens Britannia, ca. Tribunalia Angliæ*, to whome I referre you. The kings exchequer which now is setled in *Westminster*, was in diuers countries of *Wales, anno* 27. *H.* 8. *ca.* 5. but especially *ca.* 26.

Escheate (*Eschaeta*) commeth of the French (*escheoir*, i. *cadere, accidere*,

dere,excidere,and signifieth in our common lawe, any lands or other profits, that fall to a Lord within his maner by way of forfeiture,or the death of his tenēt, dying without heire generall or especiall , or leauing his heire within age or vnmaried, *Magna chart.ca.* 31. *Fitzh. nat.br.fol.* 143.*T.&c. Escheate* is also vsed some time for the place or circuit within the which the king or other Lord hath escheates of his tenents.*Bracton li.* 3.*tract.2.cap.* 2.*& pupilla oculi parte* 5.*ca.*22. *Escheate* thirdly,is vsed for a writ,which lieth, where the tenent hauing estate of fee simple in any lands or tenements holden of a superiour lord, dieth seised without heire generall or especiall . For in this case the Lord bringeth this writ against him that posesseth these lands after the death of his tenent,and shall thereby recouer the same in liew of his seruices.*Fitzh.nat. br.fol.* 144. These that we call *Escheats*,are in the kingdome of *Naples* called Excadentiæ or *bona excadentialia*: as:*Baro locat excadentias eo modo quo locatæ fuerūt ab antiquo: ita quod in nullo debita servitia minuantur, & non remittit gallinam debitam* : *Iacobutius de Franchis in præludiis ad feudorum vsum,tit.*1.*nu.*29.*& nu.*23.*v.Marantæ singularia,verbo Excadentia.* And in the same signification, as we say the fee is escheated, the Feudists vse (*feudum aperitur. li.*1.*feud.titulo.*18.§.2. *ti.*15. *& ti.*26.§.4.

Escheatour(*Escaetor*)commeth of (*Escheate*) and signifieth an officer that obserueth the *Escheates* of the king in the countie, whereof he is *Escheatour*, and certifieth them into the *Escheqver*:This officer is appointed by the *L. treasurer*, and by leters patents from him, and continueth in his office but one yeare, neither can any be *Escheatour* aboue once in 3. yeares.*anno.*1.*H.* 8.*cap.*8.*& anno* 3.*eiusd.ca.* 2. See more of this officer and his authoritie in *Cromptons Iustice of peace*.See *an.* 29.*Ed.*1.The forme of the *Escheatours* oath, see in the Register original.*fol.*301 . *b. Fitzh.* calleth him an officer of record.*nat.br.fol.*100.*C.* because that which he certifieth by vertue of his office, hath the credit of a record. *Officium escaetriæ*, is the escheatourship. *Register. orig.fo.*259.*b.*

Escuage (*Scutagiū*) commeth of the French (*Escu.* i. *clypeus*)a bucler or sheild.In our common lawe , it signifieth a kinde of knights seruice,called seruice of the shield, whereby the tenent holding is bound to follow his Lord into the *Scottish* or *Welsh* warres,at his owne charge: for the

the which see *Chyvalrie* . But note that *Escuage* is either vncertaine or certaine. *Escuage* vncertaine,is properly *Escuage*,and knights seruice,being subiect to homage fealtie,ward and mariage,so called,because it is vncertaine how often a man shalbe called to followe his lord into those wars,and againe what his charge wilbe in each iourney. *Escuage* certaine, is that which yearely payeth a certaine rent in lieu of all seruices,being no further bound then to pay his rent, called a knights fee, or halfe a knights fee, or the fourth part of a knights fee,according to his land & this leeseth the nature of knights seruice, though it hold the name of *Escuage*, being in in effect, *Soccage. Fitzh. nat. br. fol.*84.C.

Esnecy (*AEsnecia*) is a prerogatiue giuen to the eldest coparcener, to choose first after the inheritance is diuided.*Fleta.li.* 5. *ca.* 10.§.*in diuisionem.*

Esplees (*Expletia*) seeme to be the full profits that the ground or land yeldeth, as the hay of the medowes, the feede of the pasture, the corne of the earable, the rents, seruices, and such like issues: *Ingham*. It seemeth to proceede from the latine (*expleo*) The profits comprised vnder this word,the Romans call properly *accessiones. Nam accessionum nomine intelligũtur ea generaliter omnia, quæ ex re, de qua agitur, orta sunt,veluti fructus, partus, & omnis causa rei, & quæcunque ex re procedunt. l.* 2.*π.* **De** *in diem adiectio. li.* 50. *π. Ad Trebel. l.*61. §. *hiis etiam. π. de furt.* See the new Terms of law.

Esquier(*Armiger*) is in leters little altered from the french (*Escuier.* i. *scutiger*) It signifieth with vs a gentleman, or one that beareth armes, as a testimony of his nobilitie or gentrie. *S. Thomas Smith* is of opinion, that at the first, these were bearers of armes to Lords and Knights,and by that had their name and dignity. Indeede the french word is sometime translated (*Agaso*) that is, a boy to attend or keepe a horse, and in ould English writers, it is vsed for a lackey or one that carieth the shield or speare of a knight. *Mast. Camden in his Britannia pag* : 111. hath these words of them: hauing spoken of Knights: *Hiis proximi fuere Armigeri, qui & scutiferi, hominesq; ad arma dicti, qui vel a clypeis gentilitiis, quæ in nobilitatis insignia gestant: vel quia principibus & maioribus illis nobilibus ab armis erant, nomen traxerunt. Olim enim ex hiis duo vnicuique militi seruiebant, galeam clypeumque gestabant. &c.* Hotoman in the sixth chapter of his disputatiõs vpon the feods saith, that these which the

French men call *Escuiers*) were a militarie kinde of vassall haueing *ius scuti*, which is as much to say (he there interpreteth him selfe) as that they bare a shield, and in it the ensignes of their family, in token of their gentility or dignity.

Essendi quietum de telonio, is a writ that lieth for Citizens or burgesses of any city or towne, that haue a charter or prescription to exempt them from tolle, through the whole realme, if it chaunce they be any where exacted the same. *Fitzh. nat. br. fol.* 226. *Register fol.* 258.

Essoine (*Essonium*) commeth of the French (*Essonie* or *exonnie*. i. *causarius miles*) he that hath his presence forborne or excused vpon any iust cause, as sicknesse or other incumbrance. It signifieth in our common lawe, an alledgement of an excuse for him that is summoned, or sought for to appeare and answer to an action reall, or to performe suite to a court baron, vpon iust cause of absence. It is as much as (*excusatio*) with the Ciuilians. The causes that serue to *Essoine* any man summoned, be diuers & infinite: yet drawne to fiue heads, whereof the first is (*vltra mare*) the second (*de terra sancta*) the third (*de malo veniendi*) which is also called the common Essoine the fourth is (*de malo lecti*) the fifth (*de seruitio Regis*) For further knowledge of these, I referre you to *Glanvile* in his whole first booke, and *Bracton li.* 5. *tractat.* 2. *per totum.* and *Brittan ca.* 122. 123. 124. 125. and to *Horns mirrour of Iustices, li.* 1. *ca. des Essoinis*, who maketh mention of some more *Essoines* touching the seruice of the king celestiall, then the rest doe, and of some other points not vnworthie to be knowne. Of these *essoines* you may reade farder in *Fleta l.* 6. *c.* 8. & *seqq.* & that these came to vs frõ the *Normans*, is well shewed by the *Grand Custumarie*, where you may find in a maner all said, that our lawyers haue of this mater, *cap.* 39. 40. 41. 42. 43. 44. 45.

Essoines and *profers*, *anno* 32. *H.* 8. *cap.* 21. See *Profer*.

Essonio de malo lecti, is a writ directed to the Shyreeue, for the sending of 4. lawfull knights to view one that hath essoined him selfe *de malo lecti. Register. orig. fol.* 8. *b.*

Establishment of dower, seemeth to be the assurance of dower, made to the wife by the husband or his freinds, before or at mariage. And assignement is the setting it out by the heire afterward, according to the Establishment. *Britton. cap.* 102. & 103.

Estandard or Standard, commeth

meth of the French (*Estandart*) or *Estendart*. i. *signum, vexillum*. It signifieth an Ensigne in warre, as well with vs as with them. But it is also vsed for the principall or standing measure of the King, to the scantling whereof, all the measures through the land, are or ought to be framed by the Clerk of the market, *Aulneger*, or other officer according to their functions, For it was established by the statute of *Magna charta*. *anno* 6. *H*. 3. *ca*. 9. that there should be but one scantlin of weights or measures thorough the whole realme, which is sithence confirmed by *Anno* 14. *Ed*. 3. *ca*. 12. and many other statutes, as also that all should be fitted to the *Standard* sealed with the kings seale. It is not called a *Standard* without great reason: because it standeth constant and immoueable, and hath all other measures comming toward it for their conformitie, euen as souldiours in field haue their Standard or colours for their direction in their march or skirmish. Of these Standards and measures, reade *Britton*. *cap*. 30.

Estate, commeth of the French (*Estat*. i. *conditio*) and signifieth especially in our cōmon lawe, that title or interest, which a man hath in lands or tenements, as estate simple, otherwise called fee simple, and estate conditionall or vpon condition, which is (as *Litleton* saith, *li*. 3. *ca*. 5.) either vpon condition indeede, or vpon condition in lawe. *Estate* vpon condition in deede is, where a man by deede indented infeoffeth another in fee, reseruing to him and to his heires yearelie a certaine rent paiable at one feast or at diuers, vpon condition that if the rent be behind, &c. that it shall be lawfull to the feoffour and to his heires, to enter in the lands or tenements, &c. *Estate* vpon condition in lawe, is such as hath a consideration in the lawe annexed to it, though it be not specified in writing. For example, if a man graunt to another by his deed, the office of a Parkership for terme of his life, this estate is vpon condition in the lawe, or imploied by lawe. *viz*. if the *Parker* so long shall wel and truly keepe the parke, &c. I reade also of an estate particular, which is an estate for life or for yeares. *Parkins Surrenders*. 581.

Estopel, seemeth to come from the French (*estouper*. i. *oppilare, obturare, stipare, obstipare*) and signifieth

fieth in our common lawe, an impediment or barre of an action growing from his owne fact, that hath or otherwise might haue had his action: for example: A tenent maketh a feofment by collusion to one: the Lord accepteth the seruices of the feoffee: by this he debarreth himselfe of the wardship of his tenents heire. *Fitz. nat. br. fo.* 142. *K.* Diuers other examples might be shewed out of him and *Brooke h. titule* Sir *Edward Cooke. lib.* 2. *casu Goddard fol.* 4. *b.* defineth an *estopel* to be a barre or hindrance vnto one to pleade the truth, and restraineth it not to the impediment giuen to a man by his owne act onely, but by anothers also. *li.* 3. *The case of Fines. fol.* 88. *a.*

Estovers (*Estoverium*) commeth of the French (*estouver.* i. *fovere*) and signifieth in our common lawe, nourishment or maintenance: for example: *Bracton. lib.* 3. *tractat.* 2. *cap.* 18. *num.* 2. vseth it for that sustenance, which a man taken for felonie, is to haue out of his lands or goods for himselfe and his family, during his imprisonment: and the statute *anno* 6. *Ed. prim. cap.* 3. vseth it for an allowance in meate or cloath. It is also vsed for certaine allowances of wood, to be taken out of another mans woods. So is it vsed *West.* 2. *cap.* 25. *anno* 13. *Edw.* 1. *M. West parte* 2. *symbol. titulo Fines. sect.* 26. saith, that the name of *Estovers* containeth house-bote, hay-bote, and plow-bote: as if he haue in his graunt these generall words: *De rationabili estoverio in boscis, &c.* he may thereby clayme these three.

Estrepement, or *Estripament*, (*estrepementum*) commeth of the French word (*estropier.* i. *mutilare, obtruncare*) the which word the French men haue also borowed of the Italians, or rather Spaniards, with whome (*Estropear*) signifieth to set vpon the racke. It signifieth in our common lawe, spoile made by the tenent for terme of life, vpon any lands or woods, to the preiudice of him in the reversion, as namely in the statute *anno* 6. *Ed.* 1. *ca.* 13. And it may seeme by the deriuation, that *Estrepament* is properly the vnmeasurable soaking or drawing of the heart of the land by ploughing or sowing it continually, without manuring, or other such vsage as is requisite in good husbandrie. And yet (*Estropier* signifying *mutilare*) it may no lesse conueniently be applied to those, that cut downe trees or loppe them farder then the lawe will beare. This signifieth also a writte, which lieth in two sorts, the one is, when a man hauing an action depending (as a fordom,or *dum fuit infra ætatem,* or writ of right, or any such other) wherein the demandant is not to recouer dammages, sieweth to inhibite the tenent for making waste, during the suite. The other sort is for the demaundant, that is adiudged to recouer seisin of the land in question, and before executiō siewed by the writ *Habere facias seisinam,* for feare of waste to be made before he can get possession, sieweth out this writ: See more of this,in *Fitzh. nat. br. fol.* 60. & 61. See the *Register orig. fol.* 76. and the *Regist. iudicial. fol.* 33.

Estreate (extractum vel extracta) commeth of the French (*Traict*) which among other things signifieth a figure or resemblance: and is vsed in our common lawe, for the copie or true note of an originall writing. For example, of amerciaments or penalties set downe in the rolles of a court, to be leauied by the Bayliffe or other officer, of euery man for his offence. See *Fitzh. nat. br. fol.* 75. H. *I. K. & 76. A.* And so is it vsed *Westm.* 2. *cap.* 8. *anno* 13. *Edw.* 1.

Estrey (extrahura) in our common law signifieth any beast not wilde, found within any Lordship, and not owned by any man. For in this case, if it being cried, according to lawe, in the market townes adioyning, shall not be claimed by the owner within a yeare and a day, it is the Lords of the soyle. See *Britton cap.* 17. See *Estrayes* in the Forest, *anno* 27. *H.* 8. *cap.* 7. New booke of Entries. *verbo. Trespas concernant estrey.*

Evidence, (Evidentia) is vsed in our lawe generally for any proofe, be it testimonie of men or instrument. Sir *Thomas Smith* vseth it in both sortes. *lib.* 2. *cap.* 17. in these words: Evidence, in this signification, is authenticall writings of contracts after the maner of *England,* that is to say, written, sealed, and deliuered. And *lib.* 2. *cap.* 23. speaking of the prisoner that standeth at the barre, to pleade for his life, and of those that charge him with felonie, he saith thus: then he telleth what he can say: after him likewise all those, who were at the apprehension of the prisoner, or who can giue any Indices or tokens, which we call in our language (*Evidence*) against the malefactour.

Examiner in the *Chauncerie* or *Starre-chamber*, (*examinator*) is an Officer in either Court, that examineth the parties to any suite vpon their oathes, or witnesses producted of either side: whereof there be in the Chauncerie two.

Exception (exceptio) is a stoppe

or stay to an action, being vsed in the ciuill and common lawe both alike, and in both diuided into dilatorie and peremptorie. Of these see *Bract. lib.5. tract.5. per totum*, and *Britton cap.91.92.*

Exchaunge, (excambium, vel cambium) hath a peculiar signification in our common lawe, and is vsed for that compensation, which the warrantor must make to the warrantee, valewe for value, if the land warranted be recouered from the warrantee. *Bracton lib. 2. cap. 16. & li.1. cap. 19.* It signifieth also generally as much as (*Permutatio*) with the Ciuilians, as the Kings Exchaunge, *anno 1. H. 6. cap. 1. & 4. & anno 9. Ed. 3. stat. 2. cap. 7.* which is nothing else, but the place appointed by the king for the exchaunge of bullion, be it gold or siluer, or plate, &c. with the Kings coine. These places haue bene diuers heretofore as appeareth by the saide statutes. But now is there only one, *viz.* the tower of *London* conioyned with the mint. Which in time past might not be, as appeareth by *anno 1. Henrici 6. ca.4.*

Exchequer, see *Eschequer.*

Excheatour, see *Escheatour.*

Excommunication, (excommunicatio) is thus defined by *Panormitan*: *Excommunicatio est nihil aliud, quàm censura à Canone, vel Iudice ecclesiastico prolata & inflicta, priuans legitima communione sacramentorum, & quandoque hominum.* And it is diuided *in maiorem & minorem, Minor est, per quam quis à Sacramentorum participatione conscientia vel sententia arcetur. Maior est, quæ non solùm à Sacramentorum, verùm etiam fidelium communione excludit, & ab omni actu legitimo separat & diuidit. Venatorius de sentent. excom.*

Excommunicato capiendo, is a writ directed to the Shyreeue, for the apprehension of him that standeth obstinately excommunicated for fortie dayes: for such a one not seeking absolution, hath or may haue his contempt certified or signified into the Chauncerie, whence issueth this writ, for the laying of him vp without baile or mainprise, vntill he conforme himselfe. See *Fitz. nat. br. fol. 62. & anno 5. Eliz. cap. 23.* and the *Regist. orig. fol. 65. 67. & 70.*

Excõmunicato deliberando, is a writ to the vnder shyreeue, for the deliuery of an excõmunicate person out of prison, vpon certificate from the Ordinary of his conformitie to the iurisdiction ecclesiasticall. See *Fitzh. nat. br. fol. 63. A.* and the Register *fol. 65. & 67.*

Excommunicato recipiendo, is a writ whereby persons excommunicate, being for their obstinacie committed to prison, and vnlawfully

lawfully deliuered thence, before they haue giuen caution to obey the authority of the church, are commaunded to be sought for and laide vp againe. *Register orig. fo. 67. a.*

Executione facienda, is a writ commaunding execution of a iudgement: the diuers vses wherof, see in the table of the register iudiciall. *verbo Executione facienda.*

Executione facienda in Withernamium, is a writ that lyeth for the taking of his catell, that formerly hath conueyed out of the county the catell of another, so that the bayliffe hauing authority from the shyreeue, to repleuy the cattell so conueighed away, could not execute his charge. *Register originall, fol. 82. b.*

Execution (*Executio*) in the common law, signifieth the last performance of an act, as of a fine, or of a iudgement. And the execution of a fine, is the obtaining of actuall possession of the things contained in the same, by vertue thereof: which is either by entry into the lands, or by writ: whereof see *West* at large, *parte. 2. Symbol. titulo Fines. sect:* 136. 137. 138. Executing of iudgements, and statutes, and such like, see in *Fitzh. nat. br. in Indice. 2. Verbo Execution. S. Ed. Coke. vol: 6. casu Blumfield. fo. 87. a.* maketh two sorts of executions, one finall, another with a (*quousque*) tending to an end. An execution finall is that, which maketh mony of the defendants goods, or extendeth his lands, and deliuereth them to the plaintife. For this the party accepteth in satisfaction: and this is the end of the suite, and all that the kings writ commaundeth to be done. The other sort with a (*Quousque*) is tending to an end, and not finall, as in the case of (*capias ad satisfaciendum &c.*) this is not finall: but the body of the party is to be taken, to the intent and purpose to satisfie the demaundant: and his imprisonment is not absolute, but vntill the defendant doe satisfie. *Idem, ibidem.*

Executour (*Executor*) is he, that is appointed by any man, in his last will and testament, to haue the disposing of all his substance, according to the content of the said will. This Executor is either particular or vniuersall. *Particular,* as if this or that thing onely be committed to his charge. *Vniuersall,* if all. And this is in the place of him, whom the Ciuilians call *haeredem,* and the law accounteth one person with the party, whose executor he is, as hauing all aduantage of action against all men, that he had, so likewise being subiect to euery mans action, as farre as himselfe was. This executor had his beginning in the ciuill lawe, by the constitutions of the Emperours, who first permitted those, that thought good by their wils to bestowe any thing vpon good and godly vses, to appoint whome they pleased, to see the same performed, and if they appointed none, then they ordained, that the bishop of the place should haue authoritie of course, to effect it. *l. 28. C. de Episcopis & clericis*. And from this in mine opinion, time and experience hath wrought out the vse of these vniuersall executors, as also brought the administration of their goods that die without will, vnto the Bishop.

Exemplificatione, is a writ granted for the exemplification of an originall, see the *Register original. fol.* 290.

Ex grui querela, is a writ that lieth for him, vnto whome any lands or tenements in fee within a city, towne or borough, being deuisable, are deuised by will, and the heire of the deuisour entreth into them, and deteineth them from him. *Register originall. fol.* 244. *Old nat. br. fol.* 87. See *Fitzh. nat. br. fol.* 198. *L.*

Exigendarie of the common banke (*Exigendarius de banco communi*) is otherwise called *Exigenter. anno* 10. *H. 6. cap.* 4. and is an officer belonging to that court, for the which see *Exigenter.*

Exigent (*Exigenda*) is a writ, that lyeth where the defendant in an action personall, cannot be found, nor any thing within the county, whereby to be attached or distrained, and is directed to the Shyreeue, to proclaime and call fiue county daies one after another, charging him to appeare vnder the paine of outlawrie. *Termes of the law*. This writ lyeth also in an indictment of felony, where the party indicted cannot be found: *Smith de Rep. Angl. li. 2. ca.* 19. It seemeth to be called an *Exigent*: because it exacteth the party, that is, requireth his expearance or forthcomming, to answer the lawe, for if he come not at the last daies proclamation, he is saide to be *quinquies exactus*, and then is outlawed. *Crompton Iurisd. fol.* 188. and this *M. Manwood* also setteth downe for the law of the forest. *parte* .i. of his forest lawes *pag.* 71. *See the new booke of* Entries, *verbo Exigent*.

Exigenter (*Exigendarius*) *anno* 18. *H. 6. ca. 9.* is an officer of the court of common plees, of whom there be foure in number: They make all Exigents and proclamations in all actions, where proces of outlawrie doth lie, and writs of *superfedeas*, as well

well as the protonotaries, vpon such exigents, as were made in their offices.

Ex mero motu, are words formally vsed in any charter of the Prince, whereby he signifieth, that he doth that which is cōtained in the charter of his owne will and motion, without petition or suggestion made by any other. And the effect of these words are to barre al exceptions, that might be taken vnto the instrument wherein they be contained, by alledging that the Prince in passing that charter, was abused by any false suggestion: *Kitchin fol.* 151.

Exoneratione secta, is a writ that lyeth for the kings ward, to be disburdened of all suite,&c. to the Countie, Hundred, Leet, or court Baron, during the time of his wardship. *Fitz. nat. br. fol.* 158.

Ex parte latis, is a writ that lyeth for a Bayliffe or Receiuer, that hauing Auditours assigned to heare his accompt, cannot obtaine of them reasonable allowance, but is cast into prison by them. *Regist. fol.* 137. *Fitzh. nat. br. fol.* 129. The maner in this case is, to take this writ out of the Chauncerie directed to the Shyreeue, to take foure mainperuours to bring his bodie before the *Barons* of the *Echequer* at a day certaine, & to warn the Lord to appeare at that time: Newe Tearmes of the lawe. *verb. Accompt.*

Expectant, is vsed in the common lawe with this word (*fee*) and thus vsed, it is opposite to Fee-simple. For example, lands are giuen to a man and his wife in franke mariage, to haue and to hold to them and their heires. In this case they haue Fee simple. But if it be giuen to them and the heires of their body, &c. they haue tayle and fee expectant. *Kitchin fol.* 153. *Mathæus de afflictis* vseth the Adiectiue (*expectativa*) substantiuely in the same signification. *Decis.* 292. *num.* 2. *pag.* 412.

Explees. See *Espleese*.

Expeditate (*expeditare*) is a word vsuall in the Forest, signifiing to cut out the balles of the great dogges feet, for the preseruation of the Kings game. Euery one that keepeth any great dogges not expeditated, forfeiteth to the king 3. shillings 4. pence. *Crompt. iurisd. fol.* 152. *M. Manwood* vseth the same word, *parte prim.* of his Forest lawes, *pag.* 205. and *pag.* 212. he setteth downe the manner of expeditating dogges heretofore, *viz. Quòd tres ortelli abscindantur sine pellota de pede anteriori.* i. that the three clawes of the forefoot on the right side, shall be cut off by the skinne, whereunto he also ad-

addeth out of the ſame ordinance, called the Aſſiſe of the Foreſt, that the ſame maner of expeditating of dogges, ſhall be ſtill vſed and kept, and none other. *Quære* whence it groweth, that *M. Crompton* and hee differ: the one ſaying, that the ball of the foote it cut out, the other that the three foreclawes are pared off by the skinne:

Expenſis militum levandis, is a writ directed to the ſhyreeue, for levying the allowance for Knights of the Parlament. *Regiſter originall. fol.* 191. *b.*

Expenſis militum non levandis ab hominibus de antiquo dominico, nec à natiuis, is a writ whereby to prohibite the Shyreeue from levying any allowance for the Knights of the Shire, vpon thoſe that hold in auncient demeſn, &c. *Regiſt. orig. fol.* 261. *b.*

Extend (*extendere*) commeth of the French (*eſtendre*. i. *dilatare, diſpandere, diſtendere*) and ſignifieth in our common lawe, to valew the lands or tenements of one bound by ſtatute, &c. that hath forfeited his bond, to ſuch an indifferent rate, as by the yearely rent the obligour may in time be paide his debt. The courſe and circumſtances of this ſee in *Fitzh. nat. br. fol.* 131. *Brief d'execution ſur ſtatut Merchant.*

Extendi facias, is a writ ordinarily called a writ of extent, whereby the valew of lands, &c. is commaunded to be made and leavied in divers caſes, which ſee in the table of the *Regiſter originall.*

Extent (*extenta*) hath two ſignifications, ſometime ſignifiing a writ or commiſſion to the ſhyreeue for the valuing of lands or tenements. *Regiſter iudiciall* in the Table of the booke: ſometime the act of the Shyreeue or other Commiſſioner, vpon this writ. *Brooke titulo. Extent. fol.* 313.

Extinguiſhment, in our common law, ſignifieth an effect of conſolidation. For example, if a man haue due vnto him a yearely rent out of any lands, and afterward purchaſe the ſame lands, now both the property and rent are conſolidated, or vnited in one poſſeſſour, and therefore the rent is ſaid to be extinguiſhed. In like maner it is, where a man hath a leaſe for yeares, and afterwards buyeth the property: this is a conſolidation of the property and the fruites, and is an extinguiſhment of the leaſe, See the terms of lawe.

Extirpatione, is a writ Iudiciall, that lyeth againſt him, who after a verdict found againſt him for land, &c. doth maliciouſly ouerthrow any houſe vpon it, &c. and it is two-fold; one *ante iudicium*,

cium, the other *post iudicium*: Register *iudiciall fol.* 13. 56. 58.

Extortion (*Extortio*) signifieth in our common law, an vnlawfull or violent wringing of mony or mony worth from any man. For example, if any officer by terrifiing any the kings subiects in his office, take more then his ordinary duties, he committeth, and is inditeable of extortion: To this (by *M. Wests* iudgment) may be referred the exaction of vnlawfull vsurie, winning by vnlawfull games, and (in one word) all taking of more then is due, by colour or pretence of right; as excessiue tolle in millners, excessiue prices of ale, bread, victuals, wares, &c. *West parte.* 2. *Simbol. titulo. Indictments sect:* 65. *M: Manwood* saith, that extortion is *Colore officii*, and not *virtute officii. parte.* 1. of his forest lawes, *pag.* 216. *M. Crompton* in his Iustice of peace *fol.* 8. hath these words in effect: wrong done by any man is properly a trespas: but excessiue wrong done by any is called extortion: and this is most properly in officers, as Shyreeues, Maiors, Bayliffes, Eschcatours, and other officers whatsoeuer, that by colour of their office worke great oppression, and excessiue wrong vnto the Kings subiects, in taking excessiue rewarde, or fees, for the execution of their office. Great diuersity of cases touching extortion, you may see in *Cromptons* Iustice of peace. *fol.* 48. *b.* & 49. & 50. *See* the difference betweene *colore officy*, & *virtute vel ratione officy*. *Plowd. casu. Dives. fol.* 64. *a.* This word is vsed in the same signification in Italy also. For *Cavalcanus de brachio regio, parte* 5. *num.* 21. thus describeth it. *Extortio dicitur fieri, quando Iudex cogit aliquid sibi dari quod non est debitum, vel quod est vltrà debitum: vel ante tempus petit id, quod post administratam iustitiam debetur.*

Extreats. See *Estreats.*

Eyre. See *Eire.*

F

FAculty, (*facultas*) as it is restrained from the original and actiue signification, to a particular vnderstanding in lawe, is vsed for a priuiledge, or especiall power graunted vnto a man by fauour, indulgence, and dispensation, to do that which by the common lawe he cannot doe: as to eate flesh vpon daies prohibited, to mary without bans first asked, to hold two or more ecclesiasticall liuings, the sonne to succeede the father in a benefice, and such like. And for the graunting of these, there is an especiall officer vnder the Archbishop of *Canterbury*, called (*Magister ad facultates*) the Master of the faculties.

Fag.

Fag. anno. 4. Ed. 4. *cap.* 1.

Faint and false action, seeme to be *Synonima* in *Litleton. fol.* 144. For (*faint*) in the French tongue signifieth as much as (*fained*) in English.

Faint pleader (*falsa placitatio*) commeth of the French (*feint*) a participle of the verbe (*feindre.* i. *simulare, fingere*) and (*pledoir.* i. *placitare.*) It signifieth with vs, a false couenous, or collusory maner of pleading, to the deceipt of a third partie. *anno* 34. & 35. *H.* 8. *cap.* 24.

Faire, alias, Feire, (*feria*) commeth of the French (*foire*) and signifieth with vs, as much as (*Nundinæ*) with the Ciuilians: that is a solemne or greater sort of market, granted to any towne by priuiledge, for the more speedie and commodious prouision of such things, as the subiect needeth, or the vtterance of such things, as we abound in, aboue our owne vses and occasions: both our English and the French word seeme to come of (*Feriæ*) because it is alwaies incident to the priuiledge of a Faire, that a man may not be arested or molested in it for any other debt, then first was contracted in the same, or at least was promised to be payed there. *an.* 17. Ed. 4. *cap.* 2. & *anno* 1. *R.* 3. *cap.* 6.

Faire pleading, see *Beau pleader*.

Faitours, seemeth to be a French word antiquated, or something traduced. For the moderne French word is (*faiseur.* i. *factor*) It is vsed in the statute *anno* 7. *R.* 2. *cap.* 5. And in the euill part, signifying a bad doer. Or it may not improbably be interpreted an idle liuer, taken from (*faitardise*) which signifieth a kind of numme or sleepy disease, proceeding of too much sluggishnesse, which the Latines call (*veternus.*) For in the said statute it seemeth to be a Synonymon to Vagabound.

Falke land, alias, Folke land. See *Copi-hold* and *Free-hold.*

False imprisonment, (*falsum imprisonamentum*) is a trespasse cōmitted against a man, by imprisoning him without lawefull cause: it is also vsed for the writ which is brought vpon this trespasse. *Fitz. nat. br. fol.* 86. *K.* & 88. *P. v. Broke h. t.* See the new booke of Entries. *verbo. False imprisonment.*

Falso iudicio, is a writ, that lyeth for false iudgement giuen in the county, Hundred, Court Baron, or other courts being no court of record, be the plea reall or personall. *Register originall fol.* 15: *Fitzh. nat. br. fol.* 17. See the new booke of *Entries. verbo False iudgement.*

False prophecies. See *Prophecies.*

Falso returno breuium. is a writ lying

lying against the Syreeue, for false returning of writs. *Register indic. fo.* 43. *b.*

Falsifie, seemeth to signifie as much, as to proue a thing to be false. *Perkins Dower.* 383. 384. 385.

Farding, or farthing of golde. seemeth to be a coine vsed in auncient times, containing in valew the fourth part of a noble. *viz.* twenty pence siluer, and in weight the sixth part of an ounce of gould, that is, of fiue shillings in siluer, which is threepence and something more. This word is is found *anno* 9. *H.* 5. *stat.* 2. *ca.* 7. thus: Item that the king doe to be ordained good and iust weight, of the noble, halfe noble, and farthing of gould, with the rates necessary to the same, for euery city, &c. by which place it plainly appeareth, to haue bene a coine, as well as the noble and halfe noble.

Farding deale aliàs Farundell of land (*Quadrantata terræ*) signifieth the fourth part of an acre. *Crompt Iurisd fol.* 220. *Quadrantata terræ.* is read in the register *orig. fol.* 1. *b.* where you haue also *Denariata & obolata, solidata, & librata terra*, which by probabilitie must rise in proportion of quantitie from the farding deale, as an halfepeny, peny, shilling, or pound rise in valew and estimation: then must *obolata* be halfe an acre, *denariata* the acre, *solidata* twelue acres, & *librata* twelue score acres, and yet I find (*viginti libratas terræ vel reditus. Regist. original. fol.* 94. *a & fol.* 248. *b.* Whereby it seemeth, that *librata terra*, is so much as yeeldeth twenty shillings *per annum*, and *centum soliditas terrarum tenementorum & redituum. fol.* 249. *a.* And in *Fitz. nat. br. fol.* 87. F. I find these words: *viginti libratas terræ vel reditus*, which argueth it to be so much land as twenty shillings *per annum.* See *Furlong.*

Fate or Fat: is a great wooden vessell, which among brewers in *London*, is ordinarily vsed at this day, to measure mault by, containing a quarter, which they haue for expedition in measuring. This word is read *anno* 1. *H.* 5. *cap.* 10. *& anno* 11. *H.* 6. *cap.* 8.

Fealtie (*fidelitas*) commeth of the French (*feaulte.* i. *fides*) and signifieth in our cómmon lawe, an oath taken at the admittance of euery tenent, to be true to the Lord, of whom he holdeth his land. And he that holdeth land by this onely oath of fealty, holdeth in the freest maner, that any man in *England* vnder the king may hold: because all with vs that haue fee, hold (*per fidem & fiduciam*) that is, by fealtie at the least. *Smith de Repub. Anglor. li.* 3.

cap. 8. for, *fidelitas est de substantia feudi,* as *Dwarenus* saith *de feud. cap. 2. num.* 4. and *Mathæus de afflictis decis.* 320. *num.* 4. *pag.* 465. saith, that *fidelitas est substantiale feudi, non servitium.* The particulars of this oath, as it is vsed among the feudists, you may reade well expressed by *Zasius* in his Tractate *de feudis. part. 7. num. 15. & 16.* which is woorth the comparing with the vsuall oath taken here in our part of *Britannie*. This fealtie is also vsed in other nations, as the *Lombards* and *Burgundians. Cassanæus de consuet. Burgund. pag.* 419. & 420. And indeed the very first creation of this tenure, as it grew from the loue of the lord toward his followers, so did it bind the tenent to fidelitie, as appeareth by the whole course of the feods. And the breach thereof is losse of the fee. *Duarenus in Commentariis feudorum cap.* 14. *num.* 11. & *Wesenbecius in tract. de feudis cap.* 15. *num.* 4 & *seqq. Antonius Contius in methodo feudorum cap. Quibus modis feudum amittitur.* Hotoman in his Commentaries (*De verbis feudalibus*) sheweth a double fealtie: one generall, to be performed by euery subiect to his prince: the other speciall, required only of such, as in respect of their fee are tyed by this oath toward their landlords: both we may reade of in the grand Custumary of *Normandy*, being of course performed to the *Duke*, by all resient within the Dutchie. The effect of the words turned into latine by the Interpreter, is this: *Fidelitatem autem tenentur omnes residentes in Provincia Duci facere & servare: Vnde tenentur se ei innocuos in omnibus & fideles exhibere, nec aliquid ipsum incommodi procurare: nec eius inimicis præbere contra ipsum consilium vel iuvamen: & qui ex hoc inventi fuerint ex causa manifesta, notabiles & traditores Principis reputantur. Et omnes eorum possessiones perpetuæ Principi remanebunt, si super hoc convicti fuerint vel damnati: Omnes enim in Normania tenentur Principi fidelitatem observare. Vnde nullus homagium vel fidelitatem alicuius potest recipere, nisi salva Principis fidelitate. Quod etiam est in eorum receptione specialiter exprimendum. Inter Dominos autem alios & homines fides taliter debet obseruari, quod neuter in personam alterius personalem violentiam, seu percussionis iniectionem cum violētia, debet irrogari. Si quis enim eorū ex hoc fuerit accusatus in curia & conuictus, feudum omne debet amittere &c.* This fealty speciall, is with vs performed either by free men or by vileines. The forme of both see *anno* 14. *Ed.* 1. *stat.* 2. in these words: when a freeman shall doe fealty to his

lord,

lord, he ſhall hould his right hand vpon a booke, and ſhal ſay thus: Heare you my lord *R.* that I. *P.* ſhalbe to you both faithfull and true, and ſhall owe my fealty to you for the land that I hould of you at the terms aſſigned: So help me god and all his ſaints. When a villaine ſhall doe fealty vnto his lord, he ſhall hould his right hand ouer the booke, and ſhall ſay thus: Heare you my lord. *A.* that I. *B.* from this day forth vnto you ſhalbe true and faithfull, and ſhall owe you fealty for the land that I hould of you in villenage, and ſhalbe iuſtified by you in body and goods: So helpe me god & all his Saints. See the *Regiſter originall. fol.* 302. *a.*

Fee (Feodum, aliàs Feudum) commeth of the *French*) *Fief.* i. *prædium beneficiarium, vel res clientelaris*) and is vſed in our common lawe, for all thoſe lands which we hold by perpetuall right: as *Hotoman* well noteth *verbo Feodum. de verbis feudalibus*: our auncient lawyers either not obſeruing whẽce the word grew, or at the leaſt not ſufficiẽtly expreſſing their knowledge, what it ſignified among them, from whome they tooke it, *Feudum* whence the word *(Fief)* or fee commeth, ſignifieth in the *German* language *(beneficium cuius nomine opera quædam gratiæ teſtificandæ cauſa debentur, Hotoman diſput. ca.* 1. And by this name goe all lands & tenements, that are held by any acknowledgement of any ſuperioritie to a higher Lord. They that write of this ſubiect, doe diuide all lands and tenements, wherein a man hath a perpetuall eſtate to him and his heires, &c, into *Allodium & Feudum. Allodium* is defined to be euerie mans owne land, &c. which he poſſeſſeth meerely in his owne right, without acknowledgement of any ſeruice, or paiment of any rent vnto any other, and this is a propertie in the higheſt degree, and of ſome it is called *(allaudium ab a privatma particula, & laudum vel laudatio, vt ſit prædium cuius nullus author eſt niſi deus. Eſt enim laudare, vel Nouio teſte, nominare. Quod & Budæus docuit ad Modeſtinum. l. Herennius* 63. *π. de hære. inſtitu. Prateus. verbo. Allaudium. Hotoman in verb. feuda. Feudum* is that, which we hold by the benefite of another, and in the name whereof we owe ſeruice, or pay rent, or both, to a ſuperior lord. And all our land here in *England* (the Crowne land which is in the kings owne hands in the right of his crowne, excepted) is in the nature of *Feudum* or fee, for though many a man hath land by deſcent from his Auncestors, and many another hath dearely bought land for his money, yet is the land of such nature, that it cannot come to any, either by discent or purchase, but with the burthẽ that was laid vpon him, who had novel fee, or first of all receiued it as a benefite from his Lord, to him and to all such, to whome it might discend, or any way be conueied from him. So that if we will reckon with our host (as the proverbe is) there is no man here, that hath *directum dominium*. i. the very propertie or *demaine* in in any land, but the prince in the right of his crowne. *Camd. Britan. pag.* 93. for though he that hath fee, hath *ius perpetuum, & vtile dominium*: yet he oweth a dutie for it: & therefore is it not simply his owne. Which thing I take those words, that we vse for the expressing of our deepest right in any lands or tenements, to import: for he that can say most for his estate, saith thus: I am seised of this or that land or tenement in my demaine, as of fee. *Seisitus inde in dominico meo vt de feudo*, and that is as much, as if he said, it is my demaine or proper land after a sort: because it is to me and mine heires for ever: yet not simply mine, because I hold it in the nature of a benefite from another. yet the statute *anno* 37. *H.* 8. *ca.* 16. vseth these words of lands invested in the crowne: but it proceedeth from the ignorance of the nature of this word (fee) for fee cannot be without fealty sworne to a superiour, as you may reade partly in the word (*Fealtie*) but more at large in those that write *de feudis*: and namely *Hotoman*, both in his commentaries and disputations. And no man may graunt, that our king or Crowne oweth fealty to any superior but God onely. Yet it may be said, that land, &c. with vs is termed fee in two respects; one, as it belongeth to vs and our heires for ever: and so may the Crowne land be called Fee: the other, as it holdeth of another, which is and must be farre from our Crowne. *Briton ca.* 32. defineth fee to this effect. Fee is a right consisting in the person of the true heire, or of some other, that by iust title hath purchased it. *Fleta* saith that *Feudum est quod quis tenet ex quacunq; causa sibi & hæredibus suis, siue sit tenementum, siue reditus, qui non proveniunt ex camera, & alio modo dicitur feudum, sicut eius qui feoffat, & quod quis tenet ab alio: sicut dicitur: talis tenet de tali tot feuda per servitium militare. li.* 5. *ca.* 5. §. *Feudum autem*. And all that write *de feudis*, doe hold that (*Feudatarius*) hath not an entire propertie in his fee: Nay, it is held by right learned men, that these fees were at the first invention or creation of of them , either all or some of them temporarie, and not perpetuall and hereditarie. *Iacobutius de Franchis in præludio feud.ca. 2.nu.*133. The diuisions of (fee) in diuers respects are many, and those though little knowne to vs in England, yet better worthie to be known, then we commonly thinke. But for our present purpose, it is sufficient to diuide *Fee* into two sorts: *Fee absolute*, otherwise called simple: and *Fee conditionall*, otherwise termed fee tayle: *Fee* simple (*Feudum simplex*) is that, whereof we are seised in these generall words (to vs and our heires for ever.) Fee *tayle* (*Feudum talliatum*) is that, whereof we are seized to vs and our heires with limitation, that is , the heires of our body, &c. And fee taile is either generall or speciall . Generall is, where land is giuen to a man and the heires of his body. The reason whereof is giuen by *Litleton ca.*2.*li* 1. because a man seised of land by such a gift, if he marie one or more wiues , and haue no issue by them, and at the length marie another, by whome he hath issue, this issue shall inherit the land: Fee taile speciall is that, where a man and his wife be seised of lands to them, and the heires of their two bodies. The reason is likewise giuen by *Litleton* in the same place, because in this case, the wife dying without issue, and he marying another, by whome he hath issue, this issue , cannot inherit the land, being specially giuen to such heires, &c. this Fee taile hath the originall, from the statute of *Westm.* 2. *cap.* 1. which was made *anno* 13 *Ed.*1. yet see *Bracton. li.*2.*ca.*5.*nu.*3. *hiis verbis. Item quædam absoluta & larga, & quædam stricta & coarctata, sicut certis hæredibus* to whome adde *Plowden, casu Will.on.fo.* 235.*a.b.* & *seqq.* for before that statute, all land giuen to a man and his heires, either generall or speciall, was accompted in the nature of fee: and therefore held to be so firmely in him to whome it was giuen: that, any limitation notwithstanding, he might alienate and sell it at his pleasure: much like that which the Civilians call (*Nudum præceptum*) binding rather by way of counsell and aduice, then compulsion or restrainte: And this thing seeming vnreasonable to the wisedome of our realme, because so a man meaning well to this or that posterity of himselfe or his freinds, might be forthwith deceiued of his intention , the said statute was made for redresse of this inconvenience, wereby it is ordained, that if a man giue lands in fee, limiting the heires to whome it shall descend, with a reversion to himselfe or his heires for default, &c. that the forme and true meaning of his gift, shalbe obserued. Wherefore in what conscience our lawyers haue inuented meanes, so easily to cut off this forme of gift, it is to be considered. *He* that hath fee then, holdeth of another by some dutie or other, which is called seruice, and of this seruice and the diuersitie thereof, See *Chivalrie* and *Seruice*. He that will learne from what fountaine these feuds or fees did first spring let him read *Antonius* Contius his first chapter *de methodo feudorum*, where he shal receiue great light for his guide into so obscure a dungeon. *See Liege.* This word, (*Fee*) is sometime vsed with vs, for the compas or circuit of a Lordship or maner. *Bracton. lib. 2. cap.* 5. in these words: *In eadem villa & de eodem feodo.* Thirdly it is vsed for a perpetuall right incorporeall: as to haue the keeping of prisons in fee. *old. nat. br. fol.* 41. Foster in fee *eod. fol:* 6. *R*ent granted in fee. *eod. fo.* 8 Shyreeue in fee. *ann* 28. *Ed pri. stat.* 3. *ca.* 8. Lastly fee signifieth a reward or ordinarie dutie, that a man hath giuen him for the execution of his office, or the performance of his industrie in his art or science: as the lawyer or the phisitian is said to haue his fee, when he hath the consideration of his paines taken, the one with his client, the other with his patient.

Fee expectant, is by the feudists termed *feudum expectatiuum*, or *expectatiua*, substantiuely vsed, *Matheus de Afflictis decis.* 292. *nu.* 2. *pag.* 417. See *expectant.*

Fee *ferm* (*feudi firma*) is a compound of Fee. whereof see (*Fee*) and (*ferm.* i. *colonia, villa, prædium rusticum*, of (F*erme*) commeth Fermier *du prince.* i. *manceps, redemptor publicorum vectigalium, Publicanus.*) Feeferm signifieth in our common lawe, land held of another in fee, that is in perpetuitie to himselfe and his heires, for so much yearely rent, as it is reasonably worth, more or lesse, so it be the fourth part of the worth, *old tenures*, See exposition of the statute of *Glocester anno* 6. *Ed. pri.* without homage, fealtie or other seruices, other then be especially comprised in the feoffment, but by F*itzh.* it seemeth that the third part of the value may be appointed for the rent, or the finding of a chaplaine to sing diuine seruice, &c. *nat. br. fol.* 210. *C.* And the nature of it is this, that if the rent be behind and vnpaid for the space of two yeares, then the feoffour or his heires haue action to recouer the lands as their demesnes: *Britton. ca.* 66. *nu.* 4. but obserue out of *West. symbol. parte* 1. *lib.* 2. *sect.* 463.

that

that the feofment may containe feruices and fuite of court, as well as rent: and the author of the new terms of law, faith, that *Feeferm* oweth fealtie, though not expreffed in the feofment, for that fealtie belongeth to all kind of tenures: This is neere the nature of that, which among the Civilians is called (*ager vectigalis, qui in perpetuum licetur*. i. *hac lege vt quam diu pro eo vectigal pendatur. tam diu neq; ipfis qui conduxerunt, neq; iis qui in locum eorum fucceflerunt, auferri eum liceat*. *l*. 1. π. *fi ager vectigalis*, &c.

Feed: (*Fcida alias Faida*) fignifieth in the German toung *Guerram*. i. (*capitales inimicitias vel bellum*) *Hotoman difputat: de feudis ca*. 2. *B*. *Fœmina dicitur faidam non facere. gloff: in* §. *vlt*. De *lege Conradi lib*. 2. *de feudis*, by reafon that women by the law, are not fubiect to warfare, to battell or proclamatiō made for that caufe. *Skene de verbo: fignif. verbo Affidatio*. *M. Lamberd* in his explication of *Saxon* words writeth it (*Feeth*) and faith likewife, that it fignifieth *capitales inimicitias*, and alfo that (*Feud*) vfed now in Scotland and the north parts of England, is the fame, and that is, a combination of kindred to reuenge the death of any of their blood againft the killer and all his race.

Felonie (*Felonia*) feemeth to come of the french (*Felonnie .i. impetuofitas, atrocitas, immifericordia*) *Felonia* (faith *Hotoman de verbis feudalibus*) *non prafcisè contumaciam vafalli in dominum, huiufque in vafallum perfidiam fignificat, verum quoduis capitale facinus*. And againe. *Felonia Gothis & Longobardis dicitur quod Germanis hodie Schelmarey, latinis Scelus*. *S*. *Ed. Cooke* faith thus. *Ideo dicta eft felonia qua fieri debet felleo animo*. *li*. 4. *fo*. 124. *b*. *Hoftienfis in fua fumma titulo*, De *feudis*, and others fpeak of this to this effect. *Felonia, aliàs Fallonia eft culpa vel iniuria, propter quam vafallus amittit feudum Sed hec refpicit dominum feudi. Eft & alia fallonia qua non refpicit dominum, fc. quando vafallus interficit fratrem vel filium fuum, vel filium fratris, vel aliud crimen commifit quod parricidii appellatione continetur. & plures aliæ falloniæ tam refpicientes dominum, quàm alios propter quas feudum amittitur ibi notantur*. We account any offence felonie that is in degree next vnto petit treafon, and comprifeth diuers particulars vnder it, as murder, theft, killing of a mans felfe, *Sodometrie*, rape, wilfull burning of houfes, and diuers fuch like, which are to be gathered efpecially out of ftatutes, whereby many offences are dayly made felonie, that before were not. Felonie is difcerned from lighter

ter offences by this, that the punishment thereof is death. Howbe it this is not perpetuall. For *petit larcenie* (which is the stealing of any thing vnder the valew of twelue pence) is felony, as appeareth by *Broke titulo Coron. num.* 2. his reason is, because the indictment against such a one must runne with these words, (*felonicè cepit*) and yet is this not punished by death though it be losse of goods. Any other exception I know not, but that a man may call that *felony*, which is vnder petit treason, and punished by death. And of this there be two sorts: one lighter, that for the first time may be releeued by cleargie, another, that may not. And these you must also learne to know by the statutes: for Cleargie is allowed, where it is not expressely taken away. Of these maters reade Stawnfords first booke of his *pl. cor.* from the end of the second Chapter, to the 39. and the statutes whereby many offences be made felonie, since he writ that learned booke. See also *Lamberds Iustice of peace, lib.* 2. *cap.* 7. in a Table drawne for the purpose. As also *lib.* 4. *cap.* 4. *pag.* 404. and *Crompton* in his iustice of peace. *fol.* 32. *&c.* Felonie is also punished by losse of lands not entayled, and goods or chatels, as well real as personall: and yet the statutes make difference in some cases touching lands, as appeareth by the statute, *anno* 37 *H.* 8. *cap.* 6. Felonie ordinarily worketh corruption of bloud, though not, where a statute ordaineth an offence to be felonie, and yet withall saith, that it shall not worke corruption of bloud. As *anno* 39. *Eliz. cap.* 17. How many wayes felonie is cōmitted, see *Cromptons Iustice of peace. pag.* 32. *&c.*

Feyre. See *Fayre.*

Felo de se, is he that committeth felonie by murthering himselfe. See *Cromptons Iustice of peace. fol.* 28. and *Lamberds Eirenarcha. lib.* 2. *cap.* 7. *pag.* 243.

Fencemoneth, is a moneth, wherein it is vnlawful to hunt in the Forest, because in that moneth the female Deere do faune: and this moneth beginneth 15. dayes before Midsomer, and endeth 15. dayes after. So that to this moneth there be 31. daies. See *Manwood parte prim.* of his Forest lawes. *pag.* 86. but more at large *parte secunda. cap.* 13 *per totum.* It is also called the defence moneth, that is, the forbidden moneth, and the word defence is vsed in like sort. *West.* 2. *cap.* 47. *anno* 13. *Ed.* 1. in these words: All waters where Salmons be taken, shall be in defence for taking of Salmons from the Natiuitie, &c.

Fennycricke, or rather *Fenegreeke*, (*Fœnum Græcum*) is a medicinall plant or herbe, so called, because it groweth like hey, and commeth out of Greece. Of this you may reade more in *Gerrards herball. lib. 2. cap.* 483. The seede therof is reckoned among drugs, that are to be garbled. *an.* 1. *Iacob. cap.* 19.

Feofment (*feoffamentum*) by the opinion of *Sir Thomas Smith de Repub. Anglor. lib.* 3. *cap.* 8. and *M. West part. prim. symbol. lib.* 2. *sect.* 280. is descended from the Gottish word (*feudum*) which you haue interpreted in (*fee*) and signifieth (*donationem feudi.*) But (as *M. West* also addeth) it signifieth in our common lawe, any gift or graunt of any honors, castels, maners, mesuages, lands, or other corporall and immoueable things of like nature, vnto another in fee simple, that is to him and his heires for euer, by the deliuerie of seisin and possession of the thing giuen, whether the gift be made by word or writing. And when it is in writing, it is called a deed of feofment, and in euery feofment the giuer is called the Feaffour (*feoffator*,) and he that receiueth by vertue thereof, the Feoffee (*feoffatus*) and *Litleton* saith, that the proper difference betweene a feoffour and a donour is, that the feoffour giueth in fee-simple, the donour in fee-taile. *lib.* 1. *cap.* 6.

Feodarie, *aliàs*, *Feudarie*, *aliàs*, *feudatarie*, (*feudatarius*) is an officer authorized and made by the master of the Court of wards and liueries, by leters patents vnder the seale of that office. His function is to be present with the Eschcater at the finding of any office, and to giue euidence for the king as well cōcerning the valew, as the tenure, and also to surrey the land of the ward, after the office found, and to rate it. He is also to assigne the kings widowes their dowers and to receiue all the rents of the wards lands, with in his circuit, and to answer them to the Receiuer of the court of wardes and liueries. This officer is mentioned *anno* 32. H. 8. *cap.* 46.

Ferdfare, *significat quietantiam eundi in exercitum. Fleta libr. pri. cap.* 47.

Ferdwit, *significat quietantiam murdri in exercitu. Fleta libr. prim. cap.* 47.

Ferm (*firma*) commeth of the French (*Ferme*. i. *colonia, villa, prædium,*) and signifieth with vs, house or land, or both, taken by Indenture of lease, or lease parol. It may likewise not vnaptly be coniectured, that both the French and English word came from the Latine (*firmus*) for *(locare ad firmum)* I find somtime to signifie with others, as much as (to set or let to farme) with vs. The reason whereof may be in respect of the sure hould they haue aboue tenents at will. *v. vocabul. vtriusque iuris. verbo Afflictus.* The authour of the new Termes of lawe, deriueth this word from the Saxon *(feormian)* which signifieth to feed or yeeld victuall. For in auncient time the reseruations were as well in victuals as money, which I leaue to the iudgemet of the Reader. How many wayes ferme is takẽ, see *Plowden. casu Wrothesley. fol.* 195. *a. b.*

Feudarie. See *Feodarie.*

Fieri facias, is a writ iudiciall, that lyeth at all times within the yeare and day, for him that hath recouered in an action of debt or dammages, to the Shyreeue, to command him to leuie the debt or the dammages of his goods, against whome the recouerie was had. This writ hath beginning from *Westm. 2. cap.* 18 *anno* 13. *Ed.* 1. See *old nat. br. fol.* 152. See great diuersitie thereof in the Table of the *Register iudiciall. verbo. Fieri facias.*

Fifteenth (Decimaquinta) is a tribute, or imposition of mony laide vpon euery city, borough, and other towne through the realme, not by the polle, or vpon this or that man, but in general, vpon the whole city or towne; so called, because it amounteth to one fifteenth parte of that, which the city or towne hath bene valued at of ould. This is now a dayes imposed by parlament: and euery towne through the realme, great or lesse, knoweth what a fifteenth for themselues doth amount vnto, because it is perpetuall: whereas the subsidie, which is raised of euery particular mans lands or goods, must needs be vncertaine, because the estate of euery seuerall man is so ticklish and vncertaine. And in that regard am I driuen to thinke that this fifteenth is a rate auncienly laide vpon euery towne, according to the land or circuit belonging vnto it. whereof *M. Camden* hath many mentions in his *Britannia.* In stead of the rest take a fewe *page.* 168. of *Wels* in Somerset shire he writeth thus. *Quo tempore, vt testatur censualis Angliæ liber, Episcopus ipsum oppidum tenuit, quod pro quinquaginta hidis geldauit*: And *pag.* 171. of *Bathe. Geldabat pro viginti hidis, quando Schira geldabat.* thirdly, *pa.* 181. of ould *Sarisbury* thus: *pro quinquaginta hidis geldabat.* and these rates were taken out of Domes day in the Eschequer. so that this seemed in ould time, to be a yearely tribute in certainty, whereas now, though the rate be certaine, yet it is not leuied but by Parlament. See *Taske*, see *Quinsieme*.

Filazer (*Filazarius*) commeth of the french (*Filace*. i. *filum*, *filacium*) it is an officer in the common plees, whereof there be 14. in number: they make out all originall proces, as well reall as personall and mixt: and in actions meerely personall, where the defendauts be returned or sommoned, there goeth out the distresse infinite vntill apparence. If he be returned *Nihil*, then proces of *Capias infinite*, if the plaintife will, or after the third *Capias*, the plaintife may goe to the Exigenter of the Shire, where his originall is grounded, and haue an Exigent and proclamation made: And also the *Filazer* maketh foorth all writs of viewe in causes, where the view is prayed: he is also allowed to enter the imparlance, or the generall issue in common actions, where apparence is made with him, and also iudgement by confession in any of them before issue be ioyned, and to make out writs of execution thereupon. But although they entred the issue: yet the protonotarie must enter the iudgement, if it be after verdict. They also make writs of *Supersedeas*, in case where the defendant appeareth in their offices, after the *Capias* awarded.

Filctale. See *Sothale*.

File (*filacium*) is a threed or wyer, whereon writs, or other exhibits in courts, are fastened for the more safe keeping of them.

Finders. *anno* 18. *Ed*. 3. *stat*. 1. *cap*. *vnico*. *anno* 14. *R*. 2. *cap*. 10. seeme to be all one with those, which in these dayes we call searchers.

Fine (*finis*) commeth of the French (*fin*. i. *finis*) and hath diuers applications in our commō lawe: sometime being vsed for a formall or ceremonious conueyance of lands or tenements, or (as *West* saith, *titulo* Fines. *sect*. 25.) of any thing inheritable, being *in esse tempore finis*, to the end to cut off all controuersies. *West parte* 2. *symb*. *sect*. 1. defineth a fine in this signification: couenants made before Iustices, and entred of Record. And out of *Glanvile* thus *lib*. 8. *cap*. 1. *Finis est amicabilis compositio & finalis concordia, ex consensu & licentia Domini Regis, vel eius Iusticiariorum*. And *lib*. 9. *cap*. 3. *Talis concordia finalis dicitur, eo quod finem imponit negotio, adeò vt neutra pars litigantium ab eo de cætero poterit recedere*. And out of *Bracton*, *lib*. 5. *tract*. 5. *cap*. 28. *num*. 7. thus: *Finis ideò dicitur finalis concordia, quia imponit finem litibus, & est exceptio peremptoria*. The authour of the new termes of lawe, defineth it to be a finall agreement had betweene persons concerning any land or rent, or other thing, whereof any suite or writ is betweene them hanging in any court. See the new booke of Entries, *verbo Fines*. This fine is of so high a nature, that *Bratton.lib. 3. cap. 7. num. 3.* hath these words of it. *Item immediatè pertinet ad Regem querela finis facta in curia Domini Regis, & non obseruata. Et est ratio, quia nemo potest finem interpretari nisi ipse Rex, in cuius curia fines fiunt*. See also *anno 27. Ed. prim. stat. prim. cap. prim.* The Civilians would call this solemne contract *transactionem iudicialem de re immobili*, because it hath all the properties of a transaction, if it be considered in his originall vse. *v. Wesemb. parat. titulo de transact.* For it appeareth by the writers of the common lawe aboue named, that it is nothing but a composition or concord acknowledged and recorded before a competent Iudge, touching some hereditament or thing immoueable, that earst was in controuersie betweene those, that be parties to the same concord: and that for the better credit of the transaction, being by imputation made in the presence of the king, because it is leuied in his Court: and therefore doth it bind women couert being parties, and others whom ordinarily the lawe disableth to transact, onely for this reason, that all presumption of deceipt or euill meaning is excluded, where the king is priuy to the acte. But discourse of wit and reason, hath in time wrought other vses of this concord, which in the beginning was but one: as namely, to secure the title that any man hath in his possession against all men: to cut off intayles, and with more certaintie to passe the interest or the title of any land or tenement, though not controuerted, to whome we thinke good, either for yeares or in fee. In so much that the passing of a fine, in most cases, now is it but *mera fictio iuris*, alluding to the vse for the which it was invented, and supposing a doubt or controuersie, where in truth none is: and so not onely to worke a present prescription against the parties to the concord or fine, and their heires, but within fiue yeares against all others, not expressly excepted (if it be leuied vpon good consideration, and without Couin) as women couert, persons vnder 21. yeares, or prisoners, or such as be out of the realme at the time when it was acknowledged.

ledged. Touching this mater, see the statutes. *anno* 1. *Rich.* 3. *cap.* 7 *anno* 4. *H.* 7. *cap.* 24. *anno* 32. *H.* 8. *cap.* 36. & *anno* 31. *Elizab. ca.* 2. This fine hath in it fiue essentiall parts: the originall writ taken out against the conizour: the kings licence giuing the parties libertie to accord, for the which he hath a fine called the Kings siluer, being accompted a part of the Crownes reuenew. Thirdly, the concord it selfe, which thus beginneth: *Et est concordia talis, &c.* Fourthly, the note of the fine, which is an abstract of the original concord, and beginneth in this maner: *Sc. Inter R. querentem. &* S. *& E. vxorem eius, deforciantes, &c.* Fifthly, the foot of the fine, which beginneth thus: *Hac est finalis concordia facta in Curia domini Regis, apud Westm. à die Pasche in quindecim dies, anno &c.* So as the foote of the fine includeth all, containing the day, yeare, and place, and before what Iustice the concord was made. *Coke vo. 6. casu Teye. fol.* 38. *& 39.* This fine is either single or double: A single fine, is that by which nothing is graunted or rendred backe againe by the Cognizeesse to the Cognizours, or any of them. A double fine containeth a graunt and render backe againe, either of some rent, common, or other thing, out of the land, or of the land it selfe, to all or some of the Cognizours, for some estate, limiting thereby many times Remainders to straungers, which be not named in the writ of couenant. *West vbi supra, sect.* 21. Againe, a fine is of the effect, deuided into a fine executed, and a fine executory. A fine executed is such a fine, as of his owne force giueth a present possession (at the least in law) vnto the Cognizee, so that he needeth no writ of (*Habere facias seisinam*) for the execution of the same, but may enter; of which sort is a fine (*sur cognizance de droit come ceo que il ad de son done*) that is vpon acknowledgement, that the thing mentioned in the concord be *ius ipsius cognizati, vt illa qua idem habet de dono Cognitoris. West. sect.* 51. *K.* and the reason of this seemeth to be, because this fine, passeth by way of release of that thing, which the cognizee hath already (at the least by supposition) by vertue of a former gift of the cognizour. *Cokes* reports *li.* 3. the case of fines *fo.* 89. *b.* which is, in very deed, the surest fine of all. *Fines executorie* be such, as of their owne force doe not execute the possession in the Cognizeesse, as *fines sur cognizance de droit tantùm. fines sur done,* graunt, release, confirmation, or render. *For* if such fines be not leuied, or such render made vnto them, that be in possession at the time of the fines leuied, the cognizees must needs sew writs of (*Habere facias seisinam*) according to their seuerall cases, for the obtaining of their possessions, except at the leuying of such executory fines, the parties, vnto whom the estate is by them limited, be in possession of the lands passed thereby: for in this case such fines doe inure by way of extinguishment of right, not altering the estate or possession of the Cognizee, but perchaunce bettring it. *West. vbi supra, sect.* 20.

Touching the forme of these fines, it is to be considered vpon what writ or action the concord is to be made, and that is, most commonly, vpon a writ of couenant: and then first there must passe a paire of indentures betweene the Cognizour and Cognizee, whereby the Cognizour couenanteth with the cognizee, to passe a fine vnto him, of such or such things by a day set down. And these indentures, as they are first in this proceeding, so are they saide to lead the fine; vpon this couenant, the writ of couenant is brought by the Cognizee against the cognizour, who therevpon yeeldeth to passe the fine before the Iudge, and so the acknowledgement being recorded, the cognizour and his heires are presently concluded, and all straungers not excepted, after fiue yeares once passed. If the writ wherevpon the fine is grounded, be not a writ of couenaunt, but of *warrantia charta*, or a writ of right, or a writ of *mesn*, or a writ of custome and seruices (for of all these fines may also be founded. (*West. vbi supra, sect:* 23.) then this forme is obserued: the writ is serued vpon the party that is to acknowledge the fine, and then he appearing doth accordingly: See *Dier, fo.* 179. *nu.* 46.

This word (*fine*) sometime signifieth a summe of money, paide for an Income to lands or tenements let by lease: sometime an amends, pecuniarie punishment, or recompence vpon an offence committed against the king and his lawes, or a Lord of a maner. In which case, a man is said *facere finem de transgressione cum Rege, &c. Regist. Iud. fol.* 25. *a.* and of the diuersity of these fines with other mater worth the learning, see *Cromptons Iustice of peace, fol.* 141. *b.* 143. 144. and *Lamberds Eirenarcha libro.* 4. *ca* 16. *pa.* 555. But in all these diuersities of vses, it hath but one signification; and that is a finall conclusion or ende of differences betweene parties. And in this last sence, wherein it is vsed for the ending and remission of an offence, *Bracton* hath

hath it *li.2.ca.15. nu.* 8. speaking of a common fine that the Countie payeth to the king, for falsse judgemẽts or other trespasses, which is to be assessed by the Iustices in Eyre before their departure, by the oath of knights and other good men, vpon such as ought to pay it: with whome agreeth the statute *anno. 3. Ed. pri.ca.*18. There is also a common fine in leetes. See *Kitchin.fo.* 13.*a.v.common fine.* See *Fleta.l.*1. *ca.*48.

Fines pro licentia concordandi, anno 21.H.8.*c.*1. See *Fine.*

Fine force, seemeth to come of the french adiectiue (*fin*) and the substantiue (*force.*i.*vis*) The adiectiue (*fin*) signifieth sometime as much as craftie, wilie or subtill, sometime as much as, artificiall, curious, singular, exact, or perfect. as (*Rien contrefaict fin.* i. *nihil simulatum aut ad imitationem alterius expressum, potest esse exactum, vel ita absolutum, quin reprehensionem vel offensionem incurrat*, as is set downe in that worke, truly regal, intituled *βασιλικον δῶρον.pa.*115. so that this (*fine force*) with vs, seemeth to signifie an absolute necessitie or constreint, not avoidable. and in this sence it is vsed, *old. nat. br. fol.* 78. and in the statute *anno.* 35. H. 8.*ca.*12. *in Perkins Dower. fo.*321. and *Plowden.fo.* 94. *Coke. vol.6.fol.*111.*a.*

Fine adnullando levato de tenemento quod fuit de antiquo dominico, is a writ to Iustices, for the disanulling of a fine levied of lands holding in auncient demesn, to the preiudice of the Lord: *Register originall.fol.*15.*b.*

Fine capiendo pro terris,&c. is a writ lying for one, that vpon conviction by a Iury hauing his lands and goods taken into the kings hand, and his body committed to prison, obteineth fauour for a summe of money &c. to be remitted his imprisonment, and his lands and goods to be redeliuerd vnto him. *Register.orig.fo.*132.*a.*

Fine levando de tenementis tentis de Rege in capite,&c. is a writ directed to the Iustices of the cõmon plees, whereby to licence them to admit of a fine for the sale of land holding in *capite, Regist. originall,fol.*167.*a.*

Fine non capiendo pro pulchre placitando, is a writ to inhibit officers of courts, to take fines for faire pleading, *Register original.fol.*179. See *Beau pleder.*

Fine pro redisseisina capienda,&c. is a writ, that lieth for the release of one laid in prison for a redisseisin, vpon a reasonable fine. *Register. originall fol.*222.

Finarie. See *Blomarie.*

Finours of gold and siluer, be those that purifie and part those metals from other courser, by fire

fire and water. *anno*.4.H.7.*ca*.2. They be also called parters in the same place, sometime departers.

Fireboote, for the composition looke H*ayboote*. It signifieth allowance or *Estovers* of woods, to maintaine competent fire for the vse of the tenent.

First fruites (primitiæ) are the profits of every spirituall liuing for one yeare, giuen in auncient time to the Pope throughout all Cristendome: but by the statute *anno* 26.H.8.*cap*.3. translated to the Prince, for the ordring whereof, there was a court erected, *an*. 32.*H*.8.*ca*.45. but this court was dissolued. *anno.pri.Mar.sess*.2. *ca*. 10. & sithence that time, though those profits be reduced againe to the crowne, by the statute *anno 1.Eliz.ca*.4. yet was the court neuer restored, but all maters therein wont to be handled, were transferred to the Exchequer. See *Annats*.

Fishgarthe, *anno* 23.*H*.8.*ca*.18.

Fitche, See *furre*.

Fitzherberd, was a famous lawyer in the daies of King *Henry* the eight, and was chiefe *Iustice of the common plees*, he wrot two worthie bookes, one an abridgement of the common lawes, another intituled *de Natura brevium*.

F*ledwit*, commeth of the Saxon word (F*led*) that is a fugitiue, & wit, which some make but a termination, signifiing nothing of it selfe: how be it others say, it signifieth a reprehension, censure, or correction: It signifieth in our auncient lawe, a discharge or freedome from amercements, when one hauing been an outlawed fugitiue, commeth to the peace of our Lord the King, of his owne accord. *Rastall, Exposition of words*: or being licensed: *Newe termes of lawe*. See *Bloodwit*, and *Childwit*: See *Fletwit*.

Fleete(*Fleta*) is a famous prison in *London*, so called (as it seemeth) of the riuer, vpon the side whereof it standeth, *Camden Britannia, pag*. 317. Vnto this none are vsually committed, but for contempt to the king and his lawes, or vpon absolute commaundemēt of the king, or some of his courts, or lastly vpō debt, when men are vnable, or vnwilling to satisfie their creditours.

Flemeswit or rather (*Flehenswit*) commeth of the Saxon word (*Flean*) which is a contract of (*Flegen*) that is, to flie away. It signifieth with our lawyers, a libertie or charter, whereby to chalenge the catel or amercements of your man a fugitiue: *Rastall Exposition of words*. See *Bloodwit*. *Fleta* writeth this word two other waies, as (*Flemenesfre-*

vie or *Flemesfreicthe*, and interpreteth it, *habere catalla fugitivorum.li.1 ca.47.*

Fleta, is a feigned name of a learned lawyer, that writing a booke of the common lawes of England and other antiquities in the *Fleete*, termed it thereof *Fleta*: He seemeth to haue liued in *Ed.* the 2. time and *Edw.* the 3. *idem, li.1.ca.20.§.qui ceperint.li. 2. ca.66.§.item.quod nullus.*

Fletwit, aliàs Fredwit. Skene de verborum significatione.verb. Melletum. saith, that (*Flichtwit*) is a libertie to courts, and to take vp the amercements *pro melletis.* he giueth the reasō because (*Flicht*) is called *Fliting* in french (*Melle*) which sometime is conioyned with hand-strookes: And in some bookes *Placitum de melletis*, is called the moote or plee of beating or striking.

F*light See Finer.*

Florences, anno 1.R.3.ca. 8. a kinde of cloth so called.

Flotsen aliàs (Flotzam) is a word proper to the sease, signifiing any goods that by shipwrecke be lost, and lie floting or swimming vpon the toppe of the water, which with *Letson* and *lagon* and *shares* be giuen to the *Lord Admirall*, by his leters patents. Ietson is a thing cast out of the shippe being in daunger of wrecke, and beaten to the shore by the waters, or cast on the shore by the marriners. *Coke vol.6.fo.106.a. Lagon aliàs Lagam vel Ligan, is* that which lyeth in the bottome of the sea, *Coke ibi.* Shares* are goods due to more by proportion.

Foder (*fodrum*) signifieth in our English tongue, a course kinde of meate for horses and other catell. But among the Feudists, it is vsed for a prerogatiue that the prince hath, to be provided of corn and other meate for his horses by his subiects towards his wars, or other expeditions. *Arnoldus Clapmarius. de arcanis imperii.lib. 1.ca. 11.* And reade *Hotoman de verbis feudalibus. litera.F.*

Folgheres, or rather *Folgers*, be folowers, if we interpret the word according to the true signification: *Bracton* saith it signifieth, *eos qui alii deserviunt. lib. 3. tract.2.cap.10.*

Folkmoote, is a *Saxon* word, compounded of *Folk.i.populus* & *Gemettan.i.convenire.* It signifieth (as *M.Lamberd* saith in his explication of Saxon words, *verbo* (*Conuentus*) two kind of Courts, one nowe called the countie court, the other called the *Shyreeues turne*: This word is still in vse among the Londoners, and signifieth *celebrem ex omni ciuitate conuentum*: *Stowe* in his Suruey of *London.* but *M. Manwood* in his first part of forest lawes. *pag*. 111. hath these words. *Folkemote* is the court holden in London, wherein all the folke and people of the citie did complaine on the Mayor and the Aldermen, for misgouernment within the citie.

Forbarre, is for euer to depriue. *an.9.Ric.2.ca.2.*

Force (*Forcia*) is a french word, signifiing (*vim, nervositatem, fortitudinem, virtutem*) in our common lawe, it is most vsually applied to the euill part, and signifieth vnlawfull violence. *West* thus defineth it: *Force* is an offence, by which violence is vsed to things or persons. *parte 2.symbol. titulo. Inditements. sect. 65.* where also he diuideth it thus: *Force* is either simple or compound. *Simple* is that which is so committed, that it hath no other crime adioyned vnto it; as if one by force doe onely enter into an other mans possession, without doing any other vnlawfull act there. Mixt force, is that violence, which is committed with such a fact, as of it selfe onely, is criminall; as if any by force enter into another mans possession, and kill a man, or rauish a woman there, &c. he farder diuideth it into true force, and force after a sort, and so proceedeth to diuers other braunches worth the reading, as forcible entry, forcible deteining, vnlawfull assembly, *Rowtes, Riots, Rebellions, &c.*

Forcible deteining or withholding of possession, is a violent act of resistance by strong hand of men weaponed with harnes, or other action of feare, in the same place or else where, by which the lawfull entrie of Iustices or others is barred or hindred. *West parte 2. symbol. titulo Inditements, sect. 65.M.* of this see *Cromptons Iustice of peace, f.58.b &c. vsq; ad 63.*

Forcible entrie (*Ingressus manu forti factus*) is a violent actuall entrie into an house or land, &c. or taking a distresse of any person weaponed, whither he offer violence or feare of hurt to any there, or furiously driue any out of the possession thereof: *West parte 2 symbol. titulo Inditements, sect. 65.L.* of this see *Cromptons Iustice of peace, fol.58.b.59. &c. vsq; 63.* It is also vsed for a writ grounded vpon the statute. *anno 8.H.6.ca.9.* whereof reade *Fitz. nat.br.* at large, *fol.* 248. See the newe booke of Entries, *verbo Forcible Entrie*, see *Lamb. definitiõ in certen cases. Eiren.l.2.c.4.p.*145.

Forein (*Forinsecus*) commeth of the french (*Forain*.i *exterus, externus*) it is vsed adiectiuely in our common lawe, and ioyned with diuers substantiues in sences not vnworthy the exposition, as *Forein* mater, that is mater trible in another countie, *pl. cor.*

fol.

*fo.*154.or mater done in another countie, *Kitchin.fol.* 126. *Forein plea* (*forinsecum placitum*).i. a refusal of the Iudge as incompetent, because the mater in hand was not within his precincts, *Kitchin.fol.*75.*& anno* 4.*H.*8. *ca.* 2.*& anno* 22.*eiusdem.ca.* 2.*&* 14. *Forein* aunswer, that is, such an answer, as is not triable in the countie where it is made. *anno* 15.*H.6.ca.*5.*Forein seruice* (*forinsecum servitium*) that is such service, whereby a meane Lord holdeth ouer of another, without the compasse of his owne fee. *Brooke. titulo Tenures.f.*251. *nu.*12.*&* 28.*& Kitchin,fol.* 209. or else that which a tenent performeth, either to his owne Lord, or to the Lord paramount out of the fee. For of these seruices, *Bracton* speaketh thus, *lib.* 2.*cap.*16.*nu.*7. *Item sunt quædam seruitia, quæ dicuntur forinseca, quamvis sunt in charta de feoffamento expressa & nominata: & quæ ideo dici possunt forinseca, quia pertinent ad Dominum Regem, & non ad dominum capitalem, nisi cum in propria persona profectus fuerit in seruitio: vel nisi cum pro seruitio suo satisfecerit domino* Regi *quocunq; modo, & fiunt in certis temporibus, cum casus & necessitas evenerit, & varia habent nomina & diuersa: Quandoq; enim nominantur forinseca, large sumpto vocabulo, quod seruitium domini* Regis, *quandoq; scutagium, quandoq; seruitium domini Regis, & ideo forinsecum dici potest, quia fit & capitur foris, siue extra seruitium quod fit Domino capitali.v.Broke Tenures* 28. 95. *Forein seruice*, seemeth to be knights seruice or Escuage vncertaine. *Perkins* Reseruations 650. *Forein attachement* (*Attachiamentum forinsecum*) is an attachement of foriners goods, found within a libertie or citie, for the satisfaction of some citizen, to whome the said foriner oweth money.

Forein Apposer (*forinsecarum oppositor*) is an officer in the exchequer, to whom all shyreeues and baylifes doe repaire, by him to be opposed of their greene waxe, and from thence draweth downe a charge vpon the shyreeue and baylife to the clerk of the pipe.

Forest (*Foresta*) is a french word, signifing a great or vast wood. *Lieu forestier & sauuage: locus syluestris & saltuosus.* The writers vpon the common law define it thus: *Foresta est locus vbi feræ inhabitant vel includuntur. glos. in ca. cum dilecti. extra. de donatio. &* Felinus *in ca.* Rodolphus. *versu, quid autem Foresta. extra de rescriptis.* speaketh to the same effect. Some other writers doe say, it is called *foresta, quasi ferarum statio, vel tuta mansio ferarum.* But as it is taken with vs, *M.*

Manw. in his secõd part of forest lawes, *cap.* 1. *nu.* 1. thus defineth it: A Forest is a certaine territorie of wooddy grounds & fruitfull pastures, priviledged for wild beasts, and foules of forest, chace, and warren, to rest and abide in, in the safe protection of the King, for his princely delight and pleasure: which terrioritie of ground so priuiledged, is meered and bounded with vnremoueable markes, meeres, and Boundaries, either knowne by mater of record, or else prescription, and also replenished with wild beasts of Venerie, or chase, and with great coverts of vert, for the succour of the said wild beasts, to haue their aboad in: for the preseruation & continuance of which said place, togither with the vert and venison, there are certaine particular lawes, priviledges, and officers, belonging to the same, meete for that purpose, that are onely proper vnto a forest, and not to any other place. The same definiton he hath *parte* 1. *pag.* 139. which though it haue many superfluities, yet it well expresseth the nature of the thing, especially the explication adioyned, which there is set downe by the said author in both places in his first part *pag.* 16. where he fetcheth a forest from such overgrowne antiquitie, alledging for it the second booke of Kings, *ca.* 2. *ver.* 24. & *ca.* 19. *vers.* 23. and the 104. psalme *vers.* 20. the 131. *ver.* 6. he taketh licence to sport himselfe. for though our english translation haue the word forest, to expresse the vastnes of the desert, yet if we looke to the originall Idiome, we shall finde no more reason to call those places forests, thẽ either chases or parks.

The maner of making forests, as the same author well setteth downe, *parte.* 1. *pag.* 142. is this. The king sendeth out his commissiõ vnder the broad seale of England, directed to certaine discreete persõs, for the view, perambulation, meering & bounding of the place, that he mindeth to afforest; which returned into the chauncerie, proclamation is made throughout all the Shire, where the ground lieth, that none shal hunt or chace any maner of wilde bests within that precinct, without the kings speciall licence, after which he appointeth ordinances, lawes, and officers, fit for the preseruation of the vert and venison: and so becommeth this a forest by mater of record. The properties of a forest are these in speciall, first, a forest, as it is truly and strictly taken, cannot be in the hands of any but the king: the reason is giuen by *M. Manwood,* because none hath power to graunt commission to a Iustice in *Eire* for the forest, but the king. *parte.* 1.

pag.87. The second propertie, be the courts, as the Iustice seate every three yeare, the Swainemoote thrice every yeare: *Idem eodem pag*.90.& *parte* 2.*ca*. 1.*nu*. 4. & 5. and the attachement, once every fortie daies.*Idem eod. pag*.92.The third propertie may be the officers belonging vnto it, for the preservation of the vert and venison, as first the Iustices of the forest, the warden or keeper,the verders, the foristers, Agistours, Regarders, Bailiffes, Bedels and such like, which you may see in their places. See *Manwood part*.2.*ca*.1.*nu*. 4.& 5. But the cheife propertie of a forest,both by *M. Manwood. parte* 1.*pa*.144. and *M. Crompton pag*. 146. is the Swainmote, which(as they both agree) is no lesse incident vnto it, then the court of *Pyepowders* to a faire. Other courts and offices are not so requisite,in those forests that are in the hands of subiects,because they be not truly forests: but if this faile,then is there no thing of a forest remaining, but it is turned into the nature of a chace.See *Chace*.I reade of thus many forests in *England*. The forest of *Windsour in Berkshire*: *Cambd.Britan.pag*. 213. of *Pickering.Crompton* 190. of *Shirwood idem fol*.202.of *Englewood in Cumberland. anno*. 4. *H*.7.*ca*.5.& *Crompton fol*.42. of *Lancaster*. *Idem.fol*.196. of *Wolemore.Stones Annals.pag*. 462. of *Gillingham*. *Idem. pag*. 113. of *Knaresborow.anno*.21.*H*.8.*ca*. 17. of *Waltham. Camd. pag*.328. of *Breden. Idem,pag*. 176. of *Whitehart Idem, pag*. 150. of *Wiersdale*. I*dem pag*. 589.*and Lownsedall ibidem.of Deane.Idem.pag*. 266. & & *anno* 8.*H*.6.*ca*.27.& *anno* 19. H.7. *cap*. 8. *of Saint Leonards in Southsex. Manwood parte*. 1.*pa*. 144. *of Waybridge & Sapler*. I*dem.eodem. pa*. 63. *of Whitvey. pag*.81.*of Fekenham,Camd.pa* 441. *of Rockingham*. I*dem pag*. 596. *Forest de la mer. Idem.pag*. 467. *of* Huckstowe.*Idem pa*.456.*of Haye. Manwood part*.1.*pag*.144.*of Cantselly*, *eadem pag*. *of Ashdowne* in the county of Sussex.*anno*.37.*H*. 8. *ca*. 16. *Forests of Whittlewood* and *Swasie* in the countie of *Northampton. anno* 33.*H*.8.*ca*. 38.*of Fronselwood in com. Somerset. Cooke li*. 2.*Cromw.case.f*.71.*b*. I heare also of the forest of *Exmore, in* Devonshire. There may be more which he that listeth, may looke for.

*Forester (forestarius)*is a sworn officer of the Forest, appointed by the Kings leters patents, to walke the forest both earely and late, watching both the vert and venison, attaching and presenting all trespassers against them, within their owne bayliwicke or walke: whose oath you may see in *Crompton*.

fol. 201. And though these letters patents be ordinarily graunted, but *quam diu bene se gesserint*, yet some haue this graunt to thē and their heires, and thereby are called *Foristers* or *Fosters in fee. Idem, fol.* 157. & 159. *Et Manwood parte prima. pag.* 220. whome in Latine *Crompton* calleth *Foristarium feudi. fol.* 175.

Foreiudger, (*forisiudicatio*) signifieth in the common lawe, a iudgement, whereby a man is depriued, or put by the thing in question. It seemeth to bee compounded of (*fors.* i. *præter*) & (*iuger.* i. *iudicare.*) *Bracton lib.* 4. *tract.* 3. *cap.* 5. hath these words: *Et non permittas quòd A. capitalis dominus feudi illius, habeat custodiam hæredis, &c. quia in Curia nostra forisiudicatur de custodia, &c.* So doth *Kitchin* vse it. *fol.* 209. and *old nat. bre. fol.* 44. & 81. and the statute. *anno* 5. *Ed.* 3. *cap.* 9. and *anno* 21. *R.* 2. *cap.* 12. *Foriudicatus* with authors of other nations signifieth as much as (*banished*) or as (*deportatus*) in the auncient Romaine lawe, as appeareth by *Vincentius de Franchis, decis.* 102. *Mathæus de Afflictis. lib.* 3. *feudorum. Rub.* 31. *pag.* 625.

Foregoers be pourveyours, going before the king or queene, being in progresse, to prouide for them, *anno* 36. *Ed.* 3. *cap.* 5.

Forfeiture, (*forisfactura*) commeth of the French word (*forfaict.* i. *scelus*) but signifieth in our language, rather the effect of transgressing a penall lawe, then the transgression it selfe: as forfeiture of Escheates. *anno* 25. *Ed.* 3 *cap.* 2. *Statut. de Proditionibus*. Goods confiscate, and goods forfeited differ. *Stawnf. pl. cor fol.* 186. where those seeme to be forfeited, that haue a knowne owner, hauing committed any thing whereby he hath lost his goods; and those confiscate, that are disavowed by an offendour, as not his owne, nor claymed by any other. I thinke rather, that forfeiture is more generall, and confiscation particular, to such as forfeit onely to the Princes Exchequer. Reade the whole chapter. *lib.* 3. *cap.* 24. Full forfeiture (*plena forisfactura*) otherwise called (*plena vita*) is forfeiture of life and member, and all else that a man hath. *Manwood parte prim. pag.* 341. The Canon Lawyers vse also this word. For *forisfacta sunt pecuniaria pœnæ delinquentium. Glos. in cap. Præsbyteri, extra. de pœnis.*

Forfeiture of mariage, (*forisfactura maritagii*) is a writ lying against him, who houlding by knights seruice, and being vnder age and vnmaried, refuseth her, whome the Lord offereth him, without his disparagement, and marieth another. *Fitzh nat. br. fol.* 141.

141.*H.I. K.L. Register orig. fol.* 163.*b.*

Forseng, quietantiam prioris prisæ designat: in hoc enim delinquunt Burgenses Londonenses, cum prisas suas ante prisas regis faciunt. Fleta *lib.* 1. *cap.* 47.

Forgerie. See here next following, *Forger of false deeds.*

Forger of false deedes, commeth of the french (*Forger*).i. *accudere, fabricare, conflare,* to beate one an anvile, to fashion, to bring into shape, and signifieth in our common law, either him that fraudulently maketh and publisheth false writings, to the preiudice of any mans right, or else the writ that lyeth against him, that committeth this offence. *Fitzh. nat. br. fol.* 96. *B. C.* calleth it a writ of deceite. See Tearmes of law, *verbo Forger.* and *Wests Simbol. parte.* 2. *Indictments, sectio.* 66. See the new booke of Entries. *verbo* Forger. *de faits.* This is a branch of that which the ciuilians call *crimen falsi: Nam falsarius est, qui decipiendi causa scripta publica falsificat. Speculator. de crimine falsi. Falsi crimen proprie dicitur, quod vtilitatis priuatæ causa factum est. Connanus li.* 5. *ca.* 7. *nu.* 4. *Ad esse falsitatis tria requiruntur: mutatio veritatis, dolus, & quod alteri sit nocivum. Quorum si alterum desit, falsitas non est punibilis. Hostiensis, & Azo in suis summis.*

Forister. See *Forester.*

Formdon (*Breve formatum donationis*) is a writ that lyeth for him, that hath right to any lands or tenements by vertue of any entayle, growing from the statute of *Westm.* 2. *cap.* 1. It lyeth in three sorts, and accordingly is called *forma donationis*, or *formdon* in the descender: *formdon* in the reverter, or *formdon* in the remainder. *Formdon* in the descender lyeth for the recouery of lands, &c. giuen to one and the heyres of his bodie, or to a man and his wife, and the heyres of their two bodies, or to a man and his wife being cosin to the donour, in franke mariage, and afterward alienated by the Donee. For after his decease his heyre shall haue this writ against the tenent or alienee. *Fitz. nat. br. fol.* 211. He maketh three sorts of this *formdon* in the descender: The first is, in the maner now expressed: the second is, for the heire of a coparcener, that alienateth and dieth. *fol.* 214 The third is called by him (*In simul tenuit*) *fol.* 216. which lyeth for a coparcener or heire in Gauelkind, before partition against him, to whome the other coparcener or heire hath alienated and is dead. *Formdon* in the reuerter, lyeth for the donour or his heires, where land entayled to certaine and their issue, with

condi-

condition for want of such issue to reuert to the donour and his heires, against him to whom the Donee alienateth, after the issue extinct, to which it was entayled. *Fitzh. nat. br. fol.* 219. Formdon in the remainder lyeth, where a man giueth landes in tayle, the remainder to another in tayle, and afterward the former tenent in tayle dieth without issue of his bodie, and a stranger abateth, then he in the remainder shall haue this writ. *Fitz. nat. br. fol.* 217. See the *Register original. fol.* 238. 242. 243. of this see the new booke of Entries. *verb. Formdon.*

Forsechoke, seemeth to signifie originally as much as *forsaken* in our moderne language, or (*derelictum*) with the Romaines. It is especially vsed in one of our statutes, for land or tenements seised by the Lord, for want of seruices due from the tenent: and so quietly held and possessed beyond the yeare and day. As if we should say, that the tenent which seeing his land or tenements taken into the Lords hand, and possessed so long, taketh not the course appointed by lawe to recouer them, doth in due presumption of lawe disavow or forsake whatsoeuer right he hath vnto them. See the statute *anno* 10. *Ed.* 1. *cap. vnico.*

Forstall, is to be quit of amerciaments and catels arrested within your land, and the amerciaments thereof comming. New termes of lawe.

Forstalling (*forstallatio*) is partly french, for (*Estaller*) is in that tongue, as much as (*merces exponere, expedire, explicare*) or to shew wares in a market or faire. It signifieth in our common law, the buying or bargaining for any victuals or wares comming to be sould toward any faire or market, or from beyond the seas toward any city, port, hauen, creeke, or roade of this realme, and before the same be there. *anno.* 51. *H.* 3. *stat.* 6. *West. parte* 2. *Simbol. titulo indictments. sect.* 64. *Forstaller, in Cromptons Iurisdiction, fol.* 153. is vsed for stopping of a deere broken out of the forest, from returning home againe, or laying betweene him and the forest, in the way that he is to returne: See *Regratours* and *Engrossers*. See *Cromptons Iustice of peace. fol.* 69. *a.* The author of the new terms of law defineth it thus. *Forstalling* (*Forstallamentum*) is the buying of corne, cattell, or other merchandies by the way, as it commeth toward the faire or market to be sould, to the intent to sell the same againe at a more high and deere price. *Fleta* saith thus of it, *significat obtrusionem viæ vel impedimentum*

mentum transitus & fuga auertiorum, li. 1. cap. 47.

Fortescue, was a learned Lawyer, & Lord *Chauncelor* in *Henry* the 6. dayes: who writ a booke in the commendation of our common lawes.

Fortlet (forteletum) commeth nere the french *(fortelet.i. valenticulus, forticulus)* and signifieth in our common lawe, a place of some strength. *old nat. br. fol.* 45. This in other countries is written *(fortalitium)* and signifieth *(castrum.) Scraderus select. & practabil. quæst.* §. 12. *nu.* 7. & 8.

F*other*, is a weight of twenty hundred, which is a waine or cart loade. *Speight* in his *Annot.* vpon *Chawcer.*

Fourche (Afforciare) seemeth to come of the french, *(fourcher.* i. *titubare linguâ)* and signifieth in our common lawe, a putting off, prolonging, or delay of an action. And it appeareth no vnpleasant metaphor: for as by stammering we draw out our speech, not deliuering that we haue to say in ordinary time, so by fourching we prolong a suite that might be ended in a shorter space. To fourch by essoine. *Westm.* 1. *cap.* 24. *anno* 3. *Ed. prim.* where you haue words to this effect: *Coparceners, Iointtenants*, and Tenents in common, may not fourch by essoine, to essoine seuerally, but haue only one essoine, as one sole tenent may haue. And *anno* 6. *Ed.* 1. *ca.* 10. you haue it vsed in like sort.

Foutgeld, is a word compounded of these two German words *(fous.* i. *pes*, and *(gyldan.* i. *solvere)* and it signifieth an amercement for not cutting out the balles of great dogges feet in the forest. See *Expeditate*. And to be quit of *footegeld* is a priuiledge to keepe dogges within the forest, vnlawed, without punishment or controlment. *Cromptons Iurisdict. fol.* 197. *Manwood parte pri.* of his forest lawes, *pag.* 86.

Fowles of warren. See *Warren.*

Founder, is he that melteth mettall, and maketh any thing of it, by casting it into a mold, &c. *anno* 17. *Rich.* 2. *cap.* 1. deriued of the verbe *(fundere)* to powre.

Franchise, (libertas, franchesia) commeth of the french *(franchise)* so signifiing: it is taken with vs for a priuiledge, or an exemption from ordinarie iurisdiction, and sometime an immunitie from tribute. It is either personall or reall. *Cromp. Iurisd. fol.* 141. that is belonging to a person immediatly, or else by meanes of this or that place, or court of immunitie, whereof he is either chiefe or a member.

In what particular things franchises commonly consist, See *Britton cap.* 19. Franchise royall *anno* 15. *R.2.cap.4.* & *anno* 2. *H.* 5.*cap.* 7. *in fine*, seemeth to bee that, where the kings writs runne not: as *Chester* and *Durham*, they are called Seignories royall. *an.* 28. *H.* 6. *cap.* 4. The authour of the new Termes of lawe saith, that *franches royall* is, where the King graunteth to one and his heires, that they shall be quit of tolle or such like: See *franchise* in the new booke of Entries. See *Bracton lib.* 2. *cap.* 5. See *Sac.*

Frank almoine (*libera* Eleemo-*zyna*) in french (*frank Ausmone*) signifieth in our common lawe, a tenure or title of lands. *Britton cap.* 66. *nu.* 5. saith thus of it: *Franke almoyne* is lands or tenements bestowed vpon God, that is, giuen to such people, as bestow themselues in the seruice of God, for pure and perpetuall almes: whence the feoffours or giuers cannot demaund any terrestriall seruice, so long as the lands. &c. remaine in the handes of the feoffees. With this agreeth the grand custumary of *Normandie. cap.* 32. Of this you may reade *Bracton* at large. *lib.* 2. *cap.* 5. & 10. See *Fitzh. nat. br. fol.* 211. See the new booke of Entries. *verbo. Franke Almoine.* But *Britton* maketh another kind of this land, &c. which is giuen in almes, but not free almes: because the tenents in this are tyed in certain seruices to the feoffor, *Britton vbi supra.*

Frank bank (*francus bancus*) in true french, (*franc banc*) signifieth, word for word, a free bench or seate: and among our lawe writers, it seemeth to be vsed for copyhold lands, that the wife being espoused a virgin, hath after the decease of her husband for her dower. *Kitchin fol.* 102. *Bracton lib.* 4. *tract.* 6. *cap.* 13. *nu.* 2. hath these wordes: *Consuetudo est in partibus illis, quòd vxores maritorum defunctorum habeant francum bancum suum de terris sockmannorum, & tenent nomine dotis. Fitzher.* calleth it a custome, whereby in certaine cities the wife shall haue her husbands whole lands, &c. for her dower. *Nat. br. fol.* 150. *P.* See *Plowden casu Newis. fol.* 411.

Frank chase, (*Libera chasea*) is a libertie of free chase, whereby all men hauing ground within that compasse, are prohibited to cut downe wood, or discouer, &c. without the view of the forester, though it be his owne demesne. *Cromptons Iurisdictions, fol.* 187.

Frank fee (*feudum francum, seu liberum*) is by *Brooke tit. Demesn. num.* 32. thus expressed: That which is in the hand of the King or Lord of any maner, being

being auncient demesn of the Crowne (*viz.* the *Demesnes*) is called *frank fee*, and that which is in the hands of the tenents, is auncient demesn onely: see the *Register original.fol.* 12. *a.* Whereby it seemeth, that that is frank fee, which a man holdeth at the common lawe to himselfe and his heires, and not by such seruice as is required in auncient demesn, according to the custome of the maner. And again, I find in the same booke, *fol.* 14. *b.* a note to this effect, that the lands which were in the handes of king *Edward* the Saint, at the making of the booke called *Doomesday*, is auncient demesn: and that all the rest in the realme is called frank fee: with the which note *Fitzherb.* agreeth, *na. br. fol.* 161. *E.* So that all the land in the realme, by this reason, is either auncient demesn, or frank fee. The new expounder of the lawe termes defineth frank fee, to be a tenure in fee simple, of lands pleadable at the common lawe, and not in auncient demesn: See *Fachineus. lib.* 7. *cap.* 39. who defineth *feudum francum esse, pro quo nullum seruitium præstatur Domino*: with whom agreeth *Zasius de feudis. parte* 12. saying, that therefore it is *feudum improprium, quia ab omni servitio liberum.*

Frank ferme (*Firma libera*) is land or tenement, wherein the nature of fee is chaunged by feofment, out of knights seruice, for certaine yearely seruices, and whence neither homage, wardship, mariage, nor releife may be demaunded, nor any other seruice not contained in the feofment. *Britton. ca.* 66. *nu.* 3. see *Fee ferme.*

Frank *law* (*libera lex*) See *Cromptons Iustice of peace, fol.* 156. *b.* where you shall finde what it is, by the contrary. For he that for an offence, as conspiracy, &c. leeseth his franke lawe, is said to fall into these mischiefs: first, that he may neuer be impaneled vpon any iury, or assise, or otherwise vsed in testifiing any truth. Next, if he haue any thing to doe in the kings court, he must not approch thither in person, but must appoint his attourney. Thirdly, his lands, goods, and chatels must be seised into the kings hands: and his lands must be estreaped, his trees rooted vp, and his body committed to prison. For this, the said authour citeth the booke of Assises *fo.* 59. *Conspiracy.* F. 11. 24. *Ed.* 3. *fo.* 34. *See Conspiracy.*

Frank mariage (*liberũ maritagiũ*) is a tenure in taile speciall, growing from these words in the gift comprised: *Sciant &c. me M. H. de W. dedisse & concessisse, & præsenti charta mea confirmasse I. A. filio meo & Margeriæ vxori eius, filiæ veræ T.N. in liberũ maritagium vnum messuagium &c. West parte* i. *Symbol. li.* 2. *sect.* 303. The effect of which words is, that they shall haue the land to them, and the heires of their bodies, and shall doe no fealty to the donour, vntill the fourth degree. See new Terms of law. *Glanuile li* 7. *ca.* 18. *& Bracton li.* 2. *ca.* 7. *nu.* 4. where he diuideth *maritagium, in liberum & seruitio obligatum.* See *Mariage. Fleta* giueth this reason why the heires doe no seruice vntill the fourth discent, *ne donatores vel eorum hæredes, per homagii receptionem, a reuersione repellantur.* And why in the fourth discent and downeward, they shall doe seruice to the donour, *quia in quarto gradu vehementer præsumitur, quòd terra non est pro defectu hæredum donatariorum reversura, libro tertio. ca.* 11. *in princ.*

Frankpledge (Franciplegium) is compounded of *(Franc* .i. *liber)* and *(pleige* .i. *fideiussor)* and signifieth in our common law, a pledge or surety for free men. For the auncient custome of England for the preseruation of the publique peace, was that euery free borne man, at fourteene yeares of age, after *Bracton* (religious persons, clerks, knights, and their eldest sonnes excepted) should finde suerty for his truth toward the King and his subiects, or else be kept in prison, whereupon a certaine number of neighbours became customably bound one for another, to see each man of their pledge forthcomming at all times, or to answere the transgression committed by any broken away. So that whosoeuer offended, it was forthwith inquired in what pledge he was, and then they of that pledge, either brought him forth within 31. daies to his aunswere, or satisfied for his offence. This was called *Frankpledge, causa qua supra.* and the circuit thereof was called *Decenna,* because it commonly consisted of 10. houshouldes: And euery particular person thus mutually bound for himselfe and his neighbours, was called *Decennier,* because he was of one *Decenna* or another: This custome was so kept, that the shyreeues, at euery county court, did from time to time take the oaths of yonge ones, as they grew to the age of 14. yeares, and see, that he were combined in one dozen or another. whereupon this braunch of the shyreeues authority was called *visus Franciplegii,* view of frankpledge. See the statute for view of Frankpledge, made *anno.* 18. *Ed.* 2. See *Decennier, Leete vew of Frankpledge,* and *Freoborghe.* That this disci-

pline

pline is borowed by vs of the Romane Emperours or rather *Lombards*, appeareth most manifestly in the second booke of *Feuds. ca.* 53. vpon which if you reade *Hotoman*, with those authors that he there recordeth, you will thinke your labour well bestowed. Reade more of this. *viz.* what articles were wont to be inquired of in this court, in *Hornes mirrour of Iustices li.* 1. *ca. de la veneu des francs pleges*, and what these articles were in auncient times, see *in Fleta. li.* 2. *ca.* 52.

Fredwit See Fletwit.

Free chapell (*libera Capella*) by some opinion, is a chapell founded within a parish for the seruice of God, by the deuotion and liberalitie of some good man, ouer and aboue the mother Church, vnto the which it was free for the parishioners, to com or not to come, & edowed with maintenance by the founder, and therevpon called free: I haue heard others say, and more probably, that those only be free chapels, that are of the Kings foundation, and by him exempted from the Iurisdiction of the Ordinarie: but the King may licence a subiect to found such a chapell, and by his charter exempt it from the Ordinaries visitation also. That it is called free in respect it is exempted from the iurisdiction of the *Diocesan*, appeareth by the Register originall. *fol.* 40. & 41. These chapels were all giuen to the King: with chaunteries *anno.* 1. *Ed.* 6. *ca.* 14. *Free chapell of Saint Martin le grand. anno.* 3. *Eduardi* 4. *capite quarto. & anno.* 4. *Eduard. quarti ca.* 7.

Free hould (*liberum tenemetum*) is that land or tenement, which a man holdeth in fee, fee taile, or at the least, for terme of life, *Bract. li.* 2. *ca.* 9. The newe expounder of the lawe termes saith, that free hold is of 2 sorts. Freehould in deede, and freehold in lawe: Freehold in deede, is the reall possession of land or tenements in fee, fee tayle, or for life. Freehould in lawe, is the right that a man hath to such land or tenements before his entry or seisure. I haue heard it likewise extended to those offices, which a man holdeth either in fee or for terme of life. *Britton* defineth it to this effect. *Frank tenement* is a possession of the soile, or seruices issuing out of the soile, which a free man holdeth in fee to him and his heires, or at the least, for tearme of his life, though the soile be charged with free seruices or others. *ca.* 32. *Free hold* is sometime taken in opposition to villenage. *Bract. li,* 4. *ca.* 37. & 38. *M. Lamberd* (in his expliplication of Saxon words, *verbo Terra ex scripto*) saith, that land in the Saxons time was called either *Bockland*, that is holden by booke or writing: or *Folcland*, that is holden without writing: The former, he reporteth, was held with farre better conditions, and by the beter sort of tenents, as noble men and gentlemen, being such as we nowe call free hould: the later was commonly in the possession of clownes, being that which wee nowe call at the will of the Lord: I finde in the Register iudiciall. *fol.* 68. *a.* and in diuers other places, that he which holdeth land vpon an execution of a Statute merchant, vntill he be satisfied the debt. *tenet vt liberum tenementum sibi & assignatis suis.* and *fol.* 73. *b.* I reade the same of a tenent *per elegit*; where I thinke the meaning is not, that such tenents be freehoulders, but as freehoulders for their time, that is vntill they haue gathered profits to the value of their debt. *Freehoulders* in the auncient lawes of Scotland, were called *Milites. Skene de verb. signif. verb. Milites*: The *D. & Student* saith, that the possession of land, after the lawe of England, is called *franck tenement, or free hould. fol* 97. *a.*

Frenchman (*Francigena*) was wont to be vsed for euerie outlandish man. *Bracton. lib.* 3. *tract.* 2. *cap.* 15. *See* Englecerie.

Frendwite, vel Infeng, significat quietantiam prioris prisæ ratione convivii, Fleta li. 1. *ca.* 47.

Frendles man, was wont to be the Saxon word for him, whome we call an outlawe. And the reason thereof I take to be: because he was vpon his exclusion from the kings peace and protection, denied all helpe of freinds, after certaine daies. *Nam forisfecit amicos. Bract. li.* 3. *tract.* 2. *ca.* 12. *nu.* 1. whose words are these. *Talem vocant Angli (vtlaugh) & alio nomine antiquitùs solet nominari, sc: Frendles man: & sic videtur quod forisfecit amicos: & vnde si quis talem post vtlagariam & expulsionem scienter paverit, receptaverit, vel scienter cōmunicaverit aliquo modo, vel receptauerit, vel occultauerit, eadem pœnâ puniri debet, quâ puniretur vtlagatus: ita quòd careat omnibus bonis suis & vita, nisi Rex ei parcat de sua gratia.*

Fresh disseisin (*Frisca disseisina*) commeth of the french (*Fraiz. i. recens*) and (*disseisir .i. posessione eiicere*) It seemeth to signifie in our common law, that disseisin that a man may seeke to defeate of himselfe, and by his owne power, without the helpe of the king or his iudges, *Britton. ca.* 5. & that is such disseisin, as is not aboue 15. daies olde. *Bract. li.* 4. *ca.* 5. whome you may reade at large

large of this mater, concluding that it is arbitrarie, and so doth *Britton.ca.65.* but *ca.43.* he seemeth to say, that in one case it is a yeare. See him also *ca.44.*

Fresh fine, is that which was levied within a yeare past, *Westm. 2. cap. 45.an.13.Ed.1.*

Fresh force (Frisca fortia) is a force done within 40. daies, as it seemeth by *Fitzh. nat. br. fol. 7.C.* For if a man be disseised of any lands or tenements, within any city or borough, or deforced from them after the death of his auncester, to whome he is heire: or after the death of his tenent for life or in taile: he may within 40. daies after his title accrued, haue a bille out of the chauncerie to the Mayor, &c. See the rest.

Fresh suite (recens insecutio) is such a present and earnest following of an offendour, as neuer ceaseth from the time of the offence committed or espied, vntill he be apprehended. And the effect of this, in the pursuite of a Felon, is, that the partie persiewing shall haue his goods restored him agine: whereas otherwise they are the kings. Of this see *Stawnf pl.cor.li.3.ca.10.& 12.* where you shall finde handled at large, what suite is to be accounted fresh, and what not. And the same author in his first booke, *cap. 27.* saith, that fresh suite may continue for seuen yeres, See *Cookes reportes.l.3.Rigewaies case. Fresh suite*, seemeth to be either within the view or without: for *M. Manwood* saith, that vpon fresh suite within the view, trespassers in the forest may be attached by the officers persiewing them, though without the limits and boundes of the forest. *parte 2.ca.19.nu.4.fol.121.*

Freoborgh: aliàs Fridburgh: aliàs Frithborg (Frideburgum) commeth of two Saxon words *(Freo. i. liber, ingenuus)* and *(borgh.i. fideiussor)* or of *(Frid. i pax) & (Borgha.i. sponsor)* This is otherwise called after the French *(Franck pledge)* the one being in vse in the *Saxons* time, the other sithence the Conquest: wherefore for the vnderstanding of this, reade *Franck pledge.* That it is all one thing, it appeareth by *M. Lamberd* in his explication of Saxon words, *verbo Centuria* and againe in the lawes of King *Edward* set out by him, *fol. 132.* in these words: *Praeterea est quaedam summa & maxima securitas, per quam omnes statu firmissimo sustinentur: viz. vt vnusquisq; stabiliat se sub fideiussionis securitate, quam Angli vocant (Freoborghes) soli tamen Eboracenses, dicunt eandem (Tienmannatale) quod sonat latine decem hominum numerum. Haec securitas hoc modo fiebat, quòd de omnibus villis*

lis totius regni sub decennali fideiussione debebant esse universi: ita quòd si unus ex decem forisfecerit, novem ad rectum eum haberēt: quòd si aufugeret, daretur lege terminus ei 31. dierum: ut quæsitus interim & inventus, ad iustitiam Regis adduceretur, & de suo illico restauraret damnum quod fecerat. Et si ad hoc forisfaceret, de corpore suo iustitia fieret. Sed si infra prædictum terminum inveniri non posset, &c: as in the booke: *Bracton* maketh mention of (*Fridburgum. lib.* 3. *tract.* 2. *cap.* 10. in these words: *Archiepiscopi, Episcopi, Comites, & Barones, & omnes qui habent Soc, & Sak, Tol, & Team, & huiusmodi libertates, milites suos & proprios servientes, armigeros sc. dapiferos, & pincernas, camerarios, coquos, pistores, sub suo Fridburgo habere debent. Item & isti suos Armigeros, & alios sibi servientes. Quòd si cui forisfecerint, ipsi domini sui habeant eos ad rectum, et si non habuerint, solvant pro eis forisfacturam. Et sic obseruandum erit de omnibus aliis, qui sunt de alicuius manupastu.* Out of these words, I learne the reason, why great men were not combined in any ordinarie dozeine, and that is, because they were a sufficient assurance for themselues and for their meniall seruants: no lesse then the tenne were one for another in ordinarie dozeins. See *Frank pledge*: see *Skene de verborum significatione. verbo. Freiborgh. Fleta* writeth this word (*frithborgh*) and vseth it for the principall man, or at the least, for a man of euery dozein. *Frithborgh* (saith he) *est laudabilis homo testimonii liber vel servus, per quem omnes iuxta ipsum commorantes firmiori pace sustententur sub stabilitate fideiussionis eius vel alterius per denarium numerum, unde quilibet quasi plegius alterius: ita quod si unus feloniam fecerit, novem tenentur ipsum ad standum recto præsentare. lib. 1. ca.* 47. §. *Frithborgh.* See *Roger Hoveden, parte poster. suorum annal. in Henrico secundo. fol.* 345. *a.b.*

Frier (*frater*) commeth of the French (*frere*) there be foure orders reckoned of them. *anno* 4. *H.* 4. *cap.* 17. *viz.* Minours, Augustines, Preachers, and Carmelites, the foure principall orders, of which the rest descend. See in *Zechius de rep. ecc. pag.* 380 Looke *Linwood. titulo de relig. domibus. cap.* 1. *verb. Sancti Augustin.*

Frier observant (*frater observans*) is an order of Franciscans: for the better vnderstanding of whom, it is to be noted, that of those 4. orders mentioned in the word (*Frier,*) the *Franciscans*, are *minores tam Obseruantes quàm Conventuales & Capuchini. Zechius de Repub. Eccl. tract. de regular. cap.* 2. These Friers obseruant, you find spoken of *anno* 25. *H.* 8.

H. 8. *cap.* 12. who be called obſervants, becauſe they are not combined together in any cloyſter, covent, or corporation as the Conuentuals are: but only tye themſelues to obſerue the rites of their order, and more ſtrictly then the Conuentuals doe: and vpon a ſingularitie of zeale, ſeparate themſelues from them, liuing in certaine places, and companies of their owne chuſing. And of theſe you may reade *Hoſpinian. de orig. & progr. Monachatus. fol.* 878. *cap.* 38.

Friperer, is taken from the French (*fripier*) *interpolator*, one that ſcowreth vp and cleanſeth old apparell to ſell againe. This word is vſed for a baſtardly kind of broker. *anno* 1. *Iaco. cap.* 21.

Frithborgh, ſee *Freeborgh.*

Frithſoken, ſignifieth ſurety of defence, as *Saxon* ſaith in the deſcription of *England, cap.* 12. It ſeemeth to come of theſe two Saxon words, *frith*, or *frid*, or (*fred.*) i. *pax*, & (*ſoken.* i. *quærere.*) *Fleta* tearmeth it *frithſokne*, *vel forſokne*, yeelding this reaſon, *Quòd ſignificat libertatem habendi franci plegii.*

Fuer (*fuga*) commeth of the French (*fuir*, i. *fugere*) though it be a verbe, yet it is vſed ſubſtantiuely in our common law, and is twofold: *fuer in feit*, (*in facto*) when a man doth apparently and corporally flie, and *fuer in ley*, (*in lege*) when being called in the countie, he appeareth not vntill he be outlawed: for this is flight in interpretation of law. *Stawnf. pl. cor. lib.* 3. *c.* 22.

Fugitiues goods, (*bona fugitiuorum*) be the proper goods of him that flyeth vpon felonie, which after the flight lawfully found, do belong to the king. *Coke vol.* 6. *fol.* 109. *b.*

Furlong, (*ferlingum terræ*) is a quantitie of grounde containing twenty lugs or poles in length, and euery pole 16 foote and a halfe, eight of which furlongs make a mile, *anno* 35. *Ed.* 1. *cap.* 6. It is otherwiſe the eighth part of an acre. *See Acre.* In the former ſignification the *Romanes* call it (*ſtadium*,) in the later (*iugerum.*) This meaſure which wee call a pole, is alſo called a perch, & differeth in length, according to the cuſtome of the countrey. See *Perch.*

Furre (*furrura*) commeth of the French (*fourrer.* i. *pelliculare*) to line with skinnes. Of furre I find diuers ſtrange kinds in the ſtatute. *anno* 24. H. 8. *cap.* 13. as of ſables, which is a rich furre of colour betweene blacke and browne, being the skinne of a beaſt called a Sable, of quantitie betweene a Polecat and an ordinarie cat, and of faſhion like a Polecat, bred in *Ruscia*, but most and the best in *Tartaria*. Lucerns, which is the skinne of a beast so called, being nere the bignes of a wolfe, of colour betweene red and browne, something mayled like a cat, and mingled with blacke spottes, bred in *Muscovie* and *Ruscia*, & is a very rich furre. Genets, that is the skinne of a beast so called, of bignes betweene a cat and a wesell, mayled like a cat, and of the nature of a cat, bred in *Spaine*. Whereof there bee two kinds, blacke, and gray, and the blacke the more precious furre, hauing blacke spots vpon it hardly to be seene. Foines, is of fashion like the Sable bred in *Fraunce* for the most part: the toppe of the furre is blacke, and the ground whitish. Marterne, is a beast very like the Sable, the skinne something courser, it liueth in all countries that be not too cold, as *England*, *Ireland*, *&c.* and the best be in *Ireland*. Miniuer, is nothing but the bellies of Squirels, as some men say: others say, it is a litle vermin like vnto a Wesell milke white, and commeth from *Muscovie*. Fitch, is that which we otherwise call the Polecat here in *England*. Shankes, be the skinne of the shanke or legge of a kind of Kidde which beareth the furre, that we call Budge. Calaber, is a litle beast, in bignes about the quantitie of a squirell, of colour gray, and bred especially in high *Germanie*.

G

GAbell (*gabella, gablum*) commeth of the French (*gabelle*. i. *vectigal*) and hath the same signification among our old Writers, that (*gabelle*) hath in *Fraunce*, for *M. Camden* in his *Britannia*. *pag*. 213. speaking of *Wallingford*, hath these words: *Continebat* 276. *hagas.* i. *domos reddentes novem libras de gablo*: and *pag*. 282. of *Oxford*, these: *Hæc vrbs reddebat pro telonio & gablo, & aliis consuetudinibus per annum, Regi quidem viginti libras, & sex sextarios mellis: Comiti verò Algaro decem libras. Gabella* (as *Cassanæus* defineth it, *de consuetu. Burgund. pag*. 119. *Est vectigal quod solvitur pro bonis mobilibus, id est, pro hiis quæ vehuntur*, distinguishing it from *Tributum*, *quia Tributum est propriè, quod fisco vel Principi solvitur pro rebus immobilibus*.

Gage, (*vadium*) commeth of the French (*gager*. i. *dare pignus, pignore certare*) and is it selfe a French word nothing chāged, but in pronunciation. It signifieth with vs also a pawne or pledge. *Glanvile lib*. 10. *cap*.6. where he saith thus: *Quandoque res mobiles ponuntur in vadium, quandoque res immobiles*, and a litle after that, thus: *Invadiatur res quandoque ad terminum, quandoque sine termino. Item quandoque invadiatur res aliqua in mortuo vadio, quandoque non.* And from that chapter to the end of the twelfth in the same booke, he handleth this only thing. Though the word *(gage)* be retained as it is a substantiue, yet as it is a verbe, the vse hath turned the *G.* into *W.* so as it is oftener written *(wage:)* as to wage deliuerance, that is, to giue securitie that a thing shall be deliuered. For if he that distrained, being siewed, haue not deliuered the catell that were distrained, then he shall not onely avow the distresse, but *(gager deliuerance)* i. put in suretie, that he will deliuer the catell distrained. F*itzh. nat. br. fol.* 74. *D. & 67.* F. whome see also *fol. 67.* F. *G.* yet in some cases, he shall not by tyed to make this securitie: as if the catell died in pound. *Kitchin fol.* 145. or if he claime a propertie in the catell siewed for. Termes of the lawe. To wage lawe what it is, see in his place. *verbo. Lawe.* See *Mortgage.*

Gager deliuerance. See *Gage.*

Gayle. See *Gaoll.*

Gainage, (Wainagium) is neere to the French *(Gaignage.* i. *quæstus, lucrum,)* and signifieth in our common lawe, the land held by the baser kind of Sokemen or villeines. *Bract. lib.* 1. *cap.* 9. where he hath these words, speaking of seruants: *Et in hoc legem habent contra dominos, quòd stare possint in iudicio contra eos de vita & membris propter sæuitiam dominorum, vel propter intolerabilem iniuriam. Vt si eos distruant, quòd salvum non possit eis esse Wainagium suum. Hoc autem verum est de illis servis, qui tenent in antiquo dominico coronæ.* And againe, *lib.* 3. *tract.* 2. *cap.* 1. *Miles & liber homo non amerciabitur nisi secundum modum delicti secundum quod delictũ fuit magnum vel parvum, & salvo contenemento suo: Mercator verò, non nisi salva mercandiza sua: & villanus, non nisi salvo Wainagio suo.* This in *Westm.* 1. *cap. 6. an.* 3. *Ed. prim.* is called *Gaynure:* and againe, *cap.* 17. and *in magna charta, cap.* 14. it is called wainage. I find it in the *old. nat. br. fol.* 117. called *Gainor. viz.* in these words: The writ of *Aile* was *præcipe, &c. quòd reddat vnam bovatam terræ, & vnam bovatam marisci:* and the writ was abated for that the oxegang is alwaies of a thing that lyeth in gainor. I thinke this word was vsed of lands vsually plowed, because they that had it in occupation, had nothing of it but the profit and fruite raised of it by their owne paines, toward their sustenance, nor any other title, but at the Lords will. Gainor again in the same booke, *fol.* 12. is vsed for a Sokeman, that hath such land in his occupation. In the 32. chapter of the Grand Custumarie of *Normandie: Gaigneurs* be *ruricolæ qui terras eleemozinatas possident*: and *Britton* vseth gainer, for to plow or till, *fol.* 65. *a.* & 42. *b. West parte* 2. *symbol. titulo*, *Recoueries. sect.* 3. hath these words: *A pracipe quod reddat*, lyeth not in *Bovata marisci.* 13. Ed. 3. *fol.* 3. nor *de selione terræ. Ed.* 1. for the vncertaintie: because a selion, which is a land, sometime containeth an acre, sometime halfe an acre, sometime more, and sometime lesse. It lyeth not of a garden, cotage, or croft. 14. *Assis.* 13. 8. *H.* 63. 22. *Ed.* 4. 13. *de virgata terræ.* 41. 43. 13. *Ed.* 3. *de fodina, de minera, de mercatu.* 13. *E.* 3. for they bee not in demesn: but in gaine, &c. Lastly, in the statute of Distresses in the Exchequer. *anno* 51. *H.* 3. I find these words. No man of religion, nor other, shall be distreined by his beasts that gaine the land.

Galege, (*galicæ*) seemeth to come of the French, (*galloches*) which signifieth a certaine kinde of shoo worne by the *Gaules* in foule weather of old times. I find it vsed for some such implement. *anno* 4. *Ed.* 4. *cap.* 7. & *anno* 14. & 15. H. 8. *cap.* 9. where it is written plainely. *Galoches.*

Galingal (*cyperus*) is a medicinall herbe, the nature and diuersitie whereof is expressed in *Gerards herball. lib.* 1. *cap.* 22. The roote of this is mentioned for a drugge to be garbled. *anno* 1. *Iaco. cap.* 19.

Gallihalpens, were a kind of coine forbidden by the statute. *anno* 3. *H.* 5. *cap.* 1.

Galloches. See *Galege.*

Gals, (*Gallæ*) be a kind of hard fruite like a nutte, but rounder, growing of the tree called in latine (*galla.*) The diuers kinds and vses whereof *Gerard* expresseth in his Herball. *lib.* 3. *cap.* 34. This is a drugge to be garbled. *anno* 1. *Iaco. cap.* 19.

Gaol, (*gaola*) commeth of the French (*Geole.* i. *caveola*) a cage for birds, but is metaphorically vsed for a prison. Thence commeth (*Geolier*) whome we call *Gayler* or *Gaoler.*

Garbe (*garba*) commeth of the French (*garbe, aliàs, gerbe* i. *fascis.*) It signifieth with vs, a bundle or sheafe of corne. *Charta de foresta. cap.* 7. and *garba sagittarum*, is a sheafe of arrowes. *Skene de verb. signif. verbo, Garba.*

Garbling of bow-staues. anno 1. *R.* 3. *cap.* 11. is the sorting or culling out the good from the bad.

bad. As garbling of spice, is nothing but to purifie it from the drosse and dust that is mixed with it. It may seeme to proceed from the Italian *(garbo)* that is, finenesse, neatnesse.

Gard, *(Custodia)* commeth of the *French*, *(garde)* being all of one signification. It signifieth in our common lawe, a custodie or care of defence: but hath diuers applications: sometimes to those that attend vpon the safetie of the Prince, called Yeomen of the Guard: somtime to such as haue the education of children vnder age, or of an Idiot: sometime to a writte touching wardshippe. Which writs are of three sorts: one called a right of guard or ward, in French, *droit de gard, Fitzh. nat. br. fol.* 139. the second is *eiectment de gard. Idem fol.* 139. *L.* the third, is *rauishment de gard. Idem fol.* 140. *F.G.* See *Gardein*, see *Ward*.

Gardein (Custos) commeth of the *French (gardien,)* and yet the German *(Warden)* is neare vnto it. It signifieth generally him, that hath the charge or custodie of any person or thing: but most notoriously him, that hath the education or protection of such people, as are not of sufficient discretion, to guide themselues and their owne affaires, as children and Idiots: being indeede as largely extended, as both *(Tutor* and *Curator)* among the Civilians. For whereas *Tutor* is he, that hath the gouernment of a youth, vntill he come to 14. yeares of age, and *Curator*, he that hath the disposition and ordering of his substance afterward, vntil he attaine to 25. yeares: or that hath the charge of a franticke person during his lunacie: the common Lawyers vse but onely *Gardien* or *Gardian* for both these. And for the better vnderstanding of our English lawe in this thing, you must know, that as *tutor* is either *testamentarius*, or *à Prætore datus ex lege Atilia*, or lastly, *legitimus*: so we haue three sortes of *Gardeines* in *England*: one ordained by the father in his last will, another appointed by the Iudge afterward, the third cast vpon the Minor by the lawe and custome of the land. Touching the first, a man hauing goods and chatels neuer so many, may appoint a gardein to the bodie or person of his child, by his last will and testament, vntill he come to the age of fourteene yeares, and so the disposing or ordering of his substance, vntill what time he thinketh meet, and that is most commonly to the age of 21. yeares. The same may he do, if he haue lands to neuer so great a valew, so they hold not *in capite* of the king, nor of any other Lord, by knights seruice. And in the former case, if the father appoint no Gardein to his child, the Ordinarie may appoint one to order his moueables and chatels, vntill the age of 14. yeares: at which time he may chuse his guardian, accordingly as by the the ciuill lawe he may his *Curator*. For we hold all one rule with the Ciuilians in this case: and that is, *Invito curator non datur*. And for his lands, if he hold any by copie of court rolle, commonly the Lord of the fee appointeth him a guardian, vntill he come to the age of 14. yeres, and that is one, next of kind to the Minor of that side, that can hope for least profit by his death. If he hold by charter in socage, then the next of kind on that side by which the land commeth not is the guardian: and hereupon called *guardian in socage*. And that which is said here of socage seemeth to be true likewise in *petit sergeantie. anno vicesimo octauo. Edvardi primi. statuto primo.* And the reason of this, *Fortescue* giueth in his booke, intituled, *A commendation of the politique lawes of England. cap.* 44. *viz.* because there might be suspition, if the next kinsman on that side by which the land descendeth, should haue the custody and education of the child, that for desire of his land, he might be entised to worke him some mischiefe. Lastly, if a man dye seised of lands, holding by knights seruice, leauing his heire in minoritie, that is, vnder 21. yeares: the *Lord* of the fee hath, by law, the custodie both of the heire and his land, vntill he come to age. See the statute, *anno* 28. *Ed. prim. statut. prim.* And the reason of this, *Fortescue* likewise giueth, for that hee to whom by his tenure he oweth knights seruice, when he can performe it, is likeliest to traine him vp in martiall and ingenious discipline, vntill he be of abilitie. But *Polidore Virgil* in his Chronicle, *lib.* 16. saith, that this was *Nouum vectigalis genus excogitatum*, to helpe *Henry the third*, being oppressed much with pouertie, by reason he receiued the kingdome much wasted by the wars of his auncestours: and therefore needing extraordinarie helpe to vphold his estate: yet the 33. chapter of the Grand Custumary maketh mention of this to haue bene vsed by the *Normans*: and I thinke this the truer opinion. Here it is to be obserued, whether land in knights seruice hold *in capite*, or of another *Lord*, or some of the King, and some of another. If of the king, whether of the king alone or not, all is

one

one. For the king in this case is guardian to the heires both person and land by his prerogatiue. *Stawnf prarog. cap.* 1. If he hould of a common *Lord*, it is either of one alone or more; if of one onely, then is he guardian of both person and lands; if of more, then the *Lord* of whome he houldeth by the elder tenure, is guardian of the person, and euery one of the rest hath the custodie of the land holden of him selfe. If the prioritie of the tenure cannot be discerned, then is he guardian of the person, that first happeth him. Termes of the lawe. *Stawnf. vbi supra.* whom you may reade more at large: which Author *fol.* 19. maketh mention of *gardeyn in feit*, and *Gardeyn in drou*: that is, in deed, and in lawe: I take the first to be him that hath purchased, or otherwise obtained the ward of the *Lord* of whom the land holdeth: the second, him that hath the right by his inheritance and seignorie. *old. nat. br. fol.* 94 Then is there *gardein per cause de gard*, which is he that hath the wardship of a Minor, because he is guardian of his *Lord* being likewise in minoritie. *Stawnf. vbi supra. fol.* 15. Of this you may reade *Skene de verb. signif. verbo Varda.* by whom you may learn great affinitie, and yet some difference betweene the lawe of *Scotland*, and ours in this point.

Guardia, is a word vsed among the *Feudists*, for the *Latine* (*custodia*,) and *guardianus seu guardio dicitur ille, cui custodia commissa est. lib. Feudo.* 1. *titulo.* 2. & *tit.* 11.

Gardeyn of the spiritualties, (*Custos spiritualium, vel spiritualitatis*) is he to whom the spirituall iurisdiction of any Diocesse is committed, during the vacancy of the see. *anno* 25. *H.* 8. *cap.* 21. And I take, that the guardeyn of the spiritualties, may be either Guardeyn in lawe, or *Iure Magistratus*, as the Archbishop is of any *Dioces* within his prouince, or guardian by delegation, as he whom the Archbishop or Vicar generall doth for the time depute.

Gardeyn of the peace, (*Custos pacis.*) See *Conservatour of the peace.*

Gardeyn of the Cinque ports, (*Gardianus quinque portuum*) is a Magistrate that hath the iurisdiction of those hauens in the east part of *England*, which are commonly called the Cinque ports, that is, the fiue hauens: who there hath all that iurisdiction, that the Admirall of *England* hath in places not exempt. The reason why one Magistrate should be assigned to these few hauens, seemeth to to be, because they in respect of their situation, auncient'y required a more vigilant care, then other hauens, being in greater daunger of invasion by our enemies, by reason that the sea is narrower there then in any other place. *M. Camden* in his *Britannia, pag.* 238. saith, that the *Romaines*, after they had setled themselues and their Empire here in *England*, appointed a Magistrate or gouernour ouer those East partes, whom they tearmed *Comitem littoris Saxonici per Britanniam*, hauing another that did beare the same title on the opposite part of the sea: whose office was to strengthen the sea coasts with munition, against the outrages and robberies of the Barbarians. And farder signifieth his opinion, that this Warden of the Cinque ports, was first erected amongst vs, in imitation of that Romaine policie. *See Cinque ports*.

Gare, *anno* 31. *Ed.* 3. *cap.* 8. is a course wooll full of staring haires, as such as groweth about the pesill or shankes of the sheepe.

Garnishment, commeth of the French (*Garnir.* i. *instruere.*) It signifieth in our common lawe, a warning giuen to one for his appearance, and that for the beter furnishing of the cause and court. For example, one is siewed for the detinew of certaine euidences or charters, and saith, that the euidences were deliuered vnto him not onely by the plaintiffe, but by another also: and therefore prayeth, that that other may be warned to pleade with the plaintiffe, whether the said conditions bee performed yea or no. And in this petition he is said to pray garnishment. New booke of Entries. *fol.* 211. *colum.* 3. *Termes of the lawe. Cromptons Iurisd. fol.* 211. which may be interpreted either warning of that other, or else furnishing of the court with parties sufficient, throughly to determine the cause: because vntill he appeare and ioyne, the defendant (as *Fitzh.* saith) is, as it were, out of the court. *nat. br. fol.* 106. *G.* and the court is not prouided of all parties to the action. I am the bolder thus to interpret it, because I find *Britton* in the same mind. *cap.* 28. where he saith, that contracts be some naked, and *sans* garnment, and some furnished, or to vse the literall signification of his word, appareled: but a naked obligation giueth no action, but by common assent. And therefore it is necessarie or needfull, that euery obligation be appareled. And an obligation ought to be appareled with these fiue sortes of of garnements, &c. Howbeit, I reade it generally vsed for a warning in many places, and namely, in *Kitchin fol. 6. Garnisher le court*, is to warne the court. And reasonable garnishment in the same place, is nothing but reasonable warning: and againe, *fol.* 283. and many other authours also. *B*ut this may be well thought a Metonymie of the effect, because by the warning of parties to the court, the court is furnished and adorned.

Garrantie. *S*ee *Warrantie.*

Garter (Garterium) commeth of the french (*Iartiere* or *Iartier* .i. *periscelis*, *fascia poplitaria)* It signifieth with vs both in diuers statutes, and otherwise, one especiall garter, being the ensigne of a great and noble societie of knights, called knights of the garter. And this is καθ᾽ ἐξοχὴν, as *Poeta* among the *Gracians* was *Homer*, among the *Romanes Virgill*, because they were of all others the most excellent. This high order (as appeareth by *M. Camden pag.* 211) and many others, was first instituted by that famous king *Edward* the third, vpon good successe in a skirmish, wherein the kings garter (I know not vpon what occasion) was vsed for a token. I know that *Polidore Virgill* casteth in an other suspition of the originall: but his groundes by his owne confession grew from the vulgar opinion: yet as it is, I will mention it as I haue read it. *Edward* the third king of England after he had obtained many great victories: King *Iohn* of *Fraunce*, King *Iames*, of Scotland, being both prisoners in the tower of London at one time, and king *Henry* of *Castile*, the bastard expulsed, and *Don Pedro* restored by the prince of *Wales*, did vpon no weighty occasion first erect this order in *anno* 1350. *viz.* He dauncing with the Queene, and other ladies of the court, tooke vp a garter that happened to fall from one of them: whereat some of the lords smiling, the king said vnto them, that eare it were long, he would make that garter to be of high reputation, & shortly after instituted this order of the blew garter, which euery one of the order is boũd daily to weare, being richly decked with gold and pretious stones, and hauing these words written, or wrought vpon it: *Honi soit qui mal y pence.* which is thus commonly interpreted: euill come to him that euill thinketh: but I thinke it might be better thus: *S*hame take him that thinketh euill. See knights of the garter. *M. Fearne* in his glory of generosity agreeth with *M. Camden*, and expreslier setteth downe the victories, whence this order was occasioned: whatsoeuer cause of beginning it had, the order is inferior to none in the world, consisting of 26. martiall and heroicall nobles, whereof the king of *England* is the cheif, and the rest be either nobles of the realme or princes of other countries, friends and confederates with this realme; the honour being such, as Emperours and Kings of other nations, haue desired and thankfully accepted it: He that will reade more of this, let him repaire to *M. Camden*, and *Polidore*, and *M. Fern. fol. 120. vbi supra.*

The Ceremonies of the chapter proceeding to election, of the inuestures and robes: of his installation, of his vowe with all such other obseruances, see in *M. Segars* new booke, intituled *Honour militarie and ciuile. li. 2. ca. 9. fo. 65.* Garter also signifieth the principall king at armes, among our English *Heralds* created by king *Henry* the 5. *Stow. pa.* 584.

Garthman, anno 13. *R. 2. stat.* 1. *ca.* 19. & *anno.* 17. *eiusd. cap.* 9.

Gavelet, is a speciall and auncient kinde of *Cessauit* vsed in *Kent,* where the custome of Gavill kind continueth: whereby the tenent shall forfeit his lands and tenements to the Lord of whome he holdeth, if he withdraw from him his due rents and seruices. The new Expounder of lawe Termes, whom reade more at large: I reade this word, *anno* 10. *Ed. 2. cap. vnico.* where it appeareth to be a writ vsed in the *Hustings* at *London.* And I find by *Fleta,* that it is vsed in other liberties, as the *Hustings* of *Winchester, Lincolne, Yorke,* and the *Cinque ports. lib. 2. cap.* 55. *in principio.*

Gavelkind, is, by *M. Lamberd* in his Exposition of Saxon words, *verbo. Terra ex scripto,* compounded of three Saxon words, *gyfe, cal, cin: omnibus cognatione proximis data.* But *M. Verstegan* in his restitution of decayed intelligence, *cap.* 3. calleth it *(Gavelkind) quasi,* giue all kind, that is, giue to each child his part. It signifieth in our common lawe a custome, whereby the lands of the father is equally diuided at his death amongst all his sons, or the lād of the brother equally diuided among the brethren, if he haue no issue of his owne, *Kit. fol.* 102. This custome is said to be of force in diuers places of *England,* but especially in *Kent,* as the said *Authour* reporteth, shewing also the cause why Kentish men rather vse this custome, then any other prouince. *viz.* because it was a composition made betweene the Conquerour and them, after all

England beside was conquered, that they should enioy their auncient customes, whereof this was one. For *M. Camden* in his *Britannia, pag.* 239. saith in expresse words thus: *Cantiani eâ lege Gulielmo Normano se dediderunt, vt patrias consuetudines illæsas retinerent, illamq́; inprimis quam Gavelkind nominant. Hac terræ quæ eo nomine censentur, liberis masculis ex æquis portionibus dividuntur: vel fœminis, si masculi non fuerint:* adding more worth the noting, *viz. Hanc hæreditatem, cùm quintum decimum annum attigerint, adeunt, & sine Domini consensu, cuilibet, vel dando, vel vendendo alienare licet. Hac filii parentibus furti damnatis in id genus fundis succedunt, &c.* This custome in diuers gentlemens lands, was altered at their owne petition, by Act of Parlament. *anno* 31. *H.* 8. *cap.* 3. But it appeareth by 18. H. 6. *cap. pri.* that in those daies there were not aboue thirty or forty persons in *Kent*, that held by any other tenure. See the new Termes, *Gavelet*, and *Gavelkinde*.

Gawgeour, *(gaugeator)* seemeth to come of the French *(Gawchir.* i. *in gyrum torquere.)* It signifieth with vs an Officer of the Kings appointed to examin all tunnes, hogsheades, pipes, barels, and tercians of wine, oile, hony, butter, and to giue them a marke of allowance, before they bee sold in any place. And because this marke is a circle made with an iron instrument for that purpose: it seemeth that from thence he taketh his name. Of this office you may find many statutes: the first whereof is, *anno* 27. *Ed.* 3. commonly called the statute of prouision, or *Purveyours. cap.* 8.

Geld, signifieth with the *Saxons, pecunia vel tributum.* See Gyld.

Genets, *aliàs, Ienets.* See *Furre.*

Gentleman, (generosus) seemeth to be made of two words, the one French, *(gentil.* i. *honestus, vel honesto loco natus:)* the other Saxon *(Mon)* as if you would say, a man well borne. The *Italian* followeth the very word, calling those *(gentil homini)* whom we call G*entlemen*. The *Spaniard* keepeth the meaning, calling him *Hidalgo*, or *Hyo d'algo*, that is, the son of some man, or of a man of reckoning. The Frenchmen call him also *gentil houme:* so that gentlemen bee those, whom their bloud and race doth make noble and knowne. εὐγενεῖς, in Greeke, in Latine, *Nobiles. Smith de Repub. Anglor. lib.* 1. *cap.* 20. vnder this name are all comprised that are aboue Yeomen: so that Noblemen be truly called gentlemen.

But by the courſe and cuſtome of *England*, Nobilitie is either *maior* or *minor:* the greater containes all titles and degrees from Knights vpward: the leſſer all from Barons downward. *Smith vbi ſupra.cap.* 21. The reaſon of the name, as I take it, groweth from this, that they obſerue *gentilitatem ſuam,* that is, the race & propagation of their blood, by giuing of armes, which the cōmon ſort neither doth, nor may doe. For by the coate that a gentleman giueth, he is knowne to be, or not to be deſcended from thoſe of his name, that liued many hundred yeares ſince. Howbeit, that this is neglected, where ſubſtance faileth to maintaine the countenance. For many of great birth fall to pouerty, whoſe poſteritie liuing and labouring in want, haue ſmall encouragement to looke after the titles of their aunceſters, and ſo in time ſlippe into the number of the ignoble ſort: yet if they by their vertue or fortune, can againe aduaunce themſelues to ſufficient abilitie, the Herald out of his obſeruations can reſtore them to the coat of their progenitors, and now and then helpe them to one, that their aunceſtors neuer ware. *Gentiles homines,* ſee in *Tiraquel. de Nobilitate. cap.* 2. *pag.* 53. *Tully* in his *Topickes* thus ſaith of this mater. *Gentiles ſunt, qui inter ſe eodem ſunt nomine ab ingenuis oriundi, quorum maiorum nemo ſeruitutem ſeruiuit, qui capite non ſunt diminuti.* And in the firſt booke of his *Tuſc. queſtions,* hee calleth *Tullum Hoſtilium,* one of the kings of *Rome, gentilem ſuum.*

Generall Iſſue. vid. Iſſue.

Geſtu & fama, is a writ. *Lamb. Eirenarcha. lib.* 4. *ca.* 14. *pag.* 531.

Gygge milles, were for the fulling of woollin cloth and forbidden, *anno* 5. *Edward.* 6. *cap.* 22.

Gild: alias Geld (Gildare) commeth from the Saxon word *(Gildan)* i. *ſoluere, Lamb.* in his explica: of Saxon words ſaith *verb. Contubernalis.* It is vſed as a verb, and as a ſubſtantiue alſo, and as it is a ſubſtantiue, it is latined *Gilda* and ſignifieth a tribute, or ſometime an amercement, or thirdly a fraternity or company, combined together by orders and lawes made among themſelues by the princes licence. *M. Camden* citeth many antiquities, by which it appeareth to ſignifie a tribute or taxe, as *pa.* 135. 139. 159. 168. 178. *M. Crompton* in his iuriſdictions, *fol.* 191. ſheweth it to be an amercement, as footgeld, and *fol.* 197. he interpreteth it to be a preſtation within the foreſt, in theſe words: To be quit of all manner of *Gelds*. is to be diſcharged of all

maner

manner of prestations to be made for gathering of sheues of corne, of lambe, and of wolle to the vse of *Foresters*. Againe *M. Camden pag*. 349. diuiding Suffolke into three parts, calleth the first *Gildable*, because tribute is thence gathered; the second *libertatem S. Edmundi:* The third *libertatem* S. *Etheldredæ*. And the statutes: *anno* 27. *Ed*. 3. *stat*. 2. *ca*. 13. *& anno* 11. H. 7. *ca*. 9. vse *Gildable* in the same sense, and so doth the statute *anno* 27. H. 8. *ca*. 26. From this *M. Lamberd, vbi supra*, is likewise perswaded, that the common word *(Gild)* or *(Gildhall)* doth proceede, being a fraternity or communalty of men gathered into one combination, supporting their common charge by a mutuall contribution: And in the regiſter originall, *fol*. 219. *b*. I reade *Gildam mercatoriam*, that is the *Gilde* merchaunt, which I haue heard to be a certaine liberty or priuiledge belonging to Merchants, whereby they are enabled to hould certaine plees of land within their owne precincts. This word *(Gildes)* or *(Guildes)* is so vsed *anno* 37. *Ed*. 3. *ca*. 51. *& anno* 15. *R*. 2. *cap*. 5. And *Gildhalda Teutonicorum*, is vsed for the fraternity of easterling merchaunts in London, called the *stilyard anno* 22. H. 8. *cap. octauo*.

Ginger (Zinziber) is a spice well knowne, being the roote of a plant that groweth in hot countries, as *Spaine, Barbary, &c*. The true forme whereof you haue expressed in *Gerards herball. li*. 1. *ca*. 38. This is a spice whose roote is to be garbled. *anno* 1. *Iaco. ca*. 19.

Ginny peper (piper de Ginnea) is otherwise called *Indian peper*, of the place whence it commeth. The nature and farder description whereof you haue in *Gerards herball. lib*. 2. *ca*. 66. This you haue mentioned among drugs and spices to be garbled, in the statute .i. *Iaco. ca*. 19.

Gisarms: anno 13. *Ed*. 1. *stat*. 3. *cap*. 6. is a kinde of weapon. *Fleta* writeth it *Sisarmes. lib*. 1. *ca*. 24 §, *item quod quilibet*.

Glaunce Ore, Plowden casu Mines. fo. 320. *b*.

Glanuill was a learned lawyer, that was Chiefe Iustice in *Henry* the seconds dayes, and writte a booke of the common lawes of *England*, which is the auncientest of any extant touching that subiect. *Stawnf. prarog. cap. prim. fol*. 5. He was then called in Latine *Ranulphus de Glanvilla*. He died in *Richard* the first his daies at the citie of *Acres* in the coast of *Iury*, being with him in his voyage to the holy land. *Plowden. casu. Stowel. fol*. 368. *b*.

Goe, is vsed sometime in a speciall signification in our cõmon lawe: as to go to God, is to be dismissed the court. *Broke titulo. Fayler de records. num. 1.* Goe forward, seemeth also to be a signe giuen by a Iudge to the Sergeant or Counceler, pleading the cause of his client, that his cause is not good. For when he standeth vpon a point of lawe, and heareth those words of the Iudges mouth, he taketh vnderstanding, that he looseth the action. *Smith de Repub. Anglo. lib. 2. cap. 13.* To go without day, is as much as to be dismissed the court. *Kitchin fol. 193.*

Good behauiour. See Good *abearing*.

Good *abearing*, (*Bonus gestus*) is, by an especiall signification, an exact cariage or behauiour of a subiect, toward the king and his liege people, whereunto men vpon their euill course of life, or loose demeanure are sometimes bound. For as *M. Lamberd* in his E*irenarcha. lib. 2. cap. 2.* saith: he that is bound to this, is more strictly bound then to the peace: because, where the peace is not broken without an affray, or batterie, or such like: this suretie (*de bono gestu*) may be forfeited by the number of a mans company, or by his or their weapons or harnesse: Whereof see more in that learned Writer in the same chapter, as also in *M. Cromptons Iustice of peace. fol.* 119. *b.* 120. 121. 122. 123. 124. 125. 126. 127.

Good country, (*Bona patria*) is an Assise, or Iury of country men or good neighbours: *Skene de verbo. signif. verbo, Bona patria.*

Graffer (*grafarius*) signifieth as much as a notarie or scriuener. It commeth of the French (*greffier. i. scriba, actuarius.*) This word is vsed in the statute *anno.* 5. *H.* 8. *c.* 1.

Graines (*grana paradisi, alias Cardamomum*) is a spice medicinable and wholesome, whereof you may see diuers kindes in *Gerards herball, l.* 3. *ca.* 148. These are cõprised among merchãdise that be to be garbled. *an.* 1. *I. c.* 19.

Grand assise. See *Assise.* and *Magna assisa.*

Grand Cape. see *Cape* and *Attachment.*

Grand Sergeanty: See *Chyvalrie.* & *Seargeantye:*

Grand distresse: (*Magna destrictio*) is a distresse taken of all the lands, and goods, that a man hath within the county or baywicke, whence he is to be distrained: *Fleta. li.* 2. *ca.* 69. §. *penult:* See *Distresse.* This word is vsed *anno* 51. H. 3. *ca.* 9. This falleth out when the defendant hath been attached, and yet appeareth not vpõ his attachment; or whẽ he appeareth & afterward makes default. For then the Shyreeue is commanded to distreine the Defendant, by all his goods and

and chatels, and to anſwer the king the iſſues of his lands.

Grange (grangia) is a houſe or building, not onely where corne is laide vp, as barns be, but alſo where there be ſtables for horſes, ſtalles for oxen and other catell, ſties for hogs, and other things neceſſary for husbandry, *Lindwood ca. item omnes de iudiciis verbo, Grangiis, in gloſſa:*

Graunt (Conceſſio, grantum) Glanvile. ſignifieth ſpecially in our common law, a gift in writing of ſuch a thing, as cannot aptly be paſſed or conueyed by word only: as rent, reverſions, ſeruices, advowſens in groſſe, common in groſſe, villein in groſſe, tythes, &c. or made by ſuch perſons, as cannot giue but by deede, as the king and all bodies politique: which differences be often in ſpeech neglected, and then is it taken generally for euerry gift whatſoeuer, made of any thing by any perſon, and he that graunteth it, is named the grauntour, and he to whome it is made, the Grauntee. *Weſt. parte .i. ſymbol. lib. 2. ſect.* 334. A thing is ſaid to lie in graunte, which cannot be aſſigned with out deede. *Coke l. 3. Lincolnes Coll. caſe f. 63. a.*

Greate men, are ſometimes vnderſtood of the laity of the higher houſe of parlament, as *anno.* 43. Ed. 3. *ca. 2.* & *anno* 8. *R. 2. in procem.* and ſometime of the knights &c. of the lower houſe, as *anno* 2. *R.* 2. *ſtat. 2. in princip.*

Gree, commeth of the French (*Gré*). i. *ſententia, beneplacitum.* It ſignifieth in our common law, contentment or good liking: as to make gree to the parties, is to ſatisfie them for an offence done. *anno* 1. *Rich. 2. cap.* 15.

Greachbreach, is breaking of the peace. *Saxon* in the deſcription of England. *ca.* 11. *v. Raſtal. titulo. expoſition of words.* The new expounder of lawe termes writeth it (*Grichbreach*) and giueth it the ſame ſignification. See *Greve.*

Greene hewe, is all one with vert. *Manwood parte 2. of his foreſt lawes. cap. 6. nu. 5. See Vert.*

Greene waxe, ſeemeth to be vſed for eſtretes deliuered to Shyreeues out of the exchequer, vnder the ſeale of that court, to be levied in the county, *anno* 42. Ed. 3. *ca. 9.* & *anno* 7. H. 4. *cap.* 3. See *Forein appoſer.*

Greue (præpoſitus) is a word of power and authoritie, ſignifiing as much as *Dominus*, or *præfectus. Lamberd in his expoſi. of Saxon words, verbo Præfectus.* Where he ſeemeth to make it all one with (*Reve*) as I thinke vndoubtedly it is: The *Saxon* word is *Gerefa* whereof we haue diuers words compounded, as *Shyreeue. Portgreave, &c.* which were wont of the Saxons to be written *Scyrgerefa:*

resa: Portgeresa See.*Shyreeue* and *Portgreve*. See *Roger Hoveden parte poster. suorum annal. fo.* 346. *b.* where he saith thus: *Greue dicitur, ideo quod iure debeat grithe.* i. *pacem ex illis facere, qui patriæ inferunt Væ.i. miseriam vel malum.*

Grithbreach, is a breach of peace. For *Grith is a word of the old Angles*, signifiing peace. *Roger Hovedin parte poster. suorum annal. fo.* 346.*b.* See *Greachbreach.*

Grills *anno* 22.*Ed.*4.*ca.*2.

Grocers, be merchants that ingrosse all merchandize vendible *anno* 37.*Ed.*3.*ca.*5.

Groome, anno 33. *H.* 8. *ca.*10. (*Valletus*) is the name of a seruant that serueth in some inferiour place. *M. Verstegan in his restitution of decayed intelligence* saith, that he findeth it to haue beene in times past a name for youths, who albeit they serued, yet were they inferiour to men seruants, and were sometimes vsed to be sent on foote of errands, seruing in such manner as lackies doe nowe.

Groome, anno 43.*E. ca.*10. seemeth to be an engine to stretch wollen cloth withall after it is wouen.

Guydage (Guydagium) is that which is giuen for safe conduct through a strange territorie. *Cassan: de consuet. Bourg. pag.* 119. whose words be these. *Est Guidagiũ quod datur alicui, vt tutò conducatur per loca alterius.*

Guylde, See *Gyld.*

Guylhalda Teutonicorum. See *Gild.*

Gule of August (*Gula Augusti*) *anno* 27. *Ed.* 3. *stat.* 3. *cap. vnico* *Fitzh. nat. br. fol.* 62.*I. alias* Goule *de August. Plowd. casu Mines, fo.* 316.*b.* is the very day of Saint *Peter ad vincula*, which was wont, and is still within the limits of the Roman church, celebrated vpon the very Kalends of *August*. Why it should be called the gule of August, I cannot otherwise coniecture, but that it commeth of the latine (*gula*) or the French (*gueule*) the throate. The reason of my coniecture is in *Durands rationali diuinorum li.* 7. *ca. de festo Sancti Petri ad vincula*, who saith that one *Quirinus a tribune*, hauing a daughter that had a disease in her throat, went to *Alexander* then Pope of *Rome* the sixt from Saint Peter, and desired of him to borow or see the cheines that Saint *Peter* was cheined with vnder *Nero*: which request obteined, his said daughter kissing the said cheine, was cured of her disease and *Quirinus* with his family was baptised. *Tunc dictus Alexander papa* (saith *Durand*) *hoc festum in Kalendis Augusti celebrandum instituit, & in honorem beati Petri ecclesiam in vrbe fabricavit, vbi vincula ipsa reposuit, & ad vin-*

vincula nominavit ; & Kalendis Augusti, dedicavit. In qua festivitate, populus illic ipsa vincula hodie osculatur. So that this day being before called onely the Kalends of *August*, was vpon this occasion afterward termed indifferently either of the instrument that wrought this miracle, Saint *Peters day ad vincula*, or of that part of the maiden, wheron the miracle was wrought, the *Gule of August*.

Gultwit, seemeth to be compounded of (*Gult*. i. *noxa*) and *wit*, which is said by some skilfull men, to be an auncient termination of the words in the Saxon tongue, signifiing nothing in it selfe, but as (*dom*) or (*hood*) and such like be in these english words (*Christendom*) and (*Manhood*) or such others: others say, and it is true, that wit signifieth blame or reprehension. *Gultwit* (as *Saxon* in his description of England *ca*. 11. doth interpret it) is an amends for trespas.

Gust (*Hospes*) is vsed by *Bracton* for a straunger or guest, that lodgeth with vs the second night: *lib*. 3. *tracta*. 2. *ca*. 10. In the lawes of Saint *Edward* set forth by *M. Lamberd, num*. 27. it is written *Gest*: of this see more in *Vncothe*.

Gumme (*gummi*) is a certaine clammie or tough liquor that in maner of a swetie excrement, issueth out of trees, and is hardened by the sunne. Of these ther be diuers sorts brought ouer seas, that be drugs to be garbled, as appeareth by the statute *anno* 1. *Iaco. ca*. 19.

Gutter tyle, alias corner tyle, is a tile made three corner wise, especially to be laid in gutters, or at the corners of tyled houses, which you shall often see vpon douehouses at the foure corners of their roses. *anno* 17. *Eduardi* 4. *ca*. 4.

H A

H*Abeas corpus*, is a writ, the which a man indited of some trespas before Iustices of peace, or in a court of any franchise, and vpon his apprehension being laid in prison for the same, may haue out of the kings bench, thereby to remooue himselfe thither at his owne costs, and to answer the cause there, &c. *Fitzh. nat. br. fol*. 250. *H*. And the order is in this case, first to procure a (*Certiorari*) out of the Chaũcerie directed to the said Iustices for the remoouing of the Inditemẽt into the kings bench, and vpon that to procure this writ to the Shyreeue, for the causing of his body to be brought at a day, *Register iudiciall. fol*. 81. where you shall finde diuers cases, wherein this writ is vsed.

Habeas corpora, is a writ that li-

H A

eth for the bringing in of a Iurie, or so many of them, as refuse to come vpon the *(venire facias)* for the tryall of a cause brought to issue. *old nat br. fol.* 157. See great diuersitie of this writ, in the table of the Register Iudiciall. *verbo, habeas corpora.* & the new booke of Entries. *verbo eodem.*

Habendum, is a word of forme in a deede of conueyance, to the true vnderstanding whereof you must knowe, that in euery deede of conueyance, there be 2. principall parts, the premisses, and the *habendum.* The office of the premisses is, to expresse the name of the grauntour, the grauntee, and the thing graunted or to be graunted. The office of the *(habendum)* is to limite the estate, so that the generall implication of the estate, which by construction of lawe passeth in the premisses, is by the *(habendum)* controlled and qualified. As in a lease to two persons, the *(habendum)* to one for life, the remainder to the other for life, altereth the generall implication of the ioynt tenancie in the freehould, which should passe by the premisses, if the *(Habendum)* weare not. *Cooke. vol.2. Bucklers case.fo.* 55. See *Vse.*

Habere facias seisinam, is a writ Iudicial, which lyeth, where a man hath recouered lands in the kings court, directed to the Shyreeue, and commaunding him to giue him seisin of the land recouered. *old nat. br. fol.* 154. *Termes of the lawe*: whereof see great diuersity also in the table of the *Register Iudiciall, verb. Habere facias seisinā.* This writ is issuing sometime out of the Records of a fine executorie, directed to the *Shyreeue* of the countie, where the land lyeth, & commanding hi n to giue to the Cognizee or his heires, seisin of the land, whereof the fine is leuied. which writ lyeth within the yeare after the fine, or Iudgemēt vpon a *(scire facias)* and may be made in diuers formes. *West. parte.2.symb. titulo Fines. sect.* 136. There is also a writ called *Habere facias seisinam, vbi Rex habuit annum, diem, & vastum*, which is for the redeliuery of lands to the Lord of the fee, after the king hath taken his due of his lands, that was conuicted of felonie. Register.*orig. fol.* 165.

Habere facias visum, is a writ that lyeth in diuers cases, where view is to be taken of the lands or tenements in question. See *Fitzh. nat. br. in Indice. verbo, (View)* See *Bracton. li.5. tract.3. ca. 8. & lib.5. parte.2. ca.11.* See *view.* See the *Register. Iudiciall. fol.* 1. 26, 28. 45. 49. 52.

Haberiects (Hauberietus pannus

nus) magn. chart. ca. 25. *& pupilla oculi. parte.* 5. *ca.* 22.

Hables, is the plurall of the French (*hable*) signifiing as much as a porte or hauen of the sea, whence ships doe set forth into other countries, and whether they doe arriue, when they returne from their voyage. This word is vsed. *anno* 27. *Hen.* 6. *cap.* 3.

Hærede deliberando alii qui habet custodiam terræ, is a writ directed to the Shyreeue, willing him to commande one hauing the body of him, that is ward to another, to deliuer him to him, whose ward he is by reason of his land. *Register. originall. fol.* 161. *b.*

Hærede abducto, is a writ that lyeth for the lord, who hauing the wardship of his tenent vnder age by right, cannot come by his body, for that he is conueyed away by another. *old. nat. br. fol.* 93. See *Rauishment de Gard*, and *Hærede rapto, in* Regist. *orig. fol.* 163.

Hæretico comburendo, is a writ that lyeth against him, that is an heretike. *viz.* that hauing beene once conuinced of herisy by his Bishop, and hauing abiured it, afterward falleth into it againe, or into some other, and is therevpon committed to the secular power. *Fitzh. nat. br. fol.* 269.

Haga, is vsed as a kinde of latine word for a house. I finde in an auncient booke sometime belonging to the abbey of Saint *Augustines* in *Canterbury*, that king *Stephen* sent his writ to the Shyreeue and Iustices of *Kent*, in this maner. *Stephanus Rex Anglorum vicecomiti & Iusticiariis de Kent salutem. præcipio quòd faciatis habere ecclesiæ sancti Augustini & monachis hagam suam quam Goscceoldus eis dedit, ita bene & in pace & iustè & quietè & liberè, sicut eam eis dedit in morte sua coram legalibus testibus, &c.*

Hagbut, See *Haque* and *Haquebut*.

Haye *boote*, seemeth to be compounded (Haye. i. *Sepes*) and (*Bote*. i. *compensatio*) The former is french, and the second is Saxon. And although it doe fall out sometime, that our words be so compounded: yet is it rare. wherefore it may be thought peraduenture to come as well from (*Hag*) and (*boote*) which be bothe saxon words. It is vsed in our common lawe for a permission to take thorns and freeth to make or repaire hedges.

Halfe haque, See *Haque.*

Half *merk* (*dimidia merka*) seemeth to signifie a noble. *Fitzh: nat: br: fol:* 5. where he saith that in case a writ of right be brought and the seisin of the Demaundant, or his auncester alleaged, the seisin is not trauersable by the Defendant, but he may tender or proferre the halfe merke for the inquirie of this seisin, which is as much to say in plainer termes, that the Defendant shall not be admitted to deny, that the Demandant or his auncester, was seised of the land in question, and to proue his deniall: but that hee shal be admitted to tender halfe a merke in money, to haue an inquirie made, whether the Demandant, &c. were so seised or not. And in this signification I reade the same words in the old English *natura breuium, fol.* 26. *b. viz.* Know ye, that in a writ of right of *Advouzen* brought by the king, the defendant shall not proferre the halfe merke, ne iudgement finall shall be giuen against the king, &c. Wherof *Fitz. vbi supra. M.* giueth the reason, because in the kings case, the defendant shall bee permitted to trauerse the seisin by licence obtained of the Kings Sergeant. To this effect see Fitz. *nat. br. fol.* 31. *C.D.E.*

Halfe seale, is vsed in the Chauncerie for the sealing of Commissions vnto *Delegates*, appointed vpon any appeale in ecclesiasticall or marine causes, *an.* 8. *Elizab. cap.* 5.

Halfe tongue. See *Medietas linguæ.*

Halymote, aliâs, Healgemot, is a Court Baron. *Manwood parte prim.* of his Forest lawes. *pag.* 111. and the etymologie is the meeting of the tenents of one hall or maner. *M. Gwins preface to his reading*, which for the esteeme thereof, is by copies spred into many mens hands.

Hallage, is a fee due for cloths brought for sale to *Blackwell hal* in *London. Coke vol.* 6. *fol.* 62. *b.*

Hamlet (*Hameletum*) is a diminutiue of (*Ham*) which signifieth *habitationem. Camden. Brit. pag.* 149. & 354. The French (*hameau.* i. *viculus*) is also nere vnto it. *Kitchin* hath *Hamel* in the same sence. *fol.* 215. who also vseth *hampsel* for an ould house or cotage decayed. *fol.* 103. *Hamlet* (as *Stowe* vseth it in *Ed.* 3.) seemeth to be the seate of a *Free holder*. For there he saith, that the said king bestowed two maners and nine hamlets of land vpon the monasterie of *Westminster*, for the keeping of yearely obits for his wife Queene *Eleanor* deceased.

Hameling of dogges, or *hambling of dogges*, is all one with the expeditating of dogges. *Manwood parte prim.* of his Forest lawes. *pag.* 212. & *parte* 2. *cap.* 16. *num.* 5. where he saith, that this is the auncient terme that Foristers vsed for that mater, whence this word might be be drawne, I dare not resolue: but it is not improbable, that *hameling* is *quasi*, *hambalding*, that is, keeping at home, which is done by paring their feete so, as they cannot take any great delight in running abroade. See *Expeditate*.

Hampsell. See *Hamlet*.

Hamsoken, see Homesoken. *M. Skene de verb: significa:* writeth it Haimsuken, and deriueth it from (*Haim*) *a German* word, signifiing a house or dwelling, and (*Suchen*) that is to seeke, search, or persiew. It is vsed in Scotland for the crime of him, that violently, and contrary to the kings peace, assaulteth a man in his owne house: which (as he saith) is punishable equally with rauishing of a woman. *significat quietantiam misericordiæ intrationis in alienam domum vi & iniustè. Fleta. lib. pri. cap.* 47. See *Homesoken*.

Hand in and *Hand* out. *anno* 17. *Ed.* 4. *cap.* 2. is the name of an vnlawful game.

Hand full, is foure inches by the standard. *anno* 33. *H.* 8. *cap.* 5. &c.

Hankwit alias (*Hangwit*) or (*Hengwit*) commeth of the Saxon words (*Hangen* .i. *pendêre*) and (*wit*) whereof reade in *Gultwit*: *Rastall* in the title, Exposition of words saith, it is a liberty graunted vnto a man, wherby he is quit of a felon or theefe hanged without iudgement, or escaped out of custodie. I reade it interpreted, *mulcta pro homine iniustè suspenso*. Or whether it may be a libertie, whereby a Lord chalengeth the forfeiture due for him, that fordoeth himselfe within his fee or not, let the Reader consider. See *Bloodwit*.

Hanper, (*haneperium*) *haneper of the Chauncerie. anno* 10. *R.* 2. *cap. prim.* seemeth to signifie as *fiscus* originally doth in *Latine*. See *Clerke of the Hanaper*.

Hanse, (as *Ortelius* in the Index of his Additament to his *Theater, verb. Ansiatici.* saith,) is an old *Gothish* word. Where he sheweth not the interpretation. It signifieth a certaine societie of Merchants, combined together for the good vsage and safe passage of merchandies from kingdome to kingdome. This societie was, and (in part) yet is, endued with many large priuiledges of princes, respectiuely within their territories. It had foure principall seates, or staples: where the Almaine or Dutch Merchants being the erectours of this societie, had an especiall house, one of which was here in *London*, called *Gildhalda Teutonicorum*, or in our common language, the *Steelyard*. Of this you may reade more in the place of *Ortelius* aboue mentioned.

Happe, commeth of the french (Happer.i. *rapio, cum quadam velocitate capio*) and the french seemeth to come from the greeke ἁρπάζω. It signifieth in our common lawe the same thing: as to happe the possession of a deede poll. *Litleton. fol.* 8.

Haque, is a handgunne of about three quarters of a yard long, *anno.* 33. H. 8. *ca.* 6. & *a.* 2. *et.* 3. *Ed.* 6. *ca.* 14. There is also the halfe haque or demy hake. See H*aquebut*.

Haquebut, is that peece of artilery or gunne, which we otherwise call an harquebuse, being both french words. *anno.* 2. & 3. *Ed.* 6. *ca.* 14. & *anno* 4. & 5. *Ph.* & *Ma. ca.* 2.

Hariot, *aliàs, Heriot (heriotum)* is the saxon *(heregeat)* a litle altered, which is drawn from *(here .i. exercitus)* and a *(heriot)* in our Saxons time signified a tribute giuen to the lord for his better preparation toward war. *Lamb.* in his expl. of Saxon words. *verbo. hereotum.* The name is still reteined, but the vse altered: for whereas, by *M. Lamb.* opinion *vbi supra,* it did signifie so much as Releife doth now with vs: now it is taken for the best chatell that a tenent hath at the houre of his death, due vnto the lord by custome, be it horse, oxe, kettle, or any such like. *M. Kitchin* distinguisheth betweene *heriot* seruice and *heriot custom. fol.* 133. & 134. for interpretation whereof, you shall finde these words in *Brooke. titulo hariot. nu.* 5. *Hariot* after the death of the tenent for life, is *hariot* custome. For *hariot* seruice is after the death of tenent in fee-simple. The new Expounder of the lawe termes saith, that *hariot* seruice (in some mans opinion) is often expressed in a mans graunt or deed, that hee holdeth by such seruice to pay *hariot* at the time of his death, that holdeth in fee simple. *Hariot custome* is, where *hariots* haue bin payed time out of mind by custome. And this may be after the death of the tenent for life. See *Plowden. fol.* 95. *b.* 69. *a. b.* *Bracton* saith, that *heriotum, est quasi Releuium. lib.* 2. *cap.* 36. See *Reliefe.* But *Britton. cap.* 69. saith, that *heriot* is a reward made by the death of a tenent, to any Lorde, of the best beaste found in the possession of the tenent deceased, or of some other according to the ordinance or assignement of the party deceased, to the vse of his Lord. which reward toucheth not the Lord at all, nor the heire, nor his inheritance, neither hath any comparison to a Releife: for it proceedeth rather of grace or good-

goodwill then of right, and rather from villeins then free men. See *Dyer,fol.* 199. *nu.* 58. to the same effect. This in Scotland is called *Herrezelda.* compounded of *herr.* i. *dominus, herus.* and *zeild.*i. *gift.* *Skene de verbo. signif. verbo Herrezelda.*

Hart, is a stagge of 5. yeares old compleate. *Manwood parte 2. of his forest lawes. cap.* 4. *nu.* 5. which he hath out of *Budæus de philologia. li.* 2. And if the King or Queene doe hunt him, and he escape away aliue, then afterward he is called a Hart royall. And if the beast by the Kings or Queenes hunting be chased out of the forest and so escape: proclamation is commonly made in the places there about, that in regard of the pastime, that the beast hath shewed to the King or Queene, none shall hurt him, or hinder him from returning to the forest; and then is he a Hart royall proclaimed. *Idem. eodem.*

Hauberk, commeth of the French (*Haubert.*i. *lorica*) whereupon he that holdeth land in France by finding a coate or shirt of mayle, and to be readie with it, when he shall be called, is said to haue *Hauberticum feudum.* whereof *Hotoman* writeth thus: *Hauberticum feudum gallicâ linguâ vulgò dicitur pro(loricatum)* .i. *datum vasallo ea conditione, vt ad edictum loricatus siue cataphractus præsto sit. Nam vt lorica latinis propriè & minus vsitatè est tegmen de loro factum, quo maiores in bello vtebantur, quemadmodum* Seruius Honoratius *scribit in libro Æneidũ* 11 *frequentissimè autem pro ærea armatura integra vsurpatur. sic apud Gallos Haubert propriè loricam annulis contextam significat, quam vulgus Cotte de maille appellat. Hæc Hot. in verbis feudal. verbo* Hauberticum *feudum.* Hauberk with our awncesters seemeth to signifie, as in France, a shirt or coate of mayle and so it seemeth to be vsed, *anno* 13. *Ed. pri stat.* 3. *ca.* 6. Though in these daies the word is otherwise written as (*Halbert*) and signifieth a weapon well enough knowne.

Haward alias Hayward, seemeth to be componnded of two french word (*Hay*.i. *sepes*) & *Garde* .i. *custodia*) It signifieth with vs, one that keepeth the common heard of the towne: & the reason may be, because one part of his office is to looke that they neither breake nor croppe the hedges of inclosed grounds. It may likewise come from the german (*herd.*i. *armentũ* & (*bewarren.*i. *custodire*). He is a sworne officer in the Lords court: and the forme of his oath you may see in *Kitchin. fol.* 46.

Haw-

Hawkers, be certaine deceitfull felowes, that goe from place to place, buying & selling, brasse, pewter, and other merchandise, that ought to be vttered in open market. The appellation seemeeth to growe from their vncertaine wandering, like those that with hawkes seeke their game, where they can finde it. You finde the word. *anno*. 25. *H.* 8. *ca.* 6. *& anno* 33. *eiusdem*. *cap. quarto.*

H*eadborow*, is compounded of two words: (*Heofod.* i. *caput*) and (*Bor-he.*i. *pignus*) It signifieth him, that is cheife of the franckpledg: and him that had the principall gouernment of them within his owne pledge. And as he was called H*eadborowe*, so was he also called *Borowhead*, *Bursholder*, *Thirdborow*, *Tithing man*, *Cheife pledge*, or *Borowelder*, according to the diuersitie of speach in diuers places. Of this see *M. Lamberd* in his explication of Saxon words. *verbo Centuria*. and in his treatise of Constables. and *Smith de* Repub. *Anglo. lib.* 2. *cap.* 22. It nowe signifieth Constable. See *Constable.*

Healfang, is compounded of two Saxon words (*Hals.*i. *collū*) and (*fang.*i. *capere*, *captivare*). See *Pylorie*.

Heire(*Hæres*) though, for the word, it be borowed of the latine; yet, it hath not altogether the same signification with vs, that it hath with the Civilians, for whereas they call him (*hæredem*) *qui ex testamento succedit in vniuersum ius testatoris:* the cõmon lawyers call him heire, that succeedeth by right of blood, in any mans lands or tenements in fee, for there is nothing passeth with vs *iure hæreditatis*, but onely fee. Moueables, or chatels immoueable, are giuen by testament, to whom the testator listeth, or else are at the disposition of the Ordinarie, to be distributed as he in conscience thinketh meete, G*lossa in Provinciali constitut*. *Ita quorundam. De testamentis. verbo. Ab intestato.* And whether a man enioy moueable goods and chatels, by will or the discretion of the Ordinarie, he is not with vs called an heire: but onely he that succeedeth either by testament, or right of bloud in fee. *Cassanaus in consuetud. Burg. pag.* 909. hath a distinction of *hæres*, which in some sort well accordeth with our lawe: For he saith, there is *hæres sanguinis*, *& hæreditatis*. And a man may be *hæres sanguinis* with vs, that is, heyre apparent to his father, or other auncester: and yet may vpon displeasure, or meere will be defeated of his inheritance, or at the least, the greatest part thereof.

Heyre loome, seemeth to bee com-

compounded of (*heire*) and (*loome*) that is, a frame, namely to weaue in. The word by time is drawne to a more generall signification, then at the first it did beare, comprehending all implements of houshold, as namely, tables, presses, cupbords, bedsteedes, wainscots, and such like, which by the custome of some countries, hauing belonged to a house certaine descents, are neuer inventaried after the decease of the owner, as chatels, but accrew to the heyre with the house it selfe. This word is twice metaphorically vsed in that diuine speech, made by that most worthy & complete noble man the Earle of *Northampton*, against that hellish, vgly, and damnable treason of gunpowder, plotted to consume the most vertuous King that euer raigned in Europe, together with his gratious Queene, and pretious posteritie, as also the three honorable estates of this renowned kingdome.

Heck, is the name of an Engine, to take fish in the riuer of *Owse* by *Yorke*. *anno* 23. *H.* 8. *cap.* 18.

Heinfare, alias, hinefare, (*discessio famuli à domino*) the word is compounded of (*hine*) a seruant, and (*fare*) an old English word, signifing a passage.

Henchman, or *heinsman*, is a German word signifying (*domesticum, aut vnum de familia.*) It is vsed with vs, for one that runneth on foote attending vpon a man of honour or worship. *anno* 3. *Ed.* 4. *cap.* 5. *anno* 24. *Henric.* 8. *cap.* 13.

Hengwite, significat quietantiã misericordiæ de latrone suspenso absque consideratione. Fleta lib. prim. cap. 47. See *Hankwit*.

Herau'd, (*heraldus*) is borowed by vs of the French (*herault*) and in *M. Verstegans* iudgement proceedeth originally from two Dutch words (*here.* i. *exercitus*) and (*healt.* i. *pugil magnanimus,*) as if he should be called (the Champion of the armie) hauing by especiall office to chalenge vnto battell or combate. With vs it signifieth an officer at armes, whose function is to denounce warre, to proclaime peace, or otherwise to be employed by the King in martiall messages or other businesse. The *Romaines* called them plurally (*Feciales.*) *M. Stow* in his Annals deriueth them from *heroes. pag.* 12. which hee hath from other that writ of that subiect, whose coniecture I leaue to the reader. Their office with vs, is described by *Polydore. lib.* 19. in this sort: speaking of the knights of the Garter, hee saith: *habent insuper Apparitores ministros, quos heraldos dicunt: quorum præfectus armorum Rex vocitatur:*

tatur: hy belli & pacis nuncii. Ducibus, Comitibusq; à Rege factis insignia aptant, ac eorum funera curant. He might haue added farder, that they be the Iudges and examiners of gentlemens armes, that they marshall all the solemnities at the coronations of princes, manage combats, and such like. There is also one and the same vse of them with vs, and with the French nation, whence we haue their name. And what their office is with them, see *Lupanus lib. prim. de Magist. Francorum, ca. Heraldi.* There be diuers of them with vs: whereof three being the chiefe, are called Kings at armes. And of them *Garter* is the principall, instituted and created by *Henry* the fifth. *Stowes annals. pag.* 584. whose office is to attend the knights of the Garter at their solemnities, and to marshall the solemnities of the funerals of all the greater nobility, as of *Princes, Dukes, Marquises, Earles, Vicounts,* and *Barons*, yet I finde in *Plowden, casu Reniger, & Fogassa*, that Ed. the fourth graunted the office of the king of *Heralds*, to one *Garter cum feudis & proficuis ab antiquo, &c. fol.* 12. *b.* The next is *Clarentius*, ordained by *Edward* the fourth. for he attaining the *Dukedome* of *Clarence* by the death of *George* his brother, whom he beheaded for aspiring to the crowne, made the *Herald*, which properly belonged to the *Duke* of *Clarence*, a King at armes, and called him *Clarentius*. His proper office is, to marshall and dispose the funerals of all the lesser nobility, as knights, and Esquires, through the Realme of the south side of *Trent*. The third is *Norroy*, or *Northroy*, whose office is the same on the north side of *Trent*, that *Clarentius* hath on this side, as may well appeare by his name, signifiing the northern king, or king of the north parts. Beside these, there be sixe other properly called *Heralds* according to their originall, as they were created to attend *Dukes, &c.* in marshall executions. *viz. York, Lancaster, Somerset, Richemond, Chester, Windlesour*. Lastly there be foure other called marshals or poursiwants at armes, reckoned after a sort, in the number of *Heralds*, and doe commonly succeede in the place of the *Heralds* as they dye, or be preferred: and those be *Blew Mantle, Rougecrosse, Rougedragon*, and *Percullis*. The (*feciales*) among the Romans were priests, *Nam Numa Pompilius diuini cultus institutionem in octo partes diuisit, & ita etiam sacerdotum octo ordines constituit, &c. Septimā partem sacra constitutionis collegio eorum adiecit, qui Feciales vocantur. Erant autem ex*

optimis

optimis domibus viri electi, per omne ipsi vitæ tempus sacrati, quorum partes in eo versabantur, vt fidei publicæ inter populos præessent: neq; iustum aliquod bellum fore censebatur: nisi id per Feciales esset indictum. Qui vt Festus ait, a faciendo, quòd belli pacisque facienda apud eos ius esset, Feciales dicti sunt. Corasius miscel. iuris ciui. li. 1. ca. 10. *nu.* 12.

Herbage (*herbagium*) is a french word, and signifieth in our common lawe, the fruit of the earth prouided by nature for the bitte or mouth of the catell. But it is most commonly vsed for a liberty that a man hath to feede his catell in another mans ground, as in the forest, &c. *Cromptons Iurisdiction. fol.* 197.

Herbenger commeth of the french (Heberger) or (*Esberger*) (*hesberger*) .i. *hospitio excipere.* It signifieth with vs, an officer of the princes court, that allotteth the noble men, and those of the household their lodgings. It signifieth also in *Kitchin*, an Inkeeper. *fol.* 176.

Hereditaments (*hereditamenta*) seeme to signifie all such things immoueable, be they corporeall or incorporeall, as a man may haue to himselfe and his heires, by way of inheritance. *v. anno* 32. H. 8. *ca.* 2. or not being otherwise bequeathed, doe naturally and of course descend to him which is our next heire of blood, and fall not within the compas of an executour, or administratour, as chatels doe.

Heriot. See *Hariot.*

Hide of land (Hida *terræ*) *Saxonicè* (H*idelandes*) is a certaine measure or quantitie of land, by some mens opinion, that may be plowed with one plowe in a yeare: as the author of the newe Termes saith, *verbo Hidage.* by other men, it is an hundred acres. By *Beda* (who calleth it *familiā*) it is as much as will maintaine a familie. *Crompton in his Iurisdict. fol.* 220. saith, that it consisteth of an hundred acres: euery acre in length 40. perches, and in breadth 4. perches, everie perch 16. foote and a halfe. and againe, *fol.* 222. A hide of land conteineth an hundred acres, & 8. hides or 800. acres, conteine a knights fee. Of this reade more in *M. Lamberds Explica: of Saxon wordes, verbo* Hyda *terræ* . See *Carue.*

Hide and *gaine. old. nat. br. fol.* 71. *Coke. lib.* 4. *Tirringhams case.* signifieth earable land. See Gainage.

Hidage (Hi*dagium*) is an extraordinarie taxe, to be paide for euery hide of land, *Bracton li.* 2. *c.* 6. writeth thus of it: *Sunt etiam quædam communes præstationes, quæ seruitia non dicuntur, nec de consuetudine veniunt nisi cum necessitas in-*

teruenerit, vel cum Rex *venerit: sicut sunt Hidagia, Coragia, & Carvagia: & alia plura de necessitate & ex consensu communi totius Regni introducta, & quæ ad Dominum feudi non pertinent, &c.* of this reade the new expounder of lawe termes, who saith that hidage is to be quit, if the king shall taxe all the lands by hides, and yet also graunteth it to be the taxe it selfe, saying that it was wont to be an vsuall kind of taxing as well for prouision of armour, as payments of money.

H*inefare*. See *Heinfare*.

H*idel*. i. H. 7. *ca*. 6. seeemeth to signifie a place of protection, as a Sanctuarie.

Hierlome, See *Heirlome*.

Hine, seemeth to be vsed for a Seruant at husbandrie and the master hine a seruant that ouerseeth the rest. *anno*. 12. R. 2. *ca. quarto*.

Hob*lers (Hobellarii)* are certaine men, that by their tenure are tyed to maintaine a little light nagge, for the certifiing of any inuasion made by enemies, or such like perill toward the Sea side, as *Porchmouth, &c.* of these you shall reade. *anno* 18. *Ed*. 3. *stat*. 2. *cap*. 7. & *anno* 25. *eiusdem. stat*. 5. *ca*. 8.

H*oghenhine*, is he that commeth guestwise to a house, and lieth there the third night. After which time he is accounted of his familie in whose house he lieth: and if he offend the kings peace, his host must be answerable for him. *Bracton lib*. 3. *tract*. 2. *cap*. 10. In the lawes of *King Edward* set forth by *M. Lamberd*, he is called *agenhine*. wheare you may reade more of this mater.

Hithe (H*ithe*) is a petit hauen to land wares out of vessels or boates. new booke of Entrise. *fol*. 3. *colum*. 3.

Hoggeshead, is a measure of wine or oyle containing the fourth parte of a tunne. that is 63. gallons. *anno*. i. R. 3. *ca*. 13.

Hoistings. See *Hustings*.

Homage (*Homagium*) is a french word, signifiing (*fidem clientularem*.) for in the originall grants of land and tenements by way of fee, the lord did not onely tie his tenents or feed men to certaine seruices: but also tooke a submission with promis and oathe, to be true and loyall to him, as there lord & benefactour. This submission was and is called homage: the forme wherof you haue in the second statute *anni*. 17. *Ed*: 2. in these words: when a free man shall doe homage to his Lord, of whome he holdeth in chiefe: he shall hold his hands together betweene the hands of his lord, and shall say thus : I become your man from this day forthe for life, for member, & for wordly honour, and shall owe you my faith for the land I hold of you: sauing the faith, that I doe owe vnto our Soueraigne Lord the king, and to mine other Lords. And in this maner the Lord of the fee, for which homage is due, taketh homage of euery tenent, as he commeth to the land or fee. *Glanvile. lib. 9. ca. 1.* except they be women, who performe not homage but by their husbands, (yet see *Fitzherbert.* that saith the contrary in his *natura br. fol. 157. F.*) Reade *Glanuile* more at large in the said first chapter, with the second, third & fourth; The reason of this *M. Skene* giueth *de verbo. significatione, verbo Homagium. viz.* because Homage especially concerneth seruice in warre. He saith also, that consecrated Bishops, doe no homage, but onely fidelitie: the reason may be all one. And yet I find in the *Register. orig. fol. 296. a.* that a woman taking liuerie of lands holden by knights seruice, must doe homage, but not being ioyntly infeoffed, for then shee doth only fealtie. And see *Glanuile* in the ende of the first chapter of his nineth booke touching Bishops consecrated, whome he denieth to performe homage to the king for their Baronie, but onely fealty. *Fulbeck* reconcileth this, *fol. 20. a.* in these words. By our lawe a religious man may doe homage, but may not say to his Lord. *Ego devenio homo vester*, because he hath professed himselfe to be onely Gods man, but he may say, I doe vnto you homage, and to you shall be faithfull & loyall. See of this *Britton. cap. 68.* Homage, is either new with the fee, or aunceftrell: that is, wheare a man and his auncesters, time out of minde, haue held their lands by homage to their Lord, whereby the Lord is tied to warrant the land vnto his tenent. *newe Termes of the lawe.* This homage is vsed in other countries as well as ours, & was wont to be called *Hominium.* See Hotom. *de verbis feudalibus, verbo. Homo. Skene* diuideth it into *ligium & non ligium. de verb. signifi. verbo Homage.* for the which see *Leige*, and *Hotoman, disputatione de feudis tertia. Homage* is sometime vsed for the Iurie in the *Courte Baron, Smith de Repub. Anglo. lib. 2. cap. 27.* The reason is, because it consisteth most commonly of such, as owe homage vnto the Lord of the fee. And these of the Feudists are called *pares curiæ, siue curtis, siue domus, sic dicuntur enim connassalli siue compares, qui ab eodem patrono feudum receperunt, vel qui in eodem territorio feudum habent. Hotoman.* Of this homage you may read in the 29. *c.* of the *Grand Custumarie of Normandie*, where you shall vnderstand of other sorts of homage vsed by them, & straunge vnto vs. whereunto ioyne *Hotoman. disputat. de feudis*, in diuers places & namely *columna* 860. *C. his verbis. Deinceps de nota hominii & feudalitiæ subiectionis videamus. Omnium quidem video esse commune, vt dexteras tanquam in fœderibus iungerent: plerumq; etiam vt dexteris aversis, osculum praberent, interdum, vt ambas manus iunctas patrono contrectandas praberent: supplicum & dedititiorum nomine, qui velatas manus porrigebant.* and *pag.* 861. *his verbis. Multis Galliæ atq; etiam Angliæ moribus constitutum est (Quod ex Anglico Littletonio intelleximus) vt hominium seruili & supplici veneratione, ac planè tanquam a dedititiis præstetur. Nam vasallus discinctus, nudo capite, ad pedes sedentis patroni proiectus, ambas manus iunctas porrigit: quas dum Dominus suis manibus amplectitur, hæc verba pronunciat. Here, venio in tuum hominium & fidem, & homo tuus fio ore & manibus; tibiq; iuro ac spondeo fidelem me tibi futurum eorum feudorum nomine, quæ tuo beneficio accepi, &c.* Whereunto you may adde him, *colum.* 819. *G.* 822. *F.* & 857. *B.* & *D.* & *F.* Of homage in Scotland, reade *M. Skene, de verb. signif. verbo Homagium.* to whome you may also ioyne a plentifull discourse *in speculo Durandi.* commonly called (*speculator*) among the Civilians, *titulo De Feudis.*

Homagio respectuando, is a writ to the Escheatour commaunding him to deliuer seisin of lands to the heire, that is at full age, notwithstanding his homage not done, which ought to be performed before the heire haue liuerie of his lands, except there fall out some reasonable cause to hinder it. *Fitzh. nat. br. fol.* 269.

Homine eligendo ad custodiendam peciam sigilli pro Mercatoribus editi, is a writ directed to a corporation, for the choice of a new man to keepe the one part of the seale, appointed for statutes Merchant, when the other is dead, according to the statute of *Acton Burnel. Register. orig. fol.* 178. *a.*

Homine replegiando, is a writ for the bayle of a man out of prison: which, in what cases it lyeth, and what not, See *Fitz. nat. br. fol.* 66. See also the *Register orig. fol.* 77. See the new booke of Entries. *verb. Homine replegiando.*

Homine capto in Withernamium, is a writ to take him, that hath taken any bondman or woman, and led him or her out of the countie, so that he or shee cannot

not be repleuied according to lawe. *Register orig. fol.* 79.*a*. See *Withernam*.

Homicide (homicidium) is the slaying of a man: and it is diuided into voluntarie, or casuall: homicide voluntarie is that, which is deliberated, and committed of a set mind, and purpose to kill: homicide volūtary, is either with precedent malice, or without. The former is murder, and is the felonious killing through malice prepensed of any person liuing in this realme vnder the Kings protection. *West. part.* 2. *simbol: tit. Inditment. sect:* 37. *&c. vsque ad* 51. where you may see diuers subdiuisions of this mater. See also *Glanuile. lib* 14. *cap:* 3. *Bract. l:* 3. *tra:* 2. *c.* 4. 15. *&* 17. *Brit. c.* 5. 6. 7. See *Muder. Mans slaughter & Chaūce medley*.

Homesoken, aliâs Hamsoken (Hamsoca) is compounded of (*Ham.* i. *habitatio*) and (*Soken*. i. *quærere*) It is by *Bracton. lib.* 3. *tract:* 2. *c:* 23. thus defined. *Homesoken dicitur inuasio domus contra pacem* Domini *Regis*. It appeareth by *Rastall* in the title. Expositiō of of words: that in auntient times some men had an immunitie to doe this: for he defineth *Homesoken* to be an immunitie from amercements for entring into houses violently, and without licence. which thing seemeth so vnreasonable, that me thinketh he should be deceiued in that his exposition. I would rather thinke it should be a libertie, or power graunted by the king to some common person, for the cognisance or punishment of such a trangression. for so I haue seene it interpreted in an old note that I haue giuen me by a frend, which he had of an expert man toward the *Exchequer*, but of what authoritie I know not. See *Hamsoken*.

Hondhabend, is compounded of two Saxon words (*Hond* .i. *hand*, and *habend*. i. *hauing*) and signifieth a circumstance of manifest theft, when one is deprehended with the thing stollen in his hand. *Bracton. lib.* 3. *tract.* 2. *ca.* 31. *&* 54. who also vse the (*handberend*) for the same, *eodem cap.* 8.

Honour (honor) is, beside the generall signification, vsed specially for the more noble sort of seigneuries: whereof other inferiour Lordships, or maners doe depend by performance of customes and seruices, some or other, to those that are Lords of them. And I haue reason to think that none are honours originally, but such as are belonging to the King. How be it they may afterward be bestowed in fee vpon other nobles. The maner of creating these honours may in part be gathered out of the statutes *anno* 31. *H.* 8. *cap.* 5. where *Hampton court* is made an honour. and *anno* 33. *eiusdem. cap.* 37. & 38. whereby *Amptill* and *Grafton* be likewise made honours. and *anno* 37. *eiusdem ca.* 18. whereby the King hath power giuen by his leters patents, to erect foure seuerall honours. Of *Westminster*, of *Kingston* vpon *Hull*, *Saint Osithes* in *Essex*, and *Dodington* in *Berkshire*. This word is also vsed in the selfe same signification in other nations. See *ca. licet causam. extra de probationibus*. and *Minsinger* vpon it. *nu.* 4. In reading I haue obserued thus many honours in England: The honour of *Aquila. Camden. Britan. pag.* 231. of *Clare. pag.* 351. of *Lancaster. pag.* 581. of *Tickhill. pag.* 531. of *Wallingford, Notingham, Boloine. Magna charta. cap:* 31. of *West Greenewish, Camd: pag.* 239. of *Bedford. pupil. oculi. parte.* 5. *cap.* 22. of *Barhimsted. Brooke, titulo Tenure. nu.* 16. of *Hwitam. Camd pag.* 333. of *Plimpton. Cromptons Iurisd. fol.* 115. of *Creuecure*, and *Hagenet Fobert. anno* 32. *H.* 8. *cap.* 48. of *East Greenewish.* of *Windsour* in *Berkshire*, and of *Bealew* in *Essex. anno* 37. *H.* 8. *ca.* 18. of *Peverell* in the county of *Lincolne. Register orig. fol.* 1.

Horngeld, is compounded of *Horn* and *Gildan* or *Gelder*. i. *Soluere.* It signifieth a taxe within the forest to be paid for horned beasts. *Cromptons Iurisd. fol.* 197. And to be free thereof, is a priuiledge graunted by the king vnto such as he thinketh good. *Idem, ibidem.* and *Rastall* in his exposition of words.

Hors de son fee, is an exception to auoide an action brought for rent, issuing out of certaine land by him that pretendeth to be the Lord, or for some customes and seruices. for if he can iustifie that the land is without the compas of his fee, the action falleth. *v. Brooke. hoc titulo.*

Hospitallers (*Hospitalarii*) were certaine knights of an order, so called, because they had the care of hospitals, wherein Pilgrims were receiued. to these Pope *Clement* the fift transferred the *Templers*, which order, by a councell held at *Vienna* in Fraunce, he suppressed for their many and great offences, as he pretended. These *Hospitallers* be now the knights of Saint *Iohn* of *Malta. Cassan: gloria mundi. parte.* 9. *consderat.* 5. This constitution was also obeyed in *Ed.* the 2. time here in England, and confirmed by Parlament. *Tho. Walsingham. in historia Ed.* 2. *Stowes annals. ibidem.* These are mentioned *anno* 13. *Ed.* 1. *ca.* 43. & *anno* 9. *H.* 3. *ca.* 37.

Hostelers (Hostellarius) commeth of the french (*Hosteler*.i. *Hostes*) and signifieth with vs, those that otherwise we call Inkeepers,*an. 9. Ed. 3. stat. 2. c.* 11.

Hotchepot(in partem positio) is a word that commeth out of the lowecountries,where(*Hutspot*)signifieth flesh cut into pretie peeces,and sodden with herbs or roots, not vnlike that which the Romans called *farraginem. Festus.* Litleton saith that literally it signifieth a pudding mixed of diuers ingredients: but metaphorically a commxtion or putting together of lands, for the equall diuision of them being so put together. Examples you haue diuers in him.*fo.*55.and see Briton,*fol:* 119. There is in the Ciuile law *collatio bonorum* answerable vnto it, whereby if a child aduaunced by the father in his life time,doe after his father decease, chalenge a childs part with the rest,he must cast in all that formerly he had receiued,and then take out an equall share with the others. *De collatio:bonorum.π.lib:* 37. *titulo.* 6.

Housebote,is compounded of *House*, and *Bote*.i.*compensatio*. It signifieth estovers out of the Lords woode to vphould a tenement or house.

Houserobbing, is the robbing of a man in some part of his house,or his booth,or tēt in any faire or market,and the owner, or his wife, children,or seruants, being within the same. for this is felonie by *anno*.23.H:8. *cap*. i. and.*anno*.3.*Ed*.6.*cap* 9.yea, now it is felonie thoughe none be within the house.*anno*. 39. *Eliz: ca*.15. See *Burglarie*. see *West. part*.2. *sym.tit*.Inditemēts,*sect*:67.

Hudegeld,significat quietantiam transgressionis illatæ in seruum transgredientem.Fleta lib.i. *ca*: 47. *Quære* whether it should not be *Hindegeld*.

Hue,and Crie(*Hutesium & Clamor*) come of 2. french words:(*Huier*)and (*Crier*) both signifiing to shoute or cry a loude. *M. Manwood,parte*. 2. of his forest lawes. *ca*: 19. *nu*. 11. saith,that *Hew* is *latine*, meaning belike the *Interiection*: but vnder reformation,I think he is deceiued;this signifieth a pursuite of one hauing committed felonie by the high way, for if the party robbed,or any in the companie of one murdered or robbed, come to the *Constable* of the next towne,and will him to raise Hiew and Crie, or to make pursuite after the offēdour,describing the partie, and shewing as neere as he can, which way he is gone:the Constable ought forthwith to call vpon the parishe for aide in seeking the felon: and if he be not found theare, then to giue the next Constable warning, and he the next, vntill the offender be apprehended, or at the least, vntill he be thus persued to the sea side. Of this reade *Bracton.lib: 3. tracta: 2. ca. 5. Smith de Repub: Anglo: lib: 2. cap:* 20. and the statute *anno.* 13. *Ed.* 1. statute of *Winchest.c.3.&.a.* 28. *Ed: 3.c:* 11. *& anno.* 27. *El: c:* 13. The *Normans* had such a persuite with a Crie after offenders as this is, which they called *Haro*: whereof you may reade the *Grand Custumarie, cap.* 54. Some call it *Harol*: the reason whereof they giue to be this, that there was a *Duke* of *Normandy* called *Rol*, a man of great iustice and seueritie against grieuous offenders: and that thereupon when they follow any in this persuite, they crie *Ha-Rol*, as if they should say, *Ah Rol* where art thou that wert wont to redresse this, or what wouldst thou doe against these wretches, if thou now wert liuing. But in truth I thinke it commeth, from *Harier.* i. *flagitare, inquietare, vrgere. Hue* is vsed alone. *anno* 4. *Ed. pri. Stat.* 2. This the Scots call *Huesium* and *M. Skene de verbo. signif. verb. Huesium*, saith, that it commeth of the french *Oyes.* i. *Audite.* making one etymologie of this and the crie vsed before a proclamation, The maner of their hue and cry, as he there describeth it, is that if a robberie be done, a horne is blowne, and an out crie made: after which, if the partie flie away, and not yeeld himselfe to the *Kings Bayliffe*, he may be lawfully slaine, and hanged vp vpon the next gallowes. Of this *Hue* and crie, see *Cromptons Iustice of peace. fol.* 160. *b.*

Huissers. See *Vshers.*

Hundred (*Hundredum*) is a part of a shire, so called originally, because it conteined ten tithings called in latine *Decennas.* These were first ordeined by *king Alfred* the 29. *king* of the *West Saxons. Stowes Annals pag.* 105. of these thus speaketh *M. Lamb. in his explica. of Saxon words. verbo, Centuria: Aluredus rex, vbi cum Guthruno Daco fœdus inierat, prudentissimum illud olim a Ietrone Moysi datum secutus consilium, Angliam primus in satrapias, Centurias, & Decurias, partitus est. Satrapiam, shire a shyran (quod partiri significat) nominavit: Centuriam,* Hundred: *& Decuriã, Toothing siue Tienmantale.* i. *Decemvirale collegium appellavit: atq; iisdem nominibus vel hodie vocantur, &c.* And againe afterward: *Decrevit tum porro Aluredus liberæ vt condicionis quisq; in Centuriam ascriberetur aliquam, atq; in Decemvirale aliquod conijceretur collegium. De minoribus negotiis Decuriones vt iudicarent: ac si quæ esset res difficilior, ad Centuriam deferrent: difficillimas deniq; & maximi momenti* *lites, Senator & præpositus in frequenti illo ex omni satrapia conventu componerent.* Modus *autem indicandi quis fuerit, Ethelredus* Rex, *legum, quas frequenti apud Vanatingum senatu sancivit, capite* 4. *his fere verbis exponit. In singulis centuriis comitia sunto, atq; liberæ conditionis viri duodeni, ætate superiores, unà cum præposito, sacra tenentes iuranto, se adeo virum aliquem innocentem haud damnaturos sontemve absoluturos.* This forme of diuiding counties into *Hun*dreds for beter gouernment, howsoeuer it is attributed to King *Alfred* here with vs: yet he had it from Germanie, whence he and his came hither. For there *centa* or *centena* is a iurisdiction ouer a hundred townes, and conteineth the punishment of capitall crimes. *Andræas Kitchin. in his tractate, de sublimi & regio territorii iure. ca.* 4.*pa.*123. where he also sheweth out of *Tacitus, de situ & moribus Germa.* that this diuiuision was vsuall amongst the Germans before his daies. By this you vnderstand the original and old vse of Hundreds, which hold still in name, and remaine in some sort of combination, for their seuerall seruices in diuers respects, but their iurisdiction is abolished, and growne to the countie court, some few excepted, which haue beene by priuiledge annexed to the crowne, or graunted vnto some great subiect, and so remaine still in the nature of a Fraunchise. And this hath beene euer sithence the *stat. anno* 14. Ed. 3. *stat.* 1. *ca.* 9. whereby these *H*undred courts formerly fermed out by the Shyreeue to other men, were reduced all, or the most part, to to the countie court, and so haue and doe remaine at this present. So that where you read now of any hundred courts, you must know, that they be seuerall fraunchises, wherein the Shyreeue hath not to deale by his ordinarie authoritie, except they of the Hundred refuse to doe their office. See *West. parte.* 1. *symbol. lib.* 2. *sect.* 288. See. *Turn.* The newe expounder of lawe termes saith, that the latine H*undredum* is sometime vsed for an immunitie or priviledge, whereby a man is quit of mony or customes due to the gouernours, or Hundreders.

H*undreders* (H*undredarii*) be men empaneled or fit to be empaneled of a Iurie vpon any controversie, dwelling within the *H*undred where the land lieth, which is in question, *Cromptons Iurisdict. fol.* 217. & *anno* 35. H*enrici* 8. *cap.* 6. It signifieth also him that hath the Iurisdiction of a hundred, and holdeth the hundred court. *anno* 13. *Ed. pri.*

*ca.*38.*anno.*9.*Ed.*2.*stat.*2.*& anno* 2.*Ed.*3.*ca.*4.and sometime is vsed for the Bayliffe of an hundred.*Hornin his mirrour of Iustices, li.*1.*ca del office del coroner.*

H*undredlaghe*, signifieth the *H*undred courte, from the which all the officers of the Kings forest were freed by the charter of *Canutus. ca.*9. *Manwood. parte.*1. *pag.*2.

H*uors*, See *Conders.*

Huseans , commeth of the French(*houseaux*)i.*ocrea*,a boote. It is vsed in the Statute *anno.* 4. *Ed.*4.*ca.*7.

Hustings (*Hustingum*) may seeme to come from the *French* (H*aulser.*i.*tollere* , *attollere*,*suberigere*) for it signifieth the principall and highest court in *London. anno* 11.H.7.*ca.*21.*& Fitzh. nat. br.fol.*23.See *anno.*9.Ed.*pri.ca. vnico.* Other Cities and townes also haue had a court of the same name, as *Winchester*, *Lincolne*,*Yorke*,and S*heppey*, and others,where the Barons or Citizens haue a record of such things as are determinable before them. F*leta. libro* 2. *cap.* 55.

Husfastene, is he that holdeth house and land,*Bracton lib.* 3.*tractat.*2.*ca.*10.*H*is words be these, *Et in franco plegio esse debet omnis, qui terram tenet & domum, qui dicuntur Husfastene,& etiam alii qui illis deseruiunt,qui dicuntur* F*olgheres,&c.*

I A

IArrock: *anno* 1 *Ri.* 3. *ca.* 8. is a kinde of cork so called.

Identitate nominis, is a writ that lyeth for him who is vpon a *Capias* or *Exigent*, taken and committed to prison for another man of the same name: whereof see the forme and farder vse, in *Fitzh. nat. br.fol.* 267. see the *Register originall,fol.* 194.

Idiot, and he that afterward becometh of insane memory, differeth in diuers cases, *Coke. fol.* 154. *b. lib.*4. *S*ee here following *Idiota inquirenda.*

Idiota inquirenda vel examinanda,is a writ that is directed to the excheatour or the *S*hyreeue of any county, where the king hath vnderstanding that there is an *Idiot*, naturally borne so weake of vnderstanding, that he connot gouern or mannage his inheritance, to call before him the party suspected of Idiocie,& examin him: And also to inquire by the oaths of twelue men, whether he be sufficiently witted to dispose of his owne lands with discretion or not, and to certifie accordingly into the Chauncery: For the king hath the protection of his subiects,& by his prerogatiue the gouernmēt of their lands and substance, that are naturally defe-

defectiue in their owne discretion: *statut. de prærogatiua Regis editum anno* 17. *Ed.* 2. *cap.* 8. wherof read *Stawnf. prærog. cap.* 9. and of this writ, read *Fitzh. nat. br. fol.* 232. see the *register orig. fol.* 267.

Ietzon se *Flotzon.*

Ieofaile, is cópoúded of 3. french words, *I' ay faille:* i. *ego lapsus sum:* & signifieth in our commō lawe, an ouer-sight in pleading, touching the which you haue a statute *anno* 32. H. 8. *cap.* 30. whereby it is enacted, that if the Iury haue once passed vpon the issue, though afterward there be found a *Ieofaile* in the pleading, yet iudgement shall likewise be giuen according to the verdict of the Iury. See *Brooke, tit. Rrepleder*: the author of the new tearms of law saith, that a *Ieofaile* is when the parties to any suite, haue in pleading proceeded so farre, that they haue ioyned issue, which shalbe tried or is tried by a Iury or inquest: and this pleading or issue is so badly pleaded or ioyned, that it will be errour if they proceed: then some of the said parties may by their councell shew it to the court, as well after verdict giuen and before iudgement, as before the Iury be charged: the shewing of which defects before the Iury charged, was often when the Iury came into the court to trie the issue, then the councell which will shew it, shall say: this inquest you ought not to take, and if it be after verdict, then he may say: to Iudgement you ought not to goe: and because of this many delayes grew in suites, diuers statutes are made to redresse them: *viz.* 32. H. 8. *c.* 30. & others in Q. *Elizabethes* daies, and yet the fault litle amended.

Ignoramus, is a word properly vsed by the grand Enquest empaneled in the inquisition of causes criminall and publique: and writen vpon the bill, whereby any crime is offered to their cósideration, when as they misslike their euidence, as defectiue or to weake to make good the presentment. The effect of which word so written is, that all farder inquiry vpon that party for that fault, is thereby stopped, and he deliuered without farder aunswer. It hath a resemblance with that custome of the auncient Romans: where the Iudges, when they absolued a person accused, did wright *A.* vpon a litle table prouided for that purpose. i. *Absoluimus*: if they iudged him guilty, they writ *C. id est. Condemnamus*: if they found the cause difficult and doubtfull, they writ. *N. L. id est. Non liquet. Asconius Pedeanus in oratio. pro Milone. Alexander ab Alexandro. Genial. dierum, li.* 3. *ca.* 14.

Ikenild streate, is one of the four famous wayes that the Romans made in England, taking the beginning *ab Icenis*, which were they that inhabited *Northf. Southf.* and *Cambridg shyre*, *Camd. Britan. fol.* 343. See *Watlingstreat*.

Imparlance (*interlocutio vel interloquela*) is a petition made In court vpon the count of the Demanndant by the tenent, or declaration of the plaintife, by the defendant, whereby he craueth respight, or an other day to put in his aunswer, See *Brooke*, *titulo Continuance*: See *Dies datus*: Imparlaunce seemeth to be generall or speciall: speciall imparlaunce is with this clause *saluis omnibus aduantagiis tam ad iurisdictionem curiæ, quàm breue & narrationem. Kitchin: fol.* 200. Then generall in reason must be that, which is made at large without inserting that or the like clause. See *Emperlaunce*

Impeachment of Waste, (*impetitio vasti*) commeth of the french (*empeschement* .i. *impedimentum*) and signifieth with vs, a restraint from committing of waste vpon lands or tenements: See *Waste*.

Implements, commeth of the french (*emploier*, i: *insumere in re aliqua*) it signifieth with vs, things tending to the necessarie vse of any trade or furniture of houshould.

Impost, is a french word signifiing *tribute*, comming of the verb (*imposer*) i: *iniungere*, *irrogare*, it signifieth with vs, the taxe receiued by the prince for such merchandise, as are brought into any heauen from other nations: *anno.* 31. *Elizabeth. cap:* 5. and I thinke it may in some sort be distinguished from customs, bicause custom is rather that profit, which the prince maketh of wares shipped out of the land: yet may they be confounded.

Improuement, *See Approue.*

In casu consimili. is a writt: *See casu consimili.*

In casu prouiso: is a writt: *See casu prouiso.*

Incident (*incidens*) signifieth a thing necessarily depending vpon another as more principall: For example, a *court Baron* is soe incident to a maner, and a court of *pieporders* to a faier, that they cannot be seuered by graunt: for if a maner or faire be graunted, these coutts cannot be reserued. *Kitchin. fol:* 36.

I*ncroche* (*incrociare*) Se *encrochments*. *Admirals*, and their deputies doe incroche to themselues Iurisdictions, &c: *anno.* 15. *Rich:* 2. *ca:* 3.

Indenture (*indentura*) is a writing comprising some contract betwene two, and being indented in the toppe aunswerably to another, that likewise con-

conteineth the same contract: this the *Latines* called σύγγραφον, or σύγγραφη, which among the ciuilians, is defined to be *scriptura inter creditorem & debitorem indentata, in cuius sciscura literis capitalibus hæc dictio συγγραφη, or plurally τα συγγραφα scribitur.* and it differeth from χειρόγραφον, *quia hoc manu vnius tantùm, puta debitoris scribitur, & penes debitorem relinquitur pruinc. constitut. de offic: archidiaco: cap: pri: verbo In scriptis. vid. Gothofr: in notis ad l.27 §. 3. ff. ad leg. Corn. de fals.*

Indicauit, is a writ or prohibition that lieth for a patron of a church, whose Clerk is defendant in court Christian, in an action of tithes commenced by another clerke, and extending to the fourth part of the church, or of the tithes belonging vnto it. for in this case, the suite belongeth to the kings court, by the statute *Westm: 2: cap: 5.* wherfore the patron of the defendant, being like to be preiudiced in his church and aduowzen, if the plaintife obteine in the court Christian, hath this means to remoue it to the kings court; the *Register originall fol. 35. b.* see *ould. nat: br. fol. 31. & the register fol: 35.* and *Britton. cap: 109. fol. 260. A.*

Indictment (Indictamentum) see *indightment.*

Indiuisum, is vsed in the common law, for that which two houlde in common without particiō. *Kitchin. fol. 241.* in these words: he houldeth *pro indiuiso, &c:*

Indorsment (indorsamentum) signifieth in the common law, a condition writen vpon the other side of an obligation: *West: part: 2. simbol: sect: 157.*

Infang, alias infeng, significat quietantiam prioris prisæ ratione conuiuij, Fleta l: 1. cap: 47.

Infangthef, or Hinfangthefe, or Infangtheof, is compounded of 3. *Saxon* words: the preposition (*In*) (*fang or fong*) to *take* or *catch*, & (*thef*) it signifieth a priuiledge or libertie graunted vnto Lords of certaine maners, to iudge any theeife taken within there fee. *Bracton. lib. 3. tracta. 2. cap. 8.* In the lawes of King *Edward*, set out by *M. Lambard: nu. 26.* you haue it thus described: *Infangthefe, Iustitia cognoscentis latronis sua est, de homine suo, si captus fuerit super terram suam: Illi verò qui non habent has consuetudines, coram iusticia regia rectum faciant in Hundredis, vel in Wapentachiis, vel in Scyris:* The definition of this fee alsso in *Britton: fol: 90. b.* and *Roger Houeden. parte poster. suorū annalium. fol. 345. b. & M. Skene de verborum significatione, verbo Infangthefe,* who writeth of it at large, reciting diuersitie of opinions touching this and *outfangthefe: Fleta* saith that (*infangtheef*) for soe he writeth it, *dicitur latro captus in terra alicuius seisitus aliquo latrocinio de suis propriis hominibus, libro* 1. *cap:* 47:§ *Infangthecfe.*

Information, See Enditement: See the new termes of lawe.

Informer(*informator*) in french (*informateur*) is an officer belonging to the exchequer or kings bench, that denounceth or complaineth of those that offend against any penall statute. They are otherwise called promotors, but the men being bashfull of nature, doe blush at this name: these among the Ciuilians are called *delatores.*

Informatus non sum, is a formall aunswer or of course made by an atturney, that is commaunded by the court to say what he thinketh good in the defence of his client, by the which he is deemed to leaue his client vndefended, and so iudgement passeth for the aduerse party. See the new booke of Entries. *titulo Non sum informatus.* and Iudgement 12.

Ingressu, is a writ of entrie, that is, whereby a man seeketh entry into lands or tenements; it lyeth in many diuers cases wherit hath as many diuersities of formes. See *Entry*: this writ is also called in the particular, *precipe quod reddat*: because those be formall words in all writs of entry. The writs as they lye in diuers cases, are these described in the *old natura breu*: *Ingressu ad terminum qui preteriit, fol.* 121. *originall* Regist. *fol.* 227. which lyeth where lands or tenements are let to a man for terme of yeares, and the tenent houldeth ouer his terme: *Ingressu dum non fuit compos mentis. fol.* 223. *original: regist: fol.* 228. which lyeth where a man selleth land or tenement when he is out of his wits, &c. *Ingressu dum fuit infra ætatem, fol.* 123. *Register originall fol.* 228. which lyeth where one vnder age selleth his lands, &c. *Ingressu super desseisina in le quibus fol.* 125. Regist. *orig. fol.* 229. which lyeth where a man is disseised and dyeth, for his heire against the disseisour. *Ingressu in per fol.* 126. *original register fol.* 229. *Ingressu sur cui in vita, fol.* 128. *originall Register fo.* 239. both which see in *Entry*: *Ingressu causa matrimonii prælocuti. fol.* 130. *original register fol.* 233: which see *causa matrimonii prælocuti. Ingressu in casu proviso, f.* 132. *Register original. fo.* 235. which see *casu pro viso. Ingressu cui ante diuortium. fol.* 130. *original register fol.* 233. for which see, *cui ante diuortium: Ingressu in consimili casu, fol.* 233. *originall Register fol.* 236. for which *see Consimili casu. Ingressu sine consensu capituli, fol.* 128. *original*

ginal register, fol. 230: for which see *Sine assensu capituli. Ingressu ad communem legem. fol.* 132. *originall register, fol.* 234. which lyeth, where the tenent for terme of life or of anothers life, tenent by curtesie, or tenent in Dower maketh a feofment in fee, & dyeth; he in the reuersion shall haue the foresaid writ against whomsoeuer that is in the land, after such feofment made.

Ingrossing of a fine, is making the indentors by the chirographer, and the deliuery of them to the party vnto whom the cognisance is made. *Fitzh. nat. br. fol.* 147. *A.*

Ingrosser (ingrossator) commeth of the frence *Grosseur:* i. *crassitudo.* or *Grosier.* i. *Solidarius venditor,* it signifieth in the common law, one that buieth corne growing, or dead victuall, to sell againe, except barly for mault, oats for oatemeale, or victuals to retaile, badging by licence, and buying of oiles, spices, and victualls, other then fish or salte. *anno.* 5. *Edward:* 6. *cap:* 14. *anno.* 5. *Elizab: cop:* 14. *anno.* 13. *Elizab. cap:* 25. these be *M. Wests.* words, *parte.* 2. *simbol: titulo Inditements: sect.* 64. howbeit this definition rather doth belong to vnlawfull ingrossing, then to the word in generall. see *Forstaller.*

Inheritance (hæreditas) is a perpetuity in lands or tenements to a man and his heirs. For *Littleton cap:* 1. *lib:* 1: hath these words: and it is to be vnderstand, that this word *(inheritance)* is not onely vnderstand where a man hath inheritance of lands and tenements by discent of heritage, but also euery fee simple or fee taile that a man hath by his purchase, may be said inheritance: for that, that his heires may inherit him: Seuerall inheritance is that, which two or moe hould seuerally, as if two men haue land giuen them to them and the heires of their two bodies, these haue ioynt estate during their liues, but their heires haue seuerall inheritance. *Kitchin fol:* 155. See the new terms of law. *verbo Enheritance:*

Inhibition (Inhibitio) is a writt to inhibit or forbid a Iudge from farder proceding in the cause depēding before him: *See Fitzh: nat: br: fol:* 39. where he putteth prohibition and inhibition together: inhibition is most commonly a writ issuing out of a higher courte Christian to a lower and inferiour, vpon an *Appeale. anno.* 24 *H.* 8. *cap:* 12. and prohibition out of the kings courte to a court Christian, or to an inferiour temporall court.

Iniunction (iniunctio) is an interlocutory decree out of the Chācerie, sometimes to giue possession vnto the plaintife, for want of apparence in the defendant, sometime to the Kings ordinary court, and somtime to the court Christian, to stay proceeding in a cause vpon suggestion made, that the regour of the law, if it take place, is against equitie and conscience in that Case. see *West: parte. 2. simb: titulo proceeding in Chauncery sect: 25.*

Inlawgh (Inlagatus) vel homo sub lege) signifieth him that is in some frank pledge, of whome take *Bractons* words, *l. 3. tracta: 2. cap.* H. *nu. 5. Minor verò, & qui infra ætatem duodecim annorũ fuerit, vtlagari non potest nec extra legem poni: quia ante talem ætatem non est sub lege aliqua, nec in decenna, non magis quam fœmina. quæ vtlagari non potest quia ipsa non est sub lege.* i. *Inlowghe anglicè: sc: in franco plegio siue decenna sicut masculus duodecim annorum & vlteriùs, &c. Inlaughe, significat hominem subiectum legi, Fleta li.* i. *cap. 47.*

Intagary (Inlagary) is a restitution of one outlawed, to the kings protection, and to the benifite or estate of a subiect. *Bracton: lib. 3 tarcta: 2 cap. 14. nu. 6.7.8. Britton cap: 13.*

Inmates, are those that be admitted to dwell for their mony iointly with another mã, though in seuerall roomes of his mantiõ house, passing in and out by one doore, and not being able to maintaine themselues. which are inquiralle in a leete. *Kitchin. fol: 45* where you may reade him at large who be properly Inmates in intendment of law, and whoe not.

Imprision, anno 18 *Ed: 3 statu: 4: cap vnico.* seemeth to signifie so much as an attempt, comming of the french *empris)* which is all one with *(enterpris)* an enterprise.

Inquirendo, is an authoritie giuen to a person or persons, to inquire into some thing for the kings aduantage, which in what cases it lieth, see the *Register originall, fol.* 72.85.124.265.266. 179.267.

Inquisition (Inquisitio) is a maner of proceeding in maters criminall, by the office of the Iudge, which *Hostiensis* defineth thus: *Inquisitio nihil aliud est quàm alicuius criminis manifesti ex bono & æquo Iudicis compentis canonicè facta inuestigatio, ca. qualiter. de accusatio.* in the *Decretales* : this course we take here in England by the great Enquest before Iustices in *Eyre*: See *Eyre.* and the places in *Bracton* and *Britton* there noted; Inquisition is also with vs, vsed for the King in temporall causes and profits, in which kinde it is confounded with office: *Stawnf. prærog. fo. 51.* See *Office.*

Inrolement (Irrotulatio) is the regi-

registring, recording or entring of any lawful act in the rowles of the chauncerie, as recognisance acknowledged, or a statute or a fine leuied. See *West. parte 2. symbol. titulo Fines. sect.* 133.

Insimul tenuit, is one species of the writ called a *Formdon*. See *Formdon*.

Intakers, be a kinde of theeues in *Ridesdall. anno. 9. H. 5. ca. 8.* so called, as it seemeth, because they dwelling within that libertie, did receiue in such booties of catell or other things as the out parters brought in vnto them. See *Out parters*.

Interdiction (*Interdictio*) is vsed in the common lawe, in the same signification that it hath in the canon lawe, where it is thus defined: *interdictio est censura ecclesiastica prohibens administrationem diuinorum: c. quod in te: de pœnitent: & remiss.* in the Decretals: and thus is it vsed. *anno. 24. H. 8. cap. 12.*

Interpleder, See *Enterpleder*.

Intrusion (*Intrusio*) by *Bracton lib. 4. cap. 2.* is thus defined: *Intrusio est, vbi quis (cui nullum ius competit in re nec scintilla Iuris, possessionem vacuam ingreditur, quæ nec corpore nec animo possidetur, sicut hæreditatem iacentem antequam adita fuerit ab hærede, vel saltem a domino capitali ratione custodiæ, vel ratione eschaetæ si forte hæredes non existant, vel si post mortem alicuius per finem factum, vel per modum donationis, vbi successio sibi locum vendicare non possit, vel si post mortem alicuius qui tenuit ad vitam debeat tenementum reverti ad proprietariũ, ponat quis se in seisinã antequã tenemẽtũ illud veniat ad illũ ad quem pertinere deberet ex prædictis causis*, with whome agreeth *Fleta lib. 4. cap. 30. §. 1. & 2.* See *Britton cap. 65.* to the same effect. See the newe booke of Entries. *verbo Entrusion*. See *Entrusion*. See *disseisin*: the author of new Terms of lawe would haue intrusion especially after the tenent for life is deceased. *verbo, Abatement.* and abatement in all other cases: But I finde not any latine word for abatement but *intrusio*, so that I rather thinke these 2. english words to bee *synonyma*: and *Fleta cap. suprà citato*, seemeth direct against this his opinion.

Intrusione, is a writ that lyeth against the intruder: *Register: fol.* 233.

Inuentarie (*inuentarium*) is a description or repertory orderly made of all dead mens goods and catels prized by foure credible men or more, which euery executor or administrator ought to exhibite to the Ordinary, at such times as he shall appoint the same. *West. parte prim: Simb: lib: 2. sect: 696.* where likewise you may see the forme: This Inuentary proceedeth from the ciuill law; for whereas by the auncient law of the Romans, the heire was tyed to aunswer all the testators debts, by which meanes heretages were preiudiciall to many men and not profitable: *Iustinian* to encorage men the better to take vppon them this charitable office, ordained, that if the heire would first make and exhibite a trew Inuentary of all the testatours substance comming to his hand, he should be no furder charged, then to the valew of the Inuentarie: *l. vlt. Cod. de Iure deliberando.*

Inuest (Inuestire) commeth of the french word (*Inuester*) and signifieth to giue possession. Here *Hotoman de verbis feudalibus, verbo Inuestitura: Inuestitura barbarum nomen, barbaricam quoq; rationem habet. Nam vt ait* Feudista, *lib. 2. titulo. 2. Inuestitura proprie dicitur quando hasta vel aliquod corporeum traditur à domino;* with vs we vse likewise to admit the tenents by deliuering them a verge or rodd into their hands, and ministring them an oath, which is called Inuesting: others define it thus: *Inuestitura, est alicuius in suum ius introductio.*

Inure, signifieth to take effect: as the pardon inureth: *Stawnf: prærog: fol.* 40. *See Enure.*

Ioynder, is the coupling of two in a suite or action against another: *Fitzh. nat. br fol.* 118. H. 201. H. 221. & *H.* in many other places, as appeareth in the *Index. verbo Ioynder.*

Ioynt tenents (simul tenentes) liber intrationum, titulo Formdon in vieu. 3. be those that come to and hould lands or tenements by one title *pro indiuiso*, or without partition. *Litleton lib.* 3. *cap.* 3. and termes of law: See *Tenents in common.*

Ioyning of issue (Iunctio exitus) See *Issue.*

Iointure (Iunctura) is a couenant, whereby the husband or some other freind in his behalfe assureth vnto his wife, in respect of mariage, lands or tenements for terme of her life, or otherwise, See *West: part: 2. Symbol. lib. 2. titulo Couenants. sect.* 128. and the new expositiō of the law terms: it seemeth to be called a Ioynture, either because it is granted *ratione iuncturæ in matrimonio*, or because the land in franke mariage, is giuen ioyntly to the husband and the wife, and after to the heirs of their bodies, whereby the husband and wife be made ioynt tenents during the couerture. *Coke li.* 3. *Butler & Bakers case. f.* 27. *b.* See *franckmariage. Ioynture,* is also vsed as the abstract of ioynt tenents. *Coke lib.* 3. the Marques of *Winchesters* case. *fol.* 3. *a. b. Iunctura,* is also by

Bra-

Bracton and *Fleta* vsed for ioyning of one bargaine to another. *Fleta lib.* 2. *ca.* 60. touching the selfe same thing: and therefore ioynture in the first signification, may be so called, in respect that it is a bargaine of liuelyhood for the wife: adioyned to the contract of mariage.

Iourn Choppers, anno 8. *Hen.* 6. *cap.* 5. be regraters of yarn. Whether that we now call (yarne) were in those daies called (iourn) I cannot say: but (choppers) in these daies are well knowne to be chaungers: as choppers of churches, &c.

Iourneyman, commeth of the French (*Iournee*) that is a day or dayes worke. which argueth that they were called Iourneymen, that wrought with others by the day, though now by statute it be extended to those likewise, that couenant to worke in their occupation with another by the yeare. *anno quinto Elizabeth. cap. quarto.*

Issue (*Exitus*) commeth of the French (*Issir*: i. *emanare*) or the substantiue (*Issue*: i. *exitus, euentus*) It hat diuers applications in the common lawe: sometime being vsed for the children begotten betweene a man and his wife: sometime for profits growing from an amercement or fine, or expenses of suite: sometime for profits of lands or tenements: *West*: 2. *anno.* 13. *Edw. prim. cap.* 39. sometime for that point of mater depending in suite, wherupon the parties ioyne and put their cause to the triall of the Iury: and in all these it hath but one signification, which is an effect of a cause proceeding. as the children be the effect of the mariage betweene the parents: the profits growing to the king or Lord from the punishment of any mans offence, is the effect of his transgression: the point referred to the triall of twelue men is the effect of pleading or processe. *Issue*, in this last signification, is either generall or speciall: Generall issue seemeth to be that, whereby it is referred to the Iury to bring in their verdict, whether the defendant haue done any such thing, as the plaintife layeth to his charge. For example: if it be an offence against any statute, and the defendant pleade: *not culpable*: this being put to the Iury, is called the generall issue: and if a man complaine of a priuate wrong which the defendant denieth, and plead no wrong nor disseisin, and this be referred to the 12. it is likewise the generall issue. *Kitchin. fol.* 225. See the *Doctor* and *Student. fol.* 158 *b.* the speciall issue then must be that, where speciall mater being alleadged by the defendant for his defence, both the

the parties ioyne therevpon, and so grow rather to a demurrer, if it be *quæstio Iuris*, or to tryall by the Iurie, if it be *quæstio facti*, see the new booke of Entries: *verbo, Issue*.

Iuncture see *Iointure*.

Iure patronatus, See the newe booke of Entries, *verbo Iure patronatus in quare impedit. fol.* 465. *col.* 3.

Iurie (*Iurata*) commeth of the french (*Iurer: i iurare.*) it signifieth in our common lawe, a companie of men as 24. or 12. Sworne to deliuer a truth vpon such euidẽce, as shalbe deliuered them touching the matter in question. Of which triall who may and who may not be empaneled, see *Fitzh. nat. br. fol.* 165. *D*. And for beter vnderstanding of this point, it is to be knowne, that there be. 3. maner of trials in England: one by Parliament, another by battle, and the third by Assise or Iurie: *Smith de repub. Anglorum. lib:* 2. *cap:* 5. 6. 7. touching the 2. former reade him, and see Battell, and Combat, and Parlament: the triall by Assise (be the action ciuile or criminall, publick or priuate, personall or reall) is referred for the fact to a Iurie, and as they finde it, so passeth the Iudgement. and the great fauour that by this the King sheweth to his subiects more then the princes of other nations, you may reade in *Glanuil. lib:* 2: *cap:* 7. where he called it *Regale beneficium clementis principis de consilio procerum populis indultum, quo vitæ hominũ, & status integritati tam salubriter consulitur; vt in iure, quod quis in libero soli tenemento possidet, retinendo, duelli casum declinare possint homines ambiguum, &c*: see the rest. This Iury is not vsed onely in circuits of Iustices errant, but also in other courts and maters of office, as if the *Escheatour* make inquisition in any thing touching his office, he doth it by a Iury or inquest: if the *Coroner* inquire how a subiect found dead, came to his end: he vseth an inquest. the Iustices of peace in ther quarter Sessions, the Shyreeue in his county and Turne, the baylife of a Hundred, the *Stewarde* of a court Leete or court Baron, if they inquire of any offence, or descide any cause betweene party and party, they doe it by the same maner. *So* that where it is said that all things be triable by Parlament, *Battell*, or assise; Assise in this place is taken for a Iury or Enquest, empaneled vpõ any cause in a court, where this kind of triall is vsed: and though it be commonly deemed, that this custome of ending and desciding causes proceede from the *Saxons* and *Brittons*, and was of fauour permitted vnto vs by the Conquerour: yet I finde by the grand *Customarie* of *Normandie. cap*:24.that this course was vsed likewise in that countrie . For Assise is,in that Chapter, defined to be an assembley of wise men, with the Bailife in a place certaine at a time assigned 40.daies before. wherby Iustice may be done in causes heard in the court:of this custome also and those Knights of *Normandie* *Iohannes Faber* maketh mention, in the *Rubrique* of the *title de militari testamento* in *Institut*. this Iury, though it appertaine to most courts of the common law,yet is it most notorious in the half yeare courts of the Iustices errants, commonlie called the great assises,and in the quarter Sessions, and in them it is most ordinarily called a Iurie. And that in ciuile causes: wheras in other courts, it is oftener tearmed an enquest, and in the court *B*aron the Homage.In the generall Assise there are vsually many Iurise, bicause there be store of causes both ciuil and criminall commonly to be tried, wherof one is called the Grand Iury and the rest petit Iuries:whereof it seemeth there should be one for euery *Hundred*, *Lamb*.*Eirenar*:*l*.4.*cap*.3.*pa*. 384.The Grand Iurie consisteth ordinarily of 24. graue and substantiall gentlemen, or some of them yeomen chosen indifferently out of the whole shyre by the *Shyreeue*, to consider of all bils of Inditement preferred to the court:which they doe either approoue by writing vpon them these words: *billa vera*: or disallowe by writing: *Ignoramus*: such as they doe approoue, if they touch life and death, are farder referred to another Iury to be considered of, because the case is of such importance. but others of lighter moment are vpon their allowance, without more worke fined by the bench, except the party travers the Inditement, or chalenge it for insufficiencie, or remooue the cause to a higher court by certiorarie, in which 2. former cases it is referred to another Iurie, and in the latter transmitted to the higher. *Lamb*.*Eire*.*l*.4.*c*.7. & presently vpon the allowance of this bill by the Grand Enquest, a man is said to be indighted.Such as they disallowe, are deliuered to the benche,by whome they are forthwith cancilled or torne.The petit Iury consisteth of.12.men at the least,& are Empanelled, as well vpon criminall as vpon ciuile causes. those that passe vpon offences of life and death,doe bring in their verdict either *guiltie* or not *guiltie*, wherevpon the prisoner, if he be be found guiltie, is said to be conuicted, and so afterward receaueth his iudgment and condemnation: or otherwise is acquited and sett Free: of this reade *Fortes: cap:* 27. those that passe vpon ciuile causes reall, are all, or so many as can conueniently be had, of the same hundred, where the land or tenement in question doth lie, and 4. at the least: And they vpon due examination bring in their verdict either for the demaundant, or Tenent. of this see *Fortesc. cap.* 25. 26. according vnto which, iudgement passeth afterward in the court where the cause first began: and the reason hereof is, because these Iustices of Assise, are in this case, for the ease of the cuntry, onely to take the verdict of the Iurie, by the vertue of the writ called (*nisi prius*) and so returne it to the court where the cause is depending See (*Nisi prius.*) Ioyne with this the chapter formerly cited out of the custumary of *Normandie*, and that of King *Etheldreds* lawes mentioned by *Maister Lamberd*, *verbo Centuria*. in his explication of Saxon words; and by these two words you shall perceiue, that as well among these *Normans*, as the *Saxons*, the men of this Iury were associats and Assistants to the Iudges of the court, in a kind of equality; whereas now a daies they attend them in great humility, and are, as it were, at their commaund for the seruice of the court: the words set downe by *M. Lamberd* are these: *In singulis centuriis comitia sunto, atq; liberæ condicionis viri duodeni ætate superiores, unà cum præposito sacra tenentes, iuranto, se adeo virum aliquem innocentem haud condemnaturos, sontemve absoluturos*: to this ioyne also the 69. chapter of the saide custumarie. See *Enquest*. See 12. *men*. See *Lamberds Eirenarch. lib.* 4. *cap.* 3. *p.* 384.

Iuris vtrùm, is a writ, that lyeth for the incumbent, whose predecessour hath alienated his lands or tenements. the diuers vses of which writ, see in *Fitzh. nat. br fol.* 48.

Iurisdiction (*Iurisdictio*) is a dignity which a man hath by a power to doe Iustice in causes of complaint made before him. And there be two kinds of Iurisdictions, the one that a man hath by reason of his fee, and by vertue thereof doth right in all plaints concerning his fee: The other is a Iurisdiction giuen by the prince to a baylife: this diuision I haue in the Custumary of *Normandy*, *cap.* 2. which is not vnapt for the practise of our common welth, for by him whom they call a baylife, we may vnderstand all that haue commiſſion from the prince to giue iudgement in any cauſe: The ciuilians diuide *iuriſdictionem* generally vnderſtand in *imperium & iuriſdictionem*: and *imperium in merum & mixtum*. Of which you may reade many eſpeciall tractats writen of them, as a mater of great difficulty and importance.

Iuſtes, commeth of the French (*Iouſtes* .i. *decurſus*) and ſignifieth with vs, contentions betweene Martiall men by ſpeares on horſbacke. *anno* 24. *H.* 8. *cap.* 13.

Iuſtice (*Iuſticiarius*) is a French word, and ſignifieth him, that is deputed by the king, to do right by way of iudgement. the reaſon why he is called Iuſtice and not *Iudex*, is becauſe in auncient time the latine word for him was (*Iuſticia*) and not (*Iuſticiarius*) as appeareth by *Glan. lib.* 2. *cap.* 6. Roger *Houeden parte poſter. ſuorum annalium, fo.* 413. *a.* and diuers other places, which appellation we haue from the *Normans*, as appeareth by the grand cuſtumary. *cap.* 3. and I doe the rather note it, becauſe men of this function ſhould hereby conſider, that they are or ought to be, not (*Iuſti*) in their iudgements, but in abſtract (*ipſa iuſticia*) how be it I hould it well, if they performe their office in *concreto*. Another reaſon why they are called *Iuſticiary* with vs and not *Iudices*, is, bicauſe they haue their authority by deputation, as Delegates to the king, and not *iure magiſtratus*; and therefore cannot depute others in their ſteed, the Iuſtice of the *Foreſt* onely excepted, who hath that liberty, eſpecially giuen him by the ſtatute *anno.* 32. *H.* 8. *cap.* 35. for the Chanceller, Marſhall, Admirall, and ſuch like are not called *Iuſticiarii* but *Iudices*: of theſe Iuſtices you haue diuers ſorts in England, as you may perceaue heare following. The maner of creating theſe Iuſtices, with other appertenences reede in *Forteſcu. cap.* 51.

Iuſtice of the Kings bench (*Iuſticiarius de Banco regis*) is a Lord by his office, and the cheife of the reſt. wherefore he is alſo called *Capitalis Iuſticiarius Angliæ*, his office eſpecially is to heare and determine all plees of the crowne: that is, ſuch as concerne offences committed againſt the crowne, dignitie, and peace of the *King*; as treaſons, felonies, mayhems and ſuch like, which you may ſee in *Bracton, lib.* 3. *tractat.* 2. *per totum*: and in *Stawnf. treatiſe intituled the plees of the crowne*, from the firſt chapter to the 51. of the firſt Booke. But either it was from the beginning, or by time it is come to paſſe, that he with his aſſiſtans, heareth all perſonall actions, and reall alſo, if they bee incident to any perſonall action depending before them: See *Cromptons Iuridict. fol. 67.&c.* of this court *Bracton lib. 3. cap. 7. nu. 2.* ſaith thus: *placita verò ciuilia in rem & perſonam in Curia Domini Regis terminanda, coram diuerſis iuſticiariis terminantur: Habet enim plures curias in quibus diverſæ actiones terminantur; & illarum curiarum habet vnam propriam, ſicut aulam regiam, & iuſticiarios capitales qui proprias cauſas Regis terminant, & aliorum omnium per querelam vel per priuilegium ſiue libertatam; vt ſi ſit aliquis qui implacitari non debeat, niſi coram Domino rege.* This Iuſtice (as it ſeemeth) hath no patent vnder the broad ſeale. For ſo *Crompton* ſaith *vbi ſupra.* He is made onely by writ, which is a ſhort one to this effect. *Regina Iohanni Popham militi ſalutē. Sciatis quod conſtituimus vos Iuſticiarium noſtrum capitalem, ad placita coram nobis terminandum, durante beneplacito noſtro, Teſte, &c.* And *Bracton* in the place nowe recited, ſpeaking of the common plees, ſaith, that *ſine warranto iuriſdictionem non habet*, which (I thinke) is to be vnderſtood of a commiſſion vnder the great *Seale.* This court was firſt called the kings bench, becauſe the King ſate as Iudge in it in his proper *Perſon*, and it was moueable with the court. See *anno* 9. *H.* 3. *cap.* 11. more of the Iuriſdiction of this court ſee in *Crompton vbi ſupra*. See *Kings bench*. The oath of the Iuſtices ſee in the ſtatute. *anno* 18. *Ed.* 3. *ſtat.* 4. See *Oathe.*

Iuſtice of common plees (*Iuſticiarius communium placitorum*) is alſo a Lord by his office, and is called (*Dominus Iuſticiarius communium placitorum*) and he with his aſſiſtants originally did heare and determine all cauſes at the common lawe, that is, all ciuil cauſes betweene common perſons, as well perſonall as reall, for which cauſe it was called the court of common plees, in oppoſition to the plees of the Crowne or the Kings plees, which are ſpeciall and appertaining to him onely. Of this, and the Iuridiſdiction hereof, ſee *Cromptons Iuriſdiction. fo.* 91. This Court was alwaies ſetled in a place, as appeareth by the ſtatute *anno* 9. H. 3. *cap.* 11. The oath of this Iuſtice and his aſſociats, ſee *anno* 18. *Ed.* 3. *ſtat.* 4. See *Oath.*

Iuſtice of the Foreſt (*Iuſticiarius Foreſtæ*) is alſo a Lord by his office, and hath the hearing and determining of all offences, within the *Kings* foreſt, committed againſt *Veniſon* or *Vert*, of theſe there bee two, whereof the one hath Iuriſdiction ouer al the foreſts, on this ſide *Trent*: the

the other of all beyond. The cheifest point of their Iurisdiction, consisteth vpon the articles of the *Kings Charter*, called *Charta de Foresta*, made *anno* 9. *H*. 3. which was by the *Barons* hardly drawne from him, to the mitigation of ouer cruell ordinances made by his predecessors. *Reade M. Camdens Britan. pag.* 214. See *Protoforestarius*. The Court where this Iustice sitteth and determineth, is called the Iustice seate of the Forest, held euery three yeares once, whereof you may reade your fill in *M. Manwoodes* first part of Forest lawes. *pag.* 121. & 154. & *pag.* 76. *He* is sometimes called Iustice in Eyre of the forest. See the reason in *Iustice in Eyre*. This is the only Iustice that may appoint a deputy *per statutum anno* 32. *H*. 8. *cap*. 35.

Iustices of Assise (*Iusticiarii ad capiendas Assisas*) are such as were wont by speciall commission to be sent (as occasion was offered) into this or that county to take Assises; the ground of which polity, was the ease of the subiects: For whereas these actions passe alway by Iury, so many men might not without great hinderance be brought to London, and therefore Iustices for this purpose were by commission particularly authorised, and sent downe to them. And it may seeme that the Iustices of the common plees had no power to deale in this kinde of busines, vntill the statute made *anno* 8. *Rich*. 2. *cap*. 2. for by that they are enhabled to take Assises, and to deliuer *Gaols*. And the Iustices of the kings Bench haue by that statute such power affirmed vnto them, as they had one hundred yeares before that: Time hath taught by experience, that the beter sort of Lawyers being fittest both to iudge and plead, may hardly be spared in terme time to ride into the country about such busines: and therefore of later yeares it is come to passe, that these commissions (*ad capiedas Assisas*) are driuen to these two times in the yeare out of terme, when the Iustices and other may be at leasure for these controuersies also: whereupon it is also fallen out, that the maters wont to be heard by more generall Commissions of Iustices in Eyre, are heard all at one time with these Assises: which was not so of ould, as appeareth by *Bracton*, *lib*. 3. *c*. 7. *nu*. 2. *Habet etiam Iusticiarios itinerātes de comitatu in Comitatum, quandoq; ad omnia placita, quandoq; ad quædam specialia, sicut Assisas &c. & ad Gaolas deliberandas, quandoq; ad vnicam vel duas, & non plures*. And by this meanes the *Iustices* of both benches, being iustly to be accounted the fitteſt of all others, and others their aſſiſtants, as alſo the *Sergeants* at law may be imployed in theſe affaires, who as graueſt in yeares, ſo are they ripeſt in iudgement, and therefore likeſt to be voide of procialitie, for being called to this dignity, they giue ouer practiſe *anno* 8. *R*. 2. *cap*. 3. but this alway to be remembred, that neither Iuſtice of either bench, nor any other, may be Iuſtice of Aſſiſe in his owne country, *anno* 8. *Rich.* 2. *cap.* 2. & *anno* 33. *H*. 8. *cap*. 24. laſtly, note that in theſe daies, though the ſelfe ſame men diſpatch buſines of ſo diuers natures, and all at one time, which were wont to be performed by diuers, and at ſeuerall times, yet they doe it by ſeuerall commiſſions. *Cromptons Iuriſdictions. fo.* 210. For thoſe who be in one word called Iuſtices of circuit, and twice euery yeare paſſe, by two and two, through all Englād, haue one cōmiſſion to take Aſſiſes, another to deliuer *Goales,* another of *oyer* and *terminer.* That Iuſtices of Aſſiſe, and Iuſtices in Eyre did auncienty differ, it appeareth *an.* 27. *Ed.* 3. *cap.* 5. and that Iuſtices of Aſſiſe, & Iuſtices of *goale* deliuery were diuerſe, it is euident by *anno* 4. *Ed.* 3. *cap.* 3. The oath taken by Iuſtices of aſſiſe, is all one with the oath taken by the Iuſtices of the kings bench. *Ould abridgement of ſtatutes. titulo Sacramentum Iuſticiariorum.* See *Oath.*

Iuſtices of oyer and terminer, (*Iuſticiarii ad audiendum & terminandum*) were Iuſtices deputed vpon ſome eſpeciall or extraordinary occaſion, to heare and determine ſome or more cauſes. *Fitzherberd* in his *natura breuium* ſaith, that the commiſſion *d' oyer* and *terminer,* is directed to certaine perſons vpon any great aſſembly, inſurrection, hainous demeanure, or treſpaſſe committed. And becauſe the occaſion of granting this commiſſion ſhould be maturely wayed, it is prouided by the ſtatute *anno* 2. *Ed.* 3. *cap.* 2. that no ſuch commiſſion ought to be graunted, but that they ſhalbe diſpatched before the Iuſtices of the one bench or other, or Iuſtices errāts, except for horrible treſpaſſes, & that by the eſpecial fauour of the *King*. The forme of this cōmiſſion, ſee in *Fitzh. natura breu. fol.* 110.

Iuſtices in Eyre (*Iuſticiarii itinerantes*) are ſo termed of the French (*Erre.* i. *iter*) which is an old word, as (*a grand erre.* i. *magnis iteneribus*) prouerbially ſpoken. the vſe of theſe in auncient time, was to ſend them with commiſſion into diuers counties, to heare ſuch cauſes eſpecially, as were termed the plees of the crowne, and therefore I must imagine they were so sent abroad for the ease of the subiects, who must els haue beene hurried to the kings bench, if the cause were too high for the countie court. They differed from the Iustices of *oyer* and *terminer*, because they (as is aboue said) were sent vpon some one, or fewe speciall cases and to one place: whereas the *Iustices in Eyre*, were sent through the prouinces and counties of the land, with more Indefinite and generall commission, as appeareth by *Bracton, lib.* 3.*cap.* 11. 12. 13. and *Britton cap.* 2. And againe they seeme to differ in this, because the Iustices of *oyer* and *terminer* (as it is before said) were sent vncertainly, vpon any vproare or other occasion in the country: but these in *Eyre* (as *M. Gwin* setteth downe in the preface to his reading, were sent but euery seuen yeare once; with whome *Horn in his myrrour of Iustices*, seemeth to agree. *lib.* 2. *cap. queux poient estre acteurs, &c.* and *lib.* 2.*c. des peches criminels &c. al suyte de Roy, &c.* and *lib.* 3.*c. de Iustices in Eyre*. where he also declareth what belonged to their office. These were instituted by *Henry* the 2. as *M. Camden* in his *Britannia* witnesseth *pag.* 104. And Roger *Hoveden, parte posteri. annalium. fo.* 313. *b.* hath of them these wordes: *Iusticiary itinerantes constituti per Henricum secundum.* i. *qui diuisit regnum suum in sex partes, per quarum singulas tres Iusticiarios itinerantes constituit, quorum nomina hac sunt, &c.*

Iustices of Gaol deliuery (*Iusticiarii ad Gaolas deliberandas*) are such as are sent with commission, to heare and determine all causes apperteining to such, as for any offence are cast into the *Gaol*, part of whose authoritie is, to punish such, as let to mainprise those prisoners, that by lawe be not bayleable by the statute *de finibus, cap.* 3. *Fitzh. nat. br. f.* 251. These by likelyhoode in auncient time, were sent to countries vpon this seuerall occasion. But afterward Iustices of *Assise* were likewise authorised to this, *anno.* 4. *Ed.* 3. *cap.* 3. Their oath is all one with other of the kings Iustices of either bench. *Ould Abridgement of statutes. titulo Sacramentum Iusticiariorum.* See *Othe*.

Iustices of labourers, were Iustices appointed in those times, to redresse the frowardnesse of labouring men, that would either be idle, or haue vnreasonable wages. See *anno* 21. *Edwardi* 3. *cap. primo. anno* 25. *eiusd. cap.* 8. *& anno* 31. *eiusdem cap.* 6.

Iustices of *Nisi prius*, are all one now a daies with Iustices of Assises: for it is a common *Ad*iournment of a cause, in the common plees to put it off to such a day, *Nisi prius Iusticiarii venerint ad eas partes, ad capiendas Assisas*: and vpon this clause of *A*diournment, they are called Iustices of *Nisi prius*, as well as Iustices of *A*ssises; by reason of the writ or action that they haue to deale in: their commission you may see in *Cromptons Iurisdictions fol.* 204. yet *M. Crompton* maketh this difference betweene them, because Iustices of Assise haue power to giue iudgement in a cause, but Iustices of *Nisi prius*. only to take the verdict. But in the nature of both there functions this seemeth to be the greatest difference, because Iustices of *Nisi prius* haue to deale in causes personall as well as reall, wheras Iustices of *A*ssise, in strict acception, deale only with the possessory writs called *Assises*.

Iustices of trial bastō, alias of trayl baston, were a kind of Iustices appointed by King *Edward* the first vpon occasion of great disorder growne in the Realme, during his absence in the *Scottishe* and *French* warres, they are called in the ould *nat. bre. f.* 52. Iustices of triall *Baston*, but by *Holynshed* and *Stow* in *Edw. pri.* of Traile baston, of trailing or drawing the staffe as *Holinshed* saith. Their office was to make inquisition through the Realme by the verdict of substantiall Iuries vpon all officers, as *Mayors Shyreeues, B*ailifes, escheatours & others, touching extortion, briberies and other such greeuances, as intrusions into other mens lands, and Barratours that vsed to take mony for beating of men, and also of them whom they did beate; by meanes of which inquisitions many were punished by death, many by ransome, aud so the rest flying the *R*ealme, the land was quieted, & the king gained greate riches toward the supporting of his wars. Inquire farder of the name. *Baston* is thougt by some to be the beame of a paire of Scoales or waights. and this is in this place metaphorically applied to the iuste peising of recompence for offences committed. *My* poore opiniō is, that the etymology of this title or addition groweth from the French *(treilles)* i. *cancelli*, barres or letises of what thing soeuer, a grate with crosse bars, or of the singuler *(treille)* i. *pargula*, an house arbour, a raile or forme, such as vines runne vpon, and *(Baston)* a staffe or pole, noting thereby that the Iustices emploied in this commission, had authothoritie to proceede without any solemne iudgement seate in any place either compassed in with railes, or made booth or tent-wise, set vp with staues or poales without more worke, wheresoeuer they could apprehend the malefactors they sought for. See, *lib. Assisarum. fol.* 141.57.

Iustices of peace (*Iusticiarii ad pacem*) are they that are appointed by the kinges commission, with others, to attend the peace in the County where they dwell: of whom some vpon speciall respect are made of the *Quorum*, because some busines of importance may not be dealt in without the presence or assent of them, or one of them. Of these it is but folly to write more, because they haue so many thinges perteining to their office, as cannot in fewe words be comprehended. And againe Iustice *Fitzherberd* some time sithence, as also *M. Lamberd* and *M. Crompton* of late haue written bookes of it to their great commendatiō, and fruitfull benefit of the whole *Realme*. See also *Sir Thomas Smith de repub: Angl: lib:* 2. *cap.* 19. They were called *Gardians* of the peace, vntill the 36. yeare of King *Edward* the third, *cap.* 12. where they be called Iustices. *Lamb.* *Eirenarcha. lib.* 4. *cap.* 19 *pag.* 578. There oathe see also in *Lambard. lib.* 1. *ca.* 10.

Iustices of peace, &c. within liberties, Iusticiarii ad pacem infra libertates, be such in cities and other corporate townes, as those others be of any countie: and their authoritie or power is all one within their seueral precincts *anno.* 27. H. 8. *ca.* 25.

Iusticies, is a writ directed to the Shyreeue, for the dispatch of iustice in some especiall cause, wherewith of his owne authoritie he cannot deale in his Countie Courte. *lib.* 12. *cap.* 18. wherevpon the writ *de excommunicato deliberando*, is called a Iusticies in the old *nat. bre. fol.* 35. Also the writ *de homine replegiando. eodem: fol.* 41. Thirdly the writ *de secunda superoneratione pasturæ. eodem: fol.* 73. *Kitchin fol.* 74. saith, that by this writ called *Iusticies*, the Shyreeue may hold plee of a greate summe, whereas of his ordinary authoritie he cannot hold plees but of summes vnder 40. shillings. *Crompton fo.* 231. agreeth with him. It is called a *Iusticies*, because it is a commission to the Shyreeue *ad Iusticiandum aliquem*, to doe a man right, and requireth noe returne of any certificat of what he hath done. *Bracton. lib.* 4. *tracta.* 6. *cap.* 13. *nu.* 2. maketh mention of a *Iusticies* to the *Shyreeue* of *London*, in a case

case of *Dower*. See the newe booke of *Entries, Iustices*.

Iustification(Iustificatio) is an vpholding or shewing a good reason in courte, why he did such a thing as he is called to answere: as to iustifie in a cause of Repleuin. *Broke. titulo Repleuin*.

K E

KEeper of the great *Seale(Custos Magni Sigilli)* is a L. by his office and called Lord Keeper of the great Seale of England, &c. & is of the Kings priuy Councell, vnder whose hands passe al charters, Commissions, and graunts of the King strengthened by the great or broad Seale. Without the which Seale, all such Instruments, by Lawe are of no force. for the King is in interpretation and intendment of Law, a Corporation, and therefore passeth nothing firmely, but vnder the said Seale. This Lord Keeper by the statute *anno* 5. *Elizabethæ Cap.* 18. hath the same and the like place, authority, preeminence, Iurisdiction, execution of Lawes, and all other Customes, Cōmodities, and Aduantages, as hath the Lord Chaunceler of England for the time being.

Keeper of the priuy Seale (Custos priuati Sigilli) is a Lord by his office, vnder whose hands passe all Charters signed by the Prince, before they come to the broad or great Seale of England. *He* is also of the Kings priuy Councell. *He* seemeth to be called Clerke of the priuy Seale. *anno* 12. *R* 2. *Cap.* 11. But of late daies, I haue knowne none to beare this office, by reason the Prince thinketh good, rather to keepe this Seale in his owne hands, and by priuate trust to commit it to his principall Secretary, or some such one of his Councell, as he thinketh fit for that function.

Keeper of the Touch. anno 2. *H.* 6. *cap.* 14. seemeth to be that officer in the kings mint, which at this day is termed the master of the assay. See *Mint*.

Keeper of the Forest (Custos Forestæ) is also called cheife Warden of the Forest. *Manwood part. pri.* of his Forest Lawes, *pag.* 156. *&c.* & hath the principall gouernmēt of all things belonging thereunto: as also the check of all officers belonging to the Forest. And the *Lord Cheife Iustice in Eyre* of the Forest, when it pleaseth him to keepe his Iustice Seate, doth 40. daies before, send out his generall Summons to him, for the warning of all vnder-officers, to appeare before him at a day assigned in the Summons. This See in *Manwood Vbi Supra*.

King (Rex) is thought by *M. Cam-*

Camden in his *Britan. pag.* 105. to be contracted of the Saxon word *Cyninge*, signifiing him that hath the highest power & absolute rule ouer our whole Land. and thereupon the King is in intendment of Lawe cleared of those defects, that common persons be subiect vnto. For he is alwaies supposed to be of full age, though he be in yeares neuer so young. *Cromptons Iurisdictions. fol.* 134. *Kitchin. fol.* i. He is taken as not subiect to death, but is a Corporation in himselfe that liueth euer. *Crompton ibidem.* Thirdly, he is aboue the Law by his absolute power. *Bracton lib. pri cap.* 8. *Kitchin fol.* 1. and though for the beter and equall course in making Lawes he doe admitte the 3. estates, that is, Lords Spirituall, Lords temporall, and the Commons vnto Councell: yet this, in diuers learned mens opinions, is not of constreinte, but of his owne benignitie, or by reason of his promise made vpon oath, at the time of his coronation. For otherwise were he a subiect after a sort and subordinate, which may not bee thought without breach of duty and loyaltie. For then must we deny him to be aboue the lawe, and to haue no power of dispensing with any positiue lawe, or of graunting especiall priuiledges and charters vnto any, which is his onely and cleare right, as *Sir Thomas Smith* well expresseth *lib. 2. cap. 3. de Repub. Anglican.* and *Bracton. lib. 2. cap.* 16. *num.* 3. and *Britton, cap.* 39. For hee pardoneth life and limme to offendours against his crowne and dignitie, except such as he bindeth himself by oath not to forgiue. *Stawnf. pl. cor. lib. 2. cap.* 35. And *Habet omnia iura in manu sua. Bracton. lib. 2. cap.* 24. *num. prim.* And though at his coronation he take an oath not to alter the lawes of the land: Yet this oath notwithstanding, hee may alter or suspend any particular lawe that seemeth hurtfull to the publike estate. *Blackwood in Apologia Regum, c.* 11. See *Oath of the king.* Thus much in short, because I haue heard some to be of opiniō, that the lawes be aboue the king. But the kings oath of old you may see in *Bracton, lib.* 3. *cap. 9. nu.* 2. for the which looke in *Oath of the King.* The kings oath in English, you may see in the old abridgement of Statutes, *titulo, Sacram. Regis.* Fourthly, the kings only testimonie of any thing done in his presence, is of as high nature and credit as any Record. Whence it cōmeth, that in all writs or precepts sent out for the dispatch of Iustice, he vseth none other witnesse but himselfe, alwaies vsing these words vnder it, *Teste me ipso.*

Lastly, he hath in the right of his crowne many prerogatiues aboue any common person, be he neuer so potent or honourable: whereof you may reade your fill in *Stawnf.* tractate vpon the *Statute* thereof made, *anno* 17. *Ed.* 2. though that con-taine not all by a great number. What the kings power is, reade in *Bracton.lib.* 2. *cap.* 24. *nu.prim.* & 2.

King of Heradls (*Rex Heraldorũ* is an officer at *Armes*, that hath the preeminence of this Society. *See* Herald. This officer of the *Romans* was called *Pater Patratus.*

Kings Bench (*Bancus Regius*) is the Court or Iudgment seate where the Kinge of England was wont to sitte in his owne person: and therefore was it moueable with the court or kings Houshould. And called *Curia domini Regis*, or *Aula Regia*, as *M. Gwine* reporteth in the preface to his readings; and that, in that and the Exchequer, which were the only courts of the king, vntill *Henry* the thirds daies, were handled all maters of Iustice, as well Ciuill as Criminall. whereas the court of common plees might not be so by the statute: *anno* 9. *H.* 3. *cap.* 11. or rather, by *M. Gwins* opinion, was presently vpon the graunt of the great charter seuerally erected. This court of the Kings bench was wont in auncient times to be especially exercised in all Criminall maters & plees of the crowne, leauing the handling of priuate contracts to the cownty court. *Glanuil. lib.* 1. *cap.* 2. 3.4. & *li.* 10. *cap.* 18. *Smith de Repub: Anglicana, lib.* 2. *cap.* 11. and hath president of it, the Lord Cheife Iustice of England, with three or foure Iustices assistaunts, four or fiue as *Fortescu* saith, *cap.* 51. and officers thereunto belonging, the clearke of the crowne, a *Pranatory* or *Protonotari*, and other sixe inferior ministers or Atturnies. *Camd: Britan: pag.* 112. See *Latitat:* How long this court was moueable, I finde not in any wrighter: But in *Brittons* time, who wrot In K. *Ed:* the 1. his daies, it appeareth it followed the court, as M. *Gwin* in his said preface wel obserueth out of him. *See Iustice of the Kings Bench.*

Kings siluer, is properly that mony, which is due to the king in the court of common plees in respect of a licence there graunted to any man for passing a fine. *Coke vol.* 6. *fo.* 39. *a.* & 43. *b.*

Kintall of woad, iron &c. is a certaine waight of merchandize to the valew of a hundred, or something vnder or ouer, according to the diuers vses of sundry nations. This word is mentioned by by *Plowden* in the case of *Reniger* and *Fagossa*.

Knaue, is vsed for a man seruant. *a.* 14. *Ed.* 3. *stat.* 1. *ca.* 3. And by *M. Verstigans* iudgemét, in his Restitutió of decaied intelligence. *ca.* 10. it is borowed of the dutch (*cnapa*) cnaue or knaue, which signifie all one thing: and that is some kinde of officer or seruant: as (*scild-cnapa*) was he, that bore the weapon or shield of his superior, whom the latines call (*armigerum*) and the French men (*escuyer.*)

Knight (*Miles*) is almost one with the Saxon (*Cnight*.i. *Administer*) and by *M. Camdens* iudgment, *pag.* 110. deriued from the same. with vs it signifieth a gentleman, or one that beareth Armes, that for his vertue and especially Martiall prowers, is by the King, or one hauing the Kings authority, singled (as it were) from the ordinary sort of gentlemen, and raised to a higher accompt or steppe of dignity. This among all other nations, hath his name from the Horse: Because they were wont in auncient time, to serue in warrs one horsbacke. The Romans called them *Equites*, the Italians at these daies terme them *Cauallieri*. The French men *Cheualiers*. *The German*, Reiters. *The Spaniard Caualleros*, or *Varones a Caualło*. It appeareth by the statute *anno* 1. *Ed.* 2. *cap.* 1. that in auncient times, gentlemen hauing a full knights fee, and houlding their land by knights seruice, of the king, or other great person, might be vrged by distresse, to procure himselfe to be made knight, when he came to mans estate for the answerable seruice of his Lorde in the Kings warres. To which point you may also reade *M. Camden* in his *Britannia*. *pag.* 111 But these customes be not nowe much vrged: this dignity in these dayes being rather of fauour bestowed by the Prince vpon the worthier sort of gentlemen, then vrged by constraint. The maner of making knights (for the dignitie is not hereditarie) *M. Camden* in his *Britan. pag.* 111. shortly expresseth in these words: *Nostris verò temporibus, qui Equestrem dignitatem suscipit, flexis genibus educto gladio leuiter in humero percutitur. Princeps his verbis* Gallicè *affatur: Sus vel sois Cheualier au nom de Dieu.* id est, *Surge, aut, Sis* Eq*ues in nomine Dei.* The solemnitie of making Knights among the Saxons, *M. Stow* mentioneth in his *Annals. pag.* 159. See the priuiledges belonging to a knight in *Fernes* Glorie of Generositie. *pag.* 116. Of these knights there be two sorts: one spirituall, another temporall. *Cassanaeus in gloria mundi. parte* 9. *Considerat.* 2. of both these sorts, and of many ſubdiuiſions, reade him in that whole part. The temporall or ſecond ſort of knights *M. Ferne* in his Glorie of generoſitie. *pag.* 103. maketh threefold here with vs. Knights of the ſword, Knights of the Bath, and Knights of the ſoueraigne Order, that is, of the Garter: of all which you may reade what he ſaith. I muſt remember that mine intent is but to explain the termes eſpecially of our common lawe. Wherefore ſuch as I find mentioned in Statutes, I will define as I can. M: *Skene de verb. ſignificat. verbo Milites*, ſaith, that in the auncient lawes of *Scotland*, Freeholders were called *Milites*. Which may ſeem to haue bene a cuſtome with vs alſo by diuers places in *Bracton*, who ſaith, that knights muſt be in Iuries, which turne Freeholders doe ſerue.

Knights of the Garter, (*Equites Garterii*) are an order of knights, created by *Edward* the third, after he had obtained many notable victories, (king *Iohn* of *Frannce*, and king *Iames* of *Scotland* being both his priſoners together, and *Henry* of *Caſtile* the baſtard expulſed out of his Realme, and *Don Petro* being reſtored vnto it by the Prince of *Wales*, and Duke of *Aquitane*, called the blacke Prince) who for furniſhing of this honorable Order, made a choice out of his owne realme, and all Chriſtendome, of the beſt and moſt excellent renowned Knights in vertues and honour, beſtowing this dignitie vpon them, and giuing them a blew Garter, decked with gold, pearle, and precious ſtones, and a buckle of gold, to weare daily on the left legge onely, a kirtle, gowne, cloake, chaperon, a coller, & other ſtately and magnificall apparell both of ſtuffe and faſhion, exquiſite and heroicall, to weare at high feaſtes, as to ſo high and princely an order was meete. Of which Order, he and his ſucceſſours, kings of *England*, were ordained to be the Soueraignes, and the reſt fellowes and brethren to the number of 26. *Smith de Republ. Angl. libro primo. cap.* 20. I haue ſeene an auncient monument, whereby I am taught that this Honourable companie is a Colledge or a Corporation, hauing a common Seale belonging vnto it, and conſiſting of a Soueraigne *Gardian* which is the King of *England*, that alwaies gouernes this order by himſelfe or his Deputie, of 25. Companions called Knights of the *Garter*, of 14. ſecular Chanons that be Prieſts, or muſt be within one yeare after their admiſſion: 13. *Vicars* alſo *Prieſts*, and 26. poore Knights, that haue

haue no other sustenance or meanes of liuing but the allowance of this house, which is giuen them in respect of their daily praier to the Honour of God, and (according to the course of those times) of Saint *George*. There be also certaine officers belonging to this order, as namely the Prelate of the *Garter*, which office is inherent to the Bish: of *Winchester* for the time being, the Chaunceler of the *Garter*, the *Register*, who is alwaies Deane of *Windesour*. The principall King at *Armes* called *Garter*, whose chiefe function is to manage and marshall their Solemnities at their yearely feasts and Installations. Lastly, the Vsher of the *Garter*, which (as I haue heard) belongeth to an Vsher of the *Princes chamber*, called *Blacke rod*. There are also certaine ordinances or Constitutions belonging vnto this Society, with certaine forfeitures, and sometime penances for the Breakers of them; which constitutions concerne either the solemnities of making these Knights, or their duties after their Creation, or the Priuiledges belōging to so high an order, but are too large for the nature of this poore *Vocabularie*. The site of this Colledge, is the Castle of *Windesoure*, with the Chapel of *Saint George*, erected by *Edward* the third, and the Chapter house in the said Castell. Howbeit the yearly Solemnity or profession may be, and is, by the Soueraignes direction, performed at the Court, wheresoeuer it lyeth, vpō Saint *Georges day*. *M. Camden* saith, that this order receiued great ornament from *Edward* the 4 See *Fearns* glory of *Generosity.pag.* 120. See *Garter*. *Hospinian* in his booke *de origine & progressu Monachatus*, maketh mention of this honourable order, terming it by ignorance of our tongue *ordinem Carteriorum equitum*, and *Charteriorum equitum*. which you may reade. *cap.* 307. as also *Bernardus Girardus* in his historie, *libr.* 15. *ca.* 185.

Knights of the Bath (*milites balnei, vel de balneo*) are an order of Knights made within the Lists of the *Bath*, girded with a sword, in the ceremonie of his Creation. *Ferns* glorie of *generosity.pag.* 105. These are spoken of, *anno.* 8. *Ed.* 4. *cap.* 2. But I had an ould monument lent me by a freind, whereby it appeareth, that these Knights were soe called of a *Bath*, into the which (after they had bine shauen and trimmed by a *Barber*) they entred, and thence, the night before they were Knighted, being well bathed, were taken againe by two Esquiers com-

commanded to attend them, dried with fine linnen cloathes, and so apparelled and ledde through many solemne Ceremonies. *viz.* Confessing their sinnes, watching and praying all night in a church or chappell, with many other,) to the order of Knighthood the next day. So that by the same reason these seemed to be termed Knights of the *Bathe*, by which Knights made out of the feild in these daies are called knights of the *Carpet*, because in receiuing their order they commonly kneele vpon a *Carpet*.

Knights of the order of Saint Iohn of Ierusalem (*milites Sancti Iohannis Heirosolumitaui*) were otherwise called the Knights of the *Rhodes*, being an order of Knighthood, that had beginning about the yeare of the Lord. 1120. *Honorius* then Pope of *Rome*. *Cassanaus de gloria mundi, parte.* 9. *Considerarione* 4. & *M.Fern.* in his glorie of *Generosity: pag.* 127. they had their primarie foundation and cheife aboad first in Hierusalem, and thẽ in *Rhodes*, where many of thẽ liued vnder their *Principall* called the *M. of Rhodes.* vntill they were expelled thence by the Turke, *anno* 1523. sithence which time their cheife seate is at *Malta*, where they haue done great exploits against the Infidels, but especially in the yeare 1595. These, though they had their beginning & especialest abode first at Ierusalem and next in Rhodes, yet they encreased both in number and Reuenues, liuing after the order of Friers vnder the Rule of *Saint Augustine* and were dispersed into *France, Spaine, Alvern, Campany, Englãd, and Ireland*. Of these mentiõn is made in the *stat: anno.* 25. H. 8. *ca.* 2. & *anno* 26. *eiusdem, cap. secundo*, and it appeareth that they in England had one generall prior, that had the gouernment of the whole order within England & Scotland. *Reg. orig. fol.* 20. *b.* But toward the ende of *Henrie* the eights daies, they in England and Ireland being found ouer much to adhere to the *B.* of *Rome* against the King, were suppressed, and their Lands and goods referred by Parlament to the Kings disposition. *anno.* 32. *H.* 8. *cap.* 24. The Occasion and the propagation of this order more especially described, you may reade in the Treatise intituled the Booke of *Honour* and *Armes, lib.* 5. *cap.* 18. written by *M. Rich. Ihones.*

Knights of the Rhodes, anno. 32. H. 8. *ca.* 24. See *Knights of the order of Saint Iohn*,

Knights of the Temple (otherwise called Templers) *Templa-*

plarii was an order of *Knight*hood created by *Gelasius* the Pope, about the yeare of our *Lord*.1117. and so called, because they dwelt in a part of the buildings belonging to the Temple. These in the beginning dwelling not far from the Sepulchre of the *Lord* entertained Cristian straungers and *Pilgrims* charitably, and in their armour ledde them through the *Holy Land*, to view such things, as there were to be seene, without feare of Infidels adioyning. This Order continuing and increasing by the space of 200. yeares, was farre spred in Christendome, and namely here in England. But at the last, the cheife of them at *Hierusalem*, being (as some men say) found to fall away to the *Sazarens* from Christianity, and to abound in many vices, the whole Order was suppressed by *Clemens quintus*, which was about *King Ed*. the 1. daies, and their substance giuen partly to the *Knights* of the Rhodes, and partly to other Religious. *Cassan: de gloria mundi, parte 9. Consid.* 5. and See *anno prim: Ed. 1. cap. 42.* Others wright that in truth their destruction grewe from leaning to the Emperour against the Pope of Rome, what soeuer was pretended. *Ioach. Stephanus De iurisdictione. lib. 4. cap. 10. nu. 18.* See *Templers*.

Knights of the Shire (*Milites Comitatus*) otherwise be called *Knights* of the Parlament, and be two *Knights*, or other gentlemen of worth, that are chosen in *pleno Comitatu*, by the free holders of euery *Countie* that can dispend 40. shillings *per annum*, and be Resient in the shire, *anno* 10. H, *6. cap. 2. & anno* 1. *H. 5. cap.* 1. vpon the Kings writ, to be sent to the Parlament, and there by their counsell to assist the common proceedings of the whole Realme. These when euery man that had a *Knights* fee, were custumarily constreined to be a *Knight*, were of necessity to be *milites gladio cincti*, for so runneth the tenour of the writ at this day. *Cromptons Iurisdict. fol. pri.* But nowe there being but fewe *Knights* in comparison of former times, & many men of great liuing in euery county, Custome beareth that Esquiers may be chosen to this office. *anno* 23. *H. 6. ca. 6.* so that they be resient within the countie, *anno H. 6. cap. 7. & anno 1. H. 5. cap. prim.* For the obseruations in choice of these knights, see the statutes *anno 7 H. 4. cap. 15. & anno 11. eiusdem, cap. 1. & anno 6.* H. *6. cap. 4. & anno* 23. H. *6. cap.* 15. and the new booke of Entries. *verbo Parlament nu.* 1. Their expences during the Parlament are borne by the Countie.

County, *anno* 35. *H.* 8. *cap.* 11.

Knight Marshiall (Marescallus hospitii Regii) is an officer in the kings house, hauing iurisdiction, and cognisance of any transgression within the kings house and verge, as also of contracts made within the same house, whereunto one of the house is a partie. *Register orig. fo.* 185. *a. b. & fo.* 191. *b.* whereof you may there reade more at large.

Knights fee, (Feudum militare) is so much inheritaunce, as is sufficient yearely to maintaine a knight with conuenient reuenew which in *Henry* the .3. daies was fifteene pounds. *Camdeni Britan. pag.* 111. or 680. acres of land, or 800. acres. *eodem:* But *S. Thomas Smith* in his *Repub. Angl. lib. pri. cap.* 18. rateth it at fourtie pound. And I finde in the statute for knights *anno pri. Ed.* 2. *cap pri.* that such as had 20. pound in fee or for terme of life *per annum*, might be compelled to be knights. *M. Stowe* in his *annals, pag.* 285. saith, that there were found in England at the time of the Conqueror 60211. Knights fees: others say 60215. whereof the religious houses before their suppression were possessed of 28015. Knights fee, is sometime vsed for the rent, that a knight payeth for his fee to his Lord, of whom he houldeth. And this is an vncertaine summe, some houlding by fortie shillings the sheild, some by twenty shillings as appeareth by *Bracton. lib.* 5. *tract: pri. cap.* 2.

Knighten Gylde, was a *Gylde* in London consisting of 19. knights, which king *Edgar* founded, giuing vnto them a portion of void ground lying without the walls of the city, now called *Portesoken ward.* Stow. in his *Annals, pag.* 151.

L

Laborariis, is a writ that lieth against such, as hauing not whereof to liue, doe refuse to serue, or for him that refuseth to serue in summer, where he serued in winter: *orig. Register, fol.* 189. *b.*

Laches, commeth of the French (*lascher* .i. *laxare*, or *lasche.* i. *frigidus, ignavus, flaccidus*) it signifieth in our common law, negligence: as no *laches* shalbe adiudged in the heire within age, *Litleton fol.* 136. and *old nat. br. fol.* 110. where a man ought to make a thing, and makes it not, I of his *laches* cannot haue an Assise, but I must take mine action vpon the case.

Lagon, See *Flotzon*.

Laised listes, *anno* i. R. 3. *cap.* 8.

Land tenent, *anno* 14. *Ed.* 3. *stat.* 1. *cap.* 3. & *anno* 23. *eiusdem.* cap

cap. 1. & 26. *eiusdem, stat.* 5. *cap.* 2. See *Terre-tenent*, & *anno* 12. *R.* 2. *cap.* 4. & *anno* 4. *H.* 4. *cap.* 8. it is ioyned with this word (*Possessor*) as *Synonymon. v. anno* 1. *H.* 6. *cap.* 5. See *Terretenent*.

Lanis de crescentia Wallie traducendis abq; custuma, &c. is a writ that lyeth to the customer of a porte, for the permitting one to passe ouer wolles without custome, because he hath paid custome in *Wales* before, *Register, fol.* 279.

Lapse (*Lapsus*) is a slippe or departure of a right of preseting to avoide benefice, from the originall patron neglecting to present within six monethes, vnto the Ordinary. For we say that benefice is in lapse or lapsed, wherevnto he that ought to present, hath omitted or slipped his oportunitie, *anno* 13. *Eliz. cap.* 12. This lapse groweth as well the Patron being ignorant of the auoydance, as priuie, except onely vpon the resignation of the former Incumbent, or the depriuation vpon any cause comprehended in the statute, *anno* 13. *Eliz. cap.* 12. *Panor: in cap. quia diuersitatem. nu.* 7. *de concess: prebend. Rebuffus de devolut: in praxi beneficiorum: Lancelotus de collation: lib.* 1. *Institut. canon:* §. *Tempus autem.* In which cases the Bishop ought to giue notice to the *Patron*.

Larceny (*Laricinium*) commeth of the French (*Larcen .i. furtum, detractio alicui*) It is defined by *West. parte.* 2. *Symbol. titulo Inditements*, to be theft of personall goods or chatels, in the owners absence: and in respect of the things stollen, it is either great or small. *Great Larceny* is, wherin the things stolne, though seuerally, exceede the value of 12. pence, and *petit Larceny* is when the goods stolne exceede not the value of 12. pence, hitherto *M. West.* But he differeth from *Bracton. lib.* 3. *tract.* 2. *c.* 32. *n.* 1. Of this see more in *Stawnf. pl. cor. l.* 1. *cap.* 15. 16. 17. 18. 19.

Laghslite, is compounded of (*lah .i. lex*) and (*slite .i. ruptum*) and signifieth *mulctam rupta vel violata legis. Lamb: explicat. of Saxon words, verbo Mulcta.*

Last, is a Saxon word, signifiing a burden in generall, as also particularly a certaine weight: for as we say a last of hering, so they say *Ein last corns, last wines*, &c. thence commeth lastage, which see in *Lestage*. A last of hering conteineth 10. thousand, *anno* 31. *Ed.* 3. *stat.* 2. *cap.* 2. a last of pitch and tarre, or of ashes, conteineth 14. barrels. *anno.* 32. H. 8. *cap.* 14. a last of hides, *anno* 1. *Iac. cap.* 33. conteineth 12. dozen of hides or skins.

Latitat, is the name of a writ whereby all men in personall actions are called originally to the *Kings* bench. *Fitz.nat.br.fo.* 78. M. *And* it hath the name from this, because in respect of their beter expedition, a man is supposed to lurke, and therefore being serued with this writ, he must put in securitie for his appearance at the day, for *latitare, est se malitiose occultare animo fraudandi creditores suos agere volentes. l. Fulcimus* §. *Quid sit latitare.* π. *Quibus ex causis in possessionem eatur*: But to vnderstand the true original of this writ, it is to be knowne, that in auncient time, whilest the kings bench was moueable, and followed the court of the *King*, the custome was, when any man was to be siewed, to send forth a writ to the Shyreeue of the county where the Court lay, for the calling him in: and if the Shyreeue returned, *non est inventus in baliva nostra, &c.* then was there a second writ procured foorth, that had these words, (*testatum est eum latitare, &c.*) and thereby the *S*hyreeue willed to attach him in any other place where he might be found. Now when the tribunall of the Kings bench came to be setled at *Westminster*, the former course of writ was kept for a long time, first sending to the *S*hyreeue of *Midlesex* to summon the party, and if he could not be found there, then next to apprehend him wheresoeuer. But this seeming too troublesome for the subiect, it was at last deuised, to put both these writs into one, and so originally to attache the party complained of vpon a supposall or fiction, that he was not within the county of *Middlesex*, but lurking else where, and that therefore he was to be apprehended in any place else, where he was presumed to lye hidden, by a writ directed to the Shyreeue of the county where he is suspected to be: and by this writ a man being brought in, is committed to the Marshall of that court, in whose custodie when he is, then by reason he is in the same countie where the *K*ings bench is, he may be siewed vpon an action in that court, wheras the original cause of apprehending him must be a pretence of some deceit or contempt committed, which most properly of old belonged to the cognizance of that court. I haue bene enformed, that the bringing of these actions of trespas so ordinarily to the kings bench, was an inuention of Councelers, that because onely *S*ergeants may come to the common plees barre, found a meanes to set themselues on worke in that court. The forme of this writ is such: *Iacobus* Dei *gratia Angliæ, Franciæ, Scotiæ, & Hiberniæ Rex, fidei defensor, &c. Vicecomiti Cantabrigiæ salutem. Cum Vicecomiti nostro Midlesexiæ nuper preceperimus, quòd caperet Thomam T. & Wilielmum W. si inuenti fuissent in balliua sua, & eos saluo custodiret, ita quòd haberet corpora eorum coram nobis apud Westminster die veneris proximo post octavas Sanctæ Trinitatis, ad respondendum Roberto R. de placito trangressionis; cumq; vicecomes noster Midlesexiæ, ad diem illum nobis retornauerit, quod prædicti Thomas T. & Wilielmus W. non sunt inuenti in balliua sua, super quo ex parte prædicti Roberti in curia nostra coram nobis sufficienter testatum est, quòd prædicti Thomas & Wilielmus latitant & discurrunt in comitatu tuo. Idcirco tibi præcipimus quòd capias eos, si inuẽti fuerint in balliua, tua & eos salvo custodias, ita quod habeas corpora eorum coram nobis apud Westminster, die Martis proximo post tres septimanas, eodem Trinitatis, ad respondendum præfato* Roberto *de placito prædicto, & habeas ibi tunc hoc breve. Teste Iohanne Popham apud Westminster.* Roper.

Launcegay, anno. 7. Rich. *secundi. cap.* 13.

Law (lex) cometh of the *Saxon (lah)* the generall significatiõ is plaine, only this I thought to note, that the law of this land hath beene variable. For first *Dunwallo Mulmutius* otherwise *Molincius* a Brittaine, that being Duke of *Cornwall* reduced the whole land formerly seuered by ciuile wars, into the state of a *Monarchy*, made certaine wholsome lawes, which long after were called *Mulmutius* lawes, and by *Gyldas* translated out of the *Bryttish* tongue into latine. *Stow in his Annals, pag.* 16. Of these there remaine yet certaine heads, recorded by our historiographers, as followeth. 1. *vt Deorum templa, & ciuitates hominum consequantur tantam dignitatem, ne quis illò confugiens extrahi possit, antequàm ab eo quem læserat, veniam impetraverit.* 2. *vt huiusmodi privilegium immunitatis habeant etiam ipsæ viæ, quæ ducunt ad templa & ad vrbes.* 3. *Imo & iumenta quoq; illa, quæ rei rusticæ subueniunt.* 4. *Deniq; colonorum aratra ipsa tali prærogativa libertatis perfruantur.* 5. *Hoc amplius, vt ne qua terra vacaret culturâ, neve populus inopia rei frumentariæ premeretur, aut ea minueretur, si pecora sola occuparent agros qui ab hominibus coli debent.* 6. *Constituit quot aratra qualibet diœcesis haberet: ac pœnam statuit iis, per quos ille numerus aratrorum foret diminutus:* 7. *Item vetuit, bovem aratorem pro debito pecuniæ, assignari debitoribus, si alia bona debitoris essent. Ita fore, ne compendii*

dii causa homines pecuarii agros incultos redderent: sic etiam fore, ne quid earum rerum, quas natura prabet, hominibus usquam deesse posset. Rich. Vitus historiarum Britannia. li. 3. nu. 1. And of these lawes we finde no obscure remanets in our lawes now in vse: See *Magna charta. ca. 1: & ca. 14.* See *Sanctuary.* See *Peace*. Then was there a lawe called *Merchenlage*, whereby the *Mercians* were gouerned, being a kingdome in the heart of the land, conteining those countries, that be nowe called *Northampton* shire, *Leycester* shire, *Rutland* shire, *Lincolne* shire, *Nottingham* shire, and *Derby* shire. *Camd. Britan. pag.* 94. whose power was great in the *Heptarchy* of the *Saxons*, vntill at the last they were conquered by the west *Saxons*, and made subiect to them. *Polydor. in Angl. Hist. lib.* 5. But whereas the name of these lawes sauoureth of the Saxons time, it is reported by others that *Martia* a very learned Queene and wife to *Quintelinus* a Britton king, was the author of them, long before the *Saxons* set foote in England. *Rich. Vitus. histo. Britan. li. 3. nu.* 14. who also saith that *Alphred* the Saxon *King* translated both these, and also those of *Mulmutius* into the English or Saxon tongue. Thirdly, there was the lawe of the west *Saxons*, called west *Saxenlage*, and the lawe of the *Danes* when they set foote into the Realme, called *Denelage*. And of these lawes, *Edward* made one lawe, as some write, whereby he ruled his kingdome. But *M. Camd. vbi supra*, speaking nothing of *Mulmutius* lawes, saith out of *Geruasius Tilburiensis*, that of the other three *William* the Conquerour chose the best, and to them adding of the *Norman* lawes, such as he thought good, he ordeined lawes for our kingdome, which we haue at this present, or the most of them.

Lawe hath an especiall signification also, wherein it is taken for that which is lawfull with vs, and not els where. As tenent by the courtesie of *England*. *anno* 13. *Ed.* 1. *cap.* 3. and againe, to wage lawe, *vadiare legem*, and to make lawe, *facere legem. Bracton lib. 3. tract. 2. cap.* 37. is to chalenge a speciall benefite, that the lawe of this *Realme* affordeth in certaine cases: whereof the first, *sc. vadiare legem*, is to put in securitie, that he will make lawe at a day assigned, *Glanuile lib.* 1. *cap.* 9. and to make law is to take an oath, that he oweth not the debt chalenged at his hand, and also to bring with him so many men as the court shall assigne, to avowe vpon their oath, that in there consciēces he hath sworne truly. And this lawe is vsed in actions

actions of debt, without ſpecialty, as alſo where a man comming to the court, after ſuch time, as his tenements for default be ſeiſed into the Kings hands, will denie himſelfe to haue beene ſummoned, *Glanuile lib. 1. cap. 9. & 12.* and See *Bracton vbi ſupra. nu. 1. v. Kitchin. fol. 164* See the newe expoſition of lawe Termes *verbo (Ley)* this is borrowed from *Normandie*, as appeareth by the grand Cuſtumarie, *cap. 85. But Sir Edward Cooke* ſaith, it ſpringeth originally from the iudiciall lawe of god, *li. 4.* of his reports, *Slades caſe, fol. 95. b.* alleaging the *22. cap.* of *Exodus, verſu. 7.* Whether ſo or not, the like cuſtome is among the Feudiſts: by whome they that come to purge the defendant, are called *(Sacramentales.) libro feud. 1. tit. 4. §. 3. & titulo 10. & titulo. 26.*

Lawe of armes (ius militare) is a law that giueth precepts & rules how rightly to proclaime warre, to make and obſerue leagues & truce, to ſet vpon the enemie, to retire, to puniſh offendours in the campe, to appoint ſouldiers their pay, to giue euery one dignitie to his deſert, to diuide ſpoiles in proportion, and ſuch like, for farder knowledge wherof, reade thoſe that write *de iure belli.*

Lawe day, ſignifieth a leete *Cromptons Iuriſdict. fol. 160.* and the county court, *anno 1. Ed. 4. cap. 2.*

Lawles man, is he *qui eſt extra legem, Bracton lib. 3. tract. 2. cap. 11. nu. 1.* See *Outlawe.*

Lawe of Marque, See *Repriſalles.* This word is vſed *anno 27. Ed. 3, ſtat. 2. ca. 17.* and groweth from the German word *March.* i. *limes*, a bound or limite. And the reaſon of this appellation is, becauſe they that are driuen to this lawe of repriſall, do take the goods of that people of whome they haue receiued wrong, and cannot get ordinary iuſtice, when they can catch them within their owne territories or precincts.

Lawe Merchant, is a priuiledge or ſpeciall lawe differing from the common lawe of England, and proper to merchants and ſummary in proceeding, *anno 27. Ed. 3. ſtat. 8. 9. 19. & 20. anno 13. Ed. 1. ſtat. tertio.*

Lawing of dogs (expeditatio canum) See *Expeditate*. Maſtifs muſt be lawed euery three yeare. *Cromptons Iuriſd. fol. 163.*

Leaſe (leſſa) commeth of the French *(laiſſer. i. linquere, relinquere, omittere, permittere:)* It ſignifieth in our common lawe, a dimiſe or letting of lands or tenements or right of common, or of a rent or any hereditament vnto another, for terme of yeares or of life, for a rent reserued. And a lease is either written, called a lease by Indenture, or made by word of mouth, called a lease paroll. See the newe Termes of the lawe. The party that letteth this lease, is called the leassour, and the partie to whom it is let, the leassee. And a lease hath in it sixe points: *viz.* words importing a dimise, a leassee named, a commencement from a day certaine, a term of yeares, a determination, a reseruation of a rent. *Coke vol. 6. Knights case. fol.* 55.*a.*

Leete (*leta*) is otherwise called a lawe day, *Smith de Republ. Anglor. lib.* 2. *cap.* 18. the word seemeth to haue growne from the Saxon (*Lethe*) which as appeareth by the lawes of king *Edward* set out by *M.* Lamberd. *num.* 34. was a court or iurisdiction aboue the Wapentake or Hundred, comprehending three or foure of them, otherwise called *Thryhing*, and contained the third patt of a Prouince or Shire. These iurisdictions one and other be now abolished, and swallowed vp in the Countie court, except they be held by prescription. *Kitchin. fol.* 6. or charter in the nature of a franchise, as I haue said in (*Hundred.*) The libertie of Hundreds is rare, but many Lordes, together with their courts Baron, haue likewise *Leetes* adioyned, and thereby do enquire of such transgressions, as are subiect to the enquirie and correction of this Court: whereof you may read your fill in *Kitchin*, from the beginning of his booke to the fifth chapter, and *Briton. cap.* 28. But this court, in whose maner soeuer it be kept, is accompted the kings court, because the authoritie thereof is originally belonging to the Crowne, and thence deriued to inferiour persons, *Kitchin fol.* 6. Iustice *Dyer* saith, that this *Leete* was first deriued from the Shyreeues *Turn. fol.* 64. And it enquireth of all offences vnder high treason, committed against the Crowne and dignitie of the king; though it cannot punish many, but must certifie them to the Iustices of *Assise*, *per Statut. anno* 1. *Ed.* 3. *cap. vlt. Kitchin fol.* 8. but what things bee onely inquirable, and what punishable, see *Kitchin* in the charge of a court *Leet*, *fol.* 8. 9. 10. 11. 12. 13. 14. 15. 16. 17. 18. 19. 20. See also the *Statute anno* 18. *Ed.* 2. The Iurisdiction of Bayliffes in the *Dutchy* of *Normandie*, within the compasse of their Prouinces, seemeth to be the same, or very neare the same, with the power of our

Leete. *cap.* 4. of the grand Custumarie.

Legacie (*legatum*) is a particular thing giuen by last will and testament. For if a man dispose or transferre his whole right or estate vpon another, that is called *Hæreditas* by the Ciuilians, and he to whome it is so transferred, is tearmed *hæres.* Howbeit our common Lawyers call him Heire, to whom all a mans lands and hereditaments doe descend by right of bloud. See *Heire.* See *Hereditaments.*

Leproso amouendo, is a writ that lyeth for a Parish, to remoue a Leper or Lazar, that thrusteth himselfe into the company of his neighbours, either in church or other publike meeting, and communeth with them to their annoyance or disturbance. *Regi. orig. fol.* 267. *Fitz. nat. br. fol.* 234.

Lestage, aliàs lastage, (*lastagium*) proceedeth from the Saxon word (*last.* i. *onus*) and is a custome chalenged in Faires & markets for carying of things. *Rastals* Exposition of words: or a custome chalenged in cheapings or Faires. *Saxon* in the description of *England, cap.* 11. *Lastage. anno* 21. *R.* 2. *cap.* 18. seemeth to be the Ballance of a shippe. *Fleta* tearmeth it *Lesting,* saying, *quòd significat acquietantiā Lestagii. lib.* 1. *cap.* 47. §. *Lesting.*

Leters of exchaunge, (*litera Cambitoria, vel litera Cambii*) *Regist. orig. fol.* 194. *a.*

Leters patents (*litera patentes*) be writings sealed with the bread Seale of *England*, whereby a man is authorized to do or enioy any thing that otherwise of himselfe he could not. *anno* 19. *H.* 7. *cap.* 7. And they be so tearmed of their forme, because they be open with the Seale hanging, readie to be shewed for the confirmation of the authoritie giuen by them. If any will say, that leters patents may bee graunted by common persons, I will not greatly contend. For I find that to be true in *Fitzh. nat. br. fol.* 35. *E.* Howbeit they bee called rather patents in our cōmon speech, then Leters patents. Leters patents to make Denizens. *anno* 32. *H.* 6. *cap.* 16. yet for difference sake, the kings leters patents be called leters patents royall. *anno* 2. *H.* 6. *cap.* 10. There is likewise a writ patent. *Fitzh. nat. br. fol.* 1. *& seqq.*

Leuari facias, is a writ directed to the Shyreeue, for the leuying of a Summe of money vpon lands and tenements, of him that hath forfeited a recognizance, &c. *Regist. origin. fol.* 298. *b.* & 300. *b.*

Leuari facias damna de disseisitoribus, is a writ directed to the Shyreeue, for the leauying of dam dammages, wherein the diſſeiſour hath formerly beene condemned to the diſſeiſee. *Regiſt. fol.* 214. *b.*

Leuari facias reſiduum debiti, is a writ directed to the *Shyreeue*, for the leuying of a *Remanent* of a debt vpon lands and tenements, or chatels of the debtor, that hath in part ſatisfied before, *Regiſt. orig. fol.* 299.

Leuari facias quando vicecomes returnavit quòd non habuit emptores, is a writ commaunding the *Shyreeue* to ſell the goods of the debtor, which he hath alreadie taken, & returned that he could not ſell them, and as much more of the debtours goods, as will ſatisfie the whole debt. *Regiſt. orig. fol.* 300. *a.*

Leter of Atturney, (litera Atturnatus) is a writing, authorizing an Atturney, that is, a man appointed to do a lawfull act in our ſteedes, *Weſt. parte prim. ſymbol. lib.* 2. *ſect.* 559. It is called in the ciuile lawe *(mandatum*, or *procuratorium)* There ſeemeth to be ſome difference betweene a leter of Atturney, and a warrant of Atturney. For whereas a leter of Atturney is ſufficient, if it be ſealed and deliuered before ſufficient witneſſe: a warrant of Atturney muſt be acknowledged and certified before ſuch perſons, as fines bee acknowledged in the country, or at the leaſt before ſome Iuſtice or Sergeant, *Weſt. parte* 2. *ſymbol. titulo* Recoveries. *ſect.* 1. *F.* See the ſtatute, *anno* 7. *R.* 2. *cap.* 14.

Leters of Marque. See *Marque* and lawe of *Marque.* See *Repriſals.* ſee *a.* 14. *Hen.* 6. *cap.* 7.

Leters patents of ſummons for debt: anno 9. *H.* 3. *cap.* 18.

Leuy (Leuare) commeth of the French *(Leuer.* i. *alleuare, attollere)* It is vſed in our common law, for to ſet vp any thing, as to leuy a mill. *Kitchin, fol.* 180. or to caſt vp, as to leuy a ditch. *Old. nat. br. fol.* 110. or to gather and exact, as to leuy mony. See *Leuari facias.*

Libell (Libellus) literally ſignifieth a litle booke, but by vſe it is the originall declaration of any action in the ciuill lawe. *anno* 2. *H.* 5. *cap.* 3. & *anno* 2. *Ed.* 6. *cap.* 13. it ſignifieth alſo a criminous report of any man caſt abroad, or otherwiſe vnlawfully publiſhed in writing, but then for difference ſake it is called an infamous libel, *famoſus libellus.*

Libello habendo. See *Copia libelli deliberanda.*

Libera Chaſea habenda, is a writ Iudiciall, graunted to a man for a free chace belonging to his maner, after he hath by a Iury prooued it to belong vnto him. *Regiſter Iudiciall, fol.* 36. & 37.

Liberate, is a warrant iſſuing out of the Chāucery to the Treaſurer,

surer, Chamberlaines, and Barons of the Exchequer, or clerk of the Hamper, &c. for the payments of any annuall pension or other summes graunted vnder the broad seale. *v. Brooke. titulo Taile d'Exchequer. nu. 4. orig. Reg. fol. 193. a. b.* or sometime to the shyreeue .*&c. n. br. f. 132.* for the deliuery of any lands or goods taken vpon forfeits of a Recognisaunce. *Fitzh. nat. br. fol. 131. & 132. v. Coke. li. 4. Fulwods case, fo. 64. 66. & 67.* It is also to a Gaoler from the Iustices for the deliuery of a prisoner, that hath put in baile for his appearaunce. *Lamb.* Eirenarch. *lib. 3. cap. 2.*

Libertate probanda, is a writ that lyeth for such, as be chalendged for slaues, and offer to proue themselues free, to the Shyreeue, that he take security of them for the prouing of their freedome before the Iustices of *Assise*, and prouide, that in the meane time they be quiet from their vexations, that chalenge them for slaues. *Fitz. nat. br fol. 77.* See *Natiuo habendo.*

Libertatibus allocandis, is a writ that lyeth for a citizen or Burges of any citie, that contrarily to the liberties of the city or towne whereof he is, is impleaded before the kings Iustices, or Iustices errants, or Iustice of the Forest, &c. that refuseth or deferreth to allow his priuiledge *Orig. Regist. fol. 262. Fitz. nat. br. fol. 229.*

Libertatibus exigendis in itinere, is a writ, whereby the king willeth the Iustices in *eyre*, to admit of an *Atturney* for the defence of another mans libertie, &c. before them. *Regist. origin. fol. 19. b.*

Libertas (libertas) is a priuiledge held by graunt or prescription, whereby men enioy some benefite or fauour beyond the ordinarie subiect. *Liberties* royal what they be, see in *Bracton. lib. 2. cap. 5. Broke hoc titulo.* See *Franchise.*

Librata terræ, containeth foure oxegangs, and euery oxegange 13. acres. *Skene de verb. signif. verbo* Bovata *terræ.* See *Farding-deale of land.*

Licence to go to election, (Licentia eligendi, Regist. *fol. 294.)* See *Conge d'eslire.*

Licence to arise, (licentia surgendi) is a libertie giuen by the Court to a tenent, that is essoyned *de malo lecti* in a reall action. For the lawe is, that in this case he may not arise out of his bed, or at least goe out of his chamber, vntill he haue bene viewed by Knights thereunto appointed, and so vpon view of his sicknesse, haue a day assigned him to appeare, or else lye, vntill he be licenced by the court to arise. And the reason of this is, as I take it, because it may appeare, whether he caused himselfe to be essoyned deceitfully yea or not: And therefore if the demaundant can prooue, that he be seene out of his chamber, walking vp and downe his grounds, or els going abroad vnto any other place, before he be viewed or haue licence of the court, he shalbe adiudged to be deceitfully essoyned, and to haue made default. Of this see *Bracton, lib. 5. tract. 2. cap. 7. 10. & 12.* and *Fleta, li. 6. cap. 10. Horne* in his second booke of his mirrour, *ca. des Essoines*, saith that the aduerse party may graunt *licentiam surgendi* to his aduersary thus essoyned: And if he will not, the king vpon iust cause, may.

Licentia surgendi, is the writ whereby the tenent essoyned *de malo lecti*, obteineth liberty to rise. See *Licence to arise*. See the *Register, fol.* 8.

Licentia transfretandi, is a writ or warrant directed to the keepers of the Port at *Douer, &c.* willing them to let some passe quietly ouer sea, that hath formerly obteined the kings licence thereunto, *Reg. Orig fol.* 193. *b.*

Lieftenent (*locum tenens*) is a French word, signifiing as much as (*Legatus*) it is compounded of (*Lieu.* i. *Locus*) and (*tenir.* i. *tenere*) It signifieth with vs him, that occupieth the kings place, or representeth his person, as the Liefetenent of the Kings of Ireland. *anno* 4. *H.* 5. *cap.* 6. so is it vsed *anno* 2. & 3. *Ed.* 6. *cap.* 2. whence that officer seemeth to take his beginning. But I read also in *M. Manwoods* first part of forest lawes. *pag.* 113. that the lord cheife Iustice in *Eyre* of the Forest: and the cheife warden also, haue their Liefetenents in the forest. So that though a Leiftenent be most ordinary and most properly vsed for the Depute of the king: yet is it sometime extēded to ther deputes that be but Liefetenents to the King.

Liefetenent of the *Ordinance*, *anno* 39. *El. ca.* 7.

Liege, (*ligius*) is a word borowed from the *Feudists*, and hath two seuerall significations in our common lawe: sometime being vsed for Liege Lord. *anno* 34. & 35. *H.* 8. *cap.* 1. & *anno* 35. *eiusdem, cap.* 3. and somtimes for Liege man. *anno* 10. *R.* 2. *cap. vnico.* & *anno* 11. *eiusdem. cap. prim.* Liege Lord is he, that acknowledgeth no superiour. *Duarenus in Comment. de Consuetud. Feudorum, cap.* 4. *num.* 3. Liege man is he, that oweth legeancie to his liege Lord. *M. Skene de verb. sign. verbo Ligeantia*, saith, that it is deriued from the Italian word, (*liga*) i. a band, league, or obligation, in whom read more of this mater.

Ligeancie, is such a duty or fealtie, as no man may owe or beare to more then one Lord. *Idem, eodem. num.* 4. I find also this definition of ligeancie in the grand Custumarie of *Normandy, cap.* 13. *Ligeantia est, ex qua Domino tenentur vasalli sui contra omnes homines qui mori possunt & viuere, proprii corporis præbere consilii & auxilii iuvamentum, & ei se in omnibus innocuos exhibere, nec ei adversantium partem in aliquo confouere. Dominus etiam eosdem tenetur regere, protegere & defensare: eosque secundum iura & consuetudines, & leges patriæ pertractare:* this is otherwise called *legietas, Cassan: de Consuetud: Burgund: pag.* 420. & 421. This word is vsed in the statutes of our realm: as the kings liege people. *anno* 14. *H.* 8. *c.* 2. Of the oath of leageancy, *Iacobutius de Franchis in præludio feudorum, cap.* 2. *nu.* 138. hath these words: *Præstatur hoc Ligeum Homagium in manibus Regis vel imperatoris, genibus flexis, positis manibus iunctis in manibus Domini, dicendo: Ego iuro homagiũ tibi Dom. vt a modo sim homo ligeus vester, cont.. omnem hominem, qui potest viuere: verba sunt pulchra Andr. de Isern: in cap.* 1. *in verbo omnem. Colum: prima. de noua forma fidelita: & hoc ligeum Homagium videmus præstari domino Regi tantum: quia cùm per id efficiatur homo solius illius, cui iuratur, vt dixit Hostiensis in cap. ex diligenti. de Symon: alii non potest præstari.* i. *quia illius solius esse similiter non potest: Non n. esse potest duorum in solidum. l. si vt certo.* §. *si duobus vehiculum. ꝛc: commodati. secundùm And: in dicto cap:* 1. §. *omnem. & Bald: hic in* 7. *diuis & Aluar. in* 13. *diuisione.) Non ligeum verò dicitur, quando quis iurat fidelitatem Domino, excepta aliqua persona, viz. domino superiori, vel antiquiore: Hactenus Iacobutius.* where you may reade more touching this point: as also in *Hotomans disputations de feudis, pag.* 816. *fol.* 820. *&c.*

Ligeance (*Ligeantia*) See *Liege* It sometime signifieth the dominions or territoritie of the Liege Lord: as *anno* 25. *Ed.* 3. *stat.* 2. Children borne out of the Ligeance of the King.

Lierwit *est mulcta adulteriorum. Fleta li.* 1. *ca.* 47. It is vsed for a libertie whereby a Lord chalengeth the penalty of one that lyeth vnlawfully with his bond woman. See Lotherwit.

Limitation *of Assise* (Limitatio *assisæ*) is a certaine time set downe by statute, within the which a man must alledge himselfe or his auncester to haue bin seised of lands, sewed for by a writ of Assise. See the statute of *Merton, cap.* 8. *anno* 20. *H.* 3. and *West.* 1. *cap.* 38. and *an.* 32. *H.* 8. *c.* 2. & *an.* 1. *M.* 1. *p. c.* 5. See also

Theloals digest of writs lib. 10. *cap.* 2. So it is vsed in the *old. nat. br. fol.* 77. in these words: the writ *de consuetudinibus & seruitiis* lyeth, where I or mine Auncesters after the limitation of Assise, were not seised of the Customes, &c. But before the *Limitation* of Assise wee were seised, &c.

Lindwood, was a Doctor of both Ciuill and Canon lawes, and Deane of the Arches, he was Embassadour for *Henry* the fiueth into *Portingall, anno* 1422. as appeareth by the preface to his commentarie vpon the *Prouincialls*.

Litleton, was a lawyer of great accompt, liuing in the daies of *Edward* the fourth, as appeareth by *Stawnf. prærogat: cap.* 21. *fol.* 72. he wrot a booke of great accompt, called *Litletons* tenoures, which *Hotoman* in his commentary *de verbis feudalibus. verb. Foedum*, thus commendeth. *Stephanus Pasquerius excellenti vir ingenio, & inter Parisienses causidicos dicendi facultate præstans, libellum mihi Anglicanum* Litle*tonum dedit, quo Feudorum Anglicorum* Iu*ra exponuntur, ità inconditè, absurdè, & inconcinnè scriptum, vt facilè appareat verum esse, quod Polidorus Virgilius in Anglica historia scribit, stultitiam in eo libro cum malitia & calumniandi studio certare*.

Litera ad faciendum attornatum pro secta facienda: see in the *Regist: originall, fol.* 172. *Litera de annua pensione, eodem,* 266. & 307. *Litera patens ac faciendum generalē atturnatum quia infirmus, eodem, fol.* 21. *Litera per quam dominus remittit curiam suam Regi, eodem. fol.* 4. *Litera de requestu, eodem, fol.* 129. *Litera canonici ad exercendam iurisdictionem loco suo, fo.* 305. *Litera patentes ad conferendum beneficia, domino in remotis agente. fol.* 305. *Litera ad innotescēdum recuperationem Regis de ecclesia omnibus quorum interest, fol.* 305. *Litera patentes regis quod Abbas ad totam vitam suam possit facere Atturnatos generales, f.* 21. *Literæ procuratoriæ; fol.* 205. 306. *Litera Regia deprecatoria pro annua pensione, fol.* 307. All these you may see in their places, & vnderstand the meaning of them, as occasion shall require.

Liverie (Liberatura) is drawne from the French *(livree* i. *insigne, gestamen, Centuriale discrimen, nota centurialis, turmalis)* or els from *(livrer.* i. *tradere)* and accordingly hath 3. significations. In one it is vsed for a suite of cloth or other stuffe, that a gentleman giueth in coates, cloakes, hats or gownes, with cognisaunce or without, to his seruants or followers, *anno* 1. *Rich.* 2. *cap.* 7. & *anno* 20. *eiusdem, cap.* 1. & 2. & *anno* 7. *H.* 4. *ca.* 14. & *anno*

anno 8. *Ed.* 4. *ca.* 2. & *anno* 7. *eiusdem, ca.* 14. & *anno* 13. *eiusdem, ca.* 3. & *a.* 8. *H.* 6. *ca.* 4. & *anno* 8. Ed. 4. *ca.* 3. & *anno* 3. *H.* 7. *ca.* 1. & 12. & *anno* 11. *eiusdem, ca.* 3. & *anno* 19. *eiusdem, cap.* 14. In the other signification, it betokeneth a deliuery of possession vnto those tenents, which hould of the king in *capite*, or in knights seruice: for the king by his prerogatiue hath *primier seysini* (or the first possession) of all lands and tenements so houlden of him. *anno* 52. H. 3. *cap.* 16. & *an.* 17. *Ed.* 2. *cap.* 3. that is, when any such tenent dyeth, the king foorthwith entreth, and holdeth it vntill the heire do his homage, and so pray his land to be deliuered vnto him. Which act in the king is called Liuerie: and liuerie in this signification is either generall or speciall. *Stawn. prærog. fol.* 12. & *cap.* 3. Liuerie generall seemeth to be that, which is made in general words, and therefore may easily be missued. Liuerie speciall is that, which containeth in it a pardon of ouersights committed by the tenent in sewing out his liuerie, by which pardon the missuing is dispensed with. *Stawnf. pag.* 67 *cap. Trauers.* 20. See the Institutes and grounds of the common lawe. *cap.* 30. of generall and speciall liueries. Liuerie in the third signification is the writte which lyeth for the heire to obtaine the possession or seisin of his lands at the kings handes: which see in *Fitz. nat. br. fol.* 155.

Liuerie of seisin (deliberatio seisinæ) is a deliuerie of possession of land or tenement, or other things corporeall, (for of things incorporeall no liuerie of seisin may be) vnto one that hath right or a probabilitie of right vnto them. For as *Bracton* saith: *Traditio debet esse vestita & non nuda, sc. quod traditione præcedat vera causa vel putatiua, qua transeat Dominicum. lib.* 2. *cap.* 18. *num* 3. *West parte prim. symbol. li.* 2. *sect.* 196. calleth this a ceremonie in the common lawe, vsed in the conueyance of lands or tenements, &c. where you may see the vsuall forme hereof particularly set downe, whereunto ioyne the new exposition of law tearmes.

Lieutenent. See *Liestenent.*

Lieutenent of the tower, seemeth to haue bene an officer vnder the Constable. *anno Henr.* 4. *cap.* 15.

Locus partitus, signifieth a diuision made betweene 2. townes or counties, to make triall in whether the land or place in question lieth. *Fleta lib.* 4. *cap.* 15. *num.* 1.

Locall (localis) signifieth in our common lawe, as much as tyed or annexed to a place certaine: Example: the thing is locall and annexed to the *Freehold.* *Kitchin fol.* 180. and againe in the same place: *An* action of trespasse for battery, &c. is transitorie and not locall: that is, not needfull that the place of the batterie should bee set downe as materiall in the declaration: or if it be set downe, that the defendant should trauerse the place set downe, by saying, he did not commit the batterie in the place mentioned in the declaration, and so auoide the action. *And* againe, *fol.* 230. the place is not locall: that is, not materiall to be set down in certaintie. *And* the gard of the person and of the landes differeth in this, because the person being transitorie, the lord may haue his *rauishment de garde*, before he be seised of him, but not of the land, because it is locall. *Perkins Graunts* 30.

Lobbe, is a great kinde of north sea fish. *anno* 31. *Ed.* 3. *stat.* 3. *cap.* 2.

Lodemanage, is the hire of a *Pilot* for conducting of a ship from one place to another.

Loichfish, as *Lob. Ling. Cod. anno* 31. *Ed.* 3. *stat.* 3. *cap.* 2.

Lode works, is one of the works belonging to the Stannaries in *Cornwall*: for the which reade *M. Camdens Britan*: in his title of *Cornwal. pa.* 119. See *Streme work.*

Lollards (*Lollardi*) were in accompt and reputation of those times, Heretiks that abounded heere in England, in the daies of *Edward* the third, and *Henry* the fifth. *anno* 2. *H.* 5. *cap.* 7. whereof *Weekleife* was the cheife, as *Stowe* saith in his *Annalls*: *pag.* 425. who by his report, went barefooted and baslely clothed, to wit in base russet garments downe to the heeles: they preached, and especially against *Monks* and other religious men. Of these reade more in him and others that writ of those times. The name *Lindwood* deriueth a *lolio: quia sicut lolium inficit segetes: sic Lollardi multociens inficiunt fideles simplices inter quos conuersantur. in ca. finali: de Hæreticis verbo Lollardiæ*: But *Tritemius* in his chronicle, deduceth the name from one *Gualter Lolhard* a *German* as the first author of that sect, liuing about the yeare of our redemption. 1315.

Lord (*Dominus*) by *M. Camdens* opinion, is a contract (of *Lafford*) which is the Danish word for *Dominus*. It is a word of honour with vs, and is vsed diuersly. Sometime being attributed to a man, that is noble by birth or creation, which sort are otherwise called Lords of the Parlament. Sometime to those that be so called by the courtesie of *England*, as all the sonnes of a Duke, or the eldest sonne of an Earle.

Earle. Sometime to men honorable by office, as lord chiefe Iustice, &c. and sometime to a meane man that hath fee, and so consequently the homage of tenents within his maner. For by his tenents he is called Lord, and by none other, and in some places, for distinction sake, he is called Landlord. It is vsed neuerthelesse by the Writers of the common lawe, most vsually in this signification. And so is it diuided into lord aboue, and lord mesn: lord mesn, is he that is owner of a maner, and by vertue thereof hath tenents holding of him in fee, and by copy of court rolle, and yet holdeth himselfe ouer of a superiour Lord: who is called lord aboue, or lord Paramount, *old nat. br. fol.* 79. Although I thinke none simply to be accounted lord Paramount, but the Prince: because all hold either mediately or immediatly of him, and he of none. In this signification I likewise reade Very lord, and Very tenent. *eod. fol.* 42. & *Broke titulo Heriot. num.* 1. where (I thinke) very lord, is he which is immediate Lord to his tenent: and him to be very tenent to that Lord, of whom he immediately holdeth. So that if there be lord aboue, lord mesn, and tenent, the lord aboue is not very lord to the tenent, nor the tenent very tenent to the lord aboue.

Lord in grosse. Fitz. nat. br. fol. 3. is he that is lord hauing noe maner, as the king in respect of his crown. *idem, f.* 5. *F.* See him also, *fol.* 8. *A. B.* where I finde a case wherein a priuate man is lord in grosse. *viz.* a man maketh a gift in tayle of all the land hee hath, to hold of him and dyeth: his heire hath but a Seignorie in grosse.

Lorimers. anno 1. R. 3. *cap.* 12. is one of the companies in *London*, tha makeht bits for bridles of horses and such like. The name seemeth to be taken from the latine (*lorum*) and is else where writen *Lorinors.*

Lotherwit, aliâs Leyerwit, is a libertie or priuiledge to take amends of him that defileth your bondwoman without licence, *Rastall:* exposition of words. It is an amends for lying with a bondwoman. *Saxon* in his description of England. *cap.* 11. Some thinke it should be rather writen (*Legerwit*) For (*Leger*) is the Saxon word for a bedde, or (*Logherwit*) of the old word (*Logher*) being of the same signification. See *Bloodwit* and *Lyerwit.*

Lusernes, See *Furre.*

Lushborow, is a base coine vsed in the daies of *King Ed.* the 3. coined beyōd *Seas* to the likenes of English money, and brought

brought in to deceiue the *King* and his subiects. To auoide the which it was made treason for any man wittingly to bring in any such. *an.25.Ed.3.stat.4.cap. secundo.*

M

M*Acegriefs.aliàs Macegrefs.* be such as willingly buie and sell stolen flesh, *Britton, cap. 29.fo.71.b. Cromptons Iustice of peace.fo.193.a.*

Magna assisa eligenda, is a writ directed to the Shyreeue, to summon foure lawsful knights before the Iustices of Assise, there vpon their oathes to chuse 12. knights of the vicenage, &c. to passe vpon the great assise betweene A. plaintife and B. defendant, &c. *Register originall, fol.* 8.*a.*

Magna Charta, called in English the great charter, is a charter conteining a number of lawes ordained the ninth yeare of *Henry* the third, and confirmed by *Edward* the first. The reason why it was tearmed *Magna charta*, was either for that it conteined the summe of all the writen lawes in England, or else that there was another Charter called the Charter of the Forest, established with it, which in quantitie was the lesser of the two. I reade *in Holinshed*, that King *Iohn* to appease his Barons, yelded to lawes or articles of gouernment much like to this great Charter, but wee nowe haue noe auncienter writen lawe, then this, which was thought to be so beneficall to the subiect, and a lawe of so great equitie in comparison of those, which were formerly in vse, that K. *Henry* the third was thought but hardly to yeld vnto it, and that to haue the fifteenth peny of all the moueable goods both of the spiritualtie and temporaltie throughout his realme. *Holinshed* in *Henry* the third. And though this Charter consist not of aboue 37. chapters or lawes: yet is it of such extent, as all the lawe wee haue, is thought in some sort to depend of it. *Polydorus* and *Holinshed, vbi supra.*

Mahim (*Mahemium*) commeth of the old French (*Mehaigne*) as *M. Skene* saith, *de verbo.signif.verbo Machanium*, and signifieth a corporal hurt, whereby a man looseth the vse of any member, that is or might bee any defence vnto him in batel. The Canonists call it *membri mutilationem*, as the eye, the hand, the foote, the scalpe of the head, his foretooth, or, as some say, of any finger of his hand, *Glanuile lib.14. ca. 7.* See

Bra-

Bracton at large, *lib.* 3. *tracta.* 2. *cap.* 24. *nu.* 3. and *Britton cap.* 25. and *Stawnf. pl. cor. lib. pri. ca.* 41. and the newe exposition of law Termes, and the Mirrour of Iustices, *cap. d'homicid.* The grand Custumarie of *Normandie, cap.* 6. calleth it *Mahaignium,* and defineth it to be *enormem læsionem.* All agree that it is the losse of a member, or the vse thereof. And *membrum,* as Cassan: *de consuetu: Burgund. pag.* 168. defineth it out of *Baldus, est pars corporis habens destinatam operationem in corpore.* where you may reade more of this point. But if you will see it largely discussed, look *Vgolinus de irregularitatibus, ca.* 4. §. 3. 4. 5. also read *M. Skene vbi supra.*

Mainour, aliàs Manour, aliàs Meinoure, seemeth to come of the French (*Manier.* i. *manu tractare, attrectare*) or els of (*Amener.* i. *abducere*). It signifieth in our common lawe, the thing that a theefe taketh away or stealeth: as to be taken with the *mainor. pl. cor fol.* 179. is to be taken with the thing stolen about him: and againe, *fol.* 194. It was presented that a theefe was deliuered to the Vicount together with the *Mainor:* & thirdly, *fol.* 186. If a man be indited that he feloniously stole the goods of another, where, in truth, they bee his owne goods, and the goods bee brought into the court as the manour, and it be demaunded of him, what hee saith to the goods, and he disclaime them: though he be quitted of the felonie, he shall loose the goods, and againe. *fol.* 149. if the defendant were taken with the manour, and the manour bee caried to the court, they in auncient times would arraine him vpon the manour, without any appeale or inditement. I find this word vsed in the *old. nat. br. fol.* 110. in this sort: where a man maketh a thing by *mainour,* or *leuying,* or *estopping,* in such case he shall haue Assise. where it signifieth handie labour, and is but an abbreuiation of *Main-ouvrey.*

Mainovre, see *Minouerye.*

Mainprise (*Manucaptio*) is compounded of two French words (*Main.* i. *manus*) & (*prins.* i. *captus*) which is a participle of the verbe) *prendre* .i. *capere, excipere, captare*) It signifieth in our common lawe, the taking or receiuing a man into friendly custody, that otherwise, is or might bee committed to the mercie of the prison, vpon securitie giuen for his forth comming at a day assigned: as to let one to mainprise. *old nat. br. fol.* 42. is to commit him to them, that vndertake his apparence at

 the

the time appointed. And they that do thus vndertake for any, are called *Mainperuouns*, because they do receiue him into their hands. *pl. cor. fol.* 178. Of this sort is the word (*Mainpernable*) which signifieth him that hath committed such an offence, as by law he may be thus bayled. For in many cases a man is not mainparnable: whereof see *Broke, titulo Mainprise, per totum.* and *Fitz. nat. br. fol.* 249. *& seqq. M. Manwood* in the first part of his Forest lawes. *pag.* 167. maketh a great difference betweene Bayle and Mainprise. For he that is mainprised (quoth he) is alwayes said to be at large, and to goe at his owne libertie out of ward, after the day is set to mainprise, vntill the day of his appearance, by reason of the said common summons or otherwise. But otherwise it is, where a man is let to bayle to foure or two men, by the lord Iustice in *eyre* of the Forest, vntill a certaine day. For there he is alwayes accounted by the lawe to be in their ward and custody for the time. And they may, if they will, keepe him in ward, or in prison all that time, or otherwise at their will. So that he that is so bayled, shall not be said by the lawe to be at large, or at his owne libertie. Thus farre *M. Manwood.* The myrror of Iustices maketh a difference also betweene pledges and mainpernours, saying, that pledges are more generall, & that mainpernours are bodie for bodie. *lib.* 2. *cap. de trespasse venial.* and *lib.* 3. *cap. des pledges & mainpernours.* When mainprises may be granted, and when not, see *Cromptons* Iustice of peace. *fol.* 136. *&c. vsque* 141. and *Lamberd. Eiren. lib.* 3. *cap.* 2. *pag.* 336. 337. 338. 339. 340. See also *Britton fol.* 73. *a. cap. Des pledges & mainpernours:* the author of the Myrror of Iustices saith, that pledges bee those, that bayle or redeeme any thing but the body of a man, and that mainpernours be those, that free the body of a man. And that pledges therefore belong properly to reall and mixt actions, and mainpernours to personall.

Maintenance (*manutentio vel manutenentia*) is a French word, and signifieth an vpholding of a cause or person, metaphorically drawne from the succouring of a young child, that learneth to goe, by ones hand. In our common lawe, it is vsed in the euill part, for him, that secondeth a cause depending in suite betweene others, either by lending of mony, or making friends for either partie, toward his help. *anno* 32. *Henr.* 8. *cap.* 9. And when a mans act in this kinde is by lawe accounted Maintenance,

nance, and when not, see *Broke, titulo Maintenance:* and Kitchin, *fol.* 202. & *seqq.* and *Fitz. nat. br. fol.* 172. and *Cromptons Iurisdict. fol.* 38. The writ that lyeth against a man for this offence, is likewise called *Maintenance.* Termes of the lawe. *verb. Maintenance.* Speciall maintenance Kitchin, *fol.* 204. seemeth to bee maintenance most properly so tearmed. Of this see *Cromptons* Iustice of peace. *fol.* 155.*b.* and the new booke of Entries. *verbo, Maintenance.* Maintenance, *vid. Nouos terminos Iuris.*

Make (*facere*) signifieth in the common lawe, to performe or execute: as to make his lawe, is to performe that lawe which he hath formerly bound himselfe vnto, that is, to cleare himselfe of an action commenced against him by his oath, and the oathes of his neighbours. *Old nat. br. fol.* 161. *Kitchin fol.* 192. which lawe seemeth to be borowed of the Feudists, who call these men that come to sweare for another in this case, *Sacramentales.* Of whom thus saith *Hotoman in verbis feudal. Sacramentales à sacramento* i. *iuramento dicebantur ii, qui quamuis rei, de qua ambigebatur, testes non fuissent, tamen ex eius, cuius res agebatur, animi sententia, in eadem qua ille verba iurabant: illius videlicet probitate & innocentia confisi. Nam tum demum adhibebantur, cùm testes nulli extarent.* See the rest. The formall words vsed by him that maketh his lawe, are commonly these. Heare O ye Iustices, that I doe not owe this summe of money demaunded, neither all nor any part thereof, in maner and forme declared, so helpe me God, and the contents of this booke. To make seruices or custome, is nothing else but to performe them. *Old. nat. br. fol.* 14. To make oath, is to take an oath.

Maletent, in the Statute called the Confirmation of the liberties of &c. *anno* 29. *Ed. prim. cap.* 7. is interpreteted to be a tolle of 40. shillings for euery sacke of wooll. *Stow* in his Annals calleth it a *Maletot. pag.* 461 See also the Statute (*de tallagio non concedendo*) *an.* 34. *eius. stat.* 5.

Malin. See *Marle.*

Manbote signifieth a pecuniary compensation for killing of a man. *Lambard* in his exposition of Saxon words. *verbo Æstimatio.* Of which reade Roger *Houeden* also, *in parte poster. suorum annal. fol.* 344. *a. b.*

Mandamus, is a writ, that lyeth after the yere and day, whereas in the meane time the writ called (*diem clausit extremum*) hath not bene sent out to the Excheatour, for the same purpose, for the which it should formerly haue bene sent forth. *Fitzh. nat.*

br. fol. 253. *B.* See *Diem clausit extremum.* *Mandamus* is also a charge to the shyreeue, to take into the kings hands, all the lands and tenements of the kings widowe, that against her oath formerly giuen, marieth without the kings consent. *Register. fol.* 295. *b.* See *Widow.*

Mandatum, is a commaundment iudiciall of the king or his Iustices, to haue any thing done for the dispatch of iustice, wherof you shall see diuersity in the table of the Register iudiciall. *verbo Mandatum.*

Maner (Manerium) seemeth to come of the French (*manoir* .i. *domicilium, habitatio*) *M. Skene. de verbo. significatione. verbo Manerium*, saith it is called *Manerium*, *quasi Manurium*, because it is laboured with handy worke by the Lord himselfe. It signifieth in our common law, a rule or gouernmēt, which a man hath ouer such as hould land within his fee. Touching the originall of these maners, it seemeth that in the beginning, there was a certaine compasse or circuit of ground, graunted by the king vnto some man of worth (as a Baron or such like) for him and his heires to dwell vpon, and to exercise some iurisdiction more or lesse within that compasse, as he thought good to graunt, performing him such seruices, and paying such yearely rent for the same, as he by his graunt required: and that afterward this great man parcelled his land to other meaner men, inioyning them againe such seruices and rents, as he thought good, and by that meanes, as he became tenent to the king, so the inferiours became tenents vnto him. See *Perkins Reseruations* 670. and *Andrew Horns* booke intituled the mirrour of Iustices *li.* 1. *ca. du. Roy Alfred.* See the definition of a Maner. *Fu.b. fol.* 18. And this course of benefiting or rewarding their nobles for good seruice, haue our kings borowed from the Emperours of Rome, or the *Lombard* kings, after they had setled themselues in *Italy*, as may well appeare by *Antonius Contius* in *methodo feudorum, c.* i. *de origine, & libris Feudorum.* And I finde that according to this our custome, all lands houlden in fee throughout Fraunce, are diuided into *Fiefz* and *arrierfiefz*: whereof the former are such as are immediatly graunted by the king, the secōd such as the kings feudataries doe againe graunt to others. *Gregorii Syntagm. lib. 6. ca.* 5. *nu.* 3. But the inconstancy of mans estate, and the mutability of time, hath brought to passe, that those great men, or their posterity, haue alienated these Mansions and lands so giuen them

them by their Prince, and others that had none, haue by ther welth purchased many of them: and againe that many for capitall offences haue forfeited them to the king, and that thereby they still remaine in the crowne, or are bestowed againe vpon others: so that at these daies many be in the hands of mean men, such as by their skill in lawe or phisicke, by merchaundize, grazing, or such other good husbandry, haue gathered welth, and inabled themselues to purchase them of those, that by discent receiued thē from their ancestors in greater aboundance, then wit to keepe them. But who so euer possesseth these maners, the liberty belonging vnto them is reall and prediall; and therefore remaineth still, though the owners be changed. In these daies a maner rather signifieth the Iurisdiction and royalty incorporeal, then the land or site. For a man may haue a maner in grosse (as the law termeth it) that is, the right and interest of a court Baron, with the perquisites thereunto belonging: and another or others haue euery foote of the land thereunto belonging. *Kitchin. fol. 4. Brooke hoc titulo per totum. Bracton, lib: 4. ca. 31. nu. 3.* diuideth *manerium, in capitale & non capitale.* See *Bracton lib. 5. tracta. 5. ca. 28. nu. pri.* See *Fee*: The new expositor of law terms saith, that Manour is a thing compounded of diuers things, as of a house, land earable, pasture, meadow, wood, rent, advouzen, court Baron, and such like. And this ought to be by long continuance of time, to the contrary whereof mans memory cannot discerne, &c.

Mansion (Mansio) as *Bracton* defineth it, *lib. 5. cap. 28. nu. pri.* is a dwelling, consisting of one or more houses without any neighbour. And yet he graunteth forthwith, that *Mansio Mansioni possit esse vicinata.* I finde it most commonly vsed for the lords cheife dwelling house within his fee, whether it haue neighbours adioyning or not, otherwise called the capitall mesuage. *Bracton. li. 2. c. 26.* or the cheife maner place. *Mansio* amongst the auncient Romans, was a place appointed for the lodging of the Prince or souldiers in their iourney, furnished with conuenient entertainement by the neighbours adioyning. And in this sence we reade *primam mansionem*, for the first nights lodging, and so in order. It is probable that this word *(Mansion)* doth in some construction signifie so much land, as *Beda* calleth *familiam* in his ecclesiasticall history. For *Master* Lambert in his explica. of Saxon words, *ver. Hida terra*, saith, that that which he calleth *femilum*, others sithence call *Manentem vel Mansam.* (*Mansus* and *Mansum*) I reade of in the *Feudists*, which as *Hotoman* saith, in *verbis feudalibus, est neque domus, neque area, neque hortus, sed ager certi modi ac mensura.* And againe, in *Commentariis feudorum, lib. p. tit. 4. vers. de* Manso. *Agri deserti & inculti certa mensura dabantur cultoribus quasi in emphyteusin, vt culti & meliorati, feudi iure a vasallis possiderentur. In contractu autem vasalli nonnunquam incrementum.*i. *meliorationem omnem sibi recipiebant, siue per culturam, siue per inædificationem ea melioratio fieret, &c.* And *Cassanæus de consuet. Burg. pag.* 1195. defineth it thus: *Mansus est, quantum quis cum vno pari boum laborare possit.* prouing it out of *Bartolus, in li. si ita. ff. de auro & argen. legato: in fine legis.* Reade *M. Skene de verbo. sign. verbo* Mansus. I reade the latine word (*Mansia*) in the same signification, as namely in the charter graunted by King *Kanulphus* to *Ruchin* the abbot of *Abingdon*, which Sir *Edward Cooke* setteh downe in his booke *de iure Regis ecclesiastico.*

Manslaughter (*Homicidium*) is the vnlawfull killing of a man, without prepensed malice: as when two, that formerly meant no harme one to the other, meet togither, and vpon some sodaine occasion falling out, the one killeth the other. *West. par. 2. symb. titulo Inditements. sect. 44.* It differeth from murder, because it is not done with foregoing malice: & from chauncemedly, because it hath a presēt intēt to kill. And this is felony, but admitteth clergie for the first time. *Stawnf. pl. cor. lib. 1. cap. 9.* and *Britton ca. 9.* It is confounded with murder in the statute, *anno* 28. *Ed. 3. ca.* 11.

Mantyle (*Mantile*) commeth of the French (*Manteau*) and signifieth with vs a long roabe, *anno 24. Hen. 8. cap.* 13.

Manucaptio, is a writ that lyeth for a man, who taken for supition of felony, and offering sufficient Bayle for his appearance, cannot be admitted thereunto by the *Shyreeue*, or other hauing power to let to mainprise. *Fitzh. nat. br. fol.* 249. See *Mainprise*. How diuersly it is vsed, see the *Register originall*, in the table.

Manuel (*Manualis*) is a thing whereof present profit may be made. *Staunf. prærogat. fol.* 54. And a thing not manuell is that, whereof no present profit may be made, but hereafter, when it falleth, *ibid.*

Manumission (*Manumissio*) is a freeing of a villein or slaue out of his bondage. The forme of

this

this in the time of the Conquerour, M.*Lamb.* in his *αρχαιονομία.* *fol.*126. fetteth downe in these words: *Si quis velit seruum suum liberum facere, tradat eum vicecomiti, per manum dexteram, in pleno comitatu, & quietum illum clamare debet à iugo seruitutis suæ per manumissionem: & ostendat ei liberas portas, & vias, & tradat illi libera arma, scilicet lanceam & gladium: & deinde liber homo efficitur.* Some also were wont to be manumitted by charter of manumission. *vide* Brooke, *titulo Villenage fol.* 305. The newe expositour of lawe Termes maketh two kinds of manumission: one expressed, an another implied. Manumissiō expressed is, when the Lord maketh a deede to his villein to infranchise him by this worde (*Manumittere*) The maner of manumitting in old time was thus: The Lord in presēce of his neighbours tooke the bondman by the head, saying: I will that this man be free, and therewith shoued him forward out of his hands. Manumission implied, is, when the Lord maketh an obligation for paiment of mony to him at a certaine day, or sueweth him, where he might enter without suite, or granteth him an annuitie, or leaseth land vnto him by deede, for yeeres, or for life, and such like.

Manutenentia, is the writ vsed in case of maintenance, *Register originall, fol.* 182. & 189. See *Maintenance.*

Marches (*Marchia*) be the bounds and limits betweene vs and *Wales*, or betweene vs and *Scotland. anno.* 24. *Henry* 8. *cap.* 9. *Camd. pag.* 453. & 606. and the marches of Scotlād are deuided into west and midle marches *anno* 4. *H.* 5. *ca.* 7. & *anno* 22. *Ed.* 4. *cap.* 8. It seemeth to bee borowed from the German (*March.* i. *limes*) *Camd.* *Britan. pag.* 27. or it may be from the French (*Marque.* i. *signum*) being the notorious distinction of two diuers countries or territories. It is vsed in the statute *anno* 24 *Hen.* 8. *ca.* 12. generally for the precincts of the Kings dominions.

Marchers, be the noble men dwelling on the Marches of *Wales* or *Scotland:* who in times past (as M. *Camden* saith, *pag.* 453.) had their priuate lawes, much like as if they had beene Kings, which now be worne out. Of these Marchers you may reade, *anno* 2. *H.* 4. *cap.* 18. & *anno* 26. *Hen.* 8. *cap.* 6. & *anno* 1. *Ed.* 6. *cap.* 10. where they are called Lord Marchers. See *anno* 27. *Hen.* 8. *cap.* 26. howe these were extinguished.

Mareshall (*Mariscallus*) is a French word, signifying as much

as

as *Tribunus Celerum*, or *Tribunus militum* with the auncient Romanes, or Πολέμαρχος with the Grecians, or ἵππαρχος. *Tiraquel. de Nobilitate, ca.* 8. *p.* 42. *nu.* 17. The french word may seeme also (among many other that they haue, to proceede from the German M*arschalk*. i. *equitum magister*. which H*otoman in verbis feudalibus, verbo* M*arschalkus*, deriueth from the old word (*March*) signifiing a house, with whome agreeth L*upanus*, *de Magistratibus Franciæ, lib. pri. ca. Marschallus*. Others make it of these two Saxon words. (*Mar*. i. *equus* and *scalch*. i. *præfectus*) or as *M. Verstegan* saith, from (*Mare*) the generall appellation of all horses, as (*hors*) is now in Englishe, and (*Scalc*) which, in the auncient language of the Netherlanders, he affirmeth to signifie a kind of seruant, as *Scalco*, doth at this day among the Italians, being originally a *Dutch* word. with vs there be diuers officers of this name: but one most noble of all the rest, who is called *Lord* or *Earle* Marshall of England, of whome mention is made in diuers statutes, as *anno.* 1. *H.* 4. *ca.* 7. & 14. & *anno.* 13. *Rich.* 2. *ca.* 2. His office consisteth especially in maters of warre and armes, as well with vs as in other countries. whereof you may reade in L*upanus vbi supra.* and *Tilius. li.* 2. *ca. de Conestabili, Mariscallo. &c.* But he that will knowe the office of our Lord Marshall, had neede beside the fewe statutes which concerne him, to read his commission, and also to haue acces to the Heradls, who out of their antiquities are able to discouer much, that by prescription belongeth vnto this office. The next to this is the Marshal of the Kings house, whose especiall authoritie is, according to *Britton* and M. *Gwin* in the preface to his reading, in the Kings place to heare and determine all plees of the Crowne, and to punish faults committed within the verge, & to heare and determine suites betweene those of the kings houshold, and others within the verge. *Cromptons Iurisdict. fol.* 102. of him you may reade *Fitzh. nat. br. fol.* 241. *B.* and *anno.* 18. *Ed.* 3. *statut.* 2. *ca.* 7. & *anno* 27. *Ed.* 3. *stat.* 2. *c.* 6. & *an.* 2. *H.* 4. *c.* 23. & *a.* 15. *H.* 6. *c.* 1. *Fleta* saith, that the office of the Marshall of the kings house belongeth to the Earle of *Northf.* in fee, and that he may appoint (with the Kings consent) a Knight vnder him to execute the office. which office he also describeth to be especially to execute the iudgements & decrees of the Steward, & to haue the keeping of the prisoners. *li.* 2. *cap.* 4. and read farder of his office in the 5. chapter of of the said booke, which is to dispose of the Lodging in the Kings houshold vnder the Chamberlaine, and to cleere the Verge of strumpets, &c. *anno 5. Hen. 3. statut. 5.* Then be there other inferiour officers of this name: as Marshall of the Iustices in *Eyre, anno 3. Ed. 1. ca. 19.* Marshall of the Kings bench, *anno 5. Ed. 3. ca. 8.* and this is he which hath the custodie of the prison, called the Kings bench in *Southwarke. Fitzh. nat. br. fol.* 251. I. And these inferiour Marshalls be either *ad placitum*, or in fee, *Kitchin. fol.* 143. I finde also in *Fleta li. 2. ca. 15.* mention of a Marshall of the *Kings* hall, whose office is, when the tables be prepared and clothes laide, to call out both those of the houshold and straungers, according to their worth, and decently to place them, to reiect vnworthy persons, to knowe the number of the hall, and to testifie it at the next accompt, to see dogs kept out, to saue the almes from filching, to see silence kept, and euery man competently serued with meate and drinke, and when the courte remoueth, to appointe euery one of the houshold his lodging. There is also a Marshall of the eschequer. *anno. 51. H. 3. sta. 5.* to whome the courte committeth the custody of the kings debters during the terme time, to the end they may be farder imprisoned, if they cleere not their debts. He also assigneth Shyreeues, eschetators, customers, and collectors, their auditours before whome they shall accompt. He hath all inquisitions taken before escheators *virtute officii*, deliuered vnto him, to be deliuered by him to the treasurers Remembrancer.

Mareshalsee (*Marescaltia*) is the Court of the Marshall or (word for word) the seate of the *Marshall*, of whome see *Cromptons Iurisdict. fol.* 102. It is also vsed for the prison in *Southwarke*, the reason whereof may be, because the Marshall of the kings house was wont perhaps to sit there in iudgment. See the statute *anno 9. R. 2. cap. 5. & anno 2. Hen. 4. ca. 23.*

Martiall lawe, is the law that dependeth vpon the voice of the king, or the kings leiuetenent in warres. For how be it, the king for the indifferent and equall temper of lawes to all his subiects, doe not in time of peace make any lawes but by the consent of the three estates in Parlament: yet in warres by reason of great daungers rising of small occasions, he vseth absolute power: in so much as his word goeth for law. And this is called Martiall law. *Smith de repub: Angl: li. 2. c. 3.* See *Law of armes.*

Mariage (*Maritagium*) signifieth not onely the coupling together of man and wife, but also the interest of bestowing a ward or a widow in mariage. *Magna charta, ca: 6. anno 9. He. 3.* and *Bracton lib. 2. ca. 3.* and also it signifieth land giuen in mariage, *Bracton li. 2. ca. 34. & 39.* And in this signification the same authour saith, that *Maritagium est aut liberum aut seruitio obligatum. li. 2. ca. 7. nu. 3. & 4. Liberum maritagium dicitur, vbi donator vult, quòd terra sic data, quieta sit & libera ab omni seculari seruitio, quod ad Dominum feudi possit pertinere: et ita quòd ille, cui sic data fuerit, nullum omninò inde faciat seruitium vsq; ad tertium hæredem, & vsq; ad quartum gradum: ita quòd tertius heres sit inclusivus.* See the rest. See also *Skene de verbo. significatione, verbo Maritagium,* who is worth the reading.

Maritagio amisso per defaltam, is a writ for the tenent in frank mariage, to recouer lands, &c. whereof he is deforced by another. *Regist. fol. 171.*

Maritagio forisfacto, is a writ. See *Forisfactura Maritagii.*

Marke, (merca) commeth of the Saxon *(Mearc)* which signifieth a peece of mony worth thirty siluer pence. *Lamb. explicat.* of *Saxon* words. *verbo, Mancusa:* what it now signifieth in our coyne euery man knoweth. But in auncient times I find a merke of gold, which was the quantitie of eight ounces. *Stowes annals. pag. 32.* and againe, *pag. 691.* 12. merkes of golde Troy weight, the which was 200. pounds of English mony, after which rate euery merke valued 16. pounds, 13. shillings, 4. pence. *M. Skene de verbor. signific. verbo, Merke.* saith, that *in tractatu de ponderibus & mensuris,* a Mercke signifieth an ounce weight, or halfe a pound, wherof the dramme is the eighth part, like as the ounce is the eighth part of a marcke: citing *Cassanæus de consuet. Burgund. Rub. prim. §. 7. verbo. Solz Turnoys. hiis verbis. Solidus (inquit) in iure capitur pro auro, quorum 72. faciunt libram auri, & duodecim vnciæ faciunt libram, & octo vnciæ mercā.*

Market (mercatus) commeth of the French (*marche. i. emporium, forum nundinarium*) it signifieth with vs, the same thing, and also the liberty or priuiledge whereby a towne is enabled to keepe a market. *Oldnat. br. fol.* 149. So doth *Bracton* vse it, *lib. 2. cap. 24. num. 6. & lib. 4. cap. 46.* where he sheweth, that one market ought to bee distant from another *sex leucas & dimidiam, & tertiam partem dimidiæ.* The reason thereof both he and *Fleta* giueth in these wordes: *Quia omnes rationabiles dietæ constant*

ſtant ex 20. milliaribus. Diuidatur ergo dieta in tres partes: prima autē matutina detur euntibus verſus mercatum: ſecunda detur ad emendum & vendendum: quæ quidem ſufficere debet omnibus, niſi ſint forte mercatores ſtatarii qui merces depoſuerint & expoſuerint venales, quibus neceſſaria erit prolixior mora in mercatu: & tertia pars relinquitur redeuntibus de mercatu ad propria. Et quæ quidem omnia neceſſe erit facere de die, non de nocte, propter inſidias & incurſum latronum, vt omnia ſint in tuto, &c. lib. 4. cap. 28. §. Item refert.

Marle, is a kind of ſtone or chalke, which men in diuers countries of this Realme, caſt vpon their land to make it the more fertile. It is ſome where called *Malm. anno* 17. *Edward*. 4. *cap*. 4.

Marque, ſeemeth to bee a French word ſignifying *notam, vel ſignum*, or elſe to come from the German (*march*. i. *limes*) it ſignifieth in the auncient ſtatutes of our land, as much as repriſals, as *anno* 4. *H*. 5. *cap*. 7. Marques and Repriſals are vſed as *Synonyma*. And leters of Marque are found in the ſame ſignification in the ſame chapter. The reaſon may be, becauſe the griefes wherevpon theſe leters are ſought and graunted, are commonly giuen about the bounds and limits of euery contrey: or at leaſt the remedie for the ſame is likeſt there to bee had by ſome ſodaine inrode, & happing of ſuch recompence of the iniurie receiued, as may moſt conueniently be lighted vpon. See *Repriſals*. See *Marches*.

Marquis (*Marchio*) by the opinion of *Hotom. verbo Marchio, in verbis feudalibus*, commeth of the *German* March. i. *limes*, ſignifiing originally as much as (*Cuſtos limitis*) or (*Comes & præfectus limitis*) of theſe *Zaſius* thus writeth: *de Marchione nihil compertū eſt, niſi quod Gothicum vocabulum putamus*. And afterward thus: *Huiuſmodi Marchionum* (*ſiue vt nos appellamus*) *Margraphiorum origo in limitaneos, præpoſitos, ſiue duces referenda: Margraphii dicti quod limitibus, quos vulgò marken appellamus, graphii, id eſt præpoſiti fuerunt, &c*. For in thoſe teritories, that haue naturally noe bounds of great ſtrength or defence, there is neede of wiſe and ſtout men toward their borders, for the keeping out of neighbour enemies. But here in England though we haue a Lord warden of the marches northward, and a warden of the cinque ports toward the ſouth eaſt, and were wont to haue Lo. *Marchers* between vs and Wales, that ſerued this turne, yet thoſe which we call Marquiſes, are lords of more dignity, without any ſuch charge: and are in honour and accompt next vnto *Dukes*. At this day I know but one in *England*, and that is the *Marquis* of *Winchester*, being of that noble familie of the *Powlets*. See *Cassaneus de consuetud. Burg. pag.* 15.

Marrow, was a lawyer of great accompt, that liued in *Henry* the seuenth his daies, whose learned readings are extant, but not in print. *Lamb*. Eiren. *li. pri. cap.* 1.

Marterns, see *Furre*.

Master of the Rols (*Magister rotulorum*) is an Assistāt vnto the Lord Chauncelour of England in the high court of Chauncery, and in his absence heareth causes there, and giueth orders. *Crompt. Iurisd. fol.* 41. His title in his patent (as I haue heard) is *Clericus paruæ bagæ, custos rotulorum & domus conuersorum*. This *domus conuersorum*, is the place where the rols are kept, so called because the Iewes in auncient times, as they were any of them brought to christianity, were bestowed in that house separatly from the rest of their nation. But his office seemeth originally to haue sprong, from the safe keeping of the Roules or records of inditements passed in the kings courts, and many other things. He is called clerke of the rols, *anno* 12. *R. 2. ca. 2.* and in *Fortescue* his booke, *cap.* 24. and no where master of the rols, vntil *anno* 11. *Hen. 7. cap.* 20. and yet *anno* 11. *eiusdem, cap.* 25. he is also called clerk. In which respect, *Sir Thomas Smith, li. 2. ca.* 10. *de Repub. Angl.* well saith that he might not vnfitly be called (*Custos Archiuorum*). He seemeth to haue the bestowing of the offices of the sixe clerks. *anno* 14. & 15. *Hen. 8. cap.* 8.

Master of the mint, *anno* 2. *Hen. 6. cap.* 14. he is now called the Warden of the mint, whose office, see in *Mint*.

Master of the court of Wards and Liueries, is the cheife and principall officer of the court of wards and liueries, named and assigned by the king, to whose custodie the seale of the court is committed. He at the entring vpon his office, taketh an oath before the Lord Chauncelour of England, well and truly to serue the King in his office, to minister equal iustice to rich & poore, to the best of his cunning, witte, and power, diligently to procure all things, which may honestly and iustly be to the kings aduātage and profit, and to the augmentation of the rights and prerogatiue of the crowne, truly to vse the kings seale appointed to his office, to endeauour to the vttermost of his power, to see the king iustly aunswered of all such profits, rents, reuenewes, and issues, as shall yearely rise, grow, or be due to the king in his office from time to time, to deliuer with speed such as haue to do before him, not to take or receiue of any person any gift or reward in any case or mater depending before him, or wherein the king shall be party, whereby any preiudice, losse, hinderance, or disherison shall be or grow to the king, *a.33.H.8.c.33.*

Master of the horse, is he that hath the rule and charge of the kings stable, being an office of high accompt, and alwaies bestowed vpon some Noble man both valiant and wise. This Officer vnder the Emperours of *Rome*, was called (*comes sacri stabuli.*) The Master of the horse is mentioned. *anno 39. Eliz. cap. 7. & anno prim. Ed. 6. cap. 5.*

Master of the posts, is an Officer of the Kings court, that hath the appointing, placing, and displacing of all such through *England*, as prouide post horse for the speedie passing of the kings messages and other businesse, in the through-fayre townes where they dwell: as also to see that they keepe a certaine number of conuenient horses of their owne, and when occasion is, that they prouide others, wherewith to furnish such, as haue warrant from him to take post horses, either from or to the seas, or other borders, or places within the Realme. He likewise hath the care to pay them their wages, and make their allowance accordingly, as he shall thinke meete. This officer is mentioned, *anno 2. Ed. 6. cap. 3.*

Master of the armorie, is he that hath the care and ouersight of his Maiesties armour for his person or horses, or any other prouision or store thereof in any standing Armories: with command, and placing or displacing of all inferiour Officers thereunto appertaining. Mention is made of him. *anno 39. Eliz. cap. 7.*

Master of the Iewel house, is an Officer in the Kings houshould, of great credit, beeing allowed bouge of court, that is, diet for himselfe and the inferiour Officers. *viz.* Clerks of the Iewell house, and a speciall lodging or chamber in court, hauing charge of all plate of gold, of siluer double or parcell guilt, vsed or occupied for the Kings or Queenes board, or to any Officer of accompt attendant in court, and of all plate remaining in the Tower of *London*, of cheynes and loose Iewels not fixed to any garment. Mention is made of this Officer. *anno 39. Eliz. cap. 7.*

Master of the Kings houshould, (*magister hospitii*) is in his iust title called grand Master of the kings

Kings houſhould, and beareth the ſame office that he did, that was wont to be called *Lord Steward* of the kings moſt honorable houſhould. *anno 32. H. 8. ca. 39.* Whereby it appeareth, that the name of this Officer was then chaunged, and *Charles* Duke of *Suffolke*, Preſident of the Kings Councell, then enioying that office, was ſo to be called euer after, ſo long as he ſhould poſſeſſe that office.

Maſter of the Ordinance. anno 39. El. cap. 7. is a great Officer, to whoſe care all the Kings Ordinance and Artillerie is committed, being ſome great man of the Realme, and expert in marſhall affaires.

Maſter of the Chauncery (*Magiſter Cancellariæ*) is an aſſiſtant in Chauncerie to the Lord Chaunceler or Lord Keeper of the broad ſeale in maters of iudgement. Of theſe there be ſome ordinarie, and ſome extraordinarie: of ordinarie there be twelue in number, whereof ſome ſit in court euery day thorough each Terme, and haue committed vnto them (at the Lord Chauncelers diſcretion) the interlocutorie report, and ſometimes the finall determination of cauſes there depending.

Maſter of the Kings muſters, is a martiall officer in all royall armies moſt neceſſarie, as well for the maintaining of the forces complete, well armed and treined, as alſo for preuention of ſuch fraudes, as otherwiſe may exceedingly waſte the *Princes* treaſure, and extreamly weaken the forces. He hath the ouerſight of all the captaines and bands, and ought to haue at the beginning deliuered vnto him by the Lord Generall, perfect liſts and rolles of all the forces both horſe and foot, Officers, &c. with the rates of their allowances ſigned by the Lord Generall, for his direction and diſcharge, in ſignifying warrants for their full pay. This Officer is mentioned in the ſtatue, *anno 2. Ed. 6. cap. 2.* and *Muſter maſter generall, anno* 35. *Eliz. cap.* 4. who ſo deſireth to reade more of him let him haue recourſe to *Maſter Digs his Stratioticos.*

Maſter of the Wardrobe (*magiſter garderobæ*) is a great and principall officer in Court, hauing his habitation and dwelling houſe belonging to that office, called the *Wardrobe* neere P*uddle-wharfe* in *London*. He hath the charge and cuſtodie of all former Kings and Queenes auncient robes, remaining in the Tower of *London*, and all hangings of Arras, Tapeſtrie, or the like, for his Maieſties houſes, with

with the bedding remaining in ſtanding wardrobes, as *Hampton* court, *Richmond,&c.* He hath alſo the charging and deliuering out of all either Veluet or Scarlet allowed for liueries, to any of his Maieſties ſeruants of the priuie chamber, or others. *Mention* is made of this officer. *anno.* 39. *Eliz.ca.*7.

Mater *in deede, and mater of record*, are ſaid to differ. *old.nat. br.fol.* 19. where mater in deede, ſeemeth to be nothing elſe, but a truth to be prooued, though not by any Record: and mater of Record, is that which may be proued by ſome Record. For example, if a man be ſiewed to an exigent, during the time he was in the kings warres, this is mater in deede, and not mater of record. And therefore (ſaith the booke) he that will alledge this for himſelfe, muſt come, before the *Scire facias* for execution be awarded againſt him. For after that, nothing will ſerue but mater of Record; that is, ſome errour in the proceſſe appearing vpon the Record. *Kitchin fol.* 216. maketh alſo a difference betweene mater of Record, and a ſpecialitie, and nude mater; where he ſaith, that nude mater is not of ſo high nature, as either a mater of Record or a ſpeciality, otherwiſe there called mater in deede; which maketh mee to thinke, that nude mater is a naked allegation of a thing done, to be proued only by witneſſes, and not either by Record, or other ſpeciality in writing vnder ſeale.

M*auger*, is ſhuffled vp of two French words (*Mal*) and (*Gre*) *id eſt, animo iniquo*) it ſignifieth with vs as much as in deſpight, or in deſpight of ones teeth. as the wife mauger the huſbande, *Litleton fol.* 124. that is, whether the huſbund will or not.

M*eane* (*Medius*) ſignifieth the middle betweene two extreames, and that either in time or dignitie. Example of the firſt: His action was meane betwixt the diſſeiſin made to him and his recouerie: that is in the *interim.* Of the ſecond there is Lord Meane and Tenent. See *Meſn.*

M*eaſe* (*Meſuagium*) ſeemeth to come of the French (*Maiſon*) or rather (*Meix*) which word I finde in *Caſſanæus de conſuetu. Burgund.pag.* 1195. and interpreted by him *Manſus:* what *Manſus* is, ſee *Manſiõ.* It ſignifieth a houſe. *Kitchin fol.* 239. and *Fitzb.nat.br. fol.* 2.C. See *Meſuage.*

M*ed'eſe. Cromptons Iuſtice of peace, fol.* 193. is that which *Bracton* calleth (*medletum*) *li.* 3. *tract.* 2. *ca.* 35. It ſeemeth to ſignifie quarels, ſcuffling, or brawling, & to be deriued from the French

meſ-

(*mesler*).i. *miscere,turbare*

Meere(*Merus*) though an Adiectiue,yet is it vsed for a substantine, signifiing meere right. *Owld nat. br. fol.* 2. in these words. And knowe yee, that this writte hath but two issues: that is to say, ioyning the mise vpon the meere: And that is, to put himselfe in the great assise of our Soueraingе Lord the King, or to ioyne battell. *See Mise.*

Mesurement . See *Admesurement.*

Medietas linguæ, signifieth an enquest empaneled vpon any cause ,wereof the one halfe consisteth of Denizens, the other of straungers . It is called in English the halfe tongue, and is vsed in plees , wherein the one party is a straunger, the other a denizen. See the statute, *anno* 28. *Ed*.3.*ca*.13.*&*.*anno*, 27. *eiusdem,statu*: 2.*ca*.8. commonly called the statute of the Staple. *& anno*.8. H.6.*ca*.29. *&*.*anno* .2. *He*.5.*ca*.3.*&*.*anno*. 11. *He*.7.*ca*. 21.*&*. *anno*.1.*&*.2. *Phi*. *&*. *Mar*. *ca*.8. And before the first of these statutes was made, this was wonte to be obteined of the King by graunt made to any company of straungers, as *Lombards, Almaines, &c. Stawnf.pl. cor.lib*.3.*ca*.7.

Medio acquietando, is a writ iudiciall,to distraine a lord for the acquiting of a meane Lord from a rent, which he formerly acknowledgeth in court not to belong vnto him. *Register iudiciall,fol*. 29. *b*.

Melius inquirendo, is a writ that lyeth for a second inquiry, as what lands and tenements a man dyed seised of, where partiall dealing is suspected vpon the writ, *Diem clausit extremum. Fitzh. nat. br. fol*. 255.

Merchenlage, was one of the three sorts of lawes,out of which the Conquerour framed lawes vnto vs,mingled with those of *Normandy*. *Camd. Britan. pag*.94. who also,*pag*. 103. sheweth that in the yeare of our lord 1016. this land was diuided into three parts, whereof the west *Saxons* had one, gouerning it by the lawes called West *Saxon* lawes, and that conteined these nine shyres,*Kent*, *Southsex*,*Southrey*, *Barkeshire*, *Hamshire* , *Wilshire*. *Somerset*, *Dorset* and *Deuonshire*. the second by the *Danes*, which was gouerned by the lawes called Denelage, and that conteined these fifteene shires, *Yorke*, *Darby*, *Notingham*, *Leycester*, *Lincolne*, *Northampton*, *Bedford*, *Buckingham*, *Hertford*, *Essex*, *Midlesex*, *Northf. Southf. Cambridge*, *Huntington*. The third was possessed and gouerned by the *Mercians*, whose lawe was called *Merchenlage*. which were these eight.

eight, *Glocester, Worcester, Hereford, Warwicke, Oxenford, Chester, Salop*, and *Stafford*. See *Lawe*.

Mercy (Misericordia) signifieth the arbitrement or discretion of the King or Lord, in punishing any offence, not directly censured by the law. As to be in the grieuous mercie of the king. *anno* 11. *H.* 6. *cap.* 6. is to be in hazard of a great penaltie. See *Misericordia*.

Measondue, (domus Dei) commeth of the French *(maison de dieu)* by which names diuers Hospitals are named. You find the word, *anno* 2. *&* 3. *Philip. & Mar. cap.* 23. *in fine*.

Mese, See *Mease*.

Mesn (medius) seemeth to come from the French *(mainsnè. i. minor natu)* it signifieth in our common lawe, him that is lord of a maner, and thereby hath tenents holding of him, yet holding himselfe of a superiour Lord. And therefore it seemeth not absurdly to be drawne from the French *(mainsnè)* because the Lordship is created after the higher, whereof he holdeth. Mesn also signifieth a writ, which lyeth where there is Lord, mesn, and tenent, the tenent holding of the mesn by the same seruices, whereby the mesn holdeth of the Lord, and the tenent of the mesn is distrained by the superiour lord, for that his seruice or rent, which is due to the mesn. *Fitz. nat. br. fol.* 135. See *Mesnaltie*.

Mesnaltie (medietas) commeth of Mesn, and signifieth nothing but the right of the mesn: as, the mesnaltie is extinct. *old nat. br. fol.* 44. if the mesnalty descend of the tenent. *Kitchin fol.* 147. For farder vnderstanding wherof, take these words out of the Custumarie of Norm. *Medietate tenentur feuda, quando aliqua persona intervenit inter Dominum & tenentes. Et hoc modo tenent omnes post nati, mediante ante nato.*

Messenger of the Exchequer, is an Officer there, of which sorte there be foure in that court, that be Pursuyvants attending the lord Treasurer, to cary his leters and precepts. See *Pursuyvant*.

Mesuage (mesuagium) is a dwelling house. *West part.* 2. *symbol. titulo. Fines. sect.* 26. But by the name of a mesuage may passe also a Curtilage, a garden, an orchard, a doue house, a shoppe, a mill, as parcell of an house, as he himselfe confirmeth out of *Bracton. lib.* 5. *cap.* 28. *sect. prim.* and *Plowden fol.* 199. 170. 171. and of himselfe he auoucheth the like of a cotage, a tost, a chamber, a celler, &c. yet may they be demaunded by their single names. *Mesuagium* in Scotland, signifieth the principall dwelling place or house within a Barony, which in our land is called a maner-house. *Skene de verb. significat. verbo*, *Mesuagium*, where he citeth *Valentine Leigh*, that in his booke of Suruey he affirmeth *Mesuagium* to be the tenement or land earable, and the dwelling house or place, or court hall thereof, to be called the site, in Latine called *Situs*.

Mile (*milliare*) is a quantitie of a thousand paces, otherwise described to containe eight furlongs, and euery furlong to conteine forty lugs or poles, and euery lugge or pole to containe 16. foote and a halfe. *anno* 35. *El. cap.* 6.

Mildernix. anno 1. *Iacob. cap.* 24.

Mindbruch, is hurting of honour and worship. *Saxon* in his description of *Engl. cap.* 71.

Miniuer. See *Furre*.

Minouery. anno 7. R. 2. *cap.* 4. seemeth to be compounded of two French words (*main.* i. *manus* and (*ouvrer.* i. *operari*) and to signifie some trespasse or offence committed by a mans handie worke in the Forest, as an engyn to catch Deere. *Britton* vseth the verbe (*Meinoverer*) for to occupie and manure land. *cap.* 40. and *cap.* 62. *main-ovre*, for handy-worke. It is not vnlike, that our English (*manure*) is abbreuiated of the French.

Mint, commeth of the Germane word, (*meunk.* i. *pecunia, moneta*) and it signifieth with vs, the place where the kings coyne is formed, be it gold or siluer, which is at this present, and long hath bene, the Tower of London, though it appeare by diuers stories, and other antiquities, that in auncient times the mint hath bene allso at *Caleis, an.* 21. R. 2. *cap.* 16. *& anno* 9 *Hen.* 5. *stat.* 5. *cap.* 5. The Officers belonging to the mint, haue not bene alwaies alike. *At* this present they seeme to be these: The Warden, who is the chiefe of the rest, and is by his office to receiue the siluer of the Goldsmiths, and to pay them for it, and to ouersee all the rest belonging to this functiõ. His fee is an hundred pounds *per annum*. The master-worker, who receiueth the siluer from the Warden, causeth it to be melted, and deliuereth it to the moniers, and taketh it from them againe, when it is made. His allowance is not any set fee, but according to the pound weight. The third, is the Controller, who is to see that the mony be made to the iust assise, to ouersee the officers, and controll them, if the money be not as it ought to be: his fee is 100. merkes *per annum*. Then is the Master of the *Assaye*, who weigheth the siluer, and seeth whether it be according to standard: his yerely fee is also an hundred merkes. Then is the *Auditour* to take the accompts, and make them vp Auditor-like. Then is the *Surueyor* of the melting, who is to see the siluer cast out, and not to be altered after it is deliuered to the melter: which is after the Assay-master hath made triall of it. Then is the *Clerke* of the Irons, who seeth that the Irons be cleane, and fit to worke with. Then the Grauer, who graueth the stampes for the monies. Then the *Smyters* of Irons, who after they be grauen, smiteth them vpon the money. Then the *Melters*, that melt the Bullion, before it come to the coyning. Thē the Blanchers, who do aneale, boyle, and cleanse the money. The Porter, who keepeth the gate of the mint. The Prouost of the mint, who is to prouide for all the monyers, and to ouersee them. *Lastly*, the monyers, who are some to sheere the money, some to forge it, some to beate it abroade, some to round it, some to stampe or coyn it. Their wages is not by the day or yeare, but vncertaine, according to the waight of the money coyned by them. *Other* officers that haue bene in former time, are said nowe to bee out of vse.

Misauenture, or *misaduenture*, commeth neere the French (*mesaduenture* .i. *infortunium*.) In our common law, it hath an especiall signification for the killing of a man, partly by negligence, and partly by chaunce. As if one thinking no harme, dissolutely throweth a stone, where with he killeth another: or shooteth an arrow, &c. For in this case he committeth not felony, but onely looseth his goods, and hath pardon of course for his life. *Stawn. pl. cor. li. 1. ca.* 8. *Britton ca.* 7. distinguisheth betweene *Auenture* and *misauenture*. *Auenture* he maketh to be meere chaunce, as if a man being vpon or neere the water, be taken with some sodaine sicknes, and so fall in, and is drowned, or into the fire, and be burned to death. *Misauenture* he maketh, where a man commeth to his death by some outward violence, as the fall of a tree, or of a gate, the running of a cartwheele, the stroke of a horse, or such like. So that *misauenture in Stawnfords opinione*, is construed somewhat more largely, then *Britton* vnderstandeth it. *West parte.* 2. *Symbol. titulo Inditement, sect.* 48. maketh homicide casuall, to be meerely casuall or mixt. Homicide by meere chaunce, he defineth *sect.* 49. to be, when a man is slaine by meere fortune, against the

 mind

minde of the killer;as if one hewing, the axe flieth of the hafte, and killeth a man. And this is all one with *Brittons mifauenture.* Homicide by chaunce mixed he defineth *fect.* 50. to be, when the killers ignorance or negligence is ioyned with the chaunce: as if a man loppe trees by an high way fide, by which many vfually trauell, and caft downe a bowgh not giuing warning, &c. by which bowgh a man paffing by is flaine.

Mifcontinuance, Kitchin *fol.* 231. See *Difcontinuance.*

Mife *(mifa)* is a French word fignifiing as much as *(expenfum)* in latine, and the latine word (Mifa) is fo vfed in *Kitchin fol.* 144. and in *Weft. parte.* 2. *Simbol. titulo*, Proceedings in chauncery, *fect.* 21. F. It is vfed *anno* 2. & 3. *Ed.* 6. *ca.* 36. for a fomme of mony paid by the *Kings* tenents in certaine counties in *Wales* according to their feuerall cuftomes. In the ftatute 33. *H.* 8. *ca.* 13. it is vfed plurally, for certaine cuftumary gratuities fent to to the Lord Marchers of *Wales*, by their tenents, at their firft comming to their lands. And *anno* 4. & 5. *Phil.* & *Mar. ca.* 11. *mife* is vfed in an action of right or property, for the point whereupon the parties proceede to triall, either by Affife or battaile: as iffue is in an action perfonall; if the *Mife* be vpon battell. *Litleton fol.* 102. and in the *old nat. br. fol.* 2. you haue thefe words. Know yea that this writ hath but two iffues: that is to fay, ioyning the mife vpon the meere, and that is, to put himfelfe into the great Affife of our foueraigne Lord the King, or to ioyne battaile, See *anno* 37. *Ed.* 3. *ca.* 16. To ioyne the mife vpon the meere, is as much to fay, as to ioyne the mife vpon the cleare right, and that in more plaine terms is nothing elfe, but to ioyne vpon this point, whether hath the more right, the tenent or demaundant. *Litleton. li.* 3. *ca.* 8. *foll.* 101. *b.* This word in fome other place is vfed for a participle, fignifiing as much as *(caft or put vpon)* in englifh, which appeareth by *S. Ed. Cokes* report in *Saffins cafe. vol.* 6. *fo.* 124. *a.*

Mifericordia, is vfed in the common law, for an arbitrary punifhment. *Bracton li.* 4. *tracta.* 5. *ca.* 6. in thefe words. *Item fi quis in mifericordiam inciderit pro diffeifina, non remanebit mifericordia exigenda, fi ille qui amiferit, quafiuerit conuictionem. Kitchin. fol.* 78. out of *Glanuile* faith thus, *Eft autem mifericordia, quia quis per iuramentum legalium hominum amerciatus eft, ne aliquid de fuo honorabili contenemento amittat.* which faying you haue in a maner word for word in *Glanvile*,

lib. 9.

lib. 9. cap. 11. *Fitzherbert* saith, that it is called *misericordia*, because it ought to be very moderate, and rather lesse then the offence, according to the tenure of the great charter. *cap.* 14. This saith *Fitz.* in his *nat.br.* in the writ De *moderata misericordia, fol.* 75. *A.* I. *Misericordia* is to be quit of *Misericors*, that is, to be discharged of all maner of amercements, that a man may fall into within the Forest. *Crompton. Iurisd. fol.* 196. See *Amerciament*. See Mercy, and *Moderata misericordia.*

Miskenning. i. chaunging of speech in court. *Saxon* in the description of *Engl. cap.* 11.

Misnomer, is compounded of the *French (mes)* which in composition alwaies signifieth as much as *(amisse)* and *(nomer.* i. *nominare.)* It signifieth in our common lawe, the vsing of one name for another, or mis-tearming. *Broke, titulo Misnomer.*

Misprision (Misprisio) commeth of the French *(Mespris* .i. *fastidiũ, contemptus,)* it signifieth in our common lawe, neglect, or negligence, or ouersight: As for example, Misprision of treason, or of felony, is a neglect or light accompt shewed of treason or felony commited, by not reuealing it, when we know it to be committed; *Stawnf. pl. cor. li.* 1. *ca.* 19. which read at large: or by letting any person committed for treason or felony, or suspitiõ of either, to goe before he be indited. Also Misprision of Clerks, *anno.* 8. *He.* 6. *ca.* 15. is a neglect of Clerks in wrighting, or keeping records. Thirdly, *anno.* 14. *Ed.* 3. *ca.* 6. *statu. pri.* by misprision of Clerks no processe shalbe admitted. Misprision of treason, is the concealement, or not disclosing of knowne treason, for the which the offendours are to suffer imprisonment during the Kings pleasure, loose their goods, and the profits of their lands, during their liues. *Crompton in his Iustice of peace. cap. Misprision of felony, fol.* 40. *West. parte* 2. *symbol. titulo Inditements, sect.* 63. *in fine.* Misprision of felonie, seemeth only finable by the Iustices, before whome the party is attainted. *Crompton. Iustice of peace, vbi supra.* The Iustices of the common place haue power to assesse fines and amerciaments vpon persons offending for misprisions, contempts, or negligences, for not doing, or misdoing any thing, in or concerning fines. *West parte* 2. *symbol. titulo Fines. sect.* 133. Iustices of Assise shall amend the defaults of Clerks misprising of a sillable or leter in writing. *Cromptons Iurisd. fol.* 208. But it is to be noted, that other faults may be accompted misprisions of treasons or felonie, because certaine later statutes doe inflict that punishment vpon them, that of old hath beene inflicted vpon misprisions. whereof you haue an example. *anno* 14. *El. c.* 1. 3. of such as coine foreine coines not current in this Realme, and of their procurers, aiders, and abetters. And see the newe exposition of lawe Termes. Misprision signifieth also a mistaking, *anno* 14. *Ed.* 3. *stat. pri. ca.* 6.

Misses, See *Mise*.

Misuser, is an abuse of libertie or benefite: As, he shall make fine for his misuser. *old. nat. br. fol.* 149.

Mistery (*mysterium*) commeth of the latine (*Mysterium*) or rather from the French (*Mestier*. i. *ars, artificium*) an art or occupation.

Mittendo manuscriptum pedis finis, is a writ Iudiciall, directed to the Treasurer and Chamberlaines of the Exchequer, to search and transmit the foote of a fine, acknowledged before Iustices in *Eyre*, into the common plees, &c. *Register. fol.* 14. *a. b.*

Mittimus, signifieth a precept sent by the King out of his *Bench*, to those that haue the custodie of fines levied, that they send them by a day assigned to his Bench, *West parte* 2. *symbol. titulo Fynes sect.* 138. *F.* & 154. *B.* and also to the *Exchequer* for certificate that Iudgment is giuen for the liuerie of lands to such or such a one, out of the Kings hands: whervpō he is dismissed also out of the exchequer, *a.* 5. R. 2. *c.* 15. of diuers other vses and applicatiōs of this (*Mittimus*) see the Register originall in the table of the booke.

Moderata misericordia, is a writ that lieth for him that is amersed in court *Baron* or other, being not of Record, for any transgression or offence beyond the qualitie of a fault. It is directed to the Lord of the court, or his Bayliffe, commanding them to take a moderate amerciament of the party: and is founded vpon Magna *charta, ca.* 14. *Quòd nullus liber homo amercietur nisi secundùm qualitatem delicti, &c.* The rest touching this writ, see in *Fitzh. nat. br. fol.* 75. See *Misericordia*.

Modo & forma, are words of art in a processe, and namely in the answer of the defendant, wherby he denieth himselfe to haue done the thing layde to his charge, *modo & forma declarata. Kitch. fol.* 232. It signifieth as much, as that clause in the ciuile lawe. *Negat allegata, prout allegantur, esse vera.*

Moitye, commeth of the French (*Moitiè*) *id est, coæqua vel medi-*

medius pars) and signifieth the halfe of any thing, *Litleton. fol.* 125.

Monks clothes, anno 20. *Hen.* 6. *cap.* 10.

Moniers (*Monetarii*) *Register. original. fol.* 262. *b.* & *anno* 1. *Ed.* 6. *ca.* 15. be ministers of the *Mint*, which make and coine the Kings mony. It appeareth by some antiquity which I haue seen that in auncient times our Kings of England had mints in most of the countries of this Realme. And in the tractate of the Exchequer, writen by *Ockham*, I finde, that whereas the Shyreeues ordinarily were tyed to pay into the Exchequer the kings sterling, for such debts as they were to answer, they of *Northumberland*, and *Cumberland*, were at libertie to pay in any sort of mony, so it were siluer. And the reason is there giuen, because those two shires, *monetarios de antiqua institutione non habent.*

Monstrance de droyt, is as much to say, as shewing of his right. It signifieth in our common lawe, a suite in Chancerie to be restored to lands or tenements, that indeede be mine in right, though they were by some office found to be in possessiō of another lately dead. See *Stawnf. prærog. ca.* 21. at large, and *Brooke*, *titulo Petition.* of this also reade *Sir Edward Cookes reports, lib.* 4. *fol.* 54. *b.* &c. *the Wardens of the Sadlers case.*

Monstrauerunt, is a writ that lieth for tenents that hold freely by charter in auncient Demeane, being distreined for the payment of any tolle or imposition, contrary to their libertie, which they do or should enioy, which see in *Fitzh. nat. br. fol.* 14.

Morian, is all one in significatiō with the french (*Morion.* i. *cassis*) a head peece: which word the french man boroweth from the *Italian* (*morione*) *anno.* 4. & 5. *Phi* & *Ma. ca.* 2.

Morlinge, aliâs Mortling, seemeth to be that wolle which is taken from the skinne of a dead sheep, whether dying of the rotte, or being killed. *anno.* 27. *H.* 6. *ca.* 2. This is writen *Morkin. anno.* 3. *Iaco. ca.* 8.

Mort d'auncester, See *Assise.*

Mortgage (*Mortuum vadium, vel Morgagium*) is compounded of 2. French words (*Mort, id est, mors*) and (*Gage, id est, pignus, merces*) It signifieth in our common lawe, a pawne of land or tenement, or any thing moueable, laid or bound for mony borowed, peremptorily to be the creditours for euer, if the mony be not paide at the day agreed vpon. And the creditour holding land or tenement vpon this bargaine, is in the meane time called Tenét in mortgage. Of this we reade in the grand Custumarie of *Normandie, cap.* 113. in these wordes. *Notandum insuper est, quod vadiorum, quoddam viuum, quoddam mortuum nuncupatur. Mortuum autem dicitur vadium, quod se de nihilo redimit & acquietat, vt terra tradita in vadium pro centum solidis, quam cum obligator retrahere voluerit, acceptam pecuniam restituet in solidum. Viuum autem dicitur vadium, quod ex suis prouentibus acquiratur. Vt terra tradita in vadium pro centum solidis vsque ad tres annos, quae, elapso tertio anno, reddenda est obligatori, vel tradita in vadium, quousq; pecunia recepta de eiusdem proventibus fuerit persoluta.* Glanvile likewise *lib.* 10. *cap.* 6. defineth it thus: *mortuum vadium dicitur illud, cuius fructus vel reditus interim percepti in nullo se acquietant.* Soe you see by both these bookes, that it is called a dead gage, because whatsoeuer profit it yeeldeth, yet it redeemeth not it selfe by yelding such profit, except the whole somme borowed be likewise paid at the day. See *M. Skene. de verborum signif. eodem.* He that layeth this pawne or gage, is called the Mortgager, & he that taketh it, the Mortgagee. *West. par.* 2. *symb. titulo Fines: sect.* 145. This if it containe excessiue vsurie, is prohibited, *anno* 37. *H.* 8. *c.* 9.

Mortmaine (*Manus mortua*) is compounded of two french words (*Mort.* i. *mors*) and *Main.* i. *manus*) It signifieth in the common lawe, an alienation of lands or tenements to any corporation, guilde, or fraternitie, and their successours, as Bishops, parsons, vicars, &c. which may not be done without licence of the king, and the Lord of the maner. The reason of the name proceedeth from this, as I conceiue it, because the seruices and other profits due for such lands, as escheates, &c. comme into a dead hand, or into such a hand as holdeth them, and is not of power to deliuer them, or any thing for them backe againe. *Magna charta, cap.* 36. *& anno* 7. *Ed. prim.* commonly called (the statute of *Mortmaine*) and *anno* 18. *Ed.* 3. *statut.* 3. *cap.* 3. *& anno* 15. *Richard.* 2. *cap.* 5. *Polydor. Virgill* in the 17. booke of his Chronicles, maketh mention of this lawe, and giueth this reason of the name. *Et legem hanc manum mortuam vocarunt, quòd res semel datae collegiis sacerdotum, non vtique rursus venderentur, velut mortuae, hoc est, vsui aliorum mortalium in perpetuum adempta essent. Lex diligenter servatur, sic vt nihil possessionum ordini sacerdotali à quoquam detur, nisi Regio permissu.* But the former statutes be some thing abridged by *anno* 39. *Elizabeth cap.*5. by which the gift of lands, &c. to Hospitals is permitted without obteining of *Mortmaine*. *Hotoman* in his commentaries *de verbis feudal. verbo* Manus *mortua*, hath these words. *Manus mortua locutio est, quæ vsurpatur de ys, quorum possessio, vt ita dicam, immortalis est: quia nunquam hæredem habere desinunt. Quâ de causâ res nunquam ad priorem dominum revertitur*. N*am manus pro possessione dicitur, mortua pro immortali. Sic municipium dicitur non mori, l. An vsusfructus* 56. D. *de vsufr. legat. quoniam hominibus aliis succrescentibus, idem populi corpus videtur. l. proponebatur*. 76. D. *de Iudiciis: Hæc Hotomanus*. & read the rest. *Amortizatio, est in manum mortuam translatio Principis iussu. Petrus Belluga in speculo principum: fol.* 76. *Ius amortizationis est licentia capiendi ad manum mortuam. Idem, eodem*. where you may reade a learned tractate both of the beginning and nature of this doctrine. To the same effect you may read *Cassa. de consuetu. Burg. pag.* 348. 387. 1183. 1185. 1201. 1225. 1285. 1218. 1274. *M. Skene de verborum signif.* saith that *Dimittere terras ad manum mortuam, est idem atque dimittere ad multitudinem sive vniuersitatem, quæ nunquam moritur: idq; per ἀντίφρασιν, seu a contrario sensu*, because communalties neuer die.

Mortuary (*Mortuarium*) is a gift left by a man at his death, to his parish church, for the recompence of his personall tithes and offerings not duly payed in his life time. And if a man haue three or more catell of any kind, the best being kept for the lord of the fee, as a *Heriot*, the second was wont to be giuen to the persõ in right of the church, *cap. statutum. De consuetu. in provincial.* Touching this you haue two statutes. one *anno* 13. *Ed. pri.* commonly called, *Circumspectè agatis*: whereby it appeareth, that Mortuaries are suable in the court Christian; the other *anno* 21. *H.*8: *cap.*6. whereby is set downe an order and rate in mony for mortuaries.

Mulier, as it is vsed in the common lawe, seemeth to be a word corrupted and vsed for (*Melior*) or rather the French (*Melieur*). It signifieth the lawfull issue preferred before an elder brother borne out of matrimony: *anno H.*6. *cap.* 11. *Smith de repub. Anglo. lib.* 3. *cap.* 6. But by *Glanuile lib.* 7: *ca. pri.* the lawfull issue seemeth rather (*Mulier*) then (*Melior*) because it is begotten (*è Muliere*) and not (*ex Concubinâ*). for he calleth such issue *filios mulieratos*, opposing them to bastards. And *Britton cap.* 70. hath *frere mulier*. i. the brother begotten of the wife, opposit to *frere bastard*. This seemeth to be vsed in Scotland also, for *M.Skene de verborum signifi. verbo* (*Mulieratus filius*) saith that *Mulieratus filius*, is a lawful son begotten of a lawfull wife. *Quia mulieris appellatione vxor continetur. l. Mulieris* 13. & *ibid. glossa de verborum significatione*.

Mulmutius lawes, See *Lawe*.

Multure (*molitura, vel multura*) commeth neare the French, (*moulture*) and signifieth in our common lawe, the tolle that the miller taketh, for grinding of corne.

Murage, (*muragium*) is a tolle or tribute to be leuied for the building or repayring of publike edifices or walles. *Fitz. nat. br. fol.* 227. *D. Murage* seemeth also to be a libertie graunted by the *King* to a towne, for the gathering of money toward walling of the same. *anno* 3. *Ed.* 1. *cap.* 30.

Murder (*murdrum*) is borowed of the French, (*meurtrier. i. carnifex, homicida*) or (*meurtre. i. internecio, homicidium,*) The new Expositour of the lawe termes draweth it from the Saxon word, (*mordren*) signifying the same thing. It signifieth in our common lawe, a wilfull and felonious killing of any other vpon prepensed malice. *anno* 52. *H* 3. *cap.* 25. *West. part.* 2. *symbol. titulo, Inditements. sect.* 47. *Bracton. lib.* 3. *tract.* 2. *cap.* 15 *num. prim.* defineth it to be *Homicidium, quod, nullo præsente, nullo sciente, nullo audiente, nullo vidente, clam perpetratur*. And of the same minde is *Britton. cap.* 6. as also *Fleta, lib.* 1. *cap.* 30. yet *Fleta* saith also, that it was not murder, except it were proued the partie slaine were English, and no straunger. But as *Stawnf.* saith, *pl. cor. lib.* 1. *cap.* 2. the lawe in this point is altered, by the statute, *anno* 14. *Ed.* 3. *cap.* 4. and murder is now otherwise to be defined. When a man vpon prepensed malice killeth another, whether secretly or openly, it maketh no mater: or be he an English man, or a forainer liuing vnder the Kings protection. And prepensed malice is here either expresse or implyed: expresse, when it may be euidently proued, that there was formerly some euill will implyed: when one killeth another sodainly, hauing nothing to defend himselfe: as going ouer a style, or such like. *Crompton.* Iustice of peace, in the chapter of *Murder. fol.* 19. *b.* See *M.Skene de verbor. signif. verbo, Murdrum*. This by the Latine Interpretour of the graund Custumarie of *Normandy*, is called *multrum. cap.* 68. See *Were*.

Muster, commeth of the French

(*moustre* .i.*specimen*, *spectamen*, *exemplum*,) as, *feire moustre generale de toute son armee*, is as much as, *lustrare exercitum*. The signification is plaine. *Mustred* of record. *anno* 18. *H. 6. cap.* 19. seemeth to be *dare nomen*, or to bee inrolled in the number of the kings souldiours. *Master* of the kings musters. *anno.* 2. *Ed. 6. cap.* 2. See *Master*.

Muster master general. anno 35. *Eliz. ca.* 4. See *Master of the kings musters*.

N

NAam (*Namium*) seemeth to come from the Dutch word (*nemmen* .i. *capio*) It signifieth in our common law, the taking or apprehending of another mans moueable goods: and is either lawfull or vnlawfull. Lawfull *naam*, is nothing els but a reasonable distresse, proportionable to the valew of the thing distreined for. And this *naam* was auncienly called either *vif* or *mort*, quicke or dead, accordingly as it was made of dead or quicke chatels. Lawfull *naam* is so, either by the common law, or by a mans perticular fact: by the common law, as when one taketh another mans beasts dammage fesant in his grounds: by a mans particular fact, as by reason of some contract made, that for default of payment of an annuity agreed vpon, it shall be lawfull to distreine in such or such lands, &c. *Horns mirrour of Iustices. lib.* 2. *ca. de vee de naam.* where you may read of other circumstances required in lawfull *naam*: *viz*: of what thing, or of what things first, in what maner, on what daies, and at what houres it ought to be made; with other points worth the reading, for the vnderstanding of our law antiquities. See *Withernam*.

Nasse. anno 4. *H.* 7. *ca.* 21. seemeth to be the proper name of *Orford Hauen*. Whether it be so termed of the boates or water vessels that lye there or not, let the reader iudge. But (*nasselle*) is in French a kinde of small boat.

Natiuo habendo, is a writ that lyeth to the Shyreeue for a Lord, whose vilein claimed as his inheritance, is runne from him, for the apprehending and restoring of him to his Lord againe. *Register orig. fol.* 87. *Fitzh. nat. br. fol.* 77. See *Libertate probanda*.

Naturalization. See *Denizen*.

Ne admittas, is a writ that lyeth for the plaintife in a *Quare impedit*, or him that hath an action of *Darrein* presentment depending in the common Bench, and feareth that the Bishop will admit the clerke of the defendant, during the suite betweene them. And this writ must be sued within sixe monethes after the avoydance. Because after the sixe moneths the Bishop may present by lapse. *Register orig. fol.* 31. *Fitzh. nat. br. fol.* 37. where see the rest.

Negatiue pregnant (*Negatiua pragnans*) is a negatiue implying also an affirmatiue. As is a man being impleaded, to haue done a thing vpon such a day, or in such a place, denyeth that he did it *modo & forma declarata*: which implyeth neuer the lesse, that in some sort he did it. Or if a man be said to haue alienated land, &c. in fee, he denying that he hath alienated in fee, seemeth to confesse that he hath alienated in some other sort. *Dyer. fol.* 17. *nu.* 95. See *Brooke hoc titulo* and *Kitchin, fol.* 232. And see the new exposition of lawe terms. And read also in some Ciuilians, of *Affirmatiua pragnans*, and that is, *qua habet in se inclusiuam negatiuam. Et hoc importare videntur dictiones (Solùm & tantùm, qua implicant negatiuam) Pacianus. De probationibus. lib.* 1. *ca.* 31. *nu.* 16. *fol.* 93.

Neif (*natiua*) commeth of the French (*Naif.* i. *naturalis, vel natiuus*) it signifieth in our common law, a bond woman, *anno.* 1 *Ed.* 6. *ca.* 3. the reason is, because women become bond rather *natiuitate*, than by any other means.

Ne iniustè vexes, is a writ that lyeth for a Tenent, which is distrained by his Lord, for other seruices than he ought to make, and is a prohibition to the Lord in it selfe, commaunding him not to distreine. The especial vse of it is, where the tenent hath formerly preiudiced himselfe by performing more seruices, or paying more rent without constraint, than he needed. For in this case, by reason of the Lords seisin, he cannot avoide him in avowry: and therefore he is driuen to this writ as his next remedie, *Register orig. fol.* 4. *Fitzh. nat. br. fol* 10.

Ne *vicecomes colore mandati Regis quenquam amoueat à possessione ecclesia minus iustè. Register orig. fol.* 61.

Nient comprise, is an exception taken to a petition as vniust, bicause, the thing desired, is not conteined or comprehended in that act or deede, whereupon the petition is grounded. For example, one desireth of the court, to be put in possession of a house formerly among other lands &c. adiudged vnto him. The adverse party pleadeth, that his petitiõ is not to be granted, because thogh he had a iudgement for certaine lands and houses: yet the house into the possession wherof he desireth to be put, is not conteined among those for the which he had

had iudgement. See the newe booke of Entries. *titulo, Nient comprise*. This seemeth to be especially to hinder execution.

Nisle, anno 3. Ed.4.cap.5.

Nihil. anno. 5. *R.* 2.*stat.pri. cap.* 3. is a word set vpon a debt illeuiable, by the foreine Apposer in the Exchequer.

Nihil dicit, is a fayling to put in answer to the plee of the plaintiffe by the day assigned, which if a man do commit, iudgement passeth against him, as saying nothing why it should not.

Nisi prius, is a writ iudiciall, which lyeth in case, where the Enquest is paneled, and returned before the Iustices of the Banke, the one partie or the other making petition, to haue this writ for the ease of the contrie. It is directed to the Shyreeue, commaunding that hee cause the men impaneled to come before the Iustices in the same countie, for the determination of the cause there, except it be so difficult, that it need great deliberation. In which case it is sent againe to the Bank, *v. anno* 14. *Ed.* 3. *cap.* 15. The forme of the writ, see in *old. nat. br. fol.* 159. and in the *Regist. indic. fol.* 7. & 28. & 75. See the new booke of *Entries, verbo, Nisi prius*. And it is called (*Nisi prius*) of these words comprised in the same, whereby the Shyreeue is willed to bring to *Westminst.* the men impaneled at a certaine day, or before the Iustices of the next Assises: *nisi die Lunæ apud talem locum prius venerint, &c.* whereby it appeareth, that Iustices of Assises, and Iustices of (*nisi prius*) are differing. And Iustices of (*nisi prius*) must be one of them, before whom the cause is depending in the Bench, with some other good man of the Countie associated vnto him. *Fitz. nat. br. fol.* 240. *E.* which he taketh from the Statute of Yorke. *ann.* 12. Ed. 2. See *Westm.* 2. *cap.*30. *anno* 13. *Ed. prim. & anno* 27. *eiusdem. cap.* 4. & *anno* 2. Ed. 3. *cap.* 17. & *anno* 4. *eiusdem, cap.* 11. & *anno* 14. *eiusdem cap.* 16. & *anno* 7. *Rich.* 2. *cap.*7. & *anno* 18. *Eliz. cap.* 12.

Nobility (*nobilitas*) in *England* compriseth all dignities aboue a *Knight*. So that a Baron is the lowest degree thereof. *Smith de Repub. Anglor. lib. prim. cap.* 17. *Bartolus* in his Tractate *De Nobilitate*, which he compiled vpon the lawe, *Si vt proponis C. de dignitatibus*, *libro.* 12. rehearseth foure opinions *de Nobilitate*, but reiecteth them, and himselfe defineth it thus: *Nobilitas est qualitas illata per principatum tenentem, qua quis vltra honestos plebeios acceptus ostenditur.* But this definition is too large for vs, except we will accompt Knights and Banerets *inter plebem*, which in mine opinion were too harsh. For *Equites* among the Romanes, were in a middle ranke *inter Senatores & plebem.*

Nocumento. See *Nusance.*

Nomination (nominatio) is vsed by the Canonists, and common Lawyers, for a power that a man by vertue of a maner or otherwise, hath to appoint a Clerke to a patron of a benefice, by him to be presented to the Ordinarie. New termes of the lawe.

Non-abilitie, is an exception taken against the plaintiffe or demandant vpon some cause, why he cannot commence any suite in lawe, as a *Præmunire, Outlawrie, Villenage, Excommunication:* or because he is a stranger borne. The Ciuilians say, that such a man hath not *personam standi in iudicio. See Broke, hoc titulo.* see *Fitzh. nat. br. fol.* 35. *A. fol.* 65. *D. fol.* 77. *C.* The new Expositour of lawe termes reckoneth sixe causes of *Non-ability*: as if he be an outlawe, a stranger borne, condemned in a premunire, professed in religion, excommunicate, or a villein. Howbeit the second cause holdeth onely in actions reall or mixt, and not in personall, except he be a straunger and an enemie.

Non admittas. See *Ne admittas.*

Non-age, is all the time of a mans age vnder one and twenty yeares in some cases, or fourteen in some, as mariage. See *Broke, titulo, Age.* See *Age.*

Non capiendo clericum. See *Clerico non capiendo.*

Non clayme, Cromptons Iurisd. fol. 144. seemeth to be an exception against a man that claimeth not within the time limited by lawe, as within the yeare and day, in case where a man ought to make continuall claime, or within fiue yeares after a fine leuyed. *v. Coke. lib.* 4. *in proœmio.* See *Continuall clayme.*

Non compos mentis, is of foure sortes: first, he that is an idiot borne: next, he that by accident afterward wholy leeseth his wits: thirdly, a lunaticke, that hath somtime his vnderstanding, and sometime not: lastly, hee which by his own act depriueth himselfe of his right mind for a time, as a drunkard, *Coke lib.* 4. *fol.* 124. *b.*

Non distringendo, is a writ, comprising vnder it diuers particulars, according to diuers cases: all which you may see in the Table of the *Register original, verbo, Non distringendo.*

Non est culpabilis, is the generall

nerall answer to an action of trespasse, whereby the defendant doth absolutely deny the fact imputed vnto him by the plaintiffe, whereas in other especiall answers, the defendaunt graunteth the fact to be done, and alledgeth some reason in his defence, why he lawfully might doe it. And therefore whereas the Rhetoricians, comprise all the substance of their discourses, vnder three questions, *An sit, quid sit, quale sit*, this aunswere falleth vnder the first of the three: all other answers are vnder one of the other two. And as this is the generall aunswer in an action of trespasse, that is, an action criminall ciuily prosecuted: so is it also in all actions criminally followed, either at the suite of the king or other, wherein the defendant denieth the crime obiected vnto him. See the new booke of Entries. *titulo, Non culpabilis*, and *Stawnf. pl. coro. lib. 2. cap. 62.*

Non est factum, is an aunswer to a declaration, whereby a man denyeth that to be his deed, whereupon he is impleaded. *Broke, hoc titulo.*

Non implacitando aliquem de libero tenemento sine breui, is a writ to inhibit Bayliffes, &c. from distraining any man without the kings writ, touching his free hould. *Register, fol. 171. b.*

Non intromittendo quando breue pracipe in capite subdole impetratur, Is a writ directed to Iustices of the bench or in *Eyre*, willing them not to giue one hearing, that hath vnder the colour of intitling the king to land, &c. as houlding of him *in capite*, deceitfully obteined the writ called: *pracipe in capite.* but to put him to his writ of right, if he thinke good to vse it. *Register orig. fo. 4. b.*

Non mercandizando victualia, is a writ directed to the Iustices of Assise, commaunding them to inquire whether the officers of such a towne, doe sell victuals in grosse or by retaile, during their office, contrary to the statute, and to punish them, if they finde it true. *Register, fol. 184.*

Non molestando, is a writ that lyeth for him, which is molested contrary to the kings protection graunted him. *Register fol. 24.*

Non omittas, is a writ lying where the Shyreeue deliuereth a former writ to a Bayliffe of a fraunchis, within the which the party, on whom it is to be serued, dwelleth, & the Bayliffe neglecteth to serue it: for in this case, the Shyreeue returning, that he deliuered it to the Bayliffe, this shalbe directed to the Shyreeue, charging him himselfe to execute the kings commaundement. *Old. nat. br. fol. 44.* of this the

Reg. orig. hath three sorts. *fol.* 81. *b.* & 151. and the *Reg.* Iudiciall one, *fol.* 5. & 56.

Non ponendo in Assisis & Iuratis, is a writ founded vpon the *stat. Westm.* 2. *ca.* 38. and the *stat: Articuli super chartas, ca.* 9. which is graunted vpon diuers causes to men, for the freeing them from Assises and Iuries. See *Fitzh. nat. br. fol.* 165. See the *Register, fol.* 179. 100. 181. 183.

Non procedendo ad Assisam Rege inconsulto, is a writ to stop the triall of a cause appertaining vnto one, that is in the kings seruice, &c. vntill the kings pleasure be farder knowne. *Reg. fol.* 220. *a.*

Non residentia pro clericis Regis, is a writ directed to the Ordinary, charging him not to molest a Clerk imployed in the kings seruice, by reason of his *non residence. Register orig. fol.* 58. *b.*

Non-suite, is a renuntiation of the suite by the plaintife or demaundant, when the mater is so farre proceeded in, as the Iury is ready at the barre, to deliuer their verdict. *anno* 2. *H.* 4. *ca.* 7. See the new booke of *Entries*, *verbo* Non-suite. The ciuilians terme it *Litis renunciationem*.

Non soluendo pecuniam ad quam Clericus mulctatur pro non residentia, is a writ prohibiting an Ordinary to take a pecuniary mulct, imposed vpon a clerk of the kings for *non-residence. Regist. orig. fol.* 59.

Non tenure, is an exception to a coumpt, by saying that he houldeth not the land specified in the coumpt, or at the least, some parte of it. *anno* 25. *Ed.* 3. *stat.* 4. *ca.* 16. *West parte.* 2. *Simbol. titulo. Fines. sect.* 138. maketh mention of *non-tenure* generall, and *non-tenure* speciall. See the new booke of *Entries*, *verbo*, Non-*tenure.* where it is said, that especiall *non-tenure* is an exception, alledging that he was not tenent the day whereon the writ was purchased. *Non-tenure* generall is then by likelyhood, where one denyeth himselfe euer to haue bene tenent to the land in question.

Non sum informatus. See *Informatus non sum.*

Non sane memorie (*Non sana memoria*) is an exception taken to any act declared by the plaintife or demaundant to be done by another, wherupon he groundeth his plaint or demaund. And the contents of this exceptiō be, that the party that did that act (being himselfe or any other) was not well in his wits, or madde, when he did it. See the new booke of *Entries. titulo* Non *sane memory*. and *Dum non fuit compos mentis*. See also. *supra* Non *compos mentis*.

Non terme (*non terminus*) is the

time

time of vacation between Terme and Terme. It was wont to bee called the times or dayes of the kings peace, *Lamb*. *Archaiono. fol* 126. and what these were in the time of King *Edward* the Confessour, see there. This time was called (*Iusticium*) or (*Feriæ*) among the *Romanes*, or (*dies nefasti*) *Ferias appellari notum est tempus illud, quod forensibus negotiis & iure dicendo vacabat. Earum autem aliæ solemnes erant, aliæ repentinæ. Brisson. de verb. signif. lib. 6. vide Wesenbec: paratit. De Feriis. num. 6.*

Note of a fine, (*nota finis*) is a briefe of a fine made by the *Chirographer*, before it be engrossed. The forme whereof see in *West. part. 2. symbol, titulo. Fines. sect. 117.*

Novell assignement (*noua assignatio*) is an assignement of time, or place, or such like, otherwise then as before it was assigned. In *Broeke* you may find these wordes in effect: *titulo, Deputie. num. 12.* See *novell assignement of trespasse* in a new place after *Barre pleaded. Broke titulo, Trespasse. 122.* and, *novel assignement*. in a writ *de eiectione custodiæ. titulo, Eiectione custodiæ. num. 7.* See *Assignement*.

Nude mater. See *Mater*.

Nunne (*Nonna*) is the French word (*nonnain*) or (*nonne*) something altered, which signifieth a holy or consecrated virgin, or a woman that hath by vowe bound her selfe to a single and chast life, in some place and company of other women, separated from the world, and addicted to an especiall seruice of God, by prayer, fasting, and such like holy exercises. If we wold know whence this word came into *Fraunce*, S. *Hierome* maketh it an Egyptian word, as *Hospinian* recordeth of him, in his booke *De origine & progressu monachatus. fol.* 3.

Nuper obiit, is a writ that lyeth for a coheire being deforced by her coheire of lands or tenements, whereof the graundfather, father, vncle, or brother to them both, or any other their common auncesters, dyed seised of an estate in fee simple. See the forme of the writ, *origin. Regist. fol. 226. &c. Fitz. nat. br. fol. 197.* If the auncestour dyed seised in fee tayle, then the coheire deforced shall haue a *Formdon. Idem. ibid.*

Nusance (*nocumentum*) commeth of the French (*nuire*. i. *nocere*.) It signifieth in our common lawe, not onely a thing done, whereby another man is annoyed in his free lands or tenements, but especially the Assise or writ lying for the same. *Fitz. nat. br. fol.* 183. And this writ (*de Nocumento*) or of *Nusance*,

ſance is either ſimply *De nocumento, or de paruo nocumento*; and then it is *Vicountiel. old. nat. br. f.* 108. *&* 109. *& Fitzh. nat. br. vbi ſupra. & fol.* 184. *Britton* calleth it *Noſance.* whome alſo reade. *ca.* 61. *&* 62. *M. Manwood parte* 2 *of his foreſt lawes. ca.* 17. maketh three ſorts of *Nuſance* in the foreſt, the firſt is *Nocumentum commune*, the ſecond *Nocumentum ſpeciale*, the third *Nocumentum generale*. which reade with the reſt of that whole chapter. See the *Regiſter originall, fol.* 197. *&* 199.

Nutmegs (*nux myriſtica vel nux muſcata*) is a ſpice well knowne to all. It groweth of a tree like a peach tree, and is incloſed in two huskes, whereof the inner huske is that ſpice which we call mace. Of this who will, may reade more in *Gerards herball, lib.* 3. *ca.* 145. It is mentioned among ſpices that are to be garbled. *anno* 1. *Iaco. ca.* 19.

O

OBedientiæ, was a rent, as appeareth by *Roger Hoveden parte poſter: ſuorum annalium, fol.* 430. in theſe words: *vt ergo eis, ſc: regularibus, adimatur oportunitas evagandi, prohibemus, ne reditus, quos obedientias vocant, ad firmam teneant, &c. Obedientia* in the canon lawe is vſed for an office or the adminiſtration of an office. *ca. cùm ad monaſterium.* 6. *extra de ſtatu monacho: & cano. regula.* And therevpon the word (*obedientiales*) is vſed in the provinciall conſtitutions for thoſe which haue the execution of any office vnder their ſuperiors. *cap. pri. de ſtatu. regula.* For thus ſaith *Lyndwood* in his gloſſe vpon that word: *Hi ſunt qui ſub obedientia ſuorum prælatorum ſunt, & habent certa officia adminiſtranda interiùs vel exteriùs.* It may be that ſome of theſe offices called *obedientiæ* conſiſted in the collection of rents or penſions: and that therefore thoſe rents were by a metonymie called *obedientiæ, quia colligebantur ab obedientialibus.*

Oblations (*oblationes*) are thus defined in the canon lawe. *Oblationes dicuntur, quæcunq; a piis fidelibuſq; Chriſtianis offeruntur Deo & eccleſiæ, ſiue res ſoli, ſiue mobiles ſint. Nec refert an legentur teſtamento, an aliter donentur, cap. clerici.* 13. *quæſt.* 2. Reade more of theſe in *Duarenus. De ſacr. eccl. miniſter. ac beneſi. cap. tertio.*

Obligation (*Obligatio*) and Bill be all one, ſauing that when it is in Engliſh, it is commonly called a Bill, and when it is in Latine, an Obligation. *Weſt parte* 1. *ſymbol. lib.* 2. *ſect.* 146. True it is that a Bill is obligatorie: but we commonly call that an obli-

obligation, which hath a condition annexed. The former author in the same place saith thus farder. An obligation is a deede, whereby the obligour doth knowledge himselfe to owe vnto the Obligee, a certaine summe of money or other thing. In which, besides the parties names, are to be considered the thing due, and the time, place and maner of payment, or deliuerie. Obligations be either by mater in deede, or of record. An obligation by mater in deede is euery obligation not acknowledged & made in some court of record. Hitherto *M. West*.

Occupauit, is a writ that lieth for him, which is eiected out of his land or tenement in time of warre: as a writ of *Novel disseisin* lieth for one eiected in time of peace. *Ingham* §. *Bref de novel disseisin*.

Octo tales. See *Tales*: See *Brooke tit. Octo tales*.

Odio & atia, *anno* 3. *Ed.* 1. *ca.* 11: is a writ sent to the vndershyreeue, to inquire whither a man being committed to prison vpon suspition of murder, be committed vpon malice or euill will, or vpon iust suspition. *Register originall*, *fol.* 133. *b*. See *Bracton li.* 3. *parte* 2. *ca.* 20.

Office (*Officium*) doth signifie not onely that function, by vertue whereof a man hath some imploiment in the affaires of another, as of the King or other common person; but also an Inquisition made to the Kings vse of any thing by vertue of his office who inquireth. And therefore wee oftentimes reade of an office found, which is nothing but such a thing found by Inquisition made *ex officio*. In this signification it is vsed *anno* 33. *H.* 8. *cap.* 20. and in *Stawnfords prærog. fol.* 60. & 61. where to trauers an office, is to trauers the inquisition taken of office. And in *Kitchin fol.* 177. to returne an office, is to returne that which is found by vertue of the office, see also the newe booke of *Entries*, *verbo Office pur le Roy*. And this is by a metonymie of the effect: And there be two sorts of offices in this signification, issuing out the exchequer by commission *viz*. an office to intitle the King in the thing inquired of, and an office of instruction. which reade in *Sir Edw. Cokes reports*, *vol.* 6. *Pages case*. *fol.* 52. *a. b*. Office in fee, is that which a man hath to himselfe and his heires, *anno* 13. *Ed.* 1. *ca.* 25. *Kitchin fol.* 152. See *Clerk*.

Official (*officialis*) is a word very diversly vsed. For by sundry Ciuilians of other countries, that write in these daies, it appeareth to be applyed in many pla-

places, to such as haue the sway of temporall iustice. *Ægidius Bossius in pract. crim. tit. De officialibus corruptis, &c.* But by the auncienter ciuile lawe, it signifieth him, that is the minister or appparitor of a magistrate or Iudge. *l.* 1. §. *si quis vltro. ff. de quæstio. & Co. de filiis officialium, &c. li.* 12. In the Canon lawe, it is especially taken for him, to whome any Bishop doth generally commit the charge of his spirituall iurisdiction. And in this sence one in euery Dioces is *(officialis principalis)* whome the statutes and lawes of this Kingdome call chanceler. *anno* 32. *H.* 8. *cap.* 15. The rest, if there be more, are by the canō law called *officiales foranei. glos: in clem.* 2. *de Rescriptis*, but with vs termed Cōmissaries *(Commissarii)* as in the statute of *H.* 8. or some times *(Commissarii foranei.)* The difference of these 2. powers you may reade in *Lyndwood, titulo de sequestra posses. ca.* 1. *verbo. Officialis*. But this word *(officiall)* in our statutes and common lawe signifieth him, whom the Archdeacon substituteth in the executing of his iurisdiction. as appeareth by the statute aboue mentioned and many other places.

Officiariis non faciendis vel amovendis, is a writ directed to the magistrates of a corporatiō, willing them not to make such a man an officer, and to put him out of the office he hath, vntill enquirie be made of his maners, according to an inquisition formerly ordeined. *Register originall, fol.* 126. *b.*

Onerando pro rata portionis, is a writ that lieth for a ioint tenent, or tenent in common, that is distreined for more rent, then the proportion of his land cōmeth vnto. *Reg orig. f.* 182. *a.*

Open Lawe (*Lex manifesta, Lex apparens*) is making of Lawe. which by *Magna charta ca.* 28. Bayliffes may not put men vnto vpon their owne bare assertions, except they haue witnesses to proue their inputation.

Orchel. anno. 1. *R.* 3. *ca.* 8. *Orchall. anno.* 24. *H.* 8. *ca.* 2. & *anno.* 3. & 4. *Ed.* 6. *ca.* 2. seemeth to be all one with cork.

Ordinance of the forest (*Ordinatio Forestæ*) is a statute made touching forest causes in the 34. yeare of *Edward.* 1. See *Assise.*

Ordinarie (*Ordinarius*) though in the ciuil lawe, whence the word is taken, it doth signifie any iudge that hath authoritie to take knowledge of causes in his owne right, as he is a magistrate, and not by deputation: yet in our common lawe, it is most commonly, and for ought I remember, alway taken for him, that hath ordinarie Iurisdiction in causes ecclesiasticall. See *Brooke hoc titulo. Lindwood in cap. exterior. titulo de Constitutionibus. verbo Ordinarii,* saith *quòd Ordinarius habet locum principaliter in Episcopo, & aliis superioribus, qui soli sunt vniuersales in suis iurisdictionibus, sed sunt sub eo alii ordinarii, hii viz. quibus competit Iurisdictio ordinaria de iure, priuilegio, vel consuetudine, &c. v.c.*

Ordinatione contra seruientes, is a writ that lieth against a seruant for leauing his master against the statute: *Register originall, fol.* 189.

Ordæl (Ordalium) is a Saxon word, signifiing as much as Iudgement, in some mens opinions compounded of two Saxon words *(or)* a *priuatiue,* as (*a*) in greeke, and *(dæl .i. pars)* It signifieth as much as *expers:* but it is artificially vsed for a kind of purgation practized in auncient times: whereby the party purged, was iudged *expers criminis,* called in the canon lawe *purgatio vulgaris*, and vtterly condemned. There were of this two sorts, one by fire, another by water. Of these see *M. Lamberd in his explication of Saxon words. verbo Ordalium,* where he expresseth it at large, with such superstitions as were vsed in it. Of this you may likewise read *Holinshed in his description of Britanie fol.* 98. and also *M. Manwood, parte pri. of his forest lawes, pag.* 15. But of all the rest, *Hotoman* especially, *disput. de feud. ca.* 41. where of fiue kinde of proofes, which he calleth *feudales probationes,* he maketh this the fourth, calling it *explorationem, & huius furiosæ probationis 6. genera fuisse animadvertit, per flammam, per aquam, per ferrum candens, per aquam vel gelidam vel feruentem, per sortes, & per corpus Domini,* of all which he alledgeth seuerall examples out of historie, very worthie the reading. See *M. Skene* also *de verbor. significatione. verbo (Machamiũ).* This seemeth to haue bene in vse here with vs in *Henry* the seconds dayes, as appeareth by *Glanvile. lib.* 14. *cap.* 1. & 2. Reade also of this in *M. Verstegans* Restitution of decayed intelligence. *cap.* 3. *pag.* 63. & *seqq.*

Orfgild, aliâs, Cheapegild, is a restitution made by the *Hundred* or Countie, of any wrong done by one that was *in plegio. Lamberd. Archaion. pag.* 125. & 126.

Orgeis, anno, 31. *Ed.* 3. *stat.* 3. *cap.* 2. is the greatest sort of North sea-fish, now adaies called *Organ ling.*

Oredelfe, is a liberty whereby a man claimeth the Ore found in his soyle. New exposition of

Termes.

Ortelli, is a word vsed in the booke termed (*pupilla oculi*) in the chapter containing the charter of the Forest. *parte* 5. *cap*. 22. and signifieth the clawes of a dogges foote, being taken from the French, *orteils des pieds*. i. *digiti pedum*, the toes.

Osmonds, anno 32. *Henr*. 8. *cap*. 14.

Oath of the King, (*Iuramentum Regis*) is that which the King taketh at his Coronation, which in *Bracton* is set downe in these words. *Debet Rex in coronatione sua, in nomine Iesu Christi praestito sacramento haec tria promittere populo sibi subdito: Inprimis se esse praecepturum & pro viribus opem impensurum vt ecclesiae dei & omni populo Christiano vera pax omni suo tempore obseruetur. Secundò, vt rapacitates & omnes iniquitates omnibus gradibus interdicat: 3. vt in omnibus iudiciis aequitatem praecipiat & misericordiam, vt indulgeat ei suã misericordiã clemens & misericors Deus, & vt per Iustitiã suam firma gaudeant pace vniuersi.* And in the old abridgement of statutes set out in *H*. 8. daies, I finde it thus described. This is the oath that the *King* shall sweare at his coronation: That he shall keepe and maintaine the right and the liberties of the holy church, of old time graunted by the righteous Christian Kings of England, and that he shall keepe all the lands, honours, and dignities righteous and free of the Crowne of England in all maner whole, without any maner of minishment, and the rights of the Crowne hurt, decayed, or lost, to his power shall call againe into the auncient estate, and that he shall keepe the peace of the holy church and of the clergy, and of the people with good accord: and that he shall doe in all his iudgements equitie and right iustice with discretion and mercie: and that he shall graunt to hold the lawes & customes of the realme, and to his power keepe them, and affirme them, which the folke and people haue made and chosen: and the euill lawes and customes wholly to put out: and stedfast and stable peace to the people of this realme keepe and cause to be kept to his power: and that he shall graunt no charter, but where he may doe it by his oath. All this I finde in the foresaide Booke, *titulo. Sacramentum Regis*. and *Charter of pardon. quinto*.

Oth of the Kings Iustices is, that they well and truly shall serue the king, and that they shall not assent to things, that may turne to his dammage or disinheritance. Nor that they shall take no no fee nor liuerie of none but the king. Nor that they shall take gift nor reward of none that hath adoe before them, except it be meate and drinke of smal value, as long as the plee is hanging before them, nor after for the cause. Nor that they shall giue councell to none in mater that may touch the *King*, vpon paine to be at the kings will, body and goods. And that they shall doe right to euery person, notwithstanding the *Kings* letters, &c. *anno* 18. *Ed.* 3. *statut.* 4. which the old abridgement maketh to be *anno* 20. *eiusdem statuto per se.*

Otho, was a *Deacon Cardinall* of *S. Nichens in carcere Tulliani*, and *Legate* for the *Pope* heere in England, *anno* 22. *H.* 3. whose constitutions we haue at this day: *Stowes An. pa.* 303. & see the first constitution of the said Legat.

Othobonus was a *Deacon Cardinall* of *S. Adrian*, and the *Popes legate* heere in England *anno* 15. *H.* 3. as appeareth by the award made betweene the said *King* and his commons, at *Kenelworth*. his constitutions we haue at this day in vse.

Ouch, *anno* 24. *H.* 8. *ca.* 13.

Ouster le main (*Amouere manum*) word for word, signifieth to take off the hand, though in true *French*, it should be (*Oster la main*) It signifieth in the common law, a Iudgement giuen for him that tendeth a trauers, or sieweth a *Monstrance de droit*, or petition. For when it appeareth vpon the mater discussed, that the King hath noe right nor title to the thing he seised, then Iudgement shalbe giuen in the Chauncery, that the kings hands be amoued, and thereupon *Amoueas manum* shalbe awarded to the Escheatour: which is as much, as if the iudgement were giuen, that he should haue againe his land. *v.* *Stawn. prærog. ca.* 24. See *anno* 28. *Ed.* 1. *stat.* 3. *ca.* 19. It is also taken for the writ graunted vpon this petition. *Fitzh. nat. br. fol.* 256. *C.* It is written *oter le maine*, *anno* 25. *Hen.* 8. *ca.* 22.

Ouster le mer (*vltra mare*) commeth of the French (*oultre*.i. *vltra*) and (*le mer* .i. *mare*) and it is a cause of excuse or Essoine, if a man appeare not in Court vpon Summons. See *Essoin*.

Outfangthef, *aliàs vtfangthef*, is thus defined by *Bracton li.* 3. *tra.* 2. *ca.* 34. *vtfangthef dicitur latro extraneus veniens aliunde de terra aliena, & qui captus fuit in terra ipsius, qui tales habet libertates*, but see *Britton* otherwise. *fol.* 91: *b*: It is compounded of three Saxon words (*out* .i. *extra*) (*fang* .i. *capio vel captus*) and (*Thef*.i. *fur*) It is vsed in the common law, for a liberty or priuepriuiledge, whereby a *Lord* is inhabled to call any man dwelling within his owne fee, and taken for felony in any other place, and to iudge him in his owne court. *Rastals expos.* of words.

Owelty of seruices, is an equality when the tenent parauaile oweth as much to the mesn, as the mesn doth to the Lord paramont: *Fitzh. nat. br. fol.* 136 *A. B.*

Outlawry (vtlagaria) is the losse or depriuation of the benefit belonging to a subiect: that is, of the Kings protection and the Realme: *Bracton: li.* 3. *tract.* 2. *ca.* 11. *num. pri.* & *nu.* 3. *Forisfacit vtlagatus omnia quæ pacis sunt: Quia a tempore quo vtlagatus est, caput gerit lupinum, ita quòd ab omnibus interfici possit, & impunè: maxime si se defenderit, vel fugerit, ita quòd difficilis sit eius captio. & nu.* 4. *Si autem non fugerit, nec se defenderit cùm captus fuerit: extunc erit in manu domini* Regis *mors, & vita. & qui taliter captum interfecerit, respondebit pro eo sicut pro alio, v.c.*

Outeparters anno. 9. *H.* 5. *ca.* 8. seemeth to be a kind of theeues in *Ridesdall*, that ride abroad at their best aduantage, to fetch in such catell or other things, as they could light on without that liberty: some are of opinion that those which in the forenamed statute are termed out-parters, are at this day called out-putters, and are such as set matches for the robbing of any man or house: as by discouering which way he rideth or goeth, or where the house is weakest & fittest to be entred. See *Intakers*.

Owtryders, seeme to be none other but bayliffe errants, employed by the Shyreeues or their fermers, to ride to the fardest places of their counties or hundreds, with the more speede to summon to their county or hundred courts, such as they thought good to worke vpon. *anno* 14. *Ed.* 3. *stat.* 1. *ca.* 9.

Oxgang of Land (Bouata terræ) Sixe *oxgangs* of land, seeme to be so much as sixe oxen will plough. *Crompton. iurisd. fol.* 220. but an oxegang seemeth properly to be spoken of such land as lyeth in gainour, *old nat. br. fol.* 117. *M.* Skene *de verbor. significat. verbo* Bovata *terræ*, saith, that an oxen-gate of land should alway conteine 13. acres, and that 4. oxen-gates extendeth to a pound land of old extent. See *Librata terræ*.

Oyer and Terminer, (audiendo & terminando) in true French *(Ouir & terminer)* is, in the intendment of our lawe, a commission especially graunted to certaine men, for the hearing and determining of one or more causes.

causes. This was wont to be in vse vpon some sodaine outrage or insurrection in any place. *Cromptons Iurisd. fol.* 131. & 132. See *The Statute of Westm.* 2. *cap.* 29 *anno*, 13. *Ed.* 1. who might graunt this commission. And see *Fitzh. nat. br. fol.* 100. for the forme and occasion of the writ, as also to whom it is to bee graunted, and whom not. See *Broke, titulo, Oyer & determiner.*

Oyer de Record, (*Audire Recordum*) is a petition made in court, that the Iudges, for beter proofes sake, will be pleased to heare or looke vpon any Record.

P

P*Acking whites. anno*, 1. *R.* 3. *cap.* 8.

Pain fort & dure (*pœna fortis & dura*) is in true French (*peine fort & dure.*) It signifieth in our common lawe, an especiall punishment for those, that being arraigned of felonie, refuse to put themselues vpon the ordinarie triall of God and the cuntrey, and thereby are mute, or as mute in interpretation of law. This (as *Stawnf.* thinketh, *pl. cor. lib.* 2. *cap.* 60.) is founded vpon the Statute of *Westm. prim. cap* 12. *anno.* 3. *Ed. prim.* His reason is, because *Bracton*, who writ before that Parlament, maketh no mention of it: and *Britton* writing after that time, toucheth it in his 4. chapter, *fol.* 11. *viz.* in words to this effect: If they will not acquite themselues, let them be put to their penance vntill such time as they do desire triall: and let the penance bee such: *viz.* Let them be bare legged, without girdle, and without hatte or cappe, in their coate onely, and lye in prison vpon the naked earth day and night. And let them eate no bread, but of barley and branne, nor drink any other then water, and that vpon that day when they eate not. And let them be chained. *Stawnford* in his said 60. chapter of his second booke, expoundeth it more plainely and particularly in this sort. And note, that this strong and hard paine shall be such: *sc.* He shall be sent backe to the prison whence he came, and layed in some lowe darke house, where he shall lye naked vpon the earth without any litter, rushes, or other clothing, and without any raiment about him, but onely something to couer his priuie members. And he shall lye vpon his backe with his head couered and his feete. And one arme shall bee drawne to one quarter of the house with a cord, and the other arme to another quarter: and in the same maner let it be

 done

done with his legges: and let there be layed vpon his body iron and stone, so much as he may beare or more: and the next day following, he shall haue three morsels of barley bread without drinke: and the second day, he shall haue drinke three times: and as much at each time, as he can drinke, of the water next vnto the prison doore, except it be running water, without any bread. And this shall be his diet vntill he dye.

Palatine. See *County Palatine.* See *Cassan. de consuetud. Burg. pag.* 14.

Palingman, *anno* 11. *Henr.* 7. *cap.* 22.

Panell (*panellum*) commeth of the *French* (*panne.* i. *pellis*, or *paneau*) a peece or pane, as wee call it in English. It signifieth in our common lawe, a shedule or rolle, containing the names of such Iurours, as the Shyreeue prouideth to passe vpon any triall. *Register orig. fol.* 223. *a. Kitthin, fol.* 266. See *Broke*, *hoc titulo.* And thereupon the empaneling of a Iurie, is nothing but the entring of them into the *Shyreeues* rolle or booke.

Pannage (*pannagium*) is a tolle or contribution. *Fitz. nat. br. fol.* 227. *D.* See *Pawnage.*

Paramounte, *aliàs peremounte*, commeth of these two French words (*par* .i. *per*) and (*Monter* .i. *ascendere*) It signifieth in our law, the highest Lord of the fee: for there may be a Tenent to a Lord, that houldeth ouer of another Lord. And the former of those is called Lord *Mesn*, the second Lord paramount. And a Lord paramount (as it seemeth by *Kitchin, fol.* 209) consisteth only in comparison: as one man may be great being compared with a lesser, and litle being compared with a greater: and as *Genus*, among the *Logicians*, may be in diuers respects both *genus*, and *species. Fitzh. nat. br. fol.* 135. *M.* So that none seemeth simply to be Lord paramount but only the King, as *Genus summum* is simply *Genus.* For the King is patron paramount to all the benefices in England, Doctor and student: *ca.* 36. See *Parauaile, Maner.* and *Fee.*

Parauaile, *aliàs Perauaile*, is compounded of two French words (*par* .i. *per*) and (*aualler.* i. *dimittere, demittere*) It signifieth in our common law, the lowest tenent, or him that is tenent to one, who houldeth his fee ouer of another, So is it vsed. *pl. cor. fol.* 197. and *Fitzh. nat. br. fol.* 135. *M.* See *Paramounte.* See *Mesn.*

Parcell makers, are two officers in the eschequer, that make the parcels of the escheators accoumpts, wherein they charge them

them with euery thing they haue leuyed for the kings vse, within the time of their office,& deliuer the same to one of the auditors of the court,to make an accompt for the escheatour thereof.

Parceners. See *Coparceners*.

Parcinarie (*participatio*) commeth of the French (*partir*. i. *diuidiuum facere*. It signifieth in our common law, a houlding or occupying of land by more *pro indiviso*, or by ioynt tenents, otherwise called *Coparceners*, of the French (*parsonnier*. i. *partiarius*, *particeps*.) For if they refuse to diuide their common inheritance and chuse rather to hold it ioyntly, they are said to hold *in parcinarie*. *Litleton, fol.* 56.& 57. This by the *Feudists* and Lombards is termed (*adaequatio, vel paragium*.) And among the auncient Romanes *particulones*, *sic enim authore Nonio, a veteribus cohaeredes inter se dicebantur, quòd partes invicem facerent. Spigelius*.

Pardon (*Perdonatio*) is a French word, signifiing as much as *pax, venia, gratia*. It is vsed most notoriously in our common lawe, for the remitting or forgiuing of a felonious or other offence committed against the king. This pardon is two-fold: one *ex gratia Regis*, the other, *per cours del ley*, by course of law. *Stawnf. pl. cor. fol.* 47. *Pardon ex gratia Regis*, is that, which the king, in some speciall regard of the person or other circumstance, sheweth or affoordeth vpon his absolute prerogatiue or power. Pardon by course of lawe, is that which the lawe in equitie affoordeth, for a light offence, as homicide casuall, when one killeth a man hauing no such meaning. *West. parte* 2. *symbol. titulo, Inditements. sect.* 46. Of this see the new booke of Entries, *verbo, Perdon*.

Pardoners, *anno* 22. H. 8. *c.* 12. were certaine fellowes that caried about the Popes Indulgences, and sold them to such as would buy them, against whom *Luther*, by *Sleydans* report, incensed the people of *Germany* in his time, exhorting them, *ne merces tam viles tanti emerent*.

Parke (*parcus*) commeth of the French (*parquer*. i. *vallo, vel fossa circundare*.) It signifieth with vs, a peece of grounde inclosed and stored with wild beastes of chase. Which a man may haue by prescription or the kings graunt. *Cromptons Iurisd. fol.* 148. *M. Manwood parte pri.* of his Forest lawes. *pag.* 148. defineth it thus: A parke is a place of priuiledge for wilde beastes of venerie, and also for other wild beasts, that are beasts of the Forest, and of the chase, *tam sylvestres, quàm campestres*. And all those wild beastes are to haue a firme peace and protectiō there. So that no man may hurt or chase them within the park, without licence of the owner of the same. Who also *fol.* 149. saith thus: *A* parke is of another nature, then either a chase, or a warren is. For a parke must bee inclosed, and may not lye open: for if it doe, that is a good cause of seisure of the same into the hands of the king, as a thing forfeited: as a free chase is, if it be enclosed. And moreouer, the owner cannot haue action against such as hunt in his park, if it lye open. See *Forest.* See *Chase.* See *Warren.* This word *Parke, Baldwinus* deriueth *à paradiso, eumq; locum esse dicit, in quo varia animalia ad vsum voluptatis, aut venationis includuntur & possidentur, adempta naturali libertate. Ad tit. de rerum diuis. in Institutionib.*

Parco fracto, is a writ which lyeth against him, that violently breaketh a pound, and taketh out beasts thence, which, for some trespas done vpon another mans ground, are lawfully impounded. *Register originall fol.* 166. *Fitzh. nat. br. fol.* 100.

Parish (*parochia*) commeth of the greeke (*παροικία*. i. *Accolarum conuentus, accolatus, sacra vicinia*) it is vsed in the Cannon law, some time for a Bishoprick. But in our common law, it signifieth the particular charge of a secular priest. For euery church is either Cathedrall, Couentuall, or Parochiall. Cathedrall is that, where there is a Bishop seated, so called *a Cathedra*: Conuentuall consisteth of Regular clerks, professing some order of religion, or of Deane and chapter, or other colledge of spirituall men. Parochiall is that, which is instituted for the saying of diuine seruice, and ministring the holy Sacraments to the people dwelling within a certaine compas of ground neare vnto it. Our Realme was first diuided into parishes by *Honorius Archb:* of *Canterbury*, in the yeare of our Lord. 636. *Camden Britan. pag.* 104. Of these parish churches I finde there were in England in the daies of *H.* 8. the number of 45000. *Hotoman* in his disputations *de feudis. ca.* 2. maketh mention of this word (*parochia*) out of *Pomponius Latus* in these words. *Nam sic quoq; Pomponius* Latus *veterem consuetudinem fuisse scribit, eamq; ab* Imperatore *Constantino repetitam, vt Ducibus, praefectis, Tribunis qui pro augendo Imperio consenuerant, darentur agri, villaq;, vt necessaria suppeterent, quoad viuerent, quas parochias vocabant.* And a litle after: *verùm inter feuda & parochias hoc interest, quod hae plerumq; senibus, & veteranis, plerisq; emeritae militiae dabantur,*

dabantur, qui cum de Rep. bene meriti essent, publico beneficio reliquum vitæ sustentabant: aut si quod bellum nasceretur, euocati non tam milites, quàm magistri militũ viderentur. Feuda vero plurimum Iuuenibus robustis, & primo flore ætatis, qui militiæ munus sustinere poterãt: imo verò & vt possẽt & vt vellẽt, &c.

Parlament (*parlamentum*) is a French word signifiing originally as much as (*Collocutio*) or (*colloquium*) but by vse, it is also taken for those high courts of Iustice throughout the kingdome of *Fraunce*, where mens causes and differences are publikely determined without farder appeale. Whereof there be seuen in number: as *Paris*, *Tolouse*, *Gresnoble* in *Daulphene*, *Aix* in *Prouence*, *Bordeaux*, *Dijon* in *Bourgogine*, and *Roan* in *Normandy*. *Vincentius Lupanus de Magistrat. Franc. lib. 2. cap. Parlamentum. num.* 28. whereunto *Gerard de Haillon* addeth the eighth. *viz. Rhenes in Brettagne.*

In England we vse it for the assembly of the king and the three estates of the Realme, *videlicet* . the Lords Spirituall, the Lords Temporall, and commons, for the debating of maters touching the common wealth, and especially the making and correcting of lawes. which assembly or court is of all other the highest, and of greatest authoritie, as you may reade in *Sir Thomas Smith. de Repub. Anglo lib. 2. cap. 1. & 2. Camd. Britan. pag.* 112. and *Cromptons Iurisd. fol. pri. & seqq.* The institution of this court *Polydor Virgil, lib.* 11. of his Chronicles, referreth after a sort to *Henry* the first: yet confessing that it was vsed before, though verie seldome. I find in the former prologue of the Grande Custumarie of Normandie, that the Normans vsed the same meanes in making their lawes. And I haue seene a monument of Antiquite, shewing the maner of houlding this parlament in the time of King *Edward* the sonne of King *Etheldred*, which (as my note saith, was deliuered by the discreeter sorte of the Realme vnto *William* the Conquerour, at his commaundement, & allowed by him. This writing beginneth thus. *Rex est caput, principium, & finis parlamenti, & ita non habet parem in suo gradu. Et sic ex Rege solo primus gradus est. Secundus gradus est ex Archiepiscopis, Episcopis, Abbatibus, Prioribus per Baroniã tenentibus. Tertius gradus est, de procuratoribus cleri. Quartus gradus est de Comitibus, Baronibus, & aliis Magnatibus. Quintus gradus est de militibus Comitatuum. Sextus gradus est de ciuibus & Burgensibus: & ita est parlamentum*

tum ex sex gradibus. sed sciendum, licet aliquis dictorum quinq; gradu-um post Regem absens fuerit, dum tamen omnes præmoniti fuerint per rationabiles summonitiones, parlamentum nihilo minus censetur esse plenum. Touching the great authoritie of this court, I finde in *Stowes Annalls, pag.* 660. that *Henry* the sixth directing his priuie seale to *Richard Earle* of *Warwicke*, thereby to discharge him of the Captainship of *Cales*, the Earle refused to obey the priuie seale, and continued forth the said office, because he receiued it by Parlament. But one example cannot make good a doctrine. And of these two one must needes be true, that either the king is aboue the Parlament, that is, the positiue lawes of his kingdome, or els that he is not an absolute king. *Aristotle lib.* 3. *Politico. cap.* 16. And therefore though it be a mercifull policie, and also a politique mercie (not alterable without great perill) to make lawes by the consent of the whole Realme, because so no one part shall haue cause to complaine of a partialitie: yet simply to binde the prince to or by these lawes, weare repugnant to the nature and constitution of an absolute monarchy. See *Bracton, lib.* 5. *tract.* 3. *ca.* 3. *nu.* 3. *and Cassan de consuet: Burg: pag.* 335. *and Tiraquel.* in his booke *De Nobilitate, cap.* 20. *pag.* 68. *nu.* 26. See the statute *anno* 31. *H.* 8. *cap.* 8. *in proœmio*. and many excellent men more, that handle this point. That learned *Hotoman* in his *Francogallia*, doth vehemently oppugne this ground, as some other that write in corners: but he is so cleane overborne by the pois of reason, that not onely many meaner men for learning triumph ouer him in this case, but himselfe, as I haue credibly hard, vpon the sight of his fault, cried God and the world mercie for his offence, in writing that erroneous and seditious booke. The Emperours of Rome had their *semestria consilia*, & their *pretorium* or place of councell, builded by *Augustus* in his palace, and thereupon called (*palatium*) afterward termed (*consistorium*) where they, as in their principall court, did both determine the greatest sort of their causes, and also made their constitutions. And heere had they assisting them many of the wisest of their empire; whome *Augustus* first called (*consiliarios*,) *Alexander Severus* afterward (*scriniorum principes*) others after that (*palatinos*) and then (*comites consistorianos*)

anos) And these men in this respect, were indued with great honour, and enioyed many priuiledges. Yet were they but assistants to the Emperour to aduise him, not chalenging any power ouer him, or equal with him. *More* touching the course and order of this Parlament, see in *Cromptons Iurisdict. fol. pri. & seqq.* and *Vowell, alias Hooker*, in his booke purposely writen of this mater. See *King*.

Parole (Loquela) is a French word, signifying as much as *(Dictio, allocutio, sermo, vox)* It is vsed in *Kitchin, fol.* 193. for a plee in court. It is also sometime ioyned with lease, as *Lease parol*, that is *Lease per parole*. a lease by word of mouth.

Parson (Persona) commeth of the French *(Personne)*. It peculiarly signifieth with vs, the Rector of a church: the reason whereof seemeth to be, bicause he for his time representeth the church, and susteineth the person thereof, as well in siewing, as being siewed in any action touching the same. See *Fleta. lib. 6. ca.* 18. *Parson impersonee (persona impersonata)* is he that is in possession of a church, whether appropriated or not appropriated. for in the new booke of *Entries, verbo Ayde in Annuity*, you haue these words. *Et praedictus A dicit, quod ipse est persona praedicta ecclesiae de S. impersonata in eadem ad praesentationem E. patronissae, &c.* So I haue reason to thinke, that *persona* is the patrō or he that hath right to giue the benefice, by reason that before the *Lateran councell* he had right to the tithes, in respect of his liberalitie vsed in the erection or endowment of the church, *quasi sustineret personam ecclesiae*. and he *persona impersonata* to whome the benefice is giuen in the patrons right. For I reade in the *Register Iudiciall personam impersonatam*, for the Rector of a benefice presentatiue and not appropriated, *fol.* 34.*b.* and see *Dyer. fol.* 40. *nu.* 72. where he saith that a Deane and chapter be persons impersonees of a benefice appropriated vnto them. who also *fol.* 221. *num.* 19. plainly sheweth that *persona impersonata* is he that is inducted and in possession of a benefice. So that *persona* seemeth to be termed *impersonata*, onely in respect of the possession that he hath of the benefice or Rectorie, be it appropriated or otherwise, by the act of another. And yet I haue talked with men of good opinion in the common lawe, that hold onely the proprietarie of a be-a benefice to be the person personee. But if that weare true, he should rather be called person *parsonnier* . i . *partiarius vel particeps fructuum* , because the Vicare hath some parte toward his paines in seruing the cure. For (*parsonnier*) in the french tongue. is (*partiarius*) or (*particeps*)

Partes finis nihil habuerunt, &c. is an exception taken against a fine levied. *Cookes reports lib.* 3. the case of *Fines. fol*. 88. *a. b.*

Parters of gold and siluer. See *Finours.*

Partitione facienda, is a writ that lieth for those, which hould lands or tenements *Pro Indiuiso*, and would seuer to euery one his part, against him or them that refuse to ioyne in partition as Coparceners and Tenents in Gauel kind, *ould: nat. br. fol:* 142. *Fitzh. nat. br. fol.* 61. *Register orig. fol.* 76. 316. *and Register Iudiciall, fol.* 80. and the new booke of *Entrise. verbo Partition.*

Partlet, seemeth to be some part of a mans attire, as namely some loose collar of a dublet, to be set on or taken of by it selfe. without the bodies, as mens bands or womens neckirchiefs be, which are in some places, or at least haue beene within memory, called partlets. This word is reade in the statute, *anno* 24. *H*. 8. *ca*. 13. and seemeth to be a diminutiue of the word (*part.*)

Paruo nocumento, is a writ. See *Nusance.*

Passage (*Passagium*) is a French word, signifying *transitum, transitionem, meatum*. It signifieth in our common lawe, the hire that a man payeth for being transported ouer sea, *anno* 4. Ed. 3. *cap.* 7. or ouer any riuer. *Westm.* 2. *cap.* 25. *anno* 13. *Ed. pri.*

Passagio, is a writ to the keepers of ports, to let a man passe ouer, that hath license of the king. *Register originall. fol.* 193. *b.* 194. *a.*

Passeport, is compounded of two French words (*Passer*. i. *perambulare, transire*) and (*port*. i. *portus*) It signifieth with vs, a license made by any that hath authoritie, for the safe passage of any man from one place to another. *anno* 2. *Ed.* 6. *ca.* 2.

Pasuage, *pasuagium*. See *Pawnage.*

Patent (*literæ patentes*) is different from a writ, *Cromptons Iurisd fol.* 126. The Coroner is made by writ and not by patent. See *Leters patents.* See also *Literæ patentes* in the table of the Register, where you shall finde the forme of diuers patents.

Patron (*Patronus*) is vsed in

the

the Ciuile lawe, for him that hath manumitted a seruant, and thereby is both iustly accompted his great benefactor, and challengeth certaine reuerence and dutie of him during his life: see the title *De iure patronatus:* in the Digest: with the Feudists it is vsed *pro authore feudi.* *Hotom. verbo* Patro- *nus,* in his commentarie *de verbis feudal.* In the canon lawe, as also in the feuds, and our common lawe, it signifieth him that hath the gift of a benefice. And the reason is, because the gift of churches and benefices originally belonged vnto such good men, as either builded them, or els indowed them with some great part of the reuenew belonging vnto them. *De iure patronatus* in the *Decretals.* Such might well be called patrons, as builded the Church, or inriched it: but these that now haue the gift of a benefice, are more commonly patronized by the Church, though against her will, alway selling their presentations as deerely as they can: and therefore may be called *Patroni a patrocinando,* as *Mons à mouendo.* *Patronum faciunt dos, ædificatio, fundus,* saith the old verse. Of lay patrons one writeth thus. *Quod autem a supremis pontificibus proditum est, (ca. cum dilectus, extra de iure patronatus) laicos ius habere presantãdi clericos Ordinariis: hoc singulari favore sustinetur, vt allectetur laici, invitetur, & inducantur ad constructionẽ ecclesiarũ (c. quoniam. eodem) Nec omni ex parte ius patronatus spirituale censeri debet, sed temporale potius spirituali annexum. (glos. in c. piæ mentis, 16. qu. 7.)* These be *Corasius* words in his paraphrase *ad sacerdotiorum materium, parte pri. cap. 2.* and *parte. 4. cap. 6. in principio,* he thus writeth of the same mater. *Patroni in iure Pontificio dicuntur qui alicuius ecclesiæ extruendæ, aut alterius cuiuscunq; fundationis ecclesiasticæ authores fuerunt, ideoq; præsentandi & offerendi clericum ius habent. quem ecclesiæ vacanti praeesse, & in ea collatis reditibus frui velint. Acquirunt autem hoc ius, qui de Episcopi consensu vel fundant ecclesiam, hoc est, locum in quo templum extruitur, assignant, vel ecclesiam ædificant, vel etiam constructas ecclesias ante consecrationem dotant. vt non valde sit obscurum, ius patronatus quo de agimus, finire, ius esse præsentandi clericum ad ecclesiam vacantem ex gratia ei concessum, qui consentiente Episcopo, vel construxit, vel dotavit ecclesiam.*

Pannage (*Pannagium, aliàs pasnagium*) or (*pennagium*) as it is latined (*in pupilla oculi*) may be probably thought to come of the French (*panez*) or (*panets*) which is is a roote something like a parsnep, but somewhat lesse and ranker in taste, which hogs in Fraunce feede vpon, though it be eaten by men also; and the French may seeme to come of the latine (*panicium*) .i. that which men vse in the steede of bread (*Isodorus*) or (*panicium*) of the French. It signifieth in our common law, the mony taken by the *Agistors* for the feede of hogs with the mast of the kings forest: *Crompton. Iurisd. fol.* 165. *Westm.* 2. *cap.* 25. *anno* 13. *Ed. pri.* with whom *M. Manwood parte pri:* of his forest lawes agreeth in these words: *Agistment* is properly the common of herbage of any kinde of ground, or land, or woods, or the money due for the same: and *pawnage* is most properly the mast of the woods, or lands, or hedgerowes, or the money due to the owner of the same for it. But this learned man in his second part. *cap.* 12. where he writeth at large of this, driueth the word from the greeke πανήγυρις at the which (I thinke) he smiled himselfe when he set it downe. *Lindwood* defineth it thus: *Panagium est pastus pecorum in nemoribus & in syluis, vtpote de glandibus & aliis fructibus arborum syluestrium, quarum fructus aliter non solent colligi. titulo de decimis. ca. sancta. verb:* Pannagiis. *M. Skene de verborum signf.* calleth it *pannagium*, and defineth it to be the duty giuen to the king, for the pasturage of swine in his forest. The French word for the same thing is (*panage*) or (*glandee*) .i. *glandatio, vel glandium collectio, & pastio suum ex glandibus.* And we surely take it from the French, whence they had it, or what etimologie they make of it, let themselues looke.

Peace (*pax*) in the generall signification is opposite to warre or strife. But particularly it signifieth with vs, a quiet and harmlesse cariage, or behauiovr toward the king and his people. *Lamb. eirenarcha. li.* 1. *ca.* 2. *pag.* 7. And this is one way prouided for all men by oath, as you may read in *Frankpledge*, but more especially in case, where one particular man or some few goe in daunger of harme from some other. For vpon his oath made thereof before a Iustice of peace, he must be secured by good bond. See *Lamb. eirenarcha lib.* 2. *c.* 2. *p.* 77. See also *Cromptons* Iustice of peace. *fol.* 118. *b. &c. vsq; f.* 129. This amōg the Ciuiliās is called *cautio de non offendēdo. Gail, de pace publ. lib. pri. c.* 2. *nu.* 1.

Peace of God and the church, (*pax Dei & ecclesiæ*) is auncientl y vsed for that rest, which the kings subiects had from trouble and suite of law, betweene the termes. See *Vacation.*

Peace of the King. anno. 6. R. 2. *stat. pri. ca.* 13. is that peace and securitie both for life and goods, which the *King* promiseth to all his subiects or others taken to his protection. See *Suite of the kings peace*. This pointe of policie seemeth to haue beene borowed by vs from the Feudists. for in the second booke of the feuds, there is a chapter *viz.* the 53. chapter intituled thus. *De pace tenenda inter subditos, & iuramento firmanda, & vindicanda, & de pœna iudicibus apposita, qui eum vindicare & iustitiam facere neglexerint*, the contents of which chapter is a Constitution of *Fredericke* the first, as *Hotoman* there proueth, expounding it very learnedly and like himselfe. Of this kings peace, *Roger Houeden* setteth downe diuers branches, *parte poster. suorum annalium. in* Henr. 2. *fol.* 344. *a. b.* and *fol.* 430. *b.* he mentioneth a forme of an oth which *Hubert* Archbishop of *Canterburie*, and chiefe Iustice of *Englād* in *R.* the first his daies, sent through the whole realme, to be taken by the kings subiects. See *Deciners.* See *Suertie of peace.* There is also the peace of the Church, for which, see *Sanctuarie.* And the peace of the kings high way, which is the immunitie that the kings high way hath, from all annoyance or molestation. See *Watling street.* The peace of the plowe, whereby the plow and plow catell are secured from distresses. For which, see *Fitz. nat. br. fol.* 90. *A. B.* So Fayres may be said to haue their peace, because noe man may in them be troubled for any debt elsewhere contracted. See *Fayre.*

Pedage (*pedagium*) signifieth money giuen for the passing by foote or horse through any countrey. *extra de Censibus, ca. Innovamus.* I reade not this word in any English writer, but onely the author of the booke called *pupilla oculi. parte* 9. *cap* 7. *A. D.* I thinke we rather vse passage for it. *Pedagia dicuntur quæ dantur à transeuntibus in locum constitutum à principe. Et capiens pedagium debet dare saluum conductum, & territorium eius tenere securum. Baldus in vsibus Feudorum. de pa. iura. fir.* §. *Conventionales. Cassan. de consuetud. Burg. pag.* 118. hath these wordes, *Pedagium a pede dictum est, quòd à transeuntibus solvitur, &c.*

Peere (*pila*) seemeth properly to be a fortresse made against the force of the sea, for the better securitie of ships, that lye at harbour in any hauen. So is the peere of *Douer* described in *M. Camd. Brit. p.* 259. *in meo.*

Peeres (*pares*) commeth of the French (*per.* i. *par*) it signifieth in our common lawe, plurally those, that are empaneled in an Enquest, vpon any man for the conuicting and clearing him of any offence, for the which he is called in question. And the reason thereof is, because the course and custome of our nation is, to trie euery man in this case by his equals. *West prim. cap. 6. anno 3. Ed. prim.* So *Kitchin* vseth it. *fol. 78.* in these wordes: *Mais si le amerciament soit affirre per pares.* And this word in this signification, is not in vse with vs onely, but with other nations also. For *pares sunt conuasalli, quorum sententiâ vasallus propter feloniam est condemnatus. Barklaius de Regno, lib. 4. cap. 2. Et pares sunt qui ab eodem domino feudum tenent, lib. prim. Feudor. cap. 26.* But this word is most notoriously vsed for those that be of the Nobilitie of the Realme, and Lords of the Parlament, and so is it vsed in *Stawnf. pl.* of the Crowne, *lib. 3. cap. Triall per les Peeres*, being the first. The reason whereof is, because though there be a distinction of degrees in our Nobilitie, yet in all publike actions they are equall: as in their voices in Parlament, and in passing vpon the triall of any Noble man, &c. This appellation seemeth to be borowed from *Fraunce*, and from those twelue *Peeres*, that *Charles* the Great, (or *Lewis* the younger, in some mens opinion) instituted in that kingdome, which be next vnto the King, and are of like dignitie among themselues, touching their power in publike affaires. Of whome you may reade *Vincentius Lupanus de magistrat. Fraunciæ lib. 1. cap. Pares Fraunciæ.* So that we though we haue borowed the appellation, and applied it with some reason to all that are Lords of the Parlament, yet haue wee no sett number of them, because the number of our Nobles, may be more or lesse, as it pleaseth the *King*.

Pelota, is a word vsed in the booke called (*pupilla oculi*) *parte 5. cap. 22.* signifying the ball of the foot, of the French (*pelote.*) i. *pila.*

Pein fort & dure. See *Pain fort & dure.*

Pelt wooll, is the woll pulled off the skinne or pelt of dead sheepe, *anno 8. H. 6. cap. 22.*

Penon, anno 11. R. 2. cap. prim. is a Standard, Banner, or Ensigne, caried in warre. It is borowed from *Fraunce*: for *pennon* in the French language signifieth the same thing. See *Baneret*: yea reade this word, *anno 11. R. 2. cap. 1.*

Penue

Penne: See *Baye*.

Peper, (piper) is a spice known in a manner to euery childe, beeing the fruite of a plant, that is betweene a tree and an herbe: of whose diuersities and nature, you may reade *Gerards* herball, *lib.* 3. *cap.* 146. This is set among merchandize that are to be garbled. *anno*, 1. *Iacob. cap.* 19.

Peper lowse, anno, 32. *H.* 8 *cap.* 14.

Per, cui, & post, See *Entrie*.

Perambulatione facienda, is a writ, that is siewed out by two or more Lords of maners, lying neere one another, and consenting to haue their bounds seuerally knowne. It is directed to the Shyreeue, commanding him to make perambulation, and to set downe their certaine limits betweene them. Of this reade more at large in *Fitz. nat. br. fol.* 133. See *Rationabilibus diuisis*. See the *Regist. orig. fol.* 157. and the new booke of Entries, *verbo, Perambulatione facienda*.

Perche (pertica) is a French word, signifying a long pole. It is vsed with vs for a Rodde or Pole of 16. foote and a halfe in length. Whereof 40. in length and foure in bredth make an acre of ground. *Cromptons Iurisd. fol.* 222. Yet by the custome of the countrie it may be longer, as he there saith. For in the Forest of *Sheerewood* it is 25. foot, *fol.* 224. *M. Skene de verbor. signif. verbo, Particata terra*, saith, that *particata terra* is a Roode of land: where he hath also these wordes in effect: Three beere cornes without tayles set together in length make an inch: of the which cornes one should be taken of the midde ridge, one of the side of the ridge, another of the furrow. Twelue inches make a foot of measure: three foote and an inch make an elne; sixe elnes long make one fall, which is the common lineall measure, and sixe elnes long, and sixe broade, make a square and superficiall fall of measured land. And it is to be vnderstood, that one rod, one raip, one lineall fall of measure, are all one, for each one of them containeth sixe elnes in length. Howbeit, a rod is a staffe or pole of wood, a raipe is made of tow or hempe. And so much land as falleth vnder the rod or raipe at once, is called a fal of measure, or a lineal fall: because it is the measure of the line or length onely. Like as the superficiall fall is the measure both of length and bredth. *Item*, tenne fals in length and foure in bredth make a Roode; foure *Roodes* make an acre, &c. This is the measure of Scotland, whereof you may reade more in the same place.

Perdonatio vtlagariæ, in the *Register indiciall, fol.* 28. is the forme of pardon for him, that for not comming to the kings court is outlawed, and afterward of his owne accord yeldeth himselfe to prison.

Peremptorie (peremptorius) commeth of the verb (*perimere*) to cut of, and ioyned with a substantiue (as action or exception) signifieth a finall and determinate act without hope of renewing. So *Fitzh.* calleth a peremptory action, *nat. br. fol.* 35. *P. fol.* 38. *M. fol.* 104. *O. Q. R. fol.* 108. *D. G.* and *non-suite peremptorie. idem, eodem, fol.* 5. *N. F. fol.* 11. *A.* peremptory exception. *Bracton li.* 4. *ca.* 20. *Smith de rep. Anglorum, li.* 2. *ca.* 13. calleth that a peremptory exception, which can make the state and issue in a cause.

Perinde valere, is a dispensation graunted to a clerk, that being defectiue in his capacity to a benefice or other ecclesiasticall function, is *de facto* admitted vnto it. And it hath the appellation of the words which make the faculty as effectuall to the party dispensed with, as if he had bene actually capable of the thing, for which he is dispensed with, at the time of his admissiõ.

Perkins, was a learned Lawyer, fellow and bencher of the inner Temple, that liued in the daies of *Edward* the 6. and Queene *Mary*. He writ a booke vpon diuers points of the common law of very great commendation.

Permutatione Archidiaconatus & ecclesiæ eidem annexæ, cum ecclesia & præbenda, is a writ to an Ordinary commaunding him to admit a clerk to a benefice, vpon exchaunge made with another: *Register orig. fol.* 307. *a.*

Pernour of profits, commeth of the French verb (*prendre .i. accipere*) and signifieth him that taketh: as *pernour of profits, anno* 1. *H.* 7. *ca. pri. Pernour de profits*, and *cesti que vse* is all one, *Coke li.* 1. *casu Chudley. fol.* 123. *a.* See *Pernour, anno* 21. *R.* 2. *ca.* 15.

Per quæ seruitia, is a writ iudiciall issuying from the note of a fine, and lyeth for the cognizee of a maner, seignory, cheife rent, or other seruices, to compell him that is tenent of the land at the time of the note of the fine leuied, to atturne vnto him. *West parte* 2. *symbol. titulo Fines. sect.* 126. To the same effect speaketh the *old nat. br fol.* 155. See also the new booke of *Entries. verbo Per quæ seruitia.*

Perquisite (perquisitum) signifieth, in *Bracton*, any thing purchased, as *perquisitum facere. lib.* 2. *cap.* 30. *nu.* 3. *& lib.* 4. *ca* 22. Perquisites of court, be those profits that grow vnto the Lord of a maner, by vertue of his

Court Baron, ouer and aboue the certaine and yearely profits of his land, as escheats, mariages, goods purchased by villeines, fines of copie houlds, and such like. New terms of the law.

Person. See *Parson*.

Personable, signifieth as much as inhabled to hould or maineтaine plee in a court. for example: The demaundant was iudged personable to maintaine this action. *old. nat. br. fol.* 142. and in *Kitchin fol.* 214. The tenent pleaded that the wife was an alien borne in *Portingall* without the ligeance of the King, and Iudgement was asked whether shee would be answered. The plaintife saith: shee was made personable by Parlament, that is, as the Ciuilians would speake it, *habere personam standi in iudicio*. Personable is also as much, as to be of capacitie to take any thing graunted or giuen. *Plowden, casu Colthirst. fol.* 27. *b*.

Personall (*Personalis*) hath in our common lawe, one strange signification, being ioyned with the substantiue, things, goods, or Chatels: as things personall, goods personall, Chatels personall, for thus it signifieth any corporeall, and moueable thing belonging to any man, be it quicke, or dead. So is it vsed in *West, parte* 2. *symbol. titulo* Inditements, *sect.* 58. in these words. Theft is an vnlawfull felonious taking away of another mans moueable personall goods. and againe, *fol.* 61. *Larceny* is a felonious taking away of another mans moueable personal goods; & *Kitchin f.* 139. In these words: Where personall things shalbe giuen to a corporation: as a horse, a cowe, an oxe, sheepe, hogs, or other goods, &c. and *Stawnford. pl cor. fo.* 25. *Contrectatio rei alienæ*, is to be vnderstood of things personall: for in things reall it is not felony, as the cutting of a tree is not felony. The reason of this application, see in *Chatell*.

Personalty (*Personalitas*) is an abstract of personall. The action is in the personalty. *old. nat. br. fol.* 92. that is to say, brought against the right person, or the person against whome in lawe, it lieth. I find these contrary words. (*Personalitas* & Im*personalitas*) in the author of the booke called *vocabularius vtriusq; iuris*: as for example, *Personalitas significatur per has dictiones: tu, mihi, ego, tibi, cum alio significato quod probabiliter concluditur: & si nullo modo concludatur, tunc est* Im*personalitas, quia actum vitiat, prout ratio dictat. verbi gratia. Ego stipulor: constituis te mihi soluturum debitum a* Titio *mihi debitum: Tu respondes, Satisfiet. Hac Impersonalitas non contrahit obligationem*.

Persons ne Prebendaries ne seront

ront charges as quinsimes, &c. is a writ that lyeth for prebendaries or other spirituall persons, being distreined by the shyreeue, or collectours of fifteenths, for the fiftenth of their goods, or to be contributory to taxes. *Fitzh. nat.br.fol.* 176.

Pesterable wares, seeme to be such wares, as pester and take vp much roome in a shippe, *anno* 32. *H.* 8. *cap.* 14.

Peter pence (*Denarii Sancti Petri*) otherwise called in the Saxon tongue *Romefeoh*. i. the fee of Rome, or due to Rome, and also *Romescot*, and *Rome penning*, was a tribute giuen by *Inas* King of the west Saxons being in pilgrimage at Rome, in the yeare of our Lord. 720. which was a peny for euery house. *Lamberds* explication of Saxon words. *verbo Numus.* whome see also *fol.* 128. in Saint *Edwards* lawes. *nu.* 10. where it is thus writen. *Omnes qui habent* 30. *denariatus viua pecuniæ in domo sua de suo proprio, Anglorum lege dabit denariū Sancti Petri, & lege Danorum, dimidiam merkam: Iste verò denarius debet summoniri in solennitate Apostolorum Petri & Pauli, & colligi ad festiuitatem, quæ dicitur ad vincula: ita vt vltra illum diem non detineatur. Si quispiam detinuerit, ad Iusticiam Regis clamor deferatur, quoniam denarius hic Regis eleemmozina est, Iusticia verò faciat denarium reddere, & forisfacturam Episcopi & Regis. Quod si quis domos plures habuerit, de illa, vbi residens fuerit in festo Apostolorum Petri & Pauli, denarium reddat.* See also King *Edgars* lawes. *fol.* 78. *cap.* 4. which containeth a sharpe constitution touching this mater, *Stowe in his Annals, pag.* 67. saith, that he that had 20. peniworth of goods of one maner catell in his house, of his owne proper, was to giue a penie at Lammas yearly. See *Romescot.*

Petit Cape. See *Cape.*

Petit Larceny (*paruum latrocinium*) See *Larcenye.*

Petit treason (*parua tradıtio*) in true French is (*petit trahizon.* i. *proditio minor*) treason in a lesser or lower kinde. For whereas treason in the highest kinde, is an offence done against the securitie of the common wealth, *West parte* 2. *symb. titulo Inditements. sect.* 63. petit treason is of this nature, though not so expresly as the other. Examples of petit treason you shall find to be these: if a seruant kill his master, a wife her husband, a secular or religious man his prelate, *anno* 25. *Edward* 3. *cap.* 2. Whereof see more in *Staunf. pl. cor. lib.* 1. *cap.* 2. See also *Cromptons Iustice of peace. fol.* 2. where he addeth diuers other examples to those of *Staunford*. For the punishnishment of petit treason, see the statute, *anno 22.H.8.cap.14.* and *Crompton vbi supra.*

Petition (*Petitio*) hath a general signification for all intreaties made by an inferiour to a superiour, and especially to one hauing iurisdiction: But most especially it is vsed for that remedie, which the subiect hath to helpe a wrong done, or pretended to be done by the King. For the King hath it by prerogatiue, that he may not be sewed vpon a writ. *Stawnf.prar.cap. 15.* whome also read *cap. 22.* And a petition in this case is either generall, or speciall. It is called generall of the generall conclusion set downe in the same. *viz. que le Roy lui face droit & reison.* that the King doe him right and reason: wherevpon followeth a generall indorsement vpon the same. *soit droit fait aux partis.* let right be done to the partise. *Petition* speciall is where the conclusion is speciall for this or that: and the Indorsment to that is likewise speciall. See the rest *cap. 22.*

Petra lane, a stone of wooll See *Stone.*

Philiser, See *Filazer.*

Piccage (*Piccagium*) is money paid in faires for breaking of the ground to set vp boothes or standings.

Picle, aliâs pitle, seemeth to come from the Italian (*piccolo vel picciolo.i. parvus, minutus*) and signifieth with vs a little small close or inclosure.

Pienour, commeth of the French (*Pionnier .i. fossor*) and signifieth such labourers, as are taken vp for the Kings host to cast trenches, or vndermine forts *anno 2. & 3.Ed.6.cap.20.*

Piepowders court (*Curia pedis pulverizati*) cōmeth of two French words (*pied.i. pes*) and *pouldreux.i. pulverulentus*) It signifieth a court held in faires for the redres of all disorders cōmitted within them: which because it is summarie, *de plano, & sine figura iudicii*, it hath the name of dustie feete, which we cōmonly get by sitting neere the ground: of this see *Cromptons Iurisd.fol. 221.* Reade *M.Skene.de ver.signif.verbo Pedepulverosus:* which word he reporteth to signifie a vagabond, especially a merchant ,, which hath no place of dwelling, where the dust may be wiped of his feet or shooes, & therefore must haue iustice summarily ministred vnto him. *viz.* within three flowings and three ebbings of the sea. *Bract.* calleth it *Iustitiam pepoudrous, li. 5. tract. 1.ca. 6. nu. 6.* Of this court reade the statute *anno 17. Ed. 4.cap. 2.*

Pille of Foddray, in the countie of *Lancaster, an. 2.H. 6.ca.5.*

seemeth to be a creeke, and called pille by the ideom of the country for pile: for the which see *Pile*.

Pillorie(*Collistrigium, Pillorium*) commeth of the French (*Pilorie*) which may seeme to smell of the greeke, and to proceede from (πυλη) because one standing on the pillory putteth his head through a kind of doore. i. *ianua: &* ὁρῶ. i. *video*: it signifieth all one thing with it, sauing that the French is vsed for a tumbrell, as well as for that which we call the pillorie. There is a statute made of the pillorie, *anno* 51. *H*. 3. wherein you may see who were then subiect to this punishment. This was among the Saxons called *Healsfang* of (*Heals*) a necke and (*Fang*) to take, *Lamb. explication of Saxon words. verbo. Mulcta*.

Pipe (*pipa*) seemeth to be a rolle in the exchequer, otherwise called the great rolle, *anno* 37. *Ed*. 3. *ca*. 4. See *Clerke of the pipe*. It is also a measure of wine or oile conteining halfe a tunne, that is sixe score & sixe gallons, *anno* 1. *R*. 3. *cap*. 13.

Piscarie (*piscaria*) commeth of the French (*pescharie*. i. *piscatio*) It signifieth in our common lawe, a libertie of fishing in an other mans waters.

Pittle. See *Picle*.

Placard, anno 2. & 3. *Ph. & Mar. cap*. 7. is a licence whereby a man is permitted to maintaine vnlawfull games.

Plaint (*Querela*) is a French word, signifiing as much as *Questus, querimonia*. In our common law, it is vsed for the propounding of any action personall or reall in writing. So it is vsed in *Brooke, titulo. Plaint in Assise*. And the party making this plaint, is called plaintife: *Kitchin, fol*. 231.

Plea (*placitum*) commeth of the French (*ploid*. i. *lis. controversia*). It signifieth in our common lawe, that which either partie alleadgeth for himselfe in court. And this was wont to be done in French from the Conquest vntill *Edward* the 3. who ordeined them to be done in English. *a*. 36. *cap*. 15. Pleas are diuided into pleas of the Crowne, and common pleas. Pleas of the Crowne in Scotland be 4. roberie, rape, murder, and wilfull fire, *Skene de verb. sign. verb. Placitum*. with vs they be all suites in the Kings name against offences committed against his Crowne and dignitie. *Stawnf. pl. cor. cap*. 1. or against his Crowne and peace. *Smith. de Repub. Angl. li*. 2. *cap*. 9. And those seeme to be treasons, felonies, misprisions of either, and mayhem. For those onely doth that reverend

Iudge

Iudge mention in that tractat. Common pleas be those that be held betweene common persons. Yet by the former definitions, these must comprise all other, though the king be a partie. Plea may farder be diuided into as many braunches as Action, which see. For they signifie all one. Then is there a Forein plea, whereby mater is alleadged in any court that must be tried in another. As if one should lay Bastardy to another in a court Baron. *Kitchin. fo.* 75. The word (*placitum*) is vsed by the Commentours vpon the Feuds in the same signification that pleas be with vs. And (*placitare*) with them is (*litigare, & causas agere. Hotom. in verb. feudal. verb. Placitare.*

Pledge (*Plegius*) commeth of the French (*Pleige. i. fideiussor*) *Pleiger aucun.* i. *fideiubere pro aliquo.* In the same signification is *Plegius* vsed by *Glanuile. libro decimo, capite quinto,* and *Plegiatio* for the act of suretiship in the interpreter of the Grand Custumarie of *Normandie, capite* 60. *Plegii dicuntur personæ quæ se obligant ad hoc, ad quod qui eos mittit tenebatur.* And in the same booke, *capit.* 89. & 90. *Plegiatio* is vsed as *Glanuile* before doth vse it. *Salui plegii,* be vsed for *plegii, pupill. oculi, parte quint. capit.* 22. *Charta de Foresta.* This word *plegius* is vsed also for *Frank pledge* sometime, as in the ende of *William Conquerours* lawes set out by *Master Lamberd in his Archaionom. fol.* 125. in these words. *Omnis homo qui voluerit se teneri pro libero, sit in plegio, vt plegius eum habeat ad Iusticiam, si quid offenderit, &c.* And these be called capitall pledges. *Kitchin. folio decimo.* See *Frank pledge.*

Plena forisfactura, and *plena vita,* see *Forfeiture.*

Plegiis acquietandis, is a writ that lieth for a suretie against him, for whome he is suretie, if he pay not the money at the day. *Fitzh. nat. br. fol.* 137. *Regist. original.* 158.*a.*

Plenartie, is an abstract of the adiectiue (*plenus*) and is vsed by our common Lawyers in mater of benefices. Wherein *plenartie* and *vacation* be meerely contrarie. *Staunford. prerogativ. cap. octau. fol.* 32. *West. secundo, capit. quint. anno* 13. *Edvard. pri.*

Plevin (*pleuina*) commeth of the French (*pleuine .i. sponsio*)

See *Replevin.*

Plite of Lawne, *&c. anno* 3. *Ed.* 4. *cap.* 5. seemeth to be a certaine measure, as a yard, or elle, &c.

Plonkets, anno 1. *R.* 3. *cap.* 8. is a kind of wollen cloth.

P*luries*, is a writ that goeth out in the third place. For first goeth out the originall *Capias:* which, if it speed not, then goeth out the *Sicut alias* : and if that faile, then the *Pluries.* See *old nat. br. fol.* 33. In the writ *De excom. capiendo*, see in what diuersitie of cases this is vsed in the Table of the *original Regist.*

Pole. See *Perch.*

Polein, anno 4. *Ed.* 4. *cap.* 7. seemeth to be a sharpe or picked toppe set in the forepart of the shooe or boote. This fashion was first taken vp in *Richard* the seconds dayes, the pickes being made so long as they were tyed vp to the knees with siluer or golden chaines, and forbidden by *Edward* the fourth. *Stow pag.* 4.

Policie of assurance, is a course taken by those which do aduenture wares or merchandize by sea, whereby they, lothe to hazard their whole aduenture, do giue vnto some other a certaine rate or proportion, as tenne in the hundred, or such like, to secure the safe arriuall of the ship, and so much wares at the place agreed vpon. So that if the ship and wares do miscarie, the assurer maketh good to the venturer so much as he promiseth to secure, as 20. 30. 100. more or lesse: and if the ship do safely ariue, he gaineth that clearely which the venturer compoundeth to pay him. And for the more euen dealing betweene the venturer and the securer in this case, there is a certaine Clerk or officer ordained to set downe in writing the summe of their agreement, that they afterward differ not betweene themselues vpon the bargaine. This is in course Latine elsewhere called *assecuratio.* This terme you haue *anno* 43. *Eliz. cap.* 11.

Pondage. See *Poundage.*

Pone, is a writ, whereby a cause depending in the County court, is remoued to the common *Banke. old nat. br. fol.* 2. See in what diuersitie of cases it is vsed, in the table of the *Originall Register.*

Pone per vadium, is a writ commaunding the Shyreeue to take suretie of one for his appearance at a day assigned: of this see fiue sorts in the table of the *Register Iudic. verbo, Pone per vadium.*

Ponendis in Assisis, is a writ founded vpon the statute of *Westm.* 2. *cap.* 38. and vpon the statute *Articuli super chartas*, *cap.* 9. which statutes do shew, what per-

persons Vicounts ought to impanell vpon Assises and Iuries, and what not: as also what number he should empanell vpon Iuries and Inquests, which see in the *Register orig. fol. 178. a.* and in *Fitz. nat. br. fol.* 165.

Ponendo in ballum, is a writ whereby to will a prisoner held in prison, to be committed to baile in cases baylable. *Register orig. fol.* 133. *b.*

Ponendo sigillum ad exceptionem, is a writ whereby the king willeth Iustices, according to the statute of *Westm.* 2. to put their seales to exceptions laid in against the plaintiffes declaration by the defendant.

Pontage (*portagium*) is a contribution toward the maintenance or reedifying of bridges *Westm. 2. cap.* 25. *anno* 13. *Ed. pri.* It may be also tolle taken to this purpose of those that passe ouer bridges, *anno* 39. *Eliz. cap.* 24. *anno* 1. *H.* 8. *cap.* 9. and see the statute, *anno* 22. *H.* 8. *cap.* 5.

Pontibus reparandis, is a writ directed to the Shyreeue, &c. willing him to charge one or more to repaire a bridge, to whom it belongeth. *Regist. orig. fol.* 153. *b.*

Portgreue (*portgreuius*) is compounded of two words (*port*) & (*greue*) or (*graue*) i. *praefectus.* It signifieth with vs the chiefe magistrate in certaine coast townes, and as *M. Camden* saith in his *Britan. pag.* 325. the chiefe magistrate of *London* was termed by this name: in steed of whom *Richard* the first ordained two Bayliffes: but presently after him, King *Iohn* granted them a Maior for their yearely Magistrate.

Porter of the doore of the Parlament house, is a necessary officer belonging to that high court, & enioyeth the priuiledges accordingly. *Cromptons. Iurisd. fol.* 11.

Porter in the circuit of Iustices, is an officer that carieth a verge or white rodde before the Iustices in *Eyre*, so called, *a portando virgam*, *anno* 13. Ed. 1, *cap.* 24.

Porter bearing verge (*virgator*) before the Iustices of either bench, *anno* 13. *Ed.* 1. *cap.* 41. See *Vergers.*

Portemote, is a word compounded of (*port.* i. *portus*) and the *Saxon* (*Gemettan*. i. *conuenire*) or of the *French* (*mot.* i. *dictio, verbum.*) It signifieth a Court kept in hauen townes, as *Swainmote* in the Forest. *Manwood, parte prim.* of his *Forest lawes, pa.* 111. It is sometime called the *Portmoote* Court, *anno* 43. *Eliz. cap.* 15.

Portsale, *anno* 35. *H.* 8. *cap.* 7. *id est*, sale of fish presently vpon returne in the hauen.

Possession (*possessio*) is vsed two waies in our common lawe. *First* for lands and inheritance: as, he is a man of large possessions. In which signification it is also vsed among the Ciuilians *sc:* for the thing possessed, *l. possessionum: Cod. commun. vtriusq; Iudic.* Next, for the actuall enioying of that, which either in truth or pretence is ours. And in this signification there is possession indeed, and possession in lawe: *pl. cor. fol.* 198. The example there is this: Before or vntill an office to be found, the king hath onely possession in law, and not in deed, speaking of the lands escheated by the attainder of the owner. See *prerog. fol.* 54. *&*. 55. In this signification also there is an vnitie of possessiō, which the Ciuilians call *Consolidationem.* Take an example out of *Kitchin, fol.* 134. if the Lord purchase the tenancie held by Heriot seruice, then the Heriot is extinct by vnity of possession: that is, because the seigneurie and the tenancie be now in one mans possession. Many diuisions of possession you may reade in *Bracton. lib.* 2. *cap.* 17. *per totum.*

Post. See *Per.*

Post diem, is a returne of a writ after the day assigned for the returne: for the which, the *Custos breuium* hath foure pence, whereas he hath nothing, if it be returned at the day: or it may be the fee taken for the same.

Post fine, is a duty belonging to the king for a fine formerly acknowledged before him in his court which is paid by the cognizee, after the fine is fully passed, and all things touching the same wholly accomplished. The rate thereof is so much and halfe so much, as was payed to the king for the fine, and is gathered by the Shyreeue of the Countie where the land, &c. lyeth, whereof the fine was leuyed, to be aunswered by him into the Exchequer.

Post terme, is a returne of a writ, not onely after the day assigned for the returne thereof, but after the terme also, which may not be receiued by the *Custos brevium*, but by the consent of one of the Iudges: it may be also the fee which the *Custos breuium* taketh, for the returne thereof, which is twenty pence.

Postea, is a word vsed for a mater tried by *Nisi prius*, and returned into the court of common pleas for Iudgement, and there afterward recorded. See *Plowden, casu Saunders. fol.* 211. *a.* See an example of this in Sir *Edw. Cokes* reports. *volum.* 6. *Rowlands case. fol.* 41. *b.* *&* 42. *a.* See *Custos breuium.*

Post disseisin (*post disseisina*) is a writ giuen by the statute of *West.* 2. *cap.* 26. and lyeth for him that

hauing

hauing recouered lands or tenements by (*præcipe quod reddat*) vpon default, or reddition, is againe disseised by the former disseisour. *Fitz. nat. br. fol.* 190. see the writ that lyeth for this in the *Register originall*, *fol.* 208. *a.*

Posteriority, (*posterioritas*) is a word of comparison and relation in tenure, the correlatiue whereof is *prioritie*. For a man holding lands or tenements of two lords, holdeth of his auncienter Lord by prioritie, and of his later Lord by posterioritie. *Stawn. prærog. fol.* 10. & 11. when one tenent holdeth of two Lords, of the one by prioritie, of the other by posterioritie, &c. *old nat. br. fol.* 94.

Pourchas (*perquisitum*) commeth of the French (*pourchasser*, i. *sollicitare, ambire:*) it signifieth the buying of lands or tenements with money or other agreement, and not the obtaining of it by title or discent. *Coniunctum perquisitum*. Ioynt pourchase. *Regist. originall. fol.* 143. *b.*

Pour faire proclaimer, que nul eniect fimes ou ordures en fosses ou riuers pres cities, &c. is a writ directed to the Maior, Shyreeue or Bayliffe of a citie or towne, cōmanding them to proclaime, that none cast filth into the ditches or places neare adioyning: and if any be cast alreadie, to remoue it. This is founded vpon the statut, *anno* 12. *Rich.* 2. *cap.* 13. *Fitzherb. nat. br. fol.* 176.

Pourparty (*propars, propartis, vel propartia*) is contrarie to (*pro indiuiso*) For to make pourparty is to diuide, and seuer the landes that fall to *Parceners*, which before partition they hold ioyntly, and *pro indiuiso. old. nat. br. fol.* 11.

Pourpresture (*pourprestura, vel porprestura, vel paraprestura*) seemeth to come from the French (*pourpris .i. conseptum.*) It is thus defined by *Glanuile*, *lib.* 9. *cap.* 11. *Pourprestura est propriè, quando aliquid super Dominum Regem iniustè occupatur. Vt in Dominicis Regis, vel in viis publicis obstructis, vel in aquis publicis transuersis à recto cursu: vel quando aliquis in ciuitate super Regiam plateam aliquid ædificando occupauerit: & generaliter, quoties aliquid fit ad nocumentum Regii tenementi, vel Regia via, vel ciuitatis. Crompton.* in his *Iurisd. fol.* 152. defineth it thus: *Pourpresture* is properly when a man taketh vnto himself or incrocheth any thing that he ought not, whether it be in any Iurisdiction, land or fraunchis: and generally, when any thing is done to the Nusance of the kings tenents. *Et idem, eodem, fol.* 203. saith to the same effect, but more at large. See *Kitchin, fol.* 10. and *Manwood, parte prim.* of his Forest lawes, *pag.* 169. *& parte* 2. *cap.* 10. *per totum.* See *Skene de verbor. signif. verb. Purpresture.* Where he maketh three sorts of this offence: one against the King, the second against the Lord of the fee: the third, against a neighbour by a neighbour lying neare him.

Pour seisir terres la femme que tient en Dower,&c. is a writ whereby the *King* seiseth vpon the land, which the wife of his Tenent, that held *in capite*, disceased, hath for her Dowrie, if shee marry without his leaue: and is grounded vpon the statute of the *Kings* prerogatiue. *cap.* 3. see *Fitzh. fol.* 174.

Poursuyuant, commeth of the French (*poursuiure.*i. *agere, agitare, persequi*) It signifieth the Messenger of the king attending vpon him in warres, or at the counsell table, the *Starre* Chamber, Exchequer, or commission court, to be sent vpon any occasion, or message, as for the apprehension of a party accused, or suspected of any offence committed. Those that be vsed in marshall causes, be called *Poursuiuants* at armes, *anno* 24. *Hen.* 8. *cap.* 13. whereof there be foure in number of especial names, which see in *Herald.* And *M. Stowe* speaking of *Richard* the third his end. *pag.* 784. hath these words: For his bodie was naked to the skinne, notso much as one cloute about him, and was trussed behinde a Pursuyuant at armes, like a hogge, or a calfe, &c. The rest are vsed vpon other messages in time of peace, and especially in maters touching iurisdiction. See *Herald.*

Pourueyour, (*prouisor*) commeth of the French (*pourvoire* .i. *prouidere prospicere.*) It signifieth an Officer of the *King*, Queene, or other great personage, that prouideth corne and other victuall, for the house of him whose Officer he is. See *magna charta. cap.* 22. *&* 3. *Ed. prim. cap.* 7. *& cap.* 31. *& anno* 28. *eiusdem. Articuli super chartas.* 2. and many other statutes gathered by *Rastal* vnder this title.

Powldauis. anno 1. *Iacob. ca.* 24.

Power of the countie, (*posse comitatus*) by *M. Lamberds* opinion in his *Eirenar. lib.* 3. *cap.* 1. *fol.* 309. containeth the ayde and attendance of all *Knights*, gentlemen, yeomen, labourers, seruants, apprentises, and villaines: and likewise of Wardes, and of other young men aboue the age of fifteene yeeres, within the countie, because all of that age are bound to haue harnesse, by the statute of *Winchester.* But women, ecclesiasticall persons

sons, and such as be decrepit, or do labour of any continuall infirmitie, shall not be compelled to attend. For the statute 2. *H.* 5. *cap.* 8. (which also worketh vpon the same ground) saith, that persons sufficient to trauell, shall be assistant in this seruice.

Pounde (*parcus*) seemeth to signifie generally any inclosure of strength to keepe in beasts: but especially, with vs, is signifieth a place of strength to restraine catell being distrained or put in for any trespas done by them, vntill they be repleuied or redeemed. And in this signification it is called a pound *ouert*, or open pound being builded vpon the wast of some Lord within his fee, and is called the Lords pownd. For he provideth it to his vse, and the vse of his tenents. See *Kitchin. fol.* 144. It is diuided into pound open, and pound close: pound open or ouert, is not onely the Lordes pownd, but a backside, court, yarde, pasture, or else what soeuer, whether the owner of any beasts impounded may come to giue them meate and drinke without offence, for their being there, or his comming thither: pound close is then the contrary *viz.* such a one as the owner cannot come vnto, to the purpose aforesaide without offence, as some close house, or such like place.

Powndage, is a Subsidie granted to the King of all maner of merchandies of euery merchant denizen and alien, caried out of this realme, or brought into the same by way of Merchandize, to the valew of twelue pence in euery pound, *anno* 12. *Ed.* 6. *cap.* 13. *anno* 31. *Eliz. cap.* 5. *anno* 1. *Iacobi, cap.* 33.

Pray age. See *Age prier.*

Pray in ayd See *Ayd.*

Prebend (*prabenda*) is the portion, which euery member, or Canon of a Cathedrall church receiueth in the right of his place, for his maintenance. And though vse haue wrought the latine word into the nature of a Substantiue: yet I thinke it originally to be an Adiectiue, or participle, and to haue bene ioyned with (*pars* or *portio*) as (*Canonica portio*) which is in a maner all one in signification. How be it (*Canonica portio*) is properly vsed for that share which euery Canon or Prebendary receiueth yearely out of the common stocke of the Church: and *prabenda* is a seuerall benefice rising from some temporall land, or church appropriated, toward the maintenance of a Clerke, or member of a Collegiat Church; and is commonly surnamed of the place, whence, the profit groweth. And Prebends be either simple, or with dignity. Simple Prebends be those, that haue no more but the reuenew toward their maintenance: Prebends with dignity are such, as haue some Iurisdiction annexed vnto them according to the diuers orders in euery seuerall church. Of this see more in the title. *De prabendis, & dignitat:* in the Decretalls. *Alciat* saith that *(prabenda)* in the plurall number and neuter gender was auinciently vsed: as now *(prabenda)* in the singuler number and feminine gender is vsed. *parerg. ca.* 43.

Prabendary (prabendarius) is he that hath a *prebend*: See *Prabend.*

Pracept (praceptum) is diuersly taken in the cōmon law: sometime for a commaundement in wrighting sent out by a Iustice of peace, or other for the bringing of a person one or more, or records before him: of this you haue examples of diuers in the table of the *Reg. Iudiciall*: And this vse seemeth to be borowed from the customes of *Lombardy*, where *praceptum* signifieth *scripturam, vel instrumentum. Hot. in verbis feudal. & libro.* 3. *Commentariorum in libros feudorum, in prafatione.* Sometime it is taken for the prouocation, whereby one man inciteth an other to commit a felony, as theft, or murder. *Stawnf. pl. cor. fol.* 105. *Bracton* calleth it *(praceptum)* or *(mandatum) lib.* 3. *tract.* 2. *ca.* 19. whence a man may obserue three diuersities of offending in murder: *Praceptum, fortia, consilium: praceptum*, being the instigation vsed before hand, *fortia*, the assistance in the fact, as help to binde the party murdered, or robbed: *consilium*, aduise either before or in the deede. The Ciuilians vse *(mandatum)* in this case, as appeareth by *Angelus in tracta: de maleficiis. vers. Sempronium Mandatorem.*

Praceptories, anno 32. *H.* 8. *cap.* 24. were benefices in a kinde, & termed preceptories, because they were possessed by the more eminent sort of the Templers, whome the cheife master by his authoritie created and called *(praceptores Templi) Ioach. Stepha. de Iurisdict. li.* 4. *cap.* 10. *num.* 27. See *Comaundry.*

Pracipe quod reddat, is a writ of great diuersitie touching both the forme and vse, for beter declaration whereof see *Ingressu*, and *Entrie*. This forme is extended as well to a writ of right, as to other writs of entry, or possession. *old. nat. br. fol.* 13. and *Fitzh. nat. br. fol.* 5. And it is called sometime a writ of *Right close*, as a *pracipe in capite*, when it issueth out of the court of common plees for a tenent holding of the *King* in cheife, as

of

of his Crowne , and not of the King, as of any honour, castell or maner. *Register orig. fol.* 4. *b. Fitzh. nat. br. fol.* 5. F. Sometime a writ of Right patent: as when it issueth out of any Lords court, for any of his tenents deforced, against the deforcer, and must be determined there. Of this reade more at large in *Fitzh. nat. br.* in the very first chapter or writ of all his booke.

Præmunire, is taken either for a writ, or for the offence whereupon the writ is graunted. The one may well enough be vnderstoode by the other. It is therefore to be noted, that the church of *Rome* vnder pretence of her supremacie and the dignitie of Saint *Peters chaire*, grew to such an incroching, that there could not be a benefice (were it Bishoprick, Abbathy, or other) of any worth here in England, the bestowing whereof could escape the Pope by one meanes or other. In so much, as for the most part, he graunted out Mandats of ecclesiasticall liuings, before they were voide to certaine persõs by his buls, pretẽding therein a great care to see the Church prouided of a Successor before it needed. Whence it grew that these kinde of Buls were called (*Gratia expectativa*) or (*Prouisiones*) whereof you may reade a learned discourse in *Duarenus* that worthie Ciuilian in his tractat: *De beneficiis lib.* 3. *c.* 1. and in his treatise *De immunitate ecclesiæ Gallicanæ*. These prouisions, were so rife with vs, that at the last, King *Edward* the third, that heroicall Prince, not disgesting so intolerable an oppression, made a statute in the 25. yeare of his reigne, *statuto* 5. *cap.* 22. and another, *statuto* 6. *eiusdem anni. cap. pri.* and a third *anno* 27. against those that drew the Kings people out of the Realme, to answer of things belonging to the kings court; and another *anno* 28. *statu.* 2. *c.* 1. 2. 3. & 4. to the like effect: whereby he greatly restained this libertie of the Pope. Yet such was the wantonnesse that grew out of his power, & the num patiẽce of princes in those daies, that hee still advẽtured the continuance of these prouisions: in so much as King *Richard* the second made likewise a statute against them in the 12. yeare of his reigne, *cap.* 15. and the 13. yeare *statut.* 2. *ca.* 2. making mention of the said first statute of *Edward* the third, ratifiing the same, and appointing the punishment of those, that offẽded against it, to be perpetuall banishment, forfeiture of their lands, tenements, goods, and catels, as by the same doth more at large appeare. And againe in the 16.

yeare of his reigne, *cap.* 5. to meete more fully with all the shifts inuented to defraude these former statutes, he expresseth the offence more particularly, and setteth the same punishment to it, that hee ordeined in the last former statute. for there toward the ende he hath these words: If any purchase or pursiew, or do to be purchased, or pursiewed in the court of Rome, or els where, any such translations, processes, and sentences of excommunication, Buls, Instruments, or any other things, &c. After him K. *H.* the fourth in like maner greeued at this importuny by other abuses not fully mette with in the former statutes, in the second yeare of his reigne, *cap.* 3. *&* 4. addeth certaine new cases, and laieth vpon the offendours in them the same censure, whereunto for shortnes sake I referre you: admonishing likewise to adde the statute, *anno.* 9. *eiusdem. cap. pri. & anno* 7. *cap.* 9. *&* 8. *& anno* 9. *eiusdem. cap.* 8. *& anno* 3. *H.* 5. *cap.* 4. Out of which statutes haue our professors of the common lawe, wrought many daungers to the Iurisdiction ecclesiasticall, thretning the punishment conteined in the statute *anno.* 27. *Ed.* 3. *&.* 38. *eiusdem,* almost to euery thing that the court Christian dealeth in, pretending all things delt with in those courts to be the disherison of the Crowne. from the which, and none other fountaine, all ecclesiasticall Iurisdiction is now deriued: wheras in truth *Sir Tho. Smith* saith very rightly, and charitablely, that the vniting of the supremacie ecclesiasticall, and temporall in the king, vtterly voideth the vse of all those statuts. *Nam cessante ratione, cessat lex.* And whatsoeuer is now wrought or threatened against the Iurisdiction ecclesiasticall, by colour of the same, is but in emulation of one court to another: and by consequent a derogation to that authoritie, from which all Iurisdiction is now deriued, and the maintenance whereof was by those Princes especially purposed. But of this reade *Sir Thomas* Smith, *lib.* 3. *de Rep. Angl. cap.* 9.

Some later statutes doe cast this punishment vpon other offenders: as namely the statute, *anno* 1. *El. cap. primo,* vpon him that denieth the Kings supremacie the second time, &c. and the statue *anno* 13. *El ca.* 2. vpon him that affirmeth the authoritie of the Pope: or that refuseth to take the oathe of supremacie. and the statute, *anno* 13. E*l. cap.* 1. such as be seditious talkers of the inheritance of the Crowne, or affirme the *Q*ueenes *M*aiestie to be an heritique . And the word is applied most commonly to the punishment first ordeined by the statutes before mentioned, for such as transgressed them; but in later times imposed vpon other offences. for that, where it is saide that any man for an offence committed shall incurre a premunire, it is meant, that he shall incurre the same punishment, which is inflicted against those that trangresse the statute made, *anno 16.R.2.ca.* 5. which is commonly called the statute of premunire, which kinde of reference is not vnusuall in our statutes. For example, I shew onely the statute, *anno* 5. *El. ca.* 5. where it is inacted that if any man preach or teach by wrighting, that the cōmon Counsell of the Realme doe by that statute forbid flesh to be eaten, as of necessitie for the sauing of mans soule, that he shall for such preaching, &c. be punished as they be, which be spredders of false newes: hauing reference thereby to those statutes, which conteine the punishment of such offenders.

Now touching the Etymologie of this word (*Præmunire*) some thinke it proceedeth from the strength giuen to the Crown by the former statutes, against the vsurpation of forein and vnnaturall power: which opinion may receiue some ground from the statute, *anno 25. Ed. 3. stat. 6. cap. pri.* But other thinke it to grow from the verb (*Præmonere*) being barbarously turned into (*Præmunire*) which corruption is taken from the rude Interpreters of the Ciuile, and Canon lawes, who indeede doe vse the effect (*Præmunire*) many times for the efficient cause (*Præmonere*) according to our prouerb: He that is well warned, is halfe armed. And of this I gather reason from the forme of the writ, which is thus conceiued in the *old.nat.br.fol.* 143. *Præmunire facias præfatum præpositum & I. R. procuratorem, &c. quòd tunc sint coram nobis, &c.* for these words can be referred to none, but parties charged with the offence.

Præpositus villæ, is vsed sometime for the Constable of a town or petit Constable. *Cromptons Iurisdict. fol.* 205. how be it the same author *fol.* 194. seemeth to apply it otherwise. for there *quatuor homines præpositi*, be those 4. men, that for euery towne must appeare before the Iustices of the Forest in their Circuit. It is vsed sometime for a *Reeve*. See *Reeve*.

Prærogatiue of the King (*prærogatiua regis*) is that especiall

power,

power, preeminence, or priuiledge that the King hath in any kinde, ouer and aboue other persons, and aboue the ordinarie course of the common lawe, in the right of his crowne. And this word (*Prærogatiua*) is vsed by the Ciuilians in the same sense. *l. Rescriptum .6. §. 4. ff. de hono. & muner*. But that priviledge that the Roman Emperour had aboue common persons, they for the most part comprised (*sub iure fisci. ff. de iure fisci, per totum tit. & Co. li. 10. tit. 1.* Among the Feudists this is termed (*ius regalium, ius regaliorum vel a nonnullis ius regaliarum*) But as the Feudists, *sub iure regalium*, soe our lawyers (*sub prærogatiua regis*) doe comprise also, all that absolute heighth of power that the Ciuilians call (*maiestatem, vel potestatem, vel ius imperii,*) subiect only to god: which (*regalia*) the Feudists diuide into two sorts, *maiora sc. & minora regalia*. for to vse their owne words, *Quædam regalia, dignitatem, prærogatiuam, & imperii præeminentiam spectant: quædam verò ad vtilitatem, & commodum pecuniarium immediatè attinent: & hæc propriè fiscalia sunt, & ad ius fisci pertinent. Peregri: de iure fisci, li. pri. cap. 1. nu. 9.* See also *Arnoldus Clapmarius. de arcanis Imperii. lib. pri. cap. 11. & seqq.* who seemeth to make difference betwene *maiestatem, & ius regaliorũ*. Others also make those (*maiora regalia*) that appertaine to the dignitie of the prince, and those *minora*, which inrich his cofers. *Regnerus Sixtinus, de iure rega. cap. 2.* By this it appeareth, that the statute of the Kings prerogatiue made, *an.* 17. *Ed.* 2. conteineth not the summe of the Kings whole prerogatiue, but onely so much thereof, as concernes the profit of his cofers growing by vertue of his regall power and crowne. for it is more then manifest, that his prerogatiue reacheth much farder: yea euen in the maters of his profit, which that statute especially consisteth of. For example, it is the kings prerogatiue to graunt protection vnto his debtours against other creditours, vntill himselfe be satisfied. *Fitzh. nat. br. fol. 28. B.* to distreine for the whole rent vpon one tenent, that hath not the whole land. *Idem fol. 235. A.* to require the auncesters debt of the heire, though not especially bound. *Bri. cap. 28. fo. 65. b.* to seise vpon money paid by his deptour into a court, for the satisfaction of an executor. *Plowden, fol. 322. a.* to permit his deptours to siew for their debts by a (*Quo minus*) in the exchequer. *Perkins. Grawnts. 5.* to be first paid by one that oweth money both to him

him and others. *Dyer. fol. 67. nu. 26.* to take the lands of accountants into his hands for his own satisfaction. *Plowd. casu Almes. fol. 321. & 322.* to take his action of accoumpt against executors, *eodem, fol. 320.* not to be tied to the demaund of his rent. *Coke. li. 4. fo. 73. a.* Now for those regalities which are of the higher nature (all being within the compas of his prerogatiue, and iustly to be comprised vnder that title) there is not one that belonged to the most absolute prince in the world, which doth not also belong to our king, except the custome of the nations so differ (as indeede they doe) that one thing be in the one accompted a regalitie, that in another is none. Onely by the custome of this kingdome, he maketh no lawes without the consent of the 3. estates though he may quash any lawe concluded of by them. And whether his power of making lawes be restreined (*de necessitate*) or of a godly and commendable policy, not to be altered without great perill, I leaue to the iudgement of wiser men. But I hold it incontrowlable, that the king of England is an absolute king. And all learned politicians doe range the power of making lawes, *inter insignia summæ & absolutæ potestatis. Maiora autem regalia sunt hæc: clausula plenitudinis potestatis, & ex ea aliquid statuere, leges condere, ac eas omnibus & singulis dare, bellum indicere, belli indicenci licentiam alii dare, pronunciare ita vt a sententia appellari non possit, committere siue delegare alicui causam cum clausula appellatione remota, cognoscere de crimine læsæ maiestatis, legitimare per rescriptum eos qui extra legitimum matrimonium nati sunt, ad famam, honores, & natales in integrum restituere, veniam ætatis dare, creare Duces, Marchiones, Comites, regnum in feudum concedere. Huc referri potest ius erigendi scholam, quæ hodie Vniuersitas vel Academia appellatur, etiã ius creãdi doctores, gradu licentiæ aliquem insigniendi, creandi magistratus, tabelliones, siue notarios, ius dandi insignia nobilitatis, siue nobiles creandi, ius cudendæ monetæ, noua vectigalia instituendi, vel instituta vectigalia augendi; Sixtinus vbi supra.* So that those other which are mentioned in *libris feudorum,* and the interpreters of them, are (at the least for the most part) iustly called *regalia minora,* as *armandiæ, viæ publicæ, flumina nauigantia, portus, ripalia, vectigalia, moneta, mulctarum pœnarumq; compendia, bona vacantia, bona quæ indignis auferuntur, bona eorum qui incestum matrimonium contrahunt, bona damnatorum, & proscriptorum, angariæ & parangariæ, extraordinariæ*

ad

ad expeditionem imperatoris collationes, potestas creandorum magistratuum ad iustitiam exequendam, argentariæ, palatia in ciuitatibus constituta, piscationum reditus, salinarum reditus, bona committentium crimen læsæ maiestatis, thesaurus inuentus. By setting downe these regalities of both sorts, as they are accoumpted in the Empire, and other forein kingdomes, they may be the more easily compared with our kings prerogatiues, and so the differences noted betweene vs and them. And whereas some things are before reckoned both (*inter regalia maiora, & minora*) the reader must vnderstand that this may be in diuers respects. For example, the power of raising a tribute, or of coyning money is *inter maiora*: but the profit that groweth to the Prince by the one or other, is (*inter minora*) Now may there also be noted out of books a great number of prerogatiues belonging to the king of this land, which doe not bring profit to his cofers immediately, and therefore may be accoumpted *inter regalia maiora*, or at the least, in a middle or mixt nature, or *inter maiora & minora*, because by a consequent they tend to the increase of the kings exchequer. Of these such as I haue obserued in reading, I will set downe as they come to my hands, without farder curiosity in diuiding. It is the kings prerogatiue that he may not be siewed vpon an ordinary writ as tenent to lands, but by petition. *Plowd. casu Walsingham fo.* 553. to haue a cecessary consent in the appropriation of all benefices. *Idem, casu Grendon. fol.* 499. to waiue and to demurre, and to pleade to the issue, or to waiue the issue, and to demurre vpon the plee of the aduers part, yet not to chaunge the issue another terme after he and the aduers part be once at issue. *Idem, casu Willion. fol.* 23. 6. *a & casu Mines fol.* 322. *a* to be receiued in a suite before issue ioyned vpon an (*ayde prier*) *Idem, casu Dutchy of* Lancaster. *fol.* 221. *b.* to be neuer in nonage, *eodem, fol.* 218. *b.* that a man indicted may not wage battell with him. *Idem casu rimes fol.* 335. *b.* that no man vpon any right may enter vpon him being in possession, but must be put to suite. *Dyer fol.* 139. *nu.* 33. to seise the lands of his tenents that alienate without licence. *Plowd. casu.* Mines. *fol.* 322. *a.* that no subiect may wage his law against him. *Broke.* chose in action. 9. *Coke. lib.* 4. *fol.* 93. to present in the right of the youngest *coparcener* being his warde before the elder. *Plowd. casu.* Mines. *fol.* 332. *b. & fol.* 333. *a.* that a benefice by institution is not full against him. *Coke. Digbies case.fol.* 79. *a.* not to finde pledges for the persecuting of any action. For he cannot be amerced. *Fitzh.nat.br.fo.* 31. *F. & fo.*47. *C.* to sue in what court he will. *Fitzh.nat.br.f.* 7. *B. &* 32. *E.* to sue the writ *Ne admittas* after sixe monethes. *Regist. orig. fol.* 31. *a.* that a mans villein hauing remained in his auncient demesn by the space of a yeare, may not be recouered by the writ *(de natiuo habendo) Fitzh. nat. br. fol.* 79. *A.* to graunt an office with the *(habendum post mortem alterius)* Dyer. *fo.* 295 *nu.* 1. to shorten the ordinary time of summons (being 15. daies) in writ of right. *Brit. ca.* 121. to giue what honour or place he listeth to his subiects. *anno* 31. *H.* 8. *ca.* 10. to be owner of a forest. See *Forest.* to haue free warren. See *Warren.* Not to be owsted of his free hould. *Cromptons Iustice of peace. fol.* 59. *b. &* 16. *a.* to araigne a man being both a Traitor, and a Felon, rather vpon the treason, than vpon the felony, because he may haue the whole escheats. *Idem. eodem. fol.* 99. *a.* to warrant the day of appearance to his subiect being in his seruice, and summoned to appeare at a day certaine. *Fitzh. nat. br. fol.* 17. *a.* Diuers of these and many others did belong *(fisco imperatorum)* which you may finde in the *Digest: De iure fisci. & Co. lib.* 10. *tit.* 1. Besides these also many moe may be obserued to belong vnto our King out of lawes, which I leaue to their collection that are of longer reading, and more painefull industry.

Prerogatiue of the Archbishop of Canterbury, or Yorke, (prærogatiua Archiepiscopi Cantuariensis, seu Eboracensis) is an especiall preeminence, that these *Sees* haue in certaine cases aboue ordinary Bishops within their *Prouinces*. And that of the Archbishop of *Canterburie*, principally consisteth of these points.

First, in the confirmation of all elections made of Bishops by the *Deane* and Chapter of all Cathedrall Churches, as also the consecration of them.

Next, in a power of visiting his whole Prouince, of assembling Synods, of supplying the defects and negligences of inferiour Bishops, of receiuing appeales from their courtes, of assigning coadiutours to those Bishops, that grow weake and insufficient to discharge their function, of appointing Vicars generall to those that haue either none, or an insufficient man employed in that office: and of dispensing in all ecclesiasticall cases, wherein the lawes beare dispensation: of taking oath of euery Bishop, at his confirmation, to performe canonicall obedience vnto the See of *Canterburie*. But thes seem to belong vnto him by an ordinarie archiepiscopall authority.

Certaine other things there be, that appertaine vnto him more then ordinarily to other Archbishops: as the originall calling of any person in any cause belonging to spirituall iurisdiction, out of any part of his prouince, though not appealed. But this point is now limited by the Statute made, *anno* 23.*Henr*.8.*ca*.9.

The receyuing of an appeale from the lowest Iudge ecclesiasticall within his prouince immediatly. The appointing of a keeper or guardian of the spiritualties during the vacancie of any bishopricke. By which means all episcopall rites of the Dioces for that time do belong vnto him: as Visitation, Institution to Benefices, and such like.

The visitation of euery Diocesse within his prouince, when & in what order it pleaseth him. As also of all other priuiledged Churches. The probate of Testaments and graunting of administrations, in case where the party deceased hath goods of any considerable valew out of the diocesse wherein he dyeth. And that valew is ordinarily fiue pounds, except it be otherwise by composition betweene the said Archbishop, and some other Bishop: as in the Diocesse of *London* it is tenne pounds.

The probate of euery *Bishops* Testament, or the administration of his goods dying intestate, though not hauing any goods, chatels, or debts without the compasse of his owne iurisdiction. The bestowing of any one dignitie or prebend in any Cathedrall church vpon the creation of a new Bishop, that himselfe thinketh good to make choice of.

There may be more particulars of this prerogatiue, that I know not: but these may be sufficient to expresse the thing that I desire to declare. Who so desireth to reade these more at large, and other priuiledges of this Church in temporall maters, may resort to the booke intituled: *De antiquitate Britannicæ Ecclesiæ, & nominatim de priuilegiis Ecclesiæ Cantuariensis historia*: and especially to the 8. chapter of the said booke. *pa*.25.

Prerogatiue Court, (*curia prærogatiuæ Archiepiscopi Cantuariensis*) is the Court wherein all Wils be proued, and all administrations taken, that belong to the *Archbishop* by his prerogatiue, which see in *Prerogatiue*. And if any contention do grow betweene two or more touching any such will or administration, the cause is properly debated & deter-

determined in this Court. The Iudge of this Court is called *Iudex Curiæ prærogatiuæ Cantuariensis*. The Archbishop of Yorke hath also the like power and court, which is tearmed his *Exchequer*, but farre inferiour to this in countenance and profite.

Prescription (*præscriptio*) is a course or vse of any thing for a time beyond the memory of man, as the exposition of the law terms doth define it. *Kitchin fol.* 104. saith thus: Prescription is, when for continuance of time, whereof there groweth no memory, a perticuler person hath perticuler right against another perticuler person. And custome is, where by continuance of time beyond memorie, diuers persons haue gotten a right: with whome agreeth *Sir Edward Cooke, lib.* 4. *fol.* 32. *a.* And vsage is by continuance of time the efficient cause of them both, and the life of both prescription and custome. Thus saith *Kitchin*. But as in the Ciuill lawe, so I think likewise in the common, Prescription may be in a shorter time. As for example, where the Satute *anno*, 1. *H.* 8. *cap.* 9. saith, that all actions popular must be siewed within three yeares after the offence committed, and the Statute *anno*, 7. *eiusdem. cap.* 3. That foure yeares being past after the offence committed in one case, and one yeare in another, no suite can be commenced, and the Statute 31. *Eliz. cap.* 5. saith, (by way of correcting the two former statutes) that all actions, &c. brought vpon any Statute, the penaltie whereof belongeth to the King, shall be brought within two yeares after the offence committed, or else be voide. And the Satute, *anno* 39. *Eliz. cap. prim. & secund.* saith, that actions brought after two yeare by any common person, or after three yeares by the king alone for decay of husbandry or tillage, shall bee of noe force. Whosoeuer offendeth against any such Statute, and doth escape vncalled for two yeares, or three yeares, in one case of the two later of these three Statutes, may iustly be said to haue prescribed an immunitie against that action. The like may be said of the Statute made *anno* 23. *Eliz. cap. primo.* which saith, that all offences comprised in the Statute made in the 13. yeere of *Eliz. cap.* 2. are inquirable before both Iustices of peace and of Assise, within one yeare and a day, after the offence committed. Also the title that a man obtaineth by the passing of fiue yeares after a fine acknowledged of any lands or tenements, may iustly be said to be obtained by prescription. And whereas the Statute, *anno* 8. *R*. 2. *cap*.4. saith, that a Iudge or Clerke conuicted for false entring of plees, &c. may be fined within two yeares; the two yeares being ended, he prescribeth against the punishment of the saide Statute; and whereas the Statute *anno* 11. *H*. 7. saith, that he which will complaine of maintenance, or embracery, whereby periurie is committed by a Iurie, must doe it within sixe dayes, those sixe daies ended, the parties prescribe: and whereas the statute *anno prim. Ed*. 6. saith, that a man being not indicted within 3 monethes of any offences there mentioned touching Seruice and Sacraments, he shalbe cleare from thence forward: the three monethes being ended, he prescribeth: And the same may be said of the statute *anno* 5. *Ed*. 6. *cap*. 5. which saith that a man shall not be indited of any offence there mentioned touching the decay of tillage, after. 3. yeares. And whereas it is ordeined by the statute *anno* 8. *H*. 6. *cap*. 9. that those which keepe possession of lands by force after. 3. yeares possession held by themselues & their auncestours, shall not be subiect to the arbitrement of Disseisours there set down, I hould this a prescription likewise against those censures. *v. anno* 23. *H*. 6. *ca*. 15. Lastly a seruant prescribeth liberty after a yeare. *Bracton. li*. 1. *ca*. 10. *nu*. 3. and the right that is gotten in any Stray to a Lord of a maner, no man claiming it within the yeare and day after proclamation made, is an vsucapion, or prescription. See *Action perpetuall, and temporall*. And see *Cromptons Iustice of peace. fol*. 173. *b. vbi habebis festum*. But see one rule for all in *Lamb. Eirenarch. li*. 4. *ca*. 5. *pa*. 469. Of this prescription, and the learning touching the same, you may reade a solemne report in S. *Ed. Cookes*, and *Luttrels case. vol*. 4. *fo*. 84. *b. & seqq*.

Presentation (*Præsentatio*) is vsed properly for the act of a patron offering his Clerke to the Bishop, to be instituted in a benefice of his gift: the forme whereof see in the *Register originall fol*. 302. *a*.

Presentment, is a meere denuntiation of the Iurours themselues, or some other officer, as Iustice, Constable, searcher, surueiours &c. (without any information) of an offence inquitable in the court whereunto it is presented. See *Lamberd Eirenarch. lib*. 4. *ca*. 5. *pa*. 467.

President (*Præses*) is vsed in the Common law for the kings

Liuetenent in any Prouince or function: as President of *Wales*, of *Yorke*, of *Barwick*: President of the Kings Councell. *anno.* 22. *H.*8.*cap.*8.& *anno* 24.*H.* 8. *cap.* 3.& 14.

Preignotarie (*Protonotarius*) is a word that seemeth to be made either of two French words (*Prime*) or *Primier*.i.*primus*) and (*Notaire*.i. *Notarius,tabellio*,or of two *Latine* words (*præ*) & *notarius*) *quasi primus aut principalis notarius*. The office is likewise borowed from the later Romanes, who made his name of halfe Greeke, and halfe Latine, *viz* πρωτος.i.*primus* , *principalis*)and(*Notarius*). It is vsed in our common lawe for the cheife clerks of the *Kings* courts, whereof 3. be of the common pleas, and one of the Kings bench. *For* the pregnotarie of the commmon plees, *anno* 5. H. 4.*cap.* 14. is termed the cheife clerke of that court. He of the Kings Bench recordeth all actions civile sieweed in that court, as the Clerke of the Crowne office doth all criminall causes. Those of the common plees doe enter and inrolle all maner of declarations, pleadings, Assises, and Iudgements: and all actions, the same terme that the appearence is made. Also they make out all iudiciall writs, as the *venire facias* after issues ioyned, and *Habeas corpus*, for the bringing in of the Iurie, after it is returned vpon the *venire facias*. They also make forthe writs of executions, and of seisin, writs of *supersedeas*, for appearance to exigents, as well as the exigents, and writs of priuiledges, for remouing of causes from other inferiour courts of Record, in case where the partie hath cause of priuiledge: Also writs of *procedendo*, of *scire facias* in all cases, and writs to inquire of dammages: and all proces vpon prohibitions, and vpon writs of *audita querela*, and false Iudgement. Finally they inrolle all recognisances acknowledged in that court, and all common Recoueries: and may make exemplifications of any Record the same terme, before the rols be deliuered from them.

Prender, commeth of the French (*prendre*.i. *accipere, acceptare, capere, prehēdere*) it signifieth in our common lawe sometime a power, or right to take a thing before it be offered: as such things as lie in Prender, or such as lie in render. *West.parte* 2. *titulo Fines. sect.* 126. where you haue these words: If the lord graunt the seruices of his tenent by fine, or otherwise, the *Lord* before atturnment, shall haue such things as lie in prender: as the ward of the body of the heire

and

and of the land: escheats, &c. but not such things as lie in *prender*, as rents, and releifes, heriots and other seruices. For he canot avowe for them before the atturnment.

Prender de Baron, signifieth literally in barbarous French to take a husband: but it is vsed in our common lawe, as an exception to disable a woman from persiewing an appeale of murder against the killer of her former husband, *Stawnf.pl.cor. li. 3.cap.* 59. The reason whereof whether it be, because by her secōd mariage, she may iustly be thought to haue giuen vp the interest shee had in her former husband, or for that shee is now couert againe, or for both, I leaue to consideration.

Prender del profits, signifieth *verbatim* to take the profits. It signifieth substantiuely the taking of the profits. See *Cromptons Iurisdict.fol.* 185. See *Pernour of profits*.

Prest, is vsed for some dutie in money to be paide by the Shyreeue vpon his accoumpt in the exchequer, *anno* 2. & 3. *Ed.* 6.*cap*. 4.

Prest mony, is so called of the French word (*Prest.* i. *explicatus, promptus, expeditus*) for that it bindeth those, that haue receiued it, to be ready at all times appointed.

Primage, is a dutie due to the mariners and saylers for the loading of any shippe at the setting forth from any hauen, *anno* 32. *H.*8. *cap.*14.

Primier seisin (*Prima seisina*) *ad verbum* signifieth the first possession. It is vsed in the common lawe, for a braunch of the kings prerogatiue, whereby he hath the first possession of all lands, and tenements through the Realme, holding of him in cheife, whereof his tenent died seised in his demesn as of fee; and so consequently the rents, and profits of them, vntill the heire, if he be of age, doe his homage, if he be vnder yeares, vntill he come to yeares. See *Stawnf.prarog. cap.*3. and *Bracton lib.4.tract.3.cap.pri.*

Primo beneficio. See *Beneficio*.

Prince (*Princeps*) is a french word, and taken with vs diuersly, sometime for the king himselfe, but more properly for the kings eldest sonne, who is prince of *Wales*, as the eldest sonne to the French king is called *Dolphine*, both being princes by their natiuitie. *M.Fearn in the glory of generositie.pag.* 138. For *Edward* the first to appease the tumultuous spirits of the Welch men, who being the auncient *Indigenæ na* of this land, could not in long time beare the yoke of vs, whome they call strangers, sent his wife being with childe into *Wales*.where at *Carnaruan* shee was deliuered of a sonne, therevpon called *Edward* of *Carnarvan* and afterward asked the Welch men, seing they thought much to be gouerned by straungers, if they would be quietly ruled by one of their owne nation; who answering him, yea: then (quoth he) I will appoint you one of your owne country men, that cannot speake one word of English, and against whose life you can take no iust exception: and so named vnto them his sonne borne in *Carnarvan* not long before. from which time it hath continued, that the kings eldest sonne (who was before called: Lord Prince, *Stawnf. prareg: cap.* 22.*fol.* 75.) hath beene called prince of *Wales. Stowes* Annals,*pag.* 303. See *anno* 27. *H.*8. *cap.*26. & *anno* 28.*eiusdem,cap.* 3.

Principality of Chester. anno 21. *Rich.*2.*cap.*9. See *County palatine*.and *Cromptons diuers iurisdictions,fol* 137.

Prior perpetuall,or datife and removeable.anno 9. *R.* 2.*cap.* 4. and *anno* 1 Ed. 4. *cap.* 1. *paulo ante finem. Lord prior of Saint Iohns of Ierusalem, anno* 26.*H.*8.*cap.*2.

Priors aliens (*Priores alieni*) were certaine religious men borne in Fraunce, and gouerners of religious houses erected for out-landish men here in *England:* which were by *Henry* the fifth thought, no good members for this land, after such conquest obtained by him in *Fraunce*, and therfore suppressed. Whose liuings afterwards by *Henry* the 6. were giuen to other Monasteries and houses of learning. *Stowes Annals. pag.* 582. See *anno* 1. *H.* 5. *cap.* 7. but especially to the erecting of those two most famous Colledges called the Kings Colledges of *Cambridge* and *Eton.*

Prioritie, (*prioritas*) signifieth in our common lawe, an antiquitie of tenure in comparison of another not so auncient. As to hold by *Prioritie*, is to hold of a Lord more auncientlythen of another. *old. nat. br. fol.* 94. So to hold in posterioritie, is vsed by *Stawnf. prærog. cap.* 2. *fo.*11. And *Crompton* in his Iurisdiction. *fol.* 117. vseth this word in the same signification. The Lord of the prioritie shal haue the custodie of the bodie, &c. *fol.* 120. If the tenent hold by prioritie of one, and by posterioritie of another,&c. To which effect, see also *Fitz. nat. br. fol.* 142. F. *Bartolus* in his Tractate, *De insigniis & armis*, vseth these very wordes, *prioritas*, and *posterioritas*,

concer-

concerning two that beare one coate armor.

Prisage, seemeth to be that custome or share, that belongeth to the *King* out of such merchandize, as are taken at sea, by way of lawfull prize, *anno* 31 *Eliz.cap.* 5.

Prisage of Wines, anno 1. *H.* 8. *cap.* 5. is a word almost out of vse, now called *Butlerage*, it is a custome wherby the prince chalengeth out of euery barke loaden with wine, containing lesse then forty tunne, two tunne of wine at his price.

Prise (prisa) commeth of the French *(prendre.* i. *capere)* it signifieth in our Statutes, the things taken by pourveyours, of the Kings subiects. As *anno* 3. *Ed.* 1. *cap.* 7. *& anno* 28. *eiusdem.stat.* 3. *cap.* 2. It signifieth also a custome due to the King, *anno* 25. *eiusdem cap.* 5. *Regist. origin. fol.* 117. *b.*

Prisoner (priso) commeth of the French *(prisonnier)* and signifieth a man restrained of his libertie vpon any action ciuill or criminall, or vpon commaundement. And a man may be prisoner vpon mater of Record, or mater of fact: prisoner vpon mater of Record is he, which being present in court, is by the court committed to prison, only vpon an arrest, be it of the Shyreeue, Constable, or other. *Stawnf. pl. cor. lib. prim. cap.* 32. *fol.* 34. *&* 35.

Priuie, commeth of the French *(priuè.* i. *familiaris)* and signifieth in our common lawe, him that is partaker, or hath an interest in any action, or thing: as, *priuies of bloud, old nat. br. fol.* 117. be those that be linked in consanguinitie. Euery heire in tayle is priuy to recouer the land intayled. *eodem fol.* 137. No priuitie was betweene me and the tenent. *Litleton, fol.* 106. If I deliuer goods to a man to be caried to such a place, and he, after he hath brought them thither, doth steale them, it is felonie: because the priuitie of deliuerie is determined, as soone as they are brought thither. *Stawn. pl. cor. lib. prim. cap.* 15. *fol.* 25. Merchants priuie be opposite to merchant straungers. *anno* 2. *Ed. tertii. cap.* 9. *& cap.* 14. *& ann. eiusdem, stat.* 2. *cap.* 3. The newe Expositour of lawe termes maketh diuers sorts of priuies: as priuies in estate, priuies in deed, priuies in lawe, priuies in right, and priuies in bloud. And see the examples he giueth of euery of them. See *Perkins Conditions.* 831. 832. 833. and *Sir Edward Cooke lib.* 3. *Walkers case. fol.* 23. *a. & lib.* 4 *fol.* 123. *b. &* 124. *a.* where he maketh foure kindes of priuies, *viz.* priuies in bloud, as the heire to his father, &c.

priuies in representation, as executours or administratours to the deceased: priuies in estate, as he in the reuersion, and he in the remainder, when land is giuē to one for life, and to another in fee: the reason is giuen by the *Expositour of lawe termes*, for that their estates are created both at one time. The fourth sort of priuies are priuies in tenure: as the *Lord* by escheate: that is, when the land escheateth to the *Lord* for want of heires. &c.

Priuie seale (priuatum sigillum) is a seale that the King vseth some time for a warrant, whereby things passed the priuy signet and brought to it, are sent farder to be confirmed by the great seale of England: sometime for the strength or credit of other things written vpon occasions more transitory and of lesse continuance, then those be that passe the great seale.

Priuiledge (priuilegium) is defined by *Cicero* in his oration *pro domo sua*, to be *lex priuata homini irrogata. Frerotus in paratitlis ad titulum decretalium de priuilegiis*, thus defineth it: *priuilegium est ius singulare, hoc est priuata lex quæ vni homini, vel loco, vel Collegio, & similibus aliis conceditur: cap. priuilegia, distinct: 3. priua enim veteres dixere quæ nos singula dicimus. Insit Agellius lib. 10. ca. 20. Ideoq; priuilegia modò beneficia, modò personales constitutiones dicuntur, &c.* It is vsed so likewise in our common law, and sometime for the place, that hath any speciall immunity. *Kitchin fol.* 118. in the words: where depters make fained gifts and feofements of their land, and goods to their freinds, and others, and betake themselues to priuiledges, &c. Priuiledge is either personall, or reall: a personall priuiledge is that, which is graunted to any person, either against, or beside the course of the common law: as for example, a person called to be one of the Parlament, may not be arrested either himselfe, or any of his attendance, during the time of the Parlament. A priuiledge reall is that, which is graunted to a place, as to the Vniuersities, that none of either may be called to *Westm.* hall, vpon any contract made within their owne precincts. And one toward the court of Chauncery, cannot originally be called to any court but to the Chauncery, certaine cases excepted. If he be, he will remoue it by a writ of Priuiledge grounded vpon the statute *anno* 18. *Ed.* 3. See the new booke of *Entries. verbo* Priuilege.

Probat of testaments (probatio testamentorum) is the producting, and insinuating of dead mens wils before the ecclesiasticall Iudge, Ordinary of the place, where

where the party dyeth. And the ordinary in this case is knowne by the quantity of the goods, that the party deceased hath out of the *Dioces*, where he departed. For if all his goods be in the same *Dioces*, then the Bishop of the *Dioces*, or the Archdeacon (according as their composition, or prescription is) hath the probate of the Testament: if the goods be dispersed in diuers *Dioces*, so that there be any summe of note (as fiue pounds ordinarily) out of the Dioces where the party let his life: then is the Archbishop of *Canterbury* the ordinary in this case by his prerogatiue. For whereas in ould time, the will was to be proued in euery Dioces, wherein the party diceased had any goods: it was thought conuenient both to the subiect, and to the Archiepiscopall See, to make one proofe for all before him, who was and is of all the generall Ordinary of his prouince. But there may be auncieatly some composition betweene the Archebishop and an inferiour ordinary, whereby the summe that maketh the prerogatiue, is aboue fiue pound. See *prærogatiue of the Archbishop* This probate is made in two sorts either in common forme or *per testes*. The proofe in common forme, is onely by the oath of the executour, or party exhibiting the will, who sweareth vpon his credulity, that the will by him exhibited, is the last will, and testament of the party deceised. The proofe *per testes* is, when ouer and beside his oath, he also produceth witnesses or maketh other proofe, to confirme the same, and that in the presence of such as may pretend any interest in the goods of the deceased, or at the least in their absence, after they haue beene lawfully summoned to see such a will proued, if they thinke good. And the later course is taken most commonly, where there is feare of strife, and contention betweene the kindred and freinds of the party deceased about his goods. For a will proued only in common forme, may be called into question any time within 30. yeares after by common opinion, before it worke prescription.

Procedendo, is a writ whereby a plee, or cause formerly called from a base court to the Chaũcerie, Kings bench, or cõmõ plees, by a writ of priuiledge or certiorare, is released, and sent downe againe to the same court, to be proceeded in there, after it appeareth that the defendant hath no cause of priuiledge, or that the mater comprised in the bille, be not well proued. *Brooke hoc titulo.* and Termes of of lawe: *Cooke vol.6.fol.63.a.* See *anno.21.R.2.cap.11.in fine*, leters of *procedendo* graunted by the keeper of the priuie seale. See in what diuersitie it is vsed in the table of the originall Register, and also of the Iudiciall.

Proces (*Processus*) is the maner of proceeding in euery cause, be it personall, or reall, ciuile, or criminall, even from the originall writ to the end. *Britton fol.138.a.* wherein there is great diuersitie, as you may see in the table of *Fitzh.nat.br. verbo Proces*, and *Brookes Abridgement, hoc titulo*. And whereas the writings of our common lawyers sometime call that the proces, by which a man is called into the court and no more: the reason thereof may be giuen, because it is the beginning, or the principall part thereof, by which the rest of the busines is directed, according to that saying of *Aristotle*. ἡ ἀρχὴ ἥμισυ τοῦ παντός. Diuers kinds of proces vpon Inditements before Iustices of peace: See in *Cromptons Iustice of peace. fol.133. b.134.135.* But for orders sake, I referre you rather to *M. Lamberd* in his tractat of processes adioyned to his *Eirenarcha*, who acording to his subiect in hand, diuideth criminall proces, either into proces touching causes of treason, or felonie, and proces touching inferiour offeces. the former is vsually *a capias, capias aliàs, & exigi facias*. The second is either vpon enditement, or presentment, or information: that vpon enditement or presentment, is all one, and is either generall, and that is *a venire facias*, vpon which if the partie be returned sufficient, then is sent out a *Distringas infinite* vntill he come: if he be returned with a *Nihil habet*, then issueth out a *Capias*, *Capias aliâs*, *Capias pluries*, and lastly an *Exigi facias*. The speciall proces is that, which is especially appointed for the offece by statute. for the which he referreth his reader to the 8. Chapter of his 4. booke being very different.

Processum continuando, is a writ for the continuance of a proces after the death of the cheife Iustice, in the writ of *oyer* and *terminer*. *Register originall. fol. 128. a.*

Prochein Amy (*Proximus amicus, vel propinquior*) is, word for word, a neere freind. It is vsed in our common lawe, for him that is next of kinde to a childe in his nonage, and is in that respect allowed by lawe, to deale for him in the managing of his affaires: as to be his *Gardian*, if he hold of any in socage, and in the redresse of any wrong done vnto him, be it by his *Gardian*, if he be ward and hold in Chiualrie, or any others. *Statut. West. pri. cap.* 48. 3. *Ed. pri.* and *Westm.* 2. *cap.* 15. *anno* 13. *Ed. pri.*

Prose, aliàs Prove, is vsed for an Enquest. *anno* 28. *Ed.* 3. *cap.* 13.

Proclamation (*Proclamatio*) signifieth a notice publikely giuen of any thing, whereof the King thinketh good to advertise his subiects. So it is vsed, *anno* 7. *Rich.* 2. *ca.* 6. Proclamation of rebellion is a publike notice giuen by the officer, that a man not appearing vpon a *Sub pœna*, nor an attachment in the Starre Chamber or Chauncerie, shalbe reputed a rebell, except he render himselfe by a day assigned. *Cromptons Iurisd. fol.* 92. See *Commission of rebellion.*

Proclamation of a fine, is a notice openly, and solemnly giuen at all the Assises, that shall be holden in the Countie within one yeare after the ingrossing of the fine, and not at the foure generall quarter sessions. And these proclamations be made vpon transcripts of the fine, sent by the Iustices of the Common plees, to the Iustices of Assise, and the Iustices of peace. *West. parte* 2. *symbol. titulo* Fines. *sect.* 132. where also you may see the forme of the proclamarion. *Proclamare est palā, & valde clamare*, vsed by *Tullie*, *Liuie*, and the *Civilians.* π. *Quibus ad liberta proclamare non licet.* And *Proclamator* signifieth him *qui litem intendit, vel causam agit. Cicero de oratore. lib. pri. Non enim causidicum nescio quem, neq; proclamatorem, aut rabulam hoc sermone conquirimus, &c.* I reade in *Fitzh. nat. br. fol.* 85. *C.* that the kings proclamation is sufficient to stay a subiect from going out of the Realme. See the force of proclamations. *anno.* 31. *H.* 8. *cap.* 8. see also Proclamations in diuers cases. Newe booke of *Enteries. verbo Proclamation.*

Procters of the clergie (*procuratores cleri*) are those which are chosen and appointed to appeare for cathedrall, or other Collegiat churches, as also for the common clergie of euery Dioces, at the Parlament, whose choice is in this sort. First, the king directeth his writ to the Archebishop of each province for the summoning of all Bishops, Deanes, Archdeacons, cathedrall and collegiat churches, and generally of all the clergie of his prouince, after their best discretion and iudgement, assigning them the time and place in the said writ. Then the Archebishops proceede in their accustomed course. One example may serue to shew both. The Archebishop of *Canterbury* vpō his writ receiued, directerh his leters to the Bishop of *London* as his

his Deane *provincial.* 1. §. *ſtatuimus.de pœnis & verb.tanquam in gloſ.* firſt citing himſelfe peremptorily:and then willing him to cite in like maner all the *Biſhops*, Deanes, Archedeacons, cathedrall and collegiate churches, and generally all the Clergie of his *Prouince* to the place, and againſt the day prefixed in the writ. But directeth withal that one *Proctor* ſent for euery *Cathedrall* or Collegiat Church, and two for the bodie of the inferiour Clergie of each Dioceſſe, may ſuffice. And by vertue of theſe leters authentically ſealed, the ſaid Biſhop of *London* directeth his like leters ſeuerally to the Biſhop of euery Dioceſſe of the Prouince, citing them in like ſort, and commaunding them not onely to appeare, but alſo to admoniſh the ſaid *Deanes*, and Archdeacons, perſonally to appeare, and the Cathedrall and collegiat Churches, as alſo the common Clergie of the Dioceſſe, to ſend their *Proctors* to the place, and at the day appointed: and alſo willeth them to certifie the Archbiſhop the names of all and euery ſo moniſhed by them, in a ſhedule annexed to their leters certificatorie. The Biſhops proceed accordingly, and the *Cathedrall* and collegiate churches as alſo the Clergie make choice of their *Proctors*: which done, and certified to the *Biſhop*, he returneth all anſwerably to his charge at the day. Theſe proctors of the Clergie, howſoeuer the caſe of late dayes is altered, had place and ſuffrage in the lower houſe of *Parlament*, as well as the knights, citizens, Barons of the *Cinque ports*, and Burgeſſes. *For* ſo it plainely appeareth by the Statute, *anno* 21. *R.* 2. *cap.* 2. & *cap.* 12. And ſithence they were remooued, the Church hath daily growne weaker and weaker: I pray God that in ſhort time ſhe famiſh not, but that her liberties be better maintained.

Procurator, is vſed for him that gathereth the fruites of a benefice for another man. *anno* 3. *R.* 2. *ſtat.* 1. *cap.* 2. And *procuracy* is vſed for the ſpecialtie, whereby he is authorized. *Ibid.* They are at this day in the *Weſt* parts called *Proctors*.

Profer (*profrum vel proferum*) is the time appointed for the accompts of Shyreeues, and other officers in the *Exchequer*, which is twice in the yeare, *anno* 51. *H.* 3. *ſtatut. quint.* And it may be gathered alſo out of the *Regiſter*, *fol.* 139. in the writ *De Attornato Vicecomitis pro profro faciendo.* I reade alſo of *profers*, *anno* 32. *H.* 8. *cap.* 21. in theſe words:

Trinitie terme shall beginne the Monday next after Trinity Sunday, whensoeuer it shall happen to fall, for the keeping of the essoins, profers, returnes, and other ceremonies heretofore vsed and kept. In which place *(profer)* seemeth to signifie the offer, or indeauour to proceede in action by any man, whom it concerneth so to doe. See *Briton. cap. 27. fol. 50. b. & 55. a. & fol.* 80. *b.* and *Fleta lib. 1. cap.* 38. §. *Vtlagati & seqq.*

Profer the halfe merke. See *Halfe merke.*

Profession (professio) is in the common lawe, vsed particularly for the entring into any religious Order of Friars, &c. New booke of Entries, *verbo Profession.*

Profits apprender. See *Prender.*

Prohibition, (prohibitio) is a writ framed for the forbidding of any court, either spirituall or secular, to proceed in any cause there depending, vpon suggestion, that the cognition thereof belongeth not to the said court. *Fitz. nat. br. fol.* 39. *G.* but is most vsually taken, especially in these dayes, for that writ, which lyeth for one that is impleeded in the *Court Christian,* for a cause belonging to the temporall iurisdiction, or the cognisance of the Kings court, whereby as well the partie and his Councell, as the Iudge himselfe, and the Register, are forbidden to proceed any farder in that cause: for that it appertaineth to the disinheriting of the Crowne of such right as belongeth vnto it. In how many cases this lyeth, see *Broke, hoc titulo,* and *Fitz. na. br. fol. 39. & seqq.* This writ, and the *præmunire,* might in these daies well be spared: For they were helpes to the kings inheritance and Crowne, when the two swords were in two diuers hands. Whereas now both the Iurisdictions being setled in the King, there is small reason of either, except it be to wearie the subiect by many quircks and delayes, from obtaining his right: of this prohibition, you may reade *Bracton* also, *lib.* 5. *tract.* 5. *cap.* 3. 4. 5. 6. 7. 8. 9. 10. 11. 12. who saith, that it lyeth not after sentence giuen in any cause, howsoeuer the case is altered: and againe, the statute made, *anno* 50. *Ed.* 3. which ordaineth, that aboue one prohibition should not lye in one cause. See the diuersitie of prohibitions in the table of the *original Regist.* See the new booke of Entries, *verbo, Prohibition,* and *Fitz. nat. br. fol.* 39.

Prohibitio de vasto directa parti, is a writ Iudiciall directed to the tenent, and prohibiting him from making waste vpon the land

land in controuersie, during the suite. *Register Iudiciall. fol.* 21. It is sometime made to the Shyreeue, the example whereof you haue there next following.

Pro Indiuiso, is a possession, and occupation of lands, or tenements belonging vnto two or more persons, whereof none knoweth his seuerall portion, as Coparceners before partition. *Bracton lib.* 5. *tracta.* 2. *cap. pri. nu.* 7.

Prolocutour of the conuocation house (*prolocutor domus conuocationis*) is an officer chosen by persons ecclesiasticall publiquely assembled by the kings writ at euery parlament. And as there be two houses of conuocation, so be there two prolocutours, one of the higher house, the other of the lower house, who presently vpon the first assembly is by the motion of the Bishops, chosen by the lower house, and presented to the Bishops for their prolocutour, that is, the man by whom they meane to deliuer their resolutions to the higher house, and to haue their owne house especially ordered and gouerned. His office is to cause the clerk to call the names of such as are of that house when he seeth cause, to cause all things propounded to be read by him, to gather the suffrages, and such like.

Promoters (*promotores*) be those, which in popular and penall actions doe deferre the names, or complaine of offenders, hauing part of the profit for their reward. These were called among the Romaines *Quadruplatores*, or *Delatores.* They belong especially to the Exchequer and the kings bench. *Smith de Repub: Anglo. li.* 2. *cap.* 14.

Pro partibus liberandis, is a writ for the partition of lands betweene coheires. *Register originall, fol.* 316.

Prophecies (*prophetiæ*) be in our common law, taken for wiserdly foretellings of maters to come, in certaine hidden and enigmaticall speeches. Whereby it falleth out many times, that great troubles are stirred in our common wealth, and great attempts made by those, to whom the speach framed, either by the description of his cognisance, armes, or some other quality, promiseth good successe *anno* 3. *Ed.* 6. *cap.* 15. *& anno* 7. *eiusdem. cap.* 11. *& anno* 5. *Eliza. ca.* 15. But these for distinctions sake are called false, or phantasticall prophecies.

Property (*proprietas*) signifieth the highest right that a man hath or can haue to any thing, which is no way depending vpon any other mans courtesie. And this none in our kingdome can be said

said to haue in any lands, or tenements, but onely the *King* in the right of his Crowne. Because all the lands through the realme, are in the nature of fee, and doe hould either mediately or immediately of the Crowne. *See Fee.* This word neuerthelesse is in our common law, vsed for that right in lands and tenements, that common persons haue, because it importeth as much as *(vtile dominium)* though not *(directum)*.

Proprietate probanda, is a writ. See the *originall Regist. fol.* 83. *a.&* 85. *b.* It lyeth for him, that will proue a propertie before the Shyreeue. *Brookes Propertie.* 1. For where a propertie is alledged, a replegiare lyeth not. *Idem ibidem.*

Proprietarie (proprietarius) is he that hath a propertie in any thing: but it is most notoriously vsed for him, that hath the fruites of a benefice, to himselfe and his heires or successours, as in time past *Abbots* and *Priors* had to them and their successours. See *Appropriation.*

Prorata portionis. See *Onerando pro rata portionis.*

Protection (protectio) hath a generall and a speciall signification. In the generall it is vsed for that benefite and safetie, that euery subiect, or Denizen, or alien specially secured, hath by the Kings lawes And thus it is vsed, *anno* 25. *Ed. tertii. capite.* 22. *Protection* in the speciall signification is vsed for an exemption, or an immunitie giuen by the King to a person against suites in lawe, or other vexations vpon reasonable causes him thereunto moouing, which I take to be a braunch of his prerogatiue. And of this protection, *Fitzh.* maketh two sortes in his *nat. br. fol.* 28. The first forme or sort he calleth a protectiō, *cum clausula volumus*, wherof he mentioneth foure particulars. A protection, *quia profecturus*, for him that is to passe ouer sea in the kings seruice: A protection, *quia moratur*, for him that is abroad in the Kings seruice vpon the sea, or in the marches, *anno* 7. *H.* 7. *cap.* 2. A protection for the Kings debter, that he be not siewed or attached vntill the King be payed his debt. See *anno* 15. *Ed.* 3. This some Ciuilians call *moratorium*: which see *In singularibus Marantæ, verb. Princeps. pag.* 79. *col.* 2. And a protection in the kings seruice beyond the seas, or on the marches of *Scotland*: whereof you may reade something, *anno* 1. *R.* 2. *cap.* 8. See the *Regist. orig. fol.* 23. and *Britton. cap.* 123. The second forme of protection is tearmed *cum clausula, Nolumus*: which is graunted most commonly

monly to a spirituall company for their immunitie from taking of their catell by the Kings ministers. But it may be graunted also to one man spirituall or temporall. Of these things reade the same authour: and the formes of these writs. See also in the *Register originall. fol.22. & 23.* And see the new Expositour of lawe termes, to what action the kings protection doth not extend. See also the new booke of Entries, *verbo Protection.*

Protonotarie,(protonotarius.) See *Preignetarie.*

Protestation, (protestatio) is (as Iustice *Walsh* defineth it) a defence or safegard to the partie, which maketh it from being cōcluded by the act he is about to doe, that issue cannot be ioyned vpon it, *Plowden. fol. 276. b.* whereof see the *Register original. fol. 306. b.* And see Protest.

Protest, (protestari) hath two diuers applications: one is by way of cautell, to call witnesse (as it were) or openly to affirm, that he doth either not at all, or but after a sort yeeld his consent to any act, as vnto a proceeding of a Iudge in a court, wherein his iurisdiction is doubtfull, or to answer vpon his oath farder then he by lawe is bounde. See *Plowden. casu Grasbroke. fol. 276. b.* and the Register *orig. fol. 306. b.* Another is by way of complaint to protest a mans bill: For example, if I giue mony to a Merchant in *Fraunce,* taking his bill of exchange to be repayed in *England,* by one to whome he assigneth me, if at my comming I find not my selfe satisfied to my contentment, but either delayed or denyed: then I goe into the Burse, or some open concurse of Merchants, and protest that I am deceiued by him. And thereupon if he haue any goods remaining in any mans hands within the Realme, the lawe of Merchants is, that I be paid out of them.

Prouuer (Probator) See *Approuer. anno 5. H. 4. ca. 2.* See *Approuours.*

Prouince (Prouincia) was vsed among the *Romans* for a Country without the compasse of *Italie,* gained to their subiection by the sword. whereupon the part of *Fraunce* next the *Alpes* was soe called of them, when it was in their dominion, and of that carieth the same name at this present: But with vs a prouince is most vsually taken for the circuit of an Archebishops Iurisdiction, as the Province of *Canterbury,* and the prouince of *Yorke. anno 32. H. 8. cap. 23. & anno 33. eiusdem,*

dem.cap. 31. yet it is vsed diuers times in our statutes for seuerall parts of the Realme.

Provinciall (*Provincialis*) is a cheife gouernour of an order of Friers, *anno quar. Henr. quar. cap.* 17.

Protoforestarius, was he whom the auncient kings of this Realme made chiefe of Winsour forest, to heare all causes of death, or mayhem, or of slaughter, or of the Kings deare within the Forest. *Camd. Britan. pag.* 213. See *Iustice of the Forest*.

Prove. See *Profe.*

Prouision (*Provisio*) is vsed with vs, as it is vsed in the Canon lawe, for the providing of a Bishop, or any other person of an ecclesiasticall liuing, by the Pope, before the Incumbent be dead. It is also called *gratia expectatiua*, or *Mandatum de providendo*. The great abuse whereof in the Pope through all Christendome heretofore, you may read, not only in *Duarenus de sacris ecclesiæ ministeriis, & beneficiis. lib.* 3. *cap.* 2. but also for England particularly, in diuers statuts of the Realme. *viz. anno.* 25. *Ed.* 3. *cap.* 22 *stat.* 4. & *statu.* 5. commonly called the statute *de prouisoribus.* &c. *anno.* 27. *eiusdem. cap.* 1. & *anno* 38. *eiusdem. stat.* 2. *cap.* 1. & 2. 3. 4. & *anno* 38. *eiusdem*, & *anno* 2. *Rich.* 2. *cap.* 7. & *anno* 3. *eiusdem cap.* 3. & *anno.* 7. *eiusdem. cap.* 12. & *anno* 12. *eiusdem, cap.* 15. & *anno* 13. *eiusdem, stat.* 2. *cap.* 2. & 3. & *anno* 16. *eiusdem cap.* 5. & *anno* 2. *H.* 4. *cap.* 3. & 4. & *anno* 5. *eiusdem, cap. pri.* & *anno* 7. *eiusdem, cap.* 6. & 8. & *anno* 9. *eiusdem, cap.* 8. & *anno* 3. *H.* 5. *cap.* 4. See *Præmunire.*

Provisour (*Provisor*) is he that sieweth to the court of Rome for a prouision. *old. nat. br. fol.* 143. See *Provision.*

Proviso, is a condition inserted into any deede, vpon the obseruanee wherof the validitie of the deede consisteth, which forme of condition seemeth to be borrowed from *Fraunce.* for (*Pourveu Gallicum semper conditionem inducit. Tiraquel. tomo.* 3. *pag.* 216. Our common lawyers say that it sometime signifieth but a couenant, whereof you haue a large dis- dispute in the 2. booke of *Sir Ed. Cokes reports* in the Lord *Cromwels case.* It hath also another signification in maters Iudiciall: as if the plaintife or demaundant desist in prosecuting an action, by bringing it to a triall, the defendant or tenent may take out the *venire facias* to the Shyreeue: which hath in it these words, *Proviso quòd, &c.* to this ende, that if the plain- tife tie take out any writ to that purpose, the shyreeue shall summon but one Iurie vpon them both. See *old natura breuium* in the writ *Nisi prius. fol.* 159.

Purchas. See *pourchas.*

Purfles of a womans gowne. anno 33. H. 8. *cap.* 5.

Purgation (*Purgatio*) is a cleering of a mans selfe from a crime, whereof he is probably and publiquely suspected, and thereof denounced to a Iudge. Of this there was great vse in England touching maters of felonie imputed to Clerks in former time, as appeareth by *Stawnf. pl. cor. lib.* 2. *cap.* 48. See *Clergie.* It is still obserued for mater pertaining to the ecclesiasticall court, as suspicion, or common fame of Incontinencie, or such like. *Purgatio* is either canonicall (*canonica*) or vulgar (*vulgaris*) Canonicall is that which is prescribed by the Canon lawe: the forme whereof is vsuall in the spirituall courte, the man suspected taking his oath that he is cleere, of the fault obiected, and bringing so many of his honest neighbours, being not aboue twelue, as the court shall assigne him, to sweare vpon their consciences and credulitie that he sweareth truly, or hath taken a true oath. Vulgar purgation was by fire, or water, or by combat, vsed by Infidels, and Christians also, vntill by the Canon lawe it was abolished, *tit.* 15. *de purgatione Can. & vulga. in Decretalibus.* Combat, though it be lesse in vse then it was, yet is it, and may be still practised by the lawes of the *Realme*, in cases doubtfull, if the defendant chuse rather the Combat then other triall. See *Ordel.* See *Combat.*

Purlue, is all that ground neere any Forest, which being made Forest by *Henry* the second, *Richard* the first, or King *Iohn*, were by perambulations graunted by *Henry* the third, seuered againe from the same. *Manwood. parte* 2. *of his Forest Lawes. cap.* 20. And he calleth this ground either *Pourallee.* i. *perambulationem*, or *purlieu.* and *purluy*, which he saith be but abusiuely taken for *pourallee. vbi supra. nu.* 3. But with the licence of that industrious and learned gentleman, I am bold to say, that this word may be no lesse fitly made of two French words (*pur.* i. *purus*) and (*lieu.* i. *locus*) and my reason is, because that such grounds as were by those kings subiected to the lawes, and ordinances of the Forest, are now cleered and freed from the same: for as the Ciuilians cal that *purum locum, qui sepulchrorum religioni non est obstrictus.* §. 9. *de rerum diuis in institut.*

so, no doubt, in imitation of that very point, our auncestours called this purlieu, *id est, purum locum*, because it was exempted from that seruitude or thraulldom, that was formerly laid vpon it. So (*ager purus est, qui neq; sacer, neq; sanctus, neq; religiosus, sed ab omnibus huiusmodi nominibus vacare videtur. l. 2. §. 4. ff. de religio. & sumptibus funerum.*) And therefore M. *Cromptons Purraile* is not much amisse *fol. 153. of his Iurisd.* because we may also deriue it from the French words (*pur*) and (*Allee*) that is as much to say, as a cleere, or a free walke or passage. And where it is sometime called *Pouralee*, that may and doth come from (*pur*) and (*Allee*) i. *Itio, profectio, ambulatio*) because he that walketh or courseth within that compasse, is cleere enough from the lawes, or penalties incurred by them, which hunt within the precincts of the Forest. See the *stat. anno 33. Ed. pri. stat. 5.*

Pourlue man, is he that hath groũd within the *Purlieu*, and being able to dispend 40. shillings by the yeare of free hould, is vpon these two points licensed to hunt in his owne *purlieu*. *Manwood. parte pri. of his Forest lawes. pag. 151. & 177.* but what obseruations he must vse in his hunting, see him *pag. 180 181. 186.* See him likewise *parte 2. cap. 20. nu. 5. 8. 9. &c.* See *Purlieu.*

Purpresture. See *Pourpresture.*

Pursey, anno 43. Elizabeth. cap. 10.

Purswivant. See *Poursuivant.*

Purveyours. See *Pourveyours.*

Pyker, alias Pycar, a kind of shippe. *anno 31. Ed. 3. Stat. 2. cap. 2.*

Q

QVadragesima, is the first sonday in lent, so called (as I take it) because it is the fourtith day before Easter. The sonday before that is *Quinquagesima*, the second before *Sexagesima*, the 3. *septuagesima*.

Quæ plura, is a writ, that lieth where an Inquisition hath beene made by the *Escheatour* in any countie, of such lands or tenements, as any man died seised of, and all that was in his possession be not thought to be found by the office. The forme whereof see in the *Register originall, fol. 293.* and *in Fitzh. nat. br. fol. 255.* It differeth from the writ called *melius inquirendo*, as *Fitz.* there saith, because this is granted, where the Escheatour formerly proceeded by vertue of his office: and the other, where he found the first office by vertue

tue of the writ called, *Diem clausit exercmum*. See the newe booke of *Entries. verbo. Quæ plura.*

Quærens non invenit plegium. is a returne made by the Shyreue vpon a writ directed vnto him with this condition inserted. *Si A fecerit B. securum de loquelâ sua prosequenda, &c.* Fitzh. *nat. br. fol.* 38. O.

Quæ seruicia, is a writ. See *Per quæ servitia.*

Quale ius, is a writ Iudiciall, that lieth where a man of religion hath iudgement to recouer land, before execution be made of the Iudgement. for this writ must betweene Iudgement and execution, goe forth to the Escheatour, to inquire whether the religious parson hath right to recouer, or the Iudgement is obteined by collusion betweene the Demaundant and the Tenent, to the intent the true Lord be not defrauded. See *Westm.* 2. *cap.* 32. *Cum viri religiosi, &c.* the forme of this writ you may haue in the *Register Iudiciall, fol.* 8. 16. 17. & 46. and in the *old. nat. br. fol.* 161. See the newe boke of *Entries. verbo. Quale ius.*

Quare eiecit infra terminum, is a writ, that lieth for a leassee, in case where he is cast out of his ferme before his terme be expyred, against the feoffee of the leassour, that eiecteth him. And it differeth from the *Eiectione Firmæ*, because this lyeth where the leassour after the lease made, infeoffeth another, which eiecteth the leassee. And the *Eiectione firmæ* lieth against any other Straunger, that eiecteth him. The effect of both is all one: and that is to recouer the residue of the terme. See *Fitzh. nat. br. fol.* 197. See the Register originall, *fol.* 227. and the newe booke of *Entries. verbo. Quare eiecit infra terminum.*

Quare impedit, is a writ, that lyeth for him, who hath pourchased a maner with an Advousen thereunto belonging, against him that disturbeth him in the right of his Advowsen, by presenting a Clerk thereunto, when the Church is voide. And it differeth from the writ called (*Assisa vltimæ præsentationis*) because that lieth, where a man or his Auncestours formerly presented, and this for him, that is the pourchasour him selfe. See the *Expositour* of the termes of law, and *owld nat. br. fol.* 27. *Bracton. lib.* 4. *tracta* 2. *cap.* 6. *Britton cap.* 92. *and* Fitzh. *nat. br. fol.* 32. and the *Register originall. fol.* 30. where it is said that a *Quare impedit* is of a higher nature, then *Assisa vltimæ præsentationis*; because it suppofeth both a possession and a right. See at large the

the newe booke of *Entrise.verbo. Quare impedit.*

Quare incumbrauit, is a writ, that lyeth againſt the Biſhop, which within ſixe monethes after the vacation of a benefice, conferreth it vpon his Clerke, whileſt two others be contending in law for the right of preſenting. Expoſition of the terms of law, *old. nat. br. fol.* 30. and *Fitzh. nat. br. fol.* 48. *Regiſter originall. fol.* 32.

Quare intruſit matrimonio non ſatiſfacto, is a writ that lyeth for the Lord againſt his tenent being his ward, that after couenable mariage offered him, marieth another, and entreth neuer the leſſe vpon his land, without agreement firſt made with his Lord and Gardian. *Terms of the law.*

Quare non permittit, is a writ that lyeth for one that hath right to preſent for a turne againſt the proprietary. *Fleta. lib.* 5. *cap.* 16.

Quarentine (quarentina) is a benefit allowed by the lawe of England, to the widow of a landed man deceaſed, whereby ſhee may challenge to continue in his capitall meſſuage, or cheife manſion houſe, by the ſpace of 40. daies after his deceaſe. Of this ſee *Bracton lib.* 2. *cap.* 40. And if the heire, or any other attempt to eiect her, ſhee may haue the writ *De Quarentina habenda. Fitzh. nat. br. fol.* 161. ſee *anno* 9, *H.* 3. *cap.* 7. & *anno* 20. *cap. pri.* and *Britton. cap.* 103. *M. Skene de verborum ſignificatione. verbo Quarentina viduarum*, deriueth this word from the French *Quareſme.* Who alſo haue this cuſtome called *lo quareſme des vefues* granted to widows after the deceaſe of their husbands: as he proueth out of *Tapon in his Arreſts libro* 15. *titulo des dots. cap.* 7. & *lib.* 10. *tit. Subſtitutiones cap.* 30. Of this read *Fleta* alſo *lib.* 5. *cap.* 23.

Quarentena habenda, is a writ, that lyeth for a widow to inioy her *Quarentine. Regiſter originall. fol.* 175.

Quare non admiſit, is a writ, that lyeth againſt the Biſhop refuſing to admit his Clerk, that hath recouered in a plee of *Aduowſen.* The furder vſe whereof ſee in *Fitzh. nat. br. fol.* 47. & *Regiſter originall: fol.* 32. See the new booke of *Entries. verbo quare non admiſit.*

Quare obſtruxit, is a writ, that lyeth for him who hauing a ſeruitude to paſſe through his neighbours ground, cannot inioy his right, for that the owner hath ſo ſtrengthened it. *Fleta: li.* 4. *cap.* 26. §. *Item ſi minus.*

Quarter Seſſions, is a court held by the Iuſtices of peace in euery Countie, once euery quarter. The iuriſdiction whereof of how farre it extendeth, is to be learned out of M. *Lamberds Eirenarcha. Sir Thomas Smith de Republ. Anglor. lib. 2. ca.* 19. But to these you must adde the late statutes of the Realme, for their power daily increaseth. Originally it seemeth to haue bene erected onely for maters touching the peace. But in these daies it extendeth much farder. That these Sessions shold be held quarterly, was first of all ordeined (so farre as I can learne) by the statute *anno* 25. *Ed.* 3. *stat. pri. cap.* 8. of these read *Lamberds Eirenarcha* the fourth booke throughout, where he setteth them out, both learnedly, and at large.

Quashe (quassare) commeth of the French *(quasser .i. quassare, conquassare)* it signifieth in our common law to ouerthrowe, *Bracton lib.* 5. *tracta.* 2. *cap.* 3. *nu.* 4.

Quekbord, anno 17. *Ed.* 4. *ca.* 2.

Que est mesme, signifieth *verbatim. Which is the selfe same thing.* It is vsed in our common law as a word of art in an action of trespas, or of like nature, for a direct iustification of the very act complained of by the plaintiffe as a wrong, for example, in an action of the case, the plaintiffe saith that the Lord threatned his Tenents at will in such sort, as he draue them to giue vp their tenures. The *Lord* for his defence pleadeth, that he said vnto them, that if they would not depart, he would siew them as the law would. This being the same thretning that he vsed, or, to speake artificially, *que est le mesme* the defence is good. Of this see *Kitchin* in the chapter. *Que est le mesme. fol.* 236. where you may haue many like examples.

Que estate, word for word, signifieth, *Quem statum*: It signifieth in our common law, a plee whereby a man intitling another to lands, &c. saith that the same estate that he had, himselfe hath from him: for example, in a *Quare impedit* the Plaintife alleadgeth that such foure persons were seised of lands, whereunto the Advowsen in question was appendant in fee, and did present to the Church, and afterward the Church was voide, *Que estat del, &c.* that is which estate of the foure persons, he saith also, that he hath nowe during the vacation, by vertue whereof he presently, &c. *Brooke titulo Que estate. fol.* 175. & 176. But it is harder to knowe when this *Que estate* is to be pleaded, then to vnderstand what it is, as by him may appeare. See the new booke of *Entries. verbo. Que estate.*

Queene (Regina) is either shee that houldeth the Crowne of this

Realme

Realme by right of blood, or els shee that is maried to the King. In the former signification shee is in all construction the same that the King is, and hath the same power in all respects. In the other signification shee is inferiour, and a person exempt from the King. For shee may siew and be siewed in her owne name. Yet that shee hath, is the Kings, and looke what shee looseth, so much departeth from the King. *Stawnf: prærog: cap. 2. fol.* 10. *in fine.* See *Kitchin fol.* 1. *b.* See *Cooke lib.* 4. *Copy-hould cases, fo.* 23. *b. Augusta* was the like among Romaines, how be it not *eiusdem iuris* in all things.

Queenes siluer. See *Kings siluer.*

Quem reditum reddat, is a writ Iudiciall, that lyeth for him to whom a rent seck, or rent charge is graunted by fine leuied in the Kings Court, against the Tenent of the land, that refuseth to atturne vnto him, thereby to cause him to atturne. See *old: nat. br: fol.* 156. and *West. parte 2. Simbol: titulo Fines. sect:* 125. See the new booke of *Entries* . *Verbo Quem reditum reddit.*

Querela friscæ fortiæ, is a writ. See *Fresh force.*

Querela coram Rege *& consilio discutienda, & terminanda*, is a writ, whereby one is called to iustifie a complaint of a trespasse made to the king and himselfe before the King & his counsell. *Register originall, fol.* 124. *b.*

Questus est nobis, *&c.* is the forme of a writ of Nusance, which by the statute *anno* 13. *Ed. pri. cap.* 24. lieth against him, to whome the house or other thing that breedeth the Nusance, is alienated, wheras before that statute, this actiõ lay onely against him, that first leuied the thing, to the hurt of his neighbour . See the *Statute.*

Quia improvide, seemeth to be a supersedeas graunted in the behalfe of a clerke of the Chawncerie siewed against the priuiledge of that court, in the common plees, & persiewed to the exigẽd. See *Dyer. f.* 33. *n.* 18.

Quid iuris clamat, is a writ Iudiciall issuing out of the Record of the *Fine*, which remaineth with the *Custos breuium* of the common place , before it be ingrossed (for afterward it cannot be had) and it lieth for the Grauntee of a *Reversion*, or Remainder, when the particular tenent will not atturne. *West. parte. 2. symbol. titulo. Fines. sect.* 118. whome see farder. See the *Register* Iudiciall, *fol.* 36. 57. And the newe booke of *Entries. verbis Quid iuris clamat* .

Quinquagesima Sunday, is alway the next Sabbath before Shrouetide, so called, because it is the fiueteth day before Easter.

Easter. The reasons of this appellation who so desireth to know, hee may finde diuers such as they bee, in *Durandi Rationali diuinorum*, *capit. De Quinquagesima. Sexagesima Sunday* is the next Sabbath before *Quinquagesima*, so called in the opinion of the said authour, because the number of sixtie consisteth of sixe times tenne: sixe hauing reference to the sixe workes of mercie, and tenne to the tenne commandements. *Septuagesima* is the next before *Sexagesima*, and is instituted and so called, as *Durand* likewise saith, for three things: and (to vse his owne words,) *Primò, propter redemptionem* Sabbathi, *vel secundum alios, quinta feria, in qua sancti Patres statuerunt ieiunari. Secundò, propter repraesentationem, quoniam repraesentat septuaginta annos captiuitatis Babilonicae. Tertiò, propter significationem, quoniam per hoc tempus significatur deuiatio, exilium, & tribulatio totius humani generis ab Adam vsq; ad finem mundi: quod quidem exilium sub reuolutione septem dierum peragitur, & sub septem millibus annorum includitur.* But of these three dayes, you may reade him at large, that haue a mind to learne of him. I onely take occasion to note, what time of the yeare they be, because I find them spoken of in our ancient lawe writers, as *Britton ca.* 53. and such like.

Quite claime (*quiete clamantia, vel quieta clamantia*) is a release or acquiting of a man for any action, that he hath, or might haue against him. *Bracton lib.* 5. *tract.* 5. *cap.* 9. *num.* 9. & *lib.* 4. *tractat.* 6. *cap.* 13. *num. prim.*

Quitance (*quietantia*,) see *Acquitance.*

Quid pro quo, is an artificiall speech in the common lawe, signifying so much as the Greeke συν'αλλαγμα, among the Ciuilians, which is a mutuall pretestation or performance of both parties to a contract: as a horse and tenne pound betweene the buyer and the seller. *Kitchin, fol.* 184.

Quinsieme (*Decima quinta*) is a French word, signifying a fifteenth. It is vsed in our common lawe, for a taxe laid vpon the subiects, by the Prince. *an.* 7. *H.* 7. *cap.* 5. so tearmed, because it is rated after the fifteenth part of mens landes or goods. See *Fifteenth* and *Taxe.* The *Fifteenth* (as *Crompton* saith in his *Iurisdict. fol.* 21.) is leuied more commonly in these dayes by the yards of land: and yet in some places by goods also: and note also, that he there saith, that it is well knowne by the *Exchequer* rolle, what euery towne through *England* is to pay for a *Fifteenth*. Sometime this this word *Quinsieme* is vsed for the fifteenth day after any feast, as *Quinsieme* of S. *Iohn Baptist. anno 13. Ed. prim cap. 3. & anno decimo octauo. eiusd. capit. prim.*

Quòd ei deforciat, is a writ that lyeth for the tenent in tayle, tenent in dower, or tenent for terme of life, hauing lost by default, against him that recouered, or against his heire. *Exposition of termes.* See *Broke hoc tit.* See the *Regist. original. fol. 171.* and the new booke of Entries. *verbo Quod ei defortiat.*

Quod permittat, is a writ, that lyeth for him that is disseised of his commune of pasture, against the heire of the disseisour being deade. *Termes of lawe. Briton cap.* 8. saith that this writ lyeth for him, whose auncestour died seised of commune of pasture, or other like thing annexed to his inheritance, against the *Deforceour*. See *Broke hoc titulo.* See the *Register origin. fol. 155.* and the new booke of Entries. *verbo, Quòd permittat.*

Quod Clerici non eligantur in officio Balliui, &c. is a writ, that lyeth for a Clerke, which by reason of some land he hath, is made, or in doubt to be made either Bayliffe, Bedell, or *Reeue*, or some such like officer. See *Clerico infra sacros, &c.* See the *Register orig. fol. 187. Fitz. nat. br. fol. 175.*

Quòd Clerici beneficiati de Cancellaria, &c. is a writ to exempt a Clerk of the Chauncerie from contribution toward the Procters of the Clergie in Parlament. *Register originall: fol. 261. a.*

Quòd persona, nec Præbendarii, &c. is a writ, that lieth for spirituall persons, that are distrained in their spirituall possessions for the payment of the fifteenth with the rest of the parish. *Fitz. nat. br. fol. 176.*

Quòd non permittat. See *Consuetudinibus, & seruiciis.*

Quo iure, is a writ, that lyeth for him that hath land, wherein another chalengeth commun of pasture time out of mind. And it is to compell him to shewe by what title he challengeth this commune of pasture. *Fitzh. nat. br. fol.* 128. Of this see *Briton* more at large, *cap.* 59. see the *Register origin. fol. 156.* and the newe booke of Entries. *verbo Quo iure.*

Quo minus, is a writ, that lyeth for him, which hath a graunt of housebote, and heybote, in another mans woods, against the graunter making such waste, as the grauntee cannot

cannot enioy his graunt. *old nat. br. fol.* 148. Termes of lawe: see *Brooke, hoc titulo.* See *Kitchin fol.* 178. *b.* This writ also lyeth for the Kings fermer in the Exchequer, against him to whom he selleth any thing by way of bargaine touching his ferme. *Perkins Graunts.* 5. For he supposeth, that by the breach of the vendee he is disabled to pay the king his rent.

Quo warranto, is a writ that lyeth against him, which vsurpeth any *Frawnchis* or libertie against the king, as to haue wayfe, stray, faire, market, court Baron, or such like, without good title. *old. nat. br. fol. 149.* or else against him that intrudeth himselfe as heire into land. *Bracton, lib. 4. tractat.* 1. *cap.* 2. *num.* 3. See *Broke hoc titulo.* You may reade of this also. *anno 18. Ed. prim. Stat.* 2. & 3. & *anno* 30 *eiusdem.* And the new booke of Entries. *Quo warranto.*

R

RAcke vintage, *anno 32. H.* 8. *cap.* 14. is a second vintage or voyage for wines by our Merchants into *Fraunce, &c.* For rackt wines, that is, wines clensed and so purged, that it may be and is drawne from the leese. From this voyage our *Merchants* commonly returne about the end of December, or beginning of Ianuarie.

Radknights. See Rodeknights.

R*an*, is a Saxon word, signifying so open a spoiling of a man, that it cannot be denied. *Lamb. Archan. fol.* 125. defineth it thus: R*an dicitur aperta rapina, qua negari non potest.*

Ran*some,* (*redemptio*) commeth of the *French* (*rançon*) or (*rençon*) i. (*redemptio.*) It signifieth properly with vs, the summe paid for the redeeming of a Captiue: and sometime a great summ of money to be paid for the pardoning of some heinous crime. *anno pri. H.* 4. *cap.* 7. Note that when one is to make fine, and Ransome, the Ransome shal be treble to the Fine. *Cromptons Iustice of peace. fol.* 142. *a.* and *Lamb. Eirenarch*: *lib.* 4. *ca.* 16. *pa.* 556. *Horne* in his mirrour of Iustices, maketh this difference betweene amerciament, and ransome, because ransome is the redemption of a corporall punishment, due by law to any offence, *lib.* 3. *cap. de amerciament taxable.*

Rape (*rapus vel rapa*) is a part of a county, signifiing as much as a Hundred. As *Southsex* is diuided into sixe parts, which by a peculiar name are called *rapes*: *viz.* the Rape of *Chichester*, of *Arundell*, of *Brember*, of *Lewis*, of *Peuensey*, of *Hastings. Camden: Britan.*

Britan.pag. 225. whom also see *pag.* 229. These parts are in other places called Tithings, Lathes, or Wapentakes. *Smith de Repub. Anglo. lib.* 2. *ca.* 16.

Rape (raptus) is a felony committed by a man in the violent deflowring of a woman, be shee ould, or young: *Britton: cap.* 1. whereof *West. parte.* 2. *Simbol. titulo* Inditements, *secto:* 54. hath these words: *Copulation violent*, is termed, a rape, or rauishment of the bodie of a woman against her will: which is carnall knowledge had of a woman, who neuer consented thereunto before the fact, nor after. (And this in Scotland ought to be complained of the same day, or night that the crime is committed. *Skene de verborum significa. verbo* Raptus. his reason. *quia lapsu diei hoc crimen præscribitur*) This offence is with vs Felony in the principall, and his ayders. *anno* 11. *H.* 4. *cap.* 13. *anno pri. Ed.* 4. *cap. pri. Westm.* 2. *cap.* 13. (But *Fleta* saith that the complaint must be made within fourty daies, or els the woman may not be heard. *lib.* 3. *cap.* 5. §. *Præterea.* And carnall knowledge of a woman vnder tenne yeares ould is felony. *anno.* 8. *Elizab. cap* 6. Thus far *M. West:* of the diuersity of Rapes, see *Cromptons Iustice of peace. fol.* 43. *b.* & 44. See Rauishment. The ciuile lawe vseth (*raptus*) in the same signification. And (*rapere virginem vel mulierem, est ei vim inferre & violere. Co. li.* 9. *de raptu virgines.*

Raptu hæredis, is a writ lying for the taking away of an heire houlding in *Soccage*, and of this there be 2. sorts, one when the heire is maried, the other when he is not; of both these see the *Register originall. fol.* 163. *b.*

Rastall, was a Lawyer of reuerend accoumpt, that liued in Queene *Maries* daies, and was a Iustice of the common plees. He gathered the statutes of the land into an Abridgement, which carieth his name at this day. He is also the author of the new booke of *Entries.*

Ratification (*ratificatio*) is vsed for the confirmation of a Clerk, in a prebend, &c. formerly giuen him by the Bishop, &c. where the right of patronage is doubted to be in the King. Of this see the *Register originall: fol.* 304.

Rationabili parte bonorum, is a writ that lyeth for the wife against the Executours of her husband, denying her the third part of her husbands goods after debts and funerall charges defrayed. *Fitzh. nat br. fol.* 222. Who there citeth the 18. chap. of *magna charta*, and *Glanuile*, to proue, that according to the common law of England, the

goods

goods of the deceased, his debts first paid, should be diuided into three parts, whereof his wife to haue one, his children the second, and the Executours the third. *Fitzherbert* saith also, that this writ lyeth as well for the children, as for the wife. And the same appeareth by the *Register originall fol: 142.b.* I haue heard some learned men say, that it hath no vse, but where the custome of the country serueth for it. See the new booke of *Entries, verbo: Rationabili parte: et Rationabili parte bonorum.*

Rationabilibus diuisis, is a writ, which lyeth in case, where two Lords in diuers townes haue their seigneuries ioyning together, for him, that findeth his waste, by litle and litle, to haue bene encroched vpon within memory of man, against the other that hath encroched, thereby to rectifie the bounds of their seigneuries. In which respect *Fitzherbert* calleth it, in his owne nature, a writ of right. The *old natura breuium* saith also, that this is a Iusticies, and may be remoued by a *pone* out of the county to the common Bank: See farder the forme and vse of this writ in *Fitzh. nat. br. fol.* 128. and in the *Register, fol.* 157. *b.* and the new booke of *Entries. verbo. Rationabilibus diuisis.* The ciuilians call this *Iudicium finium regundorum.*

Rauishment, raptus commeth of the French (*rauissement .i. direptio, ereptio, raptio, raptus, raptura*) and signifieth in our law, an vnlawfull taking away either of a woman, or of an heire in ward. Sometime it is vsed also in one signification with rape, *viz.* the violent deflowring of a woman, See *Rape*. And thereupon is the writ called *Rauishment de gard*, otherwise called *de hærede abducto*, lying for the Lord, whose tenent by reason of his tenure in Knights seruice being his ward, is taken and conueied from him. See *Fitzh. natu br.* in the writ *De recto de custodia. fol.* 140. *F.* See also the *old nat br. fol.* 92. 93. & 94. See the new booke of *Entries. verbo. Rape, & Rauishment de gard.*

Rawe, anno 4. *Ed.* 4. *cap.* 1.

Raunge, commeth of the French (*Ranger .i. astituere, ordinare*) or else the Substantiue (*Rang. i. ordo, series*) It is vsed in our common lawe, both as a verbe (as to Raunge) and also as a substantiue (as to make Rawnge) *charta de Foresta, cap.* 6. The word is appropriated to the Forest, signifiing the office of the Rawnger. The Rawnger is a sworne officer of the Forest (of which sort there seeme to be twelue) *charta de Foresta. cap.* 7. whose authoritie is partly declared in his oath, set downe by *M. Manwood parte pri. of his Forest lawes, pag.* 50. in these words: You shall truly execute the office of a *R*awnger in the *P*urlieuse of *B*. vpon the borders of the kings Forest of *W*. you shall rechase, and with your hound driue backe again the wild beasts of the Forest, as often as they shall raunge out of the same Forest into your *P*urlieuse. You shall truly present all vnlawfull hunting, and hunters of wild beasts of venerie, as well within the purlieuse, as within the Forest. And these and all other offences you shall present at the *K*ings next court of Attachements, or *S*wainmote, which shall first happen, so helpe you God. But the same author setteth downe his office more particularly in his second part *c.*20.*n.* 15.16.& 17. The summ wherof is this. A *R*aunger is an officer of the Forest, or to the *F*orest, but not within the forest, hauing no charge of vert, but only of venison that commeth out of the forest into his charge, or part of the pourallee, to safe conduct them back againe. And therfore in those forests that haue no pouralleeses, there be no Rawngers, but Foristers serue the turne. This Raunger is made and appointed by the King his leters patents vnder the great seale, and for his better incouragement in his dutie, he hath a yearely fee of 20. pound or 30. pound paid out of the Exchequer, and certaine fee Deere both redde and falow. *H*is office consisteth cheifely in these three points *ad perambulandum quotidie per terras deafforestatas, ad videndum, audiendum & inquirendum, tam de malefactis, quàm de malefactoribus in Ballina sua: ad refugandum feras* Forest*æ tam veneris quàm chaseæ de terris deafforestatis, in terras afforestatas:* and, *ad presentandũ omnes transgressiones Forestæ n terris deafforestatis factas, ad proximas curias illius Forestæ tentas.*

Rawnsom. See R*ansom.*

R*ay*, seemeth to be a word attributed to cloth neuer coloured or died. *v. anno* 11. *H.*4. *cap.*6.

Realtie. See *Royaltie.*

Re*asonable ayde* (*Rationabile auxilium*) is a duty that the *L*ord of the fee claimeth holding by Knights seruice or in soccage to *Marye* his daughter, or to make his sonne *K*night. *Westm.* 1.*cap.* 39. See A*yde.* See *Brooke titulo* Re*asonable aide.*

Reattachement (R*eattachiamentum*) is a second attachement of him, that was formerly attached, and dismissed the court without day, as by the not cõming of the Iustices, or some such like causualtie. *Brooke tit. Reattachment*; where he maketh a

Reat-

Reattachment generall and a Reattachment speciall. Reattachment general seemeth to be, where a man is reattached for his appearance vpon all writs of Assise lying against him. *Brooke eodem nu.* 14. Then speciall must be for one, or more certaine, Register Iudiciall, *fol.* 35. See the newe booke of *Entrise. verbo* R*eattachment*.

Rebellion (Rebellio) is a French word signifiing the taking vp of armes against the *King* or present estate. This French commeth from the *Latine (Rebellio)* which signifieth a second resistance of such as being formerly ouercome in battaile by the Romanes, yeelded themselues to their subiection. The French men and we vse it generally for the traiterous taking vp of armes against the estate, be it by naturall subiects, or by others formerly subdued. Reade more of this. *lib.* 3. *feudorum cap.* 51. and *Hotoman* vpon the same chapter. *See the writ of* R*ebellion*. Rebell is sometime attributed to him that wilfully breaketh a lawe. *anno* 25. *Ed.* 3. *cap.* 6. *& anno* 31. *eiusdem, stat.* 3. *c.* 2. sometime to a villein disobeying his *Lord, a.* 1. *R.* 2. *c.* 6.

Rebellious Assembly, is a gathering together of 12. persons or more, intending or going about, practising, or putting in vre vnlawfully of their owne authoritie to chaunge any lawes, or statutes of this *R*ealme, or to destroy the inclosure of any park, or ground inclosed, or bankes of any fisheponds, pale, or conduict, to the intent the same shall remaine voide, or to the intent vnlawfully to haue common, or way in any of the said grounds, or to destroy the Deere in any Park, or any warrẽ of conies, or douehouses, or fish in any pondes, or any house, barnes, mils, or bayes, or to burne stacks of corne, or to abate rents, or prices of victuals, *an. pri. Mar c.* 12. *& an.* 1. *Eliza. cap.* 17. See *West. parte* 2. *symbol. titulo* I*nditements. Sectio* 65. And *Cromptons* I*ustice of peace. f.* 41. *b.*

R*ebutter*, commeth of the French *(Bouter. i. pellere, impellere, propellere, intrudere)* and signifieth in our common lawe the same thing. For example, a man giueth land to him and the issue of his body, to another in fee with warranty. And the *Donnee* leaseth out this land to a third for yeares. The heire of the *D*onour impleadeth the tenent, alleadging that the land was intailed to him. The *D*once commeth in, and by vertue of the warrantie made by the Donour, repelleth the heire, because though the land were intailed to him: yet he is heire to the warranty likewise;

wiſe; and this is called a *Rebutter*. See *Brooke. titulo Barre: nu.* 13. And againe if I graunt to my tenent to hould *sine impetitione vaſti*, and afterward I implede him for waſte made, he may debarre me of this action, by ſhewing my graunt, and this is likewiſe a Rebutter. *Idem,eodem, nu.* 25. See the newe booke of *Entries,verbo Rebutter.*

Renant,anno 32.H. 8.*ca.*2.

Recaption (*Recaptio*) ſignifieth a ſecond diſtreſſe of one formerly diſtreined for the ſelfe ſame cauſe,and alſo during the plee grounded vpon the former diſtreſſe. It likewiſe ſignifieth a writ lying for the party thus deſtreined,the forme, and farder vſe whereof, you may ſee in *Fitzh.nat.br.fol.* 71. and the *Regiſter orig. fol.*86.and the *Regiſter Iudiciall,fol.*69.and the new booke of *Entries.verbo.* Recaption.

Receyver(*Receptor*,or *Receptator*) generally and indefinitely vſed, is as with the Ciuilians,ſo alſo with vs, vſed commonly in the euill part for ſuch as receiue ſtollen goods from theeues, and conceale them.*l.*1 .*ff.de receptatoribus*, but annexed to other words,as the receiuer of rents, &c. it ſignifieth many times an officer of great accoumpte, belonging to the king or other great perſonage. *Cromptons Iuriſdict. fol.* 18. There is alſo an officer called the *Receiuer of Fynes*,who receiueth the mony of all ſuch, as compound with the King in the office of the finances for the buying of any lands, or tenements houlden in *Capite. Weſt.parte* 2.*ſymbol.titulo Fines.ſect.* 106. Receiuer of all offices accounptable. *anno.* 1.*Ed.*4.*ca.*1.

Receiuer generall of the Duchy of Lancaſter,is an officer belonging to the Duchy court , that gathereth in all the reuenewes and fines of the lands of the ſaid Duchy , and of all forfeitures and aſſeſments, or what elſe is thence to be receiued.

Receiuer generall of the court of Wards and liueries,is an officer belonging to that court,that is to receiue all rents, reuenewes and fines of the lands belonging to his maieſties wards, as alſo the fines for licences to the Kings widowes to mary , of *ouſter le main* ſued out , and for idiots and lunatikes land , and finally all other profits whatſoeuer in mony ariſing to his maieſtie out of or by reaſon of the court of wards and lyveries.

*Receiuer generall of the Muſter rolles.anno.*35.*El.ca.*4.

Receiuer generall of the Duchie of Lancaſter of the wards,and liveries,anno 39.*Elizab.cap.*7.

Receyt.See *Reſceit.*

Recluse (*Reclusus*) is he, that by reason of his order in religion, may not stirre out of his house or cloyster. *Litleton fol.* 92.

Recognisance (*Recognitio*) commeth of the French (*Recognoisance*. i. *agnitio, recognitio*) and in our common lawe is thus defined. A Recognisance is a bond of record, testifiing the recognizour to owe vnto the recognizee a certaine summe of money, and is knowledged in some court of record, or before some Iudge or other officer of such court, hauing authoritie to take the same: as the Masters of the Chancerie, the Iudges of either Bench, Barons of the Exchequer, Iustices of peace, &c. And those that be meere recognisances are not sealed, but inrolled. And execution by force thereof is of all the recognisours goods, and chatels, except his draught beasts, and implements of husbandrie, and of the moitie of his lands, *West. parte prim. symb. lib.* 2. *titulo Recognisances. sect.* 149. And of these you may see there great diuersitie of presidents.

Note farder, that a Recognizance, though in the speciall signification, it do but acknowledge a certaine debt, and is executed vpon all the goods, and halfe the lands of the recognisour: yet by extention it is drawne also to the Bonds, commonly called *Statute Merchant*, and *Statute of the Staple*: as appeareth by the *Register original. fol.* 146. 151. & 252. and by *West. vbi supra*, and others. See *Statute Merchant*, and *Statute Staple*.

Recognisance hath yet another signification, as appeareth by these wordes in the statute, *West.* 1. *c.* 36. *anno* 3. *Ed.* 1. It is prouided also and agreed, that if any man be attainted of disseisin done in the time of our King that now is, with roberie of any maner of goods, or moueables, by recognisance of Assise of *nouel disseisin*, the iudgement shall, &c. In which place it is vsed for the verdict of the twelue men empaneled vpon an Assise, which twelue are also called recognitours of the Assise, *Litleton fol.* 72. So also *Bracton* calleth them *lib.* 5. *tractat.* 2. *cap.* 9. *num.* 2. in these words: *In essonio vero reddendo exigentur omnes illi, quos causa tetigerit: sicut particeps, Warantus, & alii vt supra. Recognitores in Assisis, Iuratores in Iuratis, Inquisitores in Inquisitionibus, &c.* And againe, *lib.* 3. *tract. prim. cap.* 11. *num.* 16. See the Statute *anno* 20. *Ed. prim. stat.* 4. See the newe book of Entries, *ver. Recognisance*.

Recognitione adnullanda per vim & duritiem facta, is a writ to the Iustices of the common Bench, for the sending of a record, touching a recognisance, which the recognisour suggesteth to be acknowledged by force and hard dealing, that if it so appeare, it may be disanulled. *Register original. fol.* 183. *a. b.*

Recognitours (recognitores) is a word vsed for the Iurie empaneled vpon an assise. The reason why they be so called, may be, because they acknowledge a disseisin by their verdict. See *Bracton lib.* 5. *tract.* 2. *cap.* 9. *nu.* 2. & *lib.* 3. *tract. prim. cap.* 11. *num.* 16.

Record, (recordum) commeth of the Latine *(recordari.)* The word is both French and English, and in both tongs signifieth an authenticall or vncontroulable testimonie in writing. *Britton cap.* 27. and *Lamb. Eirenarch. lib.* 1. *cap.* 13. In the Grand Custumarie of *Normandie*, there are seuerall Chapters of diuers records, expressing whose presence in each of the Courts, is sufficient to make that which is enacted to be a record. *viz.* the 102. chapter, where you haue wordes to this effect. The record of the Kings Court, is a record of things done before the King. All things done before the King, so he haue one other witnesse. This record may he and other make: if he himselfe will not make it, it may be made by three others. And his person may not bee impeached (or excepted against) either in this or any other thing. The next chapter. *viz.* the 103. sheweth how many persons suffise to make a record in the Exchequer. The next how many in an assise, &c.

I find not that wee in our Courts (especially the Kings Courts) stand much vpon the number of recorders or witnesses for the strength of the testimonie which the record worketh: but that we take it sufficient which is registred in each Court. *Glanvile lib.* 8. *cap.* 8. *Bracton lib.* 3. *tract.* 2. *cap.* 37. *num.* 4. *Britton* in the Proeme of his booke, saith, that the Iustices of the Kings Bench haue a record, the Coroner, Vicount, Iustices of the Exchequer, Iustices of Goale deliuerie, the Steward of *England*, Iustices of *Ireland*, Iustices of *Chester*, Iustices assigned by the Kings leters patents, in those causes they haue commission to take knowledge of. All which (as I take it) must be vnderstood with that caueat of *Brooke, titulo (Record) num.* 20 & 22. that an act committed to writing in any of the Kings Courts,

Courts, during the terme wherein it is written, is alterable, and no record: but that terme once ended, and the said act duly enrolled, it is a record, and of that credit, that admitteth no alteration, or proofe to the contrarie. Yet see *Sir Edward Cookes* Reports *lib.* 4. Rawlins *case. fol.* 52.*b. ann.* 12. *Ed.* 2. *cap.* 4. It is said, that two Iustices of either Bench haue power to record Non suites, & Defaults in the countrey. It appeareth by Bracton, *lib.* 5. *tract.* 2. *c.* 1. *&* 11. that *quatuor milites habent recordum*, being sent to view a partie essoined *de malo lecti*, and *lib.* 5. *tract.* 1. *cap.* 4. *nu.* 2. that *Seruiens Hundredi habet recordum in testimonio proborum hominum.* And in the Statute of *Carleil*, made *anno* 15. *Ed.* 2. it is said, that one *I*ustice of either Bench with an Abbot, or a *P*rior, or a Knight, or a man of good fame and credence, hath a record in the view of one that is said by reason of sicknesse, to be vnable to appeare personally for the passing of a fine. And *anno* 13. *H.* 4. *cap.* 7. *&* *anno* 2. *H.* 5. *cap.* 3. that two Iustices of peace, with the Shyreeue, or Vndershyreeue haue power to record, what they find done by any in a ryot, or route, &c.

That which is before mentioned out of *Britton* touching the Shyreeue, seemeth to be limited by *Fitzh: nat. br. fol:* 81. *D.* Who alloweth him a *R*ecord in such maters onely, as he is commaunded to execute by the Kings writ, in respect of his office. And thence it commeth that *Kitchin fol.* 177. saith, that the Escheatour, and Shyreeue be not Iustices of record, but officers of record. In which words he signifieth, that their testimony is authenticall onely in some certaine things that are expresly inioyned them by vertue of their Commission, as ministers to the King in his higher Courts, whereas Iustices of record haue in generality a record for all things within their cognisance done before them as Iudges, though not expresly or particularly commaunded. *Fitzherbert* in his *Nat: br. fo.* 82. *in principio*, something explaneth this point, writing to this effect: Euery act that the Shyreeue doth by vertue of his commission, ought to be taken as mater of record, no lesse then the Iustices of peace. His reasons be two: the former, because his patent is of record: the other, because he is a conseruatour of the peace. And then he addeth, that the plees held before him in his County be not of record. Yet is the county called a Court of record. *Westm.* 2. *ca.* 3. *anno* 13. *Ed.* 1. But it seemeth by Britton. *cap.* 27. that it is onely in these causes, whereof the Shyreeue houldeth plee by especiall writ; and not those that he houldeth of course or custome. And in that case also it may be gathered out of the same authour, that he hath a record, but with the testimony of those annexed, that be suiters to the Court. Which seemeth to agree with *Bractons* words aboue specified. *Seruiens Hundredi habet recordum in testimonio proborum hominum.* And to this purpose read *Glanuile. lib.* 8. *cap.* 8. 9. & 10. One Iustice vpon view of forcible detinew of land, may record the same by statute. *anno* 15. *R.* 2. *cap.* 2. the Maior, and Constables of the Staple, haue power to record recognisances of debt taken before them. *anno* 10. *H.* 6. *ca.* 1.

Brooke, titulo (Record) seemeth to say, that no court ecclesiasticall is of record: how truly, it is to be inquired. For Bishops certifiing bastardy, bigamy, excommunication, the vacancy or plenarty of a Church, a mariage, a diuorce, a spirituall intrusion, or whether a man be professed in any religion, with other such like, are credited without farder enquiry or controlment. See *Brooke, titulo Bastardy.* See *Fleta. lib*: 6. *ca.* 39. 40. 41. 42. *Lamb. eirenarcha*: *lib*: *pri. cap.* 13. *Glanuile. li.* 7. *ca.* 14. & 15. the *Register originall*: *fol.* 5. *b. Bracton. lib.* 5. *tracta.* 5. *ca.* 20. *nu.* 5. *Britton ca.* 92. 94. 106. 107. & 109. *Doct.* and *Stud. li.* 2. *ca.* 5. but especially *Cosius apologie, parte pri. ca.* 2. And a testament shewed vnder the seale of the Ordinary is not trauersable. 36. *H.* 6. 31. *Perkins Testament.* 491. *Fulb. paral. fol.* 61. *b.* But it may be that this opinion groweth from a difference betweene that law, whereby the court Christian is most ordered, and the common law of this land. For by the ciuile or canon law no instrument, or record is held so firme, but that it may be checked by witnesses able to depose it to be vntrue. *Co. plus valere quod agitur quàm quod simulate concipitur. ca. cum Iohannes.* 10. *extra*: *de fide instrumentorum.* Whereas in our common law against a record of the Kings Court, after the terme wherein it is made, no witnes can preuaile. *Britton. ca.* 109. *Coke lib.* 4. *Hindes case. fol.* 71. *lib. assisarum fol.* 227. *nota.* 21. This reconciliation may be iustified by *Brooke* himselfe. *titulo, Testaments. num.* 4. 8. & 14. and by *Glanuile, lib.* 8. *cap.* 8.

The King may make a court of record by his graunt. *Glanuil. li.* 8. *ca.* 8. *Britton cap.* 121. as for example, Queene *Elizabeth* of worthy memory by her Charter dated. 26. *Aprilis. anno* 3. *regni sui* made the Consistory Court of the

the Vniuersity of *Cambridge* a Court of record.

There are reckoned among our common lawyers three sorts of records: *viz:* A record iudiciall, as attainder, &c. A record ministeriall vpon oath, as an office found. A record made by conueyance by consent, as a fine, deede enrolled, or such like. *Coke. li.* 4. *Andrew Ognels case. fo.* 54. *b.*

Recordare facias, or *recordari facias*, is a writ directed to the Shyreeue, to remoue a cause depending in an inferiour court, to the Kings bench, or common plees, as out of a court of auncient Demesn, Hundred, or Countie, *Fitz. nat. br. fol.* 71. B. out of the countie Court. *idem, fo.* 46. B. or other courts of record. *idem fol.* 71. C. & 119. *K.* Howbeit, if you will learne more exactly, where, and in what cases this writ lyeth, reade Brooke in his *Abridgm. titulo*, Recordare & *pone*. It seemeth to be called a *recordare*, because the forme is such, that it commaundeth the Shyreeue to whom it is directed, to make a record of the proceeding by himselfe, and others, and then to send vp the cause. See the *Register, verbo*, Recordare, in the Table of the originall Writs. See *Certiorari*. See *Accedas ad Curiam*.

Recorder (*recordator*) commeth of the French (*recordeur. i. talis persona qua in Ducis Curia à iudicio faciendo non debet amoueri.*) *Grand Custumarie of Norm. cap.* 107. & 121. Whereby it appeareth, that those which were necessarie Iudges in the Duke of *Normandies* Courts, were called *Recorders*: and who they were, is shewed in the ninth chapter of the said booke. And that they, or the greater part of them, had power to make a record, it is euident in the chapter 107. Here in *England* a Recorder is he, whome the Maior or other Magistrate of any citie, or towne corporate, hauing Iurisdiction, or a Court of record within their precincts by the *Kings* graunt, doth associate vnto him for his beter direction in maters of Iustice and proceedings, according vnto lawe. And he is for the most part a man well seene in the common lawe.

Recordo & *processu mittendis*, is a writ to call a Record, together with the whole proceeding in the cause, out of one court into the *Kings* Court. Which see in the Table of the *Register orig.* how diuersly it is vsed.

Recordo vtlagariæ mittendo, is a writ Iudiciall, which see in the *Register iudicial. fol.* 32.

Recouerie (*Recuperatio*) cõmeth of the French) *Recouvrer. i. Recuperare*. It signifieth in our commõ lawe, an obteining of any thing by Iudgement, or triall of lawe, as *evictio* doth among the Ciuilians. But you must vnderstand, that there is a true recouerie and a feigned. A true *Recouerie* is an actuall, or reall recouerie of any thing, or the value thereof by Iudgement: as if a man siewed for any land, or other thing moueable or immoueable, and haue a verdict, and Iudgement for him. A feigned recouerie is (as the Ciuilians call it) *quadam fictio iuris*. a certaine forme, or course set downe by lawe, to be obserued for the beter assuring of lands or tenements vnto vs. And for the beter vnderstanding of this, reade *West. parte 2. symbol. titulo Recoveries. sect. pri.* who saith, that the end, and effect of a Recouerie, is to discontinue and destroy estates Tayles, *Remainders*, and Reuersions, and to barre the former owners thereof. And in this formality there be required 3. parties, *viz.* the *Demaundant*, the Tenent, and the Vowchee. The Demaundant is he that bringeth the writ of Entrie, and may be termed the Recouerer: The Tenent is he, against whom the writ is brought, and may be termed the *Recoveree*. The Vowchee is he, whom the tenēt vowcheth, or calleth to warrantie for the land in demaund. *West. vbi supra.* In whom you may reade more touching this mater.

But for example to explane this point, a man that is desirous to cut of an estate tayle in lands or tenements, to the end, to sell, giue, or bequeath it, as him self seeth good, vseth his frend to bring a writ vpon him for this land. He appearing to the writ saith for him selfe, that the land in question came to him or his auncesters from such a man or his auncester, who in the conueiance thereof, bound him selfe and his heires to make good the title vnto him or them to whome it was conueied. And so he is allowed by the court to call in this third man to say what he can for the iustifiing of his right to this land, before he so conveied it. The third man commeth not: wherevpon the land is recouered by him that brought the writ: and the tenent of the land is left for his remedie to the third man that was called and came not in to defend the tenent. And by this meanes the entayle which was made by the tenent, or his auncester, is cut of by iudgement herevpon giuen: for that he is pretended to haue no power to entaile that land, whereunto he had no iust title, as now it appeareth: because it is evicted, or recouered from him.

This kinde of recouery is by good opinion, but a snare to deceiue the people. *Doctor & Stud. ca. 32. dial. pri. fol. 56. a.* This feigned Recouery is also called a common Recouery: And the reason of that *Epitheton* is, because it is a beaten and common path to that end, for which it is ordeined, *viz.* to cut of the estates aboue specified. See the new *booke of Entries verbo. Recouery.*

I saide before, that a true recouery is as well of the value, as of the thing: for the beter vnderstanding whereof, know, that (In valew) signifieth as much as (*Illud quod interest*) with the Ciuilians. For example, if a man buy land of an other with warranty, which land a third person afterward by suite of lawe recouereth against me, I haue my remedie against him that sould it me, to recouer in value, that is, to recouer so much in mony as the land is worth, or so much other land by way of exchaunge. *Fitzh. nat. br. fol.* 134. K. To recouer a warranty. *old. nat. br. fol.* 146. is to proue by judgement that a man was his warrant against all men for such a thing.

Recto, is a writ, called in English, a writ of Right, which is of so high a nature, that whereas other writs in reall actions, be onely to recouer the possession of the land, or tenements in question, which haue beene lost by our auncester, or our selues, this aimeth to recouer both the seisin, which some of our Auncesters, or wee had, and also the propertie of the thing, whereof our Auncester died not seised, as of fee: and whereby are pleaded, and tried both the rights togither, *viz.* as well of possession, as property. Insomuch as if a man once loose his cause vpon this writ, either by Judgement, by *Assise*, or batell, he is without all remedie, and shall be excluded (*per exceptionem Rei iudicatæ*) *Bracton lib. 5. tract. 1. cap. 1. & seqq.* where you may reade your fille of this writ.

It is diuided into two *species*: *Rectum patens*, a writ of right patent, and *Rectum clausum*, a writ of right close. This the Ciuilians call *Iudicium petitorium*. The writ of right patent is so called, because it is sent open, and is in nature the highest writ of all other, lying alwaies for him that hath fee simple in the lands, or tenements sewed for, and not for any other. And when it lieth for him that chalengeth fee simple, or in what cases, See *Fitzh. nat. br. fol. pri.* C. whome see also. *fol. 6.* of a speci-

ſpeciall writ of right in *London*, otherwiſe called a writ of right according to the Cuſtome of *London*. This writ is alſo called *Breue magnum de Recto. Regiſter originall.fol. 9, A.* B. and *Fleta li.5. cap. 32.* §.1.

A writ of right cloſe, is a writ directed to a Lord of *auncient Demeſn*, and lieth for thoſe, which hould their lands and tenements by charter in fee ſimple or in fee taile, or for terme of life, or in dower, if they be eiected out of ſuch lands, &c. or diſſeiſed. In this caſe a man or his heire may ſiew out this writ of Right cloſe directed to the L. of the Auncient *Demeſn*, commanding him to doe him right, &c. in his court. This is alſo called a ſmall writ of right. *Breve parvum, Regiſter originall.fol.9. a. b.* and *Britton, cap.* 120. *in fine.* Of this ſee *Fitzh.* likewiſe at large. *nat. br. fol.* 11. & *ſeqq.*

Yet note that the writ of right patent ſeemeth farder to be extended in vſe, then the originall inuention ſerued: for a writ of Right of *Dower*, which lieth for the tenent in Dower, and onely for terme of life, is patent, as appeareth by *Fitzh. nat. br. fol.7.E.* The like may be ſaid of diuers others that doe hereafter followe. Of theſe ſee alſo the table of the *originall Regiſter. verbo Recto.* This writ is properly tried in the Lords court betweene kindſmen, that claime by one title from their Auncester. But how it may be thence remoued, and brought either to the Countie, or to the kings court, ſee *Fleta, lib.6.cap.*3.4.& 5. *Glanvile* ſeemeth to make euery writ, whereby a man ſieweth for any thing due vnto him, a writ of right. *lib.* 10.*ca.* 1 *lib.* 11. *cap.*1. *lib.*12.*cap.*1.

Recto de dote, is a writ of Right of Dower, which lieth for a woman, that hath receiued part of her Dower, and purpoſeth to demaund the Remanent in the ſame towne, againſt the heire, or his Gardian, if he be ward. Of this ſee more in the *old nat. br. fol.* 5. and *Fitzh. fol.* 7. *E.* and the *Regiſter* originall, *fol.* 3. and the newe booke of *Entries, verbo* Droyt.

Recto de dote vnde nihil habet, is a writ of right, which lieth in caſe, where the husband hauing diuers lands or tenements, hath aſſured no dower to his wife, and ſhe thereby is driuen to ſiew for her thirds agianſt the heire or his Gardian, *old.nat. br. folio* 6. *Regiſter originall, fol.* 170.

Recto de rationabili parte, is a writ that lieth alway, beweene priuies of bloud, as brothers in *Gauel-kind*, or ſiſters, or other Coparceners, as Nephewes or

Nee-

Neeces, and for land in Fee simple. For example, if a man lease his land for tearme of life, and afterward dyeth, leauing issue, two daughters, and after that the tenent for terme of life likewise dyeth: the one sister entring vpon all the land, and so deforcing the other; the sister so deforced, shall haue this writ to recouer her part. *Fitz. nat.br.fo. 9. Register origin. fol. 3.*

Recto *quando Dominus remisit*, is a writ of right, which lyeth in case, where lands or tenements that be in the Seigneurie of any Lord, are in demaund by a writ of right. For if the Lord hold no Court, or otherwise at the prayer of the Demandant, or Tenent, shall send to the Court of the King his writ, to put the cause thither for that time (sauing to him another time the right of his Seigneurie) then this writ issueth out for the other partie, and hath this name from the words therein comprised, being the true occasion thereof. This writ is close, and must be returned before the Iustices of the common Bancke. *old. nat.br. fol. 16. Regist. orig. fol.4.*

Recto *de Advocatia Ecclesia*, is a writ of right, lying where a man hath right of *Advouzen*, and the Parson of the Church dying, a straunger presenteth his Clerke to the Church, & he not hauing moued his action of *Quare impedit* nor *darrein presentment* within sixe monethes, but suffered the straunger to vsurpe vpon him. And this writ he only may haue, that claimeth the Aduowzen, to himselfe and to his heires in fee. And as it lyeth for the whole aduowzen: so it lyeth also for the halfe, the third, the fourth part. *old. nat. br. fol. 24. Register originall. fol. 29.*

Recto de custodia terrae & haeredis, is a writ that lyeth for him, whose Tenent houlding of him in Chiualry, dyeth in his nonage, against a straunger, that entreth vpon the land, and taketh the body of the heire. The forme, and farder vse whereof see in *Fitzh. nat. br. fol. 139.* and the *register originall: fol. 161.*

Recto sur disclaimer, is a writ that lyeth, where the Lord in the kings court, *sc:* in the common plees, doth avow vpon his tenent, and the Tenent disclaimeth to hould of him, vpon the disclaimer he shall haue this writ: and if the Lord auerre, and proue, that the land is houlden of him, he shall recouer the land for euer. *old. nat. br. fo. 150.* which is grounded vpon the statute, *Westm. 2. ca. 2. anno 13. Ed. pri.* which statute beginneth. *Quia Domini feudorum, &c.*

Rector, is both Latine, and English, signifiing a Gouernour. In the common law *rector ecclesiæ parochialis*, is he that hath the charge, or cure of a parish Church: *qui tantum ius in ecclesia parochiali habet, quantum prælatus in ecclesia collegiata. ca. vlt: De locat; & Conduct: in glos: verbo Expelli potuissent.* In our common law, I heare that it is lately ouer ruled, that *rector ecclesiæ parochialis* is he, that hath a personage, where there is a vicarage, endowed: and he that hath a personage without a vicorage, is called *persona*. But this distinction seemeth to be new and subtile *præter rationem*. I am sure *Bracton* vseth it otherwise, *lib: 4. tracta: 5. ca. pri.* in these words. *Et sciendum quod rectoribus ecclesiarum parochialium competit Assisa qui instituti sunt per Episcopos, & Ordinarios vt personæ.* Where it is plaine, that *rector* and *persona* be confounded. Marke also these words there following: *Item dici possunt rectores Canonici de ecclesiis præbendatis. Item dici possunt rectores, vel quasi, Abbates, Priores & alii, qui habent ecclesias ad proprios vsus.*

Rectus in curia, is he that standeth at the barre, and hath no man to obiect any offence against him. *Smith de repub: Angl: li. 2. c. 3.* see *a. 6.* R. 2. *sta. 1. c. 12.*

Reddendum, is vsed many times substantiuely for the clause in a lease, &c. Whereby the rent is reserued to the leasour. *Coke lib. 2. Lord Cromwels case. fol. 72. b.*

Redisseisin (redisseisina) is a disseisin made by him, that once before was found, and adiudged to haue disseised the same man of his lands, or tenements. For the which there lyeth a speciall writ, called a writ of *redisseisin. old: nat. br. fol.* 106. *Fitzh. nat. br. fol.* 188. See the new booke of *Entries. verb. Redisseisin.*

Redisseisina, is a writ lying for a *redisseisin. Reg. orig. fo.* 206. 207.

Reddicion, is a iudiciall confession, and acknowledgement that the land or thing in demaũd belongeth to the demaundant, or at the least, not to himselfe. *a.* 34. & 35. *H.* 8. *ca.* 24. *Perkins Dower.* 379. 380.

Redubbours, be those that buy cloth, which they know to be stollen, and turne it into some other forme or fashion. *Britton. cap.* 29. *Cromptons Vicount, fol.* 193. *a.*

Reentry, cõmeth of the French (*reentrer* .i. *rursus intrare*, and signifieth in our common law, the resuming, or taking againe of possession, which we had earst forgone. For example, if I make a lease, of land, or tenement I doe thereby forgoe the possession, and if I doe condition with the *Leassee*, that for non payment of the rent at the day it shalbe lawfull for me to reenter, this is as much as if I conditioned to take againe the lands &c. into mine owne hands, and to recouer the possession by mine owne fact without the assistance of Iudge or proces.

Reere countie. See Rier *Countye*.

Reextent, is a second extent made vpon lands, or tenements, vpon complaint made, that the former extent was partially performed. *Brooke, titulo. Extent.fol.* 313.

Regard (*regardum*) is borowed of the French (*Regard*) or *Regardure* .i. *aspectus, conspectus, respectus*.) and though it haue a generall signification of any care or diligence: yet it hath also a speciall acceptance, and therein is vsed onely in maters of the Forest: and there two waies: one for the office of the *Regarder*, the other for the compasse of ground belonging to the *Regarders* office or charge. *Cromptons Iurisd. fol.* 175. *199*. Touching the former, thus saith *M. Manwod, parte pri.* of his Forest lawes. *pag.* 198. The Eire, generall sessions of the Forest, or Iustices seat, is to be houlden, and kepte euery third yeare: and of necessity before that any such sessions or Iustices seate can be houlden, the *Regarders* of the Forest must make their Regard. And this making of the Regard must be done by the kings writ. And the Regard is, (as he afterward there saith) to goe through the whole Forest, and euery Bayliwicke of the same, to see and enquire of the trespasses of the Forest: which he compriseth in these 4. *viz. ad videndendum. ad inquirendum, ad imbreviandum, ad certificandum*. Of euery of which braunches you may reade there his exposition.

Touching the second signification, the compas of the *Regarders* charge is the whole Forest, that is, all that ground, which is parcell of the Forest. For there may be woods within the limits of the Forest, that be no parcell thereof, and those be without the *Regard*, as the same author plainely declareth, *parte pri. pag.* 194. and againe *parte* 2. *cap.* 7. *nu.* 4. where he sheweth the difference between these words: (*Infra Regardum*) or (*Rewardum*) & *Infra Forestam*.

Regarder (*Regardator*) commeth of the French (*Regardeur*) .i. *spectator*) & signifieth an officer of the Forest. *Cromptons Iurisdict. fol.* 153. where it is thus defined. *A* Regarder is an officer of the Forest, appointed to survew all other officers. He saith there also, that this officer was ordeined in the beginning of

King *Henry* the seconds daies. *M. Manwood* in his first part of *Forest lawes. pag.* 188. thus defineth him. A Regarder is an officer of the Kings Forest, that is sworne to make the Regard of the *Forest*, as the same hath been vsed to be made in auncient time. And also to view and inquire of all offences of the Forest, as well of vert as of venison, and of all concealements of any offences or defaults of the Foresters, and of all other officers of the Kings Forest, concerning the execution of their offices. He saith there also, that a Regarder may be made either by the Kings leters patents, or by any one of the Kings Iustices of the Forest, at his discretion in the generall *Eyre*, or at such time, as the Regard is to be made, by vertue of the *Kings* writ, directed to the *Shyreeue* of the Countie for that purpose. The forme of which writ he there setteth downe.

After that pag. *192.* he setteth downe his oath in these words. You shall truly serue our souereigne *Lord* the King in the office of a Regarder in the Forest of *Waltham*. You shall make the Regard of the same in such maner, as the same hath beene accustomed to be made. You shall raunge through the whole forest, and through euery Bailiwicke of the same, as the *Foresters* there shall lead you to view the said forest. And if the foresters will not, or doe not know how to lead you, to make the regard or raunge of the Forest, or that they will conceale from you any thing that is forfeited to the King, you your selues shall not let for any thing: but you shall see the same forfeiture, and cause the same to be inrolled in your rolle. You shall inquire of all wastes, pourprestures, and Asserts of the Forest, and also of concealements of any offence, or trespasse in the *Forest*. & all these things you shall to the vttermost of your power doe, so helpe you God. Then you may reade farder the particulars of his office. *eadem, pag.* 195. *And pag.* 207. he saith that their presentments must be vpon their view, and so recorded, and that the Regarders of themselues haue power to heare and determine the fine, or amerciament for expeditating of dogs. See *Regard*.

Regio assensu, is a writ whereby the *King* giueth his *Royall* assent to the election of a Bishop or Abbot. *Register origin. fol.* 294. *b.*

Registrie) *Registrum*) commeth of the French (*Registre.* i. *liber, librarium, codex ratiocinarius, ephemeris, commentarius*) it signifieth

fieth with vs the office,or books, or rolls, wherin are recorded the proceedings of the Chauncerie, or any spirituall courte.The writer, and keeper whereof is called the Register,in latine, *Registarius*. *Register* is also the name of a booke, wherein are expressed all the formes of writs vsed at the common lawe, called the Register of the Chauncerie. *anno* 13. *Ed. prim. cap.* 24. Some say it is tearmed *Registrum quasi Regestum. Prateus.*

Regrator (*regratator*) commeth of the French (*regratter* i. *desquamare.*) *Regratter quelque vielle robe & la faire neufue*) is to scoure or furbush an old garment and to make it new againe. Also (*regratteur*) signifieth as much as (*Mango*) in Latine: which kind of men sold children, and to sel them the beter, *mentiendi coloris artem optimè callebant. Martialis & Plinius.* This word in our cōmon lawe,did auunciently signifie such as bought by the great, and sold by retayle. *anno* 27. *Ed.* 3. *stat. prim. ca.* 3. but now it signifieth him, that buyeth and selleth any wares, or victuals in the same market, or faire, or within 5. miles thereof. *anno* 5. *Ed.* 6. *cap.* 14. *anno* 5. *Eliz. cap.* 12. *anno* 13. *Eliz. cap.* 25. See *Forestallers* and *Engrossers*.

Rehabere facias seisinam quando Vice comes liberavit seisinam de maiore parte, quam deberet, is a writ Iudiciall. *Regist. Iudicial, fol.* 13.51.There is another writ of this name and nature. *eodem fol.* 54.

Reioynder (*reiunctio*) signifieth in our common lawe,asmuch as *Duplicatio* with the Ciuilians, that is, an exception to a replication. For the first answer of the Defendant to the Plaintiffes bill, is called an exception: the plaintiffes aunswer to that, is called a Replication:and the Defendants to that,Duplication in the ciuill lawe, and a Reioynder with vs; especially in Chauncerie. *West.parte* 2. *symb. titulo Chauncerie. sect.* 56. where he citeth these words out of *Spigelius. Est autem reiunctio seu duplicatio, vel allegatio, quæ datur reo ad infirmandum replicationē actoris, & confirmandum exceptionem Rei.*

Relation(*relatio*) *idem quod fictio iuris*, to make a nullitie of a thing from the beginning,(for a certaine intent) which had essence, *Cooke lib.* 3. *Butler & Baker. fol.* 28. *b.* which in playner termes may be thus expounded. Relation is a fiction of the lawe, whereby something is (for a speciall purpose) imagined neuer to haue bene, which in

 truth

truth was. Reade the rest.

Release (*relaxatio*) commeth of the French *Relasche*. i. *cessatio, relaxatio, laxamentum*) and in our common lawe is thus defined: A *Release* is an Instrument whereby estates, rights, titles, entries, actions, and other things be some time extinguished, some time transferred, sometime abridged, and sometime enlarged. *West. parte prim. symbol. lib.* 2 *sect.* 509. And there is a *Release* in fact, and a release in lawe. *Perkins Graunts* 71. A release in fact seemeth to be that, which the very words expressely declare. A Release in lawe is that, which doth acquite by way of consequent, or intendment of lawe. An example whereof you haue in *Perkins vbi supra*. Of these, how they be auaileable, & how not, see *Litleton* at large. *li.* 3. *cap.* 8. *fol.* 94. of diuers sortes of these *Releases* see the newe booke of *Entries*. *verbo Release*.

Reliefe (*relevium*) commeth of the French (*relever*. i. *relevare*) and signifieth in our common lawe, a certaine summe of money, that the tenent holding by knights seruice, grand sergeantie, or other tenure, for the which homage or regall seruice is due, or by soccage, for the which no homage is due, and being at full age at the death of his auncestour, doth pay vnto his *Lord* at his entrance. *Bracton lib.* 2. *cap.* 36. giueth a reason why it is called a *Reliefe*. *viz. quia hæreditas, quæ iacens fuit per antecessoris decessum, relevatur in manus hæredum, & propter factam relevationem, facienda erit ab hærede quædam præstatio, quæ dicitur* R*elevium*. Of this you may read *Britton. cap.* 69. in a maner to the same effect. Of this also speaketh the *Grand Custumary of Normandie, cap.* 34. to this effect: It is to be knowne, that the Lord of the fee ought to haue reliefe of the lands, which be held of him by homage, when those die, of whom he had homage. And that this is not onely proper to vs in *Eng.* or *Normandie*, appeareth by *Hotoman* in his Commentaries, *de verbis feud. verbo Relevium*, who there defineth it thus: *Relevium est honorarium, quod novus vasallus patrono introitus causa largitur, quasi morte vasalli alterius, vel alio quo casu feudum ceciderit: quod iam à novo sublevetur*: and farder speaketh of it, that which is worth the reading, and containeth great knowledge of antiquitie. See the like definition *in Marante singularibus. verbo Relevium*. For the quantitie of this reliefe, see the *Great charter, cap.* 2. in these words: If any of our *Earles* or *Barons*, or any other our tenents, which hold of vs in chiefe by knights seruice, dye, and at the time of his death his heire is of full age, and oweth to vs reliefe, he shall haue inheritance by the old *Reliefe*: that is to say, the heire, or heires of an *Earle* for one whole *Earl*dome one hundred pound: the heire or heires of a Baron for one whole Baronie, one hundred merkes: the heire or heires of a Knight, for one whole Knights fee, one hundred shillings at the most. And he that hath lesse, shall giue lesse, according to the old custome of the fees. Reade also *Glanvile lib. 9. cap. 4. fol. 68.* who saith, that in his dayes the Reliefe of a Baronie was not certaine. The heire in francke soccage, when he commeth to his full age, after the death of his auncester, shall double the rent that he was wont to pay to the Lord, and that shall be in place of reliefe. *old nat. br. fol. 94.* Somewhat more hereof you may reade in *anno 28. Ed. prim. statut. prim.* and *Kitchin fol. 145. ca.* Reliefe. and *Glanvile lib. 7. cap. 9.* The *Feudists* also write of this at large. Among others *Vincentius de Franchis decis. 121.* saith, that *Relevii solutio est quædam extrinseca præstatio à consuetudine introducta, quæ non inest feudo, quodque soluitur pro confirmatione, seu renouatione investitura & possessionis.* See *Heriot.* This *Leo* the Emperour *Novella 13.* calleth εἰσδεκτικόν. By the auncienter ciuile lawe it is termed *(introitus) l. penult. §. Alumno. ff. de legatis. Skene de verb. signif.* saith, that Reliefe is a French word from the *Latine relevare*, which is to releeue or take vp that which is falen. For it is giuen by the tenent, or vassall being of perfect age, after the expiring of the wardeship to his Lord, of whome he holds his land by *Knights* seruice, that is, by ward and reliefe; and by payment thereof he relieues, and (as it were) raiseth vp againe his lands, after they were fallen downe into his superiours hands by reason of wardship, &c.

Remainder (remanentia) signifieth in our common law, a power or hope to inioy lands, tenements, or rents after the estate of another expired. For example, a man may let land to one for terme of his life, and the Remainder to another for terme of his life. *Litleton cap. Atturnment: fol: 113.* And this Remainder may be either for a certaine terme, or in fee simple, or fee taile, as might be proued by many places in the law writers. But in steed of the rest, take *Brooke, titulo Done & Remainder, fol: 245. Glanuile. lib. 7. ca. pri: in fine* hath these words: *Notan-*

Notandum quod nec Episcopus, nec Abbas, quia eorum Baroniæ sunt de eleemozina Domini Regis, & antecessorum eius, non possunt de Dominicis suis aliquam partem dare ad remanentiam sine assensu & confirmatione Domini Regis. Where it appeareth that *Dare ad remanentiam* is to giue away for euer. To the same effect doth he vse it *cap. 9. eiusdem libri* in these words, speaking of the Lords of maners during the minority of their wards. *Nihil tamen de hæreditate, de iure alienare possunt ad remanentiam.* In the like sort doth *Bracton* vse it. *lib. 2. cap. 23. in fine*: and also *lib. 4. tracta. 2. cap. 4. nu. 4.* See the new booke of *Entries. verbo* Remainder.

Remembrancers of the Exchequer (*Rememoratores*) be three officers, or clerks, one called the Kings *Remembrancer. anno 35. El. cap. 5.* The other the Lord Treasurers Remembrancer, vpon whose charge it seemeth to lye, that they put all Iustices of that court, as the Lord Treasurer and the rest, in remembrance of such things, as are to be called on, and delt in for the Princes behoofe. The third is called the Remembrancer of the first fruites. Of these you may read something. *anno 5. Rich. 2. stat. pri: cap. 14. & 15.* to the effect aboue specified. These *anno 37. Ed. 3. cap. 4.* be called clerks of the *Remembrance*. It seemeth that the name of this officer is borowed from the Ciuilians, who haue their (*Memoriales*) *qui sunt notarii Cancellariæ in regno subiecti officio Quæstoris. Lucas de penna. C. lib. 10. tit. 12. nu: 7.* The kings *Remembrancer* entreth in his office all recognicances taken before the *Barons* for any the Kings debts, for apparences, or for obseruing of orders. He taketh al bonds for any of the kings debts, or for apparance, or for obseruing of orders, and maketh proces vpon them for the breach of them. He writeth proces against the collectors of customes, subsidies and fiueteenthes, for their accompts. All informations vpon penall statutes are entred in his office. And all maters vpon English bils in the Exchequer chamber are remaining in his office. He maketh the bils of compositions vpon penall lawes: taketh the stalments of debts: maketh a record of a certificate deliuered vnto him by the clerk of the Starrechamber of the fines there set, and sendeth them to the pipe. He hath deliuered vnto his office all maner of indentures, fines, and other euidences whatsoeuer, that concerne the assuring of any lands to the Crowne. He yearely in *crastino animarum* readeth in open court the statute for the elections of *Shyreeues*, and giueth those that chuse them their oath: he readeth in open court the oath of all the officers of the court, when they are admitted.

The treasurers remembrancer maketh proces against all *Shyreeues*, eschcators, receiuers, and bayliffs for their accoumpts. He maketh proces of (*fieri facias*) and extent for any debts due to the King, either in the pipe, or with the auditors. He maketh proces for all such reuenew as is due to the King by reason of his tenures. He maketh a record, whereby it appeareth whether Shyreeues and other accountants pay their profers dew at Easter and Michelmas. *He* maketh another record, whereby it appeareth, whether Shyreeues and other accountants keepe their daies of prefixion. All extreats of fines, issues, and amerciaments set in any courts of *Westminster*, or at the assises, or sessions, are certified into his office, and are by him deliuered to the clerk of extreats to write proces vpon them. He hath also brought into his office all the accoumpts of customers, controllers, and other accoumptants to make thereof an entry of record.

The Remembrancer of the first fruites, taketh all compositions for first fruites and tenthes: and maketh proces against such as pay not the same.

R*emittere*, commeth of the French (*remettre* .i. *restituere, reponere*) and signifieth in our common law, a restitution of one that hath two titles to lands or tenements, and is seised of them by his later title, vnto his title that is more auncient, in case where the later is defectiue. *Fitz. nat. br. fol.* 149. *F. Dyer fol.* 68. *nu.* 22. This in what case it may be graunted to any man, see in *Brooke, titulo Remitter*: and the terms of law. The *Doctor* and *Student* of this mater hath these words: if land discend to him that hath right to that land before, he shalbe remitted to his beter title, if he will. *capite nono. fol.* 19. *b.* See the new booke of *Entries: verbo Remitter.*

Render, commeth of the French (*Rendre*.i.*reddere, retribuere, restituere*) and signifieth in our common lawe, the selfe same thing. For example, this word is vsed in leuying of a fine. For a fine is either single, by which nothing is graunted, or rendred backe againe by the Cognizee, to the Cognizour: or double, which conteineth a graunt, or render backe againe of some rent, common,

 or

or other thing, out of the land it selfe to the Cognizor, &c. *West. parte. 2. symbol. titulo Fines. sect. 21. & 30. F.* Also there be certaine things in a maner that lie in *prender*, that is, which may be taken by the Lord, or his officer, when they chaunce, without any offer made by the tenent, as the ward of the body of the heire, and of the land, escheats, &c. and certaine that lie in *Render*, that is, must be deliuered or answered by the Tenent, as rents, reliefes, heriots, and other seruices. *Idem, eodem. sect. 126. C.* Also some seruice consisteth in seisāce, some in Render. *Perkins Reseruations. 696.*

Rent (*Reditus*) commeth of the French (*Rent*. i. *vectigal, pensitatio annua*) and signifieth with vs, a summe of mony or other consideration issuing yearly out of land or tenements. *Plowden, casu Browning. fol. 132. b. & fol. 138. a. 141. b.* There be three sorts of rents obserued by our common Lawyers: that is, Rent seruice, Rent charge, and Rent seck. Rent seruice is, where a man houldeth his land of his Lord by fealty, and certaine rent, or by fealty, seruice, and certaine rent. *Litleton lib. 2. ca. 12. fol. 44.* or that which a man, making a lease to another for terme of yeares, reserueth yearely to be paid him for the same. Termes of lawe. *verbo Rents.* who giueth this reason thereof, because it is in his libertie, whether he will distraine, or bring an action of debt. A Rent charge is that, which a man making ouer an estate of his land, or tenements to another, by deede indented either in in fee, or fee tayle, or lease for terme of life, reserueth to himselfe by the said indenture a summe of money yearely to be paide vnto him with clause of distresse, or to him and his heires. See *Litleton, vbi supra*. A Rent seck, otherwise a drie rent, is that, which a man making ouer an estate of his land or tenement, by deede indented, reserueth yeerely to be paid him without clause of distresse mentioned in the Indenture. *Litleton vbi supra*. and termes of the lawe. *verbo Rents.* see the newe expositour of lawe Termes: See *Plowden, casu Browning. fol. 132. b.* See the differences betweene a rent, and an annuitie. *Doctor* and *Student. cap. 30. dialo. primo.*

Reparatione facienda, is a writ, which lieth in diuers cases, whereof one is, where three be tenents in common, or ioynt tenents, or *pro Indiviso*, of a mille, or house which is fallen into decay, and the one being willing to repaire it, the other two will

will not. In this case, the party willing shall haue this writ against the other two. *Fitzh. nat. br. f.* 127. where read at large the form & many vses of this writ, as also in the *Regi. orig. fol.* 153. *b.*

Repeale, commeth of the French (*Rappel.* i. *Revocatio*) and signifieth in our common lawe euen the same; as the Repeale of a statute, *Rastall titulo Repeale. Brooke* vseth Repellance in this signification, *titulo Repellance.*

Repleader (*Replacitare*) is to plead againe, that which was once pleaded before. *Rastall, titulo Repleader.* See the newe booke of *Entries, verbo Repleder.*

Replegiare. See *Replevie.* See *Second deliuerance.*

Replevie (*Pleuina*) is the bringing of the writ called *Replegiari facias*, by him that hath his catel or other goods distreined by another for any cause, and putting in suerty to the Shyreeue, that vpon the deliuery of the thing distreined, he will persiew the action against him that distreined. Termes of lawe. See *Replegiare.* It is vsed also for the bayling of a man. *pl. cor. fol.* 72. 73. 74. *& West pri. cap.* 11. *& cap* 15. *anno* 3. *Ed.* 1.

Replegiare de averiis, is a writ brought by one, whose catell be distreined or put in pound vpon any cause by another, vpon surety giuen to the Shyreeue to persiew the action in lawe. *anno* 7. *H.* 8. *cap.* 4. *Fitzh. nat. br. fol.* 68. See the *Register originall*, of diuers sorts of this writ called *Replegiare.* in the table, *verbo eodem.* See also the *Register* Iudiciall, *fol.* 58. *&* 70. see also the newe boke of *Entries. verbo Replevin.* See *Dyer. fol.* 173. *nu.* 14.

Replevish (*Replegiare*) is to let one to mainprise vpon suretie. *anno* 3. *Ed.* 1. *cap.* 11.

Replication (*replicatio*) is an exception of the second degree made by the plantife vpon the first answer of the Defendant, *West. parte* 2. *symbol. titulo Chauncerie. sect.* 55. *& Westm.* 2. *anno* 13. *Ed. pri. cap.* 36. This is borowed from the Ciuilians, *De replicationibus, lib.* 4. *Institutio. titulo.* 14.

Report (*Repertus*) is in our common lawe a relation, or repetition of a case debated, or argued. which is sometime made to the court, vpon reference from the court to the Reporter, somtime to the world voluntarily, as *Ploydens reports*, & such like.

Reposition of the Forest, was an act whereby certaine forest grounds being made purlieu vpon view, were by a second view laide to the Forest againe. *Manwood, parte pri. pag.* 178.

Reprisels (*Reprisalia*) are all one in the common and Ciuill law. *Repraesalia est potestas pignorandi contra quemlibet de terra debi-*

 toris

toris data creditori pro iniuriis & damnis acceptis. *Vocabularius utriusq; iuris*. This among the auncient Romans was called (*Clarigatio*) of the verb (*Clarigo*. i. *res clare repeto*) It is called in the statute *anno* 27. *Ed*. 3 *stat*. 2. *cap*. 17. *lawe of Marque*, of the German word *March*. i. *terminus, limes*. And the reason may be, because one destitute of Iustice in another territory, redresseth himselfe by the goods belonging to men of that territorie, taken within his owne bounds.

Requests (*Supplicum libelli, Curia Requisitionum*) is a Court of of the same nature with the Chauncerie, redressing by equitie the wrongs that poore men doe suffer at their hand, whose might they are not able to withstand either in lawe or otherwise. It tooke beginning as some men thinke, by commission from King Henry the 8. before which time the Masters of Requests had no warrant of ordinary Iurisdiction, but travailed betweene the *Prince* and petioners, by direction from the mouth of the King. *Guins preface to his readings*, But see *Court of Requests*.

Resceyt (*Receptio*) seemeth to be an admission of a third person to pleade his right in a cause formerly commenced, betweene other two. See the newe booke of *Entries*. *verbo Resceit*. *v*. *Aide prier*. The Ciuilians call this *admissionem tertii pro suo interesse*. Of this you haue one example in the Termes of lawe, *viz*. if Tenent for terme of life, or tenent for terme of yeares bring an action: he in the reuersion commeth in, and prayeth to be receiued to defend the land, and to plead with the *Demandant*. Many more you may haue in *Brooke, titulo, Resceite*. *fol*. 205. See *Perkins Dower*. 448. eceit is also applied to an admittance of plee, though the controuersie be but betweene two onely. *Brooke estoppell*. in many places.

Resceyt of homage, is a relatiue to doing homage, for as the Tenent, who oweth homage, doth it at his admission to the land: so the Lord receiueth it. *Kitchin fol*. 148. See *Homage*.

Rescous (*Rescussus*) commeth of the French (*Rescourre se Rescourre du danger*. i. *asserere se ab iniuria*) It signifieth in our common law a resistance against a lawfull authoritie: as for example, if a Baylife, or other officer vpon a writ doe arrest a man, and another (one or more) by violence doe take him away, or procure his escape: this act is called, a *Rescus*. *Cassanaeus* in his booke *de consuetud. Burg*. hath the

the same word coupled with *(resistentia) fol.* 294. whereby it appeareth, that other nations do vse this word in the same signification that we doe, or the very like. It is also vsed for a writ, which lyeth for this act called in our lawyers latine *(Breue de rescussu)* whereof you may see both the forme and vse in *Fitzh. nat. br. fol.* 101. and the *register originall: fol:* 125. See the new booke of *Entries. verbo rescous.* This *rescous* in some cases is treason, and in some felony. *Crompton. Iustice fol:* 54. *b.*

Resciser *(reseisire)* is a taking againe of lands into the *Kings* hands, whereof a generall liuery, or *ouster le main* was formerly missued by any person or persons, and not according to forme and order of law. Of this see *Stawnf. prærога* : 26. where it is handled at large. See *resumption.*

Resiance (resiantia) seemeth to come of the *French (rasseoir,* see Rasseoir .i. *residere)* and signifieth a mans aboad or continuance in a place. *Old nat: br. fo.* 85. whence also commeth the participle *(resiant)* that is continually dwelling, or abiding in a place. *Kitchin, fol.* 33. It is all one in truth with Residence, but that custome of speach tyeth that onely to persons ecclesiasticall.

Reseruation, signifieth that rent or seruice which the graunter in any graunt tyeth the grauntee to performe vnto him, or them, or the Lord *Paramonte. Perkins reseruations: per totum.*

Residence *(residentia)* commeth of the *Latine (residere)* and is peculiarly vsed both in the Canon and Common lawe, for the continuance or abode of a Parson or Vicar vpon his benefice. The default whereof (except the partie be qualified, and dispenced with) is the losse of tenne pounds for euery moneth, *anno* 28. *Henr.* 8. *cap.* 13.

Resignation (resignatio) is vsed particularly for the giuing vp of a Benefice into the hands of the Ordinarie, otherwise called of the Canonists *(renunciatio.)* And though it signifie all one in nature with the word *(Surrender)* yet it is by vse more restreined to the yeelding vp of a spirituall liuing, into the hands of the Ordinarie, and *Surrender* to the giuing vp of temporall lands into the handes of the *Lord.* And a resignation may now be made into the hands of the King, as well as of the Diocesan, because he hath *supremam authoritatem Ecclesiasticam,* as the *Pope* had in time past. *Plowden. casu Grendon. fol.* 498. *a.*

Resort, is a word vsed properly in a writ of ayle, or cousenage

nage, as discent is in a writ of right. *Ingham.*

Respectu computi Vice-comitis habendo, is a writ for the respiting of a Shyreeues accompt vpon iust occasion, directed to the Treasurer and *B*arons of the Exchequer. *Register fol.* 139 *&* 279.

Respight of homage, (*respectus homagii*) is the forbearing of homage, which ought first of all to be performed by the tenent, that holdeth by homage. Which respight may be occasioned vpon diuers good reasons: but it hath the most frequent vse in such as hold by *K*nights seruice *in capite*: who because the *P*rince cannot be at leasure to take their homage, do pay into the *E*xchequer, at certaine times in the yeare, some small summe of money to be respighted, vntill the *P*rince may be at leasure to take it in person.

Responsions (*responsiones*) seeme to be a word vsed properly and especially by the knights of *S. Iohn* of *Ierusalem*, for certaine accompts made vnto them by such as occupied their landes or stockes. *anno* 32. H. 8. *cap.* 24.

Responsalis, is he that commeth for another at the day assigned for his appearance in Court, *Bracton. Fleta* seemeth to make a difference betweene *atturnatum*, *essoniatorem & responsalem*, *lib.* 6. *cap.* 11. §. *Officium*: as if *essoniator* came onely to alledge the cause of the parties absence, be he the demandant or tenent, and *responsalis* came for the tenent not onely to excuse his absence, but also to signifie what triall he meant to vndergoe, *viz.* the combat or the countrie. *lib.* 6. *cap.* 11. §. *Si autem. A* man in auncient time could not appoint an Atturney for him, without warrant from the king. *Fleta*, *eodem cap.* 13. *in fine.* See *Atturney.* This word is vsed in the Canon lawe, *Et significat procuratorem vel eum qui absentem excusat. cap. Cùm olim propter. extra. de rescript.*

Restitution (*restitutio*) is a yeelding vp againe of any thing vnlawfully taken from another. It is vsed in the common law, most notoriously for the setting him in possession of lands or tenements, that hath bene vnlawfully disseised of them, which when it is to be done, and when not, see *Cromptons Iustice of peace. fol.* 144. *b. &c. vsque* 149.

Restitutione extracti ab Ecclesia, is a writ to restore a man to the Church, which he had recouered for his sanctuarie being suspected of felonie. *Register ori. fol.* 69. *a.*

Restitutione temporalium, is a writ that lyeth in case, where a man

man being elected, and confirmed Bishop of any Diocesse, and hath the Princes royall assent thereunto, for the recouery of the temporalities, or Baronie of the said Bishopricke with the appurtenances. And it is directed from the King to the Escheatour of the Countie, the forme whereof you haue in the *Regist. origin. fol.* 294. and in *Fitz. nat. br. fol.* 169. Where you may read also, that it lyeth for those Abbots and Priors newly elected and confirmed, that were of the kings foundation.

Resummons (*resummonitio*) is compounded twice, that is, of *re, sub,* and *Moneo*: and signifieth a second summons and calling of a man to answer an action, where the first summons is defeated by any occasion, as the death of the partie, or such like. *Brook tit.* See *Resummons. fol.* 214. See of these foure sorts, according to the foure diuers cases in the Table of the *Register Iudiciall. fol.* 1. See also the new booke of *Entries, verbo.* Reattachement, & Resummons.

Resumption (*resumptio*) is particularly vsed for the taking again into the Kings hands, such land or tenements, as before vpon false suggestion, or other error, he had deliuered to the heire, or graunted by leters patents to any man. *Brooke, titulo Repellance, & Resumption. fol.* 298. Thus it is applyed, *anno* 31. *H.* 6. *cap.* 7. See *Reseiser.*

Retainer, commeth of the French (*retenir.* i. *detinere, retinere*) It signifieth in the cōmon law, a seruant not meniall nor familiar, that is not continually dwelling in the house of his Lord or Master, but onely vsing, or bearing his name, or liuery. This liuery was wont to consist of hats (otherwise hoods) badges, and other suits of one garment by the yeare. *anno pri:* R. 2. *cap.* 7. These were taken by great Lords, many times vpon pourpose of maintenance, and quarels, and therefore they haue beene iustly, for the better freedome of law, forbidden by many statutes: as namely by *anno pri:* R. 2. *cap.* 7. vpon paine of imprisonment, and greeuous forfeiture to the King: and againe *anno* 16 *eiusd. cap.* 4. & *anno* 20. *eiusdem, cap.* 1. & 2. and *anno pri. H.* 4. *cap.* 7. by the which the Lords offending herein should make ransome at the Kings will, and any Knight or Esquire hereof duly attainted, should loose his said Liuery, and forfeit his fee for euer; and any yeoman wearing the Liuery of the King, or other Lord, should be imprisoned, and make raunsome at the Kings will, onely some fewe excepted in the said statute: which statute

is

is farder confirmed, and explaned *anno* 2. *H.* 4. *cap.* 21. *&* *an.* 7. *eiusd. cap.* 14. *&* *anno* 13. *eiusd. cap.* 3. *&* *anno* 8. *H.* 6. *ca.* 4. And yet this offence was so deeply rooted, that *Edward* the fourth was driuen to confirme the former statutes, and farder to extend the meaning of them, as appeareth by the statute made *anno* 8. *Ed.* 4. *cap.* 2. adding an especiall paine of fiue pounds to euery man that giueth such *Liuery*, and as much to euery one so retained, either by writing, oath, or promise, for euery moneth. Yet is not this fault so well looked vnto, but that there is need of more pregnant lawes for the redresse thereof, or at the least beter execution of those, that be already made. These be by the Feudists called (*affidati.*) *Sic enim dicuntur, qui in alicuius fidem & tutelam recepti sunt. Neapol. constitu. li.* 3. *titulo* 7. And as our retainers are here forbidden: so are those (*affidati*) in other countries.

Retraxit, is an exception against one that formerly commenced an action, and withdrew it, or was non-suit before triall. *Brooke. titulo . Departure in despight, & Retraxit. fol.* 216. See also the new booke of *Entries*: *verbo Deperter & verbo retraxit.*

Returne (*returna*) commeth of the French (*retour.* i. *reditio, reuersio, recursus*) and in our common law, hath two particular applycations, as namely the return of a writ by Shyreeues, and Bayliffs, which is nothing but a certificate made to the Court, whereunto the writ directeth him, of that which he hath done, touching the seruing of the same writ. And this among the Ciuilians is called *Certificatorium*. Of returnes in this signification, speake the statutes of *Westm.* 2. *cap.* 39. *anno* 13. *Ed. prim.* and *Tractatus contra Vice-comites & Clericos*, with diuers other, collected by *Rastal, titulo Returne of Shyreeues*. So is the returne of an office, *Staunf. prarog. fol.* 70. a certificate into the court, of that which is done by vertue of his office: See the *Statutes of dayes in banke. anno* 51. *H.* 3. *& anno* 32. *H.* 8. *cap.* 21. And in this signification *Hilary terme* is said to haue 4. returnes. *viz. Octabis Hilarii, Quindena Hilarii, crastino Purificationis, Octabis Purificationis*: and *Easter terme* to haue 5. returnes, *viz. Quindena pasche, Tres pasche, mense pasche, Quinque pasche, & crastino Ascensionis.* And *Trinity terme* 4. returnes. i. *Crastino Trinitatis, Octabis Trinitatis, Quindena Trinitatis, Tres Trinitatis.* And *Michaelmas Terme* 8. returnes. *sc. Octabis Michaelis, Quindena Michaelis, Tres Michaelis, Mense Michaelis, Cra-*

stino animarum, Crastino Martini, Octabis Martini, Quindena Martini.

The other application of this word is in case of *Repleuy*. For if a man distraine catell for rent, &c. And afterward iustifie or avowe his act, that it be found lawfull, the catell before deliuered vnto him that was distrained vpon security giuen to follow the action, shall now be returned to him, that distrained them. *Brooke, titulo Returne d'auers & hommes. fol.* 218. you shall finde this word often vsed in *Fitzh. nat: br.* as appeareth in the word *Returne* in his table: but in all those places it hath the one or the other of these two significations.

Returno habendo, is a writ, which lyeth for him that hath auowed a distresse made of catell, and proued his distresse to be lawfully taken for the returne of the catell distrained vnto him, which before were expleuied by the party distrained, vpon suerty giuen to persiew the action. *Terms of law, verbo* Repleuin.

Returnum aueriorum, is a writ Iudiciall, graunted to one impleaded for taking the cattell of another, & vniust deteining of them *contra vadium & plegios*, and appearing vpon summons is dismissed without day, by reason that the plaintife maketh default, and it lyeth for the returne of the cattell vnto the Defendant, whereby he was summoned, or which were taken for the security of his apparence vpon the summons. *Regist er Iudiciall. fol.* 4. *a.*

Returnum irreplegiabile, is a writ iudiciall sent out of the common plees to the Shyreeue, for the finall restitution or returne of catell to the owner, vniustly taken by another as dammage seisant, and so found by the Iury before Iustices of Assise in the County. For which see the *Regist er Iudiciall fo.* 27. *a. b.*

Reue, aliâs Greue (Praefectus) is made of *Gerefa* the *Saxon* word for a gouerner. *Lamb: explica: of Saxon words, verb. Praefectus*, and that by reiecting the first sillable, which (he saith) among the *Saxons* is vsuall. It signifieth in our common law, the Bayliffe of a Fraunchis or maner, and especially in the West parts. Of this you may see *Kitchin. fol.* 43. See *Greue*. See *Shyreeue*. See also of this word *M. Verstigan* in his restitution of decayed intelligence. *cap*: 10. speaking much to the same effect.

Reuels, seemeth to be deriued from the French word (*Reueiller*. i. *excitari, vel expergefieri*) It signifieth with vs sports of daunsing, masking, comedies, tragedies, and such like vsed in the Kings house, the houses of court or of other great personages. The reason whereof is, because they are most vsed by night, when otherwise men commonly sleepe, and be at rest. In the Kings house there is an officer called the Master of these Reuils, who hath the ordering, and dispositions of these pastimes in the court.

Remenewe, is a French word, signifiing as much as *Reditio*, *Reuersio*, *Reditus*. It signifieth properly the yearely rent that groweth to euery man from his lands and possessions.

Reuersion (*Reversio*) signifieth in the comon lawe, a possibility reserued to a mans selfe and his heires, to haue againe lands or tenements made ouer conditionally vnto others, vpon the defect or fayling of such condition. The difference betweene a Remainder, and a Reversion is, that a Remainder is generall, and may be to any man but to him that graunteth, or conueieth the land, &c. for terme of life onely or otherwise: a Reuersion is to himselfe from whome the conueiance of the land, &c. proceeded, and commonly perpetuall, as to his heires also, *Litleton, fol.* 112. *in fine*. See *Cooke lib.* 2. *Sir Hugh Cholmleis case, fol.* 51.*a*. And yet a Reuersion is sometime confounded with a remainder. *Cooke li.* 2. *Tookers case, fol.* 67. *b. Plowden, casu Hille. fol.* 170.*b.* what this word Reuersion in a deede doth carie. See *Litleton lib.* 2. *ca.* 12.

Revocation (*Revocatio*) is the calling backe of a thing granted. Of these you haue diuers in the *Register originall*, as *Reuocationem brevis de audiendo & terminando. fol.* 124. *Revocationem præsentationis. fol.* 304 & 305. *Revocationem protectionis, fol.* 23. *Revocationem specialium Iusticiariorum quia, &c. fol.* 205.

Reviving, is a word metaphorically applied to rents and actions and signifieth a renewing of them, after they be extinguished: no lesse then if a man, or other liuing creature should be dead, and restored to life. See diuers examples in *Brooke titulo*. *Revivings of rents, actions, &c. fol* 223.

Re*wardum*. See *Regard*.

Reweye. anno. 43. *Elizab. cap.* 10.

Rie, is a Saxon word signifiing as much as *Regnum*, in Latine. *Camd. Britan. pag.* 346.

Riens passe per le fait, is a forme of an exception taken in some cases to an action. See *Brooke titulo Estraunger al fait or Record*.

Riens dans le gard, was a challenge to a Iurie, or Enquest within in *London*. for that foure sufficient men of liuelyhood to the yearely value of fortie shillings aboue all charges, within the same City, and dwelling and hauing within the same ward, weare not impanelled therein. But it is abrogated by the statute. *anno* 7.*H*.7.*cap*. 4.

Rier countie (*Retrocomitatus*) seemeth to come of the *French* (*Arriere*. i.*posterior*) and in the statute. *anno* 2. *Ed*. 3.*cap*. 5 is opposite to the open countie And by comparison of that statute with *Westm*.2.*cap*. 38. it appeareth to be some publique place, which the Shyreeue appointeth for the receipt of the kings money after the ende of his Countie. *Fleta* saith that it is *dies crastinus post comitatum. lib*. 2.*cap*. 67.§. *Quia Iusticiarii*.

Right Rectum. See *Recto*.

Ri*dings*, be the names of the parts or diuisions of *Yorke shire*, being three in number. *viz*. *West riding*, *East riding*, and *North riding*. *Camd. Britan. pag*. 530. This word is mentioned in the statute, *anno* 22.*H*.8.*cap*.5.& 23. H.8.*cap*. 18. and *M.West*. *parte* 2.*symbol. titulo* Inditements saith, that in Inditements within that Countie, it is requisite that the towne, and the *Riding* be expressed. *sect*. 70.*Q*.

Right in the Court. *anno* 6 R. 2.*stat*.1. *cap*.12. See Rectus *in Curia*.

Ringhead, *anno* 43. *Elizab*. *cap*. 10.

Riot (*Riottum*) commeth of the French (*Rioter*. i. *rixari*.) It signifieth in our common lawe, the forcible doing of an vnlawfull act, by three or more persons assembled togither for that purpose. *Westm.parte*.2.*symbol. titulo*, Inditements. *sect*. 65. P. The differences and agreements betweene a Riot, a Rout, and vnlawfull assembly. See in M. *Lamb. Eirenarcha, lib*. 2. *cap*.5. *&c*. See the statute. 1.*M*. 1. *cap*. 12.*& Kitchin*.*fol*.19. who giueth these examples of Riots: the breach of inclosures, or banks or conduicts, parks, pownds, houses, barnes, the burning of stacks of corne. *M. Lamberd vbi supra*. vseth these examples: to beate a man, to enter vpon a possession forcibly, See *Route*. *and vnlawfull assembly*. See also *Cromptons Iustice of peace diuers cases of* Riots, *&c. fol*. 53. See *Tribings*.

Ripiers (*Riparii*) be those that vse to bring fish from the sea coast to the inner parts of the land. *Camd.Britan.pag*.234. It is a word made of the latine (*Ripa*).

Rise (*oriza*) is a kinde of corne growing in *Spaine*, *Asia*, and *India*, with the which both good foodes and medicines be made. whereof if you desire farder knowledge, reade *Gerards herball. lib.* 1. *cap.* 52. This is mentioned among merchandize to be garbled in the statute. *anno* 1. *Iaco. cap.* 19.

Roag (*Rogus*) seemeth to come of the *French* (*Rogue*. i. *arrogans*) It signifieth with vs an idle sturdie beggar, that wandring from place to place without pasport, after he hath beene by Iustices bestowed vpon some certaine place of aboade, or offered to be bestowed, is condemned to be so called. who for the first offence, is called a *Roag* of the first degree, and punished by whipping, and boring through the grissell of the right eare with a hot yron an inch in compas: & for the secōd offence, is called a *Roag* of the second degree, and put to death as a felon, if he be aboue 18. yeares ould. *See* the statute, *anno* 14. *Elizab. cap.* 5. *&* 18. *eiusdem, cap.* 3. *& anno* 36. *cap.* 17. If you will know who be *Rogues*, and to be punished as *Rogues* by lawe, Reade *Lamberds Eirenarcha. lib.* 4. *cap.* 4. *See Rout.*

Robberie (*Robaria*) commeth of the *French* (*Robbe*. i. *vestis*) and in our common lawe, a felonious taking away of another mans goods from his person or presence, against his will, putting him in feare, and of purpose to steale the same goods. *West. parte* 2. *symbol. titulo* Inditments, *sect.* 60. This is sometime called violent theft. *Idem, eodem.* which is felonie for two pence. *Kitchin fol.* 26. and 22. *lib. Assis.* 39. *Robaria* is a word vsed also in other nations, as appeareth by the annotations vpon *Mathæus de Afflictis, decis.* 82. *nu.* 6. *pag.* 122. See *Skene verbo Reif. libro de verbo. significat.* See *Cromp.* *Iustice of peace. f.* 30. *b.*

Roberdsmen, anno 5. *Ed.* 3. *cap.* 14. *& anno* 7. R. 2. *cap.* 5. *M. Lamb.* interpreteth them to be mighty theeues. *Eirenarch. lib.* 2. *cap.* 6. *pag.* 190.

Rodknights, *aliâs* Radknights, are certaine seruitours, which hould their lands by seruing their *Lord* on horseback. *Bracton lib.* 2. *cap.* 36. *nu.* 6. saith of them, *debent equitare cum Domino suo de manerio in manerium. vel cum Domini vxore. Fleta. lib.* 3. *cap.* 14. §. *Continetur.*

Rodde (*Pertica*) is otherwise called a pearche, and is a measure of 16. foote and an halfe long, and in *Stafford Shire* 20. foote, to measure land with. See *Pearch.*

Rose tyle, aliâs Creast tyle, is that tyle which is made to lay vpon the rudge of the house. *anno* 17. *Ed.* 4. *cap.* 4.

Rogation *weeke* (*dies rogationum*) is a time well knowne to all,

all, being otherwise called *Gang* weeke. The reason why it is so termed, is because of the especiall deuotion of prayer and fasting, then inioyned by the Church to all men, for a preparatiue to the ioyfull remembrance of Christs glorious ascension, and the descension of the holy *Ghost*, in the forme of cloven tongues shortly after. And in that respect the solemnization of carnall matrimony is forbidden from the first day of the said weeke, vntill Trinitie Sunday. See *Aduent*.

Roode of land (*Roda terræ*) is a certaine quantitie of land being the fourth part of an acre. *ann. 5. Eliz. ca. 5.* See *Perch*.

Roll, *alias Roule* (*Rotulum*) commeth of the French (*Rouler*. i. *volvere*, *pervolvere*, *rotare*) whence also is the French (*Role ou Roule*. i. *volumen*, *catalogus*, *Codex*) It signifieth with vs a shedule of paper, or parchment turned, or wound vp with the hand to the fashion of a pipe. So is it vsed in *Stawnf. plees of the Crowne*, *fol.* 11. The chequer rolle of the kings house, out of the statute *anno 3. H. 7. cap.* 13. which signifieth nothing but the catalogue, wherein the names of the Kings houshould seruants are set downe. And *anno 5. Rich. 2. cap. 14. stat. pri:* there is mention made of the great Rolle of the Exchequer which seemeth otherwise to be called the pipe. The Roules is also a place destinated by *Ed.* 3. to the the keeping of the Rols, or Records of the Chauncery situat betweene the two Temples in *London*. *Camd: Britan: pag.* 321. the Master whereof is the second man in Chauncery, and in the absence of the *Lord Chaunceler*, or Keeper, sitteth as Iudge, being commonly called the *Master* of the *Rols*. See *Master of the Rols*.

Romescot, is compounded of *Rome*, and *Scot*, as you would say, the tribute due to *Rome*: it is called by *Mathæus Westmonasteriensis*, *Consuetudo Apostolica*, *à qua neque Rex*, *neque Archiepiscopus*, *vel Episcopus*, *Abbas*, *vel Prior*, *aut quilibet in regno immunis erat:* and was first graunted by *Offa* a Saxon King. *Camd. Britan. pag.* 306. See *Peter pence:* and *Roger Houeden parte poster. suorum annalium. fol.* 344. *a. in Henrico secundo*.

Roundlet, is a certaine measure of wine, oyle, &c. containing 18. gallons and a halfe, *anno* 1. *R.* 3. *cap.* 13.

Route, (*Routa*) is a French word signifying a companie, or flocke: as (*vne grande route de gents*, *ou de cerfs*. i. *grex hominum*, *longa ceruorum series*.) It signifieth in our common lawe, an assembly,

ſembly of three perſõs or more, going on about forcibly to cõmit an vnlawfull act, but yet doe it not, *Weſtm. parte 2. ſym. titulo Inditements. ſect. 65. o. M. Lamberd* thus ſaith of it: A Route is the ſame, which the *Germans* yet call Rot, meaning a band or great companie of men gathered together, and going about to execute, or executing indeed, any ryot or vnlawfull act: and (ſaith more) it is ſaid properly of the multitude that aſſembleth themſelues in ſuch diſorderly ſort, for their common quarels. As if the inhabitants of a towneſhip doe aſſemble to pull downe a hedge, or pale, to haue their common, where they ought to haue none, or to beate a man, that hath done them ſome publike offence or diſpleaſure. But the ſtatute of 18. *Ed. 3. ſtat. prim. cap. vnico.* which giueth proceſſe of outlawrie againſt ſuch as bring routes into the preſence of the Iuſtices, or in affray of the people, and the Statute of *2. Rich. 2. cap. 6.* that ſpeaketh of riding in great routes to make entrie into lands, and to beate others, and to take their wiues, &c. doe ſeeme to vnderſtand it more largely. And it is a route, whether they put their purpoſe in execution or no: if ſo be, that they do goe, ride, or moue forward after their meeting. *Broke, titulo* Riot. *4. & 5.* So (as it ſeemeth) a route ſhould be a ſpeciall kind of vnlawfull aſſembly: and a riot the diſorderly fact committed generally by any vnlawfull aſſembly. Howſoeuer it be, two things are common both to Riot, Route, and vnlawfull aſſembly: the one, that three perſons at the leaſt bee gathered together: for ſo it is commonly taken at this day, as I haue learned: the other, that they being together, do breed diſturbance of the peace, either by ſignification of ſpeech, ſhew of armour, turbulent geſture, or actuall and expreſſe violence: ſo that either the peaceable ſort of men be vnquieted, and feared by the fact, or the lighter ſort, and buſie bodies emboldened by the example. Thus farre M. *Lamberd* in his *Eirenarcha. lib. 2. cap. 5. &c.* Where you may reade more worth the noting, though too long to be copied out. See *Riot*, and *Vnlawfull aſſembly. Kitchin* giueth the ſame definition of a *Route, fol.* 20.

Rowing of clothes. anno 27. *H.* 8. *cap.* 13.

Royall aſſent (regius aſſenſus) is that approbation which the King giueth to a thing formerly done by others: as to the electiõ of a Biſhop by *D*eane and

Chap-

Chapter. Which giuen, then he sendeth an especiall writ to some person for the taking of his fealtie. The forme of which writ you may see in *Fitz. nat. br. fol.* 170. C. And also to a bill passed by both the Houses of Parlament. *Cromptons Iuris. fol.* 8. which assent being once giuen, the bill is indorsed with these wordes: *Le Roy veult*, i. it pleaseth the King. If he refuse to agree vnto it, then thus: *Le roy aduisera*. i. the King will yet thinke of it. See *Parlament*.

Royalties (*regalia vel regalitates*) be the rights of the *King*. *Iura Regis*. *Hotoman in verbis feudal: verbo. Regum Feudistæ*. And so are they vnderstoode of vs likewise, who otherwise call them the Kings prerogatiue. See *Prerogatiue*. And some of these be such as the King may graunt vnto common persons, some so high, as may not be separated from his owne Crowne *priuatiuè* as the Ciuilians terme it, though *cumulatiuè* he may. See *Bracton lib. 2. cap.* 5. These be in some sort expressed in the first of *Samuell. cap.* 8. but these generalities bee specified more at large by those Lawyers that write of this point. Among whom I especially commend *Mathæum de Afflictis* vpon the title of the *Feuds*. *Quæ sint regalia*. being the 33. title of the third booke, as some diuide them, but according to others the 56. of the second booke: where be named in the text 25. specialties of *Royalties*. See also *Hotomans* Commentaries *in lib.* 2. *Feudor. cap.* 56.

Rouge crosse. See *Herald*.

Rudge washed Kersey. i. made of fleece wooll washed onely on the sheepes backe. *anno* 35. *Eliz. cap.* 10.

S

Sables. See *Faire*.

Sac (*sacha vel Sacca*) is a Royalty or priuiledge touching plee, and correction of trespasses of men within a maner. *Rastal, titulo expos: of words*: where he addeth this reason: because (saith he) *Sac* in english is (*Encheson*) in French: as to say, for *sick sack, pour quel encheson*. i. for what hurt. That which our common lawyers call (*encheson*) the true French man termeth (*Achoise*. i. *occasionem*) as (*Achoise fort grande, occasio ampla*) or els may *encheson* come of (*Encheoir*. i. *incidere*) which we in english call an *accident*, or *incident*. But all this is farre enough from (*sac*) and from the interpretation thereof, as it is a liberty or priuiledge. *Bracton* hath the word, as *Stawnford* noteth out of him, *pl. cor: li. pri: cap:* 23. but neither of them both doe particularly interpret it. *Bractons* words be these *Lib.* 3. *tract.*

tract. 2. cap. 8. vel si sit aliquis qui de concessione Domini Regis *talem habeat libertatem (sicut sock & sack, Tolnetum; Team, Infangthefe, & Hutfanghhefe) qui inuẽtus fuerit seisitus de aliquo latrocinio, sicut Hondhabende &* Backberend; *tales habent regalẽ potestatẽ: & vnde qui tales libertates habẽt, habebũt prisonam suam de talibus, quia possunt tales in Curia sua iudicare.* Of the which mater he speaketh also in *lib. 2. cap. 24. nu. 2. & 3.* and againe *lib. 3. tracta. 2. cap. 35.* But in none of these places he giueth any interpretation of the word. *Saxon* in his description of England defineth *Sack* to be a forfeiture, as doth R*astall vbi supra. fol. 132. M. Camden* in his *Britan: pag.* 415. speaking of *Lincoln.* hath these words: *Eduardo Confessore regnante, erant (ex censuali libro loquor)* 1070. *mansiones hospitale, & duodecim Lageman habentes socam & sacam.* To all these adde *Bracton, lib. 2. cap.* 5. where he writeth thus. *Sunt & alia res quasi sacra, quæ personam* Regis *respiciunt, & aliquando transferri non possunt, nisi Iusticiariis Domini* Regis, *sicut visus Franciplegii, placita de vetito nannio, emendatio transgressionis Assisarum, Iudicium latronum, sicut de illis qui habent sock & sack, & huiusmodi omnia, quæ pertinent ad pacem, & per consequens ad Coronam.* I am informed, that the word (*sack*) in the *Saxon* tongue doth properly signifie so much as (*causa*) with the *Latines:* whence wee in *English* haue the word (*sake*) as (*for whose sake.*) *M. Skene de verbor. signif. verbo,* Sacke, writeth thus. In some old books it is called *placitum & emenda de transgressione hominum in Curia nostra.* In the lawes of king *Edward* set foorth by M. Lamberd, *fol.* 132. it is written, (*Sacha*) Sacha *antẽ est, si quilibet aliquẽ nominatim de aliquo calumniatus fuerit, & ille negauerit, forisfactura probationis vel negationis, (si euenerit) sua erit.* Which may be called the amercement payed by him, who denieth that thing, which is proued against him to be true, or affirmeth that thing, the contrarie whereof is true. Thus farre M. *Skene. Fleta* of this hath these words: *Sake significat acquietantiam de secta ad Comitatum, & Hundredum. lib. pri. cap.* 47. §. *Sake.* But by all those I find not any reason of the word, that is, why this liberty should be so called, and therefore I must leaue it to beter Antiquaries or *Linguists.* see R*og. H. part. poster. suorum annaliũ. f.* 345.

Saccus cum brochia, seemeth to be a seruice of finding a sacke and a broch to the King by vertue of a tenure, for the vse of his armie. *Bract. li. 2. c. 16. n. 6.*

Sacke of wooll, (saccus lanæ) is a quana quantitie of wooll, that conteineth 26. stone, and a stone, fourteene pounds, *anno 14. Ed. 3. stat. 1. cap. 21.* See *Sarplar.*

Sacramento recipiendo, quod vidua Regis se non maritabit sine licentia Regis, is a writ or commission to one for the taking of an oath of the Kings widowe, that she shall not marie without the Kings licence. *Register original, fol. 298. a.*

Safeconduict. See *Saulf conduict.*

Salus, is a coine of gold stamped by king Henry the sixth in *Fraunce*, which onely coine, with another of *Blanes* of eight pence a peice, was current in those places of Fraunce, where King *Henry* was obeyed. *Stowes Annals, pag. 586.*

Safe pledge (*Salvus plegius*) is a suretie giuen for a mans apparence against a day assigned, *Bracton lib. 4 cap. 2. nu. 2.* where it is also called *certus plegius.*

Sailing ware. anno prim. R. 3. cap. 8.

Sak. See Sac.

Sakebere, in Britton cap. 15. & 29. seemeth to be he that is robbed, or by theft depriued of his goods: with whome *Bracton* also agreeth, *lib. 3. tracta. 2. cap. 32. nu. 2.* in these words: *Furtum vero manifestum est, vbi latro deprehensus sit seisitus de aliquo latrocinio. sc. Hondhabende, & Backberend, & insecutus fuerit per aliquem, cuius res illa fuerit. qui dicitur Sacaburthe, &c.* or *Saibaber*, as *Stawnford* calleth it, *pl. cor. lib. pri. cap. 21.* The interpretation of this word I find not. Onely M. *Skene de verb. interpretatione. verbo.* (*Sacreborgh*) thinketh it should rather be written. *Sickerborgh*, of (*Sicker.* i. *Securus*) and (*Borgh.* i. *plegius*) signifing a sure cautioner or suretie which one findeth to another for theft. or slaughter: whereof he offereth to accuse him iudicially. For in this case it behoueth the persiewer to oblige, or binde himselfe into the hands of the officer, or before a Iudge competent with *Sicker borgh*, or sure caution, that he will persiew in forme of lawe. And by this meanes it may be, that the accuser was wont with vs to be called *Sakbere* of a circumstance, because in this case he was surely bound to persiew. *Sycker* is also an old english word, signifiing as much as sure, secure, or certaine, and see *Borowe.*

Salet, is a headpeece. *anno 4. & 5. Phil. & Mar.* it seemeth to come from the French (*Salut.* i. *Salus*).

Salmon sewse, seemeth to be the young fry of *Salmon, quasi salmon issue. anno 13. R. 3. stat. pri. cap. 19.*

Salva Gardia, is a securitie giuen by the *King* to a straunger, fearing the violence of some of his subiects, for seeking his right by course of lawe: the forme whereof see in the *Register originall. fol.* 26. *a.b.*

Sanctuarie (*Sanctuarium*) is a place priviledged by the prince, for the safegard of mens liues, that are offenders, being founded vpon the lawe of mercie, and vpon the great reuerence, honour, and deuotion, which the Prince beareth to the place, whereunto he graunteth such a priuiledge. Of this you may read a sufficient treatis in *Stawnf pl. cor. lib.* 2. *cap.* 38. This seemeth to haue taken beginning from the Cities of refuge, which *Moyses* appointed them to flie vnto for safegard of their liues, that had by casualty slaine a man. *Exodus, cap.* 21. In bastardly imitation whereof, first the *Athenians*, then *Romulus* erected such a place of immunity, which they, & he after them called *Asylum*. *Polidor: Virg: de inuentione rerum, lib.* 3. *cap.* 12. The Emperours of Rome made the places of their owne statues or Images, a place of refuge, as appeareth. *Cod. lib.* 1. *titulo* 15. *De iis qui ad statuas confugiunt*: as also the Churches: *eodem, titulo* 12. *De iis qui ad ecclesias confugiunt, &c.* But among all other nations, our auncient Kings of England seeme to haue attributed most to these Sanctuaries, permitting them to shelter such, as had committed both felonies, and treasons, so that within fourty daies they acknowledged their fault, and so submitted themselues to banishment: during which time, if any man expelled them, if he were laye, he was excommunicated, if a Clerk, he was made irregular. But after fourty daies noe man might releeue them. *Stawnf. vbi supra.* See of this the new booke of *Entries: verb* Sanctuary: and *Fleta: lib.* 1. *cap.* 29. And how by degrees they haue beene taken away, you may read partly in him, and partly in the statutes. *a.* 26. *H.* 8. *ca.* 13. *& anno* 28. *eiusdem, ca.* 7. *& anno* 32. *eiusd. ca.* 12. *& anno* 33. *eiusdem, cap.* 15. *& anno pri: Ed.* 6. *cap.* 12. *& anno.* 2. *eiusdem, cap.* 2. *& cap.* 33. *& anno* 5. *eiusdem, cap.* 10. See *Abiuration*.

Salarie (*salarium*) is a recompence or consideration made to any man for his paines or industry bestowed vpon another mans busines. So called, as *Pliny* saith, *qui tam necessarium quam sal homini*. The word you haue *anno* 23. *Ed.* 3. *ca pri.*

Salmon pipe, anno 25. *H.* 8. *cap.* 7. is an engine to catch Salmons and such like fish.

San-

Sandall, anno 2. *Rich.* 2. *cap.* 1. is a merchandize brought into England. And it seemeth to be a kinde of wood brought out of *India*. For (*Sandal*) in French so signifieth, and in latine it is called *Santalum*.

Sarcling time, or time of sarcling. Seemeth to be all one with hey seele. Or the time when the country man weedeth his corne. And it proceedeth from the latine *sarculare*, to rake or weed. Or from the French (*Sarcler*) which hath all one signification.

Sarpler (Sarplera lanæ) is a quantitie of woll. This in *Scotland* is called Serplathe, and conteineth fourescore stone, for the Lords in the counsell in *anno 1527*. decreed foure serpliathes of packed wolle to containe 16. score stone of woll, by the trafique of Merchants now vsed. The Merchants vse to fraught for their goods to *Flaūders*, by the Sack, to *Fraunce*, *Spaine*, and *England*, by the Tunne, and to *Dansken* and the *Easter* seas, by the Serpliathe. *Skene de verbo. significatione, verbo* Serpliathe. with vs in England a loade of wolle (as I haue beene informed) consisteth of 80. todde, each todde consisting of two stone, and each stone of 14. pound. And that a Sack of wolle is in common accoumpt equall with a load: and a Sarpler (otherwise called a pocket) is halfe a Sack. Further that a packe of wolle is a horse loade, which consisteth of 17. stone. two pounds. *Fleta lib.2.cap.* 12. saith that all our English measures are compounded of the peny sterling, which weigheth 32. wheate cornes of the middle sort. and that 2. of those pence make an ounce, and 12. ounces a pound in weight, or 20. shillings in number, and that 8. pound of wheat maketh a ialon or a galon as we now call it, and eight galons a bushell, and 8. bushels a common quarter. Also that 15. ounces of the quantitie aforesaid doe make a merchants pounde. And that 12. such pound and a halfe, make a stone, and that 14. stone make a waigh, and that two waighes or 28. stone, make a sack of wolle, which ought to waigh a quarter of wheate, and that 12. sacks make a last. So that a waigh, and a sarpler seemeth to be all one, but that the sarpler is the case, and the weigh respecteth the quantitie of the wolle it selfe: And that a loadé and a sacke is all one.

Saunkfin, is a phrase vsed by *Britton.cap.* 119. for the determination, or finall end, of the lineall race, or discent of a kindred.

dred. It seemeth to come from the French (*Sang*.i.*sanguis*) and *Finè*.i.*finitus*.)

Sauer de default, is word for word, to excuse a default. This is properly, when a man hauing made default in court, commeth afterward and alleadgeth good cause, why he did it, as imprisonment at the same time, or such like. *Newe booke of Entries. verbo. Sauer de default.*

Saulfe conduict (*Salvus conductus*) is a security giuen by the *Prince*, vnder the broad seale to a straunger, for his quiet comming in and passing out of the Realme, touching which you may see the statuts. *anno* 15. *H.* 6.*cap.*3.& *anno* 18. *eiusdem. ca.* 18.& *anno* 28.*H.*8. *cap. pri.* The forme of this see in the *Register originall, fol.* 25.

Staunford, was a man very learned in the common lawes of the land, wherein he wrote 2. bookes one termed the plees of the Crowne, the other the Princes prerogatiue. *He* florished in the daies of *Ed.* the sixth, and of Queene *Mary*, being in Queene *Maries* daies a Iudge, and knighted.

Scandalum Magnatum, is the especiall name of a wrong done to any high personage of the land, as *Prelates*, Dukes, Earles, Barons, and other Nobles: and also of the Chanceler, treasurer, clerk of the priuy seale, steward of the kings house, Iustice, of the one bench or of the other, & other great officers of the realm, by false newes or horrible & false messages, whereby debates and discords betwixt them and the commons, or any scandall to their persons might arise. *anno* 2.*R.*2.*cap.*5.

Scauage, otherwise called *Shewage* is a kind of tolle, or custome exacted by Maiors, Shyreeue, and Baylifs of Cities and Borough townes, of Merchants for wares shewed to be soulde within their precincts, which is forbidden by the statute. *anno* 19.*H.*7.*cap.*8. It commeth of the *Saxon* word (*Sceawe*) to behold or view, or to shewe. whence is the word (*Sceaw-stone*) a theater or shew place, a beholding place. *M. Verstegan in his restitution of decayed intelligences litera S.*

Scire facias, is a writ Iudiciall, most commonly to call a man to shew cause vnto the Court, whence it is sent, why execution of a Iudgement passed, should not be made. This writ is not graunted before a yeare and a day be passed after the Iudgement giuen, *ould nat. br fol.* 151. *Scire facias* vpon a fine, lieth after a yeare and a day from the fine levied. Otherwise it is all one with the writ *habere*

*habere facias seisinam.West.part.*2. *simb.titulo fines, sect.*137. See *an.* 25. *Edvardi* 3. *Sta.* 5. *cap.* 2. *v. anno* 39. *Eliz. cap.* 7. The Register originall and Iudiciall also in the table sheweth many other diuersities of this writ, which reade. See also the newe booke of *Entries.verb.Scire facias.*

Scyra. *Camd.Britan.pag.* 103. & 544. See *Shyre.*

Scot, seemeth to come of the French (*escot.*i. *symbolum*) *Rastall* saith it is a certaine custome, or common tallage made to the vse of the Shyreeue, or his Baylifes. *Saxon in his description of England. cap.* 11. saith thus: Scot a gadering to worke of Bailes: what he meaneth God knoweth I thinke the place is corruptly printed. *Scot* (saith *M. Camden* out of *Mathewe of Westm:*) *illud dicitur, quod ex diuersis rebus in vnum aceruum aggregatur.* In the lawes of *William* the Conquerour, set forth by *M.Lamberd: fol.* 125. you haue these words, *Et omnis Francigena, qui tempore Edwardi propinqui nostri fuit in Anglia, particeps consuetudinum Anglorum, quod dicunt aue blote, & aue scote persoluantur secundum legem Anglorum.*

Scot and *Lot. anno* 33. *H.* 8. *ca.* 19. signifieth a custumary contribution laid vpon all subiects after their hability. *Roger Houeden* writeth it *Aulote & Auscote, in principio Henrici secundi.*

Scotall (*Scotalla*) is a word vsed in the Charter of the Forest. *ca.*7. in these words, as *Pupilla oculi* hath them, *parte* 5. *cap.* 22. *Nullus Forestarius vel Bedellus, faciat Scotallas, vel garbas colligat, vel aliquam collectam faciat. &c. M. Manwood parte pri. of his Forest lawes.pag.* 216. thus defineth it. A Scotall is where any officer of the Forest doth keepe an alehouse within the *Forest*, by colour of his office, causing men to come to his house, and there to spend their mony, for feare of hauing displeasure. It seemeth to be compounded of *Scot* and *Ale.*

Scutagio habendo, is a writ that lieth for the King or other Lord against the Tenent, that houldeth by knights seruice, (wherein homage, fealtie, and escuage be conteined) being to make a viage to warre against the Scots, or French men. For in those cases, this writ issueth out to all such tenents to serue by themselues, or a sufficient man in their place, or else to pay, &c. See *Fitzh. nat. br. fol.* 83. It is vsed in the Register originall, for him to recouer escuage of others, that hath either by seruice or fine performed his owne to the King. *fo.*88. *a.*

Sealer (*Sigillator*) is an officer in Chauncerie, whose dutie is to ſeale the writs and inſtruments there made.

Seane fiſh, anno 1. *Iacob. ſeſ.* 1. *cap.* 25. *Seane fiſh, ibidem,* ſeemeth to be that fiſh which is taken with a very great and long net called a ſeane.

Second deliuerance (*Secunda deliberatione*) is a writ that lyeth for him who after a returne of catel repleuied adiudged to him that diſtreined them, by reaſon of a default in the party that replevied, for the repleuying of the ſame catell againe, vpon ſecuritie put in for the redeliuerie of them, if in caſe the diſtreſſe be iuſtified. New booke of Entries. *verbo, Replevin in ſecond deliuerance. fol.* 522. *col.* 2. *v.* Dyer *fol.* 41. *n.* 4. 5.

Secta ad Curiam, is a writ that lyeth againſt him, who refuſeth to performe his ſuite either to the Countie, or Court Baron. Fitz. *nat. br. fol.* 158.

Secta facienda per illum qui habet eniciam partem, is a writ to compell the heire that hath the elders part of the coheires, to performe ſeruice for all the coparceners, *Regiſt. origin. f.* 177. *a.*

Secta molendini, is a writ lying againſt him, that hath vſed to grind at the mille of *B.* and after goeth to another mille with his corne. *Regiſter origin. fol.* 153. *Fitz. nat. br. fol.* 122. But it ſeemeth by him, that this writ lyeth eſpecially for the Lord againſt his franke Tenents, who hold of him by making ſuite to his mill, *eodem.* See the new book of Entries. *verbo Secta ad molendinum.* By likelihood this ſeruice is alſo in *Fraūce.* For *Balduinus ad titulum de ſervitutibus prædiorum, in Inſtitut.* hath theſe words: *Bannalis mola nova & barbara ſervitutis ſpecies eſt, qua hodie paſſim ruſtici coguntur vna mola, quam bannalem vocamus, vnoque furno vti ad quæſtum Domini, qui fortaſſe præeſt iuriſdictioni eius pagi.*

Sectam preferre, eſt teſtimonium legalium hominum qui contractui inter eos habito interfuerint præſentes producere. Fleta lib. 2. *cap.* 63. §. *Nullus.* And *ſecta* is vſed for a witnes. *Idem, lib.* 4. *cap.* 16. §. *final. Habes tamen ſectam vnam vel plures, &c.*

Secta ad Iuſticiam faciendam, is a ſeruice due for a mans fee to be performed, being by his fee bound thereunto. *Bracton. lib.* 2. *cap.* 16. *num.* 6.

Secta vnica tantum facienda pro pluribus hæreditatibus, is a writ that lyeth for that heyre that is diſtreined by the Lord to more ſuites then one, in reſpect of the land of diuers heires deſcended vnto him. *Regiſter orig. fol.* 177. *a.*

Sectis non faciendis, is a writ, that lyeth for one in wardſhip to to be deliuered of all suites of Court during his wardship, *Register origin. fol.* 173. *b.* See other vse of this writ, *eodem, fol.* 174. touching women that for their dower ought not to performe suite of Court.

Secunda superoneratione pasturæ, is a writ that lyeth, where measurement of pasture hath bene made, and he that first surcharged the common, doth againe surcharge it, the measurement notwithstanding. *Register origin. fol.* 157. *old nat. br. fol.* 73.

Secundarie, (*secundarius*) is the name of an Officer next vnto the chiefe Officer: as the Secundarie of the fine Office: the Secundarie of the Counter: which is (as I take it) next to the Shyreeue in *London* in ech of the two Counters. Secundarie of the office of the priuie seale. *anno* 1. Ed. 4. *cap.* 1. Secundaries of the Pipe two: Secundarie to the Remembrancers, two, which be Officers in the Exchequer. *Camden. pag.* 113.

Securitatem inueniendi, quòd se non diuertat ad partes exteras sine licentia Regis, is a writ that lyeth for the King against any of his subiects, to stay them from going out of his kingdome. The ground whereof is this, that euery man is bound to serue and defend the Commonwealth, as the King shall thinke meet. *Fitz. nat. br. fol.* 85.

Securitate pacis, is a writ that lyeth for one, who is threatened death or daunger, against him that threateneth, taken out of the Chauncerie to the Shyreeue: whereof the forme and farder vse you may see in the *Register origin. fol.* 88. *b.* and *Fitzh. nat. br. fol.* 79.

Se defendendo, is a plee for him that is charged with the death of another, saying that he was driuen vnto that which he did, in his owne defence, the other so assaulting him, that if he had not done as he did, he must haue beene in perill of his owne life. Which daunger ought to be so great, as that it appeare ineuitable. As *Stawnford* saith in his plees of the Crowne. *li.* 1. *ca.* 7. And if he doe iustifie it to be done in his owne defence, yet is he driuen to procure his pardon of course from the Lord Chanceler, and forfeiteth his goods to the King. As the said authour saith in the same place.

Seignior (*Dominus*) is borowed of the French (*seigneur*) It signifieth in the generall signification, as much as Lord: but particularly it is vsed for the Lord of the fee, or of a maner, euen as (*Dominus*) or (*senior*) among the Feudists, is he, who graunteth a a fee or benefite out of his land to to another. And the reason is,(as *Hotoman* saith) because hauing graunted the vse and profite of the land to another: yet the propertie. i. *(Dominium)* he still reteineth in himselfe. *See Hotoman in verbis feudal. verbo* Dominus, *& Senior.* Seignior in grosse, seemeth to be he that is *Lord*, but of no maner, and therefore can keepe no court. *Fitz.nat. br. fol.* 3. *b.* See *Seignorie.*

Seignourage. anno 9. *H.* 5. *stat.* 2. *cap.* 1. seemeth to be a regalitie or prerogatiue of the king, whereby he challengeth allowance of gold and siluer brought in the masse to his Exchange, for coyne.

Seignorie (Dominium) is borowed of the *French (seigneury.* i. *ditio, dominatus, imperium, principatus, potentatus.)* It signifieth peculiarly with vs, a Maner, or Lordship. *Seignorie de soke mans. Kitchin fol.* 80. *Seignorie* in grosse, seemeth to be the title of him that is not *Lord* by meanes of any maner, but immediatly in his owne person: as *Tenure in capite*, whereby one holdeth of the King, as of his Crowne, is *seignorie in grosse:* because it is held of the king for the time being, and not of the King, as of any honour, maner, &c. *Kitchin, fol.* 206. See *Seignior.*

Seisin (seisina) is borowed of the French *(seisine.* i. *possessio,)* and so it signifieth in our common lawe: and to *seise*, is to take possession. *Primier seisin (prima seisina)* is the first possession. See *Primier seisin*, of the French word *(seisir)* is made a Latine *(seisire,)* vsed by the Canonists. *cap. Clericis.* §. *Nos igitur non semel de immunitate Ecclesiæ, num.* 6. as also the Ciuilians. *Guido. Pap. singula.* 865. *Seisire est etiam possessionem tradere. Tiraquellus in Tractatu.* Le *mort saisit le vif. pag.* 53. *num.* 3. *Seisin* with our common *Lawyers*, is two fold: seisin in fact, and seisin in lawe. *Perkins* Dower. 369. 370. Seisin in fact is, when a corporall possession is taken: seisin in lawe, is when something is done, which the lawe accompteth a seisin, as an Inrolment. Seisin in lawe, is as much as a right to lands and tenements, though the owner be by wrong disseised of them. *Perkins Tenent per le courtesie.* 457. 478. And it seemeth by *Ingham*, that he who hath had an houres possession quietly taken, hath *seisin de droit, & de claime*, whereof no man may disseise him by his owne force or subtiltie, but must bee driuen to his action. §. *Bref de novel disseisin. Sir Edward Cooke lib.* 4. calleth it *seisin in lawe*, or *seisin actuall. fol.* 9. *a.* The Ciuilians call the one *ciuilem possessionem*, the other *naturalem.*

Seisina

Seisina habenda quia Rex habuit annum, diem, & vastum, is a writ that lyeth for the deliuery of *seisin* to the Lord, of his land, or tenements, that formerly was conuicted of felony, after the King in the right of his prerogatiue hath had the yeare, day, and wast. *Reg. orig. fol.* 165. *a.*

Selion (selio) is borowed of the French (*sellon*.i. *terra elata inter duos sulcos*) in Latine (*Porca*) in english a *Ridge*, or land. It signifieth euen so with vs also: and is of no certaine quantity, but some time conteineth an acre, sometime halfe an acre, sometime more, and sometime lesse. *West. parte* 2. *symbol: titulo. Recouery : sect:* 3. Therefore *Crompton* in his Iurisdictions: *fol:* 221. saith, that a selion of land cannot be in demaund, because it is a thing vncertaine.

Seneshall (senescallus) is a French word, but borowed from *Germany*, being (as *Tilius* saith) compounded of *Schal*.i. *servus, aut officialis*, and (*Gesnid*. i. *familia*) we english it a *Steward*. As the high *Seneshall*, or *Steward of England*: *pl. cor: fol.* 152. High *Seneshall* or *Steward*, and *South seneshall*, or vndersteward. *Kitchin fol.* 83: is vnderstood for a steward, or vndersteward of Courts. *Seneshal de l'hostel de Roy*, Steward of the Kings houshold. *Cromptons Iurisdictions. fol.* 102.

Senescallo & Mareshallo quod non teneant placita de libero tenemento, &c. is a writ directed to the Steward or Marshall of *England*, inhibiting them to take cognisance of any action in their court, that concerneth either Freehold, dept, or couenant. *Register orig. fol.* 185. *a.* 191. *b.*

Senie, aliâs, Sene, (*sena*) is a leafe of a medicinable herbe, that bringeth foorth stalkes of a cubite high, purging phlegmaticke, cholericke, and also melancholicke humors, without great violence. The farder vse whereof you may reade in *Gerrards Herbal. lib.* 3. *cap.* 8. This is mentioned among other drugs and spices to be garbled. *anno* 1. *Iacob. cap.* 19.

Septuagesima is a sunday certaine, and alwayes the third sabbath before Shrouesunday, from the which vntill the Octaues after Easter, the solemnizing of mariage is by the Canon lawes forbidden. The reason whereof is giuen, for that all this time vntill Easter, is a time of mourning for the fall of *Adam*, and for the miserie of man thereof insuing. And Easter with the Octaues thereof is a time of Christs glorification, and so of ours also in him, for his, and by him our conquest ouer death and sinne.

And that therefore all carnall affection ought, during that ſpace, to be wholy mortified in vs See *Quinquageſima*, ſee *Aduent*, ſee *Rogation weeke*.

Sequatur ſub ſuo periculo, is a writ, that lyeth, where a ſummons *ad warrantizandum* is awarded, and the Shyreeue returneth, that he hath nothing, whereby he may be ſummoned. For then goeth out an (*Aliâs*) and (*Pluries.*) And if he come not at the (*Pluries*) then ſhall go out this writ. *old nat. br. fol.* 163.

Sequeſtration (*ſequeſtratio*) is a ſeparating of a thing in controuerſie from the poſſeſſion of both thoſe that contend for it. And it is double: voluntarie, or neceſſarie. Voluntarie, is that which is vſed by the conſent of each partie. Neceſſarie is that, which the Iudge of his authoritie doth, whether the parties will or not. It is vſed alſo for the act of the ordinarie diſpoſing of office, the goods and chatels of one deceaſed, whoſe eſtate no man will meddle with. *Dyer. fol.* 232. *num.* 5. *& fol.* 256. *num.* 8. *& fol.* 160. *nu.* 42. *& fol.* 271. *num.* 26. As alſo in the gathering of the fruites of a Benefice voide, to the vſe of the next incumbẽt. *anno* 28. *H.* 8. *cap.* 11. *Forteſcue cap.* 50. and in diuers other caſes.

Sequeſtro habendo, is a writ iudiciall for the diſſoluing of a ſequeſtration made by the Biſhop, at the *Kings* commaundement, of the fruites of a benefice, thereby to compell the Parſon to appeare at the ſuite of another: for the Parſon vpon his apparence may haue this writ, for the releaſe of the ſequeſtration. *Regiſt. Iudicial. fol.* 36. *a.*

Sergeant (*ſeruiens*) commeth of the French (*ſergeant.* i. *ſatelles, accenſus*) a man of the Guard, a kind of ſouldier, ſo called, becauſe he was *ſæpè accitus ad res neceſſarias in exercitu peragendas. Calepin.* M. *Skene de ver. ſign. verb. Seriant*, hath theſe words: Sergeant commeth from Sergent: *quæ eſt vox compoſita de* (*Serrer*) *quod eſt, includere, & gent, quod pro gente, populo vel plebe vſurpatur. Itaque Seriandus dicitur, qui iuſſu magiſtratus, quemlibet de populo reum criminis in carcerem conijcit, ſeu includit.* This word *Sergeant* is diuerſly vſed in our law, and applyed to ſundrie offices and callings. Firſt, a Sergeant at lawe, (or of the coyfe) is the higheſt degree taken in that profeſſion, as a Doctor is in the ciuill lawe. And to theſe, as men beſt learned, and beſt experienced of all others, is there one court ſeuered, to plead in by themſelues: (and that is the Court of common-plees) where the common lawe

lawe of *England* is most strictly obserued. These are made by the Kings *mandat*, or writ, directed vnto them, commaunding them vpon a great penaltie, to take vpon them that degree by a day certaine therein assigned. *Dyer fol.* 72. *num.* 1. see *Counte.* And of these one is the Kings Sergeant, being commonly chosen by the King out of the rest, in respect of his great learning, to pleade for him in all his causes: as namely, in causes of treason. *pl. cor. lib.* 3. *cap. prim.* And of these there may be more if it so please the King. This is called in other Kingdomes, *Aduocatus Regius. Cassan. de consuet. Burgund. pag.* 850. With what solemnitie these Sergeants be created, reade *Fortescue, cap.* 50. This word Sergeant seemeth to be vsed in *Britton* for an Officer belonging to the Countie: who, in his first chapter speaking of Appeales made before the Coroner, hath these words in effect: And then let the Coroner cause his appeale to be entred, and the names of his sureties. And afterward let commaundement be giuen to the Sergeant of the countrie, where the felonie was committed, that he haue the bodie of the persons appealed at the next Countie. And it is probable, that this officer was all one with him, whom *Bracton* in his fifth booke *cap.* 4. *num.* 2. calleth *Seruientem Hundredi*: of whome he hath these words: *Post probationem defaltæ, faciet seruiens* Hundredi *incontinenti summonitionem, vel affidet partibus diem, si præsentes sint, ad proximum Comitatum, &c.* This is like to be the same Officer, which in auncient time was called the Bayliffe of the Hundred, who (as is declared in *Baylife*) had the like authoritie in his Hundred, that the shyreeue had in the Countie, though inferiour to him, and to be controlled by him, as appeareth by diuers auncient presidents set downe by *Kitchin* in his tractat of Returns in Court Hundred, Court Baron, &c. I read also in *Bracton lib.* 3. *tractat:* 2. *ca.* 28. Of the Kings Sergeant, who is like to be also an officer in the County, in these words: speaking of a woman ranished, and what shee ought to doe for the persuite of the Rauisher, *& sic ire debet ad præpositum Hundredi, & ad seruientem Domini Regis, & ad coronatores, & ad vicecomitē, & ad primū comitatū faciat appellū suum.* And againe *eod. li: c:* 32. in these words: *& si sine secta cognouerit se inde esse latronem coram vicecomite, vel coronatore, vel seruiente Domini Regis, &c.* And againe *lib.* 5. *tractat:* 3. *cap.* 4. *nu.* 8. in these words. *Quid si seruiens Domini Regis dederit partibus diem* *ad Comitatum, &c.* And by *Fleta* it ſeemeth, that this terme was generall to the Shyreeue, Coroner, and Bayliffes of Counties, who in his ſixth booke. *cap:* 3. §. *1.* hath theſe worde: *Cum quis igitur ſenſerit dominum ſuum vel curiam ſuam ſibi de recto defeciſſe, tunc oſtenſo hoc vicecomiti, ſtatim præcipiat balliuo Hundredi, vel itiner.anti, vel alteri ſeruienti Regis, quòd aſſumptis ſibi liberis, & legalibus hominibus de vicineto illo, ad curiam illius domini, ſi quem habuerit accedat, &c.* And to helpe this probability, I finde that the ſteward of a maner is termed *ſeruiens manerii. Coke Vol: 4. Copyhould caſes. fo.* 21. *a.* Then is there a Sergeant at armes (*ſeruiens ad arma*) whoſe office is to attend the perſon of the *King, anno* 7 *H.* 7. *ca.* 3. to arreſt traitours, or men of worth or reckoning, that doe, or are like to contemne meſſengers of ordinary condition for other cauſes, and to attend the Lord high *Steward* of England ſitting in Iudgement vpon any Traytour, and ſuch like: *pl: cor. lib.* 3. *cap. pri:* Of theſe by the ſtatute *anno* 13. *R.* 2. *cap.* 6. there may not be aboue thirtie in the Realme. This ſort is called *del eſpee.* In the cuſtumary of *Nor. ca.* 5. which read. There be alſo ſome two of theſe Sergeants of the Parlament, one for the vpper, another for the lower houſe, whoſe office ſeemeth to ſerue for the keeping of the doores, and the execution of ſuch commaundements, eſpecially touching the apprehenſion of any offender, as either houſe ſhall thinke good to inioyne them. See *Cromptons Iuriſdictions, fol. nono.* See alſo *Vowels, aliàs Hookers* booke of the order of the *Parl.* There is one of theſe that belongeth to the Chauncery, who is alſo called a Sergeant of the Mace, as the reſt may be, becauſe they cary Maces by there office. He of the Chauncery attendeth the Lord Chauncelor, or Keeper in that court, for the meanes to call all men into that court, is either by this officer or by *ſub pœna. Weſt. pa.* 2. *ſym. tit. Chauncery Sect.* 17. Then be there ſergeants that be the chiefe officers in their ſeuerall functions within the kings houſhould, which be chiefe in their places, of which ſort you may read many named in the ſtatute *anno* 33. *H.* 8. *ca.* 12. There is alſo a more baſe kinde of ſergeant of the Mace, whereof there is a troupe in the City of London, and other townes corporate, that ſerue the Maior or other head officer, both for meſniall attendance, and mater of Iuſtice. *Kitchin fol.* 143. And theſe are called *Seruientes ad clauã.* New book of *Entries. ver. ſciro facias:*

facius: in Mainperners. f. 538. *c.* 3.

Sergeantie) *Seriantia*) commeth of the French (*Sergeant.* i. *satelles*) & signifieth in our cōmō law, a seruice due to the *King* frō his tenēt holding by such seruice. For this seruice cannot be due to any *L.* from his Tenēt, but to the King onely. And this is either grand, or petit, as you shall find at large set downe in Chivalrie. Of this also you may read *Bra l.* 2. *c.* 16. & *c.* 37. *n.* 5. 4. & *Brit.* . *c.* 66. *n.* 1. & 2. See *Seruice. M. Skene de ver. signifi.* calleth this *Sergeanterie*, defining and diuiding it as we doe in England.

Servientibus, are certaine writs touching seruants, and their Masters violating the statutes made against their abuses. which see in the *Regist. orig. fol.* 189. & 190. & 191.

Service (*seruitium*) though it haue a generall signification of dutie toward them vnto whome we owe the performance of any corporall labour, or function: yet more especially in our common lawe, it is vsed for that seruice, which the tenent by reason of his fee, oweth vnto his Lord. And so doth it signifie among the Feudists also For *Hotoman* thus defineth it. *Seruitium est munus obsequii clientelaris. verbo Servitium. De verbis feudal.* or rather declareth it so to be defined. *lib. feud.* 2. *titulo* 51. §. 8. It is sometime called seruage, as *anno.* 1. *R.* 2. *cap.* 6. This seruice is either militarie, and noble, commonly called Knights seruice: or clownishe & base, commonly called socage. of both which reade *Chiualry*, as also *socage.* and *Bracton lib.* 2. *cap.* 16. Seruice is diuided by *Britton* into personall, and reall. *cap.* 66. where he maketh wards, mariags, homage, Releifs, and such like, to be reall seruices: personall, I imagine, may those be called, that are to be performed by the person of the Tenent, as to follow his Lord into warre, &c. The Ciuilians diuide *munera* in this sort, either in *personalia*, or *patrimonalia*. Then *Bracton vbi supra num.* 7. distributeth *seruitium in intrinsecum, & extrinsecum aliàs forinsecum. & medium. Seruitium intrinsecū* is that, which is due to the capitall Lord of the maner, *Forinsecum* is that which is due to the *King*, and not to the capitall Lord, but when he goeth in his owne person to serue: or when he hath satisfied the king for all seruices whatsoeuer. And againe in the same place he saith, it is called *Fornisecum, quia sit, & capitur foris, siue extra seruitium, quod fit Domino capitali.* see *Forein seruice.* Of this reade him *vbi supra*, more at large. and *Fleta, lib.* 2. *ca.* 14. §. *Continetur.*

Seruitia quæ nec intrinseca nec forinseca sunt, Bract. handleth in the same chap. *n.*8. saying thus: *sunt etiam quædam consuetudines, quæ nec dicuntur intrinseca, nec forinseca: sed sunt quædam seruitia concomitantia, sicut seruitia regalia, & militaria, & etiam homagia: & ideo in chartis non sunt exprimenda. Quia si homagium præcesserit, & regale seruitium, sequitur exinde quod ad capitalem Dominum pertinebit Releuium, & custodia, & maritagium: siue seruitium sit militare, vel seriantia propter exercitum, &c.* Here then Reliefe, Ward, and Mariage, be those seruices, which he calleth, *nec intrinseca, nec forinseca, sed concomitantia.* Seruice is also deuided into frank seruice, and base, or villenous seruice: the one *Bracton*, calleth (*liberum seruitium*) the other (*seruitium villanum*) or (*villenagium*) *lib.*2. *cap.* 8. *nu. pri.* This *villenagium* is Socage in base tenure, as to dung the Lords ground, to serue him so many daies in haruest, to plash his hedges, &c. or els copy hould. All other seruices seeme to be frank. Seruice consisteth some in seisance, some in render. *Perkins Reseruations.* 696. Seruice seemeth also to be diuided into continuall, otherwise annuall, and casuall, or accidentall. An example of the former is the seisin of rent, and of the other, seisin of reliefe. *Sir* Ed. *Cookes reports. lib.*4. *Bevils case. fol.* 9.*a.* See *Copy hould*: See *Socage.* see *Ayde.*

Seruice secular. anno 1. *Ed.*4 *ca.* 1. which may be contrary to spirituall, *viz.* the seruice diuine commaunded to spirituall men by their founders.

Servitours of bils, seeme to be such seruāts or messengers of the marishall belonging to the kings bench, as were sent abroad with bils, or writs to summon men to that court, being now more ordinarily called *Tipstafs.*

Servitiis acquietandis, is a writ Iudiciall, that lieth for one distreined for seruices by *Iohn*, which oweth and performeth to *Robert*, for the acquitall of such seruices. *Register Iudicial, fol.*27.*a.* & 36.*b.*

Sessions (*Sessiones*) signifieth in our common lawe a sitting of Iustices in court vpon their commission: as the sessions of *oyer*, and *terminer. pl. cor. fol.* 67. Quarter sessions, otherwise called generall sessions. *anno* 5. *Elizab. cap.* 4. or open sessions, *ibidem.* Opposite whereunto are especiall, otherwise called priuie sessions, which are procured vpon some speciall occasion, for the more speedie expedition of Iustice in some cause. *Cromptons Iustice of peace. fol.* 110. what things be inquirable in generall sessions: see *Cromptons Iustice of peace, fol.* 109. Petit sessions, or statute sessions, are kept by the high Constable of euery Hundred, for the placing of seruants, *anno 5. Eli. cap. quart. in fine.*

Sessour. anno 25. Ed. 3. *cap. 6.* seemeth to signifie so much as assessing or rating of wages at this day,

Set clothes, anno. 27. Henric. 8. *cap.* 13.

Setwell, Valeriana, is a medicinal herb, the nature and diuers kinds whereof you haue in *Gerards herball, lib.* 2. *cap.* 424. The roote of this is mentioned among drugs to be garbled, *anno.* 1. *Ia. cap.* 19.

Seuerance, is the singling of two or more, that ioyne in one writ, or are ioyned in one writ. For example, if two ioyne in a writ *de libertate probanda,* and the one afterward be non-suite, here seuerance is permitted; so that, notwithstanding the non-suite of the one, the other may seuerally proceede. *Fitzh. nat. br. fol.* 78. *I.* K Of this see Brooke, *titulo seuerance, & summons. fol.* 238. For it is harder to knowe in what cases seuerãce is permitted, then what it is. There is also seuerãce of the tenents in an Assise, when as one or two, or more disseisours appeareth vpon the writ, and not the other. New booke of *Entries, fo.* 81. *col.* 4. & seuerance in attaints. *eod. fol.* 95. *col.* 2. And seuerance in debt. *verbo, debt. fol.* 220. *col.* 1. see the saide booke, *verbo Seuerance.*

Severall taile (*tallium separatum*) is that whereby land is giuen and entayled seuerally to two. For example, land is giuen to two men, and their wiues, and to the heires of their bodies begotten: the Donees haue ioynt estate for their two liues, and yet they haue seuerall inheritance: because the issue of the one shall haue his moyety, and the issue of the other, the other moyetie, *Kitchin ibidem.*

Severall tenancie (*tenura separalis*) is a plee, or exception taken to a writ, that is laide against two as ioynt, which are seuerall, *Brooke titulo, Severall tenancie, fol.* 237.

Sewantly wouen, an. 35. *El. c.* 10.

Sewar, hath two significations with vs, one applied to him that issueth or commeth in before the meate of the King, or other great personage, and placeth it vpon the table: the other to such passages, or gutters as carie water into the sea, or riuer, in lawyers Latine called *Sewera, an.* 6. *H.* 6. *c.* 5. which is also vsed in common speach for commissioners authorised vnder the broad seale to see draines, and ditches.

ditches well kept, and maintained in the marish and fenne countries, for the better conueyance of the water into the sea, and the preseruing of the grasse for feede of catell. *stat. anno* 6.H.6.*cap.* 5. It is probable to bring this word from the French *(issir)* or *(issue)* as if we should call them *(Issuers)* because they giue issue or passage to the water, &c. And the latine word *(suera)* sometime vsed in these commissions for these draines, is a competent reason of this coniecture: see *Eitzh.nat.br. in oyer* and *terminer*. Yet I finde in an old French booke conteining the officers of the King of Englands court as it was auunciently gouerned, that he whom in court we now call *Sewer*, was called *(Asseour)* which may seeme to come from the French *(Asseour)* wherein his office in setting downe the meat vpon the table is well expressed. And *Sewer* as it signifieth an officer, is by *Fleta* latined *Assessor: li.* 2.*ca.* 15. All which argueth that the descent of this word is from the French *(Asseoir)* as signifiing a disposing or placing of any thing, or (as we say in English) an assessing of any person toward the performance of a dutie.

Sexagesima. See *Septuagesima*.

Shanckes See *Furre*.

Shares. See *Flotzon*.

Shewing, is to be quit of attachment in any court, and before whom soeuer in plaints shewed and not avowed. Newe exposition of law termes. *verbo*, *Shewing*. *See Scauage*.

Shipper. anno 1. *Iac. ses.* 1. *ca.* 33. is a Dutch word, signifying the Master of the ship.

Shire, *(Comitatus, Shira)* is a Saxon word, signifying *Satrapian*, of the verbe *(scyran.* i. *partiri.)* *Lamb.* in his explication of Saxon words. *verbo Centuria*. The word is in vse so rife, that euery child vnderstandeth it. Who first thus diuided this land into shires, appeareth by *M. Camdens Britan. pa.* 102. in these words. *Nec dum tamen florente Heptarchia, Anglia ita in Comitatus diuisa, (sic enim vulgò vocant) sed postea, cum solus Aluredus rerum potiretur. Vt enim Germani maiores nostri, teste Tacito, iura per pagos vicosq; reddebant, & centeni ex plebe comites ad rem administrandam adiungebantur: sic ille (vt Ingulfi Croulandensis verbis vtar) primus Angliam in Comitatus diuisit, quod indigenæ rapinas committerent exemplo & colore Danorum. Comitatus porrò in Centurias.* i. *Hundreds, & Decimas.* i. *Tythings, distribui fecit: præcepitq; vt omnis indigena in aliqua esset Centuria, & Decima. Præfectos etiam prouinciarum, munciarum, qui antea Vicedomini vocabantur, in duo officia diuisit, viz. Iudices, nunc Iusticiarios: & Vicecomites, qui adhuc idem nomen retinent.* See the rest.

Shyreeue (Vicecomes) is compounded of these saxon words *(Scyre .i. satrapia)* and *(Reue .i. præfectus)* and accordingly he is the cheife officer vnder the King of his Shyre, or County. *See Ferme in Lacies nobility: pag.* 12. *M. Camden: pag.* 104. Thus describeth his office: *Singulis verò annis, nobilis aliquis ex incolis præficitur, quem vicecomitem, quasi vicarium comitis, & nostra lingua Shiref .i. comitatus præpositum vocamus: qui etiam comitatus, vel prouinciæ Quæstor rectè dici potest. Eius enim est publicas pecunias prouinciæ suæ conquirere, mulctas irrogatas, vel pignoribus ablatis colligere, & ærario inferre, Iudicibus præsto adesse, & eorum mandata exequi, duodecim viros cogere, qui in causis de facto cognoscunt, & ad Iudices referunt (Iudices enim apud nos, iuris solùm, non facti sunt Iudices) condemnatos ad supplicium ducere, & in minoribus litibus cognoscere. In maioribus autem ius dicunt Iusticiarii, quos itinerantes ad Assisas vocant, qui quotannis hos Comitatus bis adeunt, vt de causis cognoscant, & de incarceratis sententiam ferant. Henricus secundus hos itinerantes instituit, vel potiùs restituit. Ille (vt inquit Mathæus Parisiensis) consilio filii sui & Episcoporum constituit Iusticiarios per sex partes regni, in qualibet parte tres, qui iurarent quod cuilibet ius suum conseruarent illæsum.* Of the antiquitie and authoritie of this officer, reade *Sir Edward Cookes* Reports. *lib.* 4. *Mittons case.* The maner of appointing these *Shyreeues* in *Henry* the sixt his dayes, see in *Fortescue. cap.* 24. *fol.* 53. *b.* The name *Vicecomes* commeth from the Normans, as *Shyreeue* commeth from the Saxons. For in the fifth Chapter of the Grand Custumarie, you haue *(vicounte)* which the Latine Interpreter turneth *(vicecomitem)* whose office you shall find in that Chapter to be very like vnto ours. The forme of the Shyreeues oath see in the *Register origin. fol.* 301. *b.* Of this reade *M. Skene de verbor. signif. verbo Shyreeue*: where he largely describeth the office of the Shyreeue in *Scotland*, in a discourse woorth the reading.

Shyreeue weke of Winchester and of Essex. anno 21. R. 2. *cap.* 10. & 11.

Shire Clerke, seemeth to bee the Vndershyreeue. *anno* 11. *H.* 7. *cap.* 15. It is vsed sometime for a Clerk in the County court, deputie to the Vndershyreeue. See Sir *Edward Cookes* 4. booke of Reports in *Mittons case.*

Shire moote, see *Turne.*

Shorling, and *Morling* seeme to be words to distinguish fels of sheepe: as if *shorling* should signifie the fels after the fleeces be shorne off the sheepes backe, and *morling* the fels fleane off after they be killed or dye alone. *anno* 3. Ed. 4. *cap. prim. & anno* 4. *eiusdem, cap.* 3. *& anno* 12. *eius. cap.* 5. *& anno* 14. *eiusdem, cap.* 3.

Shot commeth of the Saxon word, *sceate*, signifying *pecuniam aut vectigal. Lamberds* explicatiō of saxon words, *verbo Primitia.*

Shrof metall.

Sicut aliàs, is a writ sent out in the second place, whereas the first sped not. *Coke libro quart. folio* 55. *b.* It is so called of these words expressed in it. For example. Iacobus *dei gratia, &c. vicecomiti Kan: salutem*: *Præcipimus tibi (sicut alias præcepimus) quod non omittas propter aliquam libertatem in Balliua tua, quin eam ingrediaris, & capias. A. B. de C. in comitatu tuo* Labourer, &c. as in the first *capias. Lamb*: in his tractat of processes in the end of his *Eirenarcha.*

Sidemen aliâs Quest men, be those that are yearely chosen according to the custome of euery parish, to assist the church wardens in the inquiry and presenting such offenders to the Ordinary, as are punishable in the Court Cristian.

Significauit, is the writ *de excommunicato capiendo*, which issueth out of the Chauncery vpon a certificate giuen by an Ordinary of a man that standeth obstinately excommunicate by the space of fourty daies, for the laying him vp in prison without bayle, or mainprise, vntill he submit himselfe to the authority of the church. And it is so called, because of the word (*significauit*) mentioned in the writ (*De excōmunicato capiendo*) whichhaue relation to the certificate, sent into the Chauncery by the Ecclesiasticall Iudge. There is also another writ in the *Register orig.* of this name, *fo*: 7. *a.* directed to the Iustices of the bench, willing them to stay any suite depending betweene such and such, by reason of any excommunication alledged against the plaintiffe: because the sentence of the Ordinarie that did excommunicate him, is appealed from, and the appeale yet hangeth vndecided. Which see: and see *Fitz. nat. br. De excommunicato capiendo. fol.* 62. *N.* but especially 66. *A.* where you may find writs of this name in other cases.

Sine assensu capituli, is a writ that lyeth in case where a Deane, Bishop, Prebendarie, Abbot, Prior or Master of Hospitall, alieneth the

the land held in the right of his house, without the consent of the Chapter, Couent, or Fraternitie. For in this case his successor shall haue this writ. *Fitzh. nat. br. fol.* 195.

Si non omnes, is a writ of association, whereby if all in cōmission cannot meete at the day assigned, it is permitted, that two or more of them may finish the businesse. *See Association.* And *Fitz. nat. br. fol.* 185. & 111. C. and *Register origin. fol.* 202. 206. & 124.

Si recognoscant, is a writ that lyeth for a Creditour against his depter for money numbred, that hath before the shyreeue in the Countie court, acknowledged himselfe to owe vnto his creditor such a summe receiued of him in *numeratis pecuniis.* The forme of the writ is this: Rex *Vicecomiti salutem. Prac. tibi quod si* A. *recognoscat se debere R.* 40. *solid. sine vlteriori dilatione, tunc ipsum distringas ad prædictum debitum eidem* R. *sine dilatione reddendum. Teste, &c.* Old *nat. br. fol.* 68.

Skawe. anno 4. *Ed.* 4. *cap.* 1.

Skyvinage. anno 27. *H.* 6. *cap.* 2. a proper name, signifying the precincts of *Caleis.*

Sluse (*exclusa*) is a frame to keepe, or let water out of a grounde.

Soc (*Soca*) is a word signifiing a power, or libertie of Iurisdiction, as appeareth by these words out of *Bracton*, *Sunt quidam Barones, & alii libertatem habentes, sc: soc, & sac, Tol & Thean, Infangthefe, & Vtfangthefe, & isti possunt iudicare in Curia sua, eum qui inuentus fuerit infra libertatem suam seisitus de aliquo latrocinio manifesto. & li.* 3. *tractat.* 2. *cap.* 8. In the lawes of King *Edward* set out by *M. Lamberd, fol.* 132. you haue these words: *Socha est quod si aliquis quærit aliquid in terra sua, etiam furtum, sua est Iusticia, si inuentum fuerit, an non. Saxon in the description of Britany, cap.* 11. saith, that *Sock* is a suite of Court and that thereof commeth *Soken. But* the signification of the word (as I haue bene credibly informed) is as much as *Inquisitio* which we in moderne English, terme (seeking) Of this (*Sok*) *Skene de verborum signific.* speaketh to this effect. *Sok* is an ould word vsed in Charters and feofments, which in sundry old bookes conteining the municipiall law of this Realme, is called *Secta de hominibus suis in curia, secundum consuetudinem Regni. So* after my opinion he that is infeoffed with *Sok* (which now we call *Sout* (but we in England *Suite*) hath power to hould courts within his owne Baronie, in which, *homines sui* ſhould giue *Soyt*. Thus farre *M. Skene*. Of this *Fleta* hath theſe words. *In huiuſmodi verò maneriis* (ſpeaking of the Kings maners) *erant olim liberi homines liberè tenentes, quorum quidam cum per potentiores è tenementis ſuis eiecti fuerant, & eadem poſtmodum in villenagium tenenda reſumpſerũt: & quia huiuſmodi tenentes cultores* Regis *eſſe dinoſcuntur, eis proviſa fuit quies ne ſectas facerent ad comitatus vel hundredos, vel ad aliquas inquiſitiones, aſſiſas vel iuratas, niſi in manerio tantùm, dum tamen pro terra, quorum congregationem tunc ſocam appellarunt. & hinc eſt quòd Socmanni hodie dicuntur eſſe. A ſoco enim derivantur, quorum tenementa ſunt villenagium domini privilegiatum, & ideo dicuntur glebæ aſcriptitii, eo quòd ab huiuſmodi glebis amoueri non deberent, quam diu ſolverent debitas penſiones: nec compelli poterunt ad huiuſmodi tenementa tenenda, contra ſuas voluntates, eo quòd corpora ſua ſunt libera. Nec obſtabit longa ſeruitutis poſſeſſio ad libertatẽ extinguendam, quamuis ad merchetum ſanguinis ſui compulſus fuerit quis pro tenemento reddendo. Nulla enim ſervitus ratione præſcriptionis temporis poteſt liberum ſanguinẽ in ſeruitutẽ reducere, non magis quam liberum tenementum poteſt ſervum in libertatem, &c.* By whoſe words it appeareth, that *Soca* is nothing elſe, but the meeting or aſſembly of theſe kinde of tenents in any place within the maner or libertie: wherefore he that hath ſoc may ſeeme to haue ſuch a maner, ſuch tenents, and ſuch a libertie belonging to his maner and tenents, as is here deſcribed. Here you ſee diuerſities of opinions touching this word, one ſaying that it is a power or libertie to ſeeke after theeues & ſtollen goods within a maner or fee, and to doe iuſtice vpon ſuch inquiſition. others that it is a libertie onely to haue ſuters to his court. other (as *Fleta*, that it conteineth both the former ſignifications, and furder that it is taken for the company of tenents which liue within ſuch a liberty; and are exempled from thoſe common ſeruices of the *Prince* and country wherunto ſubiects are ordinarily tied. This kinde of liberty is in diuers places at this day in England, and commonly knowne by the name of *ſoke* or *ſoken*. See *Soke* and *Sockmans*.

Soccage (*ſoccagium*) commeth of the French (*Soc*. i. *vomer*, a plowſhare or coulter). It ſignifieth in our common lawe a tenure of lands by or for certaine inferiour, or husbandly ſeruices to be performed to the Lord of the fee. See *Inſtituts of common lawe.* 31. As I haue shewed in (*Chivalrie*), all seruices due for land, is either knights seruice, or socage. So then, whatsoeuer is not knights seruice, is soccage: *Bracton* in his 2. booke *cap.* 35. *num. primo.* describeth it thus. *Dici poterit soccagium à Socco, & inde tenentes qui tenent in Sockagio, Sockmanni dici poterunt, eo quòd deputati sunt, vt videtur, tantummodo ad culturam, & quorum custodia, & maritagia ad propinquiores parentes iure sanguinis pertinebit. Et si aliquando inde de facto capiatur homagium, quòd pluries contingit, non tamen habebit propter hoc Dominus capitalis custodiam, & maritagium. Quia non semper sequitur homagium, licet aliquando sequatur. M. Skene de verborum significatione. verb. Sockmanria*, saith, that Sockage is a kinde of holding of lands, when a man is infeoffed freely without any seruice, ward, releife, or mariage, and paieth to his Lord such dutie, as is called petit sergeantie, or when one holdeth land in the name of burgage, or in *libera elemozina*, or otherwise in *blenche ferme, siue nomine albæ firmæ, & opponitur militi, qui tenet per seruitium militare.* Out of the place aboue named in *Bracton*, you may finde a diuision of Soccage, wherby it is termed either *Soccagium liberum*, or *villanum*. frank or free Soccage, and base, otherwise called villenage. The former is there thus defined. *Soccagium liberum est, vbi fit seruitium in denariis Dominis capitalibus, & nihil inde omnino datur ad scutum & seruitium Regis.* Where I gather that to be free soccage which paieth a certaine summe of money to the cheife Lord in regard of some tillage, or such like, and not of any Sergeantie, or eschuage. And to this effect he writeth also, *lib. 2. cap. 16. nu. 9. &c. vnde si tantum in denariis & sine scutagio vel seriantiis, vel si ad duo teneatur sub disiunctione, sc: ad certam rem dandam pro omni seruitio, vel aliquam summam in denariis, id tenementum potest dici Soccagium: si autem superaddas Scutagium, aut seruitium regale, licet ad vnum obulum vel seriantiam, illud poterit dici feudum militare.* This free Soccage, is also called common Socage, *anno* 37. H. 8. *cap* 20. Soccage in base tenure, or *villanum Soccagium*, is diuided againe in *villanum Soccagium, & purum villenagium: Villanum Soccagium est illud, de quo fit certum seruitium, idque ratione sui tenemēti, non personæ suæ. Purum villenagium est illud, in quo præstatur seruitium incertum, & indeterminatum, vbi sciri non poterit vespere, quale seruitium fieri debet mane. viz. vbi quis facere tenetur quicquid ei praeceptum fuerit*. *Bracton lib*.2. *cap*. 8. *num*. 3. The *old. nat. br. fol.* 94. maketh three parts of this diuision. *viz*. Soccage of free tenure, Soccage of auncient tenure, and soccage of base tenure. soccage of free tenure is (as the booke saith) where a man holdeth by free seruice of 12. pence by yeare, for all maner of seruices, or by other seruices yearely. Soccage of auncient tenure is of land of auncient *Demesn*, where no writ originall shall be siewed, but the writ of Right, that is called *secundum consuetudinem manerii*. Soccage of base tenure is of those that hould in Soccage, and may haue none other writ, but the *Monstraverunt*: and such Sockmen hould not by certaine Seruice. And for that are they not free Sockmen. Then againe Soccage is diuided into soccage in cheife, and common soccage. Soccage in cheife or in *capite*, is that which holdeth of the King, as of his Crowne. *Prærog. fol.* 41. Common Soccage is that, which holdeth of any other capitall Lord, or of the King by reason of some honour or maner. *Ibidem*. Burgage is also a kinde of Soccage, See *Burgage*.

Sockmans (*Sockmanni*) are such tenents as hould their lands, and tenements by Soccage tenure. And accordingly as you haue 3. kinds of Soccage, soe be there 3. sorts of sockmans. as sockmans of frank tenure. *Kitchin, fol.* 81. sockmans of auncient Demesn *ould nat. br. fol.* 11. and Sockmans of base tenure. *Kitchin vbi supra*. But the tenents in auncient Demesn, seeme most properly to be called *Sockmans*, *Fitzh. na. br. f.* 14. *B. Brit. c.* 66. *n*. 2.

Soke, *anno* 32. *H*. 8. *cap*. 15. & *cap*. 29. Of this *Fleta* saith thus *Soke significat libertatem curiæ tenentium. quam socam appellamus. lib*. 1. *cap*. 47. §. *Soke*. See Roger *Houeden, parte poster. suorum annalium. fol*. 345. *b*. and See *Soc*.

Soken (*Soca*) see *Soc*. and *Hamsoken*. *Soken* is latined *soca Register originall, fol*. 1. *a*.

Sokereue seemeth to be the Lords rent-gatherer in the Soke, or Soken, *Fleta, lib*. 2. *cap*. 55. *in principio*.

Sole tenent (*Solus tenens*) is he or shee which holdeth onely in his or her owne right without any other ioyned. For example, if a man and his wife hould land for their liues, the remainder to their son: here the man dying, the Lord shall not haue Heriot, because he dieth not sole tenent. *Kitchin, fol*. 134.

Solicitour (*Solicitator*) commeth of the French (*Soliciteur*) It signifieth in our commõ law, a man imploied to folow suites depending in law, for the beter remembrance and more ease of Atturnies, who commonly are so full of clients and busines, that they cannot so often attend the seriants and counsellers as the case may require.

Solet & Debet. See *Debet & solet.*

Solidata terræ. see *Farding deale of land.*

Sollace, anno 43. Elizabeth. cap. 10.

Sommons, aliàs summons (summonitio) commeth of the French (*semondre* .i. *vocare*) It signifieth in our common law, as much as (*vocatio in ius*) or (*citatio*) among the Ciuilians. And thence is our word (*somner*) which in French is (*semonneur* .i. *vocator, monitor*) The Custumary of *Normandie* for our (*sommons* hath (*semonse*) *ca.* 61. *summons* of the Exchequer *anno* 3. *Ed. pri: ca.* 19. *& anno* 10. *eiusdem, cap.* 9. How summons is diuided, and what circumstances it hath to be obserued. See *Fleta, lib.* 6. *cap.* 6. 7.

Solutione feodi militis Parlamenti, and *solutione feodi Burgen. Parlamenti,* be writs whereby Knights of the Parlament may recouer their allowance, if it be denyed, *anno* 35. *H.* 8. *ca.* 11.

Sontage. Stow. pag. 284. is a taske of fourty shillings laid vpon euery Knights fee.

Sorting Kerseies. 3. *Iacobi: ca:* 16.

Sothale, is a kinde of intertainment made by Bayliffes to those of their Hundreds for their gaine. Which sometime is called *Filctale.* Of this *Bracton lib.* 3. *tracta:* 2. *cap. pri.* hath these words: *De Ballivis, qui faciunt ceruisias suas, quas quandoq; vocant (sothale) quandoq; (Filctale) vt pecunias extorqueant ab eis qui sequuntur Hundreda sua, & Balliuas suas, &c.* I thinke this should rather be written *Scotale.* See *Scotale.*

Southvicont (Subvicecomes) is the vnder Shyreeue. *Cromptone Iurisdict: fol:* 5.

Sowne, is a verb neuter, properly belonging to the Exchequer, as a word of their art, signifiing so much, as to be leuiable, or possible to be gathered or collected. For example, estreats that sowne not, are such as the Shyreeue by his industry cannot get, and estreats that sowne, are such as he can gather, *anno* 4. H. 5. *ca.* 2.

Speaker of the Parlament, is an officer in that high Court, that is as it were the common mouth of the rest: and as that honourable assembly consisteth of two houses, one called the higher or vpper house, consisting of the King, the nobility, and Kings councell, especially appointed for the same, the other termed the lower or commonhouse,

con-

containing the Knights of the Shires, the citizens, barons of the cinque ports, and the burgeſses of borough townes: ſo be there alſo two ſpeakers, one termed the Lord ſpeaker of the higher houſe, who is moſt commonly the Lord Chauncelor of England, or Lord Keeper of the great ſeale: the other is called the ſpeaker of the lower houſe. And the duties of theſe two you haue perticularly deſcribed in *M. Vowels, aliàs Hookers* booke, intituled The order and vſage of keeping the Parlament.

Speciall mater in euidence. See *Generall iſſue.* And *Brooke. titulo Generall iſſue, and ſpeciall euidence.*

Spiritualties of a Biſhop (*ſpiritualia Epiſcopi*) be thoſe profits which he receiueth, as he is a Biſhop, and not as he is a Baron of the Parlament. *Stawnſ. pl. cor. fol.* 132. The particulars of theſe may be the duties of his Viſitation, his benefite growing from ordering and inſtituting Prieſts, preſtation money, that *ſubſidium charitatiuum,* which vppon reaſonable cauſe he may require of his Clergie. *Iohannes Gregorius de Beneficiis. cap.* 6. *num.* 9. and the Benefite of his Iuriſdiction. *Ioachimus Stephanus de Iuriſd. lib.* 4. *cap.* 14. *num.* 14. for theſe reckoneth *exactionem Cathedratici, quartam Decimarum, & mortuariorum, & oblationum penſitationem, ſubſidium charitatiuum, celebrationem ſynodi, collationem viatici vel commeatus, cùm* Epiſ*copus Romam proficiſcitur, ius hoſpitii, Litaniam & Proceſſionem.*

Spikenard (*ſpica nardi, vel nardus*) is a medicinall herbe, whereof you may for your farder inſtruction reade *Gerards* Herball. *lib.* 2. *cap.* 425. The fruite or eare of this (for it bringeth forth an eare like Lauender) is a drugge garbleable, *anno* 1. Iacob. *cap.* 19.

Spoliation (*ſpoliatio*) is a writ, that lyeth for an incumbent, againſt another incumbent, in caſe where the right of patronage commeth not in debate. As if a Parſon bee made a Biſhop, and hath diſpenſation to keepe his Rectorie, and afterward the patron preſent another to the Church, which is inſtituted and inducted: The Biſhop ſhall haue againſt this incumbent a writ of *ſpoliation in Court Chriſtian. Fitz. nat. br. fol.* 36. ſee *Beneuolence.*

Squalley. anno 43. *Elizab. cap.* 10.

Squyers. See *Eſquires.*

Stableſtand, is one of the foure Euidences, or preſumptions whereby a man is conuinced to intend the ſtealing of the Kings Deere in the Foreſt. *Man-*

Manwood. parte 2 of his Forest lawes. *cap.* 18. *num.* 9. the other three be these *Dogdrawe, Backbeare, Bloudie-hand.* And this *Stablestand*, is when a man is found at his standing in the Forest, with a Crosse bowe bent, ready to shoote at any *Deere*, or with a long bowe, or else standing close by a tree with Greyhounds in a lease, ready to slippe, *Idem, eodem.*

Stalkers, a kind of net. *anno* 13 *R.* 2. *stat.* 1. *cap.* 20. & *anno* 17. *eiusdem, cap.* 9.

Stallage (*stallagium*) commeth of the French (*Estaller.* i. *merces exponere, expedire, explicare.*) It signifieth in our common law, money payed for pitching of stalles in Faire or Market. See *Scavage*. This in *Scotland* is called *stallange. Skene de verbor. signif. verbo Stallangiatores.* And among the *Romaines* it was termed (*Siliquaticum*) *à siliqua, primo & minimo omnium pondere apud illam nationem.*

Stannaries (*stannaria*) commeth of the *Latine* (*stannum.*) i. *tynne*, signifying the Mines and workes touching the getting, and purifying of this mettall in *Cornewall*, and other places. Of this read *Camden. Britan. pa.* 119. The liberties of the *stannarie* men graunted by *Ed.* 1. before they were abridged by the statute, *anno* 50. *Ed.* 3. see in *Plowden. casu Mines. fol.* 327. *a.b.*

Staple (*Stapulum*) signifieth this or that towne, or citie, whether the Merchants of *England* by common order, or commandement, did carie their wolles, wol-fels, cloathes, lead, and tinne, and such like commodities of our land for the vtterance of them by the great. The word may probably be interpreted two wayes: one taking it from (*staple*) which in the *Saxon* or old English language, signifieth the stay or hold of any thing. *Lamb.* in his duties of Constables. *num.* 4. because the place is certaine, and setled: and againe, from the French (*estape.* i. *forum vinarium*) because to those places, whether our *English* Merchants brought their commodities, the French would also meete them with theirs, which most of all consisteth in wines: but I thinke this latter the truer because I finde in the Mirrour of the world written in French these words. *A Calais y auoit Estape de le laine, &c.* Which is as much to say, as the staple for wols, &c. You may read of many places appointed for this staple in the statutes of the land, according as the Prince by his Councell thought good to alter them, from the second yeare of *Ed.* 3. *cap.* 9. to the fifth of *Edw:*

the sixth. *cap*: 7. what officers the staples had belonging to them you may see *anno* 27. *Ed*. 3. *stat*. 2. *ca*. 21.

Starre chamber (*Camera stellata*) is a Chamber at *Westminster* so called (as Sir *Tho*. *Smith* coniectureth *lib*. 2. *cap*. 4.) either because it is full of windowes, or because at the first all the roofe thereof was decked with Images of guilded starres. And the later reason I take to be the trewer, because *anno* 25. *H*. 8. *ca*. 1. It is written the Sterred Chamber. In this Chamber euery weeke twice during the terme, and the very next day after terme, is there a Court held by the Lord Chaunceler or Keeper, and other honourable personages of the Realme. This Court seemeth to haue taken beginning from the statute *anno* 3. *H*: 7. *ca*. *pri*. Whereby it is ordained, that the Lord Chaunceler and Treasurer of England for the time being, and the Keeper of the Kings priuy seale, or two of them, calling to them a Bishop, and a temporall Lord of the Kings most honourable Councell, and the two cheife Iustices of the Kings Bench, and common place, for the time being, or other two Iustices in their absence, should haue power to call before them, and punish such misdoers, as there be mentioned. The faults that they punish, be *Routes*, *Riots*, Forgeries, *Maintenances*, *Embraceries*, Periuries, and such other *Misdemeanures* as are not sufficiently prouided for by the common law. It appeareth both by Sir *Tho*: *Smith lib*. 2. *de Rep*: *Anglo*: *cap*. 4. and by experience also, that at this day, the whole number of the Princes most honourable priuy Councell, and such other Barons spirituall, or temporall as be called thither by the Prince, haue place in this Court with those aboue named. Of this Court thus speaketh *M*. *Gwin* in the preface to his readings: It appeareth in our bookes of the termes of *K*. *Edward* 4. And of the report of cases hapning vnder the vsurpation of *Richard* the third that sometime the King and his Councell, and sometime the Lord Chaunceler, and other great personages, did vse to sit iudicially in the place then and yet called the *Starre Chamber*. But for as much as belike that assembly was not ordinary, therefore the next Kings, *Henry* the seuenth, and his sonne *H*. 8. tooke order by two seuerall lawes. *viz*. 3. *H*. 7. *ca*. *pri*. & 21. *H*. 8. *ca*. 2. That the Chaunceler assisted with others there named, should haue power to heare complaints against Retainours, Embraceours, misdemenures hures of officers, and such other offences, which through the power and countenance of such as do commit them, do lift vp the head aboue other faults: and for the which inferiour Iudges are not so meete to giue correction. And because that place was before dedicated to the like seruice, it hath bene euer since also accordingly vsed. Touching the officers belonging to this Court, see *Camden. pag.* 112. & 113.

Statute, (*statutum*) hath diuers significations in our common lawe. First, it signifieth a *Decree* or *act of Parlament*, made by the Prince and three estates, which is the bodie of the whole Realme. And though it borow the name from that kind of Decree, which those cities, that were vnder the Romaine Empire, made for the particular gouernment of themselues, ouer and aboue the vniuersall or common lawe of the Empire: yet in nature it commeth nearest to that which the Romaines called (*legem*) for that, as that was made by the whole people noble and ignoble: so this is ordeined by those, that represent the whole number, both of prince, and subiects, one and other, through the whole kingdome. The difference neuerthelesse was this, that *Lex* was offered to the consideration of the people by the Magistrate of the Senate, or Consull: but the bils or suggestions whence our statutes spring, are offered by any of either house, and so either passed or reiected. In this signification a statute is either generall or speciall. *Coke lib. 4. Hollands case, fol. 76. a.*

Statute, in another signification is a short speach taken for a bond; as statute Marchant, or statute staple. *anno* 5. *H.* 4. *cap.* 12. The reason of which name is, because these bonds are made according to the forme of statuts expressely, and particularly prouided for the same; which direct both before what persons, and in what maner they ought to be made. *West. parte pri. symbol. li.* 2. *sect.* 151. where he defineth a statute *M*erchant thus. A statute Merchant is a bond acknowledged before one of the Clerks of the statutes Merchant, and Maior or chiefe Warden of the citie of London, or two Merchants of the said citie for that purpose assigned, or before the *M*aior, cheife Warden, or Master of other Cities or good townes, or other sufficient men for that purpose appointed, sealed with the seale of the Depter, and of the *K*ing, which is of two peeces, the greater is keept by the ſaide Maior, cheiſe Warden, &c. and the leſſer peece thereof by the ſaide Clerks. The form of which bond, you may ſee in *Fleta.lib. 2.c.64.* §. *2.* to be ſuch; *Noverint universi me. N. de tali comitatu teneri. N. in 10. marcis ſoluendis eidem ad feſtum Pent. anno regni Regis, &c. & niſi fecero, concedo quod currant ſuper me & haredes meos diſtrictio, & pœna proviſa in ſtatuto domini Regis edito apud Weſtm. Datum London, tali die, an. ſupra dicto.* The fee for the ſame ſeale, is for ſtatutes knowledged in Faires. for euery pound an halfepeuy, and out of faires a farding. The execution vpon ſtatute Merchant, is firſt to take the bodie of the Deptor, if he be lay, and can be found: if otherwiſe, then vpon his lands, and goods: The bound is founded vpon the ſtatute, *anno* 13.*Ed. pri. ſtatut.*4. Of this alſo as of the ſtatute Staple, ſee the newe booke of *Entries. verbo. Statut Merchant.* and reade in *Fleta vbi ſupra*, more touching this mater worth the reading.

Satute ſtaple (to vſe the very words of *M. Weſt.*) is either properly ſo called, or improperly, A ſtatute ſtaple properly ſo called is a bond of Record knowledged before the Maior of the Staple, in the preſence of one of the two conſtables of the ſame ſtaple, for which ſeale the fee is of euery pouud, if the ſumme exceed not a 100.poũd, an halfepeny, & if it exceed an 100.poũd, of euery pound a farding. And by vertue of ſuch ſtatute Staple, the Creditor may forthwith haue execution of the body, lands & goods of the Depter. and this is founded vpon the ſtatute *anno* 27.*Ed.*3. *cap.* 9. A Statnte Staple improper, bond of Record, founded vpon the ſtatute *anno* 23.*H.* 8. *cap.* 6. of the nature of a proper ſtatute ſtaple, as touching the force, and execution thereof, and knowledged before one of the chiefe Iuſtices, and in their abſence before the Maior of the ſtaple, and Recorder of London. The formes of all theſe bonds, or ſtatutes, ſee in *Weſt. parte pri. ſimbol.li. 2.ſect.* 152. 153. 154. 155. Statutes is alſo vſed in our vulgar talke, for the petit ſeſſions, which are yearely kept for the diſpoſing of ſeruants in ſeruice, by the ſtatute, *anno* 5.*Eliz. cap.* 4. ſee *Recogniſance.*

Statute ſeſſions, otherwiſe called petit ſeſſions, are a meeting in euery hundred of all the ſhires in England, where of cuſtome they haue beene vſeu, vnto the which the conſtables doe repaire, and others both houſholders and ſeruants, for the de-

debating of differences between masters and their seruants, the rating of seruants wages, and the bestowing of such people in seruice, as being fit to serue, either refuse to seeke, or cannot get Masters, *anno* 5. *Eliz. cap.*4.

Statuto stapula, is a writ that lieth to take his body to prison, and to seise vpon his lands and goods, that hath forfeited a bond, called statut staple. *Register orig. fol.* 151.*a.*

Statutum de laboriis, is a writ Iudiciall for the apprehending of such laborers, as refuse to worke according to the statut. *Register Iudiciall. fol.* 27. *b.*

Statuto Mercatorio, is a writ for the imprisoning of him, that hath forfeited a bond called the statut Merchant, vntill the dept be satisfied. *Register orig. fol.* 146.*b.* and of these there is one against lay persons, *vbi supra.* and another against Ecclesiasticall. 148.

Stavisaker, staphis agria, vel herba pedicularis, is a medicinable herb, the kinde and vertues whereof, you haue set forth in *Gerards* herball, *lib.*1. *cap.* 130. The seede of this is mentioned among drugs to be garbled, *anno prim. Iacob. cap.* 19.

Stennerie, is vsed for the same that *Stannaries* be, in the statute *anno* 4. *H.* 8. *cap.* 8. see *Stannaries.*

Sterling (*Sterlingum*) is a proper epitheton for money current within the Realme. The name groweth from this, that there was a certain pure coyne, stamped first of all by the Easterlings here in England. *Stowes Annalls. pag.* 312. The which I rather beleeue, because in certaine old monuments of our English, and broken French, I finde it written *Esterling.* so *Ro. Hoveden* writeth it. *parte poster. annalium. fol.* 377. *b. M. Skene de verborum signif. verbo. Sterlingus*, saith thus: sterling is a kinde of weight conteining 32. cornes, or graines of wheat. And in the Canon law mention is made of fiue shillings sterling, and of a merke starling. *cap.* 3. *de arbitris. &c. c. constituit.* 12. *de procurator*: And the sterling peny is soe called, because it waighes so many graines, as I haue sundry times proued by experience. And by the law of England the peny which is called the sterling round and without clipping wayeth 32. graines of wheat without tailes, whereof 20. make an ounce, and 12. onnces a pound, and eight pound maketh a gallon of wine, and eight gallons make a bushell of London, which is the eight part of a quarter. Hitherto *M. Skene. Buchanan. lib.* 6. saith, that the common people thinke it so termed, of sterling a towne in Scotland. Our *Lyndwood* saith that it is called sterling of the bird which we call a sterling which as he noteth, was ingrauen in one quarter of the coine so termed. *cap.* I*tem quia. de testamentis. verbo. Centum solidos. in glos.*

Stewes, are those places, which were permitted in England to women of professed incontinencie, for the profer of their bodies to all commers: It is deriued from the French (*Estuves*.i. *thermæ, vaporarium, Balneum*) because wantons are wont to prepare themselues, to these venerous acts, by bathing themselues. And that this is not, newe, *Homer* sheweth in the 8. booke of his *Odiss*. where he reckoneth hot bathes among the effeminate sort of pleasures, Of these stewes see the statute *anno* 11. *Henric.* 6. *cap. pri.*

Steward. See *Seneschall* and *Stuward, Steward* of the Kings house *anno* 25. Ed. 3. *statute*. 5. *ca.* 21.

Stillyard (*Guilda Theutonicorum anno* 22. *H.* 8. *ca.* 8 *& anno* 32. *eiusdem ca.* 14.) is a place in *London*, where the fraternity of the *Easterling Merchants*, otherwise the Merchants of *Hawnse* and *Almaine. anno pri: Ed.* 6. *cap.* 13. Are wont to haue their aboade. see *Geld.* It is so called of a broad place, or courte, wherein steele was much sould, vpon the which that house is now founded. *Nathan Chitraus.* See *Hawnse.*

Stone of woll. (*Petra lanæ*) see *weights*. See *Sarpler.* It ought to weigh fourteene pounds, yet in some places by custome it is more. See *Cromptons Iustice of peace. fol.* 83. *b.*

Straife alias Stray. See *Estrie.*

Straites anno 18. *H.* 6. *ca.* 16.

Streme workes, is a kinde of worke in the *Stannaries*: for (saith *M. Camden titulo Cornwall pag.* 119.) *Horum Stannariorum siue metallicorum operum duo sunt genera: Alterum Lode-works, alterum streme-works vocant. Hoc in locis inferioribus est cùm Fossis agendis stanni venas sectantur & fluuiorum alueos subinde deflectunt: illud in locis editioribus, cùm in montibus puteos, quos Shafts vocant in magnam altitudinem defodiunt, & cuniculos agunt.* These you may read mentioned *anno* 27. *H.* 8. *ca.* 23.

Stirks.

Strip. See *Estreapement.*

Stuard, aliàs steward (*senescallus*) seemeth to be compounded of *steede* and *ward*, and is a word of many applications: yet alway signifieth an officer of cheife accoumpte within the place of his sway. The greatest of these is the Lord high Steward of England, whose power (if those antiquities

ties be true which I haue read) is next to the kings, and of that heighth, that it might in some sort match the *Ephori* amongst the *Lacedemonians*. The custome of our commonwealth hath vpon great consideration and policie brought it to passe, that this high Officer is not appointed for any long time, but onely for the dispatch of some especiall businesse, at the arraignment of some Noble man in the case of treason, or such like: which once ended, his commission expireth. Of the high Steward of *Englands* Court, you may reade *Cromptons Iurisdiction. fol.* 82.

I haue reade in an auncient manuscript of what credit, I know not, that this officer was of so great power in auncient times, that if any one had sought iustice in the Kings Court and not found it, he might vpon complaint thereof made vnto him, take those petitions, and reseruing them to the next *Parlament*, cause them there to bee propounded, and not onely so, but also in the presence of the King openly to rebuke the Chaunceler, or any other Iudge, or officer whom he found defectiue in yeelding iustice. And if in case the Iudge, or officer so reprehended, did alledge, that his defect grew from the difficultie of the case, insomuch as he durst not aduenture vpon it: then the case being shewed, and so found, the *Lord* steward together with the Constable of *England* there in the presence of the King and *Parlament*, might elect 25. persons, or more, or fewer, according to their discretion, and the case or cases in question, some *Earles*, some Barons, some *Knights*, some Citizens and Burgesses, which vpon deliberation should set downe, what they thought iust and equal: and their decree being read and allowed by *Parlament*, did stand as a law for euer: fardermore, if the Chaunceler or other Iudge or officer, could not well approue, that the delay of iustice complained of, grew from iust difficultie, by reason that the case in question was formerly determined by lawe or statute: then might the steward on the Kings behalfe, admonish him of his negligence, and will him to be more carefull and studious. Or if there appeared malice, or corruption, then the *King* and *Parlament* was wont to remoue him and assigne another of better hope to the place. Lastly, if the king had about him any such euill Counceller, as aduised him to things vniust, or vnanswerable to his *Maiestie*, as tending either to the disherison of the

Crowne

Crowne, publike hurt, or destruction of the subiect. The office of the Steward was, taking to him the Constable, and other great men, with some of the Commons, and giuing notice to the King of their intention, to send to that Counseler, and will him to desist from misleading the king, yea, if need so required, to charge him to stay no longer about him, but to depart from the Court, which if he neglected to performe, then they might send to the King, and will him to remoue him: and if the king refused, then they might take him as a publike enemie to the King and Realme, seise on his goods and possessions, and commit his body to safe custody, vntill the next Parlament, there to be Iudged by the whole kingdome: examples are brought of *Godwin* Earle of *Kent* in the time of King *Edward* next before the Conquerour, of *Hubert Burgh* Earle of the same County, in the reigne of *Henry* the third, and of *Peter Gaueston*, in *Edward* the seconds daies. But experience (as I said) hath found this officer more daungerous then profitable, and therefore hath time taught, though not wholly to suppresse him, yet to limite him to particular occasion, and to restraine his power. Then is there the Steward of the Kings most honourable houshould, *anno* 24. *H.* 8. *cap.* 13. whose name is changed to the name of *great Master. anno* 32. *eiusdem, cap.* 39 But this statute was repealed by *anno prim. Mar.* 2. *Parlam. cap.* 4 and the office of the Lord Steward of the Kings houshold reuiued: where you may at large reade diuers things touching his office. As also in *Fitzh. nat. br. fol.* 241. B. Of this Officers auncient power, reade *Fleta, lib.* 2. *cap.* 3. There is also a Steward of the *Marshalsea. pl. cor. fol.* 52. *& anno* 33. *H.* 8. *cap.* 12. To be short, this word is of so great diuersitie, that there is not a corporation of any accompt, or house of any honour, almost through the realme, but it hath an officer toward it of this name. A steward of a maner, or of a houshold, what he is or ought to be, *Fleta* fully describeth. *lib.* 2 *cap.* 71. *&* 72.

Straunger, commeth of the French (*estranger.* i. *alienare.*) It signifieth in our Language generally a man borne out of the land or vnknowne: but in the lawe, it hath an especiall signification for him that is not priuie or a party to an act: as a Straunger to a iudgement: *old na. br. fol.* 128. is he to whome a iudgement doth not belong. And in this signification it is directly contrarie to (*partie*) or (*priuie.*)

(*priuie.*) See *Priuie.*

Submarshall, (*submarescallus*) is an officer in the *Marshalsea*, that is, deputie to the chiefe Marshall of the Kings house, commonly called the Knight *Marshall*, and hath the custody of the prisoners there. *Cromptons Iurisdict. fol.* 104. He is otherwise called *Vnder-marshall.*

Subpœna, is a writ that lyeth to call a man into the Chauncerie, vpon such case onely, as the common lawe faileth in, and hath not prouided for: so as the partie who in equitie hath wrong, can haue none ordinary remedie, by the rules and course of the common lawe, *West. part. 2. symbol. titulo Proceedings in Chauncerie. sect.* 18. where you may reade many examples of such cases, as *sub pœna* lyeth in. There is also a *sub pœna ad testificandum*, which lyeth for the calling in of witnesses to testifie in a cause, as well in Chauncerie, as in other courts. And the name of both these proceede from words in the writ, which charge the partie called to appeare at the day and place assigned, *sub pœna centum librarum, &c.* I find mention of a common *sub pœna* in Cromptons *Iurisdict. fol.* 33. which signifieth nothing else but such a *sub pœna*, as euery common person is called by into the Chauncerie: whereas any Lord of Parlament is called by the *Lord* Chauncelers leters: giuing him notice of the suit intended against him, and requiring him to appeare. *Crompton. eodem.*

Subsidie, (*subsidium*) commeth of the French (*subside*) signifying a taxe or tribute assessed by Parlament, and graunted by the commons to be leuied of euery subiect, according to the value of his lands or goods after the rate of 4. shillings in the pound for land, and 2. shillings 8. pence for goods, as it is most commonly vsed at this day. Some hold opinion, that this subsidie is graunted by the subiect to the Prince, in recompence or consideration, that whereas the Prince of his absolute power, might make lawes of himselfe, he doth of fauour admit the consent of his subiects therein, that all things in their owne confession may be done with the greater indifferencie. The maner of assessing euery mans lands or goods, is this: first, there issueth a Commission out of the Chauncerie to some men of honour or worship in euery Countie, by vertue thereof to call vnto them, the head Constables or Bayliffes of euery Hundred, and by them the Constable and three or foure of the substantiallest housholders in euery towne within their hundred at a day certaine: which men so called, or so many of them, as the Commissioners thinke good to vse, do rate the inhabitants of their owne towne, in such reasonable maner, as they find meete, yet by the discretion of the said Commissioners. And then euery man after his value set downe, must at his time pay to the Collectour appointed, after the rate aforesaid. Yet in auncient time, these subsidies seeme to haue beene graunted both for other causes, as in respect of the Kings great trauell, and expences in warres: or his great fauours toward his subiects: as also in other maner then now they be: as euery ninth Lambe, euery ninth fleece, and euery ninth sheafe. *anno* 14. *Ed.* 3. *stat. prim. cap.* 20. And of these you may see great, varietie in *Rastals Abridgement. tit. Taxes, Tenths, Fifteenths, Subsidies, &c.* whence you may gather that there is no certaine rate, but euen as the two houses shall thinke good to conclude. Subsidie is in the statute of the land, sometime confounded with custome. *anno* 11. *H.* 4. *cap.* 7. See *Beneuolence.*

Suretie of peace, (*securitas pacis*) is an acknowledging of a bond to the Prince, taken by a competent Iudge of Record, for the keeping of the peace. *Lamberds Eirenarcha, li.* 2. *cap.* 2. *pag.* 77. This peace may a Iustice of peace commaund, either as a Minister, when he is willed so to doe by a higher authoritie, or as a Iudge, when he doth it of his owne power deriued from his commission. Of both these see *Lamberd. Eirenarcha. lib.* 2. *ca.* 2. *pag.* 77. see Peace, see *Supplicauit.*

Suffragan (*Suffraganeus*) is a titular Bishop ordeined, and assisted to aide the Bishop of the Dioces in his spirituall function. *c. Suffraganeus. Extra de electione.* For the Etimology, *Suffraganei dicuntur, quia eorum suffragiis causæ ecclesiasticæ iudicantur. Ioach. Stephanus de Iurisd. li.* 4. *ca.* 16. *nu.* 14. It was inacted *anno* 26. *H.* 8. *ca.* 14. that it should be lawfull to euery Diocesan at his pleasure to elect two sufficient men within his Dioces, and to present them to the King, that he might giue the one of them such title, stile, name, and dignity of sease in the saide statut specified, as he should think conuenient.

Suyte (*Secta*) commeth of the French (*Suite.i. affectatio, consecutio, sequela, comitatus*) It signifieth in our common law, a following of another, but in diuers senses, the first is a suite in in lawe, and is diuided into ſuite reall, and perſonall. *Kitchin, fol.* 74. which is all one with action reall and perſonal. Then is there ſuite of Court, or ſuite ſeruice; that is an attendance which a tenent oweth at the court of his Lord. *Fitzh. nat. br. in* Indice. *verbo Suite. ſuyte ſeruice* and *ſuyte reall, anno 7. H. 7. cap.* 2. The newe expoſitour of lawe Termes, maketh mention of foure ſorts of ſuites in this ſignification. Suite couenant, ſuite cuſtom, ſuite reall, and ſuite ſeruice. *Suite couenant*, he defineth to be, when your aunceſter hath couenanted with mine aunceſter, to ſiew to the court of mine aunceſters. *Suite cuſtome*, when I and mine aunceſters haue beene ſeiſed of your owne, and your aunceſters ſuite, time out of minde, &c. *Suite reall*, when men come to the Shyreeues Turne, or Leete, to which court all men are cōpelled to come, to knowe the lawes, ſo that they may not be ignorant of things declared there, how they ought to be gouerned. And it is called reall, becauſe of their allegance. And this appeareth by common exeperience, when one is ſworne: his oath is that he ſhall be a loyall and faithfull man to the King. And this ſuite is not for the land that he holdeth within the Countie but by reaſon of his perſon and his aboade there, and ought to be done twice a yeare: for default whereof he ſhallbe amerced and not diſtreined. I thinke this ſhould be called rather regall or royall, becauſe it is performed to the King for (royall). The French word in the vſuall pronuntiation commeth neere to reall, the leter (*o*) being almoſt ſuppreſſed. ſee *Leete*. *Suyte ſeruice*, is to ſiew to the Shyreeues Turn or Leete, or to the Lords court from three weekes to three weekes by the whole yeare. And for default thereof a man ſhall be diſtreined, and not amercied. And this ſuite ſeruice is by reaſon of the tenure of a mans land. Then doth ſuite ſignifie the following of one in chace, as freſh ſuite. *Weſt*. 1. *c*. 46. *a*. 3. *Ed*. 1. Laſtly, it ſignifieth a petition made to the prince, or great perſonage.

Suyte of the Kings *peace* (*ſecta pacis Regis*) *anno* 6. *R*. 2. *ſtat*. 2. *ca. pri.* & *anno* 21. *eiuſdem, cap*. 15. & *anno* 5. *H*. 4. *cap*. 15. is the perſiewing of a man for breach of the K. peace, by treaſons, inſurrectiōs, rebelliōs, or treſpaſſes.

Summoneas, is a writ Iudiciall of great diuerſitie, according to the diuers caſes wherein it is vſed, which ſee in the table of the *Regiſter* Iudiciall.

Summoner (*summonitor*) signifieth one vsed to call or cite a man to any court. These by the common lawe, ought to be *boni*, that is by *Fleta* his Iudgement, *liberi homines, & ideo boni, quia terras tenentes, quod sint coram talibus Iusticiariis ad certos diem, & locum secundum mandatum Iusticiariorum vicecomiti directum, parati inde facere recognitionem. lib.* 4. *cap.* 5. §. *Et cum.*

Summons (*Summonitio*) see *Sommons. Common Summons.* Marlb. *cap.* 18. *anno.* 52. Henric. 3. *is l.*

Summons in terra petita. Kitch. *fol.* 286. is that summons which is made vpon the land, which the party at whose suite the summons is sent forth, seeketh to haue, *Summons ad Warrantizandum.* Dyer *fol.* 69. *nu.* 35.

Sumage (*Summagium*) seemeth to be tolle for cariage on horseback, *Crompton Iurisd. fol.* 191. For where the Charter of the *Forest, cap.* 14. hath these words: for a horse that beareth loades euery halfe yeare, a halfe penny: the booke called *Pupilla oculi*, vseth these wordes: *pro vno equo portante summagium, per dimidium annum obolum.* It is otherwise called a *Seame*. And a Seame in the Westerne parts is a horse loade.

Superoneratione pasturæ, is a writ Iudiciall that lyeth against him who is impleaded in the County for the overburdening of a common with his catell, in case where he is formerly impleaded for it in the countie, and the cause is remooued into the Kings court at *Westm.*

Supersedeas, is a writ which lieth in diuers, and sundry cases, as appeareth by the table of the Register originall, and the Iudiciall also, and by *Fitzh. nat. br. fol.* 236. and many other places noted in the Index of his booke *verbo. Supersedeas.* But it signifieth in them all a command, or request to stay or forbeare the doing of that, which in apparence of law were to be done, were it not for the cause, whereupon the writ is graunted. For example: a man regularly is to haue surety of peace against him, of whome he will sweare that he is afraide, and the Iustice required herevnto cannot denie him. Yet if the party be formerly bound to the peace, either in Chauncerie, or elsewhere: this writ lyeth to stay the Iustice from doing that, which otherwise he might not denie.

Superstatutum, Ed. 3. *vers servants and labourers*, is a writ that lyeth against him, who keepeth my seruant departed out of my seruice against lawe. *Fitzh. nat. fo.* 167.

Super statuto de York quo nul sera viteller, &c. is a writ lying against him, that occupieth vitteling either in grosse or by retaile in a Citie, or Borough towne, during the time he is Maior, &c. *Fitzh. natur. bre. fol.* 172.

Super statuto, anno pri. Ed. 3. *cap.* 12. & 13. is a writ that lyeth against the Kings Tenent holding in cheife, which alienateth the kings land witout the Kings licence. *Fitzh: nat. br. fol.* 175.

Super statuto facto pour seneshall & Marshall de Roy, &c. is a writ lying against the Steward, or Marshall for holding plee in his court of freehould, or for trespasse, or contracts not made within the Kings houshold. *Fitzherbert nat. breu. fol.* 241.

Super statuto de Articulis Cleri, cap. 6. is a writ against the Shyreeue, or other officer, that distreineth in the Kings high way, or in the glebe land auncienlty giuen to Rectories. *Fitzh. nat. br. fol.* 173.

Super prærogatiua Regis, cap. 3. is a writ lying against the kings widow for marying without his licence. *Fitzherbert. nat. br. fol,* 174.

Supplicauit, is a writ issuing out the Chauncerie for taking the surety of peace against a man. It is directed to the Iustices of peace of the county, and the *Shyreeue:* and is grounded vpon the statute, *anno pri. Ed.* 3. *cap.* 16. which ordeineth that certaine persons in chauncerie shallbe assigned to take care of the peace, See *Fitzh. nat. br. fol.* 80. This writ was of old called *Breve de minis*, as *M. Lamberd* in his *Eirenarcha* noteth out of the *Register originall, fol.* 38.

Sur cui in vita, is a writ that lyeth for the heire of that woman, whose husband hauing alienated her land in fee, shee bringeth not the writ *Cui in vita* for the recouery of her owne land. for in this case her heire may take this writ against the tenent after her decease. *Fitzh. nat. br. fol.* 193. B.

Surgeon, commeth of the French (*Chirurgien*. i. *Chirurgus, vulnerarius*) signifiing him that dealeth in the mechanicall parte of phisicke, and the outward cures performed with the hand. The French word is compounded of two greeke words (χείρ. i. *manus*) and ἔργον. i. *opus*) And therefore are they not alowed to minister inward medicine. See the statut. 32. H. 8. *ca.* 4. and *M. Powltons* new abridgement, *titulo Surgeons*.

Surcharger of the forest, is he that doeth common with more beasts in the forest, then he hath right to common withall. *Manwood, parte* 2. of his forest lawes. *cap.* 14. *nu.*7.

Surplusage (*surplusagium*) commeth of the French (*surplus* .i. *corollarium, additamentum*) It signifieth in the common law, a superfluity or addition more then needeth, which sometime is a cause that a writ abateth. *Brooke, titulo. Nugation & Superfluity, fol.* 100. *Plowden casu Diue, contra Maningham, fol.* 63.*b*. It is sometime also applied to mater of accoumpt, and signifieth a greater disbursement, then the charge of the accoumptant amounteth vnto.

Surreioynder, is thus defined by *West. parte* 2. *symb. titulo.* Supplications. *sect.* 57. *A Surreioynder*, is a second defence of the plaintifes actiō, opposite to the *Defendants Reioynder*. And therefore (as he saith) *Hotoman* calleth it *Triplicationem, quæ est secunda actoris defensio, contra Rei duplicationem opposita*. Not *Hotoman* onely calleth this *triplicationem*: but the Emperour himselfe. *De Replicationibus, libro.* 4. *Institut: titulo.* 14.

Surrender (*sursum redditio*) is an Instrument testifiing with apt words, that the particular tenent of lands, or tenements for life or yeares, doth sufficiently consent and agree, that he which hath the next or immediate Remainder, or Reuersion thereof, shall also haue the particular estate of the same in possession: and that he yeeldeth, and giueth vp the same vnto him. For euery surrender ought forthwith to giue a possession of the things surrendred. *West: parte pri: lib.* 2. *sectio.* 503. where you may see diuers presidents. But there may be a surrender without writing. And therefore there is said to be a surrender in deede, and a surrender in law. A surrender in deede, is that which is really and sensibly performed. Surrender in law is in intendment of law by way of consequent, and not actuall. *Perkins Surrender.* 606.& *seqq.* as if a man haue a lease of a ferme, & during the terme, he accept of a new lease, this act is in law a surrender of the former. *Coke. vol.* 6. *fo.* 11.*b*.

Surfise (*supersisa*) *anno* 32. *H.*8. *ca.* 48. seemeth to be an especiall name vsed in the Castle of *Douer*, for such penalties, and forfeitures, as are laid vpon those that pay not their duties or rent for Castleward at their daies. *a.* 32. *H.*8. *ca.*48. *Bract.* hath it in a generall signification *lib.*5. *tract.* 3. *ca.* 1. *nu.* 8. and *Fleta lib.* 6. *ca.* 3. *in prin.*

Surueiour (*superuisor*) is compounded of two French words (*sur* .i. *super*) and *veoir* .i. *cernere intueri, despicere, prospicere, videre*) It signifieth in our common law, one

one that hath the ouerſeeing or care of ſome great perſonages lands, or works. As the *Surueiour* generall of the Kings maners. *Cromptons Iuriſd. fo.* 106. And in this ſignification it is taken *anno* 33. *H.* 8. *cap.* 39. where there is a court of *S*urueiours erected. And the *S*urueiour of the Wards and Liueries. *West parte* 2. *ſimbologr: titulo Chauncery: ſect:* 136. which officer is erected *anno* 33. *H.* 8. *ca.* 22. who is the ſecond officer by his place in the court of wards and Liueries, aſſigned and appointed by the king. His office ſeemeth eſpecially to conſiſt in the true examination of the lands belonging to the Kings wards, that the *K*ing be not deceiued. At the entrance into his office, he taketh an oath miniſtred vnto him by the Maiſter of that Court, which ſee *an.* 33. *H.* 8. *cap.* 39.

Surueiour of the Kings exchaunge, anno 9. *H.* 5. *ſtat.* 2. *ca.* 4. was an officer, whoſe name ſeemeth in theſe daies to be changed into ſome other. For I cannot learne that there is any ſuch now.

Suruiuour, is compounded of two French words (*Sur* .i. *ſuper*) and *viure* .i. *ætatem agere, viuere*) whence alſo commeth the compound (*Suruiure* .i. *ſupereſſe*) It ſignifieth in our common law, the longer liuer of two ioynt tenents. See *Brooke, titulo Ioynt tenents, fol.* 33. or of any two ioyned in the right of any thing.

Suſpenſion (*Suſpenſio*) is vſed for a temporall ſtop of a mans right, and differeth from extinguiſhment in this, that a Right of Eſtate ſuſpended reuiueth againe, but extinguiſhed it dyeth for euer. *Brooke, titulo* Extinguiſhment *and Suſpenſion. fol.* 314. Suſpenſion is alſo vſed in our common lawe, ſometimes as it is vſed in the Canon lawe, *pro minori excommunicatione.* As *anno* 24. *H.* 8. *cap.* 12. See *Excommunication.*

Suſpirall, ſeemeth to be a ſpring of water paſſing vnder the ground, toward a conduit or ceſterne. *anno* 35. *H.* 8. *ca.* 10. and to be deriued from the Latine (*ſuſpirare*) or the French (*ſouſpirer*) i. *ducere ſuſpiria.* And indeed the word it ſelf is French: for (*ſouſpiral*) in that tongue, ſignifieth (*ſpiramentum cauerna*) the mouth of a caue or den: or the tunnell of a chimney.

Swainmot, aliâs Swanimote, (*Swainmotum*) ſignifieth a Court touching maters of the Foreſt kept by the Charter of the *Fo*reſt, thrice in the yeare: *anno* 3 *Henr. octau. cap.* 18. it is called a *S*wannie-mote: what things be inquirable in the ſame, you may reade in *Cromptons Iuriſd. fol.* 180. who ſaith that this court of *S*wainemote is as incident

cident to a Forest, as the court of Piepowder is to a faire, with whome agreeth *M. Manwood parte pri. of his Forest lawes, pag.* 144. The word seemeth to be compounded of (*Swain*) and (*mot*) or (*Gemot*). For swaine, as *M. Manwood* saith *vbi supra, pag.* 111) in the Saxons tongue signifieth a *Bockland* man, which at this day is taken for a Charterer, or freeholder: and (*Gemot*) as *M. Lamberd* saith in his explication of Saxon words, *verbo Conventus*, is *Conventus*, wherevpon it is to be noted, as he saith in the same place, that the Swainemote is a court of freeholders within the Forest. Of the which you may reade him at large, *pag.* 110. *&c. vsque* 122.

T

T*Abling of fines*, is the making of a table for euery countie, where his Maiesties writ runneth, conteining the contents of euery fine, that shall passe in any one terme, as the name of the Countie, townes, and places, wherein the lands or tenements mentioned in any fine, do lye, the name of the plaintiffe and Deforceant, and of euery maner named in the fine. This is to be done properly by the *Chirographer* of fines of the common plees: who the first day of the next terme after the engrossing of any such fine, shall fixe euery of the said tables in some open place of the court of Common plees: and so euery day of the said terme during the sitting of the said court. And the said Chirographer shall deliuer to the Shyreeue of euery Countie, his Vndershyreeue or Deputie, faire writen in parchment, a perfect content of the table so to be made for that shire, in the terme that shall be next before the Assises to be holden in the same countie, or else in the meane time betweene the terme, and the said assises, to be set vp the first day, and euery day of the next assises, in some open place of the Court, where the Iustices of Assises then shall sit, to continue there so long, as they shall sit in the said court. If either the Chirographer, or Shyreeue faile herein, he forfeiteth fiue pounds. And the Chirographers fee for euery such table is foure pence. *anno* 23. *Elizab. cap.* 3. This saith, *West. parte* 2. *symbol. titulo. Fines, sect.* 130.

Taile (*Tallium*) commeth of the French (*taile*. i. *Sectura*) or the verb (*tailler*. i. *scindere*) signifiing in our common law two seuerall things, both grounded vpon one reason. *Plowden, casu Wil-*

*lion, fol.*251.*a.b.* First it is vsed for the fee, which is opposite to fee simple: by reason that it is so (as it were) minced, or pared, that it is not in his free power to be disposed of him which owneth it: but is by the first giuer cut, or diuided from all other, and tyed to the issue of the *Donee. Cooke lib.* 4. *in proœmio.* And this limitation, or taile, is either generall, or speciall. *Taile generall* is that, whereby lands, or tenements are limited to a man, and to the heires of his body begotten. And the reason of this terme is, because how many soeuer women, the tenent houlding by this title, shall take to his wiues, one after another in lawfull matrimony; his issue by them all, haue a possibility to inherit, one after the other. *Taile speciall* is that, whereby lands, or tenements be limited vnto a man and his wife, and the heires of their two bodies begotten: because if the man bury his wife before issue, and take another: the issue by this second wife cannot inherit the land, &c. Also if land should be giuen to a man and his wife, and to their sonne and heire *Iohn*, for euer: this is taile especiall. See more of this in fee. and *Litleton lib. pri: ca.* 2. and the new booke of *Entries. verbo Taile. Taile* in the other signification, is that which we vulgarly call a Tallie. For it is *vne taille de bois* a clouen peece of wood to nick vp an accoumpt vpon, for in the statute *anno* 10. *Ed. pri. cap.* 11. and *anno* 27. *eiusdem, stat. pri. ca.* 2. it is termed a *Taile*, and *anno* 38. *Ed* 3. *cap.* 5. And so in *Brooke* his *Abridgement, titulo. Taile d' Exchequer fol.* 247. See *Tayles.*

Tailes (*tallia*) are in these daies called Talleyes, well knowne what they be. Of these reade in our statutes two sorts, to haue bene vsuall in the Exchequer for a long continuance. The one is tearmed tayles of debt, *anno* 1. R. 2. *cap.* 5. which are a kind of acquittance for dept paide in to the king. For example, the Vniversitie of *Cambridge* payeth yearely ten pounds, for such things as are by their Charter graunted them in fee ferme, fiue pounds at the Annunciation and fiue at Michaelmas. He that payeth the first fiue pounds, receiueth for his discharge a taile or taley, and he that payeth the other fiue, receiueth the like. With both which, or notes of them, he repayreth to the Clerke of the Pipes office, and there in steede of them receiueth an acquittance in parchment for his whole discharge. Then be there also mentioned tayles of reward, *anno* 27. *H.* 8. *cap.* 11. & *anno* 33. & 34. *eiusdem ca.* 16. and *anno* 2. & 3. *Ed.* 6. *ca.* 4. And

4. And these seeme to be tailes, or talyes of allowances, or recompence made to Shyreeues for such maters, as to their charge they haue performed in their office, or for such monies as they by course haue cast vpon them in their accompts, but could not leauie thẽ where they were due. And these, as it seemeth by the said statute, *anno* 27. H. 8. *cap.* 11. were of old graunted in the Exchequer vnto them, vpon warrant made to the Treasurer and Chamberlaines there, by the Clerkes of the signet vpon bill assigned by the King. But sithence the statute *anno* 2. *&* 3. *Ed.* 6. *cap.* 4. what the course in this case is, I am not so well informed. Only I heare, that for some counties these tayles be still in vse, and that the warrant commeth now from the Auditour of the receipts, vnto those that make these taleys. And that the Shyreeue with them proceedeth to those who take his finall accompt, and there hath his allowance accordingly.

Taylage (tallagium) aliàs, Tallage, commeth of the French (*taille*) which originally signifieth a peece cut out of the whole: and metaphorically is vsed for a share of a mans substance payed by way of tribute. It signifieth with vs a tolle, or taxe, as *anno pri. Ed.* 2. *cap. vnico.* And *Stowes Annals. pag.* 445. Thence commeth *Tailagiers in Chawcer* for taxe, or tolle gatherers.

Taint (Attinctus) commeth of the French (*teinct.* i. *infectus, tinctus*) and signifieth either substantiuely a conviction, or adiectiuely a person convicted of felonie or treason, &c. See *Attaint.*

Tales, is a latine word of knowne signification: It is vsed in our common lawe, for a supply of men empaneled vpon a iury or enquest, and not appearing, or at their apparence, chalenged by the partie, or either partie, if there be two, as not indifferent. for in this case, the Iudge vpon petition graunteth a supply to be made by the Shyreeue of some men there present, equall in reputation to those that were impaneled. And herevpon the very act of supplying is called a *Tales de Circumstantibus.* This supply may be one or more, and of as many as shall either make defaulte, or els be chalenged by each party. *Stawf. pl. cor. lib.* 3. *ca.* 5. How be it, he that hath had one Tales, either vpon default or challenge: though he may haue another,

ther, yet he may not haue the later to conteine so many as the former, for the first Tales must be vnder the principall panell, except in a cause of Appeale, and so euery *T*ales lesse then other, vntill the number be made vp of men present in courte, and such as are without exception to the partie, or parties. Of this see *Stawnford* more at large *vbi supra*. where you may finde some exceptions to this generall rule. These commonly called (*Tales*) may in some sort, and in deede are called (*Meltores*) *viz.* when the whole Iurie is chalenged, as appeareth by *Brooke, titulo*. *Octo tales & auter tales, fol.* 105. In whome you may likewise reade many cases touching this mater.

Tales, is the proper name of a booke in the *Kings* bench office. *Coke lib.* 4. *fol.* 93. *b.*

Tallage. See *Taylage*.

Talshide. See *Talwood*.

Talwood, v. anno 34. & 35. *Henric. octau. capit.* 3. & *anno* 7. *Ed.* 6. *ca.* 7. & 43. *El. cap.* 14. *Talshide. ibidem*. It is a long kinde of shide riuen out of the tree, which shortened is made into billets.

Tartaron, anno 12. *Ed.* 4. *cap.* 3. & *anno* 4. *H.* 8. *cap.* 6.

Tasels. anno 4. *Ed.* 4. *cap.* 1. is a kinde of hard burre vsed by clothiers and cloth workers in the dressing of cloth.

Task, aliàs Taxe, by *M. Camden* following the authoritie of *Doctor Powell* (whome he greatly commendeth for his diligence in the search of antiquities) is a Britishe word signifiing tribute. *Camden. Britan. pag.* 304. And it seemeth, it is such a kinde of tribute, as being certainly rated vpon euery towne, was wont to be yearely paide. See *Gild*, and the places there cited out of M. *Camden*. Now is it not paide, but by consent giuen in Parlament, as the *Subsidie* is. And it differeth from Subsidie in this, that it is alway certaine, accordingly as it is set downe in the Chequer booke, and leuied in generall of euery towne, and not particularly of euerie man. Lastly, it is a fifteenth of that substance, that euery town was first rated at, by the number of hides of land in the same. Wherevpon it is also called a fifteenth *v. anno* 14. *Ed.* 3. *stat.* 1. *cap.* 20. for whereas *M. Crompton in his Iurisdictions*, saith that it is leuied somtime by goods, as well as by lands, as also appeareth by the statute, *anno* 9. *H.* 4. *ca.* 7. I take his meaning there to be, that though the task in the whole were at the first by the Prince proportioned by the land: Yet the townes men among themselues to make vp that summe, are at these daies sometime valued by goods. See *Fiftenth*. It seemeth that in auncient times, this task was imposed by the king at his pleasure, but *Edward* the first, *anno* 25. of his raigne, bound himselfe, and his successours from that time forward, not to leuie it but by the consent of the Realme. *anno* 25. *Ed. pri. cap.* 5. The word Task may be thought to proceede from the French (*Taux, aliàs Taxe*. i. *æstimatio, pretium*) for we call it also *Taxe*: but ouer curiously to contend in these derivatiōs, may seeme friuolous, cōsidering that many words are common to diuers peoples.

Telonium, or *Breue essendi quietum de Telonio*, is a writ lying for the Citizens of any Citie, or Bourgesses of any towne that haue a Charter, or prescription to free them from Tolle, against the officers of any town, or market constraining them to pay Tolle of their *Merchandise*, contrary to their said graunt or prescription. *Fitzh. nat. br. fol.* 226. *Hotoman lib.* 2. *commentariorum in feuda, cap.* 56. *vers. Vectigalia*, hath these words: *Telonia autem dicuntur, publicanorum stationes in quibus vectigalia recipiunt: sed apud istius generis scriptores, Telonium dicitur vectigal, quod pro pontium aut riparum munitione penditur: & plerumq; à principibus solius exactionis causa, imperatur.*

Team, aliàs Theam, is an ould Saxon word, signifiing a Royalty granted by the *Kings* charter, to a Lord of a maner. *Bracton li.* 3. *tracta.* 2. *ca.* 8. of this Saint *Edwards* lawes, *nu.* 25. say thus. *Quod si quisquam aliquid interciet (id est, penes alium defendat) super aliquem, & intercitatus, non poterit warantum suum habere, erit forisfactura sua, & Iusticia similiter de calumniatore, si defecerit. M. Skene de verborum significatione, verbo Theme.* saith, that it is a power to haue seruants and slaues, which are called *natiui, bondi, villani*; and all Baronies infeoffed with *Theme*, haue the same power. For vnto them all their bondmen, their children, goods and cattels, properly appertaine: so that they may dispose of them, at their pleasure. And in some ould authentike bookes it is writen. *Theme est potestas habendi natiuos, ita quòd generationes villanorum vestrorum, cum eorum catallis, vbicunq; inueniantur, ad vos pertineant, Theme* commeth from *Thian* .i. *seruus*, and therefore some time signifieth the bondmen, and slaues, according to an ould statute and law. *De curia de Theme.*

me. Quod si quis teneat curiam de Theme, & illa querela in illa curia mouetur, ad quam Theme *vocatur: non debet illa curia elongari, sed ibidem determinari, & omnes Theme ibi compareant.* Which is vnderstoode of the question of liberty, when it is in doubt, whether any person be a bondman or free man. Which kinde of proces should not be delayed but summarily discided. And the new expositonr of law terms. speaketh to the like effect, *verbo Them.* I read it also in an ould paper writen by an exchequer man thus translated: T*heam* .i. *propago villanorum.*

Teller, is an officer in the Eschequer, of which sort their be foure in number. And their office is, to receiue all monies due to the King, and to giue to the clerk of the Pel a bill to charge him therewith. They also pay to all persons, any money paiable vnto them by the King, by warrant from the auditour of the receipt. They also make weekely and yearely bookes both of their receipts & payments, which they deliuer to the L. Treasurer.

Templers (T*emplarii*) See *Knights of the Temple*. These whil lest they florished here in England, which seemeth to be all that time betweene *Henry* the seconds daies, vntill they were suppressed, had in euery nation a particular gouernour, whom *Brac.* calleth *Magistrū militia Tēpli:l.1.c.10.* Of these read *M. Cam.* in his *Br.p.*320. See *Hospitalers.*

Temporalties of Bishops (*Temporalia Episcoporum*) be such reuenewes, lands, and tenements, as Bishops haue had laid to their Sees by the Kings and other great personages of this land from time to time, as they are Barons, and Lords of the Parlament. See *Spiritualties of Bishops.*

Tend, seemeth to signifie, as much as to indeuour, or offer, or shew forth, to tend the estate of the party of the Demaundant, *old n.br.f.* 123. *b.* to tend to trauers. *Stawnf: prærog. fol.* 96. to tend an auertment. *Britton, cap.* 76.

Tender, seemeth to come of the French (*Tendre* .i. *tener, delicatus*) and being vsed adiectiuely, signifieth in english speech, as much as it doth in French. But in our common law, it is vsed as a verb: and betokeneth as much, as carefully to offer, or circumspectly to indeuour the performance of any thing belonging vnto vs: as to tender rent, is to offer it at the time and place where and when it ought to be paid. To tender his law of *non Summons. Kitch. fo.* 197. is to offer himselfe ready to make his law, whereby to prooue that he was not summoned. See *law*. See *make.*

Tenementis legatis, is a writ that

that lyeth to *London*, or other corporation, where the custome is, that men may demise tenements by their last will, as well as their goods and catels, to whome they list, for the hearing of any controuersie touching this mater, and for the rectifying of the wrong. *Regist. orig. fol.* 244. *b.*

Tenant, aliâs, tenent, (tenens) commeth either of the Latine *(tenere)* or of the French *(tenir)* and signifieth in our common lawe, him that possesseth lands, or tenements by any kind of right, be it in fee, for life, or for yeares. This word is vsed with great diuersitie of Epithits in the lawe, sometime signifying or importing the efficient cause of possession, as tenent in Dower: which is shee, that possesseth land,&c. by vertue of her Dower. *Kitchin, fol. 160. Tenent per statute Merchant. Idem, fol. 172.* that is, he that holdeth land by vertue of a statute forfeited vnto him. *Tenent in franck mariage. Kitchin, fol.* 158. *viz.* he that holdeth land or tenement by reason of a gift thereof made vnto him vpon mariage, betweene him and his wife. *Tenent by the courtesie.* Idem. *fol.* 159 i. he that holdeth for his life by reason of a child begotten by him of his wife being an inheritrix, and borne aliue. *Tenent per elegit.* Idem, *fol.* 172. i. he that holdeth by vertue of the writ termed *Elegit. Tenent in mortgage. idem, fol.* 38. is he that holdeth by vertue of a mortgage or vpon condition, that if the lessour pay so much money at such a day, that he may enter, and if not, that the leassee shall haue a fee simple, fee tayle, or free hould. Sometime these Epithites import the maner of admittance: as tenent by the verge in auncient demesn. *Idem. fol.* 81. is he that is admitted by the rod in a court of auncient demesne. Sometime the euidence, that he hath to shew for his estate: as Tenent by copy of court rolle, which is one admitted Tenent of any lands,&c. within a maner, that time out of the memorie of man, by the vse and custome of the said maner, haue bene demisable, and demised to such as will take the same in fee, fee-tayle, for life, yeares, or at will, according to the custome of the said maner. *West parte prim. sym. lib.2. se.646.* whom reade more at large. Againe, *Tenent by charter*, is he that holdeth by feofment in writing or other deede. *Kitchin, fol.* 57. Sometime these Epithites signifie that dutie which the tenent is to performe by reason of his tenure. As *Tenent by* Knights *seruice, Tenent in socage*, T*enent in burgage*, Tenent *in frank fee, Tenent in villenage.* Sometime they import the estate of the tenent, or his continuance in the land, as Tenent in fee simple. *Kitchin, fol. 150.* Tenent in fee taile, *Idem fol. 153.* Tenent for life, and tenent for yeares: *Idem, fol. 163.* Tenent at the will of the Lord according to the custome of the maner. *Idem fol. 132. & 165.* Tenent at will by the common law. *Idem, eodem.* Tenent vpon sufferance. *Idem, fol. 165.* Tenent of state of inheritance. *Stawnf: prærog. fol. 6.* Sometime they containe a relation toward the Lord of whom he houldeth, as Tenent in cheife .i. he that houldeth of the *King* in the right of his crowne. *Fitz. nat: br. fol. 5. F.* Tenent of the King, as of the person of the King. *Idem, eodem.* or as of some honour. *eodem:* Very tenent .i. he that houldeth immediately of his Lord. *Kitchin fol. 99.* For if there be Lord *Mesn.* and Tenent, the Tenent is very Tenent to the *mesn*, but not to the Lord aboue. *Tenent par auaile, pl. cor: fo. 197. & Fitzh. nat. br. fol. 136. D.* is the lowest tenent, and fardest distant from the Lord Paramont. It seemeth to be tenent *per auaile. See Diers commentaries fol. 25. nu. 156.* Noe tenent in right to the *Lord*, but Tenent as for the avowrie to be made, *Litleton, fol. 96.* Sometime they haue a relation betweene Tenents, and Tenents in seuerall kindes, as ioynt tenents .i. they that haue equall right in lands and tenements, and all by vertue of one title. *Litleton, li. 3. ca. 3.* Tenents in common, be they that haue equall right, but hold by diuers titles, as one or more by gift or descent, and others by purchase. *Idem, eod. cap. 4.* Particular tenent. *Stawnf. prærog. fol. 13.* that is, he which holdeth onely for his terme, as tenent in dower, tenent by the courtesie, or otherwise for life, *West parte 2. symbol. titulo. Fines. sect. 13. G.* See *anno 32. H. 8. ca. 31.* and *Cooke in Sir William Pelhams case. lib. 1. fol. 15. a.* they be termours for yeares or life. See *Plowden casu Colthirst. fol. 23. b.* Sole tenent, *Kitchin 134.* i. he that hath none other ioyned with him. If a man and his wife hold for both their liues, and the man dyeth, he dieth not sole tenent, *Idem eodem.* Seuerall tenent, is opposite to ioynt tenents or tenents in common. See *Seuerall tenencie. Tenent al præcipe,* is he, against whom the writ (*Præcipe*) is to be brought. *Cookes Reports. lib. 3. the case of fines. fol. 88. a.* Tenent in demesn, *anno 13. Ed. 1. cap. 9. anno 32. H. 8. cap. 37.* is he that holdeth the demeanes of a maner for a rent without seruice. Tenent in seruice,

seruice, *an.* 20. *Ed.* 1. *stat. pri.* is he that holdeth by seruice *v. Britton. cap.* 79. *in principio*, & *ca.* 96. Car *fealte*, &c. *vel quare* whether he may be termed tenent in demesne, that holdeth some of the Demeanes howsoeuer, and he tenent in seruice, which is a freehoulder to a maner houlding by seruice, for the free houlds of a manner are not accounted of the demesne, but onely that which the Lord keepeth in his owne hand or letteth out by copie, according to the custome of the maner. Tenent by execution *an.* 32. *Henr.* 8. *cap.* 5. is he that holdeth land by vertue of an execution vpon any statute, recognisance, &c.

Tendeheved (*decanus, vel caput decem familiarum*) of this see Roger *Hoveden, parte poster. suorum annalium. fol.* 346. *a.* See *Frank pledge.*

Tenement (*Tenementum*) is diuersly vsed in the common lawe, Most properly it signifieth a house or home stall: but in a larger signification it is taken for either house or land that a man holdeth of another. And ioyned with the adiectiue (*Frank*) in our lawyers French, it conteineth generally lands or houses, yea or offices, wherein we haue estate for terme of life, or in fee. And in this signification, *Kitchin, fol.* 41. maketh frank tenement, and base estate opposite the one to the other. In the same sort doth *Britton* vse it, through his whole 27. chapter, as also *Bracton* doeth the latine (*liberum tenentum*) *lib. pri. cap.* 5. & 6. and many other places.

Tenentibus in assisa non onerandis, &c. is a writ that lieth for him to whome a disseisour hath alienated the land whereof he disseised another, that he be not molested for the dammages awarded, if the *Disseisour* haue wherewith to satisfie them him selfe. *Register orig. fol.* 214. *b.*

Tenths (*Decima*) is that yearely portion or tribute, which all liuings ecclesiasticall doe yeeld to the king. For though the Bishop of *Rome* doe originally pretend right vnto this revenewe, by example of the high preist among the Iewes, who had tenths from the *Levites, Numb. cap.* 8. *Hieronimus in Ezechielem.* yet I read in our Chronicles that these were often graunted to the *King* by the *Pope*, vpon diuers occasions, sometime for one yeare, sometime for more, vntill by the statute, *anno* 26. *Hen.* 8. *cap.* 3. they were annexed perpetually to the Crown. See *Disms.* It signifieth also a taske leuied of the temporalty. *Holinshed. H.* 2. *f.* 111.

Te-

Tenore indictamenti mittendo, is a writ whereby the Record of an indictment, and the proces thereupon, is called out of another court into the chauncerie. *Register orig. fol.* 169.*a.*

Tenure (*Tenura*) commeth of the Norman (*Teneure*) as appeareth by the Grand Custumarie: *cap.* 28. where it is defined to this effect: Tenure is the maner, whereby tenements are houlden of their Lords. What may make a tenure and what not, see *Perkins Reseruations,* 70. And in that chapter shall you finde the most of those tenures recited, that be now vsually in England. In Scotland I finde that there be foure maner of tenures, which they call halding of land; the first is *pura eleemozina,* which is proper to spirituall men, paying nothing for it, but *deuota animarum suffragia*: the second they call Few, or few ferme, which houldeth of the King, Church, Barons, or others, paying a certaine duty called *Feudi firma.* The third is a hould in (*Blench*) as they terme it, by payment of a peny, rose, paire of guilt spurs, or some such like thing, if it be asked, in name of *Blench, id est nomine albæ firmæ.* The fourth is by seruice of ward, and relieue, where the heire being *minor,* is in the gard or custody of his Lord, togither with his lands, &c. And land houlden in this fourth maner, is called there *feudum de Hauberk,* or *Haubert.* or *feudum militare,* or *feudum Hauberticum,* or *feudum loricatum*: because it is giuen vpon condition, that the vassall possessor therof, shall come to the host with a Iack, or *Haubert* which is a coate of maile. *M. Skene de verb: significa: verbo. Haubert. Tenure* in grosse, is the Tenure in *Capite.* For the Crowne is called a Seignory in grosse, because it consisteth as a corporation of and by it selfe, not tyed to any honour, or maner. See *Cromptons Iurisd: fol:* 206. See the new booke of *Entries, verbo* Tenure.

Term (*Terminus*) signifieth with vs commonly, the bounds and limitation of time: as a lease for terme of life or terme of yeares. *Bracton lib.* 2. *cap.* 6. *nu.* 4. But most notoriously it is vsed for that time, wherein the Tribunals, or places of Iudgement are open to all that list to complaine of wrong, or to seeke their right by course of law, or action. The rest of the yeare is called vacation. Of these terms there be foure in euery yeare: during the which, maters of Iustice (for the most part) are dispatched. and this Sir *Tho. Smith lib.* 3. *de Rep. Ang: cap.* 2. reckoneth as miraculous: that in lesse time then the third part of the yeare, three Tribunals, all in one city, should certifie the wrongs of so large and populous a nation, as England is. Of these terms one is called *Hilary* terme which beginneth the 23. of Iannuary, or if that be Sunday, the next day following, and endeth the 21. of February. Another is called Easter terme, which beginneth 18. daies after Easter and endeth the munday next after Ascension day. The third is Trinity terme, beginning the Friday next after Trinity Sūday, and ending the Wedensday fortnight after. The fourth is Michaelmas terme, beginning the 9 of October, or if that be Sunday, the next day after, and ending the 28. of Nouember.

Termor (*Tenens ex termino*) is he that houldeth for terme of yeares or life. *Kitchin fol.* 151. *Litleton fol.* 100.

Terra extendenda, is a writ directed to the *Escheatour, &c.* willing him to inquire and find the true yearely value of any land, &c. by the oath of twelue men, and to certifie the extent into the Chauncerie, &c. *Regist. orig. fol.* 293. *b.*

Terris, bonis & catallis rehabendis post purgationem, is a writ that lyeth for a Clerke to recouer his lands, goods, or chatels formerly seised on, after he hath cleared himselfe of that felonie, vpon suspition whereof he was formerly conuicted, and deliuered to his Ordinarie to be purged. *Regist. orig. fol.* 68. *b.*

Terris liberandis, is a writ, that lyeth for a man conuicted by attaint, to bring the *Record* and processe before the *King*, and to take a fine for his imprisonment, and to deliuer him his lands and tenements againe, and to release him of the *Strip* and *Waste*. *Regist. orig. fol.* 232. *a.* It is also a writ for deliuery of lands to the heire after homage, and reliefe performed. *eodem fol.* 293. *b.* or vpon securitie taken, that he shall performe them. *eodem, fol.* 313. *b.*

Terris & catallis tentis vltra debitum levatum, is a writ Iudiciall, for the restoring of lands or goods to a deptour that is distrained aboue the quantitie of the dept. *Register Iudiciall. fol.* 38. *b.*

Terretenent, (*terratenens*) is he, which hath the naturall, and actuall possession of the land, which we otherwise call the occupation. *anno* 39. *Eliz. cap.* 7. For example, a Lord of a manner hath a freeholder, who letteth out his free land to another to be occupied: this occupier is called the *Terretenent*. *West. parte* 2. *symb. titulo.* Fines. *sect.* 137. *Cromptons Iurisd. fol.* 194. *Britton. cap.* 29. *Perkins feofments.* 231. And *Petrus Belluga in speculo Principum, um. Rub. 46. versiculo, Restat videre num. 9.* vseth this word *Terratenentes* in the same signification. See *Land tenents.* Yet I haue heard some learned in the lawe say, that the *Tertenent*, is the tenent in free, or copyhold, according to the custome of the maner, and opposite to tenent for terme of yeres. *Quare.*

Ters, is a certaine measure of liquide things, as wine, oyle, &c. conteining the sixth part of a Tunne. *anno 32. H. 8. cap. 14.* or the third part of a pipe.

Testament, (*testamentum.*) See *Will.*

Testatum, is a writ that seemeth especially to lye against great personages of the realm, whose bodies may not be medled with in actions of dept. And therefore if the Shyreeue return, (*nihil habet in balliva mea*) in a case of execution, another writ shall be sent out into any other Countie, where such personage is thought to haue whence to satisfie, which is termed a *Testatum*, because the Shyreeue hath formerly testified, that he found nothing in his Bayliweeke to serue the turne. See *Kitchin* in his Returnes of writs. *fol.* 287. *b.*

Teste, is a word commonly vsed for the last part of any writ: so called, because the very conclusion of euery writ wherein the date is contained, beginneth with these words, (*teste meipso, &c.*) If it be an originall writ, or if iudiciall, *teste Thom. Flemming*, or *Edovardo Cooke*, according to the Court whence it commeth. Where I may note by the way, that in *Glanvile lib. pri. cap. 6. & 13. & lib. 2. cap. 4.* I find the forme of an originall writ in the last clause to be (*teste Ranulpho de Glanvilla apud Clarindon, &c.* And diuers times in the Register *orig. Teste custode Angliæ*: as namely, in the title *Prohibition. fol. 42. a.* and *Consultation, fol. 54. b.*

Thanus, is a made Latin word of the Saxon (*thegn*) which commeth of (*thenian.* i. *alicui ministrare.*) It signifieth sometime a Noble man, somtime a free man, sometime a Magistrate, somtime an Officer, or minister. *Lamb.* in in his Explication of Saxon words. *verbo Thanus.* See the place. See *vavasour. M. Skene de verbor. signif.* saith, it is the name of a dignitie, and appeares to be equall with the sonne of an Earle. And *Thanus* was a free holder holding his lands of the King. And a man not taken with the *fang* (that is, with the maner, as we say,) accused of theft, no sufficient proofe being brought against him, must purge himselfe by the oath of 27. men, or of three *Thanes. Tha-*

nagium Regis, signifieth a certaine part of the *Kings* lands, or propertie, whereof the rule and gouernement appertaineth to him, who therefore is called *Thanus*. For *Domania Regis*, and *Thanagia, idem significant*. It is a *Dutch* word: For *(teiner)* signifieth a seruant, and *teinen* to serue. And *thane* is likewise a seruant, and *vnder-thane*, an inferiour *thane* or subiect. Thus farre *M. Skene*.

Thacktile. anno 17. Ed. 4. cap. 4. otherwise called *plaine tyle*, is that tile which is made to be layed vpon the side, and not vpon the rudge of a tyled house. *anno* 17. *Ed. 4. cap.* 4.

Theam. See *Team.*

Theft (furtum) is an vnlawfull felonious taking away of another mans moueable, and personall goods against the owners will, with an intent to steale them. *West. parte 2. symbol. titulo Inditements. sect.* 58. where also he saith, that theft is from the person or in presence of the owner, or in his absence. Theft from the person or in presence of the owner, is of two sorts: the one putting the owner in feare, the other not. *Idem, eodem, sect.* 59. The former is properly called *Robberie. ibid. sect.* 60. The new expounder of lawe termes, *verbo Larcenie*, diuideth theft into theft so simply called, and petit or litle theft. Whereof the one is of goods aboue the value of twelue pence, and is felonie, the other vnder that value, and is no felonie. But see *Felonie.*

Theftbote, is made of *(theft)* and *(boote)* i. *compensatio*, and signifieth properly the receiuing of goods from a theefe, to the end to fauour, and maintaine him. The punishment whereof is raunsome and imprisonment, and not losse of life and member. *Stawnf. pl. cor. lib. prim. cap.* 43. and the myrror of Iustices. *lib. 2. cap. des peches criminels al sute le Roye.* And yet he there maketh mention of a Record alledged, which testified a iudgement of life and member giuen in this case.

Thegue. See *Thanus*, and *Thingus.*

Them. See *Team.* It signifieth *acquietantiam amerciamentorum sequela propriorum servorum. Fleta lib. prim. cap. 47. §. Theme.*

Thelonium. See *Tholle*, and *Tholonium*, and *Tolle.*

Theolonio rationabili habendo pro Dominis habentibus Dominica Regis ad firmam, is a writ, that lyeth for him, that hath of the *Kings* demesne in fee ferme, to recouer reasonable tolle of the Kings tenents there, if that his demesn haue bene accustomed to be tolled. *Register origin. fol.*

fol. 87. *b.*

Thingus. *Cromptons Iurisd. fol.* 197. seemeth to be vsed for the Saxon *Thegne.* See *Thanus.* His words are these, speaking of a Charter or Graunt made by a Lord of a Forest. *Scietis me concessisse omnibus militibus, & omnibus thingis, & omnibus liberè tenentibus, qui manent in Foresta mea de Honore de* Lancaster, *quòd possunt, &c. Fleta* writeth it *Tlem,* & saith, *quòd significat liberum.*

Then, significat servum. Fleta li. prim. cap. 47. See *Thanus,* and *Thingus.*

Thridborow, is vsed for a constable. *anno* 28. H. 8. *cap.* 10. which also is noted by *M.* Lamberd in his Tractate intituled: The dutie of Constables, *pag.* 6. which seemeth to be corruptly vsed for the *Saxon* (*freoborh.* i. *ingenuus fideiussor,*) or (*freborhesheofod.* i. *vas primarius*) *Idem.* in his explication of Saxon words. *verbo. Centuria.*

Thrid with hawan man (*trium noctium hospes*) who if he did any harme, his host, by the lawes of Saint Edward, and of the Conquerour, was answerable for the harme. *Rogerus Hoveden parte poster. suorum annal. fol.* 345.

Thokes of fish, anno 22. Ed 4. *cap.* 2.

Tholl (*Thelonium*) *est libertas emendi, & vendendi in terra sua. Archainom. Lamb. fol.* 132. See *Toll.*

Thraue of corne, anno 2. *H.* 6. *ca.* 2. consisteth of two shookes: and euery shoke conteineth 6. sheaues. It seemeth to be a word proper to the north parts.

Thrimsa, commeth of (*Threo*) that is three, and signifieth a peece of money of three shillings. *Lamb. expli. of Saxons words. verbo Thrimsa.*

Tilsen of saten, anno 1. *H.* 8. *ca.* 14.

Tincell, commeth of the French (*Estincelle.* i. *scintilla*) or the verb (*Estinceller.* i. *scintillare*) It signifieth with vs a stuffe or cloath made partly of silke and partly of gold or siluer, so called because it glistereth or sparkleth like starres.

Tissu, is a French word signifiing as much as (wouen) Cloth of Tissue, with vs cloth of silke and siluer, or of silke, and gould wouen togither.

Tithe (*Decima*) seemeth to be an abbreuiat of (tything) being the *Saxon* (*Teothung*) a litle altered, which signifieth *Decuriam, Lamb. explica. of Saxon words. verbo. Decuria.* It signifieth in our common lawe, the tenth part of all fruites prediall, or personall, which be due to God, and so consequently to his Minister, toward the recompence of his paines taken in instructing his charge, how to liue after Gods commandements, and his continuall intercession that he doth or ought to make vnto God for their both spirituall and temporal blessings *Leuit. cap.* 27. *versu.* 30. I say the tenth part, though *Couarruvias* with other learned Canonists and Scholemen, hold the rate of tithes, not to be necessarily the tenth part of the fruites by the morall lawe of God. Yet the beter and more theologicall opinion is, that they are all deceiued, and that from their errour hath sprong much wrong to almighty God, and greate mischief to his church: & that by the law of God and nature no contrary custome ought to last any longer, then the parson and parishioner shall both thinke well of it. Wherefore those customes of paying a halfepeny for a lambe, or a pennie for a calfe by such as haue vnder seuen in one yeare, how long so euer it hath indured, is but very vnreasonable in these daies, when both lamb and calues are growne foure times deerer, and more then they were when this price was first accepted. And therefore no man dischargeth well his conscience in this point that paieth not duly the tenth of euery Lamb, euery calfe, and euery other thing titheable. For by this course the minister fareth well or euill in a proportion with his parishioner, as it pleaseth God to giue increase, whereas by any other order the one or the other shall finde want of indifferencie, as the prices of things shall rise or fall.

Tithing (*Tithingum*) is the Saxon word *Teothung* for the which see (*Tithe*) It signifieth (as *M. Lamb.* saith in his dutie of Constables) the number or company of ten men with their families cast, or knit together in a societie, all of them being bound to the King for the peaceable and good behauiour of each of their societie. Of these companies was there one cheife or principall person, who of his office was called (*Teothung man*) at this day in the West parts (*Tithingman*) But now he is nothing but a Constable. For that old discipline of Tithings is left long sithence. It signifieth also a court, *anno* 23. *Ed.* 3. *cap.* 4. & *anno* 9. *H.* 3. *cap.* 35. See *Chiefe Pledge* and *Frank pledge*, and *Decennier*. Tithing is vsed for a Court. *Magna charta, cap.* 25. and *Merton, cap.* 10.

Todde of wooll, is a quantitie conteining 28. pound in weight, or two *Stone*.

Toft (*Toftum*) is a place, wherein a mesuage hath stoode

West.parte 2. *symbol. titulo* Fines *sect.*26.

Toile, commeth of the French (*Toile*.i.*tela*) and signifieth with vs a net of cord to compasse or take Deere.

To *lange and to bred*. See *Bred*.

Tolle(*Tollere*) as it is a verbe signifieth to defeate or take away, *anno* 8.*H*.6.*cap*. 9.

Toll, aliàs Tholl (*Tolnetum, aliàs Theolonium*) is a *Saxon* word, and hath in our common lawe two significations: first it is vsed for a libertie to buy and sell within the precincts of a maner. *Lamb. Archainom. fol.*132.which seemeth to import so much as a faire or market. The words be these: *Thol(quod nos dicimus* Tho*loniū) est scilicet quod habeat libertatem vendendi & emendi in terra sua*. In the second signification it is vsed for a tribute or custome paid for passage, &c. as in Bracton. *Si cui concedatur talis libertas quòd quietus sit de Theolonio & consuetudinibus dandis per totum Regnum Angliæ in terra & mari,& quod* Theolonium *& consuetudines capiat infra libertatem suam de ementibus & vendentibus,&c,lib*.2.*cap*. 24. *num*.3. But euen there in the end of the second number he hath this word, T*oll*(as it seemeth) in the former signification also,which by these words, aboue writen folowing a little after,he interpreteth to be a libertie as well to take as to be free from T*olle*. The made *Latine* word(*Theolonium*)*Cassaneus in consuetud. Burgund.pag.*118,deriueth a T*ollendo*) but I rather thinke it commeth from the greeke (ζωλδνια) or (ζελονεῖα) .i. *vectigalium redemptio, vel etiam vectigalium exactio*) *Fleta* hath these words of it: T*ol significat acquietantiam* Theolonii *vbiq; in Regno, lib. pri. cap*. 47. *M. Skene de verb. signifi. verbo* T*oll*, saith it is a custome, and that it commeth from the Greeke word of the same signification(ζιλες) and that he who is infeoffed with T*oll*, is custome free, and payeth no custome: which is manifest by sundry ould bookes,wherein it is writen: T*oll, hoc est quod vos & homines vestri de toto homagio vestro sint quieti de omnibus mercantiis, & de* T*olneto,de omnibus rebus emptis & venditis*. Thus farre he. *Kitchin fol*.104.maketh mention of Tolle through, and Toll Trauers,his words be to this effect. Custom or prescription to haue Toll through in the high way, is not good: for it is against the common right. But to haue prescription of Tolle Trauers, is good. In which place the difference betweene the one, and the other the newe expositour of lawe terms saith to be, that tolle trauers is that mony,which is is taken for passing ouer a priuate mans ground. But this author seemeth to differ from *Kitchin* touching the lawfulnes of tolle through, saying that by reason of a bridge prouided at the cost and charge of the towne, for the ease of trauellers, he thinketh it resonable, that tolle through be exacted toward the maintenance thereof: which writer also maketh mention of tolle turn: and that he defineth to be tolle paide for beastes driuen to be sold, though they be not sold indeede. Where, I think, he must meane a tolle paide in the returne homeward from the faire or market, whether they were driuen to be sold. *Plowden, casu Willion, fo. 236.* agreeth in this definition of tolle trauers. And this the *Feudists* call parangariam, defining it to be *sumptus & labores ferendi referendiue alicuius causa a principe impositi, cùm non per viam, sed aliò versum iter suscipitur. l. 2. Co. de Episc. & cleri. a graeco* (παραγγαρεία) .i. *transitus per viam transversam. Gothofred. ad l. 4. §. 1. π. de vetera.* I finde in *Andrew Horns mirrour of Iustices, lib. 1. cap. des articles, &c.* that by the auncient lawe of this land, the buyers of corne or catell in faires or markets, ought to pay tolle to the Lord of the market, in testimony of their contract there lawfully made in open market: for that priuie contracts were held vnlawfull.

Toloneum, or Breve de essendi quietum de Toloneo, is a writ that lyeth in case, where the Citizens of any Citie, or Burgesses of any towne, be quit from tolle by the graunt of the kings predecessours, or prescription: which you haue at large in *Fitzh. nat. br. fol. 226.* See *Telonium.*

Tolt (Tolta) is a writ whereby a cause depending in a court Baron, is remoued into the county court. *Old nat. br. fol. 2.* The reason of the appellation seemeth to come from the verb *(Tollo) v: Cooke, lib. 3. in praefatione ad lectorem.*

Tonne. See *Tunne.*

Tonnage, is a custome or impost due for merchãdise brought or caried in tonns and such like vessels, from or to other nations after a certain rate in euery tonne *anno 12. Ed. 4. ca. 3. anno 6. H. 8. ca. 14. & anno pri. Ed. 6. cap. 13. anno pri. Iacobi, cap. 33.* I haue heard it also called a duty due to the Mariners for vnloading their ship arriued in any hauen after the rate of euery tonne.

Torny. See *Turney.*

Totted anno 42. Ed. 3. cap. 9. & anno 1. Ed. 6. ca. 15. is a word vsed of a dept, which the forein Apposer or other officer in the Exchequer noteth for a good

dept

dept to the *King* by writing this word(*Tot*) vnto it.

Tourn. See *Turn*.

Tout temps prist & vncore est: that is to say in English, Alway ready and is at this present: this is a kinde of plee in way of excuse or defence vnto him that is siewed for withhoulding any dept, or duty belonging to the plaintiffe. See of this *Brooke* his Abridgement, *fol*. 258.

Traile baston. See *Iustices of triall baston*.

Traitor (*traditor, proditor*) See *Treason*.

Transgressione, is a writ, called commonly a writ or action of trespas. Of this *Fitzherbert* in his *Natura bre*: hath two sorts: one *Vicountiel*, so called, because it is directed to the Shyreeue, and is not returnable but to be determined in the countie: The forme whereof differeth from the other, because it hath not these words: *Quare vi & armis, &c*. and this see in *Fitzh. nat. br. fol*. 85. *G*. The other is termed a writ of trespasse vpon the case, which is to be siewed in the common Bank, or the Kings Bench, in which are alwaies vsed these words *vi & armis, &c*. And of this you haue *Fitzh. nat. br. fol*. 92. *E*. See *Trespas*. See the diuers use of this writ in the *Register originall*, in the table.

Transcript, anno 34. & 35. *H*. 8. *cap*. 14. is the copy of any originall writen againe or exemplified.

Transcripto Recognitionis facta coram Iusticiariis itinerantibus, &c. is a writ for the certifiing of a *Recognisance*, taken before Iustices in Eire, into the Chauncery, *Register orig fol*. 152. *b*.

Transcripto pedis finis levati mittendo in Cancellariam, is a writ for the certifiing of the foote of a fine leuied before Iustices in Eyre, &c. into the Chauncerie, *eodem. fol*. 169. & *Register Iudiciall, fol*. 14.

Travers, cometh of the French (*Traverser. i. transfigere*) It signifieth in our common lawe sometime to denie, sometime to ouerthrow, or vndoe a thing done. Touching the former signification take these words in *Wests symbol. parte* 2. *titulo Chauncery, sect*. 54. An answer (saith he, speaking of an answer to a bille in Chauncerie) is that, which the Defendant pleadeth or saith in barre to avoide the plantiffes bille, or action, either by confession and avoiding, or by denying and traversing the materiall parts thereof. And againe, *sectio*. 55. A replication is the plaintiffes speech or answer to the Defendants answer, which must affirme and persiew his bille, and confesse

 and

and auoide, deny or traverse the Defendants answer. And the formall words of this trauers are in Lawyers French (*sans ceo*) in Latine (*absque hoc*) in English (without that.) See *Kitchin fol.* 227. *titulo Affirmatiue & Negatiue*. In the second signification I find it in *Stawnfords prerog.cap.* 20. through the whole chapter, speaking of trauersing an office: which is nothing else, but to proue, that an inquisition made of goods or lands by the *Eschetour*, is defectiue and vntruly made. So trauersing of an Inditement, is to take issue vpon the chiefe mater thereof: which is none other to say, then to make contradiction, or to deny the point of the Enditement. As in presentment against *A.* for a high way ouerflowne with water for default of scowring a ditch, which he and they, whose estate he hath in certain land there, haue vsed to scower and cleanse. *A.* may trauerse either the mater, *viz.* that there is no high way there, or that the ditch is sufficiently scowred: or otherwise he may trauers the cause, *viz.* that he hath not the land, &c. or that he and they whose estate, &c. haue not vsed to scoure the ditch. *Lamb. Eirenarcha. lib. 4. cap.* 13. *pag.* 521 522. Of Trauers see a whole chapter in *Kitchin, fol.* 240. See the new booke of Entries. *verbo, Trauers.*

Treason (*traditio, vel proditio*) commeth of the French, *trahison*, i. *proditio*) and signifieth an offence committed against the amplitude and maiestie of the commonwealth. *West parte* 2. *symbol. titulo Inditements. sect.* 63. by whom it is there diuided into High treason, which other call *altam proditionem*, and petit treason. High treason he defineth to be an offence done against the securitie of the common wealth, or of the Kings most excellent Maiestie: whether it be by imagination, word, or deed: as to compasse or imagine treason, or the death of the Prince, or the Queene his wife, or his sonne and heyre apparent, or to deflowre the Kings wife, or his eldest daughter vnmaried, or his eldest sonnes wife: or leuie war against the King in his Realme, or to adhere to his enemies, ayding them, or to counterfeit the Kings great Seale, priuie Seale, or money, or wittingly to bring false money into this Realme counterfeited like vnto the money of *England*, and vtter the same: or to kill the Kings Chaunceler, Treasurer, Iustice of the one bench, or of the other, Iustices in *Eyre*, Iustices of Assise, Iustices of *oyer* and *terminer*, being in his place, & doing of of his office. *anno* 25. *Ed. prim. ca.* 2. or forging of the *Kings* seale manuell, or priuy signet, priuy seale, or forrein coine current within the Realme *anno* 2. *Mar. cap.* 6. or diminishing or impairing of money current, *an.* 5. *Elizab. ca.* 11. & *anno* 14. *El. ca.* 3. & 18. *Elizab. ca. pri.* and many other actions which you may read there and in other places particularly expressed. And in case of this treason a man forfeiteth his lands, and goods to the *King* onely. And it is also called treason Paramount. *anno* 25. *Ed.* 3. *cap.* 2. The forme of Iudgement giuen vpon a man conuicted of high treason is this. The Kings Sergeant after the verdict deliuered, craueth Iudgement against the prisoner in the behalfe of the King. Then the Lord *Steward* (if the traitour haue bene noble) or other Iudge (if he be vnder a peere) saith thus: N. Earle of P. For so much as thou before this time hast bene of these treasons indited, and this day arraigned for thee same, and put thy selfe vpon God and thy peeres, and the *Lords* thy peeres haue foũd thee guilty, my Iudgement is that thou shalt from hence be conueied vnto the Tower of London, whence thou camest, and from thence drawne through the middest of *London* to *Tiburne*, and there hanged: and liuing thou shalt be cut downe, thy bowels to be cut out and burnt before thy face, thy head cut off, and thy body to be diuided in foure quarters, and disposed at the *Kings* Maiesties pleasure: and God haue mercy vpon thee.

Petit treason is rather described by examples, then any where logically defined: as when a seruant killeth his master, or a wife her husband, or when a secular or religious man killeth his prelate, to whom he oweth faith and obedience. And in how many other cases petit treason is committed. See *Cromptons Iustice of peace.* And this maner of treason giueth forfeiture of Escheats to euery *Lord* within his owne fee *anno* 25. *Ed.* 3. *cap.* 2. Of treason see *Bracton lib.* 3. *tract.* 2. *cap.* 3. *nu. pri.* & 2. Treason compriseth both high and petit treason *anno* 25. *Ed.* 3. *stat.* 3. *cap.* 4.

Treasure troue (*Thesaurus inuentus*) is as much as in true French (*Tresor trouuè*) .i. treasure found: and signifieth in our common law, as it doth in the Ciuile law, *id est, veterem depositionem pecuniæ, cuius non extat memoria, vt iam dominum non habeat. l.* 31 §. *prim. ff. de acquir. rerum Dom.* Neere vnto which definition commeth *Bracton. lib.* 3. *tract.* 2. *cap.* 3. *num.* 4. And this treasure found, though the ciuill lawe do giue it to the finder, according to the lawe of nature; yet the lawe of *England*, giueth it to the *King* by his prerogatiue, as appeareth by *Bracton vbi supra*. And therefore as he also saith in the sixth chapter, it is the Coroners office to enquire therof by the countrie to the Kings vse. And *Stawn. pl. cor. lib. pr. cap.* 42. saith, that in auncient times, it was doubtfull, whether the concealing of treasure found were felonie, yea or not: and that *Bracton* calleth it *grauem præsumptionem, & quasi crimen furti*. But the punishment of it at these dayes, as he proueth out of *Fitzh. Abridgment. pag.* 187. is imprisonment, and fine, and not life and member. And if the owner may any way be knowne, then doth it not belong to the kings prerogatiue. Of this you may reade *Britton* also, *cap.* 17. who saith, that it is euery subiects part, as soone as he hath found any treasure in the earth, to make it knowne to the Coroner of the countrie, or to the Bayliffes, &c. See *Kitchin* also, *fol.* 40.

Treasurer, thesaurarius, commeth of the French (*tresorier*) i. *quæstor, præfectus fisci*) and signifieth an Officer, to whom the treasure of another, or others, is committed to be kept, and truly disposed of. The chiefest of these with vs, is the *Treasurer* of *England*, who is a Lord by his office, and one of the greatest men of the land: vnder whose charge and gouernment is all the Princes wealth contained in the *Exchequer*, as also the checke of all Officers any way employed in the collecting of the Imposts, tributes, or other reuenewes belonging to the Crowne. *Smith de Repub. Anglor. lib.* 2. *cap.* 14. more belonging to his office, see *ann.* 20 *Ed.* 3. *cap.* 6. & *anno* 31. H. 6. *cap.* 5. & *anno* 4. *Ed.* 4. *cap. pri.* & *anno* 17. *eiusdem. cap.* 5. & *anno prim. R.* 2. *cap.* 8. & *anno* 21. H. 8. *cap.* 20. & *anno prim. Ed.* 6. *cap.* 13. Ockams Lucubrations affirme, that the Lord chiefe Iustice had this authoritie in times past: and of him hath these words: *Iste excellens Sessor omnibus, quæ in inferiore vel superiore scacchio sunt, prospicit. Ad nutum ipsius qualibet officia subiecta disponuntur: sic tamen vt ad* Domini *Regis vtilitatem iuste perueniant. Hic tamen inter cætera videtur excellens, quod potest his sub testimonio suo breve Domini Regis facere fieri, vt de thesauro qualibet summa liberetur, vel vt computetur quod sibi ex Domini Regis mandato prænouerit computandum, vel si maluerit, breve suum sub aliorum testimonio faciet de his rebus.*

This high Officer hath by vertue of his office at this day, the nomination of the *Escheatours* yeerely throughout *England*, and giueth the places of all customers, controllers, and searchers in all the ports of the Realme. He sitteth in the chequer chamber, and with the rest of the court, ordereth things to the Kings best benefite. *He* with the Barons may by statute stall depts of three hundred pounds and vnder. And by commission from his maiestie, he with others ioyned with him, letteth leases for liues or yeares, of the lands that came to the Crowne by the dissolution of Abbeys. *He* by his office giueth warrant to certaine men to haue their wine without impost. He taketh declaration of all the money payed into the Receipt of the *Exchequer*, and of all Receiuers accompts.

Then is there a *Treasurer* of the kings houshold, who is also of the priuie Councell, and in the absence of the *Steward* of the Kings houshold, hath power with the Controller and the Steward of the Marshalsea, without commission to heare and determine treasons, misprisions of treasons, murder, homicide, and bloudshed, committed within the Kings pallace. *Stawnf. pl. cor. lib.* 3. *cap.* 5. In the statute *anno* 28. *Rich.* 2. *cap.* 18. & *anno* 11. *H.* 7. *cap.* 16. mention is made of the *Treasurer* of *Calis*. In *Westm.* 2. *cap.* 8. of the Treasurer of the Exchequer. & *anno* 27. *Ed.* 3. *stat.* 2. *cap.* 18. & *ann.* 35. *Eliz. cap.* 4. Of the *Treasurer* of the Nauie, or Treasurer of the warres or garrisons of the Nauie. *anno* 39. *El. cap.* 7. *Treasurer* of the Kings chamber. *anno* 26. *H.* 8. *cap.* 3. & *anno* 33 *eiusdem cap.* 39. *Treasurer* of the warres. *anno* 7. *H.* 7. *cap. prim. anno* 3. *H.* 8. *cap.* 5. *Treasurer* of the Chauncerie. *West. parte* 2. *symbol. titulo Fines. sect.* 152. Treasurer of the Kings Wardrobe. *anno* 15. Ed. 3. *stat. prim. cap.* 3. & *anno* 25. *eiusdem, stat.* 5. *cap.* 21. whose office you haue well set foorth in *Fleta, lib.* 2. *cap.* 14. *Treasurer* of the Countie for poore souldiers. *anno* 35. *Eliz. cap.* 4. *And* most corporations through the kingdome, haue an officer of this name, that receiueth their rents, and disburseth their common expences.

Treate commeth of the French (*traire.* i. *emulgere*) and signifieth in the common lawe, as much as *taken out*, or *withdrawne*. As a Iurour was chalenged, for that hee might not dispend 40. pounds, and for that cause he was treate by the *Statute*. *old na. br. fol.* 159. that is, remoued or discharged.

Breade of treate, anno 51. *H.* 3. *Statute of breade, &c.* what it signifieth, I cannot learne.

Trespas (*Transgressio*) is a French word signifiing as much as *Mors, obitus, excessus.* The reason whereof I take to be, because in interpretation it is a passage from one place or estate to another: for in *Britton, cap. 29.* I find *trespassants* for *passengers.* In our common law and language, it is vsed for any transgression of the lawe, vnder treason, felonie, or misprision of treason, or of felonie, as may be gathered out of *Stawnf. pl. cor. fol.* 38. where he saith, that for a Lord of the Parlament to depart from the Parlament without the kings licence, is neither treason nor felonie, but trespasse. And againe, *fol.* 31. saying, that where it was wont before the statute made *anno prim. Ed. 2.* called *Statutum de frangentibus prisonam,* that the breach of prison was felonie, if it were the *Kings* prison: it is sithence but trespasse, except the prisoner were committed for felonie. But it is most commonly vsed for that wrong or dammage, which is done by a priuate man to the King, as in his Forest, *pl. cor. lib. 2. cap.* 18. or to another priuate man. And in this signification it is of two sortes: trespasse generall, otherwise termed, trespasse *vi & armis*: and trespasse especiall, otherwise called trespasse vpon the case. And this seemeth to be without force. Termes of the *Lawe.* Action vpon the case, as appeareth by *Kitchin, fol.* 176. The former I take to be called generall, because it riseth from that generall ground in lawe, that whatsoeuer is done by any priuate mans humour *vi & armis*, is an offence. The later I call especiall, because *Kitchin* calleth the other generall: and another reason may be this, because it springeth from a particular case or fact, not conteined vnder any other generall head. And the action lying for this trespasse, is otherwise called an action vpon the case, as may be gathered out of diuers places vnder the title *Trespasse,* in *Brookes* his *Abridgement.* How to distinguish the forme of these writs or actions, See *Fitz. nat. br. fol.* 86. *I. &* 87. *H. I.* In an action of trespasse, this is perpetuall, that the plaintiffe sieweth for dammages, or the valew of the hurt done vnto him by the *Defendant.* It seemeth an hard thing to distinguish these two kinds of trespasses so, as to be able to say when it is a trespasse *vi & armis*, and when vpon the case: as may well appeare to him that shall peruse this title in *Brooke.* But this is to be left to the experiēce

of

of graue and skilfull pleaders. I find moreouer in *Kitchin*, *fol.* 188 that there is a *trespasse locall*, and *trespasse transitorie*: *trespasse locall* is that, which is so annexed to a place certaine, as if the Defendant ioyne issue vpon the place, and trauers the place, onely by saying, *Absque hoc*, that he did the trespasse in the place mentioned in the declaration, and auerre it, it is enough to defeate the action. *Trespasse transitorie* is that, which cannot be defeated by the defendants trauers of the place, saying: without that I cōmitted the trespasse in the place declared: because the place is not materiall. Examples of both you haue set downe by *Kitchin*, in the place aboue named, to this effect: trauers by (*Absque hoc*) of trespasse in batterie, or goods brought in, is transitorie, and not locall: as it is of trees cut, or herbes.

And therefore in trespasse transitorie the place shall not make issue, neither is it trauersable: no more then is a trespasse vpon a case of an Assumption. *Bracton* in his fourth booke, *cap.* 34. *num.* 6. diuideth *transgressionē in maiorem & minorem*: which place reade. See also great diuersitie of trespasses in the new booke of Entries. *verbo Trespasse.*

Triall (*triatio*) is vsed in our common lawe, for the examination of all causes ciuill or criminall, according to the lawes of our Realme. Of this word *Stawn. pl. cor. lib.* 2. *cap.* 26. writeth to this effect. There was a statute made *prim. & secund.* *Philip. & Mar. cap.* 10. to this purpose. And be it furder enacted by the authoritie aforesaid, that all trials hereafter to be had, awarded or made for any treason, shal be had and vsed according to the due order and course of the common lawes of this Realme, and not otherwise, &c. By this word (*triall*) saith *Stawnf.* in that place, some vnderstand as well the inquest that indicteth a man, as the enquest vpon the arraignment, that attainteth or acquiteth him. For these two make but one entire triall, that euery man is to haue, when he is impeached of treason. But others haue answered to this, that triall in common speech, is the triall that a man is to haue, after he is indicted, and not before. For in lawe the inditement is nought, but the accusation against him, which he is to make answer vnto and that being tried, it either attainteth, or acquiteth him. So that the triall is the issue, which is tried vpon the Inditement, & not the Inditement it selfe. For that is no part of the thing which trieth, but the thing which is tried, and the offence. And so is this word Triall vnderstood in the statute, *anno* 33.*H.* 8.*cap.*23. where it saith thus: must be indighted within the shires or places, where they committed their offences, and also tried by the Inhabitants, or feeholders. So he putteth a differen ce betwene Inditement and Triall, as he doth also afterward in these words: There to be indited and tried of their offences, &c. Thus far: *Stawnf.Sir.Tho. Smith de Rep. Anglo. li 2. ca 5.* saieth, that by order and vsage of England, there are three trialls, that is.3. waies and maners, whereby absolute, and definite Iudgement is giuen: by Parlament, which is the highest, and most absolute. by battell and great Assise: which he seuerally describeth in 3. chapters folowing, though not so fully as the thing requireth. But of the great Assise, he speaketh at large in the 23. chapter of the same booke. And of these trials see more in *Stawnf.pl.cor.lib.2.cap.pri.2 & 3.* whereof he deuideth the great Assise into two sorts: one proper to Barons of the Parlament, which is by 20. or 18. of their Peeres: the other common to others of lower condition, which is by 12. men, that be neighbours to the place where the offence was committed, And of those you may read him at large in the saide chapters there following. See *Twelue men.* See *the new booke of Entrise. verbo. Triall.*

Tribing (*Tribinga, vel Trithinga*) seemeth by a place in *Edward* the confessours lawes, set out by M. *Lamberd, nu.* 34. to be the third part of a shire or prouince, otherwise called (*Leth*) which we now call (*Leete*). The same lawe doth *M. Camden* also mention, *pag.* 102. & 103. This court is aboue a court Baron, and inferiour to the Shire, or countie. This word is also vsed in the sentence of excommunication vpon the great Charter and charter of the Forest. denounced in the daies of *Edward* the first, as it is latined in the booke called *pupilla oculi. parte 5. cap. 22.* A.I. in these words: *Visus autem de franco plegio sic fiat, sc: quòd pax nostra teneatur, & quod Tribinga integra sit, sicut esse consueuit, &c.* Of this *Fleta lib.2.cap.*61.§.*final.* writeth thus; *Sciendum est quod aliæ potestates erant super Wapentakia, quæ Tritinga dicebantur, eo quòd erat tertia pars prouinciæ, qui verò super eas dominabantur, trithingreves vocabantur, quibus deferebantur causæ quæ non in Wapentakiis poterant definiri in Schiram Sicq; quòd vocatur Hun-*

Hundredum, item per variationem locorum & idiomatis, Wapentakie appellatur, & tria vel quatuor vel plura Hundreda solebant trithinga vocari: & quod in trithingis non poterant diffiniri in shiram .i. in comitatum deferebatur terminandū. Modernis autem temporibus pro vno & eodē habentur apud homines Hundreda Wapentakia & trithinga Learne whether those diuisions in Yorke-shire called ridings, be not *quasi trithings*. Of this *Roger Houeden parte post. suorum annal. fo.* 346. *b.* hath the same words in effect.

Treswell of double soled shooes, anno 2. & 3. *Ed. 6. cap. 9.* which as I haue heard should rather be written creswel, signifieth the broad edge or verge of the shoe sole round about.

Trinitie house, is a certaine house at *Deptford* which belongeth to a companie or corporation of sea-faring men that haue power by the Kings Charter to take knowledge of those that destroy sea markes, and to redresse their doings, as also to correct the faults of saylers, &c. and to take care of diuers other things belonging to nauigation and the seas *v. anno* 8. *Elizab. ca.* 13. & *anno* 35. *eiusdem, ca.* 6.

Trink, is a kind of net to fish withall. *anno* 2. *H. 6. cap.* 15.

Triours, be such as be chosen by the court to examine whether a challenge made to the panell, or any of the panell, be iust yea, or not. *Brooke titulo. Challenge. f.* 122. & *ould na. br. f.* 158.

Tritis, aliàs Tristis, is an immunitie from that attendance, in the forest, whereby euery man dwelling in the forest, is tyed to be readie, houlding of a Greyhound, when the Lord of the Forest is disposed to chace within his Forest, at such place as he shall be appointed, or els to be amerced for his default. *Manwood parte pri. of his forest lawes. pag.* 86. and *Cromptons Iurisdict. fol.* 192. & 197.

Tronage (*Tronagium*) is a kind of tolle, *Westm.* 2. *cap.* 25. *anno* 13. *Ed.* 1. taken (as it seemeth) for weying. *For* I find in *Fleta li.* 2. *cap.* 12. §. *Item vlnas* that *trona* is a beame to weigh with. See *Weight*.

Trover, commeth of the French (*Trouver.* i. *Invenire*) It signifieth in our common lawe, an action which a man hath against one that hauing found any of his goods, refuseth to deliuer them vpō demaund. See the new booke of *Entries ver. Trover*.

Troy weight (*Pondus Troiæ*, See *Weight*.

Tumbrell (*Tumbrellum*) is an engine of punishment, which ought to be in euery libertie that hath view of frank pledge, for

for the coertion of skowldes and vnquiet women. *Kitchin. fo.* 13. *a.* Newe booke of *Entries, Franchise* 2. *& Quo warranto.* 1. See *Cucking stoole.*

Tunne, is a measure of oile or wine conteining twelue score and twelue gallons, *anno* 1. *R.* 3. *cap.* 12. that is 4. hogsheads.

Tunnage. See *Tonnage.*

Turbarie (*Turbaria*) is an interest to digge turves vpon a common. *Kitchin, fol.* 94. *old. nat. br. fol.* 70. It commeth of the rude Latine word (*Turba*) which is vsed for a turfe. *Lynd, in provin. de decimis cap. finali.*

Turmerick (*Turmerica*) is a certaine roote of an herb growing in *Arabia*, as I haue bene informed, very wholsome for diuers diseases in horses, and sometime vsed for man also in the case of ieandes. It is reckoned among the garbleable drugs *anno* 1. *Iaco. ca.* 19.

Turne (*Turnum*) is the Shyreeues court kept euery yeare twice: once after Easter, and againe after Micheelmas. *Magna charta cap.* 35. and that within one moneth after each feast, *anno* 3. *Ed.* 3. *c.* 15. from this court are exempted onely, Archbishops, Bishops, Abbots, Priors, Earles, Barons, all religious men, and women, and all such as haue Hundreds of their owne to be kept. And these are not bound to appeare there except their apparence be especially required vpon some extraordinary cause, *anno* 25. *H.* 3. *cap.* 10. and *Britton, cap.* 29. It seemeth to be called the *Shyreeues Turn* of the French word (*Tour* .i. *ambitus. circuitus, vicissitudo*) and is of *Britton* called *Tour, cap.* 61. *sub fine capitis*, as if we would say (The Shyreeue his course) for (as *Britton* noteth in the said 29. chapter) that which before the Shyreeue, is called the Shyreeues Turne, is called in the court of Fraunchises and Hundreds, the view of Frank-pledge: wherein inquirie is especially made of such as be not in any dozin. with whome *Fleta* agreeth: And by *Fleta* it appeareth that this Turn was the Shyreeues course to keepe his court in euery Hundred. *lib.* 2. *cap.* 52. *in princip.* So that as the inferiour courts had their times to take knowledge of those, and other causes belonging to their cognisance: So the Shyreeue had his course or turne to doe the like at these two seuerall seasons. That if there were any defects in them, it might be redressed in these, and Gods peace and the Kings so much the more carefully obserued. This, as *Lamberd* saith, was of old called also the *Shyreeues* moote, *lib.* 4.*cap.* 4. In this court (as *Britton* saith *vbi supra*) the *Shyreeue* causeth to be found out 12. of the most sage, loyall and sufficient men of all the Hundred (for he kept his turne twice every yeare in each Hundred. *Magna charta, cap.* 35. & *Britton vbi supra*) whome he charged vpon their oathes, to present the truth touching the articles ministred vnto them, and set downe by *Britton* in the same chapter. This done he put all other to their oathes, according to their dozins and villages, truly to present vnto the former twelue all things concerning such articles, as by them they should be asked of. But sithence the Hundred courts are all called to the county by the statute *anno.* 14.*Ed.*3.*cap.* 3. *Statut.pri.*these Turnes be likewise kept in one cheife place of euery shire, and not seuerally in euery *Hundred*, as before they were. Of this you may reade more in *Britton* or in *Cromptons Iurisdiction fol.* 230. and in the *Mirrour of Iustices, lib. pri. cap. de Turnes.*

Turney (*Torneamentum*) commeth of the French (*Tournoy.* i. *Decursorium*) It signifieth a martiall exercise of Knights or Souldiers fighting one with another in disport, and is thus defined. *ca: felicis Extra de Torneamentis Torneamenta dicuntur Nundinæ vel feriæ, in quibus milites ex condicto conuenire, & ad ostentationem virium suarum, & audaciæ, temerè congredi solent.* This word is vsed in the statute, *anno.* 24. *Henric. octau. capit.* 13. and as I haue heard, it signifieth with vs in England those combats, that are made with arming swords on horsebacke And I thinke the reason of the name to proceede from the French (*Tourner.* i. *vertere*) because it consisteth much in agilitie both of horse and man.

Turno vicecomitum, is a writ, that lyeth for those that are called to the Shyreeues turne out of their owne Hundred. *Register orig. fol.* 174.

Tuain nithes gest. (*hospes duarum noctium*) *Roger Houeden, parte poster suorum annalium, fol.* 345. *b.* who if he did harme to any, his hoste was not aunswerable for it, but himselfe. See *Thrid nithes hawan man.*

Twelue men (*Duodecim homines legales*) is a number of twelue persons, or vpwards to the number of 24. by whose discretion all tryals passe both in ciuill and criminall causes, through all courts of the common law in this Realme. First for ciuile causes, when proofe is made of the mater in queſtion, as the parties and their councell thinke good, on both ſides, the point of the fact, that they are to giue their verdict of, is deliuered likewiſe vnto them, which we call the iſſue: and then are they put in minde of their oath formerly taken, to doe right betweene party and party, and ſo ſent out of the court ſeuerally by themſelues to conſider vpon the euidence of both ſides, vntill they be agreed; which done they returne to the court againe, and deliuer their verdict by the mouth of the foreman. And according to this verdict, Iudgement afterward paſſeth, either condemnatorie for the plantife, or abſolutory for the Defendant. Theſe *12.* be called 12. *milites. Glanuile, lib. 2. cap.* 14. & 15. and ſo be they in *Bracton* diuers times: but that word is altered.

In cauſes criminall there be two ſorts of Enqueſts, one called the graund *Enqueſt*, and the other the Enqueſt of life and death. The graund Enqueſt is ſo called, either becauſe it conſiſteth commonly of a greater number then 12. as of *24. 18.* or *16.* at the leaſt, or els becauſe all cauſes criminall or penall firſt paſſe through them: whereas the other Enqueſt is eſpecially appointed for one or few maters touching life and death, committed to their conſiderations. Thoſe of the grand Enqueſt are alſo called by *Bracton 12. milites lib.* 3. *tracta.* 2. *cap. pri. nu. 2.* becauſe they were wont to be Knights, as it ſeemeth, and not inferiours, except ſo many knights could not be found. *Idem eodem. num.* 1. *in fine.* And their function is to receiue all preſentments made vnto them of any offence, and accordingly to giue their generall opinion of the preſentment by writing either theſe words (*Billa vera*) vpon the bille of preſentment, which is an Inditement of the party preſented: or els this word (*Ignoramus*) which is an abſoluing of him. Now as criminall cauſes be of two ſortes, either capitall touching life and member, or finable: ſo is there a double courſe of theſe Inditements. For in cauſes onely finable, the party indited muſt either trauers the Inditement by denying it and ſo it is referred to a petit Iury, whereby he is either conuicted or diſcharged of the crime, or els he confeſſing it, the court ſetteth his fine vpon his head without more worke. But in maters of life and death, the party indited is commaunded to hold vp his hãd, & ãſwer (guilty) or (not guilty) if (guilty) he ſtandeth conuicted by his owne confeſſifession: if (not guilty) he is farder referred to the Enquest of life and death: which consider vpon the proofe brought against the prisoner, and accordingly bring in their verdict, (Guilty) or (not Guilty) So is he iudged to dye, or deliuered by the court. Of this read more in Inditement. Assise, Iury, See the statute *anno* 35. *H.* 8. *cap.* 6. & 37. *eiusdem cap,* 22. & *anno* 2. Ed. 6 *cap.* 32. & *an.* 5. *El.c.a.* 25.

V

Vacation (*vacatio*) hath an especiall signification in this kingdome, being vsed for all that time respectiuely which passeth betweene terme and terme at *London*. And when such times begunne and ended in our anncesters daies, see Roger *Hovedens annals parte posteriori fo.* 343.*a.* where you shall find that this intermission was called (*pax Dei & ecclesiæ.*)

Vaccarie, alias vacharie (*vaccaria, alias vacheria*) semeth to be a house to keepe kine in, *Fleta lib.* 2. *cap.* 41. §. *Item inquiratur* 12. and *Cromptons Iurisd. fol* 194. in these words: without warrant no subiect may haue within the *Forest* a vacarie. But in the statute *anno* 37. H. 8. *cap.* 16. I finde vacharie to be, as it were a speciall proper name of a certaine quantitie and compasse of ground within the forest of *Ashedowne*.

Valewe (*valentia, valor*) The word is in it selfe plaine enough: But I cannot omitte one place in *M. West. parte.* 2. *symbol. titulo* Inditements, *sect.* 70. *V. W.* touching the difference betweene value and price. These be his words, And the value of those things, in which offences are committed, is vsually comprised in Inditements, which seemeth necessary in thefe, to make a difference from petit larceny: and in trespas, to aggrauate the faulte, and increase the fine. But no price of things *feræ naturæ*, may be expressed, as of deere, of hares &c. if they be not in Parks and warrens, which is a liberty *anno* 8. Ed. 4. *fol.* 5. nor of charters of land. And where the number of the things taken are to be expressed in the Inditement, as of yong Doues in a Doue house, yong haukes in a wood, there must be saide (*pretii*) or (*ad valentiam*) but of diuers deade things (*ad valentiam*) and not (*pretii*) of coine not current, it shalbe (*pretii*) but of coine current, it shall neither be saide (*prety*) nor (*ad valentiam*) for the price and value thereof is certaine. But of counterfeit coine, shall bee said (*ad valentiam*) and in couterfeiting of coine shall not be said (*decem libras in dena-*

riis Dominæ Reginæ) nor (*in pecunia Dominæ Reginæ*) but (*ad instar pecuniæ Dominæ Reginæ*).

Valour of mariage (*Valore maritagii*) is a writ that lyeth for the Lord, hauing profered couenable mariage to the Infant, without disparidgement, against the Infant, comming to his yeares, if he refuse to take the Lords offer. And it is to recouer the value of the mariage, *Regist. orig. fol. 164. old. nat. br. fol. 90.*

Variance, commeth of the French (*varier*. i. *alterare*) it signifieth in the common lawe, an alteration, or change of condition after a thing done. For example, the communality of a towne make a composition with an Abbot. Afterward this towne by a graunt from the king obteineth Bayliffes. This is a variance, and in this case, if the Abbot cōmence any suite for breach of the composition, he must varie from the words of the communalty set downe in the Composition, and begin against the Bayliffes and the Communalties. *Brooke tit. Variance. fol. 292.* It is also vsed for an alteration of some thing formerly laide in a plee, which is easilier knowne what it is, then when it may be vsed as it appeareth by *Brooke* through the whole title aforesaide: See *variance* in the newe booke of Entries.

Vassall, (*vassallus*) signifieth him, that holdeth land in fee of his Lord, *Hot. verbo Feudal*: we call him more vsually a tenent in fee: whereof some owe fidelitie and seruice, and are called *vassalli iurati*: some that owe neither, and are called *vassalli iniurati*. But of this later sort, I thinke that in *England* we haue not any. Of these thus writeth *Hotoman* in his disputations vpon the Feuds, *cap. 3. Propriè is vassa dicitur, qui ab Imperatore regale feudum accepit, vassallus autem ὑποκοριστικῶς diminutivo nomine qui ab illo feudale beneficium adeptus est: quasi qui in vassi fide & cliente la est &c. M. Skene de verbor. signif. verb. Ligentia*, saith, that *vassallus* is diuided into *homologum*, & *non homologum*. *Homologus* is he that sweareth seruice with exception of a higher Lord: and *non homologus*, is he that sweareth with out exception, all one with *Ligeus*. And the same author *verb. Vassallus*, saith, that it is *vassallus*, *quasi bassallus*, *id est*, *inferior socius*. From the French (*bas*. i. *humilis, dimissus*) and the Dutch word (*gesel*. i. *socius*:) his reason is, because the vassall is inferior to his master, and must serue and reuerence him: and yet he is in maner his companion, because each of them is obliged one

one to the other. He saith farder out of *Cuiacius, lib. prim. de Feud.* that *leades, leodes, fideles, homines nostri, feudatarii, ministeriales, beneficiarii, beneficiati, vassalli,* signifie almost all one thing. And a litle after he saith thus: In the lawes of the Feuds, *vassallus* is called *fidelis, quia fidelitatem iurat.* Amongst vassals the first place of dignitie is giuen to them, that are *Duces, Marchiones, Comites,* and are called *Capitanei Regni.* The second is granted to Barons and others of like estate, and are called *Valvasores Maiores.* The third to them who are called *Gentlemen* or *Nobles* holding of Barons, which also may haue vnder them vassals that be Gentlemen. And such vassals holding in chiefe of Barons, are called *Valvasores minores* And they which hold of Gentlemen, are called *vassalli, valvassini, seu minimi valvasores.* But in this Realm (he speaketh of *Scotland*) they that hold of Barons, are called *Milites,* and they that hold of them, are called *subvassores.* Thus farre *M. Skene.*

Vasto, is a writ that lyeth for the heire against the tenent for terme of life or of yeares, for making waste, or for him in the Reuersion or Remainder. *Fitzh. nat. br. fol.* 55. *Regist. orig. fol.* 72. & 76. and *Regist. Iudic. fol.* 17. 21. 23. & 69. *v. anno* 6. *Ed. pri. cap.* 5.

Vavasour (*vavasor, aliàs, valvasor*) is one that in dignitie is next vnto *Baron. Camden Britan. pag.* 109. *Bracton lib. prim. cap.* 8 saith thus of this kind of men. *Sunt & alii potentes sub Rege, qui dicuntur Barones, hoc est, robur belli: sunt & alii qui dicuntur Vavasores, viri magnæ dignitatis. Vavasor enim, nihil meliùs dici poterit, quàm vas sortitum ad valetudinem. Iacobutius de Franchis in præludio Feudorum. tit. prim. num.* 4. *&c.* calleth them *valvasores,* and giueth this reason of it: *Quia assident valvæ* i. *portæ Domini in festis, in quibus consueuerant homines curtizare & eis reuerentiam exhibere, propter Beneficium eis collatum, sicut libertus patrono: M. Camden.* in his *Britan. pag.* 108. hath these words of them. *Primus etiam Normannorum temporibus, & Thani proximi à Comitibus in dignitate censebantur. Et valvasores maiores (si illis qui de feudis scribunt credimus) iidem fuerunt Barones.*

Venditioni exponas, is a writ Iudiciall, directed to the Vndershyreeue, commaunding him to sell goods that he hath formerly by commaundement taken into his hands, for the satisfying of a iudgement giuen in the kings Court. *Register Iudicial. fol.* 33. *b.*

Venire facias, is a writ Iudicall, and goeth out of the Record, lying where two parties plead and come to issue. *sc*: vpon the saying of the country. For then the party plaintiffe, or Defendant shall haue this writ directed to the Shyreeue, that he cause to come twelue lawfull men of the same country, to say the truth vpon the sayd issue taken. And if the Enquest come not at the day of this writ returned, then shall goe a *habeas corpora*, and after a distresse vntill they come. *old. nat. br. fol.* 157. See how diuersly this writ is vsed in the table of the *Register Iudiciall*. There is also a writ of this name, that is originall, as appeareth in the *Register orig. fol.* 200. *b.* which *M. Lamberd* in his processes annexed to his *Eirenarcha* saith to be the common proces vpon any presentment not being felony, nor especially appointed for the fault presented by statute. Whereof he setteth downe an example in the same place. See also the new booke of *Entries. verbo Enquest fol.* 253. *columna*. 1. 2. & 3.

Venire facias tot matronas. See *Ventre inspiciendo*. See *Lamb. Eirenarcha, li.* 4. *ca.* 14. *pa.* 532.

Venew (vicinetum) is taken for a neighbour or neare place. As for example twelue of the Assise ought to be of the same *Venew* where the Demaund is made. *old. nat. br. fol.* 115. and in the statute *anno* 4. *H.* 4. *ca.* 26. & *anno* 25. *H.* 8. *ca.* 6. I finde these words: And also shall returne in euery such panell vpon the (*venire facias*) sixe sufficient Hundreders at the least, if there be so many within the Hundred, where the *Venew* lyeth.

Ventre inspiciendo, is a writ for the search of a woman that saith shee is with childe, and thereby withhouldeth land from him that is the next heire at the common law. *Register originall fol.* 227. *a.*

Verdour (viridarius) commeth of the French (*verdior* .i. *Saltuarius, vel custos nemoris*) he is (as *M. Manwood parte pri*: of his forest lawes *pag* 332. defineth him) a Iudiciall officer of the Kings forest, chosen by the King, in the full county of the same shire, within the forest, where he doth dwell, and is sworne to maintaine, and keepe the Assises of the forest, and also to view, receiue, and inrolle, the Attachments and presentments of all maner of trespasses of the forest of vert, and venison. And the same authour vpon the first article of *Canutus* charter, in the beginning of the same part, saith, that these in the *Saxons* times were called (*Pagered*) being foure in number, and they chiefe

chiefe men of the forest, as then they were. Their fee was in *Canutus* time, each of them euery yeare of the *Kings* allowance, two horses, one of them with a saddle, another of them without a saddle, one sword, fiue Iauelins, one speare, one shield, and ten pounds in money. These foure (as appeareth by the said charter, *nu.* 11.) had *regalem potestatem*, and might proceede to a threefold iudgement: And if any man offered them, or any of them violence, if he were a free man, he should loose his freedome, and all that he had: if a villein, he should loose his right hand. All the officers of the forest were to be corrected and punished by them. *ibidem, nu.* 10. The verdour is made by the Kings writ. *Cromptons Iurisd: fol:* 165. the forme of which writ you haue in *Fitzh. nat. br. fol.* 164. which is directed to the Shyreeue for the choice of him in a full County, by the assent of the said County. Yet if a verdour bee sodainely sicke or dead at the time of the Iustice seate, a new may be chosen without a writ. *Manwood parte prim. pag.* 72. the office is (as *Crompton* saith) *loco allegato*) properly to looke to the vert, and to see that it be wel maintained. Also when any forfeiture is taken in the Forest before the Foristers, or other ministers: the price thereof shall be deliuered to the verdour, who is to answer for it before the Iustices in *Eyre*. And if he die, his heire is chargeable therewith. *Crompton ibidem*. The forme of his oath at his admittance you may see in *Manwoods* first part of his Forest lawes. *pag.* 51. who there calleth him *verderour. aliàs, verdictor*. You shall truly serue our Soueraigne Lord the King in the office of a *verderor* of the Forest W. you shall to the vttermost of your power, and knowledge, do for the profit of the *King*, so farre as it doth apperteine vnto you to do. You shall preserue and maintaine the auncient rights and franchises of his Crowne: you shall not conceale from his Maiestie any rights or priuiledges, nor any offence either in vert or venison, or any other thing. You shall not withdraw, nor abridge any defaults, but shal endeuour your selfe to manifest and redresse the same, and if you cannot doe that of your selfe, you shall giue knowledge thereof vnto the King, or vnto his Iustice of the Forest. You shall deale indifferently with all the *Kings* liege people: you shall execute the lawes of the Forest, and do equall right and iustice, as well vnto the poore, as vnto the rich in that appertaineth vnto your office: you shall not oppresse any person by colour thereof, for any reward, fauour or malice. All these things you shall to the vttermost of your power obserue and keepe. Their office is farder expressed, *eodem pag.* 93. which is to sit in the court of attachment, to see the attachments of the Forest, to receiue the same of the Foresters and Woodwards, that do present them, and then to enter these Attachments into their rolles.

Verdict, (veredictum) is the answer of a Iurie or Enquest made vpon any cause ciuill or criminall, committed by the court to their consideration or triall. And this verdict is two-fold: either generall or especiall. *Stawnf. pl. cor. lib.* 3. *cap.* 9. A general verdict is that, which is giuen or brought into the Court, in like generall termes to the generall issue: as in an action of *disseisin* the Defendant pleadeth, *No wrong, no disseisin.* Then the issue is this in generall, whether the fact in question be a wrong or not. And this committed to the Iurie, they vpon consideration of their euidence, come in and say, either for the plaintiffe, that it is a wrong, and disseisin: or for the Defendant, that it is no wrong, no disseisin. And againe, the prisoner at the barre pleading, Not guiltie: the Enquest in like generall termes bring in their verdict, either for the King, Guilty, or for the prisoner, *Not* guilty. A speciall verdict is that, whereby they say at large, that such a thing, and such, they find to be done by the Defendant, or *Tenent*, so declaring the course of the fact, as in their opinions it is proued: and for the qualitie of the fact, they pray the discretion of the Courr. And this speciall verdict, if it containe any ample declaration of the cause, from the beginning to the end, is also called a verdict at large. Whereof reade diuers examples in *Stawnf. pl. cor. lib.* 3. *cap.* 9. and one or two in *Litleton. fol.* 78. & 79. See the new booke of Entries, *verb. Verdict.*

Verge (virgata) may seeme to come from the French *(verger i. viridarium, hortus.)* It is vsed here in *England* for the compasse about the Kings court, that boundeth the iurisdiction of the Lord Steward of the Kings houshold, and of the the Coroner of the Kings house, and that seemeth to haue bene 12. miles compasse. *anno* 13. *R.* 2. *Stat. prim. cap.* 3. & *Fitz. nat. br. fol.* 241. *B.* and *Britton. fol.* 68 *b.* 69. *a.* and *Fleta lib.* 2. *cap.* 2. and *Sir Edward Cookes Reports. li.* 4. *fol.* 47. *a.* For this see the Sta-

tute

tute *anno* 33. *H.* 8. *cap.* 12. toward the end. But *Fleta* saith, that this compasse about the Court is called *vurgata, à virga, quam Marishallus portat vt signū suæ potestatis, lib.* 2. *cap.* 4. § *prim.* Verge hath also another signification, and is vsed for a sticke, or rodde, whereby one is admitted tenent, and holding it in his hand sweareth fealtie vnto the *Lord* of a maner: who for that cause is called Tenent by the verge. *old nat. br. fol.* 17.

Vergers, (virgatores) be such as cary white wands before the Iustices of either banke, &c. *Fleta lib.* 2. *cap.* 38. otherwise called Porters of the verge.

Very Lord, and very Tenent (verus Dominus, *& verus Tenens)* are they that be immediate Lord & Tenent one to the other; *Brooke. titulo, Hariot. fol.* 23. In the *old nat. br.* and in the writ (*Replegiare de averiis. fol.* 42. I find these words: *And* know ye that in taking of leases, six things are necessarie: that is to say, very Lord and very tenent, Seruice behind, the day of the taking, seisin of the seruices, and within his Fee. *And* know ye, that a man is not very tenent, vntill he haue atturned to the *Lord* by some seruices. *So* that by *Brooke,* the very Lord, and the very Tenent, must be immediate, and by this booke there must be an acknowledgement. *See an.* 19. H. 7. *cap.* 15. See *Tenent.*

Vert, (viride) is made of the French (*verd.* i. *viridis*) and signifieth with vs in the lawes of the Forest, euery thing that doth growe, and beare greene leafe, within the Forest, that may couer and hide a *Deere. Manwood* in the second part of his Forest lawes, *fol.* 6. *a.* and *fol.* 33. *b.* (with whom also *Crompton* agreeth, *fol.* 170. of his Iurisd.) *And* vert (as the same author saith, *eodem, fol.* 34.) is diuided into *Ouer vert,* and *Neather vert. Ouer vert,* is that, which the *Lawyers* call (*Hault bois*) and *Neather vert,* is that which they cal (*South bois.*) And of this you may reade him in his second part of *Forest* lawes. *cap.* 6. *per totum.* Where you shall find, that he diuideth vert into generall, and speciall: *Generall* is, as it is aboue defined: vert speciall, is euery tree and bush within the Forest to feed the *Deere* withall: as Peare trees, Crabtrees, *Hauthornes,* Blackbush, and such like. *And* the reason of this name is, because the offence of destroying of such vert, is more highly punished, then of any other, according to the quantity thereof. *eod ca.* 6. *nu.* 2. *fol.* 35. *a.*

Veruise, otherwise called Plonkets. *anno.* 1. R. 3. *cap.* 8. a kind of clothe.

Vesses. anno 1. *R.* 3. *cap.* 8. & *anno* 14. & 15. *H.* 8. *cap.* 11. otherwise called, Set clothes.

Vesture (vestitura) is a French word signifying a garment: but in the vse of our common lawe, turned metaphorically to betoken a possession, or an admittance to a possession. So it is taken, *Westm.* 2. *c.* 25. *anno* 13. *Ed. prim.* And in this signification is it borowed from the Feudists, with whom *(Investitura)* signifieth a deliuerie of possession by a speare, or staffe, and *vestitura*, possession it selfe. *Hotoman. in verbis feudal. verbo Investitura.*

Vesture of an acre of land. an. 4. Ed. *prim. stat. prim.* is the profit of it. & *anno* 13. Edvard. 1. *cap.* 25.

Vice-treasurer of the Exchequer 1. Iacob. 26. See *Vnder-treasurer of England.* See *Treasurer of the Exchequer.*

View of frank pledge, (visus Franci plegii) is the office which the Shyreeue in his Countie court, or the Bayliffe in his Hundred, performeth in looking to the Kings peace, and seeing that euery free man be in some pledge. This is called of *Bracton li.* 2. *ca.* 5. *nu.* 7. *in fine, Res quasi sacra, quia solam personam Regis respicit, & quòd introductus sit pro pace & communi vtilitate. eodem, ca.* 16. *nu.* 8. *in fine.* See *frank pledge*, and *Leete*, and *Decennier.* See the new booke of *Entries. verb: view of frank pledge.*

Veiours (visores) commeth of the French *(Veoyr.* i. *cernere, intueri, despicere, prospicere, videre)* and signifieth in our common lawe those, that are sent by the court to take view of any place in question, for the beter descision of the right: *old. nat. br. fol.* 112. So doth *Bracton*, vse it, *lib.* 5. *tract.* 3. *cap.* 8. *per totum.* It signifieth also those, that are sent to view such as essoine themselues *de malo lecti*, whether they be in truth so sicke, as they cannot appeare, or whether they counterfeit. *Bracton lib.* 5. *tracta.* 2. *cap.* 10. & *cap.* 14. *per totum.* Lastly it is vsed for those that are sent or appointed to view an offence, as a man murdered, or a Virgin rauished. See *View.*

Vicario deliberando occasione cuiusdam Recognitionis, &c. is a writ that lyeth for a spirituall person imprisoned vpon forfeiture of a Recognisance, without the Kings writ. *Reg. orig. fol.* 147. See *statuto mercatorio contra personam ecclesiasticam.*

Vicis & venellis mundandis, is a writ that lyeth for a Maior and Bayliffes of a towne, &c. For the cleane keeping of their streets. *Register orig. fol.* 267. *b.*

View (visus) commeth of the French

French (*veue*. i. *visus*, *aspectus*, *conspectus*, *prospectus*) and signifieth with vs, the act of viewers. For (as the author of the Termes of lawe saith) when any action reall is brought, and the Tenent knoweth not well what land it is, that the Demandant asketh, then he may pray the view: that is to say, that he may see the land, which is claimed: of this *Britton* speaketh, *cap*. 45. This point of proceeding we haue receiued from the Normans, as it appeareth by the Grand custumarie. *cap*. 66. where you shall reade to this effect. It is to be knowne that there bee diuers sorts of viewes: one of a fee, another of a man in sicknes, another of an offence, as of a man slaine, or of a Virgin deflowred: all which he describeth in that place, and againe, *cap*. 80. & 96. which are worth the reading: this view at this day is vsed in an Assise of rent seruice, rent charge, or rent seck. *Fitzh. nat. br. fol*. 178. D. and in a writ *de Curia claudenda*. *Idem, fol*. 128. *B*. In a writ of *Nusance*. Idem, *fol*. 183. L. N. O. In a writ *Quo iure*. Idem. *fol*. 128. *L*. In the writ *de rationalibus diuisis*. Idem. *fol*. 129. D. And in the writ *de secta ad molendinum*. *Idē f*. 123. *B*. See the new booke of Entries: *verbo*: View. and see *Fleta* how this view is made. *lib*. 4. *ca*. 6. See *Veiours*.

Vicechamberlaine, called vnderchamberlaine anno 13. R. 2. *stat*. 2. *cap*. 1. is a great officer in court next vnder the Lord Chamberlaine, and in his absence, hath the command and controlmēt of all officers superior & inferior whatsoeuer, appertaining to that part of his maiesties houshold, which is called the chamber, wherein is included as well the bedde chamber, as the priuy chamber, the presence and the great Chamber, and all other roomes, as galeries, &c. thereto belonging, with the Councell chamber, priuie closet, &c. And in the Lord Chamberlaines absence he keepeth his table in the great chamber, commanding and overseeing the attendance of all, to whome it appertaineth to be ready and waiting on his maiestie going to the chapell, or to speake with ambassadours, or els walking or riding forth.

Vicount, aliàs Viscount (*vicecomes*) commeth of the French (*vicompte*. i. *Procomes*) and signifieth with vs as much as Shyreeue. Betweene which two words I finde no other difference, but that the one commeth from our Conquerours the Normans, and the other from our Auncesters the Saxons, wherefore see more of this in *Shyreeue*. Vicount also signifieth a degree of nobility next vnto an Earle, which (as *M.Cam.Brita.p.* 107. saith) is an old name of office, but a newe one of dignitie, neuer heard of amongst vs, vntill *Henry* the sixth his daies. But this degree of honour is more auncient farre in other countries. *Cassan in gloria mundi, parte* 5.*consid.* 55. whome you may reade.

Vicountie, is an adiectiue made of *vicountie*, and signifieth as much, as belóging to the vicount; as writs vicountiel are such writs as are triable in the countie or Shyreeues court: *old.nat.br.fol.* 109. Of this kinde you may see diuers writs of *Nusance* set downe by *Fitzh.* in his *nat. br. fol.* 184.*b.* There be also certaine fermes called Vicountiels, which the Shyreeue for his time payeth a certaine rent for to the King, and maketh what profit he can of them. See the statutes, *anno* 33.& 34.*H*.8.*ca.* 16.& *anno* 2.& 3.*Ed.* 6. *ca.* 4. and *anno* 4. *H. quint. capite secund.*

Vi laica removenda, is a writ that lyeth for the remooving of forcible possession of a benefice kept by lay men. And this writ is graunted some time vpon the Certificate of the Bishop into the Chauncerie, that there is such a force in his Dioces: some time vpon a surmise made there of by the Incumbent himselfe, without the certificat of the Bishop, and hath a seuerall forme for either case. *Fitzh.nat.br. fol.* 54. *Register orig. fol.* 59. & 60.

Villanis Regis subtractis reducendis, is a writ that lieth for the bringing back of the kings bondmen, that haue beene caried away by others out of his maners, whereunto they belonged, *Register origin. fol.* 87.*b.*

Villein(*villanus*) commeth of the French (*vilain*.i. *illiberalis, impurus, vilis, turpis*) and signifieth in our common lawe a bondman, or as much as *Servus* among the Ciuilians. Of these there be two sorts in England, as *Sir Tho.Smith* saith in his *repub. Anglo.li.* 3. *cap.* 8. one termed a Villein in grosse, which is immediately bound to the persons of his *Lord* and his heires, the other a villein regardant to a maner, whome the Ciuilians terme (*Glebæ ascriptitium*) being bound to their Lord, as members belonging and annexed to such a maner, whereof the *Lord* is owner. This diuision is affirmed by diuers places of our common lawe writers: as in the *old. nat. br. fol.* 8. You haue these words. Know ye that a woman shall

be

be indowed with a villein in grosse,&c. and againe *fol.* 39. If a man doe menace or threaten any villeins, which are regardant to a maner, &c. *Bracton* hath another diuision of villeins, which is all one with the Ciuilians. For in his first booke, *cap.* 6.*nu.* 4. he saith thus: *Serui autem nascuntur aut fiunt*, and then thus goeth forward: *Nascuntur ex nativo & nativa alicuius copulatis vel solutis, sive sub potestate Domini constituti sint, sive extra potestatem. Item nascitur seruus, qui ex natiua soluta generatur, quamvis ex patre libero: quia sequitur conditionem matris quasi vulgò conceptus, &c.* And after diuers things deliuered of this sort, he saith againe thus: *Fiunt etiam servi liberi homines captivitate de iure Gentium: &c. Fit etiam servus liber homo pro confessionē in Curia Regis factam: vt cum liber homo sit in Curia Regis, & se cognoscat ad villanum. Item liber homo fit servus, si cum semel manumissus fuerit, ob ingratitudinem in seruitutem reuocetur. Item fit liber homo seruus, cùm ab initio clericus vel monachus factus fuerit, postea ad secularem vitam redierit. Quia talis restitui debet Domino suo.* v. *Tiraquellum de Nobilitate. cap.* 2. *pag.* 14.*num.* 54. In very many prouinces of Fraunce there be certaine men called (*homines manus mortuæ, qui tanta iuris similitudine adscriptiis, colonis coniuncti, & prope iidem videntur. Non autem serui sunt omnino, sed in territorio domini sunt, tanquam alligati, non habentes demigrandi potestatem. Itaq; serui corporis & prosecutionis vulgò dicuntur, quòd si fugerint, potest eos prosequi dominus & capere. Tributum autem isti & nonnullas commoditates domino præstant: in quibus hæc maxima, quòd ipsis vita functis sine sobole, succedit dominus vel ex toto vel ex parte. Connanus. li.* 2. *cap.* 10.*num.* 3. whose words I thought not vnfit for this place, because they expresse the nature of our villenage somthing aptly.

Villein fleeces: anno 31. *Ed.* 3. *cap.* 8. are fleeces of wolle, that are shorne from scabbed sheepe

Vidimus, anno 15. *H.6.ca.*3.

Villenage (Villenagium) commeth of *(villein)* and signifieth a seruile kinde of tenure belonging to lands or tenements; that is, a tenure of lands or tenements, by such a seruice, as villeins are fittest to performe. For euery one that houldeth in villenage, is not a villein, or a bond man. *Villenagium vel seruitium nihil detrahit libertatis, habita tamen distinctione, vtrum tales sint villani, & tenuerint in villano soccagio de dominico Domini Regis. Bracton, lib. pri. ca.* 6. *nu. pri* Britton in his 66. chapter speaketh to this effect.

effect: Villenage is a tenure of the demesns of a Lord deliuered to a Tenent at the Lords will, by villenous seruices, to improoue it to the Lords vse, and deliuered by the rodde, and not by any title of writing, or succession of inheritance, &c. And a litle after he hath words to this effect: In the maners of our auncient Demesns, there be pure villeins both by blood and tenure: the which may be cast out of their tenement, and depriued of their chatels, at the pleasure of the Lord. By which two places I gather, though villein tenure doe not alway make the Tenent a villein: yet that there is a twofold tenure called villenage: one wherin both the persō & the tenure is bound, and in all respects at the disposition of the Lord: and another, which in respect of the tenure is after a sort seruile, though the person be not bond. This is well proued by *Bracton, li.* 2. *ca.* 8. *nu.* 3. in these words. *Item tenementum non mutat statum liberi, non magis quam serui: Poterit enim liber homo tenere purum villenagium, faciendo quicquid ad villanum pertinebit, & nihilo-minus liber erit, cum hoc faciat ratione villenagii, & non persona sua: & ideo poterit, quando voluerit, villenagium deserere, & liber discedere, nisi illaqueatus sit per vxorem natiuam ad hoc faciendum, ad quam ingressus fuit in villenagium, & quæ præstare poterit impedimentum, &c.* So that a man may hould in pure villenage, and yet be a free man in respect of his person. But what is pure villenage? *Bracton* aunswereth in the words there next following: *Purum villenagium est, à quo præstatur seruitium incertum & indeterminatum, vbi sciri non poterit vespere, quale seruitium fieri debet manè. viz: vbi quis facere tenetur quicquid ei preceptum fuerit.* The other sort of villenage which is not pure, is there called of *Bracton (villanum soccagium)* which differeth from the other in this, because it is onely tyed to the performance of certaine seruices agreed vpon betweene the *Lord* and the Tenent. Whereof see *Bracton* also in the same place: by whom you may perceiue, that a man may hould *(per villanum soccagium)* and yet haue *(liberum tenementum* if he haue it to himselfe and his heires. This villanous soccage is to cary the Lords dung into his feilds, to plow his ground at certaine daies, sow and reape his corne, plash his hedges, &c. See *Soccage.*

Villenous iudgement (Villanum iudicium) is that which casteth the reproch of villeny and shame vpon him against whom it is giuen, as a Conspiratour, &c.

Stawnf:

*Stawnf:pl:cor. lib.*3.12.*f.*175. This *M. Lamb:* in his *Eirenarcha, lib.* 1. *ca.* 13. *pag.* 63. calleth villenous punishment, and saith that it may well be called infamous, because the iudgement in such a case shalbe like the auncient iudgement in Attaint (as it is said *anno* 4. *H.* 5. *Fitzh. Iudgement* 220.) and is (in 27. *lib. Assis: pl.* 59.) set downe to be, that their oathes shall not be of any credit afterward, nor lawfull for them in person to aproch the *Kings* Courts: and that their lands and goods be seised into the Kings hands, their trees rooted vp, and their bodies imprisoned, &c. And at this day the punishmẽt apointed for periury, (hauing somwhat more in it, then corporall or pecuniary paine) stretching to the discrediting of the testimony of the offender from euer after, may be partaker of this name. Thus farre *M. Lamberd.*

Virgata terræ. Register orig. fol. 167. *a.* See *yard land.*

Viridario eligendo, is a writ that lyeth for the choice of a verdour in the forest. *Register orig. fol:* 177.

Visitation of maners (Visitatio morum) was wont to be the name of the Regarders office in auncient time. *Manwood, parte pri.* of his forest lawes, *pag.* 195. See *Regarder.*

Visne (Vicinetum) signifieth a neihgbour place, or a place neere at hand *anno* 16. *R.* 2. *ca.* 6.

Visu Franciplegii, is a writ to exempt him from comming to the view of Frankpledge, that is not within the Hundred resident. For men are bound vnto this view by reason of their habitation, and not of lands held where they dwell not, *Register orig. fol.* 175.

Vitteller (victualarius) commeth of the *French,* (*victuailes.* i. *commeatus*) and signifieth with vs, him that selleth victuals. For these there is a writ in *Fitz. nat. br. fol.* 172. if they exercise their trade, bearing a magistracie in any towne corporate.

Vmple. anno 3. *Edvard.* 4. *cap.* 5.

Vncore prist, is a plee for the Defendant, being siewed for a debt due at a day past, to saue the forfeiture of his bond; saying, that he tendered the dept at the time and place, and that there was none to receiue it, and that he is now allso readie to pay the same. 7. *Ed.* 6. 83. *Dyer.* See *Vnquest prist.*

Vncuth, is a Saxon word signifying as much as (*incognitus*) It is vsed in the auncient *Saxon* lawes, for him that commeth to an Inne guest wise, and lyeth there for two nights at the most. In which case his host was not bound to answer for any offence, that he committed, whereof he was guiltlesse himselfe. But if he laid there the third night, then he was called *(guest, hospes)* and thẽ must the host answer for him, as for one of his owne familie. And if he taried any longer, then was he called *Agen hine*, that is to say, *familiaris*. Whom, if he offend against the Kings peace, his hoste was to see foorthcomming: or if he could not bring him out within a moneth and a day, he must satisfie for his offence. *Lamberd. Archaiono. fol.* 133. *num.* 7. Of this *Bracton. lib.* 3. *cap.* 10. *num.* 2. writeth thus: *Item secundum antiquam consuetudinem dici poterit de familia alicuius, qui hospitatus fuerit cum alio per tres noctes: quia primâ nocte poterit dici* Vncuth, *secundâ verò Gust, tertiâ nocte Hoghenhine, &c.* This law was made for the better preseruation of the Kings peace, and to shew in what pledge euery man was to be accompted, that trauelled by the way. *See Tuainnithes gest.*

V*nde nihil habet*, is a writ. *See Dote vnde nihil habet.*

V*nder-chamberlaine of the Exchequer*, is an Officer there, that cleaueth the taileys written by the Clerke of the Tailcys, and readeth the same, that the Clerke of the Pel and the controllers thereof may see their entrie be true. He also maketh searches for all Rcords in the Treasurie. There be two Officers there of this name.

V*nderescheatour. Subescheatour. anno* 5. *Ed.* 3. *cap.* 4. See *Escheatour.*

Vndershyreeue, (Subvicecomes) See *Shyreeue.*

Vndersitter is an Inmate. See *Inmate.*

V*ndertakers*, be such as are employed by *Pourueyours* of the King as their deputies. *anno* 2. *&* 3. *Phil. & Mar. cap.* 6. and such as vndertake any great worke, as drying of *Fennes*, &c. *anno* 43. *Eliz. cap.* 11.

V*nder-treasurer of England, (vicethesaurarius Angliæ) anno* 39. *El. cap.* 7. *& anno* 43. *eiusdem. Subsidie of the Clergie.* This Officer (as some Exchequer men thinke) was first created in the time of king *H.* the seuenth, to chest vp the Kings Treasure at the end of euery Terme, and to note the content of money in each chest, and to see it caried to the Kings *Treasurie* in the Tower, for the ease of the Lord Treasurer, as being a thing too meane for him to be troubled with, and yet meete to be performed by a man of great secrecie and trust. He in the vacancie of the Lord *Treasurers*

ſurers office, doth all things in the receipt, that the *Lord* Treaſurer doth. He nominateth the two Prayſers of all goods ſeiſed as not cuſtomed, and ordereth, whether the partie ſhall haue them at the price or not. He appointeth the Steward, Cooke, and *Butler* for the prouiſion of the Starre-chamber. But this Officer in other mens iudgment, is farre more auncient then *Henry* the ſeuenths dayes, yet named *Treaſurer* of the Exchequer in the Statutes vntill Queene *Elizabeths* time, where he is tearmed Vnder-treaſurer of *England*. Neuertheleſſe, *anno* 35 *Eliz*. he is alſo written Treaſurer of the Exchequer. Read the *Statutes*, *anno* 18. *Ed*. 3. *ſtat*. 2. *cap*. 17. & 27. *eiuſdem. Stat*. 2. *cap*. 18. 1. *Rich*. 2. *cap*. 5. 4. *Hen*. 4. *cap*. 18. 8. *H*. 6. *cap*. 17. 27. *H*. 8. *cap*. 11. with diuers other places, that ſeeme to approue this to be true.

Vnion (*vnio*) is a combining or conſolidation of two Churches in one, which is done by the conſent of the Biſhop, the *Patron*, and the Incumbent. And this is properly called an *Vnion*. *Howbeit*, that there be two other ſortes: as when one Church is made ſubiect to the other, and when one man is made Prelate of both, and when a conuentual is made *Cathedrall*, as you may reade in the Gloſſe of the chapter, *Licet. De locato & conducto*, in *Lyndwoods Prouincials*. §. *Et quia. verſu Appropriationis*. Touching Vnion in the firſt ſignification there was a ſtatute, *an*. 37. *H*. 8. *cap*. 21. that it ſhould be lawfull in two Churches, wherof the value of the one is not aboue ſixe pounds in the *Kings* bookes of the firſt fruites, and not aboue one mile diſtant from the other. Vnion in this ſignification is perſonall, that is, for the life of the Incumbent: or reall, that is, perpetuall, whoſoeuer be Incumbent.

Vnitie of poſſeſſion, is called *conſolidatio vſus fructus, & proprietatis* in the Ciuill lawe, ſignifying a ioynt poſſeſſion of two rights by ſeuerall titles. *For* example, I take a leaſe of land from one vpon a certaine rent: afterward I buy the *Fee*-ſimple. This is an vnitie of poſſeſſion, wherby the leaſe is extinguiſhed: by reaſon that I, which had before the occupation only for my rent, am become *Lord* of the ſame, and am to pay my rent to none, but my ſelfe. Alſo an Abbot being ſeated within a certaine pariſh, afterward obtaineth an appropriation of the tythes belonging to that Church, for the vſe of his houſe. Here is an vnity of poſſeſſion, by reaſon that the tythes, which before were to be paid to the Incumbẽt, are now to be paid to none but himselfe, by vertue of the appropriation.

Vniversitie, (*Vniuersitas*) is by the Ciuill lawe any bodie politicke, or corporation: but in our language it is (at the least most ordinarily) taken for those twó bodies, that are the Nourishes of learning, and the liberall Sciences, *Cambridge* and *Oxford*: endowed with great fauours, and priuiledges, for their beter maintenance, as appeareth not onely by *an*. 2. & 3. *Ph. & Mar. c*. 15. *a*. 13. *El. c*. 21. & *a*. 18. *eius. c*. 6. but much more by their seuerall charters, graunted vnto them by diuers godly and magnanimous Kings of this land.

Vnlawfull assembly, (*Illicita congregatio, illicita assemblata*) is the meeting of three or more persons together, with force to commit some vnlawfull act, and abiding stil, not indeuouring the execution thereof, as to assault or beate any person, to enter into his house or land, &c. *West. parte* 2. *symb. titulo, Inditements, sect*. 65. *M. Lam*. in his *Eirenarcha. cap*. 19. saith thus: *An* vnlawfull assembly is the companie of three persons or more, gathered togther, to do such an vnlawfull act, although they do it not indeed. *So* saith *Kitchin* in effect, *fol*. 20.

Vnques prist, is (word for word) alwaies readie. And it signifieth a *Plee*, whereby a man professeth himselfe alway ready to do or performe that, which the *Demaundant* requireth, therby to auoide charges. *For* example: a woman sieweth the tenent for her *Dower*: and he cõming in at the first day, offereth to auerre, that he was alway ready and still is, to performe it. In this case except the *Demaundant* will auerre the contrarie, he shall recouer no dammages. When this *Plee* will serue to auoide Charges, and when not, see *Kit. fol*. 243. See *Vncore prist*.

Voydance (*vacatio*) is a want of an Incumbent vpon a benefice: and this voydance is double: either in law, as when a man hath more benefices incõpetible: or indeed, as when the Incumbẽt is dead, or actually depriued. *Brooke, titulo Quareimpedit. n*. 51.

Voucher (*Aduocatio*) is a calling in of one into the Court at the petition of a party that hopeth to be helped thereby. New booke of *Entries. verbo. voucher. voucher de garantie Brit. ca*. 75. in latine (*Aduocatio ad warantizandum*) is a petition in court made by the Defendant to haue him called, of whom he or his Auncester bought the land or tenement in question, and receiued warranty for the secure inioying thereof against all men.

Brit-

Britton of this writeth a long chapter. *vbi supra*, intituling it *Garant voucher*. But *Bracton* writeth a large tractate of it, *lib.* 5. *tracta.* 4. *per totum. Litleton* also handleth it not minsingly, in the last chapter of all his Tenures. Of this you may read *Fitzh.* also in his *nat. br. fol.* 134. *De warantia charta*. All this law seemeth to haue bene brought into England out of Normandy. For in the Grand Custumary you haue likewise a chapter intituled (*vouchement de garant, cap.* 50. *id est, vocamentum Garanti*) where it is set downe, what time ought to be giuen, for the appearance of the warrant called in this case, how many warrants may be vouched, one calling in another, and diuers other points touching this doctrine. All which, and many more, you may read in *Bracton vbi supra*. A common *voucher*, a double *voucher*. *Coke lib.* 2. Sir *Hughe. Cholmleis case, fol.* 50. *b*. This is very aunswerable to the contract in the Ciuill lawe, whereby the buyer bindeth the seller, sometime in the simple value of the thing bought, sometime in the double, to warrant his secure enioying of the thing bought. But this difference I find betweene the Ciuill lawe and ours, that whereas the Ciuill lawe bindeth euery man to warrant the securitie of that which hee selleth, ours doth not so, except it be especially couenanted. The party that voucheth in this case, is called the Tenent, the partie vouched is tearmed the *Vouchee*. The writ whereby he is called, is termed *Summoneas ad warrantizandum*. And if the *Shyreeue* return vpõ that writ, that the party hath nothing, whereby he may be summoned: then goeth out another writ. *viz. Sequatur sub suo periculo*. See *Termes of the lawe. verbo* Voucher. And *Lamb.* in his Explication of Saxon wordes, *verbo Advocare*. See *Warrantie*. I reade in the new booke of *Entries*, of a *forain voucher*, which hath place properly in some *Franchise*, Countie *Palatine*, or other where one voucheth to warrantie one not dwelling within the *Franchise*. *fol.* 615. *columna*. 1. whereupon because the foreyner neede not be tryed in that Court, the record and cause is remooued to the common plees, &c. See of this *Fitz. nat. br. fol.* 6. E.

Vser de action, is the persiewing or bringing of an action, which in what place and countie it ought to be, See *Brooke, titulo Lieu & Countie. fol.* 64.

Vse (*vsus*) is in the originall signification, plaine enough: but it hath a proper application in our common lawe, and that is the profit or benefit of lands or tenements. And out of *M. Wests* first parte of his *simbol: lib. pri sect.* 48. 49. 50. 51. and 52. I gather shortly thus much for this purpose. Euery deede in writing hath to be considered the substance, and the adiuncts. Touching the substance, a deede doth consist of two principall parts, namely the premisses and the consequents. The premisses is the former parte thereof, and is commonly saide to be all that, which preceedeth the (*Habendum*) or limitation of the estate, which be the persons contracting, and the things contracted. The consequent is that which foloweth the premisses, & that is the (*Habendum*) In which are two limitations: the one of the estate, or propertie, that the party passiue shall receiue by the deede, the other of the vse: which is to expresse in the said (*Habendum*) to or for what vse, and benefite he shall haue the same estate. And of the limitation of those vses, you may read many presidents set downe by the same author in his second booke of his saide first part, *sectio.* 308. and so forth to 327. These vses were inuented vpon the statute called, *West.* 3. or *Quia emptores terrarum*, before the which statute no vses were knowne. *Perkins. Devises.* 528. And because mens wits, had in time deuised many deceits, by the setting of the possession in one man and the vse in another, there was a statute made, *anno,* 27. *H.* 8. *ca.* 1. wherby it was inacted, that the vse and possession of lands and possessions should alway stand vnited. New expositour of lawe termes, *verbo.* *Vse. v.* Coke *lib.* 1. *Chudleise case. fol.* 121. *& seqq.*

Vsher (*Ostiarius*) commeth of the French (*Huissier*.i. *Accensus, apparitor,* I*anitor*) It signifieth with vs first an officer in the Eschequer: of which sort there be foure ordinarie vshers that attend the cheife officers and Barons of the court at *Westminster*, and Iuries, Shyreeues and all other accoumptants at the pleasure of the court. Therbe also Vshers in the *Kings* house, as of the priuy chãber, &c.

Vtas (*Octava*) is the eight day following any terme or feast: as the *vtas of Sainct Michaell, the vtas of Sainct Hilary, the vtas of* Sainct *Martine*, *of* Sainct *Iohn Baptist*, of the Trinitie &c. as you may reade. *anno* 51. *H.* 3. *stat.* concerning generall daies in the Benche. And any day betweene the feast and the eighth day, is saide to be within the *vtas*. The vse of this is in the returne of writs, as appeareth by the same statute.

Vtfangthef, is an auncient Royaltie graunted to a Lord of a maner, by the King which giueth him the punishment of a theefe dwelling out of his liberty, and hauing committed theft without the same, if he be taken within his fee. *Bracton. lib.* 2. *cap.* 24. who in his third booke, *tract.* 2, *ca.* 35. seemeth rather to interpret the word, then to expresse the effect, and saith thus. *Vtfangthef dicitur extraneus latro, veniens aliunde de terra aliena, & qui captus fuit in terra ipsius, qui tales habet libertates* It seemeth to be compounded of these three words. *Vt, fang, thef.* which in our moderne *English* be, oute, take or taken, Theefe. Of this *Fleta* hath these words. *vtfangenthef dicitur latro extraneus veniens aliunde de terra aliena, & qui captus fuerit in terra ipsius qui tales habet libertates. Sed non sequitur quod possit ille hominem suum proprium extra libertatem suam captum reducere vsq; in libertatem, & ibi eum iudicare: reducere tamen poterit iudicatum, & iudicium in proprio patibulo exequi ratione libertatis: commodum tamen non video. Debet enim quilibet iuri subiacere, vbi deliquit: proprios tamen latrones & alienos iudicare possunt, dum tamen infra libertatem fuerint capti, &c.*

Vtlaghe, significat bannitum extra legem. Fleta. li. 1. *cap.* 47. *See Vtlawrie.*

Vtlagato capiendo quando vtlagatur in vno comitatu, & postea fugit in alium, is a writ, the nature whereof is sufficiently expressed in the words set downe for the name thereof. See the *Register* originall, *fo.* 133.

Vtlawrie (*vtlagaria, aliàs vtlagatio*) is a punishment for such as being called into lawe, and lawfully sought, doe comteptuously refuse to appeare. And as *Bracton* saith *li.* 3. *tract.* 2. *ca.* 11. He that is sewed must be sought, and called at 5. counties, a moneth being betweene euery countie, to answer to the lawe. And if he come not within that time, *pro exlege tenebitur cum principi non obediat, nec legi: & ex tunc vtlagabitur*: that is, as the author of the termes of lawe saith, he shalbe pronounced by the coroner, to be out of the Kings protection, and depriued of the benefit of the lawe. The effect of this is diuers (as the same Author saith). for if he be outlawed in an action personall, (he meaneth) at the suite of another in a ciuile cause: he shall forfeit all his goods and cattells to the King: if vpon felonie then he shall forfeit all his lands and tenements, that he hath in fee simple, or for terme of his life, and his goods and cattles. *Bracton: vbi supra, nu.*5. saith, that such as be outlawed vpon felonie, *ex tunc gerunt caput lupinum, ita quod sine iudiciali inquisitione ritè pereant, & secum suum iudicium portent & meritò sine lege pereunt, qui secundum legem viuere recusarunt. Et hæc ita, si cum capiendi fuerint, fugiant, vel se defendant si autem vivi capti fuerint, vel se reddiderint, vita illorum & mors erit in manu Domini Regis.* See *Horns mirrour of Iustices, lib.* 3. *cap. des fautes punishables.* Bracton saith in the place aboue specified (with whome also *Fleta* agreeth, *lib.* 1. *cap.* 27.) that a Minor or a woman cannot be outlawed. But take his owne words: *Minor verò, & qui infra ætatem.* 12. *annorum fuerit, vtlagari non potest, nec extra legem poni, quia ante talem ætatem non est sub lege aliqua, nec in Decenna, non magis quàm fœmina, quæ vtlagari non potest, quia ipsa non est sub lege.* i. *Inlaugh Anglicè, sc: in frãco plegio, sive decenna: sicut masculus,* 12. *annorum, & vlteriùs. Et ideo non potest vtlagari. Waiviari tamen bene potest, & pro derelicta haberi, cum pro felonia aliqua fugam fecerit siue ceperit. Est enim waiuium, quod nullus aduocat, nec princeps eum advocabit, nec tuebitur, cum fuerit rite Waiviata: sicut fit de masculo, qui secundum legem terræ ritè fuerit vtlagatus, &c.* To the same effect writeth *Fitz h.* in his *na. br. fo.* 161. *viz.* And because women be not sworne in leetes to the King, as men be of the age of 12 yeares or vpward: it is said, when a woman is outlawed, that shee is waiued, but not outlawed. for shee was neuer vnder the law, nor sworne vnto it. More of this you may reade in *Bracton, lib.* 3. *tracta.* 2. *cap* 12. & 13. and then in the 14. how an outlaw is inlawed againe, and restored to the Kings peace and protection. See also *Fleta, lib.* 1. *cap.* 28. *per totum.*

Vtrum. See *Assise.*

Vtter Baristers, be such as for their longe study and great industry bestowed vpon the knowledge of the common lawe, be called out of their contemplation to practise, and in the face of the world to take vpon them the protection and defence of clients. These are in other countries called, *(Licentiati in iure).* How be it in modestie they still continue themselues hearers for diuers yeares, like the scholers of *Pythagoras*, that for the first fiue yeres neuer aduentured to reason or discourse openly vpon any point of their masters Doctrine, which their silence *(a cohibendo sermone)* was termed ἐχεμυθία as *Suidas* and *Zenodorus* doe report.

Vtlepe,

Vtlepe significat escapium latronum. Fleta lib. 1. *ca.* 47.

W

WAge (*vadiare*) proceedeth of the *French* (*Gager*. i. *dare pignus* , *pignore certare*) and signifieth in our common lawe the giuing of securitie for the performing of any thing: as to wage lawe, & to wage deliuerance which see before in *Gage*. None wageth lawe against the King. *Brooke tit*. *Chose in action, num*.9.The substantiue of this verb is (*Wager*) in the latine (*vadium*) which some Feudists call (*wadium*) as testifieth *Hotoman in his Commentaries de verbis feudalibus. verbo Wadium*.See *Lawe*.

Wainage (*Wainagium, aliâs Wanagium*) signifieth as much as *peculium servorum* of the Saxon word *wonen*.i.*habitare*, & *woening*.i. *habitatio*. See. *Gamage*.

Waiue (*waiuiare*) *Register orig. fol*.277. *a*) is to forsake (*habere pro derelicto*) as the Ciuilians terme it. *Waiviare feudum suum. Bracton lib.* 2. *cap.* 7. that is to forsake . Many of the *Kings* liege people to be outlawed, and many waiued by erroneous proces. *anno* 7. *H*. 4. *ca*. 13. See *Vtlawrie*. To waiue the company of theeues. *Stawnf.pl.cor. fol*.26. To waiue his benefit. *Idem fol*. 46. to waiue the aduantage. *Idem prærog. fol*. 17. Persons attainted or waiued. *West. parte* 2. *simbol. titulo Fines, sect*: 13. *D*. This word *waiued waiuiata* properly belongeth to a woman that being siewed in law contemptuously refuseth to appeare, as outlawed doth to a man. *Register orig fo*. 132. *b*. & 277. *a*. The reason whereof see in *Fitzh. nat. br. fol*. 161. *A*. See *Weif*.

Wales (*Wallia*) is a part of England, on the west side inhabited by the offspring of the auncient *Britons* chased thither by the Saxons, being called hether by them to assist them against the might of the *Picts*. The reason of the appellation commeth from the *Saxon* (*wealh* .i. *externus, vel peregrinus*) for so the *Saxons* both called them and held them, though now to the great quiet of this kingdome they be incorporated vnto vs See *M.Lamb* explication of *Saxon* words. *verbo. Wallus*.

Walkers, seeme to be those that are otherwise called Forresters. *Crompton* in his Iurisdictions, *fol*. 154. hath these words in effect. There be *Foresters* assigned by the *King*, which be walkers within a certeine space assigned them to looke vnto.

Waiuiaria mulieris, is as much as *vtlagatio viri*. *Register originall fol*. 132. *b*. See *Waiue*.

Wapentake (*Wapentakium*) is all one with that, which we call a Hundred, as appeareth by *Bracton, lib. 3. tract. 2. ca. pri. nu. pri. in fine. Conuocentur* (saith he) *postmodum seruientes & Balliui Hundredorum, & per ordinem irrotulentur Hundredarii, siue wapentakia, & nomina seruientium, quorum quilibet affidabit, quod de quolibet Hundredo eliget quatuor milites, qui statim veniant coram Iusticiariis ad faciendum preceptum Domini Regis, & qui statim iurabunt, quòd eligent duodecim milites, vel liberos & legales homines, si milites non inueniantur, &c. M. Lamberd* in his explication of *Saxon* words, *verbo Centuria*, is of the same minde: and farder saith, that this word is especially vsed at this day in the countries be north the riuer *Trent*. And in the lawes of King *Edward* set forth by him *nu. 33.* it is most plaine in these words. *Et quod Angli vocant Hundredum, supradicti comitatus vocant wapentakium.* But there he nameth some shires of this side *Trent*, as *Warwickshire, Leicester shire*, and *Northhampton-shire*. In the words there folowing, there is a reason giuen of this appellation in these words. *Et non sine causa: Cum quis enim accipiebat praefecturam wapentakii, die statuto in loco, vbi consueuerant congregari, omnes maiores contra eum conueniebant, & descendente de equo suo, omnes assurgebant ei. Ipse verò, erecta lancea sua, ab omnibus secundum morem foedus accipiebat. Omnes enim quotquot venissent, cum lanceis suis ipsius hastam tangebant, & ita confirmabant per contractum armorum, pace palam concessa. Anglicè enim arma vocantur (wapun) & taccare confirmare: quasi armorum confirmatio. Vel vt magis expressè secundum linguam anglicanam dicamus, wapentak armorum tactus est (wapun) enim arma sonant (tac) tactus est. Quamobrem poterit cognosci, quòd hac de causa, totus ille conuentus dicitur (wapentac) eò quòd per tactum armorum suorum ad inuicem confoederati sunt.* Thus farre the booke goeth word for word. With whom *Fleta* agreeth, sauing that *Fleta* saith, that this word is vsed in all counties *be north Watlinstreete, li. 2. ca. 61. §. vniuersimode.* Take Sir *Tho: Smithes* opinion also: whose words in his second booke *de Rep: Anglo: ca: 16.* be these: *Wapentak*, I suppose, came of the *Danes*, or peraduenture of the *Saxons*. For that so many townes came by there order then into one place, where was taken a mouster of there armour and weapons: in which place, from them that could not finde sufficient pledges for their good abearing, their weapons were taken away. The statute *anno 3. Henrici 5. ca. 2. & anno 9. H. 6.*

cap.

cap. 10. & *anno* 15. *H.* 6. *ca.* 7. T. maketh mention of *Stainclife Wapentake*, and *Frendles Wapentake*, in *Crauen* in the County of *Yorke*. See *Roger Houeden, parte poster: suorum annalium, fo.* 346. *b.*

Wards and Liueries (*wardi & liberatura*) is a Court first erected in King *Henry* the eighth his time, and afterward augmented by him with the office of *Liueries*, and therefore called by him (as now it is) the Court of *wards* and *Liueries*. The chiefe of this Court is called the master of the Court, &c. To whom are ioyned the *Surueiour*, *Atturny*, and *Receiuer* of the said Court, as his Assistants: then as Ministers the *Register*, two inferiour *Atturnies* or Clerks, and a Messenger.

Ward (*Custodia*) is the *German* word, as (*Garde*) is the French. Both these be vsed among our common lawyers: the one by those that write in French, the other by those that write in English. Wherefore for your farder vnderstanding, See *Gard* and *Gardein*. Yet is *Gard* sometime vsed in the Englishbookes also: as yeomen of the *Gard*. And also the keeper of one in his minority, is not called a *warden* but a *Gardein* or *Gardian*. *Ward* hath diuers applications, as a *Ward* in *London*, latined (*warda*) which is a portion of the City committed to the especiall charge of some one of the 24. Aldermen of the city, in such sort as euery one knoweth his certaine ward assigned vnto him, and hath dwelling within the same compas some one graue Citizen for the good gouernment thereof: who is in that respect a Deputie to the said Alderman, and commonly called the Aldermans Deputie. Of these there be 25. within the citie, and one without, beside other liberties and the suburbes. *Stowes Surney of London.* Also a Forest is diuided into *wards*: *Manwood, parte prim.* of his Forest lawes. *pag.* 97. Lastly, a prison is otherwise called a *Ward*. And the heire of the Kings tenent, houlding by knights seruice, or *in capite*, or of any common person by Knights seruice, is called *Ward*, during his nonage. See *anno* 32. *H.* 8. *cap.* 46.

Warden (*Gardianus*) signifieth al one thing with the French (*Gardien.*) And therefore of this see more in *Gardien*. But it is the more vsuall word of all that writ in English, for him that hath the keeping or charge of any person or thing by office: as Wardens of Felowships in *London. anno* 14. *H.* 8. *cap.* 2. *Warden courts, anno* 31. *H.* 6. *ca.* 3. *Warden of the Marches, anno* 4 *H.* 7. *cap.* 8. *Wardens and Com-*

munaltie of the lanes contributorie to *Rochester* bridge. *anno* 18. *Eliz. cap.* 7. Wardens of peace. *anno* 2. *Ed.* 3. *cap.* 3. Statute *Northampton*. Warden of the West Marches. *Camd. Brit. pag.* 606. *W*arden of the Forest. *Manwood, parte prim. pag.* 111. & 112. *W*arden of the Aulnage. *anno* 18. H. 6. *cap.* 16. Chiefe *W*arden of the Forest. *Manwood parte prim. pag.* 42. & 43. *W*arden of the *K*ings wardrobe. *anno* 51. H. 3. *statut. quinto*. *W*ardens of the tables of the *K*ings Exchaunge, *anno* 9. *Ed.* 3. *stat.* 2. *cap.* 7. & *anno* 9. H. 5. *stat.* 2. *c.* 4. *W*arden of the rolles of the Chauncerie. *anno* 1. *Ed.* 4. *cap.* 1. & *cap.* 5. *W*arden or Clerke of the hamper of the Chauncerie. *ibid. W*arden of the kings writs, and *R*ecords of his common bench, *ibid. W*arden of the Kings armour in the tower. *anno* 1. *Ed.* 4. *cap.* 1.

Wardmote, is a court kept in euery ward in *London. anno* 32. H. 8. *cap.* 17. ordinarily called among them, the *Wardmote* Court.

Ward peny, is money to be contributed toward watch and ward.

Warantie, (*warantia*) commeth of the French (*garantie*) or (*garant*) i. *vindex litis*:) which is a word of great antiquitie with the *F*rench men, being brought first thither by the *Francogalli*. And thence do they make a Latinish verbe, *viz.* (*guarentare*) *vel, vt est in aliis libris, guarentisare*. i. *causam alterius suscipere, se defensorem profiteri*. The Feudists also vse this word (*guarentus*) *quo significatur is, qui Latinis author dicitur, & euictionem præstat. lib.* 2. *Feud. titulo* 34. §. 2. The Ciuilians haue a stipulation (*habere licere*) whereby is signified a power of perpetuall & quiet possession to be giuen: *l.* 11. § *final.* π. *de action. empt. & vend.* But this reacheth not so farre as our warrantie. *F*or the seller hereby is bound but to a kind of diligence and care to maintaine the buyer in his possession. *F*or if he be euicted, the buyer is not tyed to recōpence. *Doctores in l. stipulatio ista, Habere licere.* π. *de verb. obliga.* *W*arrantie signifieth in our common lawe, a promise made in a deed by one man vnto another for himselfe and his heires, to secure him and his heires against all men, for the enioying of any thing agreed of betweene them. And he that maketh this warrantie, is called *Warrantus* by *Bracton, lib.* 2. *cap.* 10. & 37. The Romaines called him *Auctorem*, as *Hotoman* testifieth in his Commentarie vpon *Tullies* oration *pro Aulo Cecinna. verbo, Cesennius author fundi*, whom you

may

may reade more at large. And that which we terme *vocationem warranti*, the Ciuilians call *authoris laudationem vel nominationem*. *Eimer pract. cap. 48*. This warranty passeth from the seller to the buyer, from the feoffer to the feoffee, from him that releaseth, to him that is released of an action reall, and such like. And for the forme it passeth in a clause toward the end of a deed in these wordes: *Et ego verò præfatus* I. *& hæredes mei prædictas decem acras terræ cum pertinentiis suis prefato H. hæredibus, & assignatis suis contra omnes gentes warrantizabimus in perpetuum per præsentes. West. parte prim. symbol. lib. 2. titulo Feofments. sect.* 281. *& 288*. So a release may be with a clause of warrantie. *Idem, eodem. titulo Releases. sect.* 510.

There is allso a warrant of Atturney, whereby a man appointeth another to do some thing in his name, and warranteth his action, *West. eod. sect. 181*. And these warrãts of Atturney seeme to differ from leters of Atturney, because that, whereas leters passe ordinarily vnder the hand and seale of him, that maketh an Atturney by them, before any credible witnesses: warrants of Atturney be acknowledged before such persons, by such means and in such maner, as Fines. *West. parte 2. symbol. titulo* Recoueries. *sect. prim. F.* See *Atturney*.

But these waranties in passing land from one to another, be of greatest consequent, & of more intricate vnderstanding. And therefore of these, diuers haue written at large: as *Glanvile lib. 3. per totum. Bracton lib. 5. tract. 4. per totum. Britton. cap. 105. Litleton* in the last chapter of his tenures: the forme and effect whereof *Bracton* in his second booke *cap. 16. num.* 10. declareth thus: *Et ego & hæredes mei warrantizabimus tali & hæredibus suis tantùm, vel tali & hæredibus & assignatis, & hæredibus assignatorum, vel assignatis assignatorum, & eorum hæredibus, & acquietabimus, & defendemus eis totam terram illam cum pertinentiis (secundum quod prædictum est) contra omnes gentes in perpetuum, per prædictum seruitium. Per hoc autem quòd dicit (Ego & hæredes mei) obligat se & hæredes suos ad warrantiam, propinquos, & remotos, præsentes & futuros ei succedentes in infinitum Per hoc autem quòd dicit (warrantizabimus) suscipit in se obligationem ad defendendum suum* Tenementum *in possessione rei datæ, & assignatos suos & eorum hæredes, & omnes alios, secundum quod supradictum est, si fortè tenementum datum petatur ab antiquo in* Dominico. *Per hoc autem quòd dicit (acquietabimus) obligat se & hæredes suos ad* acquie-

acquietandum, si quis plus petierit seruitii, vel aliud seruitium, quam in charta donationis continetur: per hoc autem quod dicit (Defendemus) obligat se & hæredes suos ad Defendendum, si quis velit seruitutem ponere rei datæ contra formam suæ donationis, &c. But the new expounder of law terms saith, that this warranty beginneth two waies: one by deede of law: as if one and his auncesters, haue held land of another and his auncesters, time out of minde by homage (which is called *Homage auncestrell*) for in this case, the homage cõtinually performed by the tenent is sufficient to bind the Lord to warrant his estate. The other is by deede of the party, which by deede or fine tyeth himselfe to warrant the land or tenement to the tenent. And Sir *Ed: Cooke* in the fourth booke of his reports, mentioneth the same distinction. *Nokes case, fo.* 81. *a.* calling the one a warranty in law, the other an expresse warranty. Ciuilians would call these *species, tacitam & expressam.*

Warranty (as the said author of the terms of law saith, is in two maners: warranty lineall, and warranty collaterall. But (*Litleton* saith *vbi supra*) it is threefold: warranty lineall, warranty collaterall, and warranty that beginneth by disseisin. Warranty by disseisin what it is, is partly declared in Sir *Ed. Cookes* reports, *li.* 3. *Fermors case, fol.* 78. *a.* Whether of them deuideth more aptly, let the learned iudge. For my part, I thinke that lineall and collaterall be no essentiall differences of warranty, as it is originally considered in the first warranter. For he bindeth himselfe and his heires in generall. And such be bound, be they lineall or collaterall vnto him. Therefore this diuision riseth rather from the euent of the originall warranty: *videlicet,* because it so falleth out, that the tenent, to whom the warranty was made, or his heires, when he or they be called into question for the land warranted formerly by the first feoffour, is driuen by the meanes of the first warranters death, to cal or vouch him to warranty that is his heire, and now presently liuing, be he descending or collaterall, as it falleth out. For example. *A.* infeoffeth *B.* in twenty acres land, with clause of warranty against all men. So long as *A.* himselfe liueth, he is liable to this couenant, and none els: after his discease his heire is subiect vnto it, be he his sonne, brother, vncle, or what els. And whether of these, or neither of these it will be, none knoweth vntill he be dead. Wherefore I conclude that this distinction of lineall or collate-

collaterall hath no vse originally in this contract. For (as the author of the terms of law saith) the burden of this warranty, after the death of the first warranter, falleth vpon him, vpon whom the land should haue descended, if the warranty had not bene made. And that is the next of blood to the warranter, be he in the descending or collaterall line. And therefore I resolue that this distinction groweth from an euent, after the death of him that couenanteth to warrant. But to make this plaine, I finde warranty to be vsed equiuocally: signifiing in one sort, the contract, or couenant of warranty first made, as appeareth by *Bracton* in the place formerly noted: and in another sort the very effect and performance of this contract, either by the warranter or his heires, when he or they be by the tenent thereunto vouched, or called: As also I shew out of *Bracton, lib.* 5. *tract.* 4. *ca. pri. nu.* 2. in these words. *Imprimis videndum est quid sit warrantizatio. Et sciendum quod warrantizare, nihil aliud est, quàm defendere & acquietare tenentem, qui warrantum vocabit in seisina sua, &c.* With whom agreeth *Fleta* saying that *warrantizare nihil aliud est, quam possidentem defendere, li.* 5. *ca.* 15. §. 1. & *lib.* 6. *ca* 23. *quod lege per totum*. And the former diuision of lineall and collaterall warranty, rather belongeth to warranty in this second signification then the former.

And that this way it is imperfect or at the least obscure, I thinke it not hard to declare. First to shew this I note out of *Bracton*, who may be called to warrantie. And he *lib.* 5. *tractat.* 4. *cap. pri. num.* 5. saith thus: *Videndum est quis vocari possit ad warrantum, & sciendum, quod tam masculus quam fœmina, tam minor quàm maior (dum tamen si minor vocetur, remaneat placitum de warantia in suspenso vsq; ad ætatem, nisi causa fuerit ita fauorabilis, quòd ætas expectari non debeat, sicut ex causa Dotis) Item non solum vocandus est ad warantum ille qui dedit, vel venddit: verùm etiam vocandi sunt eorum heredes descendentes in infinitum propter verba in Chartis contenta, (Ego & hæredes mei warantizabimus tali & hæredibus suis, &c.) Et in quo casu tenentur hæredes warantizare, sive sint propinqui, sive remoti, remotiores, vel remotissimi. Et quod de hæredibus dicitur, idem dici poterit de assignatis, & de illis, qui sunt loco illorum hæredũ, sicut sunt capitales Domini qui tenentibus suis quasi succedunt, vel propter aliquem defectum, vel propter aliquod delictum, sicut de eschaetis Dominorum:* By which words we perceiue that

that the burden of this warrantie is not tyed to heires only, be they in the descending or collaterall line, but that vnder this word (*Hæredes*) are comprised all such, as the first warranters lands afterward come vnto either by discent, or otherwise *ex causa lucratiua* So that if a man haue 20 children, yet if he will, and may giue his land to a straūger, leauing his childrē no land: that straunger in this case is his assigne, & is conteined vnder this word, heire. So if he commit felonie after such warrantie covenanted, and forfeit his lands to his Lord by escheate: the Lord is *quasi hæres* in this case, and lyable to the warrantie formerly passed. And in these two later cases, warranty in the secōd signification seemeth to be neither lineall, nor collaterall: at the least as *Litleton*, and the other author haue defined, or by examples expressed them.

But yet let vs define these two species, as they be. wherefore lineall warranty is that, which he is called vnto by the tenent, vpon whome the land warranted had descended, if the warranty had not beene couenanted. For example; A selleth to *B*. 20. acres land with clause of warranty, and afterward dieth leauing issue. C. soone after *B*. is impleaded for this land by *D*. and voucheth. *C*. This is called a lineall warranty: because but for it the land had descended from A. to C.

Warranty collaterall, is that whereunto he is called by the tenent vpon the couenant of him, from whome the land could not descend to the party called. For example; *B*. the sonne pourchaseth tenements in fee, whereof A. his father disseiseth him, and selleth them to C. with a clause of warranty. A being deade, C. is impleaded for the tenements, and calleth *B*. to warranty. This warranty whereunto B. is caled, is collaterall: bycause the tenements, if the warrnty had not beene couenanted by *A*. could not haue descended from him to his father A. for they were his owne by Pourchase. Many other exāples there be of this in *Litleton*. And this very case he maketh his example of warranty by disseisin, as also of warranty collaterall. which plainly argueth, that warranty by disseisin, and warranty collaterall, are not distinct members of warranty, but may be confounded: though one warranty may cary both names in diuers respects. For there is some warranty collaterall that beginneth not by disseisin. For

exam-

example. A . tenent in taile, alienateth to B.in fee, and dieth leauing issue. C. Afterward. D. brother to A. and vncle to C. releaseth to B. with warranty, and dying leaueth . C . his heire being next of blood vnto him. This warranty is collaterall, because it descendeth vpon . C. from his vncle. D. and yet it beginneth not by desseisin of his said vncle.

Warranty, hath a double effect: one to debarre him vpō whome it discendeth from the first warranter as his next of blood, from claiming the land warranted: aud another to make it good to the tenent , if by him he be vouched thereunto, or els to giue him as much other land by exchange. But as the former of these effects taketh place with all heires, except those to whome the land warranted was intailed , and that reape no equiualent benefit by the first warranter. *anno 6. Ed. pri, ca.* 3. soe the latter preiudiceth none that receiueth not sufficient land from the first warranter to make it good. *Bracton, lib*. 5. *tractat*. 4 *ca*. 8. *nu. pri. & cap*. 13. *nu*. 2. In the custumarie of Norm . *ca* . 5 . you haue *vouchement de garant*, which the Interpreter translateth, *Vocamentum Garanti*. a voucher or calling of the wartanter into the court to make good his sale or gift.

Warantia diei, is a writ lying in case, where a man hauing a day assigned personally to appeare in court to any action wherein he is siewed, is in the meane time by commaundement imployed in the *Kings* seruice, so that he cannot come at the day assigned. This writ is directed to the Iustices to this end, that they neither take nor record him in defaulte for that day. *Register originall, fol. 18.* Of this you may read more in *Fitzh. nat. br. fol.* 17. and see *Glannile, lib. pri. ca*. 8.

Warantia chartæ , is a writ that lieth properly for him who is infeoffed in land or tenements with clause of warranty , and is impleaded in an Assise or writ of *Entrie*, wherein he cannot vouche or call to warranty : for in this case his remedy is , to take out this writ against the feoffour or his heire. *Register orig. fol.* 157. *Fitzh. nat. br: fol.* 134 Of this you may likewise reade *Fleta, lib* . 6 . *ca* . 35 . and *West parte 2. simb . titulo Fines . sect.* 156.

Warrantia custodiæ, is a writ Iudiciall, that lyeth for him that is challenged to be ward vnto another, in respect of land said to be houlden in *Knights* seruice, which when it was bought by the auncesters of the ward, was warranted to be free from such thraldome. And it lieth against the warranter and his heires, Register Iudiciall, *fol.* 36.

Warrant of Atturney. See *Leter of Atturney*, and *Waranty*.

Wardwite significat quietantiam misericordiæ in casu quo non invenerit quis hominem ad wardam faciendam in castra, vel alibi. Fleta lib. 1. *cap.* 47.

Warren (*Warrenna, aliâs varrenna*) commeth of the French (*Garrenne.i. vivarium, vel locus in quo vel aves, vel pisces, vel feræ continentur, quæ ad victum duntaxat pertinent*) *Calapine* out of *Aulus Gellius. lib.* 2. *Noct. Attica: cap.* 20. A warren (as we vse it) is a prescription or graunte from the king to a man of hauing fesants, partridges, connies, and hares, within certaine of his lands, *Cromptons Iurisdict. fol.* 148. where he saith, that none can haue warren, but onely the *King*, no more then Forest or chase. Because it is a speciall priuiledge belonging to the *King* alone. And a little after he hath words to this effect: The king may graunt warren to me in mine owne lands, for fesants and partridges onely. And by this graunt no man may there chase them without my licence. And so of Hares, but not of Connies. For their property is to destroy the fruites of the earth, as to eate corne, and pille the barke of aple trees. *M. Manwood* in his first part of Forest lawes, saith thus of it: *A* warren is a fraunchise or priuiledged place of pleasure, onely for those beasts and foules that are beasts and foules of warren, *tantùm campestres & non sylvestres. viz.* For such beasts and foules as are altogether belonging to the feilds, and not vnto the woods: and for none other beasts or foules. There are but two beasts of warren, that is to say Hares and Connies: and there are also but two foules of warren, *viz.* Fesants and partridges. And none other wild beasts or birds haue any firme peace, priuiledge, or protection, within the warren. If any person be found to be an offender in any such free warren, he is to be punished for the same by the course of the common law, and by the statute. *anno* 21. *Ed.* 3. called the statute *de male factoribus in parcis & chaceis &c.* For the most parte there are noe officers in a warren, but the master of the game, or the keeper. A free warren is some time inclosed, and also the same some time doth lie open. for there is no necessity of inclosing the same, as there is of a park, for if a park be suffered to lie open, it ought to be seised into the kings hands. Thus farre *M. Manwood.*

Warscot, is the contribution, that was wont to be made towards armour in the *Saxons* time. In *Canutus* his charter of the *Forest* set out by *M. Manwood* in the first part of his Forest lawes, *num.* 9. you haue these wordes: *Sint omnes tam primarii quàm mediocres, & minuti, immunes, liberi & quieti ab omnibus prouincialibus summonitionibus, & popularibus placitis, quæ Hundred laghe Angli dicunt, & ab omnibus armorum oneribus, quod Warscot Angli dicunt, & forinsecis querelis.*

VVarwit, aliàs, VVardwit, is to be quite of giuing money for keeping of watches. New exposition of lawe termes.

VVaste (*vastum*) commeth of the *French* (*gaster*. i. *populari*. It signifieth diuersly in our common lawe, first, a spoile made, either in houses, woods, gardens, orchards, &c. by the tenent for terme of life, or for terme of anothers life, or of yeares, to the preiudice of the heire, or of him in the *Reuersion* or *Remainder*. *Kitchin fol.* 168. *&c. vsque* 172. vpon this committed the writ of waste is brought for the recouerie of the things, whereupon the waste is made. See *Vasto.* VVaste may be also made of tenents or bondmen belonging or regardant to the maner. *Regist. orig. fol.* 72. *a.* & 73. *a.* See the new booke of Entries. *verbo VVaste.* A waste of the Forest (as *M. Manwood* saith, *parte prim*. of his Forest lawes, *pag.* 172.) is most properly where any man doth cut downe his owne woods within the Forest, without licence of the king, or of the Lord chiefe Iustice in *Eyre* of the Forest. But it is also, where a man doth plow vp his owne medow or pasture, and conuerteth it vnto tillage. And of this you may reade him at large, in his second part, *cap.* 8. *num.* 4. & 5. VVaste in the second signification is taken for those parts of the *Lords* Demeins, that be not in any one mans occupation, but lye common for bounds or passages of the Lord and tenent from one place to another, and somtimes for all the *Kings* subiects. VVhich seemeth to be called waste, because the Lord cannot make such profit of it, as he doth of other of his land, by reason of that vse which others haue of it in passing to and fro. *V*pon this none may build or feed, or cut downe trees, without the Lords licence. VVaste hath a third signification, as yeare, day, and waste. *Annus, dies, & vastum*: which is a punishment or forfeiture belonging to petit treason, or felonie: whereof you may reade *Stawnf. pl. cor. lib.* 3. *cap.* 30. And see *Yeare, Day*, and *VVaste.*

VVasters. anno 5. Ed. 3. *cap.* 14 See Roberds men. See *Draw latches.*

VVastell breade, anno 51. *H.* 3. *statute of bread, and statute of pilorie.*

VVater bayliffes, seeme to bee officers in port townes for the searching of shippes, *anno* 28. *H.* 6. *cap.* 5.

Watlingstreet, is one of the 4. waies, which the Romaines are said to haue made here in *England*, and called them *Consulares, Prætorias, Militares, Publicas. M. Camden* in his Britannia, perswadeth himselfe that there were more of this sort than 4. This streete is otherwise called *Werlam streat*, (as the same author saith, and howsoeuer the Romains might make it and the rest, the names be from the *Saxons*. And *Roger Houeden* saith, it is so called, because the sonnes of *Wethle* made it, leading from the East sea to the *West. Annal. part. prior. fol.* 248. *a.* This street leadeth from *Douer* to *London*, and so to S. *Albons*, and there onward directly toward the North-west through the land, as from *Donstable* to *Westchester. anno* 39. *El. cap.* 2. the second street is called *Ikenild street*, beginning *ab Icenis*, who were the people inhabiting *Northfolke, Southfolke*, and *Cambridge shire*, as *M. Camden* declareth, *pag.* 345. The third is called *Tosse*: the reason of the name he giueth, because he thinketh it was ditched of each side. The fourth is called *Ermin street, Germanico vocabulo, à Mercurio, quem sub nomine Irmunsull.* i. *Mercurii columna, Germani maiores nostri coluerunt.* Of these reade more in the said author, *pag.* 43. & 44. *In* the description of *England* going vnder *Saxons* name, *cap.* 7. I reade that *Belinus* a *Briton* king made these 4. wayes: whereof the first and greatest he calleth *Fosse*, stretching out of the South into the North, and beginning from the corner of *Cornwel*, and passing foorth by *Deuonshire, Somersetshire*, and so along by *Tetburie* vpon *Totesw ould* besides *Couentree* vnto *Lecester*, and thence, by the wide plaines to *Newarke* and to *Lincolne* where it endeth. The second he nameth *Watling street*, comming out of the South-east toward the *Fosse*, beginning at *Dover*, and passing through the middle of *Kent* ouer *Thames* beside London nere *Westminster*, and thence to S. *Albons*, by *Donstable, Stratford*, Towceter, *Wedon*, Lilborn, *Atheriston, Gilberts hill*, now called *Wreaken*, by *Se-*

uerne

uerne, Workecester, Stratton, and so foorth by the middle of *Wales*, vnto *Cardican* and the Irish seas. The third he calleth *Erminage-street*, stretching out of the West North-west into the East South-east, from S. *Dauids* in the west *Wales* vnto *Southhampton*. The fourth he called *Rikenild street*, stretching foorth by *Worcester*, by *Wicombe, Brinningham*, *Litchfield, Derby, Chesterfield*, and by *Yorke* foorth into *Tynmouth*. But he that listeth to reade at large of these wayes, let him haue recourse to the first volume of *Halinsheds* Chronicle, and the description of *England* there, the 19. chapter. Where this antiquitie is farre otherwise declared, then by the former writer. *Henry of Huntington* likewise in the first booke of his historie, not farre after the beginning mentioneth these 4. streetes, terming them *calles Regia sublimatos authoritate, ne aliquis in eis inimicum invadere auderet, &c.*

Waterbayliffes. *anno* 28. *H.* 6. *cap.* 5. is an officer belonging to the citie of *London*, which hath the superuision and search of fish, that is brought to that citie, as also the gathering of the tolle rising from that water. He is reckoned an Esquier by his office, as the Sword-bearer, the Huntsman, and the chiefe Sergeant is. He also attendeth vpon the Lord *Maior* for the time being, and hath the principall care of marshalling the guests at his table.

Way. See *Chimin*.

Weife (*wauium*) whence it hath his originall, I cannot certainely say. But I finde the nineteenth chapter of the Grand Custumary of Normandy to be intitled (*De choses gaiues*) and latined by the interpreter. (*De rebus vaiuis*) which are there thus defined. *vaiua sunt res, vel alia, quæ nullius proprietati attributa, sine possessionis reclamatione sunt inuenta, quæ vsq; ad diem & annum seruanda sunt. Et de iis modo, quo dictum est de veriscis*, that is (*wreeks*) *ea sua esse probantibus est restitutio facienda, &c.* This weife or things weiued haue the very same signification in our common law, and be nought but things forsaken. The Ciuilians call it (*Derelictum*) or (*Quod est pro derelicto*) *Bracton* in the twelue chapter of his first booke *nu.* 10. reckoneth them *inter res quæ sunt nullius ea quæ pro waiuio habentur: sicut de aueriis, vbi non apparet Dominus*, where he also saith, *quòd olim fuerunt inuentoris de iure naturali, & iam efficiuntur principis de iure Gentium.* That this is a Regality, and belonging to the King, except it be challenged by the owner within a yeare and a day, it appeareth by *Britton* in his uenthteene chapter. Now the Kings in their times haue graunted this and such like prerogatiues vnto diuers subiects with their fees. who there likewise saith, that weifes, things lost, and estrayes, must by the Lord of the fraunchise where they are found, be caused to be cried and published in markets and churches nere about, or els that the yeare and day doth not runne to the preiudice of him that hath lost them. See *Waine*. *M. Skene de verborum signifi.verb. waife*, saith, that *waife est pecus, vel animal aberrans*, which wanders and wauerrs without a knowne master, and being found by any man within his owne bounds, must be by him proclaimed vpon diuers, and sundry market daies, at the parish church, and within the shyreeuedome. Otherwise the deteiner may be accused of theft. And it is lawfull for the owner to challenge the beast within a yeare and day. Whereby it appeareth, that in Scotland that is called a weife which we heere call a stray or estray.

Weald of Kent, is the wooddie part of the Countrie. *Camden Britannia, pag.* 247. *M. Verstegan* in his restitution of decayed intelligence saith, that Wald, Weald, and Would differing in vowell, signifie one thing, to wit a Forest. See the rest *luera*. W.

Wedding (*Nuptiæ*) commeth of the German (*wed*).i.*pignus*.and wedde in Scotland signifieth so much at this day. *Skene de verborum signifi. verbo Vadium.*

Weigh (*waga*) is a certaine waight of cheese or wooll, conteining 256. pounds of *avoyr de poyce*. See *Clove*.

Weights (*Pondera*) what they be, it is wellknowne. There be 2. sorts of them in vse with vs. The one called Troy weight, which conteineth 12. ounces in the pound, and no more: by the which, pearl, pretious stones, electuaries, & medicinal things, gould, siluer, and bread be waied: The other is called *Auer de pois*, which conteineth 16. ounces in the pound. By this all other things are waied, that passe betweene man and man by weight, sauing onely those aboue named. why the one should be called Troy weight, I haue not learned. though I reade it termed *libram & unciam Troianam*: as if it came from Troy. But *Georg. Agricola* in his learned tractate *de ponderibus & mensuris. pa.* 339. termeth the pound of 12. ownces *libram medicam*, and the other of 16. ownces *libram ciuilem*. saying thus of them both: *Medica & ciuilis libra, numero non gra-*

grauitate vnciarum differunt. The second seemeth soe to be termed by reason of the more full weight. for (*Avoir de pois*) in French, is as much to say, as to haue full weight. But by these words (*Avoir de pois*) are some time signified such marchandies as are bought and sould by this kinde of weights. the first statute of *Yorke anno* 9. *Ed*. 3. *in proœm. & anno* 27. *Ed*. 3. *stat*. 2. *ca*. 10. *& ann*. 24 *H*. 8. *ca*. 13. Of weights in Scotland. See *Skene de verb: signif. verbo Serplathe*. All our weights and measures haue their first composition from the peny sterling which ought to weigh 32. wheat corns of a middle sort, twenty of which pence make an ownce and twelue such ownces a pound or twenty shillings, but 15. ownces make the Merchants pound. *Fleta*, *li*. 2. *ca*. 12. It is not vnlike that this merchants pound, though an ounce lesse, should be all one in signification with the pound of *auoir de pois:* and the other pound, called by *Flata trone weight*, plainely appeareth to be all one with that which we now call troie weight. And I finde not Troie weight mentioned by any other that euer I read vpon this subiect, but onely our owne contry men. See *Tronage*.

Weights of Awncell, anno 14. *Ed*. 3. *stat. pri. c*. 12. See *Awncell weight*.

Were, aliàs werre signifieth as much as (*Æstimatio capitis, aut pretiũ hominis*. *M. Lam. exp*. of Saxõ words, *verbo: Æstimatio*. That is to say, so much as one paid for killing of a man. Whereby he gathereth that slaughters, and such other great offences, were more rarely committed in aunciient times, then now: when as for the multitude of offenders, death is most iustly inflicted for those crimes, that then were redressed by pecuniary mulcts. Of this see *Roger Houeden, parte poster. suorum annalium, in Henrico* 2. *fo*. 344.

Weregelt theef. significat latronem qui redimi potest. wera enim anglicè idem est in Saxonis *lingua, vel pretium vitæ hominis appretiatum. Fleta lib*. 1. *ca*. 47.

West Saxon lage, aliàs West sexenlage. See *Lawe*.

Wharfe (*wharfa*) is a broad plaine place neare to a *Creeke* or *hithe* of the water, to lay wares vpon, that be brought to or from the water to be transported to any other place. New booke of *Entries, fol*. 3. *col*. 3.

Wharfinger, is the keeper of a wharfe, *anno* 7. *Ed*. 6. *ca*. 7.

White hart siluer (*Candidi Cerui argentum*) is a tribute or mulct paid into the Eschequer out of the Forest of white hart: which (as *M. Camden* reporteth in his

Bri-

Britan. pag. 150.) hath continued from *Henry* the thirds time, and was imposed by him vpon *Thomas De-la-linde*, for killing of a most beautifull hart, which himselfe before had purposely spared in hunting.

Widow (*vidua*) seemeth to come of the French (*vide. i. inanitus, exinanitus*) or the verb (*vuider. i. inaniare*) *quasi priuata atq; orba marito. Macrobius lib. pri. saturn. ca.* 15.. draweth it from the *Hetruscan* verb (*Iduare .i. diuidere. Vnde vidua quasi valde idua .i. valde diuisa: aut vidua .i. a viro diuisa.* The signification with vs is apparent. But there is one kinde of widow, called the widow of the King, or the Kings widow (*vidua Regis*) that requireth exposition. And shee is that widow, which after her husbands death being the Kings tenent *in capite*, is driuen to recouer her Dower by a writ *De dote assignanda*. Of whom you may read *Stawnf. prærog. cap.* 4. The words of the statute of the *prærog*: made *anno* 17. *Ed.* 2. be these. *Item assignabit viduis post mortem virorum suorum, qui de eo tenuerunt in capite, dotem suam, quæ eas contingit, &c: licet hæredes fuerint plenæ ætatis, si viduæ voluerint. Et viduæ illæ ante assignationem dotis suæ prædictæ, siue hæredes plenæ ætatis fuerint, siue infra ætatem, iurabunt, quòd se non maritabunt sine licentia Regis. Tunc Rex capiet in manum suam nomine districtionis omnes terras, & tenementa, quæ de eo tenentur in dotem, donec satisfecerint ad voluptatem suam: ita quod ipsa mulier nihil capiet de exitibus, &c. quia per huiusmodi districtiones huiusmodi mulieres, seu viri eorum finem facient Regi ad voluptatem suam. Et illa voluntas tempore Regis Henrici patris Regis Edwardi æstimari consueuit ad valentiam prædictæ dotis per vnum annum ad plus, nisi vlteriorem gratiam habuerint. Mulieres, quæ de Rege tenent in capite aliquam hæreditatem, iurabunt similiter, cuiuscunq; fuerint ætatis, quòd se non maritabunt sine licentia Regis. Et si fecerint, terræ & tenementa ipsarum eodem modo capiantur in manum Domini Regis, quousq; satisfecerint ad voluntatem Regis.* Of this fee likewise the great charter *cap.* 7. whereby it appeareth that other common Lords haue the same power ouer their widowes, touching their consent, in their mariage, that the King hath. Of this you may read more in the writ *De dote assignanda. Fitzh. nat. br. fo.* 263. *C.* See also the statute *anno* 32. *H.* 8. *cap.* 46.

Windelesor. a Herald. See *Herald.*

Withernam (*vetitum Namium*) *Master* Lamberd thinketh to be compounded of (*wither. i. altera, siue secunda*) & (*Nam. i.*

pigno-

pignoris captio) marueiling much why it should so farre be depraued in the interpretation, as to be translated *(vetitum Namium.)* Reade him in the explication of *S*axon wordes, *verbo,* P*ignorari.* The concord of the thing signified with the meaning of the *L*atine words, maketh some to thinke, that it is compounded of *(wehren.* i. *veto,)* and *(nyman,)* or *nemmen.* i. *capio.)* For *withernam* in our common lawe is the taking, or driuing a distresse to a hould, or out of the countie, so that the Shyreeue cannot vpon the repleuin make deliuerance thereof to the partie distreined: In which case, the writ of *Withernam,* or *de vetito Namio* is directed to the *S*hyreeue, for the taking of as many of his beasts that did thus vnlawfully distrein, or as much goods of his, into his keeping, till that he hath made deliuerance of the first distresse. Also if the beastes be in a fortlet or castell, the *S*hyreeue may take with him the power of the countie, and beat downe the castell, as it appeareth by the Statute. *Westm. pri. cap.* 20. *Britton. cap.* 27. But *M. Lamberds* interpretation seemeth more consonant to the writ, the forme whereof is thus in part, *(Fitz. nat. br. fol.* 73.) *Tibi pracipimus quòd averia pradicti B. in Balliva tua capias in withernam, &c.* and the *Register orig. fol.* 82. *&* 83. *&* 79. *a. &* 80. *a.* and in the Re*gister Iudic. fol.* 29 *a. &* 30. *a.* Whereby it appeareth, that the Shyreeue by these words is willed to take in compensation of the former taking, so many cattell, &c. But yet this may qualifie *M.* L*amberds* maruelling, because they that translated this word into such *L*atine, seeme to haue bene deceiued by the propinquitie of the word, *(wehren)* both to the word *(withernam)* and also to the meaning. This error (if it be an error) hath a probable likelihood of descent from the *Normans,* as appeareth by the grand Custumarie. *cap.* 4. where you haue wordes to this effect: *Deficientes (sc. Balliuos) facere iusticiari, & ea, de quibus iudicium vel recordatio habet fieri in curia: debet (sc. Iusticiarius) retrahere vel recitare. Treugam dari debet facere, quod est assecuratio pacis obseruanda. Nampta iniuste capta per ius facere liberari, &c.* Here you may see *(nampta)* referred to the first taking or distresse, which is vnlawfull. *Sir Thomas Smith* in his *Repub. Anglor.* agreeth with *M. Lamberd* in these words: This *(withernam)* he (meaning *Litleton,* with whom Br*acton* also agreeth. *lib.* 2. *cap.* 5. *& lib.* 3. *tract.* 2.

cap. 36.) interpreteth *vetitum Namium,* in what language I know not. Whereas in truth it is in plaine *Dutch,* and in our old *Saxon* language (*wither nempt.* i. *alterum accipere, alterum rapere,)* a word that signifieth all one with that barbarous *Latine* word, *(Repræsalia)* when one taking of me a distresse, which in *Latine* is called *(pignus)* or any other thing,and carying it away out of the Iurisdiction, where I dwell, I take by order of him that hath iurisdiction, another of him againe, or of some other of that Iurisdiction: and do bring it into the iurisdiction, wherein I dwell: that by equall wrong *I* may come to haue equall right,&c. *Namatio animalium* in *Scotland* is vsed for the pounding of cattell, *Skene de verbor. signif. verbo, Averia:* whom also reade, *verbo,* Namare. *Withernam in Bracton lib. 3. tract. 2. cap.* 37. and also in *Westm. 2. ca.* 2. seemeth to signifie an vnlawfull distresse, made by him that hath no right to distreine. *an. 13.* Ed. *prim. cap. 2.* See the newe booke of Entries. *verbo Withernam.*

Woad, *(glastum)* is an herbe brought from the parts of *Tolouse* in *France*,& from *Spayne*, much vsed and very necessary in the dying of wollen cloth. *an 7.* H. 8. *cap. 2.* we call it *woad* of the Italian word *(guado)* or the *Germane* word *(weidt.)*

W*oodgeld*, seemeth to be the gathering or cutting of wood within the Forest, or money payed for the same, to the vse of the *F*oresters. And the immunitie from this by the *Kings* graunt, is by *Crompton* called W*oodgeld. fol.* 197.

Woodmen, seeme to be those in the Forest, that haue their charge especially to looke to the Kings woods. *Manwood parte pri.* of his Forest lawes *pag.* 193. and *Cromptons Iurisd. fol.* 146.

Woodmote court, is the Attachment of the Forest. *Manwood parte pri.* of his Forest lawes. *pag.* 95. *See Attachment.*

Woodward (Woodwardus) is an officer of the Forest, whose function you may partly gather by his oath set downe in *Cromptons Iurisd. fol.* 201. which *M. Manwood* hath also in his first part of his Forest lawes *pag.* 50. to the same effect, but something more at large, *viz.* You shall truly execute the office of a woodward of *B.* woods within the Forest of *W.* so long as you shalbe woodward there : you shall not conceale any offence either in Vert or in Venison, that shalbe committed or done within your charge: but you shall truly present the same, without any fauour, affection or reward. And if if you doe see or know any malefactors, or doe finde any Deere killed or hurt, you shall forthwith doe the verderour vnderstand thereof. And you shall present the same at the next court of the Forest: be it *Swainmote*, or court of Attachments, so help you God. Woodwards may not walke with bow and shafts, but with Forest bills. *Manwood parte pri.* of his Forest lawes *pag. 189.* and more of him *pag. 97.*

Wooldriuer, anno 2. & 3. Ph. & Ma. ca. 13. be those that buy wool abroad in the country of the sheep masters, & carry it by horse backe to the clothyers or to market townes to sell it againe.

Woolferthsod (Caput lupinum) is the condition of those, which were outlawed in the *Saxons* time, for not yelding themselues to Iustice. For if they could be taken aliue, they must haue bene brought to the King: and if they in feare of apprehension did defend themselues they might be slaine, and their heads brought to the *King*. For they carried a woolues head, that is to say: their head was noe more to be accoumpted of, then a woolues head, being a beast so hurtfull vnto man. See the lawes of *K. Edw:* set out by *M. Lamberd fol. 127.b.nu.7.* The very like whereof *Bracton* also saith *lib. 3. tract. 2. ca. 11.* See *vtlarie*. *Roger Hoveden* writeth it (*Wulueshened*) *parte poster, suorum annalium fol. 343.b.*) whom read of this mater because you shall there see what it was in those daies to violate the peace of the church.

Woolstaple, anno 51. H. 3. stat. 5. See *Staple.*

Wooll winders, be such as winde vp euery fleece of wooll that is to be packed and sould by weight, into a kinde of bundle after it is clensed in such maner as it ought to be by statute. And to auoide such deceit as the owners were wont to vse by thrusting locks of refuse wooll and such other drosse to gaine weight they are sworne to performe that office truly betweene the owner and the merchant. See the statute, *anno 8. H. 6. cap. 22. & anno 23. H. 8. ca. 17. & anno 18. Eliza. ca. 25.*

Would. See *Weald.*

Wranglands, seeme to be misgrowne trees that will neuer prooue timber. *Kitchin fol. 169. b.*

Wormseede (*semen santonicum*) is medicinal seede browght forth of that plant which in Latine is called (*Sementina*) in English, holy wormwood, whereof you may read in *Gerards Herball li. 2. ca. 435.* This is a drugge to be garbled, *anno 1. Iacob. cap. 19.*

Wreck (wreccum vel wrectum maris) is the losse of a shippe and the goods therein conteined by tempest, or other mischaunce at the sea. The Ciuilians call it (*Naufragium*) This wreck being made, the goods that were in the shippe, being brought to land by the waues, belong to the king by his prerogatiue. And therevpon in many bookes of our common lawe the very goods, so brought to land are called wreck. And wreck is defined to be those goods which are so brought to land. *Sir Ed. Coke vol. 6. relatio, f.* 106. *a.* & the statute *anno* 17. *Ed.* 2. *ca.* 11. in these words. *Item Rex habebit wreccum maris, per totum Regnum, ballenas, & sturgiones captas in mari vel alibi infra Regnum, exceptis quibusdam locis privilegiatis per Regem.* Whereby it appeareth that the *King* hath them, or such as haue by graunt this libertie or priuiledge of him. And that this statute doth but affirme the auncient lawe of the land, it appeareth by *Bracton, lib.* 2. *cap.* 5. *num.* 7. *his verbis: Sunt etiam alia res quæ pertinent ad coronã propter privilegium Regis, & ita communiõ non recipiunt libertatem, quin dari possint, & ad alium transferri. Quia si transferantur, translatio nulli erit damnosa, nisi ipsi Regi siue principi. Et si huiusmodi res alicui concessa fuerint, sicut wreccum maris, &c.* The reason of this he toucheth shortly in his first booke. *cap.* 12. *num.* 10. where he reckoneth these goods (*iure naturali*) to be (*in bonis nullius*) *quia non apparet Dominus eorum, sed iure Gentium fieri principis:* And see him also, *lib.* 2. *cap.* 24. *num.* 1. & 2. It is worth the asking to know what is a wreck, and what not in this stricter signification. And the author of the termes of lawe saith, that if any person of the shippe come to land, it is not a wreck, or the wreck is not such, that the king ought to haue the goods. with whome agreeth *S. Ed. Coke vol.* 6. *f.* 107. *a.* No, if either Dogge or Catte escape aliue to the land: the goods are the owners still, so he come within a yeare, and day to claime them. And for this the statute is plaine *Westm. pri. ca.* 4. *anno* 3. *Edw. pri.* which doctrine Fitzh. in his *nat. br. fol.* 112. *E.* extendeth thus farre, that if any of the goods be cast vpon the drie land by any in the shippe, it is no wreck subiect to the prerogatiue, for by this some of the shippe are presumed to come to land, and still to haue a custodie of the goods. *Cooke vbi supra.* This in the

Grand Custumarie of Normandie. *cap.* 17. is called *(varech)* and latined (*veriscum*) where it appeareth that the like lawe to ours was in Normandie almost in all points . But some sorts of their pretious Merchandise doe by their lawe appertaine to the *Duke* by his prerogatiue, though a iust challenge of the goods be made within the yeare and day. The Emperours of *Rome* made no advantage of this pitifull event , as appeareth: *titulo De Naufragiis* 11. *Cod.* And it appeareth that *Richard* the first had some remorse of poore sea mens miseries in this case. For he *quietum clamavit wreck suis subditis*. *Rog. Hoveden parte poster. suorum annal. fol.* 386. Of this *M. Skene de verb. signif.* speaketh to this effect: *wreck* signifieth a power, liberty, and prerogatiue appertaining to the King, or to any person, to whome the same is graunted by him by feofment, or any other disposition , to take vp and gaine such goods as are shipbroken, or fall to him by escheate of the sea.

Writ, (breue) is that with our common lawyers (in *Sir Tho. Smiths* iudgement *lib.* 2. *de Repub. Anglorum. cap.* 9.) which the Civilians call (*Actionem* , *siue formulam*) But I am rather of his iudgement, that hath added the marginall note vnto him, saying that (*Actio*) is the parties whole suite: and that (*Breue*) is the kings precept , whereby any thing is comaunded to be done touching the suite or action: as the defendant or tenent to be summoned, a distresse to be taken, a disseisin to be redressed, &c. And these writs are diuersly diuided, in diuers respects. Some in respect of their order , or maner of graunting, are termed originall, and some Iudiciall . Originall writs be those, that are sent out for the summoning of the Defendant in a personall, or Tenent in a reall action, or other like purpose, before the suite beginneth, or to begin the suite thereby Those be iudiciall , that be sent out by order of the court, where the cause dependeth, vpon occasion growing after suite begunne. *old. nat. br. fol.* 51. And Iudiciall is thus by one signe knowne from the Originall, because the *Teste* beareth the name of the chiefe Iustice of that Court whence it commeth, where the Orig. beareth in the *Teste* the name of the Prince. Then according to the nature of the action, they be personall or reall: and reall be either touching the possession, called writs of Entrie, or the property, called writs of right.

Fitzh. nat. br. sparsim per totum. Some writs be at the suite of a party, some of office. *old. nat. br. fol.* 147. Some ordinary, some of priuiledge. A writ of priuiledge is that which a priuiledged person bringeth to the court, for his exemption, by reason of some priuiledge. See *Procedendo.* See the new booke of Entrise. *verbo. priviledge.* See *Briefe.*

Writ of rebellion. See *Commission of rebellion.*

Writer of the talies (*Scriptor talliarum*) is an officer in the Exchequer being clerk to the auditour of the receipt, who writeth vpon the talies the whole letters of the tellers billes.

Y

Yard land (*Virgata terræ*) is a quantitie of land called by this name of the Saxon (*Gyrdlander* (but not so certaine a quantity, as that it is all one in all places. For in some country it conteineth 20. acres: in some 24. in some 30. as *M. Lamb.* saith in his explication of Saxon words: *verbo virgata terræ.* This yard land *Bracton* calleth (*virgatam terræ. lib. 2. cap.* 10. & 27.) but he expresseth no certainty what it conteineth.

Yere and day (*annus & dies*) is a time thought in construction of our common lawe fit in many cases to determine a right in one, and to worke an vsucapion or prescription in another. As in a case of an estray, if the owner (proclamations being made) chalenge it not within that time, it is forfeit. So is the yeare and day giuen in case of appeale, in case of descent after entry or claime; of no claime vpon a fine or writ of right at the common lawe: so of a villein remaining in auncient demeane, of the death of a man sore bruised or wounded: of protections; essoines in respect of the Kings service: of a wreck, and divers other cases *Coke. vol. 6. fol.* 107. *b.* And that touching the death of a man seemeth an imitation of the civile lawe. *Nam si mortifere fuerit vulneratus, & postea post longum intervallum mortuus sit, inde annum numerabimus secundum Iulianum. l. ait lex. ff. ad legẽ Aquil.*

Yeare, day, and waste, (*annus dies, & vastum*) is a part of the Kings prerogatiue, whereby he challengeth the profits of their lands and tenements for a yere, and a day, that are attainted of petit treason or felonie, whosoeuer be Lord of the maner, whereunto the lands or tenements do belong, and not onely so, but in the end wasteth the tenement, destroyeth the houses, rooteth vp the woods, gardens,

dens, pastures, and ploweth vp medowes, except the Lord of the fee agree with him for the redemption of such waste, afterward restoring it to the Lord of the fee. Whereof you may reade at large in *Stawnf. prærog. cap.* 16. *fol.* 44. *& seqq.*

Yoman, seemeth to be one word made by contraction of two Danish words *(yong men)* which I gather out of *Canutus* Charter of the *Forest* set out by *M. Manwood parte prim. fol. prim. num.* 2. in these words: *Sunt sub quolibet horum quatuor ex mediocribus hominibus, quos Angli (Legespend) nuncupant, Dani vero (yong men) vocant, locati, qui curam & onus tum viridis tum veneris suscipiant.* These *M. Camden* in his *Britan. pag.* 105. placeth next in order to Gentlemen, calling them *(Ingenuos)* whose opinion the statute affirmeth, *anno* 16. *R. 2. cap.* 4. whereunto adde the statute *anno* 20. *eiusdem Regis cap.* 2. *Sir Thomas Smith* in his *Repub. Anglor. lib. prim. cap.* 23. calleth him a Yoman, whom our lawes call *legalem hominem*: which (as he saith) is in English a *Free* man borne, that may dispend of his owne free land, in yerely reuenew, to the summe of forty shillings sterling. Of these he writeth a good large discourse, touching their estate and vse in this common wealth. The former etymologie of the name he liketh not, making question whether it come of the *Dutch* *(yonker)* yea or not, which in the Low countries signifieth a meane Gentleman, or a gay fellow. But he that hath added the marginall notes to that booke, seemeth to draw it from the *Saxon* *(Geman)* which signifieth a maried man. *M. Verstegan* in his restitution of decayed intelligence, *cap.* 10. writeth, that *(Gemen)* among the auncient *Teutonicks*, and *(Gemein)* among the moderne, signifieth as much, as Common, and that the first leter G. is in this word, as in many others, turned into Y. and so written *Yemen*, and that therfore Yemen, or Yeomen signifieth so much as Commoner. Yoman signifieth an Officer in the *Kings* house, which is in the middle place betweene the *Sergeant* and the Groome: as Yoman of the Chaundrie, and Yoman of the Scullerie. *anno* 33. *H.* 8. *cap.* 12. Yoman of the Crowne. *anno* 3. *Ed.* 4. *cap.* 5. *& anno* 22. *eius. cap.* 1. *& anno* 4. *H.* 7. *cap.* 7. This word *(Yongmen)* is vsed for *Yomen* in the statute. *anno* 33. *H.* 8. *cap.* 10.

Τῷ Θεῷ Δόξα.

FINIS.